The Best 1001 WordPerfect Tips Ever

WARNING: BEFORE OPENING THE DISK PACKAGE OPPOSITE, CAREFULLY READ THE TERMS AND CONDITIONS OF THE DISK WARRANTY FOUND ON THE BACK OF THIS PAGE.

About the Disk

The 3.5-inch disk that accompanies this book is packed with information discussed in the 1001 tips in this book. On the disk you will find sound files, clip art, macros, styles, and templates. As you look through the book, you will notice disk icons with filenames beneath them. These are the names of the disk files on the accompanying disk.

To maximize the space on the disk, all of the files are stored in a special zipped format that cannot be accessed directly. The disk appears to contain only three large files (TIPSDOCS.EXE, TIPSMACS.EXE, and TIPSGRPH.EXE) and a READ.ME file, but each of the three large files contains many compressed files. These compressed files have been placed in three different files because WordPerfect will look for the type of information they contain in three different locations. As you place these files on your hard disk (using the procedure described below), they will be expanded automatically into the component files and placed in the directory where WordPerfect initially expects to find them.

Since WordPerfect stores different types of files (like macros and graphics, for example) in different directories, you will want to place the unzipped version of each of the three files in different directories. The suggested locations below conform to WordPerfect's defaults. This means if you place the files in these locations and are using the default locations, you will be able to access the files easily. If you have set WordPerfect to use different locations for these file types, you can adjust the location where you place the sample files as they are unzipped. Once you pick your location, all you need to do is activate the directory where you want these unzipped files placed, and type the drive name of the disk containing the file and the name of the large sample file. For example, the accompanying disk contains clip art in the TIPSGRPH.EXE file. In order to place that clip art on drive C in the directory \WP60\GRAPHICS, switch to the \WP60\GRAPHICS directory on drive C, put the accompanying disk in drive A, and type **A:TIPSGRPH**.

Sample File	File Type	Default WordPerfect Directory
TIPSGRPH	Graphics Files (Clip Art)	\WP60\GRAPHICS
TIPSDOCS	Sound Files	\WPDOCS
	Templates	\WPDOCS
	Styles	\WPDOCS
TIPSMACS	Macros	\WP60\MACROS
	Button Bar	\WP60\MACROS

To install all of the files, you'll want to have at least 2MB of hard disk space available. You'll need to make the following sequence of entries from the DOS prompt if you are using all three default locations:

- ❏ CD \WP60\GRAPHICS
- ❏ A:TIPSGRPH
- ❏ CD \WPDOCS
- ❏ A:TIPSDOCS
- ❏ CD \WP60\MACROS
- ❏ A:TIPSMACS

If your files are stored in different locations, or if you have placed your sample disk in a drive other than drive A, you will need to make the necessary adjustments to refer to the location you are using.

In addition, the sample documents, styles, and templates use the default printer font and the fonts that come with WordPerfect. If you have not installed the fonts that come with WordPerfect or you have a different default printer font than the one used in the book, the documents will look slightly different because WordPerfect must substitute one of the fonts available on your computer. Some of the graphics files are not in WordPerfect's WPG graphics file format. When you use one of these graphics files, WordPerfect will prompt you for the format of the file. Accept WordPerfect's suggestion and either press ENTER or click Select to let WordPerfect bring the graphics file—in a different format—into the current document.

Copyright Information

The Best 1001 WordPerfect Tips Ever

Mary Campbell

Osborne **McGraw-Hill**

Berkeley New York St. Louis San Francisco
Auckland Bogotá Hamburg London Madrid
Mexico City Milan Montreal New Delhi Panama City
Paris São Paulo Singapore Sydney
Tokyo Toronto

Osborne **McGraw-Hill**
2600 Tenth Street
Berkeley, California 94710
U.S.A.

For information on translations or book distributors outside of the U.S.A., please write to Osborne **McGraw-Hill** at the above address.

The Best 1001 WordPerfect Tips Ever

1234567890 DOC 9987654

ISBN 0-07-881819-2

Acquisitions Editor
Scott Rogers

Associate Editor
Kristin D. Beeman

Editorial Assistant
Sherith Pankratz

Technical Editor
Jim Sheldon

Project Editor
Kelly Barr

Copy Editors
Judith Brown
Paul Medoff
Ann Spivack

Proofreaders
Linda Medoff
Audrey Johnson

Indexer
Elizabeth Reinhardt

Illustrator
Lance Ravella

Computer Designer
Stefany Otis

Cover Design
Communication Design
Mason Fong

Table of Contents

2
Page and Paragraph Formatting

3 Fonts and Character Appearance

4
Screen

Tip

5
Headers and Footers

Tip

6
Printing

Tip

7
Working with Blocks

Tip

8
Searching and Sorting

9
Styles

Tip

10
Date and Time

11
Working with Large Documents

14
Tables

15
Columns and Math

Tip

16
Outlines

17
Merges, Form Letters, and Templates

18
Hyphenation

Manu-
script

Tip

19 Files

20
Initial Settings

Tip

21
Macros

Tip

22
Desktop Publishing

Tip

A
WordPerfect 6 Codes

B
Macros on Disk

C
Styles and Templates on Disk

D
Graphics on Disk

Acknowledgments

Although I feel that all of my books are a cooperative effort involving many people, this book seemed to require the help of more people than usual. I would like to thank each of the many people who helped with this book, especially the following individuals:

Gabrielle Lawrence, for all of her work on so many parts of the book. She helped not only with organization but seemed to step in whenever we needed anything, including art work, macros, and a disk stretcher that let us jam even more information onto the accompanying disk so we could include sound files.

Elizabeth Reinhardt, for all of her creative ideas for illustrating tips with the clip art collection included on the accompanying disk. Elizabeth also created a great index that makes it easy to find all the information in the book.

Jim Sheldon, who is far and away the best reviewer I have ever had for a manuscript. Jim willingly spent late hours going over the manuscript to ensure that everything was perfect.

Scott Rogers, Acquisitions Editor, who was always willing to do anything possible to help with the book. Scott held a focus group session to help select the clip art collection, listened to sound files, and even helped with the vendor art.

Sherith Pankratz, for all of her help in tracking the 1001 pieces to this book and for keeping the art and other components moving through the system.

Kristin Beeman, who prepped all the chapters and helped us give it a consistent look throughout.

Kelly Barr, Project Editor, who coordinated the details to get the book successfully into production and helped us ensure that it was as accurate as possible—despite the fact that the product changed several times while this book was being written.

Jim Anderton, Lisa DiNota, Peter Haney, Gwendaline Mazzara, for their help in providing excellent examples of their products in the sound files and clip art included on the accompanying disk.

Lance Ravella and the Production Department at Osborne for their excellent work creating art and laying out pages.

CHAPTER 1

Entering a Document

A Custom WordPerfect 6 Button Bar Makes Text Entry and Editing Easier

The Button Bar at the top of the WordPerfect 6 screen is optional. If you use a mouse you may find it convenient to display the Button Bar, since, with it, WordPerfect features are only a click away. If you make the necessary selection from the View menu to display the Button Bar and are disappointed that it does not offer your favorite commands, you can create your own custom Button Bar. You can even attach macros to buttons or choose the order in which the buttons are presented. The following Button Bar was created with menu selections and macros supplied with WordPerfect:

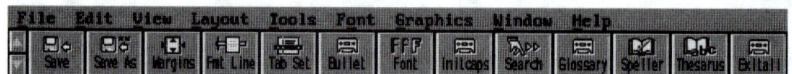

This sample Button Bar is available on the accompanying disk as EDITING.WPB.

EDITING.WPM

If you would like to use it, you can follow these steps:

1. If you install the macros on the accompanying disk, the Button Bar is automatically copied with them. If you have not yet done this, you will need to do it before proceeding.
    The .WPM and .WPB files should be copied to the WP60\MACROS directory unless you have changed your Environment settings.
2. Choose **V**iew and select Button Bar **S**etup.
3. Choose **S**elect, choose EDITING, and select OK.

Some of the buttons in this Button Bar represent menu selections; others are created from the macros distributed with WordPerfect. The buttons and the tasks they will perform for you are as follows:

Button	Name	Use
	Save	Saves the current document
	Save As	Saves the current document under the new name you specify
	Margins	Lets you change the margins
	Fmt Line	Lets you change the format of the current line
	Tab Set	Lets you change tab settings
	Bullet	Creates an entry for a bulleted list
	Font	Lets you change the font
	InitCaps	WordPerfect macro to change text to initial caps
	Search	Searches for specified text
	Glossary	Macro to allow you to use abbreviations
	Speller	Invokes the Speller
	Thesaurus	Invokes the Thesaurus
	Exit All	Macro that exits all dialog boxes and returns to edit

You can also create your own custom bar, which you can learn about in Tip 221

Move Up or Down a Set Number of Lines Quickly with the Repeat Key

Using the arrow keys to move up or down a specific number of lines can be frustrating. The automatic repeating of keypresses means you often overshoot the desired stopping place. The solution is to specify the number of lines that you want to move up or down. Follow this procedure:

1. Press the Repeat key (CTRL-R with WordPerfect 6 and ESC with WordPerfect 5.1).
2. Type a number representing the number of lines to move.
3. Press the UPARROW or DOWNARROW to indicate the desired direction.

If you want to move up six lines, press the Repeat key, type **6**, and press the UP ARROW.

WordPerfect 6's Undo Feature Can Restore Most Changes

It is easy to make a mistake while editing a document. You might accidentally delete a section of text, move the wrong paragraph, or change the formatting of the wrong section of the document. Fortunately, you can undo any of these changes if you act right away. To undo your last action:

Select **E**dit **U**ndo or press CTRL-Z.

You cannot use the Undo feature to reverse actions such as printing or writing to a file, since these tasks involve changes in other media that cannot be undone.

Liven Up Articles and Reports by Adding a Pull Quote

A *pull quote* can add visual interest to a page that contains nothing but text in reports or newsletters. A pull quote is nothing more than a phrase or a sentence in the body of the text that is duplicated in

the margin to add visual interest. To ensure that the text matches exactly, copy it rather than type it again. The result might look something like this:

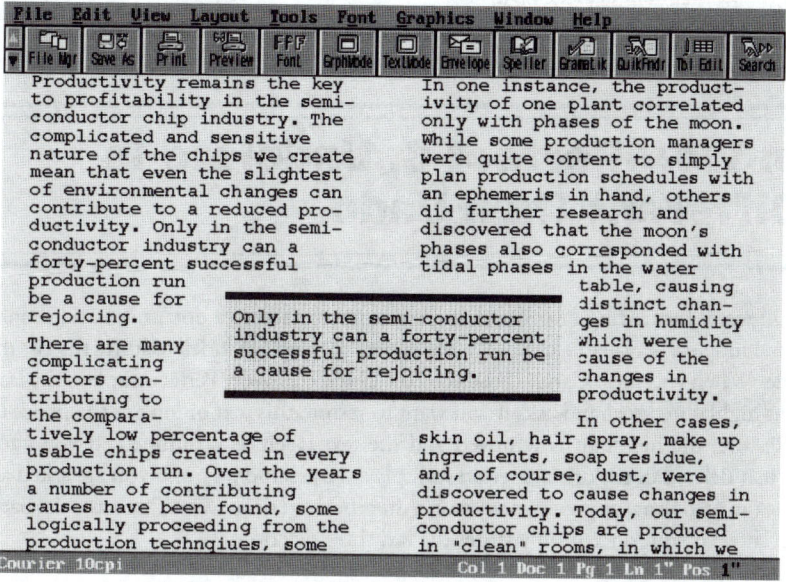

First, block the text using the Block feature (F12). Then complete the first step of the copy (Copy and Paste in WordPerfect 6) process for a block, using the menu or CTRL-F4. You then see a prompt at the bottom of your screen telling you to press ENTER to retrieve the copy of text. Next you need to set up the graphics box, following the appropriate steps for either WordPerfect 6 or WordPerfect 5.1.

WordPerfect 6 steps:

1. Select **G**raphics and then select Graphics **B**oxes.
2. Select **C**reate.
3. Select Cr**e**ate Text and press ENTER to retrieve the copied text.
4. Press F7 (Exit).
5. Select Based on Box St**y**le, highlight Text Box, and choose **S**elect.
6. Select OK. If you are using a Graphics mode view, the text box will appear beside your text clearly.

WordPerfect 5.1 steps:

1. Press ALT-F9 to activate the Graphics feature.
2. Select Text **B**ox and select **C**reate.

3. Select **E**dit and press ENTER to retrieve the copy.
4. Press F7 (Exit) twice to return to the editing screen.
5. To view the box, press SHIFT-F7 for print and then select **V**iew Document.
6. Press F7 (Exit) to exit the view.

In WordPerfect 6, Undelete Is Different Than Undo

Undo lets you reverse formatting or other changes you have made to a document and is only available in WordPerfect 6. Undelete is available in both WordPerfect 5.1 and 6. Undelete stores the last three deletions you have made. When you press Cancel or select Edit Undelete, WordPerfect displays the last text deleted at the cursor as highlighted text and asks if you want to restore this text or look at the previous deletion. If you choose **R**estore, the highlight is removed and the text is left as positioned. If you choose **P**revious Deletion, the text deleted in the prior deletion is displayed the same way, and you are asked again whether you want to restore or look at the previous deletion. After the third time, WordPerfect cycles back to redisplay the first text it showed you, since it only stores the last three deletions.

WordPerfect 6's Default Code Placement Is Different From Earlier Releases

You will notice that WordPerfect 6 handles placing many of the codes you add and removes ones that are no longer needed. This is called Auto Code Placement and may seem very different, especially if you have worked with an earlier release of WordPerfect. If you use the default settings, you do not need to be at the top of the page to change page layout options, or at the beginning of the line to change the left or right margin; WordPerfect 6 automatically moves the code to the beginning of the line.

You can change the way that WordPerfect 6 handles code placement to correspond with WordPerfect 5.1 by changing File Setup Environment Auto Code Placement.

Save Your Document Before Making Drastic Changes

If you want to try something on your document, save it; then make the changes. If you do not like the changes, you can exit the document and open it again to return to its state before the change.

Another important time to save is when you want to use one document as a model for a second document. Unless you begin by making a copy of the original file with a new name, you should immediately save under a new name. Otherwise, you might make your changes, and forget and save the revised document under the name of the original document. You can use the new File Save As command in WordPerfect 6 or use F10 or File Save in WordPerfect 5.1 and type a new name. If you do this consistently, you will never have to worry about losing your original documents.

Keep Boilerplate Paragraphs in Separate Disk Files

You can insert text from a file into the current document by retrieving the file. To save typing time, store frequently used paragraphs on disk and insert them where needed.

For example, you might have several versions of a closing paragraph used with order acknowledgments. The paragraph that you want to use may depend on whether you are responding to an order from a frequent customer or one that has not placed an order in some time. You could store the two closing paragraphs in the files FREQUENT and SELDOM. After typing a unique beginning for the letter that acknowledges the specific order and commits to a delivery date, retrieve the appropriate file. The file SELDOM, which could be used to close your letter, might look like this:

```
Please call if you have any questions or complaints about our
service or product so that we can serve you better by responding
to your specific needs. Your sales representative will be
checking in with you after you receive this order to confirm that
you received the correct products in a timely fashion. We are
glad that you have placed an order with us again. We hope to hear
from you frequently in the future.
```

Create Quick Documents with Partially Completed Forms

When you need to distribute similar documents frequently, a good idea is to store a partially completed copy that you can complete quickly. All you need to do is to fill in the needed data and you are ready to print a copy. With this approach, you can afford to invest the time in creating some pretty fancy documents. The time investment is only needed once but can be used any time you need the memo, fax cover sheet, or other similar document.

The following document is a simple form that can be used for an interoffice memo:

Tall Trees Landscaping

MEMORANDUM

To:	recipient's name
From:	your name
Date:	June 8, 1993
Re:	subject of memorandum

body of memorandum

This sample form is available on the accompanying disk as MEMOFORM. The tree graphic is one of the graphics images that comes with WordPerfect 6.

MEMOFORM

Since it is partially completed, you can save some typing time. Margin settings and other formatting options that you want are also stored with the document. You can focus completely on the needed content, rather than appearances.

New WordPerfect 6 Function Key Assignments Can Cause Confusion

With every new release of WordPerfect, some function keys are reassigned to new tasks. This is because of the growing list of tasks that WordPerfect can handle. The latest release, WordPerfect 6, has redefined some of the function keys used in WordPerfect 5.1. Some keys have totally new uses, others perform new tasks in addition to old ones, and others just have new names. Since all of these changes can create a bit of confusion, the cheat sheet that follows shows the new functions of keys that have been changed:

Key	Function
F1	Help
ALT-F1	Writing Tools
F3	Switch to
F5	File Mgr
SHIFT-F5	Date
CTRL-F5	Outline
CTRL-F6	Decimal Tab
SHIFT-F7	Print/Fax
CTRL-F7	Notes
F10	Save As
SHIFT-F10	Open/Retrieve
SHIFT-F11	WP Characters
ALT-F11	Table Edit
CTRL-F11	Tab Set
SHIFT-F12	Bookmark
ALT-F12	Envelope
CTRL-F12	Save

If you are installing WordPerfect 6 for users without training in the new release, you might want to provide this cheat sheet of new function key assignments to post next to their computers.

If you or your users are not quite ready to change to the new WordPerfect 6 key assignments, you can select File Setup Environment WordPerfect 5.1 Keyboard.

Use Abbreviations to Shortcut Entries

TIP 11

Lengthy technical terms can be tedious to type. Instead, create a unique abbreviation and use it throughout your document. Before printing the document, use a macro that looks for the abbreviation and replaces it with the technical term or name of your organization. A simple WordPerfect 6 macro to replace one abbreviation is shown here:

```
DISPLAY(Off!)
SearchFindWholeWordsOnly(Yes!)
SearchString("ab")
ReplaceString("American Bar Association")
ReplaceForward()
```

You can edit this macro to change the abbreviation and replacement text by selecting **Tools Macro Record**, specifying FIXIT, and marking the check box to edit the macro.

FIXIT.WPM

This sample macro is available on the accompanying disk as FIXIT.WPM.

You can get much more sophisticated with replacements. If you have different replacements in different documents you might want the macro to prompt you for the abbreviation and replacement text. If you work with technical terms a lot, a complete glossary might be what you need. WordPerfect supplies a glossary macro with the product. Follow these steps to add your abbreviations to this glossary.

1. With the cursor on a blank line, select **T**ools **M**acro **P**lay.
2. Type **glossary** for the macro name and select OK. The glossary definition screen appears.
3. Select **C**reate.
4. Select **A**bbreviation and type your unique abbreviation. For example, you might use "ab" to represent the "American Bar Association".
5. Select **E**xpanded Form and type the full entry.
    For the "ab" example, you might type the full entry **American Bar Association.**
6. Select OK, continue to create more entries until they are all in, and select OK again.

To type an abbreviation and have WordPerfect make the replacement from your glossary entries, follow these steps:

1. Type the abbreviation.
2. Select **T**ools **M**acro **P**lay.
3. Select or type **glossary**and the replacement is made.

In WordPerfect 6, F1 Displays Help and ESC Exits Help

TIP 12

WordPerfect 6 has redefined the use of F1 and ESC. If you were using WordPerfect 5.1, it will take a little time to get used to. If you are new to WordPerfect, you will find that the new definitions follow industry standards. The keys are used as follows:

Key	Function
F1	Invokes Help features and is equivalent to selecting **Help** **C**ontents from the pull-down menu
ESC	Cancels the current request or restores deleted text

The Repeat feature that was formerly invoked with ESC can be accessed with CTRL-R

Many WordPerfect Features Add Codes to Your Document

TIP 13

As you make changes that affect the format of characters and the layout of text, WordPerfect adds codes to your document. To remove the changes that you make, you need to delete the hidden codes. To remove a code press ALT-F3 or F11 to display the Reveal Codes screen, move to the code, and press DEL. Consult Appendix A for the meaning of any codes that you are not familiar with.

Some Codes Are Paired, Others Are Not

Appendix A lists the codes you will see in your WordPerfect 6 documents. The codes for other releases of WordPerfect are similar but are sometimes spelled a little differently and do not include all the features for the later releases. Codes can be *paired* or *nonpaired*. Paired codes are for features that are turned on and off. When you get to the first code of the pair, the feature is turned on. When you get to the second code of the pair, the feature is turned off. Nonpaired codes stay in effect until the end of the document or until the code is entered again with new settings. Tab settings, for example, are nonpaired codes.

Some features, such as centering of text on a line, are turned off by a hard return

Paired Codes Appear at the Beginning and End of Selected Text

Many of the features you use in WordPerfect add hidden codes to your document. These codes are only visible from the Reveal Codes screen. Some codes are paired and are always ended by the second code in the pair. Paired codes always sandwich the text that they affect. If you want to enter more text at the location that is affected by those codes, you can move the cursor inside the codes and type it. If you want to type text without that formatting, you can simply press RIGHT ARROW until you are past the ending code and start typing.

Check the Reveal Codes Screen to See Settings

The Reveal Codes screen codes can show you more than the fact that a feature was invoked. For example, if you can't remember the tab settings, you can look at the tab code to see the actual settings.

WordPerfect 5.1 always provides all of the detail, but that is not the default setting in WordPerfect 6. To see all the detail for the codes in WordPerfect 6 follow these steps:

1. Select **V**iew Scree**n** Setup.
2. Select **R**eveal Codes.
3. Select **D**isplay Details and select OK.

Alternatively, when you highlight a code in the Reveal Codes screen, it expands to show you all of the detail.

You Can Copy Text in Typeover Mode and the Copy Will Not Replace Any Existing Text

As you are typing, Typeover and Insert modes are quite different, unless you are adding text to the end of the document. When you type text with the cursor in the middle of text in Typeover mode, each keystroke replaces a character on the screen.

However, Copy and Move work differently. Even though Typeover may be in effect, the text that you move or copy is added to existing text without replacing it. If you want to replace text, block and delete it and then copy or move the replacement text.

Hidden Codes Can Cause Your Cursor to Stay in the Same Place

When you want to move one position to the right or left, pressing LEFT ARROW or RIGHT ARROW once seems like the obvious solution, but it might not work in WordPerfect 5.1. WordPerfect 5.1 recognizes the hidden codes that are in the text, even though you might not see them. If you look at text in the Reveal Codes screen to see the codes, you will realize that the cursor is actually moving from code to code, though in the normal document screen it does not appear to move at all.

You Can Move Codes Just as You Can Move Text

If you put a formatting code in the wrong place, you can move it to the desired location. This may be quicker than deleting it and making menu and dialog box selections again. You may, for example, intend to change the tab settings before one section of your text and accidentally place it in another location. To move the new tab settings to the new place, follow these steps:

1. Display the Reveal Codes screen by pressing ALT-F3.
2. Use drag and drop to move the codes in WordPerfect 6. In WordPerfect 5.1, block them, press CTRL-F4, select Block, select Move, and press ENTER when your cursor is in the correct location.

When you are attempting to change the effect of paired codes, you want to delete one code in the pair, block the text that should be affected, and invoke the paired code feature again.

Use Reveal Codes If Your Text Looks Strange

Since some of WordPerfect's formatting features can be invoked with a keypress, you might make a typing mistake and make an unexpected change. As you look at your text on the screen you might notice that it appears to be indented or have formatting such as boldface or underlining that you did not want. Any time your screen does not match what you expect, you should display the Reveal Codes screen. You can move to the problem code and press DEL to eliminate the problem.

Use WordPerfect 6 Text Mode for Maximum Speed When Entering Text

WordPerfect's Graphics mode gives you a good idea of what your text will look like when printed. Boldface, changes in character size, the use of different fonts, and other changes appear on your screen as you make them. You can even see graphics images that you add to your text right on the screen. If you are a good typist, you will probably find that your typing can outpace the ability of the Graphics mode screen to display your input. WordPerfect will beep and not accept any of the letters that are typed while it is beeping. This causes you to lose your concentration, since you have to stop and look at the screen to see what it has accepted. If you are doing nothing but typing text, you will want to switch to Text mode until you have your text entered. To make this change:

Select **V**iew **T**ext Mode or click the Text Mode option on the Button Bar.

In WordPerfect 6 Use the Shortcut Keys

WordPerfect 6 has added some shortcut keys that you can invoke by pressing CTRL and a letter key. Most of these options can also be selected through a menu or dialog box, but you can save some time with these combinations:

Key Combination	Effect
CTRL-A	Compose a character
CTRL-C	Copy blocked text
CTRL-F	Find QuickMark
CTRL-I	Begin or end italics
CTRL-N	Return to use of the normal font
CTRL-O	Outline Edit
CTRL-P	Insert a page number with formatting
CTRL-R	Repeat keypress that follows
CTRL-S	Play a sound clip
CTRL-T	Toggle the list or paragraph number
CTRL-V	Paste
CTRL-W	Insert a WordPerfect Character
CTRL-X	Cut blocked text
CTRL-Z	Undo the last action

Special Options Let You Delete Quickly

Although DEL and BACKSPACE work fine, they only remove one character at a time. There are quicker options when you need to delete a lot of text.

- ❏ CTRL-BACKSPACE deletes the previous word.
- ❏ CTRL-DEL deletes the current word.
- ❏ CTRL-END deletes all the characters from the cursor's position to the end of the line.
- ❏ Block your text and press DEL to remove the entire block.
- ❏ You can also delete an entire sentence, paragraph, or page quickly with CTRL-F4.

Pressing HOME Freezes the Cursor In WordPerfect 6 Graphics Mode

In Graphics mode, the cursor normally flashes on and off. When you press HOME, this flashing stops, and the cursor freezes in either the on or off position. In other words, you might not see a cursor. Don't be confused by this. WordPerfect is waiting for you to press another key, since HOME is never used by itself.

You Might Not Be Able to Undelete as Much as You Think

Be sure you understand what constitutes one deletion, since you can only use Undelete with the last three deletions. Every time you move your cursor before deleting additional text, WordPerfect considers what you remove as a new deletion. For example, you can delete four consecutive words, and they will count as one deletion. If you next delete an extra space in three different locations, they will count as three deletions. After this, all WordPerfect can undelete are the three individual spaces. The words can no longer be undeleted, since they were the fourth previous deletion.

You can think of the way this works as WordPerfect having three scrap boxes. Each deletion is placed in a box after the box is emptied of a previous entry. Once you use the three boxes, one of them must be emptied to make room when you delete again. Undelete only has the contents of these three boxes available.

The keys for undeleting text have changed. In WordPerfect 5.1 you pressed F1 (Cancel) to undo the last deletion. In WordPerfect 6 you press ESC or select Edit Undelete. Once you invoke Undelete, the next step is the same in all releases as you choose to restore or look at a previous deletion.

Deleting Either Part of a Paired Code Deletes Both Parts

TIP 26

Paired codes are codes, such as boldface or underlining, that sandwich the text that they affect. When you add these features to your text, you need to take an action to both start and stop the feature. When you want to delete the feature, you do not need two actions. You can delete either the code that started the feature or the code that indicates the ending point for the feature. Either way, the feature no longer affects the text and both the start and stop code disappear at the same time.

WordPerfect 6 Deletes Codes with Text

TIP 27

WordPerfect 6 is set to delete codes in the Reveal Codes screen only. If you are working without the Reveal Codes displayed, WordPerfect skips over the code and moves to the first character after it whether you are using DEL or BACKSPACE to delete. WordPerfect 6 will delete paired codes, but only after the last character affected by the codes is deleted.

With the entries shown here, pressing BACKSPACE causes WordPerfect to display a prompt about deleting the [Bold Off] code only in release 5.1 if the bold feature was turned off after typing the word "text":

Bold is used for some **text**

In WordPerfect 6, the second "t" is deleted instead, unless Reveal Codes is displayed. With Reveal Codes displayed, both releases work the same and delete the ending Bold code.

Deleting Codes Does Not Display a Prompt with Reveal Codes Active

WordPerfect does not prompt you before deleting codes when Reveal Codes is displayed. WordPerfect assumes that you can see both text and codes in the bottom of the screen. If you make a mistake, you can always use the Undelete feature to restore either text or codes. See Tips 5 and 25 for how to use Undelete.

Watch the Use of Back Tab in Typeover Mode

Be careful about entering text, using SHIFT-TAB to insert a back tab, and then typing more text, since the new text you type might overwrite the original text.

Use a Hard Space to Keep Two Words on the Same Line

Some words should always remain as a group. These include the following types of entries:

Entry Type	Example
Date	April 28, 1993
	April 28
	April 1993
Time	11:15 P.M.
Names and titles	John Smith
	John Smith, Sr.
	John Smith, M.D.
	Mr. Smith
Measurements	3 feet
	200 miles

You can keep these words together by inserting a *hard space* between them. To insert a hard space in any location, press HOME and then SPACEBAR.

Hard Hyphens Can Separate Sections of a Compound Word

Compound words are broken with a hyphen. A few examples are *dog-and-pony show, pay-as-you-go taxes, up-to-date numbers, hit-or-miss strategy, well-behaved boy, ice-cold, baby-sit, and step-by-step* instructions. However, since WordPerfect uses the hyphen to separate words, your compound word might be split at the end of a line or checked by Speller as two words. To make WordPerfect treat a hyphenated word as one word, use a *hard hyphen*, which you can insert by pressing HOME, -. The hidden code for a hard hyphen is a hyphen, while the hidden code for a hyphen is [- Hyphen] in WordPerfect 6 and - in WordPerfect 5.1.

Soft Page Breaks and Hard Page Breaks Function Differently

Unlike some word processors, WordPerfect automatically paginates your text, splitting the pages in appropriate locations based on the margins and other page layout options. The soft page breaks that WordPerfect adds for you move from one location in your document to another as text is added or deleted. Hard page breaks are a request to break to a new page at the current location in your document.

Hard page *breaks* are added by pressing CTRL-ENTER. This feature forces a page break in a specific location, even if text is added or deleted. Hard page breaks are used when you want to create a title page or other part of a report where you want to keep the entries on a separate page.

You Cannot Delete Soft Page Breaks

There is nothing that you can do to delete a soft page break. If you delete all the text that required the soft page break, it will go away, but you cannot move or remove it directly. If you add or delete text, WordPerfect will automatically reposition it, but you cannot do anything with it directly.

You Can Tell a Hard Page Break from a Soft Page Break by the Symbols Used

A hard page break forces a break to the next page, whether or not the current page is full. A soft page break generates a page break at the current location because the page is full. If you change the margins or add or remove text, the location of a soft page break will change while a hard page break remains in the same location. You can tell by the symbol representing the page break what type you have. A soft page break looks like this:

A hard page break looks like this:

You can also differentiate between the two on the Reveal Codes screen where the code for a hard page break is [HPg] and a soft page break is [SPg].

If you press ENTER *on the last line of a page, rather than insert [HRt], WordPerfect inserts [HRt-SPg], moving the cursor to the next page.*

Soft and Hard Returns Serve Different Purposes

You will find both hard and soft returns used in WordPerfect to indicate the end of a line. Hard and soft returns serve two very different purposes and cannot be used interchangeably.

Soft return codes are automatically inserted by WordPerfect to end lines. WordPerfect inserts them when the line you are typing approaches the margin, wrapping text down to the next line and letting you continue typing. You do not insert a soft return code. When you add or delete text or change the left or right margins, WordPerfect changes the location where lines break. WordPerfect automatically

moves the soft return code to the new location in the text, reflecting the new positions of the line breaks. For example, if you change the left and right margins from one inch each to two inches each, the line lengths are shorter. WordPerfect automatically adjusts the location of the soft returns so that the text fits within the new margins.

You insert *hard return* codes [HRt] each time you press ENTER within your document. WordPerfect cannot move these hard return codes. Because of this, the only time you should use hard return codes is to create blank lines, to end a pargarph, or to end short lines of text. Hard returns mark the end of lines and of paragraphs. Each section of text that ends in a hard return code is considered a single paragraph by WordPerfect, even if that "paragraph" is only one word long.

You do not want to use hard return codes to mark the end of each line in a paragraph. WordPerfect will wrap the text of each line, using a soft return, if you change the margins or the text. For example, the following screen shows the effect of changing the margins for a paragraph typed using hard returns at the end of each line and a second paragraph that contains a hard return only at the end.

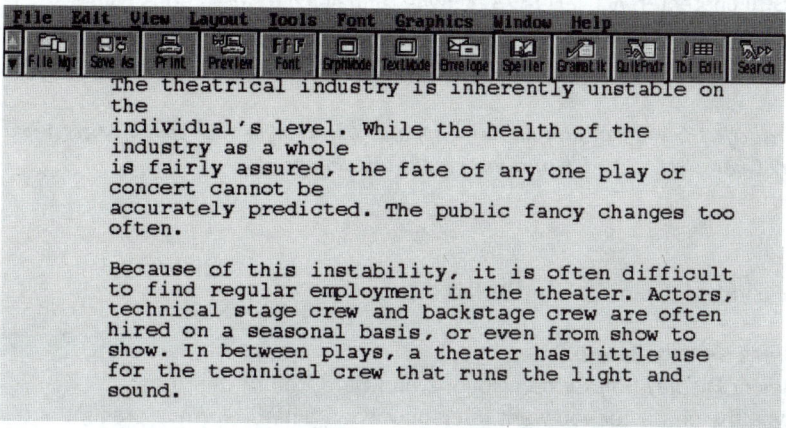

Display Hard Returns If You Are Used to Using a Typewriter

If you are used to using a typewriter, you are probably used to pressing the RETURN key at the end of each line. Though some advanced typewriters can wrap lines for you, you must watch when you are nearing the end of a line and press RETURN on most of them. This is a very bad habit to get into with

WordPerfect because WordPerfect uses word wrap to move you down to the next line of text. If you enter hard returns at the end of each line, you will quickly find that the formatting of your document is off, especially if you change font size or margins.

One way to help you remove all the unnecessary hard return codes you have entered is to display them. Usually, you have to open the Reveal Codes screen to show hidden codes, but with WordPerfect, you can assign a character to symbolize hard return codes and display that character in your text. This character will not print if you print the document, but it will appear on the screen and let you see easily where you have extra hard return codes in your document. Follow these steps in WordPerfect 6:

1. Select **V**iew Screen Setup.
2. Select **D**isplay Characters.
3. Select **H**ard Return Character and type a character in the text box. Make sure this character is not one that appears often in your documents.
   You might try pressing ALT and a number from the numeric keypad to insert an ASCII character. ALT-7, ALT-175, ALT-249, and ALT-250 are all possibilities.
4. Select OK.

In WordPerfect 6 you can also display a special character for each space. Select View Screen Setup Display Characters Space Characters to make this change.

The steps are a little different in WordPerfect 5.1:

1. Press SHIFT-F1 (Setup).
2. Select **D**isplay **E**dit Screen Options and **H**ard Return Character.
3. Type the character you want to display when a hard return is present and press ENTER.
4. Press F7 (Exit).

Avoid the Use of a Lowercase l for a 1 and an Uppercase O for 0 (Zero)

On a typewriter it is fine to type the letter l instead of the number 1. Likewise if a zero in needed, you can get by if you type the uppercase letter O.

This is never a good idea on the computer. It will not provide the results you expect if you try to resequence your data later with the Sort feature.

Slow the Key Repeat Speed If You Lose Text

When you press a key and hold it down, WordPerfect repeats the action of that key. For example, if you press the = key and hold it down, you can create a double line across your page. You may find it difficult to gauge how many characters will be added but you can control it with the Repeat option, discussed in Tip 65. However, deleting text might cause more of a problem, since you don't often know the exact number of characters that you want to delete. If you press and hold down the DEL or BACKSPACE key, you delete text that appears in your document. If the key responds too quickly, you might find that you have accidentally deleted much more text than you intended. You might find it helpful to change the cursor speed. This controls how quickly a key repeats when it is held down. This setting affects the arrow keys and any other keys that repeat when pressed, such as the letter and number keys and the deletion keys. To change the cursor speed in WordPerfect 5.1 or 6:

1. Press SHIFT-F1 (Setup) and select **E**nvironment.
2. Select **C**ursor Speed.
3. Select one of the available options. The options are expressed in terms of cps, or characters per second. Your choices are 15, 20, 30, 40, or 50 cps, or normal.
4. Press F7 to return to the document.

Terminate-and-stay-resident programs can affect the cursor speed. If you have any other program in memory, you might find that changing this setting is ineffective. To prevent errors, you might want to select Normal as your cursor speed, so that your WordPerfect setting does not conflict with the setting of any other program.

You Cannot Change Cursor Speed from WordPerfect When in Windows

If you are using WordPerfect in Windows, you will find that the cursor speed set with WordPerfect, which controls how quickly characters repeat when held down, does not actually change the cursor

speed or how fast your keys repeat. This is because WordPerfect uses the Windows setting for the speed of the key's repeat. When running WordPerfect in Windows, simply set your WordPerfect cursor speed to Normal and change the key repeat speed in the Windows Control Panel instead:

1. Select **F**ile, Se**t**up, and **E**nvironment.
2. Select **C**ursor Speed.
3. Select Normal
4. Select OK to return to the document.
5. Press CTRL-ESC to open the Active Task List, highlight Program Manager, and press ENTER.
6. Press ALT-W to open the **W**indows menu, highlight the Main program group in the menu, and press ENTER.
7. Double-click the icon labeled Control Panel in the Main program group window.
8. Double-click the icon labeled "Keyboard".
9. Select **R**epeat Rate and use the mouse to drag the scroll box in the appropriate direction.
10. Select OK, select **S**ettings, and select E**x**it to return to the Program Manager.

Some TSR (terminate-and-stay-resident) programs can interfere with your ability to change the speed of the cursor.

TIP 40 — Use Shortcuts to Move Quickly in Your Document

WordPerfect offers a number of shortcut keys that move the cursor around your document quickly. Although these keys can save time in WordPerfect 5.1, they are especially useful in WordPerfect 6 with Graphics mode, where each separate repositioning request causes WordPerfect to rewrite the screen. Pressing PGDN requires one screen rewrite whereas using the DOWN ARROW requires a rewrite for each time you press the DOWN ARROW key. These keys include the following:

Keypress	Cursor Movement
PGUP	Move the cursor to the preceding page.
PGDN	Move the cursor to the following page.

Keypress	Cursor Movement
END	Move the cursor to the end of the line.
HOME	Move the cursor in the direction of the arrow key that is pressed next. If you press the HOME key once before pressing an arrow key, the cursor moves to the edge of the screen in the direction of the arrow. Using the HOME and RIGHT ARROW key combination moves the cursor to the end of the line, rather than to the edge of the screen, if the line is not as wide as the screen. Pressing the HOME key twice before pressing the UP ARROW or DOWN ARROW key moves the cursor to the top or the bottom of the document.
CTRL-RIGHT ARROW	Move the cursor one word to the right.
CTRL-LEFT ARROW	Move the cursor one word to the left.
Gray – (Screen Up)	Move the cursor to the top of the screen. If pressed again, it moves the cursor to the previous screen.
Gray + (Screen Down)	Move the cursor to the bottom of the screen; if pressed again, moves the cursor to the following screen.
CTRL-HOME	Move the cursor to a specified character or page.

You Can Locate the Next Occurrence of a Character Quickly

41

You can quickly move the cursor to the next occurrence of a character. To do this, press CTRL-HOME, or select Edit Go to. When the Go to dialog box appears, type the character you want to locate. You must type the correct case. For example, if you type **A**, you will only find capital **A** letters, not lowercase ones. WordPerfect immediately moves the cursor to the right of the located character and closes the dialog box.

You cannot use this feature to find the next occurrence of a number, because when you enter a number in the Go To dialog box, WordPerfect thinks that you mean to move to that number page. If you do enter a number, you must press ENTER before the cursor will move, and this feature then moves you to the page with that number, or the closest page to it.

If the character you enter in the Go to dialog box is not within 2000 characters of your current location, WordPerfect makes your computer beep, because the character is too far away to find.

Create WordPerfect 6 Bookmarks to Act as Placeholders

With WordPerfect 6, you can create *bookmarks*, which act as placeholders in your text to help you move quickly between two locations. When you create a bookmark, WordPerfect inserts a hidden code, [Bookmark]. If you highlight this code in the Reveal Codes screen, the code reads [Bookmark:*name*], where *name* is the name you have assigned to the bookmark. Follow these steps:

1. Move the cursor to the location you want the bookmark to appear. If you want to apply the bookmark to a block of text, block that text.
2. Select **E**dit Boo**k**mark.
3. Select **C**reate, opening the Create Bookmark dialog box, type the name for the bookmark, and select OK. The default name is the line of text or the blocked text.
4. Select OK again to return to the document window.

You can find bookmarks quickly, which enables you to move quickly through large documents. For example, if you are creating a long report, you might want to put a bookmark at the start of every section of the report. You can move quickly between sections by finding the bookmark for the section you wanted to move to as follows:

1. Select **E**dit Boo**k**mark.
2. Highlight the bookmark you want to find in the Bookmark list box.
3. Select **F**ind. WordPerfect moves the cursor to immediately after the Bookmark hidden code.

When You Save a WordPerfect 6 Document, a Special Bookmark Is Inserted

When you save your document, WordPerfect 6 inserts a special bookmark called a *QuickMark*. You can use this feature to exit from your document and quickly return to where you left off. For example,

if you go to lunch, you might close a document to keep it from being read by others, return, retrieve the document, and find the QuickMark bookmark to return to work exactly where you left off.

There can only be one QuickMark bookmark in the document at any time. When you resave the document, or insert another QuickMark bookmark in another way, the original one is deleted.

WordPerfect offers a shortcut for finding a QuickMark bookmark. Instead of going through the menu, simply press CTRL-F to move to the location of the QuickMark bookmark in your document.

Hard Spaces Keep Together Two Words You Don't Want Separated

When you have two words that you do not want to have separated, you can insert a hard space between the two components. WordPerfect treats words separated by a hard space as a single word. For example, you might use a hard space between two elements of a name to prevent the name being treated as two words and being split at the end of the line.

While a hard space prevents two words from being separated by a soft return code, it does not control the size of that space if you are using full justification. WordPerfect will adjust the size of the space depending on how much space is needed to make the words on the line reach the left and right margins, even though it is a hard space.

The Use of Hard Hyphens Affects How WordPerfect Splits Words

If you type a hyphen character to separate compound words, WordPerfect assumes that the hyphen is where the word should be hyphenated, if it needs to be hyphenated. If you use a hard hyphen, as discussed in Tip 31, WordPerfect treats the entire entry as one word and follows its regular hyphenation procedures. Hard hyphens are added by pressing HOME and typing a hyphen (-).

When WordPerfect hyphenates a word, it first checks its hyphenation dictionary to see where it is appropriate to hyphenate the word. If a regular hyphen is in the word, this is the first place that WordPerfect will select for hyphenating the word. If WordPerfect cannot find the word in its hyphenation dictionary, it then prompts you to tell it where to hyphenate the word.

Press HOME an Extra Time to Move to a Position in Front of Codes

When you press HOME and an arrow key, WordPerfect moves the cursor to the beginning or end of the line or to the top or bottom of the screen. However, if you open the Reveal Codes screen, you will see that the cursor has not moved beyond the codes at that location. For example, if there are paragraph numbering codes at the beginning of the line, pressing HOME and LEFT ARROW moves you to the beginning of the text, but after the paragraph numbering codes. If you want to position the cursor in front of the codes, in order to insert text that is not affected by those codes, you need to press HOME a second time. If you press HOME, HOME, and LEFT ARROW, you move before the paragraph numbering code, and can enter text before the codes.

When you press HOME, HOME, and UP ARROW or DOWN ARROW, you move to the beginning or the end of the document. Again, though, you do not move past the codes at the beginning or end of the document. To do so, press HOME a third time before pressing the arrow key. You cannot move before the initial styles code at the beginning of the document, which sets the default features for the document.

Use the + and – Keys on the Numeric Keypad to Move Quickly in a Document

Two cursor-movement keys that are often forgotten are the gray + and – keys on the right side of the numeric keypad. These keys move the cursor one screen up or down, respectively. Like the other keys on the numeric keypad, these keys change function depending on the status of the NUMLOCK key. When NUMLOCK is on, these keys insert a + or a – character into the document. When NUMLOCK is off, they move the cursor.

Press CTRL-HOME and Type a Number to Move to a Specific Page in Your Document

You can use the Go to feature to quickly move to the top of a specific page in your document. To use this feature, press CTRL-HOME or select Edit Go to (Search Go to in 5.1), opening the Go to dialog box. Then type the number of the page you want to move to and press ENTER. WordPerfect moves the cursor to the beginning of that page, after the codes, and clears the dialog box from the screen. You will find this feature particularly helpful if you have a long document in which the usual cursor movement keys are too slow.

Pressing CTRL-HOME, CTRL-HOME Places the Cursor in Its Last Position

Sometimes you want to perform two different operations on the same block of text. Rather than select the text again with the mouse or arrow keys, you can use a special technique to select it quickly. After blocking the text and performing the first operation, follow these steps to select it again:

1. Press F12 or ALT-F4 to turn on Block.
2. Press CTRL-HOME, CTRL-HOME. The text selection is reblocked.
3. Perform the second operation.

You Can Align Text on a Symbol Other Than the Decimal Point

WordPerfect's decimal tabs will align with a period or decimal point. You can change this to another character. For example, you can change it to a $ if you want entries to align on this character. In WordPerfect 6, this character is set by selecting Layout Character Decimal/Align Character and typing

the character to use in place of a period. In 5.1, you select Layout or press SHIFT-F8, select **Other Decimal/Align Character**, and type the character to use. WordPerfect adds the code [Dec/Align Char] or [Decml/Algn Char:*character*,,]. The code is in effect from the point you insert it to the end of the document. When you use the decimal align character, you see a reminder that the character will be used to align entries. As a word of caution, WordPerfect uses the same alignment character for the decimal point. If you change the character, you change what WordPerfect looks for in math totals and displays in calculated results.

Suppose, for example, you have a column of times (7:30, 8:29, 9:10, and so on) that you want to align on the colons. To do this, you change the decimal align character as described above to a colon, set the decimal tab stops that you will use, and enter the times in the columns you want. After you have finished, you will want to return the decimal align character to a period so you can use math features or use the period for an alignment character again. An example of a document that does this is shown here:

```
 File   Edit   View   Layout   Tools   Font   Graphics   Window   Help
 File Mgr  Save As  Print  Preview  Font  GrphMode TextMode Envelope Speller Gramatik QuikFindr Tbl Edit Search
```

Winners of Country Cash Contest:

Song Played	Call Received	Name
11/17		
7:30 AM	7:32 AM	Ryder, Elizabeth
8:29	8:32	Landers, Lawrence
9:10	9:11	Sanders, Terry
3:22 PM	3:24 PM	Anderson, Lee
4:18	4:23	Summers, Jane
5:42	5:43	Jump, Drake
6:12	6:13	Forney, Jill
7:22	7:24	Webster, Sam
8:41	8:43	Campbell, Fran
9:23	9:24	Madsen, Justin

TIP 51   Align Codes Are Not Where You Expect to Find Them

WordPerfect handles aligning the characters at a tab stop. The only codes added to the document are the ones placed at the beginning of the text to be aligned with the next tab stop. These codes are [Lft Tab] in 6.0 or [Tab] in 5.1, [Cntr Tab], [Rgt Tab], and [Dec Tab]. WordPerfect does not add any codes at the center point that WordPerfect uses for aligning a center tab, indicating the decimal character used for a decimal tab, or at the rightmost point of text aligned at a right tab.

Use Comments to Provide Reminders

Comments are a great way to include reminders in text. You can use them to remind you to get the needed details such as a phone number or address to add to a letter. See Tip 71 for more information on comments.

Use TAB Rather Than SPACEBAR to Align Text

A tab will always indent text by the distance set by the tab stops but a space's width changes according to the font the text uses. It is difficult to have columns line up when you use the SPACEBAR rather than TAB, especially if you use a proportional font. The easiest way to see the difference is to look at the text illustrated here. The two columns on the left side were aligned using spaces and the two columns on the right side were aligned using the TAB key. You can see that the second column does not quite line up.

File Edit View Layout Tools Font Graphics Window Help				
File Mgr Save As Print Preview Font GrphMode TextMode Envelope Speller GramLik QuikFndr Tbl Edit Search				
Total Annual Commission		Total Annual Commission		
Name	Commission	Name	Commission
Bender, Sam	$13,432	Bender, Sam	$13,432
Collins, Jill	$25,234	Collins, Jill	$25,234
Johns, Ila	$21,129	Johnson, Mary	$21,129
Landers, John	$12,439	Landers, John	$12,439
Thomas, Kim	$23,329	Thomas, Kim	$23,329

The difference between using tabs and spaces is more noticeable when you are using a proportional font. You can convert from using spaces to tabs by using ALT-F2 or using the command Edit Replace in 6.0 or Search Replace in 5.1. For the text to search for, you can search for five spaces. For the text to replace the spaces with you can enter the code [Lft Tab] or [Tab].

Pressing TAB in Typeover Mode Moves the Cursor

In Typeover mode, when you press TAB, WordPerfect does not replace the character at the cursor's location with a tab. Instead, if you are in text, WordPerfect moves to the next tab stop. This can be every five or so characters depending on the font size and style. If the line is empty, or if you use TAB to go beyond the end of the line, WordPerfect adds tabs to the document but does not replace any hard or soft returns.

The Appearance of Indented Text Will Change When Tab Settings Are Altered

The tabs in a document use the tab stops in effect for that location in the document. If you change the tab stop settings, WordPerfect adjusts the document to use these new tab stops. For example, suppose you have tab stops set to every half inch and then you change them to every inch. Text that you have entered after two tab stops is now two inches from the left margin instead of one inch because the second tab stop is now two inches away, rather than one inch.

Use WordPerfect's Convert Case Feature to Change Capitalization

If you have entered text using the wrong capitalization style, you can have WordPerfect adjust the capitalization. To do this, select the block. Then select Edit Convert Case or press SHIFT-F3. At this point, you can select whether to convert every letter in the block to uppercase or lowercase letters. In WordPerfect 6, you also have a proper case choice, which makes the first letter of every word uppercase, with subsequent letters in the word lowercase.

If You Have Accidentally Entered Text Using All Uppercase Letters, Let WordPerfect Switch the Case for You

When you have accidentally pressed CAPS LOCK and typed text all in uppercase, you can block the text and change its case. You will want to block sentences starting with the second letter of the sentence so the first letter in the sentence remains uppercase. Another option is to start the selection of text at the space before the beginning of the sentence so that WordPerfect can recognize that it is the beginning of a sentence. When you convert text to lowercase with Edit Convert Case, WordPerfect leaves the first letter of a sentence as uppercase.

Changing to lowercase does not change every letter in the block. When a block has sentences in it, the first letter of each sentence remains uppercase while other letters are changed. Also, the letter I by itself remains uppercase. For example, you might have the following sentence:

I will meet Greg at 6 PM. HE AND I WILL GO OUT TO DINNER.

To fix the second sentence, move to the space before HE and block the rest of the sentence. Selecting Edit Convert Case and then Lowercase in 6.0 or To Lower in 5.1 will change the sentence to look like this:

I will meet Greg at 6 PM. He and I will go out to dinner.

Correcting Transposed Words with a Macro

Typing words in reverse order is frustrating, since you have to switch the order yourself, rather than have WordPerfect do it for you. You can use a simple macro that handles switching words for you. The macro's contents are shown here:

```
DISPLAY(Off!)
BlockOn(CharMode!)
PosWordNext
Cut
PosWordNext
Paste
```

WORD.WPM

This sample macro is available on the accompanying disk as WORD.WPM.

TIP 59 — Correcting Transposed Letters with a Macro

Another frequent cause of mistakes in a document is transposed letters. The Speller will catch some but if the entry is for a word not in the Speller, you will have to make the change yourself. You can use a simple macro that handles switching letters for you. The macro's contents are shown here:

```
DISPLAY(Off!)
BlockOn(CharMode!)
PosCharNext
Cut
PosCharNext
Paste
```

ALTW.WPM

This sample macro is available on the accompanying disk as ALTW.WPM.

TIP 60 — The Overstrike Feature Might Let You Create Some Special Characters Without a Graphics Printer

WordPerfect can create over 1500 special characters if you have a graphics printer. Characters that the printer does not support directly are created by WordPerfect. Without a graphics printer, you can only create the characters on your keyboard. Your printer might support printing two characters in a single location. If it does you can use the Overstrike feature to print two characters in the same location. You

might want to approximate the symbol for yen with a Y and an equal sign or show a zero with a slash through it by typing **0** and **/** in the same location.

To use Overstrike in WordPerfect 6, follow these steps:

1. Select **L**ayout Cha**r**acter.
2. Select Create **O**verstrike.
3. Type the characters you want to print in the same location, such as **Y =** to create a yen symbol.
4. Select OK.

To use the Overstrike feature in WordPerfect 5.1, follow these steps:

1. Press SHIFT-F8 (Format) and choose **O**ther
2. Select **O**verstrike and select **C**reate.
3. Type the characters you want to Print in the same location, such as **Y =** to create a yen symbol.

You are not limited to two characters with the Overstrike feature.

Use the WordPerfect Overstrike Feature to Create a Fraction

You can create any fraction without using the equation editor. All you need to do is start to create an overstrike character and access the font attributes needed for superscripts and subscripts. After telling WordPerfect 6 you want to create an overstrike character, you can use the following steps to create the fraction 7/8 (similar steps will handle the task in 5.1):

1. Press CTRL-F8, select **P**osition, and select Sup**r**script. WordPerfect adds the code for turning superscript on.
2. Type **7**.

3. Press CTRL-F8, select **P**osition, and select Su**p**rscript. WordPerfect adds the code for turning superscript off.
4. Press - (hyphen). In WordPerfect 5.1, a hard hyphen is needed (HOME -).
5. Press CTRL-F8, select **P**osition, and select Su**b**script.
6. Type **8**.
7. Press CTRL-F8, select **P**osition, and select Su**b**script.
8. Select OK.

 *You can use appearance attributes with Overstrike to add variety to the characters you create. Once you start to create an overstrike character, you can press CTRL-F8 to access appearance attributes. The first selection will turn the attribute on and the second will turn it off. This allows you to add bold to one character and not the others.*

ASCII Codes Can Be Used to Type Some Special Characters

You can use ALT and type a number with the numeric keypad to create any of the characters in the ASCII character set. This character set is sometimes referred to as the IBM character set. If you press ALT-1, for example, a happy face will appear, since the code for this character is 1.

WordPerfect Has Several Options for Creating a Compose Character

WordPerfect supports the use of many different characters beyond the ones on your keyboard. These include foreign characters, scientific symbols, digraphs, and diacritical marks. WordPerfect can create any of the characters found in the file CHARMAP.TST if you have a graphics printer. You can retrieve this file from your WordPerfect program directory to examine a series of character maps that look like this:

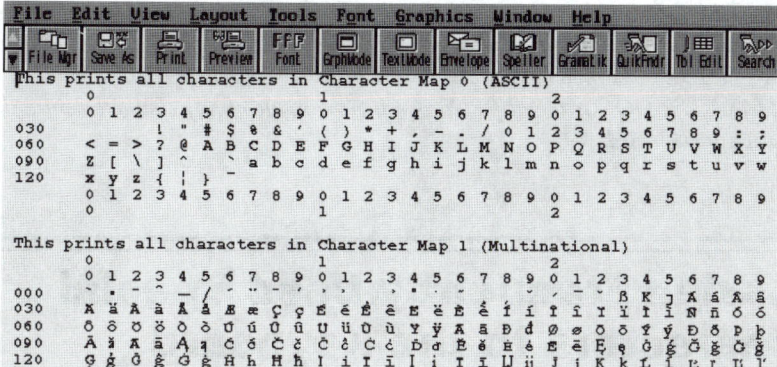

WordPerfect will create any of the more than 1500 characters in these maps graphically if your printer does not support them. The techniques that you can use for creating these compose characters depend on whether you are using WordPerfect 5.1 or WordPerfect 6. The instructions are listed separately for the two releases, due to the many differences:

WordPerfect 6 steps with CTRL-A:

1. Press CTRL-A.
2. Type two characters with no separator to have them overprint, as in **Y=** to create a yen symbol, or type the number of the character code map from WP characters and the character number, separated by a space.

WordPerfect 6 steps using WordPerfect characters:

1. Select F**o**nt WP **C**haracters or press CRTL-W.
2. Select **S**et and choose the character set you want to use.
3. Select **C**haracters, choose the desired characters, and select **I**nsert.

As an alternative in either WordPerfect 5.1 or 6, you can press ALT *and type the number representing the ASCII code from the IBM Character set that you want to use.*

WordPerfect 5.1 steps:

1. Press CTRL-V or CTRL-2 to display a Key = message.
2. Type the number of the character map, type **,** (a comma), type the character number from the map, and press ENTER.

 *CHARACTR.DOC, another file provided with WordPerfect, also displays character codes. You can display it with graphics print turned off to see which codes your printer supports. However, CHARACTR.DOC is a much longer file than CHARMAP.TXT, as it only shows one character per line. CHARACTR.DOC is useful for discovering the name of any character, since this additional information is also listed.*

Assign Frequently Used Special Characters to the Keyboard

You can create your own custom keyboard layout. This is useful if you use many special symbols and characters or if you want to assign macros to specific keypresses. A custom keyboard layout even allows you to redefine the use of the function keys. WordPerfect has several alternative keyboards that you can try. To change to another keyboard, follow these steps:

1. Press SHIFT-F1 (Setup).
2. Select **K**eyboard Layout.
3. You can select another keyboard layout at this point, edit an existing layout or create your own custom layout.

You will learn more about creating a custom keyboard in Tip 925.

Use CTRL-R to Duplicate Characters Quickly

You can duplicate characters by holding down the key you want and letting the autorepeat feature take effect, but the number of repetitions is difficult to project. A better way is to use the Repeat feature. Just press CTRL-R in WordPerfect 6 or ESC in WordPerfect 5.1 and type the character you want to have automatically duplicated eight times (WordPerfect's default repeat value is 8). Tip 67 tells you how to change the number of repeats either temporarily or permanently.

Eliminating Text Quickly with Repeat and Quick Delete

The Repeat feature (CTRL-R in WordPerfect 6, ESC in WordPerfect 5.1) can be combined with quick delete options covered in Tip 23. For example, if you want to delete the next three words, invoke the Repeat feature and press CTRL-DEL.

You Can Set a New Repeat Value with Every Use

WordPerfect's default repeat value is 8. If you request the Repeat feature (CTRL-R in WordPerfect 6, ESC in WordPerfect 5.1) instead of typing a keystroke to repeat, you can tell WordPerfect to change the repeat value. To change the repeat value for one use:

1. Press CTRL-R in WordPerfect 6 or ESC in WordPerfect 5.1.
2. Type a new repeat value that you want.
3. Type the keystroke you want to repeat.

To change the repeat value for your entire WordPerfect session, press ENTER after typing the new repeat value.

Changing the Repeat Value Allows You to Draw Lines of Equal Length

The Repeat feature (CTRL-R in WordPerfect 6, ESC in WordPerfect 5.1) is a great time saver when you need to draw many lines in a document that are all the same length. Change the repeat value and draw the lines where you need them. Follow this procedure to add the lines:

1. Position the cursor at the location of the first line.
2. Press CTRL-R in WordPerfect 6 or ESC in WordPerfect 5.1.

3. Type the new repeat value for the length of the lines and press ENTER.
4. Press CTRL-R or ESC and press the _ (underscore) key.

Make Repeated Copies Without Selecting Text Again

69

If you need to copy text to several locations, the procedure for subsequent copies does not need to duplicate the procedure for the first copy, if you make them all at the same time. In WordPerfect 6, you can continue selecting Edit Paste without telling it which text to copy again. In WordPerfect 5.1 use CTRL-F4 and select Retrieve and Block to make the additional copies.

Add Copy Editing Notes Using Document Comments

70

Comments offer an easy way to add copy editing comments to text without changing it. You might start your comment with the name of the author and include requests for editing changes in text. If you have already made the changes, this is a good way to ask the author to review the edits that you have made in sections of text.

Comments can be a good way to get the input from a number of people. Each person can add comments where needed.

You Can Change Comments Into Text

71

If you want to verify a section of text before including it in the final document or are uncertain about deleting a section of text, you might want to make it a comment. This way it will not appear in any printout, but you can restore it to the document easily if you decide to. Comments will appear on your edit screen in a box like this so you cannot forget that they are in the document:

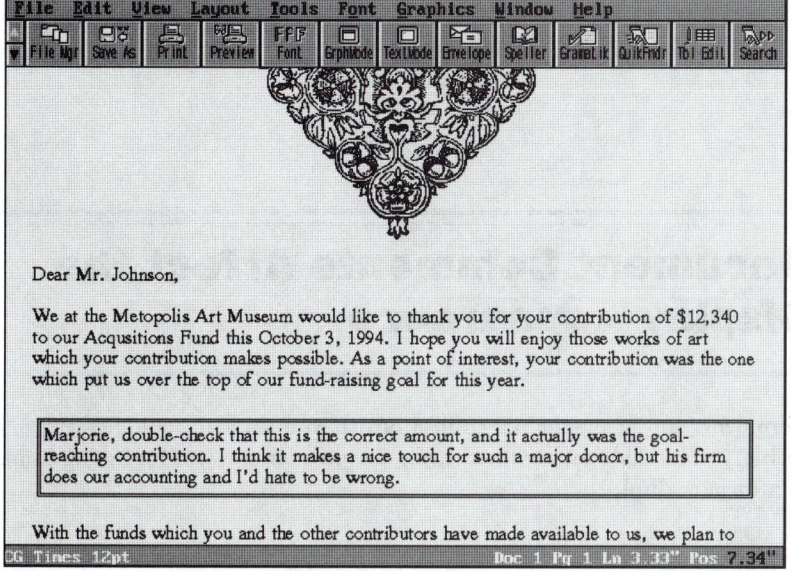

To change a section of WordPerfect 6 text into a comment:

1. Block the text.
2. Select **L**ayout Comme**n**t and select **C**reate.

To change a WordPerfect 6 comment into text:

1. Move the cursor to a location just after the comment.
2. Choose **L**ayout Comme**n**t Convert to **T**ext.

To change a section of text into a comment in WordPerfect 5.1:

1. Block the text.
2. Press CTRL-F5 and respond with Yes.

To change a WordPerfect 5.1 comment into text:

1. Move the cursor to a location just after the comment.
2. Press CTRL-F5, and then select **C**omment Convert to **T**ext.

WOODCARV.PCX

The graphic in the letterhead is available on the accompanying disk as WOODCARV.PCX.

Document Comments Affect the Display Appearance

Document comments appear on the screen in a box. If you want to look at the text without the comments visible, you can hide the comments. Tip 78 provides the steps for hiding comments if you no longer want them to display.

Document Comments Can Contain Character Enhancements

You do not have to worry about losing special formatting features when you turn a passage of text into comment. This is retained and can even be added to new comment entries if you type them. If you later turn these comments back into text, the formatting will still be there.

You Can Change Entries in Document Comments

You can edit document comments, but not from the regular typing screen. You need to select the Edit option under document comments to alter anything that appears on the screen in a documents box.

Use Document Comments to Temporarily Keep Text That Might Be Deleted Later

Don't be too quick to delete text. If you are uncertain about removing text from your document you can always make it into a comment. It will not print and can be restored easily.

Use Document Comments When You Want to Remove Text Temporarily

When you are working with a long document and want to focus on a few sections, you can mark a large section of the document as a comment and choose not to display the comments, as described in Tip 78.

To Print Comments, Make Them Text Temporarily

WordPerfect does not provide an option for printing comments within a document. If you have a lengthy comment or two, you might want a hard copy to help resolve an outstanding issue. The only way to accomplish what you want is to convert the comment to text, print the document, and then make the text back into a comment. You can make these changes with macros.

Sample macros are available on the accompanying disk as COMMENT.WPM and UNCOMMNT.WPM.

COMMENT.WPM
UNCOMMNT.WPM

To use COMMENT, block the text you want to make into a comment and run the macro COMMENT. To place an existing comment into the text, position the cursor on the comment and run the macro UNCOMMNT.

Delete the Comment Code, and You Delete the Comment Text

Any place you have a comment in your document there is a [Comment] code that precedes it on the Reveal Codes screen. If you delete this code, the comment text is also removed from the document.

If you want to keep comments, yet have them temporarily removed from the display, you can hide them. In WordPerfect 6 you would select View Screen Setup and choose Window Options, making sure that the check box for Display Comments does not contain an X. In WordPerfect 5.1 you need to select SHIFT-F1 (Setup), choose Display Edit Screen Options Comments Display, and select No.

Get Comfortable for Maximum Efficiency

If you only need to type a sentence or two you can probably stand hunched over your computer and do a good job. If you have a significant amount of typing to do, you can reduce errors and be more comfortable if you consider the following:

❑ **Type of chair** Specially designed computer chairs that place some of your weight on your knees can help you achieve an erect position that is good for your back. This type of chair does not have a backrest, as shown here:

You can get one with adjustable seat height and casters if you are willing to order a more expensive model from an office furniture store. Cheaper models are available at all the discount houses. Other models of office chairs can also meet your needs. Try out a few options before deciding on the model you can sit in for eight hours a day.

❑ Chair height Regardless of the type of chair selected, adjustable height should be a mandatory feature. When you sit in a standard office chair, your thighs should not tilt up or down and should be parallel with the floor.

❑ Monitor position Monitors should be placed slightly below the level of your eyes. Placing the monitor in a location where it does not pick up reflected light can save eyestrain. If you cannot avoid reflected light sources, buy an antiglare cover for the monitor screen.

❑ Keyboard height Your keyboard is at the right height when there is almost no upward bend to your wrists as you type. You can change the height of your chair to minimize the problem or buy wrist pads to place on the desk or table to provide support for your wrists.

❑ Paper holder A paper holder designed to hold the paper that you are typing from. You can buy stationary models that sit next to your computer or clip-on arms that attach to the computer. Rather than needing to look down at the desk as you type you can look to the side and read from the manuscript, minimizing neck strain.

CHAPTER 2

Page and Paragraph Formatting

Automatic Format Settings Affect Your Documents

Every new document you create starts off with a set of initial settings. You can change the initial settings for one document or for all new ones. The initial settings set the default settings for many WordPerfect features.

WordPerfect 6 inserts the Initial Codes style in a document automatically. This code appears as [Open Style:InitialCodes] when you reveal the document's codes. This code cannot be deleted. If you want to change them in WordPerfect 6, you need to edit the Initial Codes style. Tip 82 contains more information about changing the contents of the Initial Codes style.

WordPerfect 5.1 also has default settings that affect the appearance of your document. The initial codes do not appear as part of the document's codes. To alter the settings for WordPerfect 5.1 you need to change the Initial Settings Initial Codes on the Setup menu.

The default settings for many of WordPerfect's settings are shown here. They are almost identical for both WordPerfect 5.1 and 6.

Format	Settings for WordPerfect 5.1 and 6
Margins	Top - 1"; Bottom - 1"; Left - 1"; Right - 1"
Line Spacing	Single
Justification	Left for WordPerfect 6 and Full for WordPerfect 5.1
Font	Printer Default
Tab Settings	Every 1/2"
Page Size	8 1/2" × 11"

Maintaining the Current Document Defaults by Typing a Blank Space Before Retrieving a File

If you retrieve a file into an existing file, the existing file's initial code settings are used for the combined text from both documents. The initial code settings from the file you are retrieving are ignored. If,

however, you open a document or retrieve a file into a blank document, the retrieved or opened document's initial codes are used. If you want to use an existing document without its initial codes, press the SPACEBAR and use File Retrieve to retrieve the document. In WordPerfect 6, using File Open will always put the document in a new window. You can retrieve a document into a new document specifically to use the file without its default codes.

Use Document Initial Codes to Organize Codes and Prevent Deletion

TIP 82

The codes at the beginning of your document can clutter up the Reveal Codes screen. They can also be deleted easily. Since these are the initial settings for the document, you might find it better to move them to the Initial Codes screen. Codes put in the document's initial codes—rather than the beginning of the document's text—also affect extended text, such as headers, footnotes, and text in graphics boxes. Putting these codes in the initial codes groups them in one location and provides better organization. To transfer codes from the beginning of the document to the document's initial codes, follow these steps:

1.   Press ALT-F3 to reveal the document's codes.
2.   Block the codes that you want to move.
3.   Press CTRL-DEL, the shortcut for **E**dit **M**ove, or **E**dit Cut and Past**e**.
4.   Select **L**ayout or press SHIFT-F8 and select **D**ocument.
5.   Select **I**nitial Codes or Document Initial **C**odes, depending on the WordPerfect version you are using.
6.   Press ENTER to put the codes in the current dialog box or screen. You can also enter any other codes you want the document to use.
7.   Press F7 until you return to the document.

You Can Change Two Types of Initial Codes

TIP 83

There are two types of initial codes you can use to create default codes for your document. One feature, the Document Initial Codes, described in Tip 82, sets the codes that are the current document's initial codes. The Initial Codes Setup feature sets the codes for all new documents.

To set the Initial Codes for new WordPerfect 5.1 documents:

1. Select **F**ile Se**t**up or press SHIFT-F1.
2. Select **I**nitial Settings and Initial **C**odes.
3. Add the formatting you want to apply to the document.
4. Press F7 (Exit) until you return to the document.

To set the Initial Codes for new WordPerfect 6 documents:

1. Select **L**ayout or press SHIFT-F8.
2. Select **D**ocument and Initial Codes Se**t**up.
3. Add the formatting you want to apply to the document.
4. Press F7 until you return to the document.

With either version of WordPerfect you can, in step 3, use either the menu or function keys to add WordPerfect features you want in every new document.

Use the Easiest Way to Apply Paragraph Formatting

WordPerfect 6 offers many ways to apply paragraph formatting changes. You will want to find the methods that are easiest for you. For example, you can change indentation by pressing F4 or SHIFT-F4, or you can select from the Layout Alignment submenu (Align in WordPerfect 5.1). You can change justification for a paragraph by selecting from the Layout Justification menu (Justify in WordPerfect 5.1), by selecting from WordPerfect 6's Ribbon, or by selecting Layout Line Justification and selecting one of the options. When you have multiple methods of adding the same feature, WordPerfect adds the same code so the results are the same, regardless of the method.

Changing the Page Size Changes the Line Length Without Changing Margins

When you change the page size, the margins are not affected. If you change the paper size from 8 1/2 × 11 inches to 6 × 4 inches, the default 1-inch margins will be used unless you have changed them.

WordPerfect adjusts the line length and the number of lines that will fit on a page to correspond to the new page size. For example, when the page size is 8 1/2 × 11 inches, the line length is 6 1/2 inches (8 1/2 minus 2), and 54 lines of Courier 10cpi will fit on a page. If you change the page size to 6 × 4 inches, the line length is 4 inches (6 minus 2), and 12 lines of Courier 10cpi will fit on a page.

To set the page size in WordPerfect 5.1:

1. Select **L**ayout **P**age Paper **S**ize.
2. Highlight the page size you want to use and choose **S**elect.
3. Press F7 (Exit) to return to the document.

To set the page size in WordPerfect 6:

1. Select **L**ayout **P**age Page **S**ize/Type.
2. Highlight the page size to use and choose **S**elect.
3. Select OK to return to the document.

When you change to a smaller page size, consider changing the margins to 1/2 inch; otherwise you will have too much white space in relation to the amount of text on the page.

In WordPerfect 6, You Can Set Paragraph Margins Separately from Document Margins

When you want one or just a few paragraphs to use different margins than the rest of the document, you can change the margin settings just for those paragraphs. This is easier to do in WordPerfect 6 than WordPerfect 5. In WordPerfect 6, block to select the paragraphs. Next, select Layout Margins and enter the margins for the selected paragraphs. When you select OK, only the selected paragraphs have the different margins. If you look at the codes, you will see codes for the margins you have changed. The codes at the beginning of the modified paragraphs have a + sign and the codes at the end (the ones that return the margins to the document's primary margin setting) have a – sign.

To change the margin settings for one or just a few paragraphs in WordPerfect 5.1, you must move to the beginning of the paragraphs and add the code yourself for the new margin setting. Then move to the end of the paragraphs and add the code that returns to the previous margin setting.

To change left margins of paragraphs or both left and right margins by increments of the tab stops, move to each paragraph and press F4 *or* SHIFT-F4.

Using Different Measurements for Margins or Tab Settings

In WordPerfect, you can enter tab settings, margins, and several other sorts of distance measurements. You can use any of the measurement systems WordPerfect accepts. Initially, inches is the default setting for measurements. Any time you enter a measurement, WordPerfect assumes you are using the default measurement system. However, when you want to use a measurement system that is not the same as WordPerfect's default setting, you must tell WordPerfect what measurement system you want to use by adding a letter after the measurement. Type **c** or **p** after a margin or tab setting to specify centimeters or points instead of the default measurement (inches). (If you are using the centimeters measurement system, you can type " to tell WordPerfect that a measurement is in inches.)

Checking the Current Margin Settings If You Need To

To see the current margin settings, start the command that changes the margins and then abandon the command. In WordPerfect 5.1, select Layout or press SHIFT-F8 and select Line for left and right margins or Page for top and bottom margins. In WordPerfect 6, select Layout or press SHIFT-F8 and select Margins. You can also see the margins in Graphics or Page display mode or when you preview the document. Changing the margins uses the same Layout Margins command.

If you do not like the location of the page breaks, you might want to look at the Block Protect or Conditional End of Page features, as discussed in Tips 140 and 141. These features keep blocks of text together.

Changing Where Words Wrap by Altering the Margin Settings

TIP 89

If you want to change where words wrap on the page, you need to alter the margin setting. The right margin changes the location of the word wrap from the right edge of the paper, but changing the left margin also has an effect, since it changes the length of the line.

Be Careful of the Cursor Location When You Change Margins in WordPerfect 5.1

TIP 90

Since WordPerfect 5.1 places hidden codes at the location the cursor occupies when you are making the margin change, be sure to place the cursor exactly where you want the new margins. If you are not careful about positioning the cursor, your codes will not take effect where you expect them to.

Top and bottom margins should be changed at the top of a page. You can press CTRL-HOME, type the page number, and press ENTER to move to the top of the page. If you add a code for new top or bottom margins in the middle of the page, the change does not take effect until the beginning of the next page.

Left and right margins should be changed at the beginning of a line. You can press HOME and LEFT ARROW to move to where you want to add the code. If you add a code for new left or right margins in the middle of a line, the changes do not take effect until the next line.

WordPerfect 6 Moves Margin Settings to the Correct Location

TIP 91

WordPerfect 6 has a default auto code placement. This feature takes away the burden of positioning the cursor in exactly the right spot before changing a setting. If you are not at the beginning of a page when you change the top or bottom margin, WordPerfect moves the code to the top of the page. If you are not at the beginning of the paragraph when you change the right or left margin, WordPerfect automatically moves the code to the beginning of the paragraph.

Substructures Are Not Affected by Margin Changes in the Document

A document contains substructures that are not part of the document you enter in the main editing window. Substructures include headers, footers, watermarks, endnotes, comments, entry fields, and text in graphics boxes. Substructures are like miniature documents that have their own code settings. By thinking of them as miniature documents, you can understand why changing the margins, as well as many other WordPerfect changes, have no effect on substructures. Substructures are only affected by codes in the substructure and in the document's initial codes. Substructures in WordPerfect 6 are also affected by any codes in the substructure's style, as described in Tip 423. When you want to change a setting for both the document and the substructures (such as changing the margins), change the document's initial codes, as described in Tip 82. When you want to change the setting for just one substructure, edit it and add the code there for the new formatting change. For example, if you want a header to have different margins than the document, edit the header and change the margins there.

Adding Line Numbers to Make Discussion Easy

When you distribute a manuscript for discussion at a meeting, it is often difficult to pinpoint the location of suggested changes. You can assist in this location process if you add both page numbers and line numbers to the document. With this approach, a meeting participant can state, "I recommend changing the wording on page 7 line 22," and everyone in the group can find the location quickly.

As a rule, you will not want to number every line of the page, since the long line of numbers can be almost as confusing as the unnumbered document. Instead, space your numbers so that only every fifth line is numbered. Also, instead of numbering your entire document from the first line to last, add page numbers, and restart the line numbering at the top of each page. This keeps the line numbers small, so that they are easier to understand.

To print every fifth line number with WordPerfect 5.1:

1. Select **L**ayout **L**ine Line **N**umbering **Y**es.
2. Select **N**umber Every n Lines, type **5**, and press ENTER.
3. Press F7 (Exit) to finish.

To print every fifth line number with WordPerfect 6:

1. Select **L**ayout **L**ine Line **N**umbering **L**ine Numbering On.
2. Select Numbering **I**nterval, type **5**, and press ENTER.
3. Select OK twice.

Since the **R**estart Numbering on Each Page check box is selected or set to Yes, WordPerfect restarts counting on every page, rather than counting from the beginning of the document to the end of the document. WordPerfect will also count empty lines because the Count Blank Lines check box is selected or set to Yes. When you print a document after making these selections, the beginning of your document may look like this:

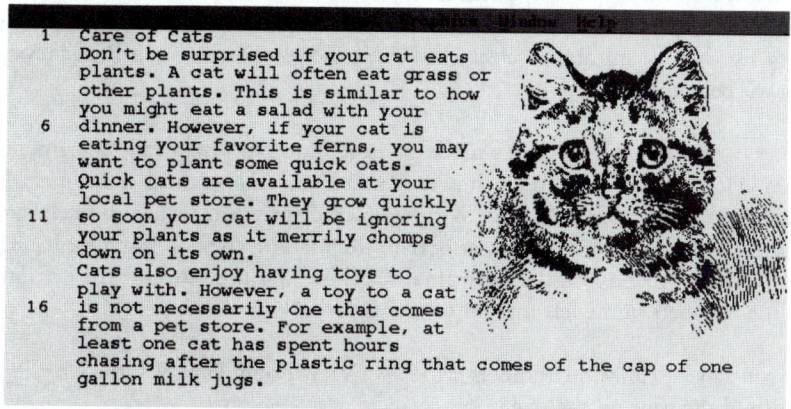

You can change where the numbers appear by selecting Position of Number and making new selections before performing step 3. You can change from starting at 1 to starting at another number. In WordPerfect 6, you can also change line numbers in other ways, including whether Arabic numbers, Roman numbers, or letters will be used, and the font the numbers will be printed in.

To turn off page numbering in WordPerfect 5.1, select Layout Line Line Numbering No and press F7 (Exit). To turn off page numbering in WordPerfect 6, select Layout Line Line Numbering, clear the Line Numbering On check box, and select OK twice.

You can use WordPerfect to add line numbers to computer programs, but you will want to use slightly different conventions. Usually every line in a program is numbered continually from beginning to end, rather than restarting on every page.

The cat picture is available on the accompanying disk as CAT.PCX.

CAT.PCX

Line Numbers Do Not Appear in Text Mode

When you add line numbering to your document, you might not see the line numbers onscreen. Both the WordPerfect 5.1 display and the WordPerfect 6 Text mode displays will not show the line numbers. If you want to see the line numbers, select File Print and View Document or Print Preview to view the document as it will be printed.

In WordPerfect 6, you can use Graphics mode or Page mode to display the document and its line numbers. Even in Graphics or Page mode, however, you might not see the line numbers. In both these modes the default magnification is Margin Width, which displays the text from the left margin to the right. Because the line numbers are set to appear in the margin, they do not appear on your screen. For the example shown in Tip 93, the horizontal scroll bar was used to shift the document's display to the left so the numbers in the left margin would appear.

Another way you can see your line numbers is to select View Zoom Page Width. WordPerfect displays the entire width of the page on the screen.

Formatting Long Quotations with Paragraph Margin Adjustments

The standard way of formatting long quotations of more than a line is to indent them from both the left and right margins using WordPerfect's Indent feature. Long quotations are set off like this and provide an attractive display:

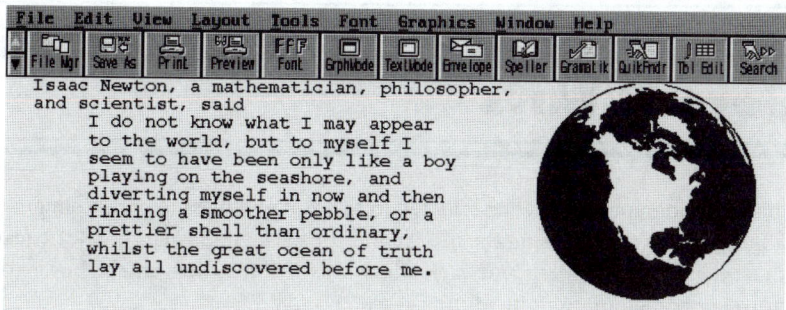

If the quotation contains many paragraphs, you might find it annoying to have to insert an indent code for each paragraph. Also, if you change tab settings elsewhere in the document, your changes can affect how the quotes following the changes are indented.

Another way to indent long quotations is to adjust the margins for those paragraphs. Do this by making an entry after selecting Layout Margins and Left Margin Adjustment or Right Margin Adjustment. Left Margin Adjustment sets the additional amount added to the left margin. Right Margin Adjustment sets the additional amount added to the right margin. When you use margin adjustments, the distance from the margins is automatic, even if you find you have to adjust the margins of your document. To change the margin adjustments:

1. Select the text to indent further.
2. Select **L**ayout **M**argins opening the Margin Format dialog box.
3. Select L**e**ft Margin Adjustment or R**i**ght Margin Adjustment.
4. Type the additional margin to add.
5. Select OK.

If you change the document's margin, the adjustment does not change, so you continue to have the same additional margin you entered in step 4. If you type a negative number, you reduce the paragraph's margins. In step 1, if you don't select a block first, the margin adjustment is in effect from the current location until you change the margin adjustment, or until the end of the document.

While you can use indent and back tab features to create adjustments to paragraph width, they always affect the document based on the current tab stop settings. Using paragraph margin adjustments lets you change paragraph widths to a location where the document has no tab stop because you are supplying the distance to increase or decrease the margin.

The globe picture is one of the graphics images that accompanies WordPerfect 6.

You Can Create Hanging Indents in Several Ways

When you create bibliographic entries or bulleted items, you will need to create hanging indents. You can create hanging indents either using the indent and the back tab or margin release feature, or using paragraph adjustments. Using indent and back tabs works well for a few entries but if you have many, you will want to use paragraph margin adjustments.

When you use indent and back tabs, the indentation will indent the paragraph in from the left margin. The back tab or margin release moves the first line in the paragraph back to the left. You can indent the paragraph with F4. This is the same as Layout Alignment Indent →. Back tab or margin release is done with SHIFT-TAB or Layout Alignment and Back Tab or Margin Rel, depending on the release. The following was created with indenting and back tab; the bullet to the left of each name is part of the hanging indent:

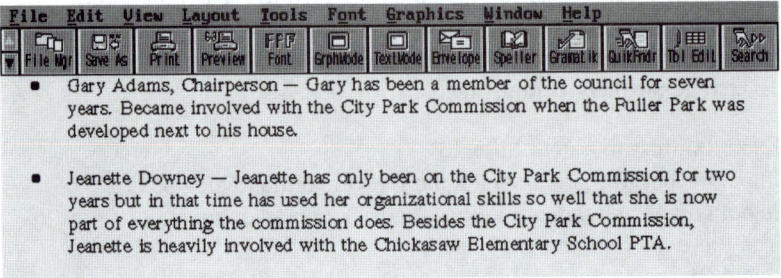

You can also get the same results using margin adjustments in WordPerfect 6. Select Layout Margins Left Margin Adjustment to set the additional amount added to the left margin. Right Margin Adjustment sets the additional amount added to the right margin. First Line Indent sets the additional amount added to the left margin and left margin adjustment for the first line of every paragraph. For the above hanging entry, type .5 after Left Margin Adjustment and –.5 after First Line Indent. The left margin adjustment and first line indent continue until you reset them both to 0. Use indent and back tab when you only have a few hanging indents to create or you are using WordPerfect 5.1. If you have many hanging indents to create, use paragraph adjustments by selecting Layout Margins.

Using Bulleted Items to Bring Out Points in a Document

To effectively call attention to the important points in your document, create a bulleted list to emphasize each point. Bullets make items in a list stand out. When you want to add the bullet character, use Compose. In WordPerfect 5.1, select Font Characters or press CTRL-V. In WordPerfect 6, select Font WP Characters or press CTRL-W. As described in Tip 63, select the character you want to use for the bullet. The following shows a few characters you might want to use as bullets.

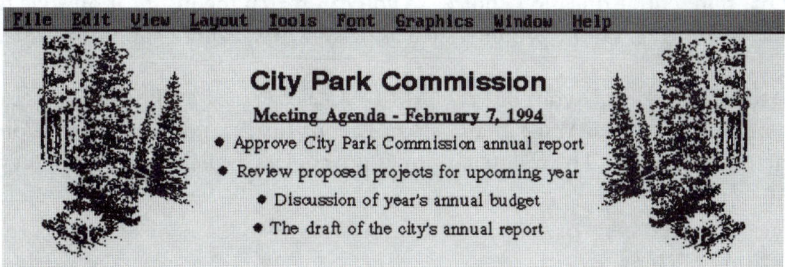

If the bulleted items run for multiple lines, you may want to add paragraph margin adjustments or indent the text. The following shows text where paragraph adjustments are used to align the text.

You might find a bulleted style easier to use than a Compose sequence.

TREES.PCX

The tree graphics image is available on the accompanying disk as TREES.PCX.

Tell WordPerfect 6 to Indent First Lines of Paragraphs

If you want all paragraphs to have their first lines indented, have WordPerfect do the indentation for you. You can select Layout or press SHIFT-F8 and select Margins. After First Line Indent, type the amount you want each line indented, usually .5 for half an inch. When you select OK, all of the paragraphs after this point will have their first line indented by the amount you entered. If you enter a negative number, the beginning of the paragraph is indented to the left.

Choose Paragraph Justification Appropriate for Your Document

WordPerfect has different justification choices so you can match the justification style to the kind of document you are creating. (Some printers, such as daisy-wheel, cannot support justification.)

To choose Justification, select Layout or press SHIFT-F8, select Line and Justification, and then select one of the justification choices. You can also select Layout Justification (Justify in WordPerfect 5.1) and select one of the options. The following shows the choices available and how you can use them in documents.

Justification	Uses
Left	Documents where you want a ragged right edge
Full	Documents where you want an even right edge
Full, All Lines	Documents where you want an even right edge, including on the last line
Center	Title pages and announcements
Right	Rightmost columns in multiple-column documents

You Can Use More Than One Alignment Option on a Line

Sometimes you will find that you want to create a line that includes text that is left-aligned, centered, and right-aligned. For example, for a header in a document you might want a title left-aligned, a chapter and page number centered, and a date or author name right-aligned. By combining the alignment options, you could create this kind of a line, as shown here:

To create this text, type **Budget Report for 1993**, press SHIFT-F6, type **Section 2, Page**, press CTRL-P for the page number, press ALT-F6 for flush right, press SHIFT-F5, and select Date Text to add the date.

Unlike the alignment options, justification options cannot be combined. Each time you select a justification option for a paragraph, it affects all of the text in that paragraph and replaces any previous justification setting.

Use the WordPerfect 6 Ribbon to Set Paragraph Justification

WordPerfect 6 offers a shortcut for setting paragraph justification with the mouse. Instead of selecting from the menu or dialog boxes, you can click the pop-up selection box in the Ribbon. This box appears in the middle of the Ribbon, beneath Font on the menu bar:

The Ribbon is available by selecting View Ribbon. This selection box offers the four standard kinds of justification: left, right, center, and full. This box does not offer the new fifth kind of justification used in WordPerfect 6, which is Full, All Lines.

Right-Justifying Blocks of Text Quickly

A shortcut for right-justifying blocks of text is to select the block and press ALT-F6. In WordPerfect 5.1, you must select Yes to confirm. At the beginning of the block, WordPerfect adds the code for right justification and at the end of the block is the code to return the paragraph justification to the previous setting.

Center Short Pages from Top to Bottom for Balance

When you look at printed pages with very little text, the text appears too close to the top margin with all the white space on the bottom part of the page. The appearance of the document is unbalanced and unprofessional. You can improve the document appearance by centering the text between the top and bottom margins.

To center a short page in WordPerfect 5.1:

1. Move to the beginning of the page you want to center.
2. Select **L**ayout or press SHIFT-F8, and select **P**age.
3. Select the **C**enter Page and **Y**es.
4. Select F7 (Exit) to return to the document.

To center a short page in WordPerfect 6:

1. Move to the page you want to center.
2. Select **L**ayout or press SHIFT-F8, and select **P**age.
3. Select the **C**enter Current Page check box.
4. Select OK.

In WordPerfect 5.1, if you are not at the beginning of the page when you perform the above steps, the page is not centered. With WordPerfect 6, which has default auto code placement, WordPerfect moves the code for centering a page to the top of the page.

Centering Single Pages or All Remaining Pages in a WordPerfect 6 Document

In WordPerfect 6, you can center either a single page or all of the remaining pages of a document. Centering a document does not change how much text fits on a document. It only shifts extra space that would be empty at the bottom and puts it at the top. If you have a document consisting of a number of short pages of text, such as one you will use to print transparencies, you might want all of those pages to be centered between the top and bottom margins of the pages. Tip 103 covers the steps for centering a single page. To center all of pages from the current page until the end of the document in a WordPerfect 6 document, follow these steps:

1. Select **L**ayout **P**age.
2. Select the Center **P**ages check box.
3. Select OK to return to the document.

To discontinue centering pages, move to the first page where you want the centering to stop and follow the same steps, clearing the Center **P**ages check box.

Centering Title Page Text Both Vertically and Horizontally

You can center text on your page both vertically and horizontally in two quick steps. You may want a title page centered both ways to give it a more professional appearance. To center a page vertically and horizontally, type the text and follow these steps.

1. Select **L**ayout **P**age and the **C**enter Current Page check box.
2. Select OK.
3. Block the text on the page.

4. Press SHIFT-F6 or select Center from the Ribbon (see Tip 101).
5. In WordPerfect 5.1, select **Y**es to the confirmation prompt.

In WordPerfect 5.1, you must block the page using ALT-F4 or F12. In WordPerfect 6, you can select Edit Select **P**age to block the entire page of text.

Centering Many Lines at Once

106

You are probably already familiar with changing the alignment of a line so that it is centered by using SHIFT-F6 or by selecting Layout Alignment Center. However, this feature is not quite as useful if you want to center a number of lines at once, because it is designed to be used to center text on a single line.

If you need to center many lines of text, block the lines and press SHIFT-F6. Just like pressing ALT-F6 on a block to change to right justification, pressing SHIFT-F6 after selecting a block changes the justification for the entire block to center justification.

Extra Tabs or Spaces Prevent Text from Centering Correctly

107

If text is center-aligned or center-justified but does not center correctly, display the document's codes. Look for extra tabs or spaces at the beginning or end of the line that you do not see in the regular document window. If there are extra tabs or spaces, WordPerfect includes them in the text that you want centered. Delete these extra codes and your text will be correctly centered.

Pressing TAB *and* SHIFT-F6 *centers the text around the tab stop, rather than across the page.*

You Might Need to Delete Alignment and Justification Codes Before Using a New Setting

Some alignment settings will not take effect until you remove a previous setting. For example, if you move to the beginning of the text "This is text" and press ALT-F6 to make the text flush right, and move to the *T* in "This" and press SHIFT-F6 to center the text, the text will not change. You need to reveal the document's codes and delete the code for the alignment or justification you do not want.

Altering the Way Text Is Adjusted for Full Justification

You can change the expansion and compression percentages to control how much WordPerfect can expand or compress the space between words and characters when using full justification. When you use full justification in your document, WordPerfect tries to stretch or compress text to fit correctly on the line. WordPerfect has, for example, certain default settings that prevent it from expanding the word "the" across the entire width of a page, or compressing it too tightly to read.

To change the compression and expansion percentages:

1. Select **L**ayout or press SHIFT-F8 and select **O**ther **P**rinter Functions.
2. Select Word Spacing **J**ustification Limits.
3. Type the minimum percent text can be compressed and press ENTER.
4. Type the maximum percent text can be expanded and press ENTER.
5. Press F7 until you return to the document.

If you want to make this change permanent, perform these steps when you change the Initial Code Setup, as described in Tip 83.

Use WordPerfect 6 Paragraph Borders to Add Lines, Color, or Shading

You can add visual impact to your documents by adding lines, color or shading to paragraphs. All of these features are created by adding paragraph borders. When you add borders, you can add lines in various shapes and sizes to any or all sides of the paragraph and assign colors to those lines. You can also add colors and patterns to the background of the paragraph. Use these features to make certain text stand out from surrounding text. To add paragraph borders to your text:

1. Move to the paragraph you want to add borders to.
2. Select **L**ayout **L**ine Paragraph **B**orders.
3. Select **B**order Style, highlight a border style, and choose **S**elect.
4. Select **F**ill Style, highlight a fill style, and select **S**elect.
5. When you have finished, select OK twice to return to the document.

You can also change the border's appearance by selecting Customize before step 5. Tip 113 has more information about border options you can change. The paragraph borders continue until you turn them off. To turn them off, move to the first paragraph in which you do not want to use borders. Select Layout Line Paragraph Borders Off. A document using borders might look like this:

The box is created with the thick line style and a 10-percent fill. Notice how the paragraph border bottom is not at the end of each paragraph. Instead, the bottom of the paragraph border is where the code that turns the paragraph's borders off is located or at the end of the page. Every paragraph between the code that starts the paragraph borders and the code that ends the paragraph borders is surrounded by the same border. The exception is a page break—WordPerfect will add the bottom of a paragraph border to the bottom of the page.

Border bottoms might not appear in Graphics mode. However, the border's bottom will appear in Page display mode, the Print Preview window, and when you print the document. In Text mode, you will not see the borders until you print or preview the document.

The image of the panda in the sample is available on the accompanying disk as PANDA.CGM.

PANDA.CGM

If Each Paragraph Needs Its Own Border, Add Each Border Separately

As the sample border in Tip 110 shows, paragraph borders span several paragraphs. When you want each paragraph to have its own border, you must add them separately. For example, you might want separate boxes for individual paragraphs, as shown here:

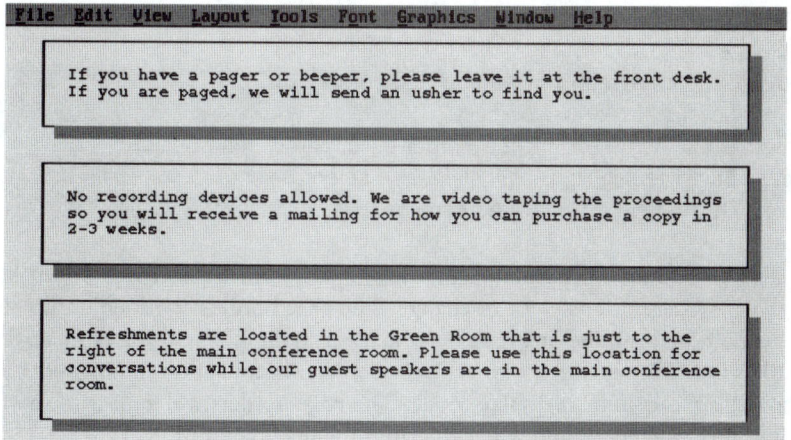

The border style and fill style are customized styles that Tip 113 describes how to create. To create the previous document:

1. Move to a paragraph.
2. Select **E**dit **S**elect **P**aragraph.
3. Select **L**ayout **L**ine Paragraph **B**orders **B**order Style.
4. Highlight the border style you want to use (Points in this case) and choose **S**elect.
5. Select OK twice to return to the document.

Adding Borders to Entire Pages in WordPerfect 6

You can add borders and colors to entire pages, as well as to paragraphs. When you add page borders to a page, you can choose the type of lines used to create the border, the type of pattern used as the background of the page, and the colors to assign to the borders and the fill. You can add borders and fill in order to make a flyer distinctive or to create a certificate.

To add page borders:

1. Move to the paragraph you want to add borders to.
2. Select **L**ayout **P**age Page **B**orders.
3. Select **B**order Style, highlight a border style, and choose **S**elect.
4. Select **F**ill Style, highlight a fill style, and select **S**elect.
5. Select OK twice to return to the document.

You can also change the border's appearance by selecting Customize before step 5. Tip 113 has more information about border options you can change. The page borders continue until you turn them off. To turn them off, move to the first page on which you want to stop using borders. Select Layout Page Page Borders Off. The top and bottom of page borders do not appear in Graphics mode; no part of the page border appears in Text display mode. The page borders will appear in the Page display mode, the Print Preview window, and when you print the document.

Creating Your Own WordPerfect 6 Border Styles

You can change the styles of the borders and fill colors used for paragraph and page borders. You can either customize the current border and fill style, or you can create your own.

To customize the current border and fill styles, select Layout Line Paragraph Borders Customize or Layout Page Page Borders Customize. From the dialog box, you can change the lines, color, spacing, shadow, corners, and fill style. The different selections and the areas of the border they affect are shown here:

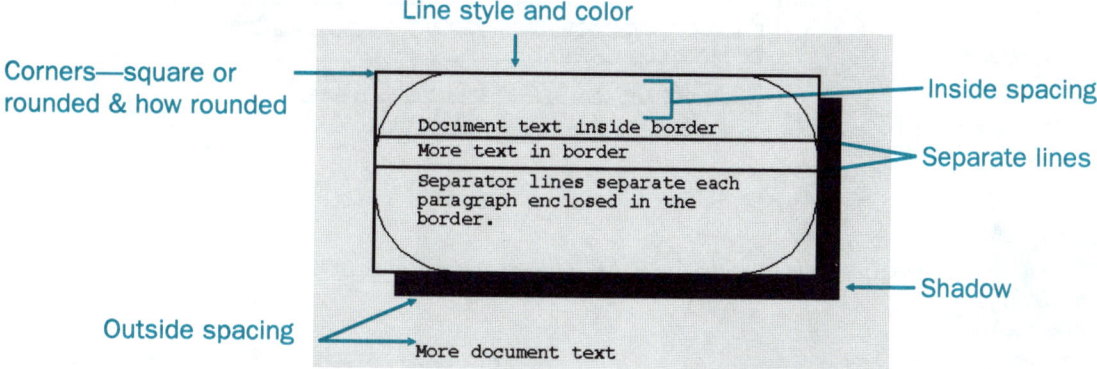

As you select from Lines, Color, Spacing, Shadow, Corners, and Fill, you can make the appropriate entries to create your own border and fill styles.

To create your own border and fill styles:

1. Select **Layout Line** Paragraph **Borders** or **Layout Page** Page **Borders**.
2. Select **Border** Style or **Fill** Style for the style to create.
3. Highlight the style closest to what you want and select **Create**.
4. Type a name for the style and select OK.
5. Select the features of the style to change and make new entries.
6. Select OK until you return to the document.

In step 5, the selections you can change depend on whether you select Border Style or Fill Style.

Once you create the style, it is available in the document any time WordPerfect prompts you for a border or fill style. Also, paragraph borders, page borders, and graphics box borders can be shared. The ones you use for one document can be used by another. If you want to share border or fill styles with other documents, save the styles in a file. Then, in the documents where you want to use the border or fill styles, select **R**etrieve and enter the name you saved the styles under. The following shows some examples of different border and fill styles:

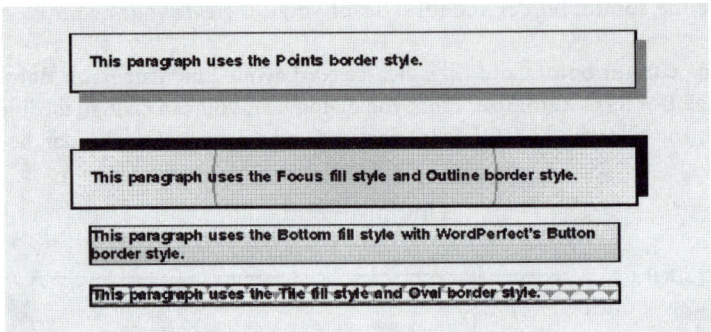

BORDERS.STY

The sample style is available on the accompanying disk as BORDERS.STY.

Use Blank Lines to Separate Sections

TIP 114

When you are creating a document with different sections, you will want to make the difference between sections clear. For example, if your sales report discusses several regions but your readers do not realize where in the text the breaks between each discussion occur, they may develop mistaken notions about sales in those regions.

One easy way to help separate sections is to add white space. If you break up your text with blank lines, the place where each section ends becomes clear: the blank lines provide a clear visual cue to the reader. You might want to include blank space at the end of each section, even if you are creating section headings, to help reinforce the change of topics.

Setting Line Spacing with Macros

When you frequently switch between two types of spacing, you can have macros that set the spacing for you. The following shows a macro that sets a document to double-spacing:

```
DISPLAY(Off!)
LineSpacing(2.0)
```

The following shows a macro that sets a document to single-spacing:

```
DISPLAY(Off!)
LineSpacing(1.0)
```

While these macros do not save many keystrokes, they can be easily used. Since these macros have the names ALTD.WPM and ALTS.WPM, you can switch between double- and single-spacing by pressing ALT-D and ALT-S.

These sample macros are available on the accompanying disk as ALTS.WPM and ALTD.WPM.

ALTS.WPM
ALTD.WPM

Line Spacing Affects Where Soft Page Breaks Are Added

WordPerfect adds soft page breaks to your document whenever the next line would fall below the bottom margin. The line spacing that you choose for a document affects where the soft page breaks will appear. For example, if you use double-spacing, there may be one line's worth of space left between the last line and the bottom margin. However, since that space is needed to maintain the double-spacing, the soft page break will be inserted at the end of the last printed line. The next line in the document must appear on the next page to maintain double-spacing.

Line Spacing Might Not Display in Text Mode

When you are in Text mode in WordPerfect, you will find that some line spacing settings do not appear to affect the display of text. For example, if you can change the line spacing to 1.25, there will be no change in how the text is displayed. However, if you enter 2 for double-spacing, the text display changes to reflect double-spacing.

Text display mode cannot display fractional line spacing. So, while Text mode will adjust to display single, double, or triple line spacing, it cannot accurately change to display 1.25 spacing. Instead, WordPerfect rounds the fractional values you enter and displays the closest available spacing. For example, for 1.25 spacing, WordPerfect displays single-spaced text. When you use 1.5 spacing, however, WordPerfect displays double-spaced text because WordPerfect rounds up to the nearest whole number.

Allow Sufficient White Space for Readability

You can fit more on a page if you narrow margins and leave no space between sections, but readability will suffer. If your readers have a choice between reading a document with sufficient white space and one crammed from edge to edge with text, many readers will choose to read the document with adequate white space. If you need more space to fit the contents of the document, look at Tip 271 for suggestions on how to fit more on a page.

Adding Extra Space Between Paragraphs

TIP 119

If you want extra space between paragraphs, have WordPerfect add the space for you. WordPerfect will add the extra space at every [HRt] code. The following shows a few paragraphs using this feature:

> File Edit View Layout Tools Font Graphics Window Help
>
> Jim Connolly will address the symposium on "Using Quality Reviews Effectively." His presentation will walk the practitioner through a typical quality review, include points that will improve the quality of your practice's audits. He will also focus on the deficiencies reviewers are finding, and modifications to your own internal quality control program to prevent deficiencies.
>
> Jim Connolly is a partner at Connolly and Jacobs. Besides the many committees he has served on, he is also a board of director for several local Fortune 500 companies. He graduated from the Wharton School of Business at the University of Pennsylvania with both his bachelors and masters degrees.
>
> Following Jim's presentation is a panel discussion on the effect of computers on internal quality control. Panel members include Sheila Jozwiak, Robert Snow, and Darlene Norris.
>
> The discussion will be followed by lunch at 12:00.

To add extra space between paragraphs in WordPerfect 5.1, follow these steps:

1. Select **L**ayout or press SHIFT-F8.
2. Select **O**ther **P**rinter Functions **L**eading Adjustment.
3. Press ENTER to leave the Primary Leading adjustment unchanged.
4. Enter the space to add between lines that end with an [HRt] code.
5. Press F7 (Exit) until you return to the document.

In step 4, you must specify a physical distance, rather than the number of lines. To create the illustrated example, the secondary leading is set to .083 (half a normal line's height).

To add extra space between paragraphs in WordPerfect 6, follow these steps:

1. Select **L**ayout or press SHIFT-F8.
2. Select **M**argins **P**aragraph Spacing.
3. Enter the line spacing to add to lines that end with an [HRt] code.
4. Select OK until you return to the document.

In step 3, you specify the number of lines. To create the illustrated example, you would enter 1.5 in step 3.

Formatting for Endnotes and Footnotes Is Set Separately from the Document Text

If you block and change the line spacing for your entire document, you may be surprised to discover later that your endnotes and footnotes do not have the new spacing. As mentioned in Tip 92, substructures such as endnotes and footnotes are not affected by most changes you make in the document. If you want to change the line spacing used by endnotes or footnotes, you have to change the spacing in the endnote or footnote or change the spacing in the initial codes.

Use a Hard Page Break, Rather Than Hard Returns, to Force a New Page

When you want to force a new page, it might seem logical to press ENTER until you reach the end of the page, and WordPerfect inserts a soft page return. The problem with this approach is that if you later edit the text or change its formatting, the page break might disappear or move.

To make sure the page breaks where you intend, add a hard page break by pressing CTRL-ENTER. A *hard page break* forces the text that follows to the new page, even if the amount of text that fits on the previous page changes.

Use Automatic Page Breaks When Needed

Sometimes you want text to start on a new page. You might want a new chapter, a table of contents, or an index to start on an odd page or an even page. For example, each chapter in this book starts on an odd page. You can tell WordPerfect that you want a page to be an odd or an even page and not worry about it any more as you edit the document. To begin a new page at any location in WordPerfect

5.1 or 6.0, you can press CTRL-ENTER to insert a hard page break. The steps for forcing an odd or even page are as follows:

1. Select **L**ayout or press SHIFT-F8 and select **P**age.
2. Select **F**orce Odd/Even Page or **F**orce Page, depending on the WordPerfect version you are using.
3. Select **O**dd or **E**ven for where you want the current page to start.
4. Press F7 to return to the document.

WordPerfect Defaults to Left-Aligned Tabs

When you are setting new tabs, WordPerfect always defaults to left-aligned tabs. You can change to any type of tab after setting the location of a tab by typing the appropriate letter for the kind of tab you want. Your first step is to select Layout Line Tab Set in WordPerfect 5.1 or Layout Tab Set in WordPerfect 6. Next, add one or more repetitive tab stops, move to the tab stop to change the alignment, and type **R**, **C**, or **D** to select Right, Centered, or Decimal.

Enter 0 Before Tab Settings of Less Than One Inch

When you are setting tabs, if you initially type a period without a preceding 0, WordPerfect will interpret the decimal point as selecting dot leader for that tab stop. So to enter a tab at a location such as .6 inches, type **0.6**. In WordPerfect 6, you can avoid this by selecting Set Tab before typing in the tab stop position.

Dot Leader Tabs Can Help Readers Match Related Entries

Dot leader tabs are designed to help a reader scan across the screen or page to related data on the other side of the page. One of the most common uses of dot leaders is in a table of contents where the subject matter appears on the left, the page number appears on the right, and the two are connected by a series of dots. There are other times when they make an attractive display. You can use dot leader tabs with entries like this to make it easy for readers to match the part number and price:

File Edit View Layout Tools Font Graphics Window Help

File Mgr Save As Print Preview Font GrphMode TextMode Envelope Speller GramatIk QuikFndr Tbl Edit Search

Silly Sam's Garden Shop Price List

Item	Part Number	Cost
Gas String Trimmer	SX-125	69.99
9" Bump Feed Weed Trimmer	82209	19.88
17" Straight Shaft Brush Cutter	ST-285BC	139.99
10 Light Tier Light Set	LX10610T25	49.50

MONBAGS1.WPM

The graphic from the example is available on the accompanying disk as MONBAGS1.WPM.

T I P 126
Combine the Dot Leader Tab Specification with Any Other Tab Type

Dot leaders are not specifically reserved for right tabs. You can make other tab stops dot leaders as well. To do this, when you set a tab stop, type . (period) to indicate that you want the tab stop to also be a dot leader, or select the Dot Leader check box in WordPerfect 6.

As an example, the dot leaders in the document shown in Tip 125 are created by making most of the tab stops dot leaders. This includes the left-aligned tab stops in the middle section. The dot leader character is changed so there are no spaces between the periods in the dot leader, as the next tip describes.

Since the dot leader feature can be added to any type of tab setting, when you set tab stops to be dot leader tabs, the L, R, or C is displayed with the same appearance as blocked text.

Changing the Appearance of Dot Leaders in WordPerfect 6

A dot leader tab gets its name from the dots that are most commonly used as leader characters. You can, however, use characters other than dots to provide variety or visual interest. You might prefer to use a dash because it follows across on the midpoint of the line. You can try out a new setting with these steps:

1. Select **L**ayout Character Dot **L**eader Character.
2. Type the character to use for the dot leader.
3. Type the number of spaces between the characters in the dot leader.
4. Select OK to return to the document.

In the following document, the dot leader is changed to a hyphen leader, with no spaces between the characters:

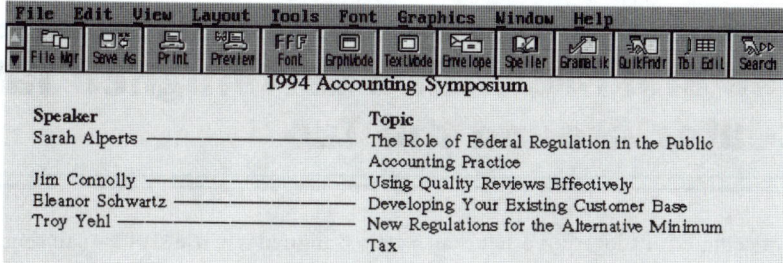

Use CTRL-F6 to Align Text with the Decimal-Alignment Character

When you press CTRL-F6 after putting any character as the first character in a line, WordPerfect aligns the text as if the next tab stop is a decimal tab. This lets you have decimal-align tabs in some lines without redefining your tab stops. In the following document, the numbers on the right side are aligned by the decimal point because CTRL-F6 was used. The tab stops have the same left alignment that you can see at the top of the document:

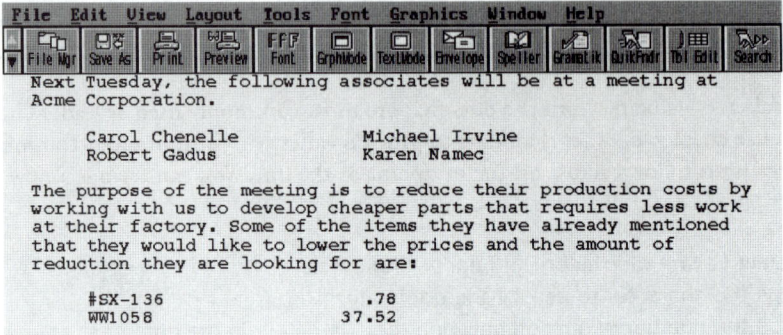

 *If you want to use a character other than a period to align characters, look at Tip 50.*

Use SHIFT-F6 with a Left-Aligned Tab to Center Around the Tab

If you want text centered at a location other than a center-aligned tab, use SHIFT-F6 to center the entry. When SHIFT-F6 is not the first entry on a line, it will center text after it. WordPerfect centers the text based on the cursor position when you press SHIFT-F6. If you want text centered over text below it, move to the center point above the text and press SHIFT-F6. For example, notice the text in the second line in this illustration:

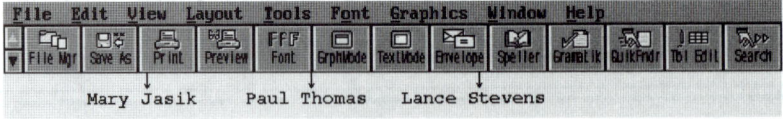

The first line of text has arrows indicating the points where the cursor moved before pressing SHIFT-F6. The second line contains text centered on these points.

Inserting Page Numbers in a Predefined Location

TIP 130

WordPerfect can quickly insert page numbers in a document in one of eight predefined locations. To insert these page numbers, select **Layout** or press SHIFT-F8, select **Page Page Numbering Page Number Position**, and select one of the predefined locations. The numbers in the diagram of the pages show you where the page numbers will appear. Press F7 until you return to the document. The page numbers will be included when you print the document.

After you insert automatic page numbers, you may be surprised that pages are breaking in different locations. Page numbers require a line to print on and a line to separate the page number from the document's text. These two lines change the location where pages split. You may want to decrease the top or bottom margin by the height of two lines to compensate for the two lines used for the page number.

Since WordPerfect 5.1 places codes at the cursor's location, you want to be at the top of the page when you add an automatic page number.

Inserting Page Numbers in Other Locations

TIP 131

In addition to inserting the page number in WordPerfect's predefined locations, you can also insert page numbers in other locations. Some of the possible locations:

- ❑ in the document
- ❑ in a header or footer
- ❑ in a graphics box

In each of these cases, the page number is added by pressing CTRL-B in WordPerfect 5.1 or CTRL-P in WordPerfect 6. For example, you can see the page number added to a graphics box in a document header here:

In this document, each page has its own graphics box for the page number.

Page Numbers Only Appear When You Print or Preview Text

If you add an automatic page number or place it in a substructure such as a header or footer, it will not appear onscreen in Text or Graphics mode. To check the page numbers, select File Print Preview. Page numbers only appear on your printout, in a preview of the printout, or in WordPerfect 6's Page display mode.

Customizing the Page Number with Words

You are not restricted to a simple number for the automatic page numbers. You can enclose the page number in dashes or add the word "Page" or other text. You might want page 9 to appear as "-9-",

"Page 9", or "MLS Page 9". You can customize the text that WordPerfect prints (along with the actual page number) with these steps:

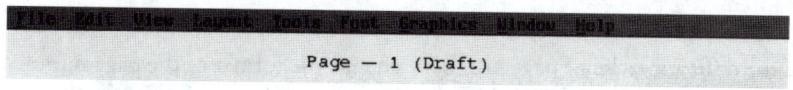

1. Select **L**ayout **P**age.
2. Select Page **N**umbering from the Page Format dialog box.
3. Select Page Number **F**ormat in 6.0 or Page Number **S**tyle in 5.1.
4. Type the text around the ^B or the [page #] code.
5. Press ENTER and press F7 until you return to the document.

The text around the ^B or [page #] is the text that appears on either side of the page number when you print the document. If you delete the ^B or [page #], you can get it back. You can add the ^B for the page number in WordPerfect 5.1 by pressing CTRL-B. You can add the [page #] for the page number in WordPerfect 6 by pressing F5 for the Number Codes and selecting **P**age Number.

As an example, the page number seen here was added by following the steps above and putting text on either side of the code for the page number:

```
 File  Edit  View  Layout  Tools  Font  Graphics  Window  Help

                    Page — 1 (Draft)
```

The appearance of the page number is set either by the default font or by changing the page number's attribute, as described in the Tip 134.

Adding Font and Attribute Formatting to Page Numbers

TIP
134

You can customize the appearance of page numbers. You can insert the page number with any text you have displaying around it, as described in Tip 133, by selecting Layout Page Page Numbering and Insert Page Number in WordPerfect 5.1 or Insert Formatted Page Number in WordPerfect 6. Then the page number information will appear with any formatting you add to that part of the document.

Another possibility is to create a header or footer that contains the page number and any character formatting you want. You can insert the page number into the document by pressing CTRL-B in WordPerfect 5.1 or CTRL-P in WordPerfect 6. The page number will use the formatting used in the header or footer.

In WordPerfect 6, you have a new set of options that you can use to add formatting to a page number. You can make all of your changes through convenient dialog box selections by selecting Layout Page Page Numbering Page Numbering Position Font/Attributes/Color to display the Font dialog box. From this dialog box, you can select the font and attributes of the formatted automatic page number. Additional changes can be made after selecting Color, where another dialog box appears and lets you choose a standard or custom color and determine the percent of shading to use.

Using Different WordPerfect 6 Page Number Levels

WordPerfect 6 has four sets of page numbers. This means you can create a document that is divided into chapters, with page numbers that include both the chapter number and the number of the page within the chapter.

To use one of the different styles of page numbers, change the format of the page number by selecting Layout Page Page Numbering and Page Number Format. In the text box, press F5 to add the codes for the different levels of page numbering. You can select Secondary Page Number to add the [scndy pg #] code, Chapter Number to add the [chpt #] code, and Volume Number to add the [vol #] code. The page number and secondary page numbers automatically increment on every page. The chapter numbers and volume numbers do not advance until you tell them to.

When you use different page number levels, mark where you want page numbers and secondary page numbers to restart with 1 and where you want to increment chapter and volume numbers. For example, if you have a document that contains chapters and you want the pages to be labeled with the chapter number and the page number within the chapter, move to the beginning of each chapter and increment the chapter number and restart the page number.

Starting a Separate Section with Any Number You Want

If you are creating a document that you will combine with others, you will want to set the page number of the first page of the WordPerfect document to match what the appropriate page number will be

when you include the WordPerfect document with the other documents. You can reset the number for the first page from 1 to any number by selecting Layout Page Page Numbering and New Page Number in WordPerfect 5.1 or Page Number in WordPerfect 6.

Suppressing Page Formatting for Selected Pages

TIP 137

You might want to prevent page numbers, headers, footers, watermarks, and other kinds of page formatting from appearing on pages you have intentionally left blank. You can also remove some—but not all—of the page formatting from a page; for instance, it's a good idea to remove a watermark from a page that you will be filling with graphics images.

To suppress some or all of the page formatting, move to the page where you want to prevent some or all of the page formatting from appearing. Then select Layout Page Suppress. From the dialog box or list of options presented, you can select whether you want to suppress one or both of the headers, one or both of the footers, one or both of the watermarks, and the page number. For page numbers, you can also temporarily display the page number in the bottom center of the page rather than its default location.

Using a Macro to Insert Page Numbers

TIP 138

You can develop macros that insert page numbers and your favorite page number style. Since you will usually insert page numbers in the same location in your documents, having a macro that inserts page numbers for you can save you time. The sample page number macro called ADD_PAGE.WPM creates page numbers that look like this:

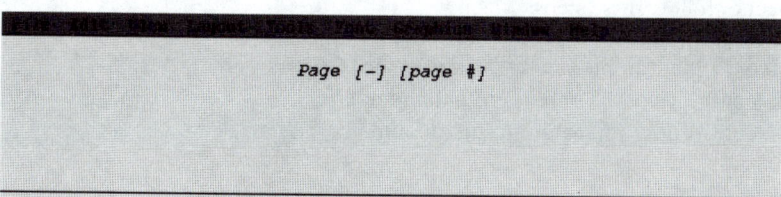

The macro has the following instructions:

```
DISPLAY(Off!)
PageNumberPosition(BottomCenter!;DontUseDefaultValues!;;;;;;;
     {Italics!})
PageNumberFormat("Page [-] [page #]")
```

ADD_PAGE.WPM

This sample macro is available on the accompanying disk as ADD_PAGE.WPM.

Widow and Orphan Protection Keep Single Lines with Other Text

When the last line of a paragraph is placed on a page by itself it is called a *widow*. When the first line of a paragraph is alone on a page it is called an *orphan*. Both widows and orphans are undesirable in printed text because they tend to interrupt the reader's train of thought. WordPerfect has a Widow/Orphan Protect feature that prevents widows and orphans from occurring. To prevent widows, WordPerfect places the last two lines of the paragraph on the next page. To prevent orphans, WordPerfect moves the first line to the next page with the rest of the paragraph text. If a paragraph contains only three lines, WordPerfect places the entire paragraph on the next page.

Follow these steps to turn on widow and orphan protection in WordPerfect 5.1:

1. Select **L**ayout or press SHIFT-F8 and select **L**ine.
2. Select **W**idow/Orphan Protection.
3. Select **Y**es and press F7 (Exit).

In WordPerfect 6, follow these steps:

1. Select **L**ayout or press SHIFT-F8 and select **O**ther.
2. Select the **W**idow/Orphan Protect check box.
3. Select OK until you return to the document.

Keeping a Group of Entries Together on a Page with Block Protect

TIP 140

Block Protect lets you keep several lines of text together on a single page. When you protect a block, a page break that would have fallen in the middle of the block is moved so that it falls before the block—keeping the text of the block on one page of the document. For example, you can use Block Protect to keep names and addresses together on a single page.

With either version of WordPerfect, first select the block that you want to appear on the same page by using ALT-F4, F12, or the mouse. Next, in WordPerfect 5.1:

> Press SHIFT-F8

To protect a selected block in WordPerfect 6:

1. Select **L**ayout **O**ther and the **B**lock Protect check box.
2. Select OK.

The Block Protect code is a paired code. The code turning the Block Protect on appears before the text to be treated as a block, and the code turning the feature off is at the end. If you enter more text between these codes, that text will also be part of the block that is to be kept together.

Using a Conditional End of Page to Keep Section Heads with Text

TIP 141

Occasionally, you may find a section heading on one page and the text that goes with the heading on the next page. (WordPerfect decided that the end of the page came immediately after that heading.) You can use the Conditional End of Page feature, as well as Block Protect (described in Tip 140), to prevent this from happening.

Block Protect requires that everything between the beginning of the block and the end of the block remains on one page. As you edit the text in the block, you are changing the number of lines kept together on a page. Conditional End of Page only requires that a specific number of lines *after* the current point be on the same page. For example, you could use Conditional End of Page on the tip titles in this book and require that they always be on the same page as the next two lines after the tip title. That way, if the text after the tip text changes, WordPerfect would not care. It would continue to count two lines beyond the tip's title to determine page break locations.

The Conditional End Of Page code is put in the line above the text you want kept with the following lines. You can go to the line above the tip's title, using this book as an example. You can decide how many lines you want to keep together. If WordPerfect cannot fit the line with the Conditional End of Page code and the number of lines set by the code on the same page, WordPerfect puts the page break before the line with the Conditional End of Page code.

To insert a Conditional End of Page code:

1. Move to the line before the first line you want to keep together.
2. Select **L**ayout or press SHIFT-F8
3. Select **O**ther **C**onditional End of Page.
4. Type the number of lines you want to keep with the following line.
5. Press F7 until you return to the document.

Positioning Text at Fixed Locations on a Preprinted Form

When you use WordPerfect to fill out a preprinted form, it is difficult to line up the text entries with the lines on the form if you are simply typing the text into a document screen. The WordPerfect Advance feature lets you lay out the form entries to your exact specifications. You can measure the form to see the exact position for each entry and specify your measurement with Advance.

After you select **L**ayout or press SHIFT-F8 and select **O**ther **A**dvance, you select the direction that you want to advance to. You can move left, right, up, or down from the cursor's current position. You can also move down or right from the page's edge. After you select the direction you want to advance, type the distance you want to advance. This is *distance*, rather than the number of lines or characters. When you return to the document, enter what you want at that location.

Since it is easier to measure when you are working with a baseline placement, you might want to set the Baseline Placement for Typesetters to Yes. This is discussed in more detail in Tip 144. After making this change, the measurement will provide the exact location where the text begins. The portion of the form shown in the following shows how you might measure the location of some entries after making this change:

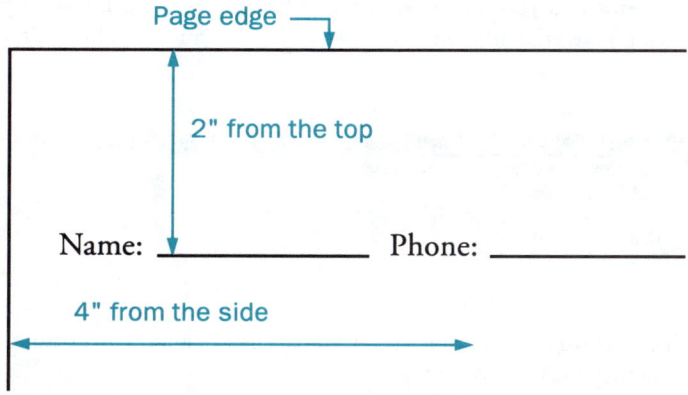

The codes in the WordPerfect document that place the name and phone number entries might look like this:

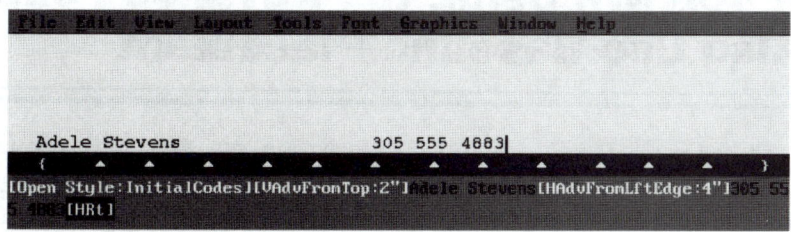

After you use the Advance feature, the position of the cursor is changed. Text entered after the Advance feature has the same relative position as text entered without the Advance feature.

The Advance feature also allows you to position text in a specific location on top of graphics images. You can set text so it does not wrap around the graphics box as described in Tip 634.

Fixed Line Height Setting Does Not Allow for Font Variations

WordPerfect's default sets a line's height to accommodate the tallest text on the line. If you change to a fixed line height, WordPerfect will not adjust the line's height as you change the height of the text on the line. This means that you may have more or less space between lines if you change the text height. The following shows the difference between automatic and fixed line height after changing the text point size to 16.

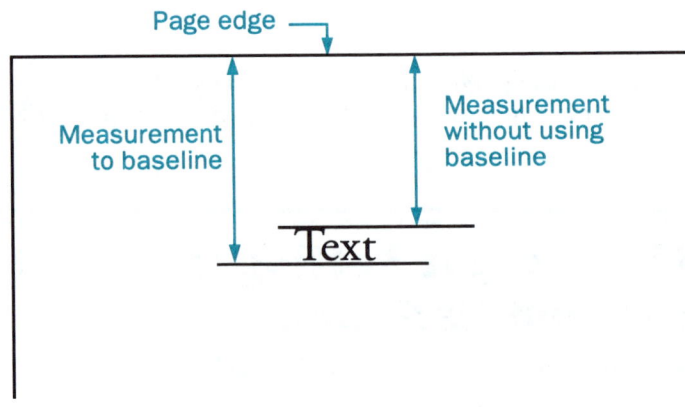

In the top two lines, WordPerfect automatically adjusts line height. The bottom two lines have their line height fixed, so they look too close together.

If You Are Using the Advance Feature, Also Use Baseline Placement

When you use the Advance feature described in Tip 142, WordPerfect measures vertical distances from the top of the page or the cursor's current location to the top of the text you are advancing. Usually you will measure distances from the top of the page or the bottom of the current location to the bottom of the text. The advantage of measuring to the bottom of the character, or the baseline, is that if the font changes height, the bottom of the characters have the same location, as shown here:

Page edge

Measurement to baseline

Measurement without using baseline

Text

To use baseline placement in WordPerfect 5.1:

1. Select **L**ayout or press SHIFT-F8 and select **O**ther **P**rinter Functions.
2. Select **B**aseline Placement for Typesetters and **Y**es.
3. Press F7 (Exit) until you return to the document.

To use baseline placement in WordPerfect 6:

1. Select **L**ayout or press SHIFT-F8 and select **D**ocument.
2. Select the **B**aseline Placement for Typesetters check box.
3. Select OK until you return to the document.

Using a Delay in WordPerfect 6 to Stop Immediate Use of a Feature

TIP 145

WordPerfect 6 automatically places codes for page formatting at the top of the current page, but there is a new setting that allows you to delay such a formatting change from taking effect. If, for instance, you want to add formatting changes that will take effect on a page after the current page, choose to delay the effect of the change. For example, when you are preparing a document, you might want the first page to have a different style than the rest. At the beginning of the document, add a delay code that will take effect after the first page. To use this feature, follow these steps:

1. Select **L**ayout **P**age **D**elay Codes.
2. Type the number of pages you want to delay the code and select OK.
3. Enter the codes that you want to be in effect later.
4. Select OK until you return to the document.

WordPerfect 6 Handles Some Delay Codes for You

TIP 146

When you notice a delay code in a document, it will—in most cases—be one that WordPerfect has added for you. For example, you may look at your document's codes and notice one that looks like this: [Delay On;[Wid/Orph:On]]. Your document contains this code where you added the feature. At the beginning of the document or the last hard page break is the [Delay;#] code. The # symbol is replaced by the number of pages difference between the two codes. Some codes WordPerfect puts at the beginning of the document. When you have selected it at another location, WordPerfect creates the delay code for you. Deleting either [Delay] code removes the feature provided by the code.

CHAPTER 3

Fonts and Character Appearance

Limit the Number of Fonts You Use in a Single Document

If you use many fonts in a single document, your readers will devote more time to the appearance of the document than its contents. A good rule of thumb is to use no more than three fonts in one document.

Use WordPerfect 6's ALLFONTS Macro to Create a Quick List of the Available Fonts

WordPerfect's ALLFONTS macro will print a sample of every font available to you in WordPerfect. You can perform this macro by selecting Tools Macro Play, typing **ALLFONTS**, and selecting OK. You will want to start in an empty document. The final result will be a listing of every font that appears when you select Font from the Font dialog box. The list depends on the printer selected and the software fonts you have installed. The beginning of a sample of the macro's output looks like this:

```
File  Edit  View  Layout  Tools  Font  Graphics  Window  Help
File Mgr  Save As  Print  Preview  Font  GrphMode  TextMode  Envelope  Speller  Gramatik  QuikFndr  Tbl Edit  Search

Font list for HP LaserJet III:

Bodoni-WP Bold (Type 1)
CG Times
CG Times Bold
CG Times Bold Italic
CG Times Italic
CommercialScript-WP (Type 1)
Courier 10 Bold (Speedo)
Courier 10 Bold Italic (Speedo)
Courier 10 Italic (Speedo)
Courier 10 Roman (Speedo)
Courier 10cpi
Courier 10cpi Bold
Courier 10cpi Italic
```

Fit the Text Style to Your Message

TIP 149

When you are choosing the font you want to use in a document, think of the document's purpose. If you are creating a document for a business proposal, you do not want to be as creative with your fonts as you would be for a party flyer you're going to distribute to your friends. You can use many fonts in WordPerfect, and it is tempting to try out the different possibilities. However, mismatching the font and the document will distract your readers. The following are a few ideas for ways to use the fonts provided with WordPerfect 6:

Bodoni	Transparencies and slides
Commercial Script	Party invitations
Dutch 801	Résumés, report headings
Helvetica	Headings
Roman	Letters

Use WordPerfect 6's Resulting Font Box to Visually Check the Font Appearance

TIP 150

WordPerfect 6's Font dialog box includes a Resulting Font box. In Graphics mode, this box shows you how the font you select will display in your document. When you change a font in WordPerfect 6, look at this box to see that your selections are providing the appearance you want.

Some fonts, especially those provided by your printer, will have a slightly different appearance when you print your document. This is because your printer does not tell WordPerfect what these fonts will look like. Therefore, WordPerfect makes a substitution with one of the fonts it does have in order to display your document on the screen. It will use the font you selected when you print the document.

Fonts Are Set Separately for Text and Extended Text

The font that you select in a document has no effect on the fonts used by headers, footers, footnotes, endnotes, page numbers, and text in graphics boxes. The fonts for these extended text items are set by the document's initial codes. If you want to change these fonts, you must either change the document's initial codes or change the font within the individual header, footer, footnote, endnote, page number, or graphics box.

WordPerfect 6 provides a library of system styles that provide default styles for a header, footer, and so on. If you change any of the styles that affect extended text, your settings will override the settings in the document initial codes.

See Tip 423 for more information on changing system styles.

Font Settings Can Be Paired or Open

When you change a font setting, WordPerfect adds either a paired or open code to the document. Paired-code settings have a code at the point the font setting is to begin, and another where the setting is to end. Open-code font settings only have a code at the beginning; the setting continues until the end of the document or until you select another font setting of the same type. Among the paired-code font settings are the following:

❑ Attributes such as Bold, Underline, Double Underline, Italics, Outline, Shadow, Small Caps, Redline, and Strikeout

❑ Positions such as Subscript and Superscript

❑ Relative font sizes such as Fine, Small, Normal, Large, Very Large, and Extra Large

Among the open-code font settings are the following:

❑ Whether underlining is done for spaces and tabs that separate words

❑ Font typeface

❑ Text color

❑ Font size set by Size in WordPerfect 6's Font dialog box

In Text Mode, the Appearance of Font Characteristics Is Reflected by Screen Color

WordPerfect's Text mode display uses colors to indicate different font characteristics. When you edit a document in WordPerfect 5.1 your document is displayed in Text mode. In WordPerfect 6, however, Text mode is just one option. You can set how the different text attributes will appear in Text mode. For each attribute, you can change the foreground color (the color of the text) and the background color (the color behind the text). To change the colors used for different font characteristics in WordPerfect 5.1, follow these steps:

1. Select **F**ile Se**t**up **D**isplay **C**olors/Fonts/Attributes **S**creen Colors.
2. Use the UP ARROW and DOWN ARROW to move to the attribute you want to change.
3. Type the letter for the foreground color.
4. Press the RIGHT ARROW and type the letter for the background color.
5. Repeat steps 2, 3, and 4 for the colors you want to change.
6. Press F7 (Exit) until you return to the document.

The screen after the selections in step 1 looks like this:

```
Setup: Colors              A B C D E F G H I J K L M N O P
                             C D E F G H I J K L M N O P
Attribute                  Foreground  Background  Sample
Normal                        H            A       Sample
Blocked                       H            E       Sample
Underline                     B            H       Sample
Strikeout                     A            D       Sample
Bold                          P            B       Sample
Double Underline              B            D       Sample
Redline                       E            H       Sample
Shadow                        B            H       Sample
Italics                       O            B       Sample
Small Caps                    E            D       Sample
Outline                       F            D       Sample
Subscript                     E            H       Sample
Superscript                   F            H       Sample
Fine Print                    A            F       Sample
Small Print                   H            F       Sample
Large Print                   E            A       Sample
Very Large Print              D            A       Sample
Extra Large Print             H            A       Sample
Bold & Underline              P            H       Sample
Other Combinations            A            G       Sample

Switch documents; Move to copy settings      Doc 1
```

To set the color of text in a Text mode screen in WordPerfect 6:

1. Select **F**ile **Se**tup **D**isplay **T**ext Mode Screen Type/Colors.
2. Select **C**olor Schemes and highlight one of the color schemes.
3. Select **E**dit.
4. Select **T**ext Attributes under Colors to Edit (if it is not already selected) to change the colors.
5. Select **A**ttributes
6. Select the attribute you want to change.
7. Select a color combination for foreground and background colors.
8. Repeat steps 6 and 7 for each attribute to change.
9. Select OK until you return to the document.

The dialog box after step 3 looks like this:

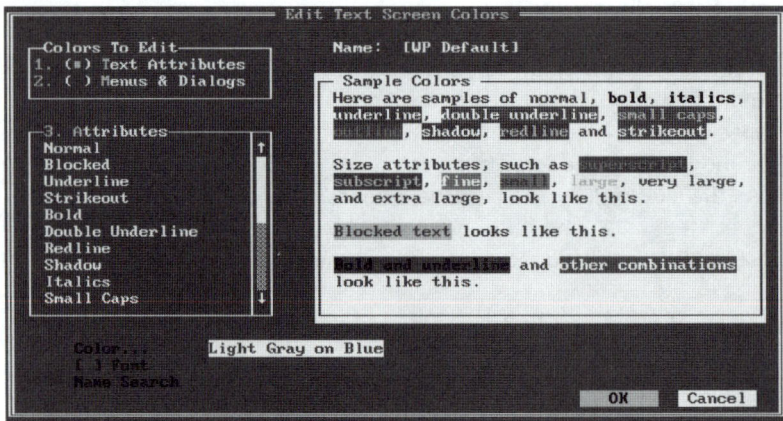

In WordPerfect 6, the color schemes you see listed at step 2 include several enclosed in brackets. These are the color schemes that WordPerfect provides and cannot be changed. You can create your own color schemes by selecting Create and supplying a name for the new color scheme.

Normal Sets Characters Back to the Default Size

You can switch off paired font settings (relative size, attributes, and position) with Font Normal. When you use this command, the end code for any paired font settings is placed to the left of the cursor's position. After you use Font Normal, the only font settings that remain in effect are open font settings.

As mentioned in Tip 152, this includes whether spaces and tabs are underlined, font typeface, text color, and font size set by Size in WordPerfect 6's Font dialog box.

Use the WordPerfect 6 Ribbon to Set the Font and Font Size

You can use the WordPerfect 6 Ribbon and your mouse to set the font typeface and size of text. When you display WordPerfect 6's Ribbon, the last two choices in the Ribbon are the font typeface and the font size. The Ribbon appears when you select View Ribbon (see Tip 200), and looks like this in Graphics mode:

The Ribbon looks like this in Text mode:

Clicking the box or arrow for the font typeface or font size selection opens a drop-down list that displays the available selections. You can double-click a selection to select the font typeface or size. With font size, you also have the option of typing the font size (assuming you type a font size available for the font). Changing the font typeface and size using the Ribbon has the same effect as if you used the Font Font command.

Set the Font Using the Font Button in WordPerfect 6's Button Bar

In addition to using the Font Font command or pressing CTRL-F8 to display the Font dialog box, you can also display the dialog box by clicking the Font button in the Button Bar. This button looks like this:

You cannot select this button with the keyboard—you must use a mouse.

Page Size and Orientation Set Portrait or Landscape Fonts

Some printers have fonts that can be used in portrait orientation and some that can be used in landscape orientation. The page size and orientation set with Layout Page Paper Size/Type sets whether a page uses portrait or landscape orientation. The list of fonts for the base font or the font you are changing to only includes the portrait or landscape orientation fonts that match the page orientation.

You Change More Than the Character Style with a Font Selection

As you change fonts, you change one or more characteristics: typeface, character style, character size, symbols in the set, horizontal spacing, pitch, or density. These are attributes of the font itself that can change when you select a new font.

Symbols in the set are the characters that the font can print without using graphics to draw the character. Some fonts include different characters, such as mathematical symbols. Horizontal spacing means how much space on the line the characters occupy. Switching to a new font that is the same size as another font can change how lines wrap because the number of characters that fits on a line changes. Horizontal spacing is also described as pitch or cpi, which is how many characters fit in one inch. Fonts that only have specific pitch settings often tell you so in the name of the font, as in Courier 10cpi.

Typefaces set to the same size in points or cpi may have different actual character sizes. For example, if you plan to use the Commercial Script - WP font, you have to increase its size so it has the same size appearance as another font with the same size settings. To show you this, the first line in the illustration below is Courier 12-point and the second line is Commercial Script - WP. The second line

looks like it is the same size. However, its actual point size has been changed from 12 to 14 points, so the two fonts appear to be the same point size:

```
Sales Distribution Map
Salesperson's Regional Distribution
```

You might also change the character style or density when you select a new font. For example, if you select Courier Italic Bold (Speedo), you are going to change the style of the font, even though you have not inserted italics or boldface hidden codes. Style refers to such qualities as italics and shadowing, while density is the weight or thickness of the lines in the characters, such as in boldface characters.

Font Menu and WordPerfect 6's Font Dialog Box Options Are the Same

TIP 159

WordPerfect 6 has the font attributes, size, and position selections both in the Font pull-down menu and in the Font dialog box that is displayed when you select Font Font. You can get the same results by changing the font attributes, size, and position selections from either location.

Use Boldface to Emphasize Text

TIP 160

When you have text that you need to emphasize, make it boldfaced. The heavier character weight will draw the reader's attention. Boldface also makes headings stand out. This is a much better option than changing the font setting to a heavier style.

WordPerfect 6 has the shortcut CTRL-B *to turn boldfacing on or off for text you are about to type or text you have selected.*

F, f

Use the RIGHT ARROW Key to End Character Attributes or Styles

You can end paired font settings such as boldface and underline by pressing RIGHT ARROW. Pressing RIGHT ARROW moves you past the code that ends the attribute, relative size, or position.

Spaces and Tabs Between Underlined Words Can Be Underlined

When there are spaces or tabs in text that is underlined, you can select whether the spaces and tabs are also to be underlined. The default setting underlines spaces but not tabs. To set whether WordPerfect 5.1 underlines spaces and tabs:

1. Select **L**ayout **O**ther.
2. Select **U**nderline.
3. Select **Y**es or **N**o for whether you want spaces underlined.
4. Select **Y**es or **N**o for whether you want tabs underlined.
5. Press F7 (Exit) to return to the document.

To set whether WordPerfect 6 underlines spaces and tabs:

1. Select F**o**nt **F**ont.
2. Select **U**nderline and select or clear the **S**paces check box.
3. Select **U**nderline and select or clear the **T**abs check box.
4. Select OK to return to the document.

WordPerfect 6 has the shortcut CTRL-U *to turn underlining on or off for text you are about to type or text you have selected.*

Italics Adds Emphasis, But Must Be Used in Moderation

Adding italics is useful for introducing new terms or adding emphasis. Don't overdo the italics, however, or your reader may end up with noticing the italics rather than the substance of the italicized text.

WordPerfect 6 has the shortcut CTRL-I *to turn italics on or off for text you are about to type or text you have selected.*

Too Much Outline and Shadow Text Is Difficult to Read

Some of the font effects, such as outline or shadow, are strictly for headings. These attributes can make headings more interesting, but you should use them only briefly because they make text harder to read.

Combining Outline and Shadow Options Makes the Text Difficult to Read

While either outline or shadow can make headings more interesting, combining the two produces results like this:

Even if you can read this you probably don't want to read too much of it. It is best not to combine these attributes.

Redline and Strikeout Show the Edits Made to a Document

When you have two documents that are similar, you can have WordPerfect compare them. In the comparison process, you have one document that you compare against a document stored on disk, even if the document is open in another window. After the comparison, the current document is displayed using redline text, which indicates text that does not appear in the document on disk, and strikeout text, which marks text in the document on the disk that was not part of the current document. To compare the documents in WordPerfect 5.1, select Mark Document Compare Add Markings. To compare the documents in WordPerfect 6, select File Compare Documents Add Markings. Then enter the name of the document to compare with the current document. You can even leave the default of the same name as the document when you want to compare the document with the version on the disk. When you select OK or press ENTER, WordPerfect performs the comparison.

A document after the comparison might look like this:

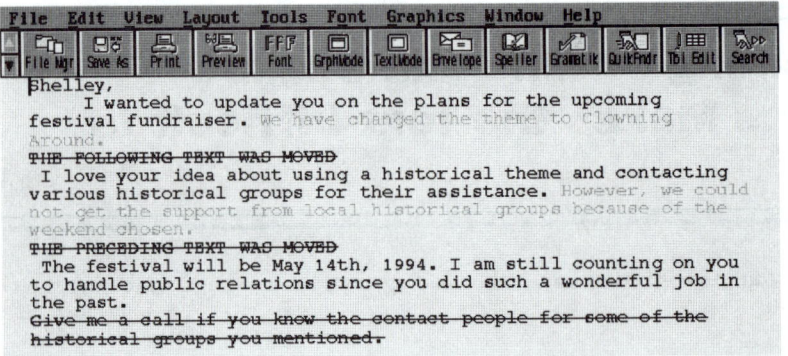

This document comparison compares DOC_SCND with the file DOCFIRST. In this document, the second and fourth sentences appear in DOC_SCND but do not appear in DOCFIRST. The last sentence appears in DOCFIRST but does not appear in DOC_SCND. The third sentence, which is not redlined but between the two strikeout indicators, is moved from one location to its current location.

Eliminating Redline and Strikeout Text in One Easy Step

TIP 167

After you have compared documents, rather than removing the strikeout and redline yourself or retrieving a new version of the file, have WordPerfect remove the redline and strikeout. To remove redline and strikeout in WordPerfect 5.1, select Mark Document Compare Remove Markings, and then select Yes to confirm that you want to remove the redline attribute and strikeout text. In WordPerfect 6, select File Compare Documents Remove Markings. Then select Remove Redline Markings and Strikeout Text and OK to remove the redline attribute from text, as well as removing all text with the strikeout attribute. In WordPerfect 6, instead of selecting Remove Redline Markings and Strikeout Text, you can select Remove Strikeout Text Only if you want to leave the redline attribute in the document.

A Marker in the Margin Can Indicate Redline Text

TIP 168

When you print a document containing redline text, the way the redline text appears in the printed copy often depends on your printer. WordPerfect's default is to use the printer selection to determine how redline text is printed. For example, a Hewlett-Packard LaserJet III prints redline text as a shade of gray. Another option lets you indicate the redline text with a character in the margin. To print redline text this way, select Layout Document Redline Method. You can select whether the printer determines how redline text is marked, or whether to indicate redlining with a character in the margin on the left side, the right side (WordPerfect 6 only), or on alternating sides for odd and even pages. In WordPerfect 5.1, if you select Left or Alternating, you can type the character to mark the redline text. In WordPerfect 6, you can select Redline Character and type the character that marks redline text.

Leave Sufficient Space for Handwritten Entries on Forms

TIP 169

When you are creating underlined areas to be filled in with handwritten entries, make sure these areas are large because handwriting is much larger than typed or printed text. This includes both horizontal and vertical space. In the following example, you can see how plenty of room is left for handwritten entries.

F, f

File Edit View Layout Tools Font Graphics Window Help

File Mgr | Save As | Print | Preview | Font | GrphMode | TextMode | Envelope | Speller | Gramatik | QuikFndr | Tbl Edit | Search

Hilson and Donald Esq.
Phone Message Form

M _____

called M _____

at _____ am/pm on _____

Will Call	Returning Call	Urgent
Please Call	Personal	Left Message

Message or Phone Number

_____

_____

PH_NOTE

This sample form for handwritten entries is stored on the accompanying disk as PH_NOTE.

You Can Hide Text in WordPerfect 6

TIP 170

Use hidden text when you have text in a document that you want to hide. In a document, hidden text does not look any different than normal text. The difference between hidden text and normal text is that you can instruct WordPerfect not to display hidden text, and the hidden text will not appear while you edit or when you print the document. (You can, if you wish, display hidden text and include it when you print the document.) To make text hidden, select Font Hidden Text and select the Hidden Text check box. Then type the text to be hidden. You can also make existing text hidden by selecting it before you select Font Hidden Text and select the Hidden Text check box.

Deciding Whether to Print Hidden Text in WordPerfect 6

TIP 171

Displaying hidden text in a document determines whether the hidden text is in a printed copy of the document. If you want the hidden text omitted from a printed copy, hide the hidden text in the document. If you want the hidden text included in a printed copy, display the hidden text in the document. To hide

or display the hidden text, select Font Hidden Text. Select the Show All Hidden Text check box if you want the hidden text to appear in the document including any printouts, or click the check box if you do not want the hidden text to appear. As an example, you might have a document that looks like this:

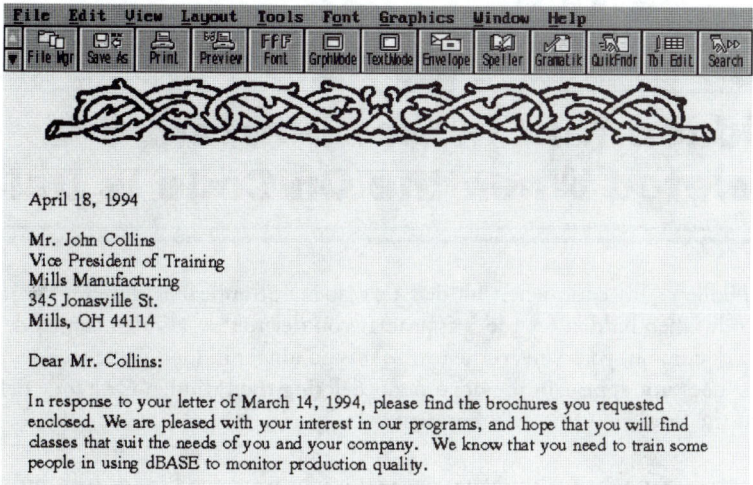

If you print this document, you will print all of the text, including the hidden text. After you hide the hidden text (the last sentence), the document will look like the following:

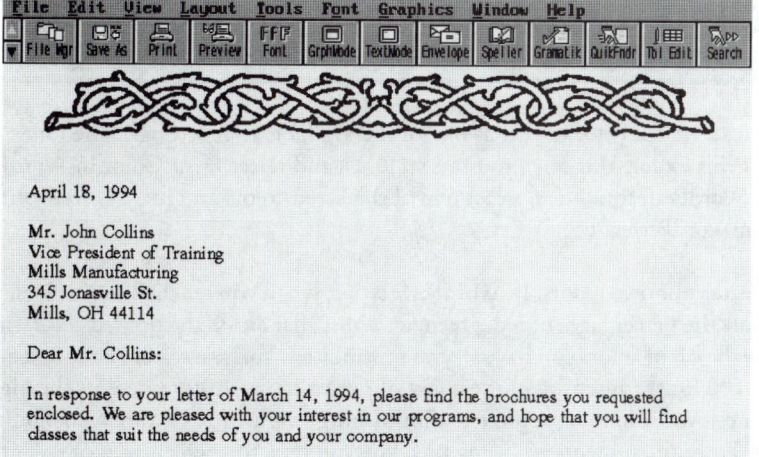

If you print this document, the hidden text will not appear on the printed copy because the hidden text does not appear onscreen at the time you began printing.

BRIAR.PCX

The letter in these illustrations includes the file BRIAR.PCX as part of the letterhead.

Hidden Text in WordPerfect 6 Is Deleted When the On Code Is Deleted

Deleting the [Hidden On] code when hidden text does not appear is different from deleting the [Hidden On] code when hidden text does appear. If you delete the [Hidden On] code while hidden text appears in a document, you convert the text so it is no longer hidden. When a document contains hidden text that does not appear in the document, deleting the [Hidden On] code deletes all of the hidden text that the [Hidden On] code represents.

If the document has many areas of hidden text, you might want the hidden text displayed. You can then block and remove both the codes and text that you want to eliminate.

Setting the Font Color

You can set the color of text as one of the available font settings. The font's color is set by selecting Font Print Color. You can also press CTRL-F8 and select Print Color in WordPerfect 5.1, or select Color in WordPerfect 6. Next, select one of the listed colors and press F7 in WordPerfect 5.1 or choose Select in WordPerfect 6.

You can also create your own colors. In WordPerfect 5.1, when you see the list of colors, you can select Other and supply the percentages of red, green, and blue that create the desired color. In WordPerfect 6, when you see the list of colors you have several possibilities. You can select Shade and enter a number between 0 and 100 for the intensity of the color you want to use. 100 represents the highest intensity of the color; the lower numbers represent diminishing intensities. Another possibility is to select Custom Color. From the subsequent dialog box, you can type the percentages of red, green, and blue to create a custom color. In the color wheel you can click the color that you want to see; by using the bar on the right you can select the darkness of the color. If you really like the color, you can select Add to Palette and supply a name for this color after Color Name.

Of course when you print the document, the text will only appear in a different color if your printer can support colors. On some printers, the different colors will print as shades of gray.

Shades of Gray Will Work on Most Black-and-White Printers

For most printers that can only print black, you can select shades of gray to print different text. When you select a color with Font Print Color and select a different color, your printer might print the text in different shades of gray. As mentioned in Tip 110, you can also add shading as a background to text by adding shading to a paragraph.

Emphasizing a Section of Text by Reversing the Colors

You can reverse the colors to have white text on a black background. This is done by changing the font's color to white. Then the paragraph, like the single line paragraph shown below, has black shading. The shading is added by selecting Layout Line Paragraph Borders Fill Style 100% Shaded Fill, then selecting OK until you return to the document. Since it is harder to read white text on black, the text should be made larger and bold. An example of this feature used for table headings looks like this:

File Edit View Layout Tools Font Graphics Window Help

Sales per Region for 1st Qtr of 1994			
	Total Sales	Average Sales per Client	Average Sales per Salesperson
Northeast	$21,456,000	$1,192,000	$2,682,000
Southeast	$34,563,300	$1,502,752	$3,142,118
Northwest	$12,432,030	$1,036,003	$2,486,406
Southwest	$43,493,400	$1,359,169	$2,899,560
Midwest	$21,304,300	$1,775,358	$2,663,038

Reverse colors do not print on all printers. You will want to preview the document to visually check that you have the results you want.

Avoid Reverse Colors or Black on Gray for Long Segments of Text

While using white-on-black letters and black letters on color or shades of gray works well in headings, too much text like this can be difficult to read, especially from a distance. Use reversed colors for headings and small sections of text as shown here:

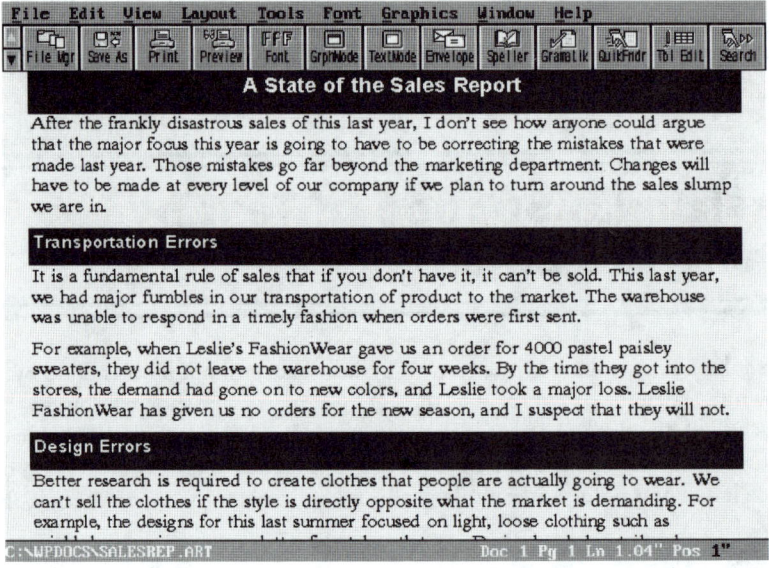

Graphics Fonts Are Available in More Sizes Than Printer Fonts

Many fonts available through your printer might only be available in specific sizes. That is why when you select Font Base Font in WordPerfect 5.1 or select Size in the Font dialog box in WordPerfect 6, you will only see specific sizes. The graphics fonts WordPerfect 6 provides are, however, available in any size. These are the fonts that have "Speedo" or "Type 1" after the font name. You may also have other graphics fonts available through your printer. Graphics fonts, also called *scalable* or *vector* fonts,

can be enlarged or reduced to fit your needs. However, they take longer to print than printer fonts. The graphics fonts available through WordPerfect have another advantage: they are shown on the screen as they will appear when printed. This is different from printer fonts, which require WordPerfect to make substitutions in order to display those fonts on the screen, as described in Tip 191.

Most Fonts Are Measured in Points, or 1/72-Inch Increments

WordPerfect can measure font sizes using different methods. Most of the time, WordPerfect measures fonts using points (1/72 inch). Some printer fonts may be measured in *pitch*, or *cpi*, which is the number of characters that fit lengthwise in an inch. Pitch and points are inversely related, since the taller a character, the higher the number of points, and the fewer characters that can usually fit on a line.

Font Sizes Can Be Set Exactly or Relatively

When you select Fine, Small, Normal, Large, Very Large, or Extra Large for font size, you are setting the font's size relative to the Normal font setting. Fonts can also be set to specific sizes. For example, when you select Font Base Font in WordPerfect 5.1, many of the selections are for specific point sizes. In WordPerfect 6, you can set a font's size using one of the relative font selections available from the Size/Position option on the Font pull-down menu or through the Font dialog box. You can also set the font's size by selecting Size in the Font dialog box and typing a new size or selecting one of the listed font sizes. Some fonts are only available in specific sizes, depending on the source of the font.

Use an Absolute Font Point Size When Applying It to the Rest of the Document

If you want to change the size of the font for the rest of the document, change the base font in WordPerfect 5.1 or change the font's size to a specific size in WordPerfect 6, rather than selecting a relative size. Relative font sizes are paired codes, so you have to select the rest of the document before you can set the new font size. In WordPerfect 5.1, when you change the base font to another size with Font Base Font, the change applies from the current location to the end of the document. In WordPerfect 6, when you select Font Font and change the font size by selecting another font in the font list or by selecting another size with Size, the change applies from the current location to the end of the document. Changing the size this way changes it with an open code rather than a paired code.

Changing the Amount of Increase in Relative Font Sizes

When you select a relative font size in WordPerfect, WordPerfect has set percentages that it uses to increase or decrease the font size relative to the normal size. You can change these percentages.

To change the percentages for relative font sizes in WordPerfect 5.1:

1. Select **F**ile Se**t**up **I**nitial Settings **P**rint Options.
2. Select **S**ize Attribute Ratios.
3. Type the percentage of normal size for each relative size.
4. Press F7 (Exit) until you return to the document.
5. Select **F**ile **P**rint **S**elect Printer.
6. Highlight your printer in the list.
7. Select **U**pdate.
8. Press F7 (Exit) until you return to the document.

In step 3, you can type different percentages for the Fine, Small, Large, Very Large, and Extra Large relative sizes, as well as the superscript and subscript attribute.

To change the percentages for relative font sizes in WordPerfect 6:

1. Select **F**ont **F**ont and Setup.
2. Select Size **R**atios.
3. Select the relative size, type the new percentage, and press ENTER.
4. Repeat step 3 for each relative size to change.
5. Select OK until you return to the document.

Step 1 above can also be performed by selecting File Print/Fax Select, highlighting the printer, and selecting Edit and Font Setup.

The change will only have an effect if the font is available in other sizes. For example, some printer fonts are only available in specific sizes. If you use some of the graphics fonts provided through WordPerfect, you have more sizes and styles available (although printing can take longer).

Status Line Increments Vary by the Size of the Font Selected

The status line's Ln measurement changes to show the vertical position of the top of the line where the text is being placed. When you change the height of the line by changing the font of characters in the line, the amount the status line increases when you move to the next line increases. For example, if you use the Bitstream Courier font and change the font size from 12 to 16 points, the line height will change from .167 inch to .223 inch. You will also notice how the status line, instead of going from 1 inch to 1.16 inches when moving from the first to the second line, will go from 1 inch to 1.22 inches.

Starting New Documents with a Different Font

WordPerfect has multiple methods for setting the font in a new document. You can set a document's initial font with one of the following selections:

- ❏ Select Layout Document Initial Font (Initial Base Font in WordPerfect 5.1).

- ❏ Select File Print Select Printer, highlight the printer, select Edit and Initial Base Font in WordPerfect 5.1. Select File Print/Fax Select Edit Font Setup Select Initial Font in WordPerfect 6.

- ❏ Select Font Font Setup Select Initial Font in WordPerfect 6.

In WordPerfect 5.1, you will see a list of the available fonts. Selecting one of these selects the initial font. In WordPerfect 6, each of these options displays the following dialog box:

F, f

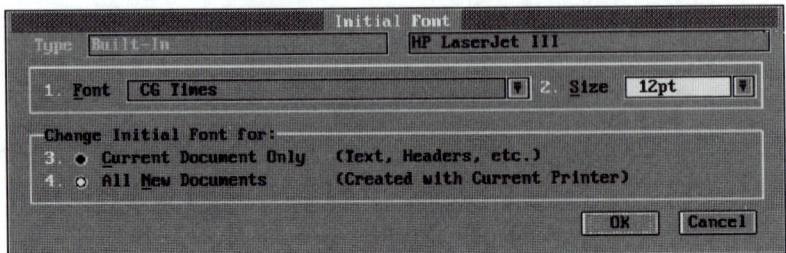

You can select Font and one of the fonts listed. If the font size varies, you can select Size and type or select an available size. You must also decide whether the Current Document Only or the All New Documents radio button is selected. Selecting the Current Document Only radio button sets the initial font for only the current document. The All New Documents radio button sets the initial font for every document created while the printer named at the top of the dialog box is selected. Selecting the font through File Print/Fax always sets the font for all new documents. Setting the font with Layout Document in WordPerfect always sets the initial font for only the current document.

You can also change a font for a single document by moving to the beginning of the document and selecting the font with Font Font. Another possibility is to select Layout Document and Document Initial Codes or Initial Codes Setup (depending on whether you want to change the current or new documents), and press CTRL-F8 or select Font Font to select one of the fonts.

Each Printer Can Have Its Own Initial Font

Setting the initial font applies to a specific printer. If you change to another printer, the initial font changes to the initial font last selected for the new printer. For example, suppose you usually use a Hewlett-Packard LaserJet III printer and have selected the Courier 10 cpi font as the initial font. If you change to a Brother HL-10DV printer, the initial font will change to a font such as Brougham 10 cpi, assuming you have not selected this printer before and changed its initial font. After you change to a different printer, you can change the initial font to the font that you want used on all documents created for that printer, as described in Tip 183.

Change Tab and Column Spacing with Display Pitch in Text Mode

Display pitch is a measurement that determines the character widths used by formats such as tab and indent, as well as column, table, and graphics box margins. It is important because these format features normally use an absolute measurement rather than a specific number of characters. It is needed in Text mode because characters are always displayed the same size regardless of the point size of the font chosen. When separated by tabs, characters with a small point size might not appear the way you would expect, even though they will print correctly. All of your columns do not appear onscreen at the same time with a font size of 4 points and columns set at 2.5, 4.5, and 6, as shown here:

```
File  Edit  View  Layout  Tools  Font  Graphics  Window  Help
er
Inc                                               Teak
                                                  Walnut
```

The reason is that the automatic display pitch shows the number of small characters that can fit in the space without overlap and therefore expands the space between columns, and all columns will not display at once. The display pitch set automatically is .025; if you change it to .9, you can see all of the columns at once, like this:

```
File  Edit  View  Layout  Tools  Font  Graphics  Window  Help
            Desk                   Henry Miller      Teak
            Chair                  All-Wood, Inc     Walnut
```

Use these steps in WordPerfect 6 to change the display pitch:

1. Select **L**ayout **D**ocument.
2. Select **D**isplay Pitch.
3. Type a value and select **M**anual.
4. Select OK and Close.

When you want the setting to be automatic, repeat the procedure but substitute a selection of Automatic in step 3.

In WordPerfect 5.1, follow these steps to make the change:

1. Select **L**ayout **D**ocument.
2. Select **D**isplay Pitch.
3. Select **N**o to turn off the automatic setting and type a new display pitch.
4. Press F7 (Exit).

Create Counters That WordPerfect 6 Updates

WordPerfect 6 can handle counters that you create within a document. You probably have already used several of WordPerfect's internal counters. As Tips 130, 460, and 599 mention, WordPerfect can number pages, footnotes, endnotes, and graphics boxes for you. WordPerfect uses counters to keep track of this kind of numbering. Using page numbers as an example, when you include the page number on a page, WordPerfect places the current value of its page number counter. When WordPerfect finishes printing the page, it adds one to the current value of the page number counter.

You can create your own counters. Counters in WordPerfect can be created, displayed in a document, and increased. You can create a counter for any document where you want WordPerfect to handle numbering. For example, in the following document, the step numbers that appear are counters. WordPerfect makes sure that the numbers are consecutive.

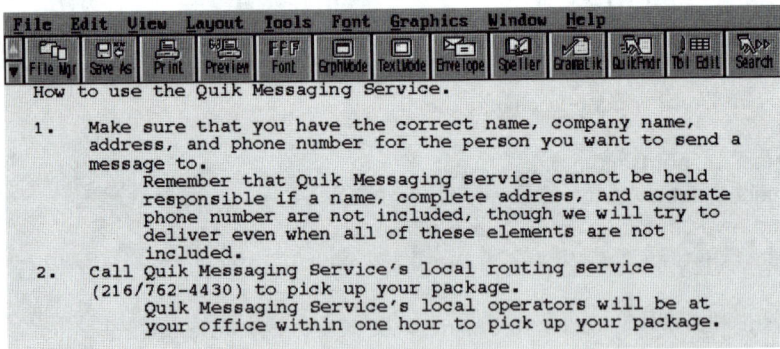

To create a counter like this one, select Layout Character Counters and Create. WordPerfect 6 shows the Create Counter Definition dialog box:

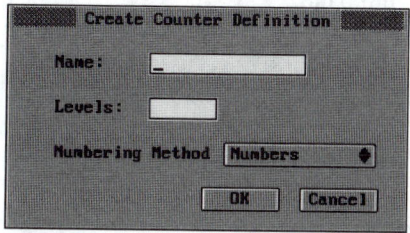

Type a name for the counter. You can also have multiple levels, just as you can have multiple levels of page numbers (as described in Tip 135). You can also select Numbering Method to select how the counters appear when you add them to the document. When you select OK to close the Create Counters Definition dialog box, the Counters dialog box appears. From this dialog box you can edit the existing counter's current value and numbering method. You can also select Increment or Decrement to increase or decrease the value of the counter highlighted under Counter.

Often when you are using counters in a document you will press F8 from the Counters dialog box to select Increment & Display to close the dialog boxes, put the counter in the document, and increase the counter so the next time you use it the counter's value is automatically one higher. When you are using a counter you can also select Display in Document when you want the counter's current value to appear without changing the current value.

Use Kerning to Decrease Space Between Characters

TIP 187

To reduce space between characters, use WordPerfect's kerning features. Kerning adjusts the space between characters so the amount of space between letters looks the same. For example, when you type **DD II** on a typewriter, there appears to be more space between the two I's than the two D's. Using a proportional font (like the one used in the book) makes the space between the characters more even. Kerning performs further adjustment. It reduces the space between specific combinations of characters. When you print a document with kerning, it prints slower because WordPerfect must make more adjustments to the placement of characters on a line. Kerning does not work with all fonts.

To use kerning in a document, select Layout Other Printer Functions **Kerning**. With Yes selected in WordPerfect 5.1 or the check box selected in WordPerfect 6, WordPerfect will kern characters. This command will affect the remainder of the document unless you block the section of text that will be kerned before performing the command.

Kerning is set through the printer files WordPerfect uses. These can be modified with the PTR program that is part of WordPerfect's utilities. Tips 314, 315, and 316 include more information about the PTR utility.

Setting Printer Spacing Between Characters and Words

The spacing between words and letters can be set by the printer, by WordPerfect's printer definition file, or by you. The default is to use the spacing setting set by WordPerfect. This is why, when you select Layout Other Printer Functions Word Spacing in WordPerfect 5.1, or Word Spacing and Letterspacing in WordPerfect 6, the current setting for Word Spacing and Letterspacing is **Optimal**. You can also select **Normal** if you want to use the default word and letter spacing set by the printer. You can select **Percent of Optimal** or **% of Optimal** (depending on your WordPerfect version) and type the percentage of the **Optimal** setting that you want to use. The final option is to select **Set Pitch** and type the number of characters you want to fit per inch. As an example, the text below shows text with different settings for word and letter spacing:

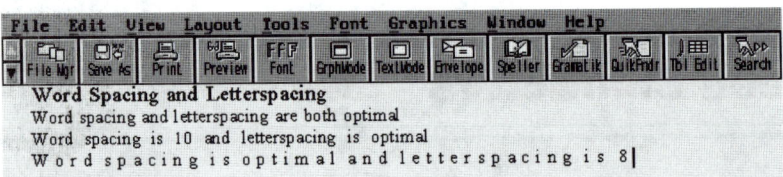

When you change the font's size, the pitch for letter and word spacing changes in proportion to the new size. Sometimes, however, the word and letter spacing is set by the printer or the selected font, so you will not be able to change the word and line spacing.

Setting WordPerfect to Use Your Printer Cartridges

You can set up WordPerfect to use any printer cartridges you have. To do this in WordPerfect 5.1, follow these steps:

1. Select **F**ile **P**rinter or press SHIFT-F7 (Exit) then choose **S**elect Printer.
2. Select **E**dit with the highlight on the printer that uses cartridges.
3. Select **C**artridges and Fonts.
4. Highlight Cartridges and select **S**elect.
5. Highlight the name of your cartridge and press * to select it.
6. Repeat step 5 for each cartridge on your printer.
7. Press F7 (Exit) until you return to the document.

To do this in WordPerfect 6, follow these steps:

1. Select **F**ont **F**ont and Setup.
2. Select Select **C**artridges/Fonts/Print Wheels.
3. Highlight Cartridges and select **E**dit.
4. Highlight the name of your cartridge and press * to select it.
5. Repeat step 4 for each cartridge on your printer.
6. Select OK until you return to the document.

Step 1 can also be performed by selecting File Print/Fax Select, highlighting the printer, and selecting Edit and Font Setup.

Printer Fonts Do Not Come in All Sizes and Might Not Support All WordPerfect Features

If you are using printer fonts, you may be limited in the WordPerfect font features you can use. Some printer fonts come in predefined sizes and cannot work with all of WordPerfect's features. For example, a font may not support italics. When you use a printer font with an attribute it does not support,

WordPerfect makes a substitution as described in Tip 191. You can see the results of the substitution when you preview the printed document or when you print it.

Appearance of Printer Fonts Is Different When the Document Is Actually Printed

Since your printer does not tell WordPerfect what the characters look like when printed, WordPerfect substitutes the printer fonts in a document with one of the software fonts it has available. One of the consequences of selecting a printer is to tell WordPerfect the fonts that your printer supplies. Selecting the printer also selects the graphics fonts that WordPerfect uses to display printer fonts. For example, when you use a Courier font available through your printer, WordPerfect knows to use its Speedo Courier font when it displays text with that font in WordPerfect's Text display mode or in Print Preview. If you do not like the substitution WordPerfect makes, you can change the font WordPerfect uses to display the text in Graphics editing mode and in the Print Preview. To make this change, follow these steps:

1. Select F**o**nt F**o**nt and Setup.
2. Select Edit **S**creen Font Mapping Table.
3. Select the printer font to change and **S**elect Screen Font.
4. Select a font from the ones listed.
5. Repeat steps 3 and 4 for each printer font to change.
6. Select OK until you return to the document.

If you want to return to the default, which allows the printer driver file to select the corresponding screen font to use with each printer font, select Auto Map Font in step 3.

Setting Printing for Any Combination of Font Typeface and Attribute

When you add an attribute to a font, WordPerfect has to check how the font will appear with that attribute. For example, if you add italics to a font, WordPerfect must adjust the font. Some fonts are not available in bold or italics, and others are only available in specific sizes. In these cases, WordPerfect must change the typeface style or make some other font change to give you the results you want.

For example, in a document using Courier 10 cpi on a Hewlett-Packard LaserJet printer, when you change the text to extra large, the font looks different, as you can see here:

```
Courier 10 cpi
Courier 10 cpi Extra Large|
```

Since the Courier 10 cpi font is only available in a specific size, WordPerfect substitutes another font that is available at a larger size, in this case CG Times. In a Hewlett-Packard LaserJet III printer, the CG Times font is scalable, so it is available in sizes ranging from .25 to 999.75 points.

The translation between the fonts you select in your document and the fonts that are used when you print the document are chosen by the printer you have selected. You can, however, override the translation if you want to change how a font with different attributes prints. For example, if you have added printer cartridges to a Hewlett-Packard LaserJet III printer, you may want to use some of the fonts available through the cartridges when you select different attributes of the printer's fonts.

You can change the font WordPerfect uses for the substitution when you add different attributes. You can make the substitutions for either printer fonts or graphics fonts, although you cannot use a graphics font (such as a Bitstream Speedo font) in place of a printer font nor can you use a printer font as a substitution for a graphics font. To make the change, select Font Font and Setup or File Print/Fax Select, highlight the printer, and select Edit and Font Setup. From the Font Setup dialog box, select Edit Automatic Font Changes for Printer Fonts to change the way a printer font is adjusted as you add different attributes or select Edit Automatic Font Changes for Graphics Fonts to change the way a graphics font is adjusted as you add different attributes. Highlight the name of the font to change and select Edit. Highlight the attribute that you want to change and select Edit again. Highlight the font to use in place of the font named at the top of the dialog box and choose Select.

WordPerfect 5.1 does this change through its PTR program. Tips 317 and 319 describe some of the many changes you can make through this program.

Using Soft Fonts Provided by Your Printer

In addition to the graphics fonts provided through WordPerfect, you might also have fonts provided by third-party software. Both the graphical fonts provided by WordPerfect and fonts provided by other software are called *soft fonts* because they are created by software. This is different than fonts built into your printer, which are called *printer fonts*. WordPerfect can use soft fonts—such as the Bitstream and TrueType fonts—that work on many different printers, as well as soft fonts specifically designed for your printer. Tips 194 and 195 discuss working with the first type of soft fonts. The second type of soft fonts are installed differently than the first.

If you are using printer soft fonts, they are either loaded once or as needed. The advantage of loading a soft font once is that it is always available as you print additional documents. The disadvantage of loading a soft font once is that it consumes printer memory that you might want to use for other purposes. With soft fonts that are loaded as needed, the advantage is that the font is in the printer's memory only while printing the document. The disadvantage of loading a soft font as needed is, of course, that it must be loaded every time you print a document using that soft font. Frequently used soft fonts should be loaded once. WordPerfect 6, unlike WordPerfect 5.1, allows you to load fonts as needed.

To add printer soft fonts to WordPerfect 5.1, select File Print Select Printer, highlight the printer, and select Edit Cartridges and Fonts. Highlight Soft Fonts and choose Select. Next, select the group of printer soft fonts you are using and choose Select. You will see a list of the different possible combinations of the font group and the different sizes available, along with the memory each font takes. Move to the fonts you want to add and press *. You can only add as many soft fonts as you have memory. When all the fonts you want are added, press F7 (Exit) until you return to the document. From the same screen you saw after you selected Cartridges and Fonts, you can also select Change Quantity and type a new amount of printer memory that you want to reserve for soft fonts.

To add printer soft fonts to WordPerfect 6, first select Font Font. Next select Setup and choose Select Cartridges/Fonts/Print Wheels, highlight Soft Font and choose Edit. Next, select the group of printer soft fonts you are using and choose Edit. If there are predefined fonts, you will see a list of the different possible combinations of the font group. If there are none, you will see the message "No predefined fonts for this font category". If the fonts display, the different sizes available, (along with the memory each font uses), will also display. Move to the fonts you want to be loaded once and press *. Move to the fonts you want to be loaded as needed and press +. You can only add as many soft fonts as you have memory. When all the fonts you want are added, select OK until you return to the document. From the same screen you saw after you selected Cartridges/Fonts/Print Wheels, you can also select Quantity and type a new amount of printer memory that you want to reserve for soft fonts.

F, f

You Must Install Soft Fonts Before You Can Use Them

At the time you install soft fonts that are not installed with WordPerfect, you are informing WordPerfect that you are using those soft fonts. The fonts will have files that need to be copied to your hard disk. Follow the font's directions for the procedure. If the font's instructions include directions for using the fonts with your version of WordPerfect, follow those directions. Once the soft fonts are installed, you might need to initialize the printer as described in Tip 280. You may also need to select the soft fonts, as described in Tip 193.

In WordPerfect 5.1, after you install the soft fonts according to the directions that accompany the soft font software, start WordPerfect. Select File Print Select Printer, highlight the printer, select Edit and Path for Downloadable Fonts and Printer Command Files. Type the directory where the files are located and press ENTER. At this point, select Cartridges and Fonts to select the fonts, pressing F7 (Exit) until you return to the document.

In WordPerfect 6, the Font Installer program handles most of the font installation. The Font Installer program can be run from the WordPerfect Installation program, from the DOS prompt by entering **WPFI**, or from within WordPerfect by selecting Font Font Setup Install Fonts. From the Font Installer program, you select the type of font, tell the program where the font files are located, mark the ones you want to add, and select Install Marked Fonts. When the fonts are installed, they are available for WordPerfect documents.

Using Bitstream, CG Intellifont, TrueType, and Type 1 Fonts from Other Sources

Bitstream, CG Intellifont, TrueType, and Type 1 fonts may be available through other packages you have on your system. You can make them available in WordPerfect as well. You need to tell WordPerfect where it can find the files the soft fonts use. Tip 194 includes more information on installing the soft font files that you find on your system.

$\mathcal{F}, f$

For example, if you have Windows 3.1 installed on your system, you can use the same Windows TrueType fonts in your WordPerfect documents. To do this, start the WordPerfect Font Installer program and select TrueType. When prompted for the location of the files, select .TTF Files and supply the location of the Windows TrueType files, which is \WINDOWS\SYSTEM, using the default Windows locations. If you have two groups of the same font files in different locations, copy them to another location and use the new location to install the fonts into WordPerfect.

To find these font files, you need to know where they are stored. Use DOS or WordPerfect's File Manager to find the files with the correct file extensions. Bitstream needs .TTF files, CG Intellifont needs .TYP and .SFS files, TrueType needs .TTF files, and Type 1 needs .TTF files. If you find these files, try using them.

If WordPerfect Cannot Find an Installed Font, Check the Directory

TIP 196

If you want to use a soft font that you have installed but you cannot find it or WordPerfect displays a message that it cannot find it, make sure that WordPerfect is looking for the font in the appropriate directory. First check which directory contains the files for the soft font.

In WordPerfect 5.1, select File Print Select Printer, highlight the printer that will use the soft fonts, and select Edit. From the Select Printer: Edit screen, select Path for Downloadable Fonts and Printer Command Files. Then type the directory where these files are on your hard disk. After pressing F7 (Exit) until you return to your document, you should be able to use the soft fonts.

In WordPerfect 6, start the Font Installer by selecting Font Font Setup Install Fonts. From the Select Font Type in the Font Installer, select the type of font. At this point you will either see the Location of Files dialog box or select Directories for Files. Select the option for the type of files and type in the directory where these files are located on your hard disk. After selecting OK and Exit until you return to your document, you should be able to use the soft fonts.

To Use an Installed Soft Font That You Cannot Find, Update the Graphic Fonts List

If you run the Font Installer program outside of WordPerfect 6, you might need to tell WordPerfect to update its tables of the fonts that are available, and update the way it should change the font when you add different attributes. You can do this by selecting Font Font Setup Update Graphics Fonts.

The other reason you might not find a soft font you have installed is that the font is not completely installed. For example, it is easy to go into the Font Installer program, select the font type, supply directory entries, mark the fonts to install and select Exit. Since Install Marked Fonts was not selected, the fonts are not properly installed. You will need to complete *all* the font installation steps before the fonts are available to WordPerfect 6.

Selecting Which of Your Printer's Built-in Fonts Are Available for Your WordPerfect Documents

You may want to remove fonts you do not use so that you can easily find the ones you do use. You can restore these fonts when you want to use them again. To change which printer fonts appear in the list of available base fonts in WordPerfect 5.1, follow these steps:

1. Select **F**ile **P**rint **S**elect Printer.
2. Highlight the printer and select **E**dit and **C**artridges and Fonts.
3. Highlight Built-In and choose **S**elect.
4. Add and remove fonts by moving to them and pressing the SPACEBAR.
   Fonts that have a * before their name will appear in the font list.
5. Press F7 (Exit) until you return to the document.

If you have soft fonts, select Soft Fonts in step 3 and select the font group before selecting which of the soft fonts are available for your documents.

To change which printer fonts appear in WordPerfect 6's Font list:

1. Select **Fo**nt **Fo**nt Setup and Select **C**artridge/Fonts/Print Wheels.
2. Highlight Built-In to modify the printer's internal fonts and **E**dit.
3. Add and remove fonts by moving to them and pressing the SPACEBAR.
    Fonts that have a * before their name will appear in the font list.
4. Select OK to complete the font selection.

If you have soft fonts, select Soft Fonts in step 2 and select the font group before selecting which of the soft fonts are available for your documents.

With both versions of WordPerfect, if you remove a printer font that a document uses, WordPerfect makes its best substitution. The document will contain a * in front of the replacement font's name. However, the document continues to remember the original font; if the original font later becomes available, WordPerfect will use it.

Selecting Which Graphics Fonts Are Available to Your WordPerfect 6 Documents

If you have an overwhelming number of graphics fonts available, you might want to remove the fonts you don't normally use so you can easily find the ones you do use. Also, if you have removed some of the fonts you have installed in WordPerfect, you might want to restore them so they are available to your documents. To change which graphics fonts appear in the Font list, follow these steps:

1. Select **Fo**nt **Fo**nt Setup and Select **G**raphics Fonts. WordPerfect lists the installed graphics fonts.
2. Add and remove fonts by moving to them and pressing the SPACEBAR.
    Fonts that have a * before their name will appear in the font list.
3. Select OK to complete the font selection.

If you remove a graphics font that a document uses, WordPerfect makes its best substitution when you open the document. When you look at the font code for the graphics font that is no longer used, you will see a * in front of the font name. The document retains the font name, so if you restore the font at a later time, the document will return to using that font.

You can add or remove all of the fonts for a particular source of font, such as all of the Bitstream fonts. Only the graphics font files that are included will appear in the list of graphics fonts that you can make available. To change the font sources that are available, follow these steps:

1. Select **F**ile **S**etup **L**ocation of Files and Graphics **F**onts Data Files. WordPerfect lists the available graphics screen font sources.
2. Add and remove fonts by moving to them and pressing the SPACEBAR Fonts that have a * before their name will appear in the font list.
3. Select OK until you return to the document.

CHAPTER 4

Screen

WordPerfect 6 Text and Graphics Mode Options Must Be Set Separately

You must set the Button Bar and Ribbon options separately for Text and Graphics modes. If you display the Button Bar in Graphics mode and then switch to Text mode, the Button Bar is not displayed. You will have to choose to display the Button Bar again if you want to show it in Text mode.

To display the Button Bar or Ribbon:

> Select **V**iew **B**utton Bar or **V**iew **R**ibbon.

Alternatively, if you want to change several options at once, use this procedure:

1. Select **V**iew Scree**n** Setup or press CTRL-F3 and then SHIFT-F1.
2. Select **S**creen Options.
3. Select the options you want displayed on the screen. For the Ribbon, select **R**ibbon (Graphics) or R**i**bbon (Text). For the Button Bar, select **B**utton Bar (Graphics) or Bu**t**ton Bar (Text).

If you are using WordPerfect 6 and there is no Button Bar visible on the screen, select View Button Bar to display it.

Use WordPerfect 6 Buttons to Switch Modes

Each of the three modes in WordPerfect 6 has its own advantages. The Text mode is the ideal way to enter text quickly since WordPerfect is not slowed down by having to redraw graphics images on the screen. As the following image shows, it can be difficult to tell exactly what the completed document will look like in Text mode; the graphics image is shown as an empty box and special font selections all appear the same size with different colors distinguishing one attribute from another:

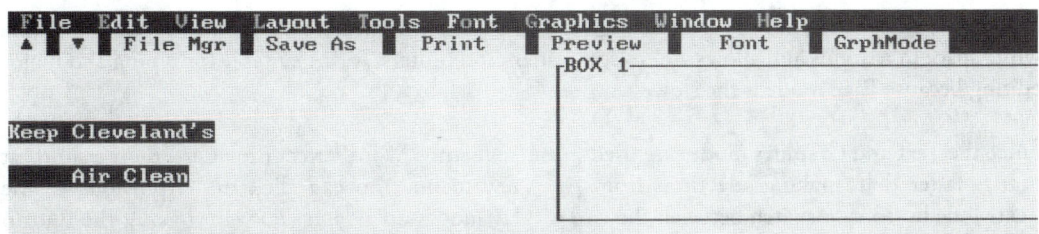

The Graphics mode lets you see how graphics images and various fonts and colors will appear when printed but is slower than Text mode. The same document can appear quite different in Graphics mode as you have a WYSIWYG (What You See Is What You Get) display, which looks like this:

Page mode shows the entire page, which gives you a better perspective of the text in relation to the white space in margins and allows you to see headers and footers. It isn't suitable for typing and major editing because Page mode is the slowest mode.

Since the Text and Graphics modes are used most frequently, WordPerfect provides a mouse shortcut that is faster than making selections from the View menu. You can click the GrphMode or the TextMode buttons to switch between the two display modes quickly. If you want to alter the Button Bar as discussed in Tip 221 you can add a button that will let you change to Page mode quickly.

Without a mouse, the quickest approach is to use the CTRL-F3 *key, and then choose Display Mode from the Screen dialog box.*

Change the Background Color When Your Eyes Tire

The default background color for WordPerfect 5.1 and Text mode in WordPerfect 6 is a bright blue. You may find that this color becomes boring, or that your eyes feel strained. Changing the background color provides variety and can ease eye fatigue.

To change the background color for WordPerfect 6:

1. Switch to Text mode.
2. Select **F**ile Se**t**up **D**isplay.
3. Select **T**ext Mode Screen Type/Colors to display the following dialog box:

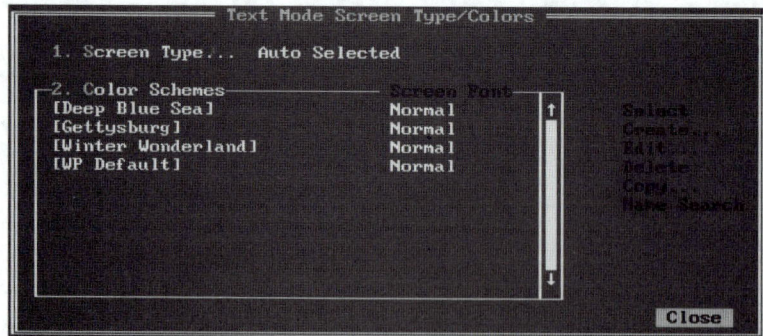

4. Select **C**olor Schemes.
5. Select **C**reate, type a name for the color scheme, and select OK.
   If you prefer to edit a color scheme you created earlier, highlight the desired scheme and choose **E**dit instead.
6. Select **A**ttributes.
7. Highlight Normal.
8. Select **C**olor.
9. Use the arrow keys to move to the color combination you want to use for normal text.
10. Select OK twice.
11. Choose **S**elect to use the newly created color scheme.
12. Select Close.

Once you create your new WordPerfect 6 color scheme, you can use macros to switch the screen color at any time. You can have two macros, one to switch to the new colors and one to switch back to the default colors. The following macro, which is named ALTN.WPM after the ALT-N combination, can be used to switch to a color scheme named "newcolor":

```
DISPLAY(Off!)
DisplayMode(Text!)
ColorSchemeSelect("newcolor")
SetupSave
```

If you create another custom color scheme you can edit the macro ALTN.WPM and replace "newcolor" with the name of your color scheme enclosed in quotes. For example if your new color scheme is called "lotsared", line three of the macro would read ColorSchemeSelect("lotsared").

A second macro to switch back to WordPerfect's default might look like this:

```
DISPLAY(Off!)
DisplayMode(Text!)
ColorSchemeSelect("[WP Default]")
SetupSave
```

Notice the square brackets inside the quotes and surrounding the name of the color scheme. All WordPerfect default color schemes require these brackets in addition to the quotes.

If you assign the macros to buttons on the Button Bar you can even switch colors with a quick click.

ALTN.WPM
ALTB.WPM

These sample macros are available on the accompanying disk as ALTN.WPM and ALTB.WPM.

To change the background colors with WordPerfect 5.1:

1. Press SHIFT-F1 (Setup) or select **F**ile Se**t**up.
2. Select **D**isplay.
3. Select **C**olors/Fonts/Attributes.
4. Select 1 **S**creen Colors.
5. Use the arrow keys to move the row for the **N**ormal attribute.
6. Type the letter that corresponds to the color in which you want text to appear from the sample at the top.
7. Press the RIGHT ARROW key to move to the Background column.
8. Type the letter that corresponds to the background color you want from the sample shown at the top.
9. Press F7 twice to continue editing your document.

Although you can change the color of various screen objects, there is no way to change the color of the background when you are in WordPerfect 6's Graphics mode.

Font Colors Do Not Appear in Text Mode

You can assign colors to blocks of text. Assuming you have a color printer, you can print that text in the assigned colors. In Graphics mode for WordPerfect 6, text assigned a color appears in that color. In Text mode, however, the text does not change to the assigned color. Colors are assigned to text in Text mode to indicate various attributes that can be applied to text (such as boldfacing, italics, and so on). Therefore, although text can be printed in color, it cannot be displayed in color. To see how your document will appear in color, either switch to Graphics mode or use the Print Preview screen.

Since there is no Graphics Mode option for WordPerfect 5.1, colors will never appear on the editing screen but will appear when printed on a color printer or in the Print Preview screen.

You Cannot Use the Arrow Keys to Move to Another Document

TIP 204

In WordPerfect 5.1 you can use both a document 1 and a document 2 window to work on two documents at once or to copy or move text between them. In WordPerfect 6, you now can use nine different document windows at the same time. Since you can size WordPerfect windows you may have more than one window onscreen at once. You might be tempted to try to move to another window using the arrow keys. After all, the text in the second window may be just below or above the window you are in. Why not use the arrow keys to move there?

You can't because arrow keys are effective only within the active window. Even if another document window lies just below the current one, when you reach the end of the current document and press the DOWN ARROW key, WordPerfect beeps and does not move to the next window. To move to another window, you must switch to it using either the menu or the keyboard.

To move to the previously active window:

> Select **W**indow **S**witch to or press SHIFT-F3

Because WordPerfect 6 can have so many open windows you need a quick way to pick from a list. To move to any open window in WordPerfect 6:

> 1.   Select **W**indow **S**witch or press F3.
> 2.   Type the number for the window you want to make active or click it.

In WordPerfect 6, the quickest way to change to another window that is displayed is to click it. Another shortcut is to press the HOME *key and type the number of the desired window, as you'll see in Tip 211.*

Ease Eye Strain by Looking Elsewhere

TIP 205

Staring at the computer screen all day is not good for your eyes. Eventually you start to feel the strain in headaches or eye fatigue. If you can type by touch, an easy solution is not to stare at the screen. If you are typing from someone's notes, you will focus on those notes. If you are writing at the keyboard or transcribing from a Dictaphone, simply look at a calendar, a print, or a blank wall. Position

your body so you can view the screen easily and check what you are typing, to make sure you haven't pressed the CAPS LOCK key or placed your fingers on the wrong keys.

Use the Highest Resolution to Improve Screen Appearance

How your screen displays the text you enter into WordPerfect is partially determined by the screen driver file. The screen driver file sets certain options concerning the resolution of the screen. Resolution means how many tiny dots of light can appear on the screen. The more dots of light, the finer or more precise the image on the screen can be. If there are fewer dots, it is hard to show small details. A screen driver also determines if you display black and white or color.

The screen driver file you select must be compatible with the actual hardware you have. If you select a screen driver for a color monitor, and yours is monochrome, you are going to have a problem. If your graphics card—the card inside your computer that translates messages from the computer and sends them to the screen—can only handle EGA screens (EGA refers to a level of resolution), then you may be able to select a VGA screen driver, but it will not improve your screen appearance. Remember, how well your monitor displays WordPerfect depends on a combination of the graphics card, the monitor itself, and the screen driver you select.

You can improve your screen display by choosing for your screen driver the highest possible setting that your hardware supports. The screen setting in WordPerfect 6 is set separately for Text mode and Graphics mode.

To change the screen driver for either mode in WordPerfect 6:

1. Select **F**ile Se**t**up **D**isplay.
2. Select **G**raphics Mode Screen Type/Colors or **T**ext Mode Screen Type/Colors.
3. Select **S**creen Type.
4. Highlight the name of the screen driver.
5. Choose **S**elect.
6. Highlight the resolution you want to use.
7. Choose **S**elect.
8. Select Close twice.

To change the screen driver for WordPerfect 5.1:

1. Select **F**ile Se**t**up **D**isplay.
2. Select **G**raphics Screen Type or **T**ext Screen Type.
3. Highlight the desired driver, and then choose **S**elect.
4. Press F7 (Exit) twice to return to your document.

In WordPerfect 6, Switch to Text Mode to Change Text Attribute Colors

In Text mode, the attributes you assign to text, such as size, boldfacing, or italics, are indicated by different colored text or backgrounds. Before you can change the display settings, you must switch to Text mode. You cannot change these settings in Graphics mode because the menu options are dimmed (indicating that they are not currently available).

Change the Colors of WordPerfect 6 Screen Elements

You can change the colors assigned to dialog box elements and other screen elements in both Graphics and Text modes by changing the current color scheme. In Text mode, color schemes also indicate how text is supposed to appear, depending on the attributes assigned to it. In Graphics mode you cannot change the color of text or its background because the colors onscreen display in the same colors that will print.

To select a new color scheme:

1. Select **F**ile Se**t**up **D**isplay.
2. Select **G**raphics Mode Screen Type/Colors or **T**ext Mode Screen Type/Colors.
3. Select **C**olor Schemes.
4. Highlight a different color scheme and choose **S**elect.
5. Select Close.

You can either use the color schemes provided or create your own color schemes. The process is a little different for Graphics and Text modes.

1. Select **F**ile Se**t**up **D**isplay.
2. Select **G**raphics Mode Screen Type/Colors or **T**ext Mode Screen Type/Colors.
3. Select **C**olor Schemes.
4. Select **C**reate, type a name, and select OK.
5. Select **S**creen Elements. If you are setting colors for Text mode, select Color to Edit and then select **M**enus & Dialogs.
6. Highlight the screen element you want to assign a new color to and select **C**olor.
7. Use the arrow keys to highlight the color you want to assign and choose Select.
8. Repeat steps 6 and 7 until you have reassigned all of the screen elements that you want to.
9. Select OK.
10. Highlight the new color scheme and choose **S**elect.
11. Select Close twice.

WordPerfect 6 Protects the Default Color Schemes

WordPerfect 6 provides four default color schemes for Text mode and four default color schemes for Graphics mode. These predefined color schemes cannot be edited or changed. You can tell which color schemes are provided by WordPerfect because once you get to the Graphics (Text) Mode Screen Type/Colors dialog box, and look at the contents of the Color Schemes list box, you will see that some of the color scheme names are enclosed within square brackets. These are the default color schemes. Except for these bracketed schemes, you can edit any color scheme.

You Can Display a Document in Two Windows but Only Save from One

You can open two copies of a document into two different document windows. WordPerfect will allow you to make changes in both windows and save one copy over another unless you use the DOS SHARE command in your AUTOEXEC.BAT file. If you try this, you will lose one set of changes. If you put the DOS SHARE command in your AUTOEXEC.BAT file, copies after the first copy of a document opened will be read-only and you will not need to worry about one set of changes overlaying another.

You can make changes to the original copy and use the second copy to reference what the document looked like before you started making changes. You can make changes to both documents and save them to different names. WordPerfect lets you save the first copy opened to the original filename. When you want to save the copy of the file in the second or later document window, you have to supply another filename. To alter your AUTOEXEC.BAT file to safeguard against making changes to two copies of the same document, enter this line in your CONFIG.SYS file:

```
C:\DOS\SHARE.EXE
```

You will need to reboot your system to have this command take effect.

Switch to a WordPerfect 6 Window by Pressing HOME and the Window's Number

WordPerfect 6 offers a shortcut for switching to another document window, if you know which window you want to switch to. Simply press the HOME key and the number of the window you want to switch to. WordPerfect quickly moves to the correct window.

Use WordPerfect 6's Options for Window Sizing and Placement

212

WordPerfect offers quick options for displaying open windows on the screen. You can tile all the windows on the screen so that each is the same size and all windows line up like tiles on the floor as shown here:

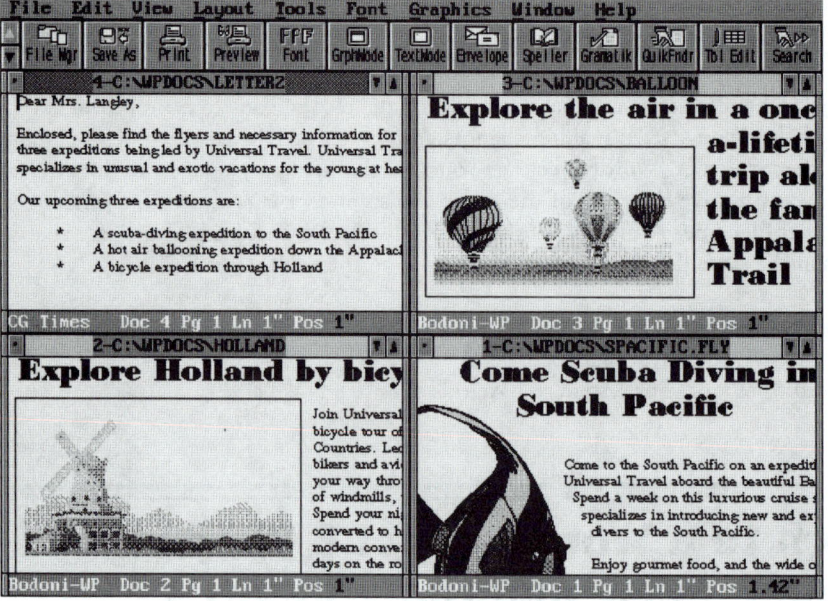

To tile all the open windows:

Select **W**indow **T**ile.

Your other option is to cascade the windows. Cascading means you layer the windows like a deck of cards with the larger part of the top window visible and just the title bars and edges of the other open windows showing like the following:

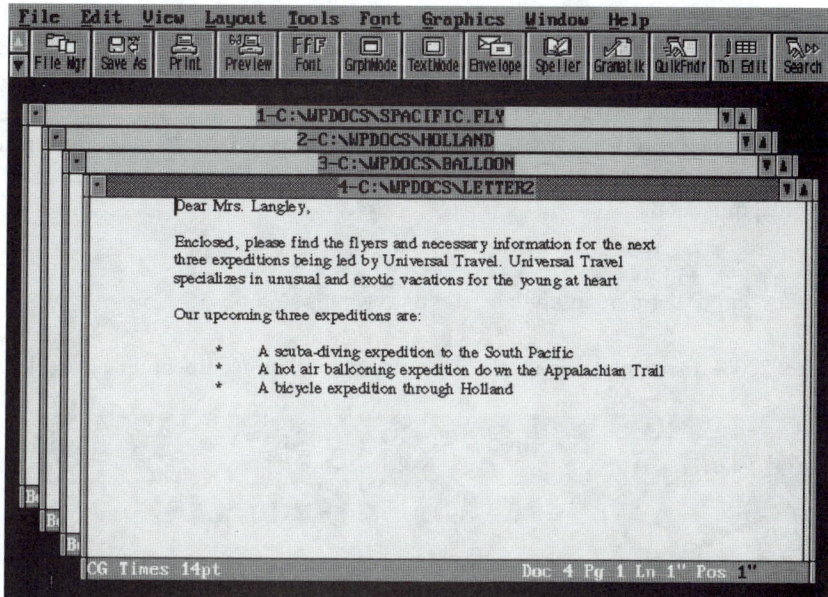

The other windows are accessible with a quick click to the edge of the desired window. To cascade windows:

Select **W**indow **C**ascade.

View a WordPerfect 6 Document at Different Levels of Magnification

TIP 213

In Graphics mode, you can view a document at varying levels of magnification. You may want to reduce the magnification to see the entire page at once and review the layout, or you may increase the magnification to view specific elements of your page, such as the alignment or placement of graphics.

With WordPerfect, you can change the magnification to one of three standards or you can select a specific percentage. The default magnification is Margin Width, in which WordPerfect calculates the magnification so that, on the screen, you see the page from margin to margin. Other standard settings are Page Width, in which WordPerfect calculates the magnification to show the entire page width, and Full Page, in which WordPerfect shrinks the image to display an entire page at a time—full width and full length.

To change the magnification:

1. Select **View Zoom**.
2. Select one of the percentages or standard widths.

When you select 200%, for example, you zoom in on a section of the document for a closer look like this:

To change the magnification percentage specifically:

1. Select **View Screen** Setup.
2. Select **Z**oom.
3. Select **P**ercentage, and type a magnification percentage, or select one of the other option buttons for the three standard magnifications.
4. Select OK.

WordPerfect 5.1 does not give you the same option but it does let you use the Print Preview feature for a closer look.

If the Text Is Unreadable, Change the Magnification or Change the Font

You may find text on your screen unreadable, either because you are using a very small font, or because it is a complicated font with many attributes, such as shadow or outline, applied to it. There are two easy ways to change the text to make it readable.

If you are working in WordPerfect 6 and the text is unreadable on the screen because it is too small, change the magnification at which the screen is displayed by selecting View Zoom, then selecting a higher percentage. Remember that if the text is unreadable on the screen because of size, it may be unreadable when you finally print it out.

A second solution, when the text is unreadable because of an elaborate font or small size, is to change the font. To change the font in WordPerfect 6:

1. Block the text.
2. Select F**o**nt **F**ont.
3. Select a font from the **F**ont selection box, enter a larger size in the **S**ize text box, or select one of the **R**elative Size options that is larger.

This solution is probably preferable to simply changing the magnification because text that is unreadable on the screen is likely to be unreadable when printed.

The solution in WordPerfect 5.1 is a little different:

1. Select F**o**nt Base F**o**nt.
2. Highlight the desired font and choose **S**elect.

You also can choose different size options from the Font pull-down menu.

You can change font mapping, thereby altering the screen fonts that various printers map fonts to. In WordPerfect 5.1, you would use the separate PTR program to make this change. In WordPerfect 6, you can either use PTR or Font Setup Edit Screen Font Mapping Table.

Set the View Percentage Using the WordPerfect 6 Ribbon

If you regularly use the Ribbon and the mouse, you can change easily the magnification at which documents are displayed. With the mouse, click on the down arrow after the first selection box in the Ribbon. A drop-down box detailing the available options appears. Double-click on the magnification you want to use.

Select the Information WordPerfect 6 Displays in the Status Line

Normally, the status line displays the current font, for unsaved documents, or the filename in the left side of the status line. WordPerfect 6 offers three customizing options for this part of the status line. You can have this portion of the status line display the default, display the current font, or display nothing at all. WordPerfect 5.1 limits you to just two choices and you must use a different set of steps to make the change.

To change the setting for the WordPerfect 6 status line:

1. Select **V**iew Scree**n** Setup.
2. Select **W**indow Options, and then select **S**tatus Line.
3. Select the option you want to use from the pop-up menu: **F**ilename, F**o**nt, or **N**othing.
4. Select OK.

To switch the status line from displaying the filename to displaying nothing (and vice versa) in WordPerfect 5.1, follow these steps:

1. Select **F**ile Se**t**up **D**isplay.
2. Select **E**dit-Screen Options.

3. Select **F**ilename on Status Line and type a **Y** or an **N** to select Yes or No.
4. Press F7 (Exit) to exit.

Increase the WordPerfect 6 Text Area by Hiding the Button Bar, Ribbon, and Menus

TIP 217

At times, you will want to be able to see more of the document at one time. You can do this by reducing the magnification, but this makes the document difficult to read. You can also increase the amount of space available for displaying the document by hiding several screen elements such as the Button Bar, the Ribbon, Reveal Codes window, or even the menu bar.

To set the menu bar to activate when you press ALT or click the right mouse button and then remove the Button Bar, Ribbon, and pull-down menu bar from display:

1. Select **V**iew Scree**n** Setup.
2. Select **S**creen Options.
3. Clear the **P**ull-Down Menus check box and activate the **A**lt key activates menus check box.
4. Clear the **R**ibbon (Graphics) check box.
5. Clear the **B**utton Bar (Graphics) check box.
6. Select OK.

Don't Hide the Menu Bar Unless You Are an Expert

TIP 218

Before you hide the menu bar to make space on your screen, make sure that you fully know WordPerfect's features, or that you have selected the option that activates the menu bar when you press the ALT key or the right mouse button. Otherwise, you may have an uncomfortable few minutes finding your documentation and learning how to activate features with the keyboard instead of with the menus.

To set the menu to activate when you press ALT:

1. Select **V**iew Scree**n** Setup.
2. Select **S**creen Options.

3. Select the **A**lt key activates menus check box.
4. Select OK.

Move the WordPerfect 6 Button Bar to a Convenient Location

When you first display the Button Bar it is located at the top of the screen, under the Ribbon and menu bar. Depending on the kind of documents you create and how you work, you may prefer to display it at some other point on the screen. With WordPerfect 6, you can move the Button Bar to any side of the screen.

To relocate the Button Bar:

1. Select **V**iew Button Bar **S**etup.
2. Select **O**ptions.
3. Under Position, you can select the **T**op, **B**ottom, **L**eft Side, or **R**ight Side option buttons.
4. Select OK.

With the Button Bar on the right your screen will look like this:

Shrink the WordPerfect 6 Graphics Mode Button Bar

The default for the Graphics mode Button Bar is to be displayed as a small picture with text underneath it. If you want to make the Button Bar smaller so that you can display more text, you can choose to display only the text or only the picture. This means that you would have a Button Bar that looks like this:

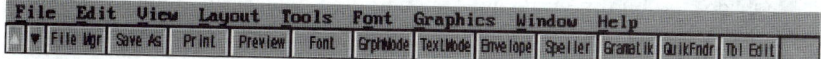

or like this:

To change the display of the Button Bar:

1. Select **V**iew Button Bar **S**etup **O**ptions.
2. Under Style, select either **P**icture and Text, Picture **O**nly, or **T**ext Only option buttons.
3. Select OK.

Change the Buttons on the WordPerfect 6 Button Bar

When you first start WordPerfect and select the Button Bar, a default Button Bar appears. This default Button Bar contains buttons of general interest. Your individual uses for WordPerfect or personal style of working may require that an entirely different set of features be used most often. You can edit the Button Bar or create a new Button Bar file with different buttons on it to maximize the usefulness of the Button Bar.

To edit the current Button Bar:

1. Select **V**iew Button Bar **S**etup **E**dit. The Edit Button Bar dialog box appears.
2. To add a menu item as a button, select Add M**e**nu Item, and then select the menu command. Press F7 when finished.
3. To add a specific feature as a button, select Add **F**eature. Highlight a feature in the Feature Button List dialog box, and then choose **S**elect.
4. To add a macro as a button, select Add Ma**c**ro, highlight a macro in the Macro Button List dialog box, and choose **S**elect.
5. To add a button for switching to another Button Bar, select Add **B**utton Bar. Then highlight a Button Bar file in the Button Bar List dialog box and choose Select.
6. To delete a button that you do not use, highlight the button in the list box, then select **D**elete Button. When WordPerfect prompts you to confirm that you want to delete this button, select **Y**es.
7. To move a button from one location to another on the Button Bar, highlight the button in the list box, and then select **M**ove Button. Highlight the button that you want the button you are moving to appear before, then select **P**aste Button..
8. When finished editing the Button Bar, select OK.

You can create a brand-new Button Bar file instead of modifying an existing Button Bar. To do this, follow these steps:

1. Select **V**iew Button Bar **S**etup.
2. Choose **S**elect.
3. Select **C**reate.
4. Type the filename for the Button Bar and select OK.
5. Follow the steps given above for editing a Button Bar to create the new Button Bar.
6. When finished creating the new Button Bar, select OK.
7. Highlight the Button Bar name in the Button Bar list box, and choose **S**elect.
8. Select OK.

You can create many different Button Bars for specific purposes. For example, you might have one Button Bar for legal documents and another for memos.

Display WordPerfect 6 Scroll Bars If You Use a Mouse

When you use a mouse, WordPerfect offers a shortcut for moving through a document quickly: you can use the scroll boxes or arrows on the scroll bars. You can display both vertical and horizontal scroll bars in both Graphics and Text modes, but each must be set individually.

To display the scroll bars:

1. Select **V**iew Screen Setup.
2. Select **W**indow Options.
3. Select **H**or. Scroll Bar or **V**ert. Scroll Bar with the desired Text or Graphics designation following them.

A scroll bar has three parts: the scroll bar arrows, the scroll bar itself, and the scroll bar box. The scroll bar box tells you the approximate location of the cursor in the document; when you move the cursor the scroll bar box moves as well. For example, when you move the cursor to the end of the document, the vertical scroll bar box moves to the bottom of the scroll bar.

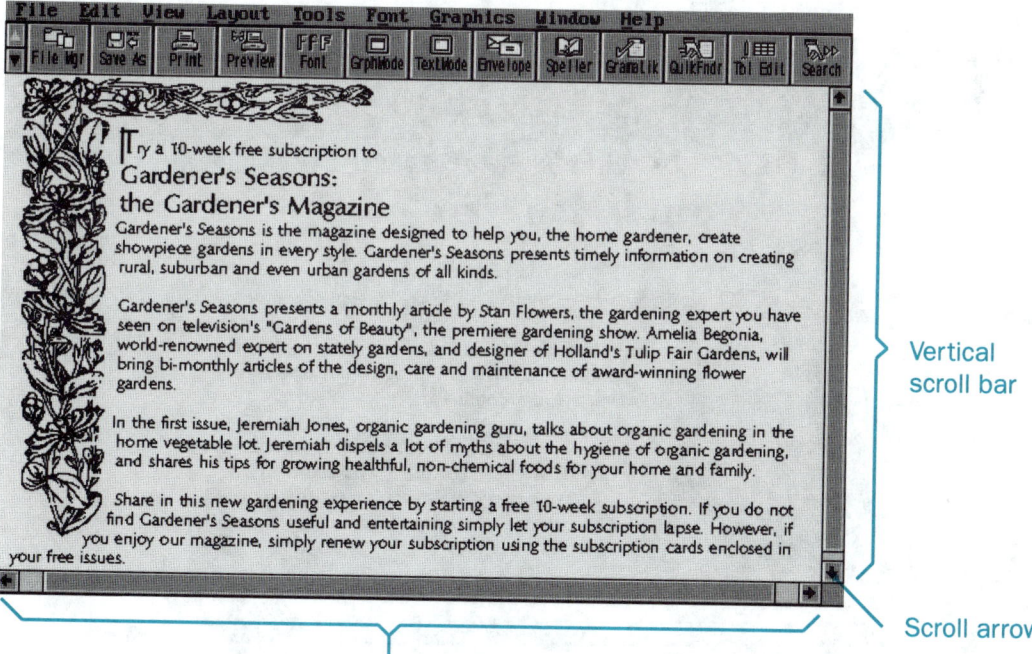

Vertical scroll bar

Scroll arrow

Horizontal scroll bar

You can move through the document using the mouse by clicking on the scroll bar arrows. You move one line (up or down) when you click the vertical scroll bar arrows, and one character (left or right) when you click the horizontal scroll bar arrows.

You also can move the scroll bar box to change your position in the document. Point the mouse pointer at the scroll bar box, and drag the scroll bar box to another position in the scroll bar. The cursor will move to an equivalent position in the document.

Note that when you first create a document, the scroll bar box is as long as the entire scroll bar. Because there is not yet any text, the cursor represents the entire document. As you add text to your document, the scroll bar box reduces in size, because a lesser amount of the document can be displayed at any one time. A large scroll bar box tells you that the document is small, while a tiny scroll bar box tells you that the document is large.

You Must Add a Frame to a Document Window Before You Can Move and Size It

Before you can size or move a document window, you must add a frame to that window. When you add a frame, borders and a title bar (which identifies the contents of the window) appear so that the window is encased on all four sides, as shown here:

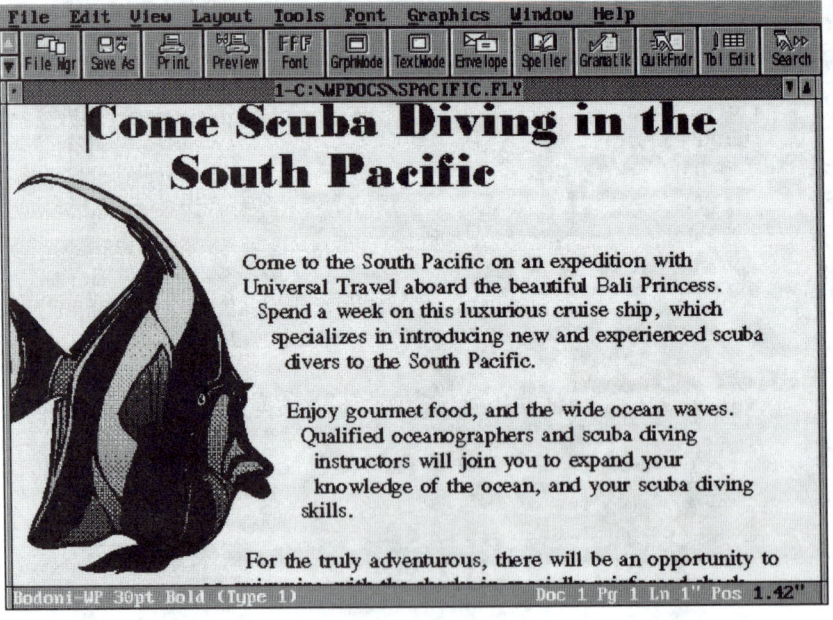

Once you have framed a window, you can easily move or size the window to fit your screen as you desire.

To frame a window:

Select **W**indow **F**rame, or press CTRL-F3 and select **W**indow **F**rame.

Use a Mouse to Size WordPerfect 6 Windows from Any Side

T^{IP}

224

You can adjust the size of a window with your keyboard after pressing CTRL-F3 and selecting **W**indow **S**ize. A dotted border displays at the edges of the window. Your adjustment must be from the lower-right corner as WordPerfect will accept only the UP ARROW key and the LEFT ARROW key when the screen is full size.

If you use a mouse, you can adjust the size of a framed window from any side or corner without invoking a menu command first. With a mouse, you also can move the document by dragging the title bar—the bar at the top that either contains the name of your document or the word "Untitled".

To size a framed window, point at the window border with the mouse until you see a double-headed arrow. Next, press the left mouse button and move the mouse to the location where you want that side of the window before releasing the button. After you drag and release the side, WordPerfect resizes the window to fit the area you define.

When you size windows with the mouse, you size using one or two sides at a time. If you point the mouse at a side, then only that side will change, so that you change the height of the window without affecting the width. If you point at a corner of the window so that you see a two-headed arrow with a diagonal orientation, both of the sides that meet at that corner will move. You will affect both the height and the width of the window at once.

When you want to move a window with the mouse, point at the title bar, the bar across the top of the window that identifies the contents of the window. Drag the title bar to change the position of the window.

Display the Margins and Tab Stops on the Screen with Reveal Codes

When you reveal the hidden codes in your document, you are probably looking for specific codes in order to delete or move them. You may not realize that you can see the current margin and tab stop settings at the same time.

The bar that separates the normal document display from the Reveal Codes screen shows the current margin and tab settings, as shown here:

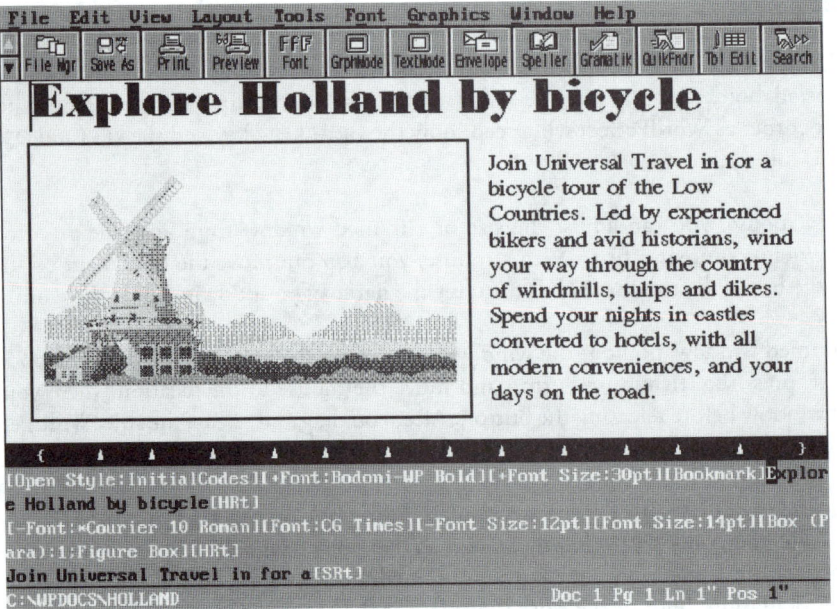

The up-pointing triangles indicate each tab stop. You cannot tell which alignment is assigned to those tab stops from this bar. The curly brackets indicate the margins. There is a tab stop set at the margin. If there is no tab stop set exactly at the margin, than the margin indicators are square brackets.

When you change the percentage of magnification at which the document is displayed, this bar changes. At all times, the markers on this Reveal Code bar will match the locations of the margins and tab stops relative to the displayed page. Therefore, as you change tab stops and margins, you can use this bar to quickly view where text will align on your page.

Change Amount of the WordPerfect 6 Screen Allocated to Display Codes

TIP 226

Sometimes you will want a very small Reveal Codes screen. At other times, you will want the Reveal Codes screen to be fairly large, and to reduce the space allotted to the normal document display. The size of the Reveal Codes screen will depend on what you are doing with your document.

To change the amount of window allocated to the Reveal Codes screen when you activate it:

1. Select **V**iew Scree**n** Setup.
2. Select **R**eveal Codes.
3. Select **W**indow Percentage, then type the percentage of the window you want allocated to the display of the Reveal Codes screen. The default is 25 percent.
4. Select OK.

Create Graphics Documents in Text Mode

TIP 227

Even if you have to use Text mode because of limited computer system memory, you can still create documents that contain graphics. You will use the same steps for creating graphics documents as you would if you were using Graphics mode. However, since Text mode cannot display graphics, instead of seeing the graphics on the screen, you will see empty boxes marking the location of the graphics. You will, of course, still need a printer capable of printing graphics.

When you create a document in Text mode (and cannot switch to Graphics mode or use the Print Preview screen because your computer cannot support graphics images on the screen), remember to print draft copies of your document more often than you do when working in Graphics mode. You will not be able to see the alignment of text around your graphics box or the actual effect of graphics elements as easily as you can when they appear on the screen. Make sure that you take the time to print and view the graphics image to ensure the most effective presentation of your document.

Set the Graphics Mode Options Correctly Even If You Use Text Mode for Most Tasks

Even if you use Text mode for most of your document editing, you still want the Graphics mode options set correctly. WordPerfect uses the Graphics mode settings for other features that use a Graphics screen, such as previewing how a document will print. If the setting for Graphics mode is off (meaning that the wrong or a less effective screen driver file is selected), your preview display may be hard to read or use.

Some Features Do Not Appear in Page Mode in WordPerfect 6

Page mode is another way of displaying your documents. When you display a document in Page mode, you see the document as it actually will print. This means that elements of the document that you do not see in Graphics mode are displayed in their proper locations. However, elements such as document comments do not appear because these elements never appear in the printed document.

Use Page Mode to See Headers and Footers in WordPerfect 6

Page mode shows the document as it will print. This means that elements such as headers and footers, as well as footnotes and endnotes, appear in the document in Page mode just as they will appear in the printed document. If you want to easily view your headers and footers to see how they relate to your document, select View Page Mode to switch to Page mode.

Determine When Document Comments Will Appear in a Document

TIP 231

Document comments let you include information of importance to the author or editor that you do not want to include in the document itself. In Graphics and Text modes, you can choose whether or not you want document comments displayed. You may want to hide document comments while you add new sections of text to your document, and then display them again when editing.

To control the display of document comments in WordPerfect 6:

1. Select **V**iew Scree**n** Setup or press CTRL-F3 and SHIFTF1.
2. Select **W**indow Options.
3. Select or clear the **D**isplay Comments check box.
4. Select OK.

To control the display of document comments in WordPerfect 5.1:

1. Select **F**ile Se**t**up or press SHIFT-F1.
2. Select **D**isplay **E**dit-Screen Options Comments Display.
3. Select **Y**es to show document comments, or **N**o to hide them.
4. Press F7 (Exit) to return to the document.

Changing Page Size May Create Some Surprising Displays in WordPerfect 6 Page Mode

TIP 232

If you change the page size to look at a label that fits three across in Page View mode, your screen may look a little different than expected. The labels are displayed against a gray background with each one added to the display as it is typed. Gray bands separate labels as they are placed next to each other, although the next row of labels are not separated from the first, as shown in the following:

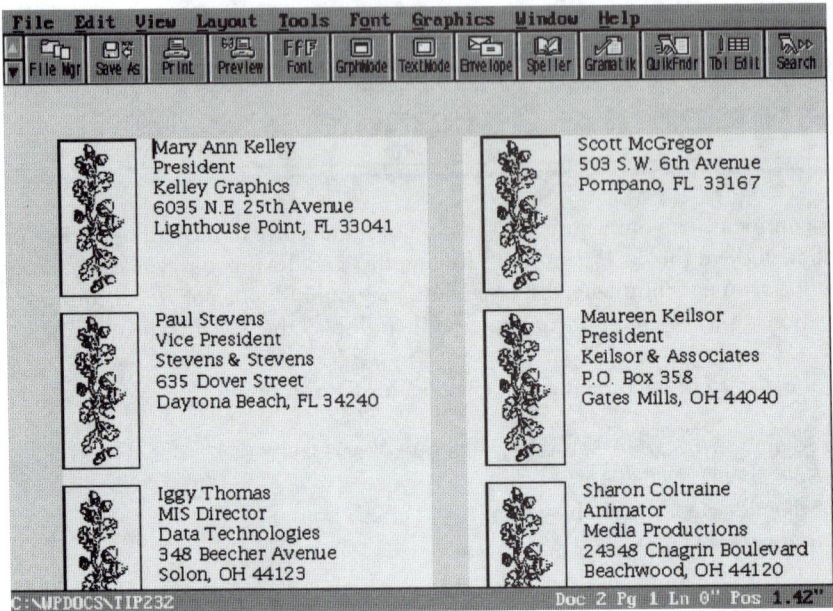

ACORN.PCX

The graphic added to the labels resides on the accompanying disk as ACORN.PCX. It was added to each label by defining its use as part of a style definition.

CHAPTER 5

Headers and Footers

Use Headers, Footers, and Watermarks Innovatively

Headers, footers, and watermarks are special features that can improve the appearance of your documents. A page can have two headers, two footers, and two watermarks. The information that appears at the top of every page is a *header*. The information that appears at the bottom of every page is a *footer*. The two different headers and footers that you can use are labeled A and B. You can select whether the A or B header or footer appears on odd pages, even pages, or both.

WordPerfect 6 also lets you add watermarks to pages. *Watermarks* can be either text or images that appear as part of the paper the document is printed on. They are added with the Header/Footer/Watermark option on the Layout menu. The use of watermarks originated from a design embedded into the paper during the papermaking process. If you buy quality paper and hold a sheet to the light, you'll see a faint emblem—that is the watermark. You can make the watermarks that you add with WordPerfect 6 faint images or more like normal printing depending on the effect you want to achieve.

Headers, footers, and watermarks can serve more than one purpose. For example, if you think of watermarks as a way to include text or graphics throughout your document, you can start using them to include newsletter titles on every page, or as a unique way to identify sections by printing the section title along one margin. Headers and footers can do more than just label the contents of pages—they allow you to put any creative message or design at the top and bottom of pages. This flyer shows a watermark used in creating an advertisement:

Both the graphics image of the plane and the text on its banner are a watermark, and the "Two Days Only" is another watermark. The graphics image could have been placed in a header just as easily. The reverse band at the bottom is a footer. The only text entered into the document is the text that appears in the middle beginning with "Start the Summer Sale" and ending with the last item description.

Do not limit yourself to the obvious. The possible uses for headers, footers, and watermarks are limited only by your imagination.

The airplane that appears as part of the watermark shown above is in the FILLIN12.CGM file on the accompanying disk. The "Two Days Only" text in the middle is in a graphics box. The text in the graphics box at the bottom is reversed, as described in Tip 175. The document that you can use as a template is in SILLY.TEM. Both are available on the accompanying disk.

FILLIN12.CGM
SILLY.TEM

Headers, Footers, and Watermarks Can Use Standard Formatting Features

TIP 234

You can use any character, paragraph, or page formatting in headers and footers that you can use in the main text of your document. For example, you can change the font size or the alignment of the text in a header or footer, as shown in this footer:

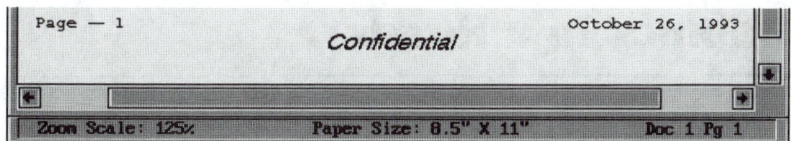

When you want your header or footer to have different formatting than the text, you need to apply those formatting changes directly to the header or footer. If you apply the formatting to the document initial codes, both the header and footer as well as the entire document are affected. The only way to change the format within the header or footer without changing the format of the body text is to edit the header or footer and apply the formatting directly. Notice that as you work with a header or footer, you can select many of WordPerfect's features. Use the function keys or the menu as you add formatting to headers, footers, and watermarks.

Changing a Document's Format Does Not Affect Headers and Footers

If you decide to change the font or margins in your document, you may simply move to the beginning of the document and insert the new settings. However, when you print the document, you will find that these changes affect only the body text of your document, not the headers, footers, or watermarks. For example, if you block all of the text in your document and change the font from Courier to Roman, your headers, footers, and watermarks will still appear in Courier font. Also, headers, footers, and watermarks will use the margins set by the document's initial codes rather than the ones set in the document.

To change initial settings so that they affect all elements in the document including headers and footers, you modify the document's initial codes. You can do this by selecting Layout Document then Initial Codes in WordPerfect 5.1 or Document Initial Codes in WordPerfect 6. Next, select the codes you want at the beginning of the document, selecting alternative fonts, margins, or any other feature.

By setting the changes as part of the Document Initial Codes, you make sure that all elements use the same basic settings—that your headers and body text use the same margins and fonts, for example. This prevents the unprofessional appearance of documents with two different fonts or margins because the changes were made to body text, but not to headers or footers.

Create Letterhead That Incorporates Graphics in a Header

Letterhead that includes your name, address, and telephone number is the norm. This type of letterhead conveys authority and conservativeness. You may want to project a slightly different image by including a company logo in your professional letterhead, or a graphics element in the letterhead of your personal stationery.

For example, you can have a letterhead in a document's header that contains only your company's name and address. You can dress this letterhead up by adding a graphics image and changing the alignment of the text to present a more innovative attitude in your stationery, as shown in the following:

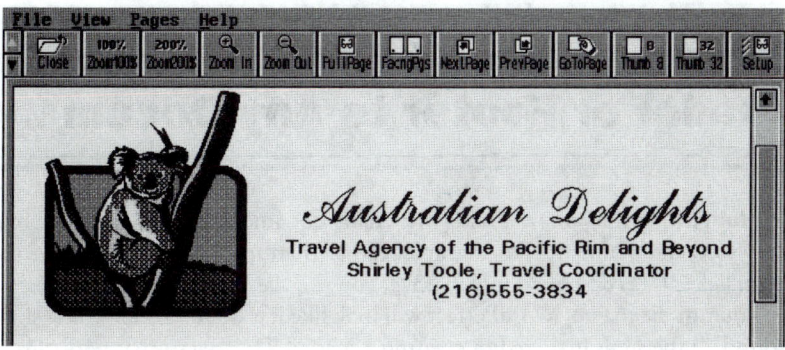

The accompanying disk includes SIDNEY.CGM, which contains the graphic used in this header.

SIDNEY.CGM

Save Frequently-Used Headers, Footers, and Watermarks in Files

If you want to use the same watermark, header, or footer repeatedly, you can save them into a file. For example, you can create a document that has no text but contains the header, footer, or watermark that you plan to use in many documents. Then save that document to a file.

When creating a document in which you will use that header, footer, or watermark, position the cursor on the page where you want to place the header, footer, or watermark. Then retrieve the file into the current document using the File **R**etrieve command. Since the only contents of the file are the header, footer, or watermark codes, you do not have to worry about changing the text in your document. All you are importing is the header, footer, or watermark. As an example, if you save the document shown in Tip 236, you can retrieve this document every time you want to use the letterhead.

Create a Macro to Add a Custom Header or Footer to Any Document

Another option for putting the same contents into many documents is to create a macro that adds the header or footer to each document. For example, rather than retrieving a document containing the header shown in Tip 236 (as described in Tip 237), you can create a macro that will add the contents for you. When you run the macro, WordPerfect will look like it is not doing anything since it performs in the background all the steps involved in creating a macro. The macro that performs this feature is given here:

```
DISPLAY(Off!)
HeaderA(Create!)
BoxCreate(FigureBox!)
BoxContentType(Image!)
BoxImageRetrieve(MakeInternal!;"C:\WP60\GRAPHICS\SIDNEY.CGM";CGM!)
BoxWidth(AutoWidth!)
BoxHeight(2")
BoxChangeStyle(UserBox!)
BoxHorizontalAlignment(AlignMargins!;Left!;0")
BoxTextFlowContour
BoxEnd(Save!)
HardReturn
HardReturn
HardReturn
HardReturn
Center
Font("CommercialScript-WP (Type 1)")
FontSize(36p)
Type("Australian Delights")
Font("Swiss 721 Roman (Speedo)")
FontSize(14p)
HardReturn
Center
Type("Travel Agency of the Pacific Rim and Beyond")
HardReturn
Center
Type("Shirley Toole, Travel Coordinator")
HardReturn
Center
```

```
Type("(216)555-3834")
SubstructureExit
```

The accompanying disk has the KOALA_HD macro that creates the heading shown in Tip 236. The macro assumes that the SIDNEY.CGM file from the accompanying disk is in the \WP60\GRAPHICS subdirectory.

KOALA_HD.WPM

Since the added image is in a header, you will need to use Print Preview to see it.

Headers and Footers Display Only at Certain Times

You do not normally see the headers and footers in your document on the screen. You will only see them in certain situations. If you want to view your headers and footers, you will have to edit them, switch to Page mode, or use the Print Preview screen.

Switching to Another Document While Editing a Header Makes Some Menu Options Unavailable

While you are editing a header, footer, or watermark, some menu options are unavailable. For instance, you may access the menu to switch to another document to transfer text or a graphic between the header, footer, or watermark, and another document. However, in the other document, you will notice that several menu options remain unavailable. For example, while you are editing a header, footer, or watermark, the Text Mode, Graphics Mode, and Page Mode options in the View menu are not available whether you have switched to another document or are entering header or footer text.

Headers and Footers Cannot Be Edited in Page Mode

When you see the headers and footers while using the Page Display mode, it is tempting to try to make changes to the headers and footers. Remember that you can edit the header or footer only by selecting Layout Header/Footer/Watermark, then Headers or Footers, and the correct header or footer, then Edit. Even though you can see the header and footer in Page mode or in the Print Preview screen, you cannot edit them there.

Use a Shortcut to Add a Page Number to a Header or Footer

Instead of using the page numbering command, you can add a page number to your headers or footers with a simple key combination. Press CTRL-B (WordPerfect 5.1) or CTRL-P (WordPerfect 6) in a header or footer and WordPerfect adds a formatted page number to the document, which of course changes for each page.

Use the Date in Headers or Footers to Easily Identify the Latest Version

If you have ever created a report or other document that required several revisions, you know how confusing it is to sort out which pages belong to the most recent revisions. On movie sets and television shows, the coordinator simply prints script revisions on different colors of paper, but this option is probably not available to you. WordPerfect lets you distinguish the latest revision of a document easily by allowing you to add a date code to a header or footer. Do this, and every page of the document

tells you when it was printed. Since date codes automatically update themselves, you won't have any extra work in adding draft numbers to your document, yet you will be able to determine easily if the page 5 you are holding goes with the first printout of the document, or the printout you did this morning.

You can mark these entries as hidden text to make it easy to use them on drafts and exclude them from a customer copy.

This macro creates a footer that contains the date, time, and a page number:

```
DISPLAY(Off!)
FooterA(Create!)
Type("Date: ")
DateCode
Center
Type("Time: ")
DateFormat("[Hour(12)#]:[Minute0#] [Am/Pm]")
DateCode
DateFormat("[Month] [Day#], [Year(4)#]")
FlushRight
Type("Page: ")
PageNumberDisplayFormat
SubstructureExit
```

When you execute this macro, the resulting footer looks like the following:

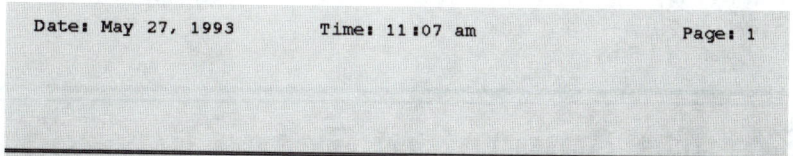

Date: May 27, 1993   Time: 11:07 am   Page: 1

The macro used to create this footer can be found on the accompanying disk in the file DATETIME.WPM.

DATETIME.WPM

Add the Filename to WordPerfect 6's Headers to Make Them Appear on the Printout

With some documents, such as invoices or supply reports, you may want to include the document name and date as part of the header or footer. Also, when you make printouts of macros or programs from WordPerfect, you will want the filename available to identify the source of the macro or program. The advantage of including the filename in a header or footer is that it will make finding the file again easier.

To add a filename to a header or footer, as well as adding it anywhere else to a document, select **Layout Other Insert Filename**. The dialog box WordPerfect presents lets you add just the filename as in MY_FILE.DOC or the path and the filename as in C:\WPDOCS\MY_FILE.DOC. The document will have the code [Filename] so if you change the location or name of the file, the new location or name appears in the document.

In order for this to work, you must remember to save the file that contains this information with the correct name.

To include a filename in WordPerfect 5.1 documents, you must type the filename yourself.

Set the Amount of Space Between the Header and the Regular Document Text

As a default, WordPerfect leaves .167 inches of space between the bottom of the header and the beginning of the document text for that page. WordPerfect also leaves .167 inches of space between the bottom of the document text and the footer. You can add more space when you want the header text to stand out more or reduce this space when you want the header and the document text to be closer together. Less space is useful when you use a graphics image in the header rather than text.

To change the amount of space:

1. Select **L**ayout **H**eader/Footer/Watermark.
2. Select **H**eaders or **F**ooters.
3. Select **S**pace Below Header or **S**pace Above Footer.
4. Type the distance you want between the header or footer and the document text.

   You can use any unit of measure and WordPerfect will convert your entry. For example, an entry of **40p** is converted to .556 inches.
5. Select OK.

WordPerfect Uses the Most Recent Header Code If It Finds More Than One

TIP 246

You can insert multiple headers, footers, or watermarks into your document. WordPerfect starts using the new header, footer, or watermarks on the page where it encounters the new code. You can use this feature to switch the header, footer, or watermark when you switch sections of a report, so that the header or footer can contain the title of the section. To replace a header or footer in WordPerfect 5.1, select Layout Page then Headers or Footers, **A** or **B** for the header or footer to change, and then select when the header or footer should appear rather than selecting Edit. To replace a header, footer, or watermark in WordPerfect 6, select Layout Header/Footer/Watermark, then Headers or Footers, **A** or **B** for the header or footer to change, and then select Create rather than Edit.

Suppress Headers and Footers on a Title Page and First Page of a Letter

TIP 247

Headers and footers are not appropriate on a title page where the focus should be the name of the document and its author. Also, the first page of a letter does not require a header or footer because the first page should already contain most of the information that the header or footer gives.

To suppress headers and footers for a single page:

1. Select **L**ayout **P**age.
2. Select **S**uppress.
3. Select the check box or select the option that you want to suppress.
   In WordPerfect 5.1, you will need to select **N**o.
4. Press F7 until you return to the document.

Use the A and B Footer and Header for Different Entries on Odd and Even Pages

WordPerfect documents can have two headers, footers, and watermarks. Each one is labeled A or B. With two headers or footers, you can alternate so that one is assigned to odd-numbered pages and the other to even-numbered pages. Use different headers and footers for odd and even pages when you are printing on double-sided pages. For example, in this book, you can see that the header on pages on the left side has different text than the header on pages on the right side.

For example, assume you want the text "Top Ten WordPerfect Tips" to appear on the inside of each page, and the page number to appear on the outside. When you are entering the header for odd-numbered pages you would left-align the title and use flush right for the page number. On even-numbered pages, you would want to left-align the page number but use flush right to align the title. Create a Header A with the settings for odd-numbered pages, and a Header B for even-numbered pages, and select the settings that ensure that those are the only pages they appear on.

In WordPerfect 5.1, create the header this way:

1. Select **L**ayout **P**age **H**eaders Header **A O**dd Pages.
2. Type the entries to appear on the top of odd pages.
3. Press F7 (Exit).
4. Select **H**eaders Header **B** Even Pages.
5. Type the entries to appear on the top of even pages.
6. Press F7 (Exit) twice.

In WordPerfect 6, create the header this way:

1. Select **L**ayout **H**eader/Footer/Watermark **H**eaders Header **A**.
2. Select **O**dd Pages and **C**reate.

3. Type the entries to appear on the top of odd pages and press F7.
4. Select **L**ayout **H**eader/Footer/Watermark **H**eaders Header **B**.
5. Select Ev**e**n Pages and **C**reate.
6. Type the entries to appear on the top of even pages and press F7.

After creating the two headers, your document appears symmetrical, as you can see in the following (the font size is oversized):

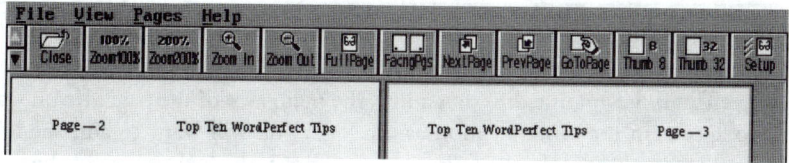

WordPerfect does not care if you use A for odd pages and B for even pages or vice versa. A and B are just labels that WordPerfect uses to distinguish the two headers, two footers, or two watermarks that a page may contain.

A Blank Header or Footer Prevents the Display of the Correct Header or Footer

TI**P** 249

When headers and footers suddenly stop appearing after a specific page, one of two things may have happened. First, the headers and footers may have been turned off. You can do this in WordPerfect 5.1 by selecting Layout Page Headers or Footers, **A** or **B**, then Discontinue. To stop a header or footer in WordPerfect 6, select Layout Header/Footer/Watermark, Headers or Footers, **A** or **B**, then Off.

The other cause may be an empty header or footer. WordPerfect uses the latest header or footer code; if you add an empty footer code, for example, the previous footer code will no longer appear. You can search for the [Header A], [Header B], [Footer A], or [Footer B] codes. Tip 350 has more information about searching a document for codes.

If you want to turn off a header or footer for a couple of pages, suppress it as described in Tip 247.

Use a WordPerfect 6 Watermark to Drop a Header Into the Text

Using a graphic, such as a logo, as part of your header catches the attention of the reader. You can get a very interesting effect if the graphic dips down into the main area of the page. If you want text from the document to appear in the same location as the logo, you will want to add the letterhead as a watermark rather than as a header. In the following document, the logo is part of the watermark:

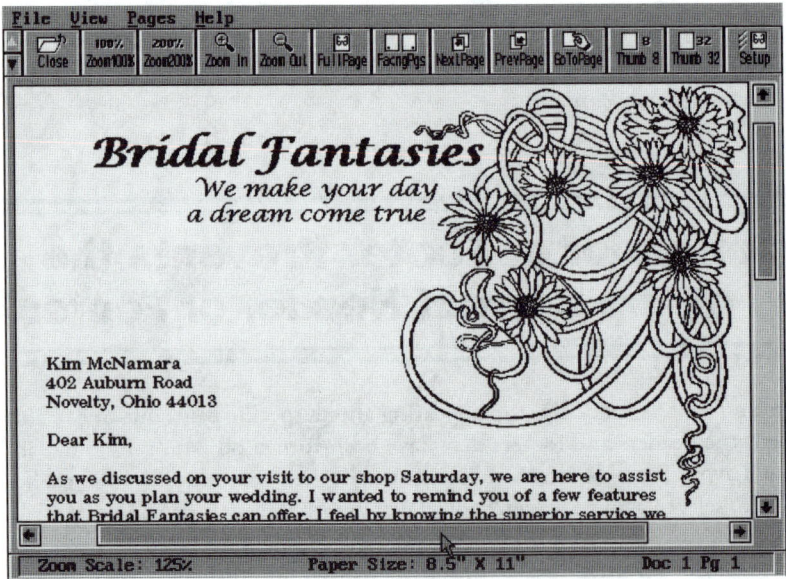

In this example, the shading of the graphics in the watermark and the text in the watermark is set to 100 percent. Tip 256 contains more information about changing the shading of the contents of a

graphics box. If you had put the same contents in a header rather than a watermark, you could not start the letter until after the bottom of the graphics.

The accompanying disk contains the DAISY.PCX image used in the document shown here.

DAISY.PCX

Create Paper Designs Without Specialty Paper By Using a Watermark

TIP 251

If you look through a paper company's catalog, you will see specialty papers for certificates, brochures, and other specific uses. As an alternative to ordering specialty papers, you can use WordPerfect 6 watermarks to create your own specialty paper.

For example, you may want to create paper with a design in the background. The design in the watermark will let you know whether you are looking at a copy or the original. (Watermarks print at the same time the document prints.)

To create your own specialty paper:

1. Select **L**ayout, **H**eader/Footer/Watermark, **W**atermarks.
2. Select Watermark **A** or Watermark **B**.
3. Select **A**ll Pages and **C**reate.
4. Select **G**raphics **R**etrieve Image.
5. Type the graphics filename for the watermark graphic and press ENTER.
6. Press F7.

Now, when you create a document with this watermark, each page will have the watermark design in the background. The watermark is lighter than the text because its shading is set to 25 percent of normal color. A document using the BACK.WPG watermark looks like the following:

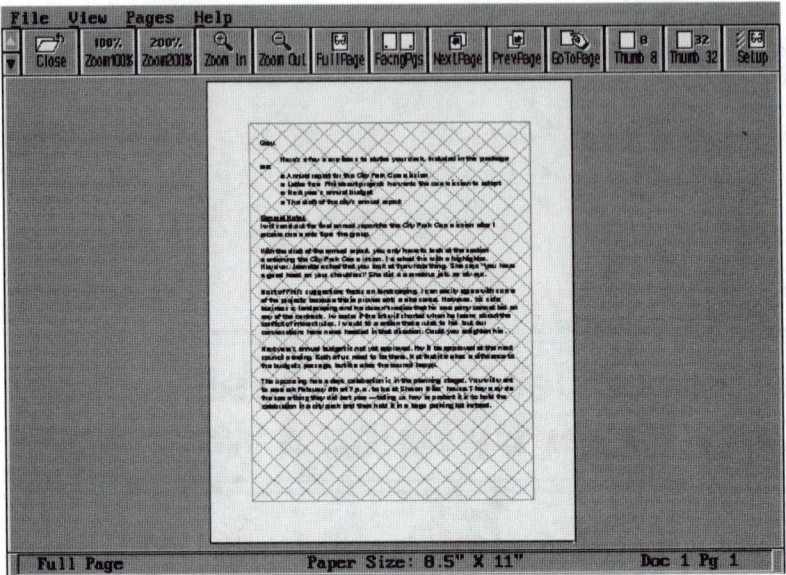

You can create other specialty papers using various graphics images, either those shipped with WordPerfect or those you purchase or create.

BACK.WPG

The accompanying disk contains the BACK.WPG file that you can use in your own watermarks.

TIP 252
Create Multiple Watermarks

In any document you have available two watermarks, Watermark A and Watermark B. You can have these watermarks appear on all pages, all even pages, or all odd pages. If you assign two watermarks to print on the same page, they will, and one image will superimpose the other.

Also, you can change the contents of Watermark A and Watermark B at any point in the document by creating a new Watermark A or B. For example, you may want to use one watermark for the text portion of your report, then use a different one for the tables that appear at the end of your report. To switch, move to the first page of the tables and create a new watermark. Remember, if you create a new Watermark A, the old Watermark A is replaced, but the old Watermark B is not.

You can use this feature to turn off watermarks. For example, you may want a watermark for the text of your report, but not for the bibliography at the end. Simply create a watermark to replace the watermark you used in the text, but leave the watermark editing screen empty. From that point until you create yet another watermark, no watermark will print. You also can discontinue using a watermark by selecting Layout Header/Footer/Watermark Watermarks, **A** or **B**, then Off.

In WordPerfect 5.1, you can create watermarks by adding a graphics box such as a User Box to a page. The user box should have the Anchor Type set to Page, the Vertical Position set to Full Page, the Horizontal Position set to Margin, Full, and the Wrap Text Around Box set to No. WordPerfect 5.1 does not have any brightness controls so you must use a graphic that is naturally light. To use a watermark like this, set it to repeat on every page.

Change the Margins to Keep Text Off a Watermark

Watermarks use the margins assigned in the Document Initial Codes. When you want to use a watermark along a side of the page, you can change the margins within the document so you do not print over the watermark. For example, if you use BCKGRD48.CGM as a watermark, the graphic appears along both sides of the page. To avoid actually printing text on this watermark, increase the left and right margins by 1 inch using the Layout Margins command while editing the main document. The results are shown in the following:

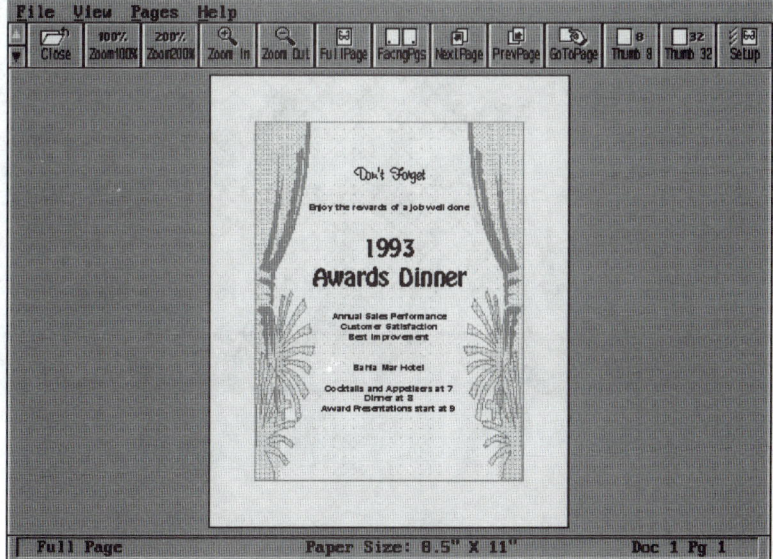

BCKGRD48.CGM

The image that appears in the watermark is in the file BCKGRD48.CGM on the accompanying disk.

Don't Make Watermark Graphics Light

TIP 254

WordPerfect handles making the contents of watermarks light. When you are creating graphics for a watermark, make it as dark as you want. If you want to change how light or dark a watermark appears in a document, use WordPerfect's features to make the change. As an example, the following illustration shows a simple watermark created with DrawPerfect. Notice how the lines are black. You can see this same watermark used in a document in Tip 251. If you created the lines in DrawPerfect using gray lines, when you used the BACK.WPG file in WordPerfect, the lines would be too light.

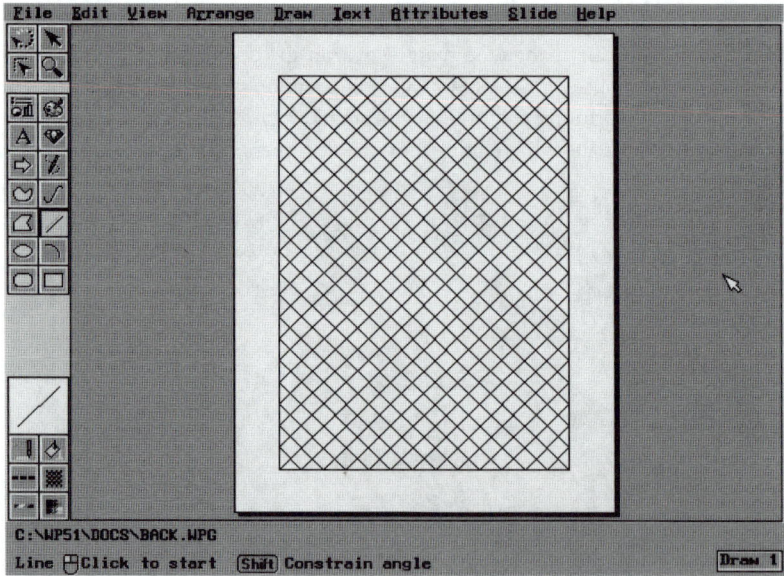

Don't Add Extra Space for Watermark Margins

When you create designs for watermarks, you do not want to add extra space to the actual image. This is because WordPerfect adjusts the size of the graphic so that it fits within the margins. If you look at the DrawPerfect screen in Tip 254, you will see how the design fills the entire drawing area. WordPerfect will scale the drawing to fit the watermark's area on the page.

You may want to adjust the margin settings from the Watermark Edit Screen in order to adjust the fit of the watermark on the page.

Change the Darkness of Watermarks to Add Emphasis

Watermarks normally print at 25 percent of the darkness of normal text or graphics because they are supposed to appear in the background. However, for special circumstances such as when creating specialty paper, you may want a watermark to have more intensity. Tips 233 and 250 showed examples of this. You can change the level of intensity separately for watermark images and for watermark text.

You have two ways to change the intensity for text in a watermark:

1. Select **L**ayout **S**tyles **O**ptions.
2. Select the List S**y**stem Styles check box and OK.
3. Highlight either Watermark A or Watermark B and select **E**dit.
4. Select Style **C**ontents.
5. Highlight the code [Char Shade Change], press DEL, then press F7.
6. Select OK, then select Close.

This method changes the initial code that appears at the beginning of watermarks. The preceding steps showed you how to set the shading level to 100 percent. The following method changes the shading of just the watermark you are editing:

1. Select **F**ont **P**rint Color **Sh**ade.
2. Type **100** and select Close.

Graphics in a watermark become darker or lighter when you change their intensity. The intensity or brightness uses a scale of 1 to –1. 1 is all white and –1 is all black. 0 is normal intensity. Watermarks normally use .25 (or 25 percent of the normal density).

You have three ways of changing the intensity of an image in a watermark. You can edit the Watermark Image Box graphics box style, or you can edit the specific image box that you have created. A third possibility is to add a graphic to a watermark as a different graphics box style so the graphic uses the shading set by the other graphics box style. Any of the three solutions will work, although the first choice changes the shading for all watermarks in a document and the other two change just the shading of the watermark you are working with.

To change the intensity of all watermarks in the document when you are not editing a watermark:

1. Select **G**raphics Graphics **B**oxes St**y**les.
2. Highlight Watermark Image Box and select **E**dit.
3. Select Image **S**ettings **C**olor Adjust **B**rightness.
4. Type the new brightness level.
5. Select OK and Close until you return to the document.

To change the intensity of a graphic in a watermark you are editing:

1. Select **G**raphics Graphics **B**oxes **E**dit,
2. Select the graphics box to edit and select **E**dit Box.
3. Select Image **E**ditor.
4. Select B**r**ightness and type the new brightness value.
5. Press F7 until you return to the watermark editing window.

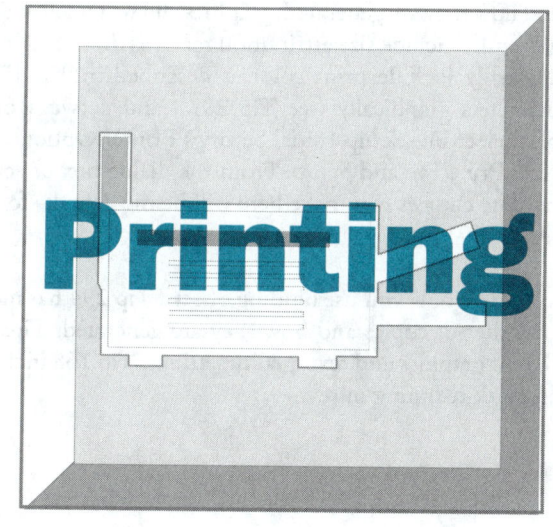

Print Settings Are Saved in Different Locations

Some print settings are saved with the document, some with the WordPerfect session, some become the new WordPerfect settings, and some return to the default once a document is printed. The print settings saved with the document only apply to the affected document. The ones that become part of the WordPerfect session last only until you leave WordPerfect. The print settings that become WordPerfect's settings remain until you select another choice for that setting. The ones that return to the default after printing must be set every time you want to use that setting.

Set the Print Settings You Want for the Defaults

Some of the print settings can be set as the defaults for all print jobs. These settings include binding offset, number of copies and how they are generated, graphics and text quality, and the redline method. WordPerfect 5.1 printing defaults include size attribution ratios as described in Tip 181. WordPerfect 6's printing defaults additionally include print color as described in Tip 173, font size, in which WordPerfect generates characters graphically (see Tip 293), and network options. To change the settings in WordPerfect 5.1, select File Setup Initial Settings Printer Options. To change the settings in WordPerfect 6, select File Print/Fax and Setup. From the dialog box or screen presented, change any options that you want. The choices you make here will be the defaults for subsequent times that you print with WordPerfect.

Tip 984 has more information on how you use binding offsets. Tip 294 has more information on the choices available for the number of copies and how they are generated. Tips 272 and 310 describe when you want to use different graphics and text quality settings. Tip 168 includes information about the different ways you can mark redlining in text.

Set Default Print Settings for New Documents Differently than for Existing Documents

TIP 259

You use a different procedure to change print settings for all documents formatted with a specific printer than to change print settings for a single document.

Most print settings that are set with the Print/Fax dialog box or after selecting File Print/Fax only affect the current document. When you change the defaults using File Setup Initial Settings Printer Options in WordPerfect 5.1 or File Print/Fax and Setup in WordPerfect 6, these changes affect all new documents. To change the printer settings for existing documents, you must make the changes within the individual documents.

What to Do When WordPerfect Prints and Your Printer Doesn't

TIP 260

Most printer problems are easy to resolve. Check this list of common printing problems to see if one of these suggestions fixes your printer.

- ❑ *Is the printer turned on?* It may sound stupid, but this is one of the two most frequent causes of printer problems.

- ❑ *Does the printer have paper?* This is the other most frequent cause of printer problems.

- ❑ *Are you using a printer switch box?* If so, check that the printer switch box is turned to the setting for your computer.

- ❑ *Is the printer ready to accept information?* Most printers have a button that turns them online. Usually, pressing this button when the printer is offline will begin the flow of information from the computer to your printer.

- ❑ *What do you see when you select Control Printer?* If the Status is Stopped, you must select Go before printing can continue.

- ❑ *Is the correct printer selected?* You can see the printer named to the right of Select Printer in WordPerfect 5.1 or in the top of the Print/Fax dialog box in WordPerfect 6. If the wrong printer is selected, you need to select the correct one. Tip 321 contains more information about selecting a printer.

❏ *Is the correct printer port selected?* The printer port tells WordPerfect which connection on the back of your computer is connected to the printer. Printer ports or connection ports have names such as LPT1 and COM1. You can see the printer port selected for a printer in WordPerfect 5.1 by selecting File Print Select Printer, highlighting the printer, and selecting Edit. In WordPerfect 6, choose Select from the Print/Fax dialog box, highlight the printer, and select Edit. If the connection is incorrect, select Port, and then select the correct one. The correct port selection depends on how your computer is set up. You always can try connecting the cable to the other port as long as you do not force a connection that wasn't designed to occur.

❏ *Is your computer connected to the printer?* This problem normally occurs when you are first setting up your printer or when you have moved furniture. A partially connected printer cable cannot send the information to the printer. You can reattach the cable using the screws or clips on the cable to secure it to your printer or computer.

❏ *Are you having problems with only specific types of WordPerfect features?* For example, if you can print using the printer's built-in fonts but can't get any cartridge fonts to print, your problem may be that the cartridge is not correctly inserted or you have not told WordPerfect that the cartridge is available (see Tip 189).

❏ *Does the printed document look correct when you preview it?* Usually, the printed document will look just like the preview of the document. If the preview contains the same mistakes as the printout, the problem is in the document rather than the printing process. This is another good reason to preview the document before you print it.

❏ *What is the location of your printer files?* WordPerfect's default is to put the .PRS and .ALL files in the \WP51 or \WPC60DOS directory. Check to see that the files are in this directory and that the location where WordPerfect looks for printer files matches their actual location. You can see and set the location of printer files by selecting File Setup Location of Files Printer Files.

❏ *What have you changed since the last time you printed in WordPerfect?* If you already have printed successfully in the current WordPerfect session, the problem lies either in something you've done differently or the document itself.

❏ *Is only one page causing problems or is every page problematic?* If the problem occurs just on one page, it's likely that a wrong code is causing the problem. Go to that page, reveal codes, and look through the page for a code that you don't think should be there. That code could be the source of the problem.

❏ *Can you print from other applications?* If you can, the problem is probably within WordPerfect. If you cannot, the problem is probably with the computer, connection, or printer.

❏ *Is there a message on your printer's display?* For example, on a Hewlett-Packard IIP+ you need to press Alt-Continue to print legal paper.

❏ *Are you working on a network?* Perhaps you have routed your output to the wrong print queue or someone ahead of you in the queue may be printing a lengthy document.

Look at WordPerfect's Notes About Your Printer

TIP 261

Since your printer may offer some interesting features that you can take advantage of with WordPerfect, the program contains notes about the different printers. These notes include how to use unusual printer features, when you need to use care with specific WordPerfect features, and warnings about WordPerfect features your printer does not support. To see these notes in WordPerfect 5.1, select File Print Select Printer then, with your printer highlighted, select Help. In WordPerfect 6, select File Print/Fax Select and, with the printer highlighted in the Select Printer dialog box, select Info. This is an example of what you might see:

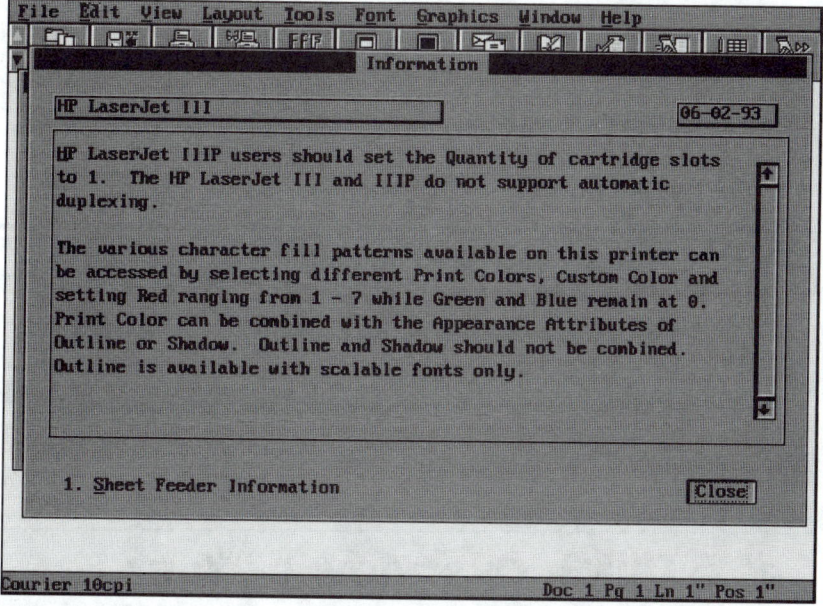

You Cannot Print Using Printer Features Your Printer Does Not Support

TIP 262

Your printer's capabilities determine what can be printed. If you cannot get a WordPerfect feature to print, check to see that your printer supports the feature (see Tip 263). While software can supplement printer features by creating graphics and fonts, some WordPerfect features still may not be available

to your printer. As Tip 261 mentions, you can view information about your printer to get a list of features your printer does not support.

Create Samples of the WordPerfect Features You Want to Use

If you want to incorporate some WordPerfect features that you aren't certain your printer will print, create a sample document to try the features. For example, before setting your document to use watermarks or graphics boxes, create a document using a page of text copied from another document.

Another method of testing how various WordPerfect features will print is to open the PRINTER.TST document in the same directory as your WordPerfect program files and print it. PRINTER.TST contains samples of different WordPerfect text attributes, fonts, a watermark, and graphics in WordPerfect 6. PRINTER.TST for WordPerfect 5.1 is limited to the features supported by 5.1 and does not contain an example of features such as watermarks.

Before Printing a Document, Preview It

You can save time and paper by previewing your document before you actually print it. Often while flipping through the pages onscreen, you will notice and fix some little detail that will save you from having to reprint the entire document.

Get a Quick Overview of Your WordPerfect 6 Document with a Thumbnail Preview

A thumbnail preview of your document shows a small version of each page in the document. This lets you see that all the pages look consistent, shows where a document has too much or too little space, and points out where your document needs more graphics if you want the document to evenly use graphics.

A thumbnail display can show from 1 to 255 pages at a time. The thumbnail display is available by selecting Print Preview, selecting View Thumbnails, and then one of the options to display a thumbnail view of 1 Page, 2 Page, 4 Page, 8 Page, 32 Page or Other. The next step, if you selected Other, is to type the number of pages you want to display at one time. You also can display a thumbnail view of 8 or 32 pages by selecting one of these two buttons in the Preview Button Bar:

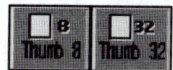

The page with the extra outline around it is the current page. This will be the page shown if you select View Full Page.

Use the Same Keys for Moving Through the Document in the Print Preview Window

As you work, several key combinations can help you move quickly through a document. You press PGUP and PGDN to move from one page to the next, HOME HOME UP ARROW or HOME HOME DOWN ARROW to move to the beginning or end of the document, CTRL-HOME to move to a specific page and the grey - and grey + key to scroll up or down on a page. All of these keys perform the same function when you use them in the Print Preview window. Use these keys to quickly move between pages in the Print Preview window.

WordPerfect 6 has several commands and Button Bar buttons that are equivalent to some of these keys. The Pages menu includes Next Page, Previous Page, and Go to Page, which are equivalent to PGDN, PGUP, and CTRL-HOME. The Button Bar buttons that provide these same features are shown in the following:

Use Different Preview Viewing Levels to Check a Document

Don't be surprised if you notice different details about a previewed document at different magnification levels. For example, if you are previewing a page with lots of text, at 200 percent preview level, you will notice the text. At 100 percent magnification, you will focus more on margins and line spacing. Using an 8-page thumbnail view as described in Tip 265, you may notice that the text is centered on the page or that you want to distribute the text more evenly over several pages.

If Your Document Uses Colors, Preview How They Will Look on Your Printer

If your printer only prints one color but your document uses several, preview the document to show how your printer will print the colors. In WordPerfect 5.1, select File Setup Display View Document Options Graphics in Black & White, then Yes. In WordPerfect 6, select File Setup from the Preview window or click the following button:

Select the View Text & Graphics in Black & White check box. Selecting No in WordPerfect 5.1 or clearing the check box returns WordPerfect to the colors the text or graphics originally contained.

You Can Customize the Button Bar in the Print Preview Window in WordPerfect 6

The Button Bar in WordPerfect 6's Print Preview window is different from the buttons available while you are editing a document. The Print Preview window Button Bar looks like this:

Close Print Preview window
Display at 100% magnification
Display at 200% magnification
Increase magnification
Decrease magnification
Show full page
Show facing pages

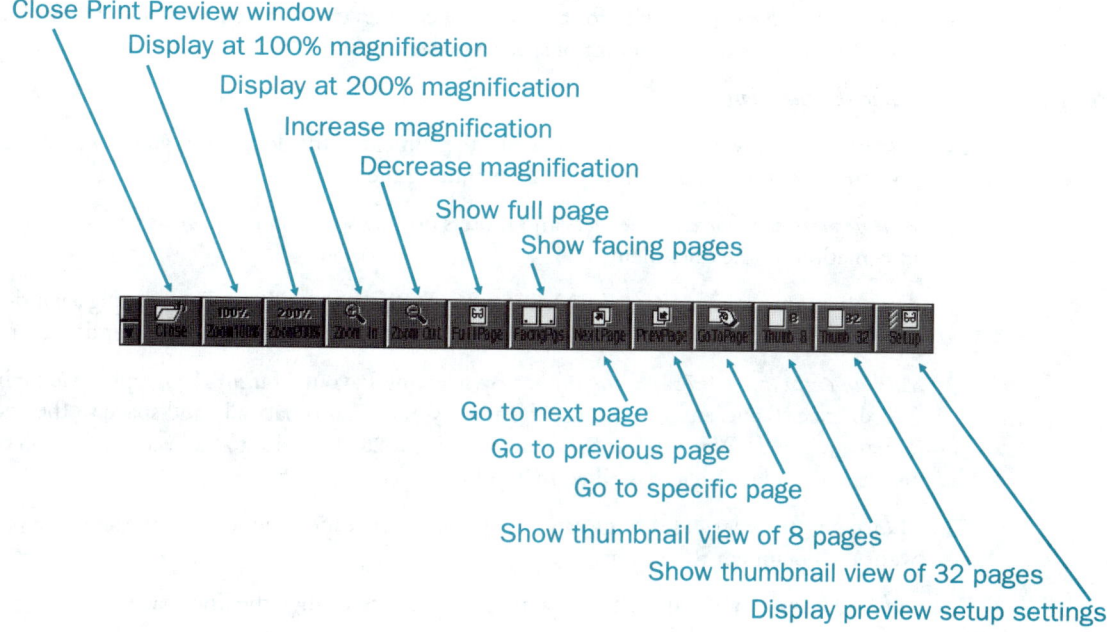

Go to next page
Go to previous page
Go to specific page
Show thumbnail view of 8 pages
Show thumbnail view of 32 pages
Display preview setup settings

Clicking the down arrow on the side of the Button Bar shows the Button Bar Edit and Button Bar Options icons. Tips 1 and 221 include more information on using these buttons and customizing the appearance of the Button Bar.

How to Spread Out the Contents of a Page

When you have extra space at the bottom of a page or you want to make a document longer, you have several options for making the document's contents fit the desired space:

❑ *Select a larger font* Changing font size by a point or a half of a point is not very noticeable but can make great changes in how much space a document occupies. This option is only available if the fonts the document uses have additional sizes available.

❑ *Select a typeface that takes up more room* Some fonts can fit more information on a line than others.

❑ *Increase margins* Larger margins mean a document's text will take up more space lengthwise on the page.

❏ *Increase line spacing* As with font sizes, small changes to line spacing are not obvious but make big changes in the amount of space a document uses.

❏ *Make the titles larger*

❏ *Add graphics* If you have graphics that fit the context of the document, you can make the document more visually stimulating by including them.

❏ *Add headers and footers* Headers and footers occupy space on the page as well as provide information on the document.

❏ *Disable hyphenation as described in Tip 826* WordPerfect will stop hyphenating a word at the end of a line, and will shift the word to the next line, thus adding space to your document.

❏ *Add an extra line between paragraphs* By selecting Layout Margin Paragraph Spacing in WordPerfect 6 and entering a larger number, you can automatically add space to the end of paragraphs. In WordPerfect 5.1, you either press ENTER twice to end each paragraph or use secondary leading as described in Tip 119.

❏ *Add more headings* Headings can clarify topics for readers while they fill the space you want the document to occupy.

❏ *Add leading* Tip 985 describes how to use leading to change the line spacing.

How to Cram More Information onto a Page

If you need to fit more information on a page, try some of these methods of conserving space:

❏ *Switch to a proportional font* Proportional fonts usually fit more lines per character than nonproportional ones. The Roman-WP font in WordPerfect 6 is an example of a font that can fit many more characters into a line than a font such as Courier.

❏ *Switch to a smaller font* Scalable fonts are especially good because you can shrink them in smaller increments than nonscalable fonts. For example, if you want to fit all of the terms of sale on the back of an invoice, you can use a scalable font to go from a 10-point font to a 9-point font. A nonscalable font may have fonts only in a few sizes such as 12, 10, and 8. Changing font size by one or half a point is not very noticeable.

❏ *Reduce margins* Smaller margins increase the space on the page for a document's text.

- ❏ *Decrease spacing* You can have spacing in smaller increments than whole lines. For example, you can switch from double-spacing to 1.5 spacing. This affects both the body of the text and footnotes.

- ❏ *Use only one space between sentences* If you habitually use two spaces between sentences and you need room, use Edit Replace in WordPerfect 6 to replace the period and two spaces with a period and one space.

- ❏ *Decrease line spacing* As with font sizes, small decrements in line spacing are not obvious but make big changes in the amount of space a document uses.

- ❏ *Make the titles smaller*

- ❏ *Enable hyphenation as described in Tip 826* Hyphenation increases the number of words that fit on a line.

- ❏ *Decrease leading* Tip 985 describes how to use leading to change line spacing.

Print Documents Without Graphics When You Just Want to Proofread Text

TIP 272

When you want to proofread just the text in your document, you can print it much faster by omitting any graphics. To print a document without its graphics, press SHIFT-F7 or select Print (Print/Fax in WordPerfect 6) from the File menu. Next, select Graphics Quality and Do Not Print before selecting Full Document. You can resume graphics printing by selecting Graphics Quality, and then Draft, Medium, or High. Note that when you omit the graphics in a document, pictures and rotated text (see Tip 631) do not print either, although text in graphics boxes will.

Printing Wide Documents

TIP 273

To print a wide document, the first thing you need to do is change the page size. This is done by selecting Layout Page, and then choosing Paper Size in WordPerfect 5.1 or Paper Size/Type in WordPerfect 6. Pick the size you want from the list given. Most of the time, you will want to change from portrait to landscape orientation. If you switch the orientation, you may notice a different set of fonts available as described in Tip 157. When you preview a document after setting its page size, WordPerfect adjusts the page size to your selection.

Printing Labels

TIP 274

WordPerfect can print labels from data you have in a document. When you print labels in WordPerfect, each page represents one label. WordPerfect handles printing the data to fit correctly on each label.

Labels are indicated very differently in WordPerfect 5.1 and 6. In WordPerfect 5.1, follow these steps to tell WordPerfect you are printing labels:

1. Select **L**ayout **P**age Paper **S**ize.
2. Select **A**dd, and then choose the page type to select a page size.
3. Make any changes to the page size as described in Tip 273.
4. Select **L**abels and **Y**es to display the Format: Labels screen.
5. Enter the measurements for the labels in the Format: Labels screen.
6. Press F7 (Exit) until you return to the document.

When you define the size of the label, you must indicate to WordPerfect the height and width of the labels, as well as the distances between the columns and rows of labels, as shown here:

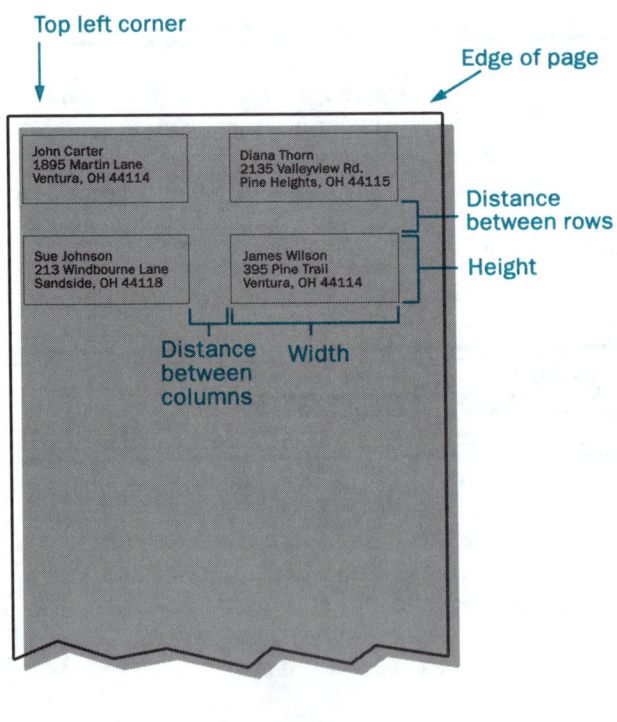

In WordPerfect 6 most of the standard label sizes already have been defined, so you do not need to take these measurements.

To tell WordPerfect you are using labels:

1. Select **L**ayout **P**age **L**abels.
2. Select one of the label sizes given in the list box. (Notice the changes in the Label Details as you move your cursor through the list.) You can limit the label sizes defined in the list by selecting Display **L**aser, Display **T**ractor-Fed, or Display **B**oth. If the size you want is not listed, select the one closest to the size of your labels and select **E**dit or choose **C**reate if you want to keep the originals intact. From the Edit Label dialog box, you can enter the information WordPerfect needs.
3. Make any changes to the Labels Printer Info dialog box. From the dialog box, you can select the source of the labels, whether you need to be prompted to load it, whether to use portrait or landscape fonts, and how the text needs to be adjusted.
4. Select OK twice to close the dialog box and return to the document.

After you tell WordPerfect you are printing a label, the page size will change so each page fits one label. When you preview the label, it will appear as it will print. This means that if a page fits three labels across and ten down, the Print Preview window will show this.

You can use the same data file that you use for a form letter. All you have to do is create a form file that has the field merge codes added and the page size defined. Tip 804 gives more information about printing labels using merge code and data files.

If you cannot fit all of the data that you want in a label, change the font. You can create a border that edges the labels when you want to check if the labels are printed correctly with Layout Page Page Borders.

Before you print out a lot of labels, print your file onto plain paper and hold each page against the labels to make sure that they align. You can use the Print Preview window to see how many labels fit on one page, and then print that many pages to have one page worth of labels.

TIP 275

Printing Envelopes with WordPerfect 6

Rather than writing or typing addresses for an envelope, have WordPerfect address the envelope for you. When WordPerfect addresses the envelope, it handles address placement. Also, you can use your address as the default so you don't have to enter a return address (unless you're using an address other than your regular one).

If you have an address in the document, WordPerfect will pick up the address as the mailing address. Alternately, you can insert the envelope address into a document on a separate page so when you print the document, you also can print the envelope.

To print an envelope:

1. Select **L**ayout En**v**elope.
2. Select **R**eturn Address, type the address you want to use, and press F7.
3. Select **M**ailing Address, type the address you want to use, and press F7.
4. Select **I**nsert or **P**rint.

In step 4, selecting Insert adds the envelope address to the end of the document so when you print the document, you can print an addressed envelope. Selecting **P**rint prints the envelope without adding anything to the current document. The first time you use this feature, after performing step 2, select Save Return Address as Default. Then, you can skip this step in subsequent documents for which you use the same return address. You do not have to perform step 3 if the current document has an address—WordPerfect automatically picks up the address and enters it below Mailing Address. WordPerfect will also handle creating POSTNET bar codes when you supply the 5-, 9-, or 11-digit code in the POSTNET **B**ar Code text box.

You also can press SHIFT-F1 for Setup when you want to set the default envelope size or to select whether you want to manually set the POSTNET bar code, have it set automatically, or not be available. When the POSTNET bar code is set to be entered automatically, WordPerfect creates it only for addresses picked up from the document.

To use WordPerfect to print envelopes for form letters, create an envelope using the merge codes in the mailing address for the data you want picked up from the data file. You can use the same data file that you use for form letters. See Tip 804 for more information about printing envelopes with the same data you use for form letters.

What to Do When the Printer Doesn't Accept Characters

TIP 276

If you select File Print (or Print/Fax in WordPerfect 6) Control Printer and you see a message that your printer is not accepting characters, the problem is usually one of three causes. Either you have the wrong definition (which you can change as described in Tip 321), your printer is not turned on, or your cable has come loose. Once you remedy the problem, you will be able to print the document. Tip 260 lists other quick fixes for common printer problems.

You Can Print Faster Using Your Printer's Fonts

TIP 277

Some fonts print faster than others. The fonts that your printer provides print faster than the fonts WordPerfect provides. Printer fonts also print faster than software fonts because the printer already has the font definitions at hand so your computer does not have to tell your printer how each character in the font is printed.

Most printers can print in two ways. In the first way, the computer tells the printer which characters to print using the information stored in the printer to set how each character appears. This is similar to how a typewriter works in that the characters are preformed and ready to be put to paper. In the second method, the computer tells the printer which dots to print in order to create the image of the character you want. This way is similar to drawing on a piece of paper in that the letters are created, not stored ready to print. The second way is the most flexible because having the ability to print dots in any location means the printer has a wider range of results. All graphics are printed with this second method. Its disadvantage is that it is slower for the printer and the computer to create each character.

Use the Print Button in the Button Bar to Print Documents

Select the Print button in the WordPerfect 6 Button Bar to quickly display the Print/Fax dialog box. The Print button in the Button Bar looks like this:

Use the Preview Button in the Button Bar to Preview Printed Documents

Select the Preview button in the WordPerfect 6 Button Bar to preview the current document just as if you selected File Print/Fax. The Preview button in the Button Bar looks like this:

If Your Printed Documents Do Not Match the Preview, Initialize the Printer

When you print a document and find it contains settings that belonged to a previous document, initialize the printer. (To initialize the printer in WordPerfect 5.1, press SHIFT-F7 (Print) or select File Print then select Initialize Printer. In WordPerfect 6, select File Print/Fax or press SHIFT-F7 then select Initialize Printer.) For example, if another program has printed something using a different printer font than the default and did not switch back the font, your subsequent documents will continue to

use the other font. While most programs handle both turning on and turning off printer settings, some programs might not.

Initializing the printer resets it to use its default settings and downloads soft fonts that you have set to be downloaded as described in Tip 193.

If a WordPerfect 6 Previewed Document Does Not Match a Printed Copy, Print the Document Graphically

Some documents that contain graphics may not print correctly unless you set WordPerfect 6 to print the job graphically. To print a job graphically, select the Print Job Graphically check box in the Print/Fax dialog box. Printing jobs graphically is slower, so do this only when a document does not print correctly and does not match the preview. Some of the types of features you will print graphically include reversed text as described in Tip 175, and overlapping text and graphics.

Choose How Much of Your Document Prints

WordPerfect has many options for printing all or a portion of a document. You can print the entire document, the document summary, one page, a range of pages, or the block you select. You select the part of the document to print by selecting an option in the first group of selections available after selecting File Print or Print/Fax. Full Document prints the pages in the document that you see in the editing screen. Page prints the current page containing the cursor. Multiple Pages prints a selected group of pages from the current document. In WordPerfect 5.1, you can type the page numbers you want printed. In WordPerfect 6, you can select Page/Label Range and type the numbers of the pages to print. WordPerfect 6 also lets you select Secondary Page(s), Chapter, or Volume when you want to print pages that have the secondary page numbers, chapter numbers, or volume numbers in the range you enter. For page numbers, secondary page numbers, chapters, and volume ranges you can enter specific numbers or a range. The following shows sample page number entries and the pages WordPerfect will print with the entries:

Page Number Entry	Printed Pages
1,3,5	Pages 1, 3, and 5
-5,7	Pages 1 through 5 and page 7
1,5-	Page 1 and page 5 through the end

WordPerfect 6 has other options in the Print Multiple Pages dialog box. You can select Document Summary when you want to print the document summary on a page before the rest of the document is printed. In WordPerfect 5.1, select File Summary and press SHIFT-F7 to print the document summary. You also can use the Print as Booklet check box when printing a booklet as described in Tip 982. Have WordPerfect print pages in reverse order with the Descending Order check box.

When you are typing the page numbers you want to print, they must be in numerical order. For example, WordPerfect will accept 1, 5, 10 but will not accept 10, 5, 1.

A "Disk Full" Message When Printing Indicates Insufficient Work Space

283

As described in Tip 287, when you print, WordPerfect puts in a temporary file the information to be sent to the printer. If you do not have enough disk space, WordPerfect cannot create this temporary information and will not print the document. You can print the document after you have deleted extra files so WordPerfect has room to create the temporary files. To correct this problem, go to DOS or the File Manager to delete files that you no longer need.

If Double-Sided Pages Are Not an Option on Your Printer, Insert the Pages into the Printer Twice

284

To print a double-sided document when your printer does not support double-sided printing, print all the odd pages, flip the paper, then print the even pages. To do this, select File Print/Fax Multiple

Pages. In WordPerfect 5.1, you will have to type the page numbers separated by commas as in **1,3,5**. In WordPerfect 6, select **Odd/Even Pages** and **Odd** and then select OK and Print.

Next, after the odd pages are printed, put the pages back into the printer so printing occurs on the opposite side of the paper. For a dot matrix printer, this means turning the paper around and rethreading it through the printer. In a laser printer, you will need to flip over the paper. A neat trick for printing on two sides of the page using a laser printer in WordPerfect 6 is to remove the pages without rearranging them, leaving page one at the bottom of the stack. If the last page is an odd-numbered page, remove this page from the stack as you put the pages back into the laser printer's feeding tray with the printing face down. Also remember to keep track of which way the top of the page should face. When you print the even pages on a laser printer when page one is at the bottom of the stack, select the **Descending Order** check box. This little trick means you do not have to rearrange pages so page one is at the top, then page three, and so on.

Next, print the even pages. Select File Print/Fax Multiple Pages. In WordPerfect 5.1, you will have to type the even page numbers separated by commas as in **2,4,6**. In WordPerfect 6, select **Odd/Even Pages** and **Even** then select OK and Print. If you plan to bind the pages, see Tip 984 about adding a binding offset.

You Can Insert Your Own Pages into a Laser Printer

TIP 285

If you are using a laser printer, you probably use the tray most of the time to feed paper into the printer. You can feed individual sheets into many models, which is useful if you want to use special paper to print a few pages. If you plan to feed paper into the printer manually, know which way you must insert a page for the text to match the top of the paper. For example, when printing on paper with a letterhead, know how to insert the paper with the letterhead so the letterhead appears on the top of the printed document. Also, if you are printing a double-sided document as described in Tip 284, know how to reinsert the pages that have been printed on one side in order to print the second side of the page correctly.

The easy way to check this is to draw an arrow on a blank sheet of plain paper, and run the page through the printer using WordPerfect to print text at the top of the page. Notice how you insert it into the printer and how it comes out, as well as the direction of the arrow and whether it is on the correct side of the page. As an example, you can insert the test page into a Hewlett-Packard LaserJet printer as shown in the following, with the arrow facing up and pointing toward the printer:

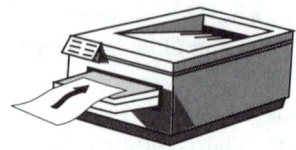

When you print a WordPerfect document containing "This is Text" in large letters, the resulting page will include the text and the arrow as shown above. From this test, you know that when you want a document to use a specific side of a page, the paper must be inserted so the front of the page is on top and the top of the page is the side closest to the printer.

There May Be a Delay Between Your Print Request and the Actual Printing

TIP 286

When you print a document, WordPerfect may need to perform some preparation work. For example, if the document requires that fonts be downloaded, the first part of the printing process will be downloading the fonts. If you are uncertain whether WordPerfect is printing the document, select **File Print** in WordPerfect 5.1 (Print/Fax in WordPerfect 6) Control Printer to see WordPerfect's listing of the documents it is printing and their status. The screen looks something like this:

```
 File  Edit  View  Layout  Tools  Font  Graphics  Window  Help
                          Control Printer
┌─Current Job──────────────────────────────────────────────────────────┐
│ Job Number: None                    Page Number:  None                 │
│ Status:     Stopped                 Current Copy: None                 │
│ Message:    None                                                        │
│ Paper:      None                                                        │
│ Location:   None                                                        │
│ Action:     Fix printer (check cable, make sure printer is turned ON)  │
│             Press "G" to continue                                       │
│ Percentage Processed: 0   [                                        ]    │
└────────────────────────────────────────────────────────────────────────┘
┌─Job  Document                    Destination──────┐  1. Cancel Job
│ 2    C:\WPDOCS\SALES93           LPT 1            │  2. Rush Job
│                                                    │  3. * (Un)mark
│                                                    │  4. (Un)mark All
│                                                    │
└────────────────────────────────────────────────────┘
┌─Text        Graphics      Copies   Priority─┐   [ Stop ]   [ Go ]
│ High        Medium        1        Normal    │
└──────────────────────────────────────────────┘   [ Network... F8 ]  [ Close ]
```

If you have a page printer (as described in Tip 308), you will experience a delay, which is caused by the printer not printing until it receives all the information it needs to print an entire page. However, when you select File Print in WordPerfect 5.1 (Print/Fax in WordPerfect 6) Control Printer, you will notice that WordPerfect is making progress in printing the document.

Changes Made to a Document That Is Printing Do Not Appear in the Printed Copy

When you print a document, WordPerfect takes all of the information that it will send to the printer and puts it in a temporary file. By having the information in a temporary file, WordPerfect can send information to the printer as fast as the printer can print it. Printers are usually slower than computers so having WordPerfect handle sending printer information in the background means you can continue working with your WordPerfect documents. Any changes you make to your WordPerfect document will not change the temporary file containing the information being sent to the printer. As a result, changes you make to a document that WordPerfect is printing do not appear in the output.

You Can Still Use Fast Save and Print from the Disk in WordPerfect 6

As described in Tip 894, you can use the Fast Save feature to quickly save a file, however, files saved with this format are not saved with all the formatting WordPerfect uses to print the document. In WordPerfect 5.1, you cannot print a document from disk that you have saved with the Fast Save feature. To print a document saved with the Fast Save feature in WordPerfect 5.1, you must open the document. In WordPerfect 6, WordPerfect will handle formatting a document saved on disk with the Fast Save feature for the current printer. This occurs in the background after you have selected Document on Disk from the Print/Fax dialog box, provided the document to print, and started the printing process. Since WordPerfect 6 handles printing documents saved with the Fast Save feature for you, WordPerfect 6 is set to automatically save documents with the Fast Save feature, unless you select otherwise.

WordPerfect 6 Will Print Documents Created with Other Programs

You don't have to use other word processors to print documents created with other programs. WordPerfect can print Ami Pro, DisplayWrite, Multimate, OfficeWriter, Word, and WordStar word processing files as well as its own files. In addition, WordPerfect can print non-word processing files such as Lotus 1-2-3 and Quattro Pro spreadsheets and .BMP and .PCX graphics. When you select Document on Disk from the Print/Fax dialog box and select the file to print, after you select Print to start printing you will see the dialog box that prompts for the format for the file. When you select the file's format, WordPerfect converts the file into a WordPerfect document and prints it.

Different Selections Start the Printing Process

You want to know when WordPerfect starts the printing process because changes you make after starting the printing process do not affect the printing tasks you have already started. WordPerfect 5.1 starts printing using all of the current print settings when you select Full Document, Page, or after completing the responses for Multiple Pages or Document on Disk. WordPerfect 6 does not start printing until you select the Print button.

You Can Print a Range of Pages from Disk

When you print a document from disk, you may not want to print all of the pages. Perhaps in flipping through a printout you realize that you need more copies of a particular page. You have to be more careful than when you print multiple pages from a document on the screen, however, because you cannot actually look at the document on the screen and check that you are printing the correct pages.

Printing a range of pages from a document saved on disk is just like printing a document on disk normally. After you select the **D**ocument on Disk option from the Print/Fax dialog box or the Print menu, WordPerfect prompts you for the name of the file on disk. Then it prompts you for the pages you want to print, in WordPerfect 5.1, or displays the Print Multiple Pages dialog box in WordPerfect 6. Simply indicate the pages you want to print and select OK to print those pages.

You Need the Password to Print a Locked File Stored on Disk

When you print a document from disk and the document is protected with a password, you can print it as long as you can supply the correct password. In WordPerfect 5.1, after you select **D**ocument on Disk and supply the filename and the pages you want to print, WordPerfect will prompt you for the password. In WordPerfect 6, WordPerfect does not start printing until you select the Print button and enter your password in the dialog box provided. Once you provide the correct password, WordPerfect will print the document.

Print Banners Faster by Enlarging the Graphical Printing of Fonts

WordPerfect prints large characters as graphics. Characters in soft fonts or graphical fonts can either be defined character by character or they can have their entire character set defined and just tell the printer which characters, from the character set to print. The first method is quicker when the document has a few large characters, but if you are printing a document that has many, for such items as banners and flyers, you will get faster results by having WordPerfect tell the printer once how each character appears and thereafter telling the printer which of those characters to use. The cutoff point between when WordPerfect defines each character and when WordPerfect defines the character set is set by the threshold point size. To change the size at which WordPerfect defines each character, select File Print/Fax and Setup. After Threshold Point Size, type the point size of the character size. Characters this size or larger have their characters defined one character at a time. When you are printing a document with lots of large characters in the same font, you will want to set the size larger than the size you use in the document.

You Can Generate Multiple Copies in Several Ways

If you want multiple copies of a document, print them by increasing the number of copies. Select **File Print** in WordPerfect 5.1 (**Print/Fax** in WordPerfect 6) **Number of Copies** and type the number of copies you want to print. In WordPerfect 5.1, the number of copies set will remain the same until you leave WordPerfect. In WordPerfect 6, the number of copies will revert to the default setting (usually one) after you leave the Print/Fax dialog box.

WordPerfect creates multiple copies in one of two ways. WordPerfect can print one copy of a document and then continue to print more copies of a document until the last copy is printed. WordPerfect also can tell the printer to print page 1 and the printer will handle printing as many copies of that page as WordPerfect tells it to before starting to print the second page. The output generated with the first method has each copy grouped together. The output generated by the second method has each page grouped together so you must collate the pages. The second method may be faster, depending on your printer. To tell WordPerfect how you want to create multiple print jobs, select **Multiple Copies Generated by** in WordPerfect 5.1 or **Generated by** in WordPerfect 6. You can select **WordPerfect** to have WordPerfect generate each copy or **Printer** to have WordPerfect send one copy of the page to the printer and let the printer handle making multiple copies. If you are on a network, you may be able to select **Network**. Network lets WordPerfect send one copy of each page to the network and have the network send repeated copies of the document to the printer.

To Reverse the Order of Printed Pages, Have WordPerfect Print the Last Page First

The output areas for some printers may hold pages so that the first page printed is always on the bottom of the stack. If you are frequently rearranging printouts to put them in the correct order, have WordPerfect print the document backward. This means that the last page is printed first and page 1 is the last page to be printed. To do this in WordPerfect 6, select **File Print/Fax Multiple Pages Descending Order** and **OK**.

You Can Change the Order in Which Documents Print

TIP 296

WordPerfect prints documents in the order you tell it to. Some printers print quickly enough so that it's never necessary to change the order of documents being printed. If you have a slow printer, though, you may need a document that's at the end of the print queue and not have time to wait for it. In that case, rearrange document order.

Select File Print (Print/Fax) then Control Printer, and WordPerfect lists all of the jobs in the print queue. The one at the top is the one WordPerfect is currently printing. The rest of the documents are waiting their turn. The document you need in a hurry is a rush job, so it moves to the top of the list. To do this, highlight the print job and select Rush Job. WordPerfect asks if you want to interrupt the current job. Select Yes to interrupt the current print job or No to move the highlighted print job to follow directly behind the current print job. When you interrupt a print job with a rush job, WordPerfect completes the current page of the current job, prints the rush job, then prints the remaining pages of the current job.

You Can Change Your Mind About Printing a Document

TIP 297

If you tell WordPerfect to print a document that you later realize you do not want printed, cancel printing of that document. Select File Print (Print/Fax) then Control of Printer. In the list of print jobs in the print queue, highlight the print job that you wish to cancel and select Cancel Job. WordPerfect asks you to confirm that you want to cancel. Select Yes. If WordPerfect has finished printing the document, you cannot undo it. Also, as mentioned in Tip 298, your document may continue to print for a moment after you cancel it.

Your Printer Will Continue to Print for a Short While After You Cancel Printing

When you print a document, the computer sends information to the printer faster than it can be printed. Your printer holds part of the document in its memory until that part is printed. Although you can cancel a print job as described in Tip 297, your printer still may have part of the document in memory. The printer will continue to print its memory's contents. Only after all of the document stored in the printer's memory is printed will the printer be told that the print job is canceled and move to the next print job. If your printer has a lot of memory, the additional amount of text printed from the document may be more than you expect.

To clear your printer's memory, turn off the printer or press its Reset button.

If a Printer Is Busy You Can Print to Disk and Print Later with DOS COPY

If you are sharing a printer with someone else and you want a document printed but not immediately, you can send information to a file instead of sending information to a printer. Later, have DOS's COPY command send to the printer the information in the file that is intended for the printer.

In WordPerfect 5.1, redirect output to a file by selecting File Print Select Printer, highlighting the printer you will later use to print the file. It is important that you select the printer you will use with the DOS COPY command. If the wrong printer is selected, you will get erroneous printouts. Select Edit Port Other, type the name of the file to use, and press F7 (Exit) until you return to the document. Once you select Full Document, Document on Disk, Page, or Multiple Pages to start printing, all of the information that WordPerfect would send to the printer is sent to the file you named after selecting Other.

In WordPerfect 6, redirect output to a file by selecting File Print/Fax Select, highlighting the printer you will later use to print the file, and selecting Edit Port, Prompt for Filename. It is important that you select the printer you will use with the DOS COPY command. If the wrong printer is selected, you will get erroneous printouts. Select OK twice and Select once to return to the Print/Fax dialog box. Once you select Print, you will see a dialog box like the following:

In this dialog box, type the name of the file that will store the information normally sent to the printer. Unless you provide a drive and directory location, the file is placed in the same location as your WordPerfect documents. When you select OK, all of the information that WordPerfect regularly sends to the printer is sent to the file you named in the dialog box.

Later, when you want to print the file, all you have to do is use the DOS COPY command from the DOS prompt in the directory the file was printed to. This is an example of a command you might use:

```
COPY PRINTOUT LPT1 /B
```

In this example, PRINTOUT is the name of the file containing the information to be sent to the printer. LPT1 is the port to send the information to, as described in Tip 260. The /B prevents DOS from assuming it has reached the end of the file too early. /B keeps sending a file's contents until all of the bytes are sent, rather than until an end-of-file character is reached.

The file you create by sending the printing information to a file rather than a printer is specifically designed to use a printer and is not designed for other purposes. If you try looking at the file in WordPerfect or with the File Manager, you will see characters you do not recognize as part of your document.

Initialize the Printer to Include Soft Fonts

When using soft fonts that must be downloaded, tell WordPerfect to download these fonts. At the same time, you are resetting the printer to use only the printer's initial settings. To download soft fonts and remove any previous printer settings, select File Print in WordPerfect 5.1 (Print/Fax in WordPerfect 6) Initialize Printer. You only need to do this once during a WordPerfect session but you'll have to redo it if you have turned your printer off then back on. Also try this method when you have printed and the soft fonts your document uses do not look correct.

If the Printout Looks Garbled, Check the Printer Selection

If your output contains strange characters or looks nothing like what you see when you preview the document, check the printer selection. Select File Print (Print/Fax) then look at the printer named to the right of Select Printer in WordPerfect 5.1 or at the top of the dialog box in WordPerfect 6. If the printer named displayed does not match your printer, change it as described next. If the correct printer is selected, check the connection between the computer and the printer for a loose cable.

In WordPerfect 5.1, if the wrong printer is selected, choose Select Printer. From the list of printers, highlight the printer to use and choose Select and you will return to the Print screen.

In WordPerfect 6, if the wrong printer appears below Current Printer in the Print/Fax dialog box, choose Select. From the Select Printer dialog box, highlight the printer you are using and choose Select.

Print Many Files at Once by Marking Them on the List Files Screen

A quick way to print multiple files is to press F5, select File List Files in WordPerfect 5.1, or select File File Manager in WordPerfect 6. From the file list, move to each file you want to print and press *. When all of the files you want to print are marked, select Print. WordPerfect asks if you want to print the marked files. Confirm that you do by selecting Yes. You will also see the prompt for printing multiple pages or the Print Multiple Pages dialog box that you can use to set several WordPerfect 6 options.

Your entries for the pages to print or the dialog box options apply to each document printed. When files have been saved with the Fast Save feature described in Tip 894, WordPerfect opens the document behind the scenes to format it for the current printer as it prints the documents. This is also the case when you print a document from WordPerfect that is not in a WordPerfect 6 format (although you will see the same prompt to select the appropriate format of the document as described in Tip 289).

Line Height Options Vary by Printer

TIP 303

Don't be surprised if you fit a different number of lines on a page when you change to a different printer. When you are using a printer font, the print sets the line height. By using a different printer, you are potentially using a different line height. When the line height is different, you will have a different number of lines on each page. If you want to ensure that you have the same number of lines print on a page, regardless of which printer you use, change the line height from automatic to fixed as discussed in Tip 143 or change the amount of leading as described in Tip 985.

Documents Must Be Reformatted If You Select Another Printer

TIP 304

Each printer has its own defaults for available printer margins, fonts, and other settings that affect how the document appears when printed. When you change the selected printer, documents formatted for the previous printer must be reformatted before they are printed. WordPerfect handles this for you so you do not have to perform any special task with each document after changing the printer. WordPerfect also has to format documents when you have saved them with the Fast Save feature as described in Tip 894. When you change the printer or open a document saved with the Fast Save feature, you will see WordPerfect's message that it is formatting the document for the selected printer.

Rotate the Printout by Changing the Page Size

TIP 305

You can print documents in either portrait orientation or landscape orientation. Portrait orientation is printed from top to bottom (so as the paper emerges from the printer, you can read it). Landscape orientation is printed from side to side (so you have to wait until the page finishes printing and turn it sideways to read it). The following shows how the text is printed using the different orientations:

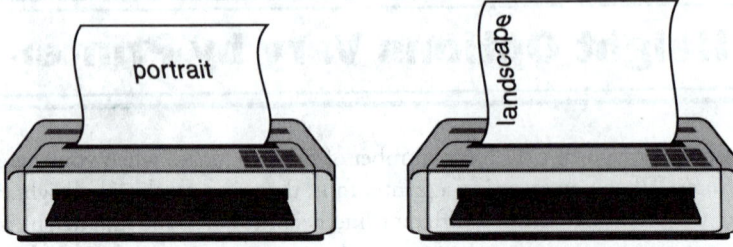

You set page orientation by setting paper size. When you select Layout **P**age Paper Size you can see both the different sizes of the actual paper and the different orientations available for each paper size. In WordPerfect 5.1, the orientation is shown in the Font Type column, with "Port" indicating portrait orientation and "Land" indicating landscape. In WordPerfect 6, the orientation appears as part of the paper name; in addition, WordPerfect 6 shows how characters are rotated with the *A* under Orientation.

Change Other Settings When You Alter the Paper Size

TIP 306

When you change a page's size, you may have several document settings that need to change because they no longer look appropriate for the page's new size. For example, if you set the page size to 5 1/2 inches by 8 1/2 inches (see Tip 273 about changing page size), you may want to decrease the margins from one inch to a half inch because the half-inch margins will look better on the smaller page size. Other possible changes include default font size and line spacing.

Share a Printer by Using a Switch Box

TIP 307

Rather than having one printer for every computer, you can have one printer shared by multiple computers. Sharing a printer lets you pool resources so you can get one good printer rather than several mediocre ones. While sharing printer capabilities is one reason for using a network, you do not need a network to share a printer when the computers are within cable distance from the printer. You can purchase a switch box specifically designed for printers. Each computer that wants to use the printer connects to the switch box rather than the printer and one cable connects the switch box to the printer. By changing the switch box's setting, you select which computer is sending information to the printer.

You can connect to a printer that's as far away as 1200 feet by using a parallel line extender at a cost of less than $100.

When using a switch box for your printer, first check that the switch box is turned to your printer if any printing problems occur.

Consider Adding Memory to Your Printer

TIP 308

If you use many downloadable fonts, you can increase the number of fonts stored in your printer's memory. Of course in WordPerfect 6, as mentioned in Tip 193, you can have downloadable fonts loaded only as needed.

Some printers are page printers in that they store all of the information for a single page before printing the page. Laser printers are an example of page printers. One advantage of adding memory to a page printer is you increase the amount of data you can fit on a page. Fitting data on a page can be a problem if a page has a lot of graphics.

If you get a message that your printer is out of memory, consider making a few memory-saving changes:

❑ Switch from graphics fonts like the ones WordPerfect provides to built-in printer fonts.

❑ Reduce the number of downloadable fonts.

❑ Reduce the size of graphics (see Tip 645). A graphic that cannot fit on one page may fit when you change its size to half a page.

❑ Reduce the Graphics Quality (dpi).

Make Laser Printer Toner Cartridges Last Longer

TIP 309

If you are using a laser printer, you can make your toner cartridges last longer. When you think a cartridge is near the end of its life, remove it from the printer, shake it from side to side, and then insert

it back into the machine. This helps to evenly spread the remaining toner in the cartridge so you don't end up with a blank streak in the middle of the page. Tip 310 has other pointers on making your toner cartridges last longer by using less toner.

Use Less Toner by Printing Lighter

You can make laser printer toner last longer by printing lighter and by printing drafts instead of letter-quality copies whenever possible. Lighter text uses less ink. It is also easier to write your changes over. You can set a document to use lighter text by moving to the top of the document and selecting **Font Print Color**. In the Color Selection dialog box, select **Shade of Color** and type a number lower than 100. When you select **OK**, the document will use that percentage less of the current color, presumably black.

The other option is to select **File Print (Print/Fax) Text Quality** and then select **Draft** or **Medium**. Text quality levels differ from printer to printer so try the various printing quality levels on your printer to see how each prints.

To print the final version of your document, use 100 percent of color and high text quality. To return to using 100 percent of the color, search for the [Char Shade Change] code and delete it. To return to high text quality, select **File Print (Print/Fax) Text Quality High**.

You Must Install a Fax Board for WordPerfect 6 with WordPerfect's Installation Program Before Using the Fax Board

Installing a fax to use with WordPerfect requires two steps. First, you must install the fax board on your computer or network, which means setting up a device driver—a program that interprets between your computer and the fax. When you get the fax board, it will include the directions you must follow to install it. Second, you must install the fax driver for WordPerfect, which means telling WordPerfect that one is available. WordPerfect can use only FaxBios-compatible fax boards.

To install a fax board driver for WordPerfect:

1. Move to the WordPerfect program directory by typing **cd\wp60** .
2. Type **install** and press ENTER.
3. Select **Y**es if you see three colored boxes, or **N**o if you do not.
4. Select **D**evice Driver (Sound, Graphics, Fax, Printer).
5. Select **F**ax Files.
6. Select the type of board that you have from the three types of fax boards that are currently supported.
7. If you select FaxBios compatible, the Install program simply displays a message that tells you to load the FaxBios driver before starting WordPerfect. After pressing a key, you are ready to continue with step 10.
8. If you select another type of fax board, the Install program prompts asks where you are installing from and where you are installing to. You can enter new directories or simply press ENTER to accept the defaults.
9. Install now prompts you for the disks it needs to install the drivers.
10. When you are finished, select **E**xit to return to the main Install menu.
11. Select **E**xit to exit the program.

Save Documents You Fax Often in an Easily Faxable File Format and Fax Them from Disk

TIP 312

If you fax certain documents repeatedly, such as resumes, price lists, or promotional material, you can save these documents in a rasterized format and then simply fax the document from disk. A *rasterized* document is one that has been converted so it can be transmitted across the phone lines to another fax machine, then printed. You can send unrasterized files only if your modem and the receiving modem both support binary file transfer.

To save a file in a rasterized format, select Fax Services in the Print/Fax dialog box. After selecting Send Fax, select Save as an image for Fax on Disk, and enter the name for the file as usual.

Use One of Several Options to Add Printer Features to Your Document

Your printer has many features that you can use in your WordPerfect documents but before you can, your printer must be provided with instructions. You can add printer instructions to your WordPerfect document in several ways. First, try to add the printer feature using the menu. For example, when you want text to be boldfaced, selecting the text and pressing F6 means that when you print the document, WordPerfect handles sending the printer instructions on turning boldfacing on and off.

If the printer feature you want in your document is not available through the menu, add a printer command to the document. In WordPerfect 5.1 you would use Format (SHIFT-F8) Other Printer Functions Printer Command. In WordPerfect 6 you use Layout Other, and then choose Printer Functions Printer Commands. In both releases you can select Command and type the code that activates the printer function or select Filename and enter a filename.

The disadvantage of using a printer command is that each printer has its own set of instructions. When you use WordPerfect menus to add printer features (such as when you boldface text), WordPerfect handles sending the correct instructions to the printer, assuming you have selected the correct printer. A printer command inserted into a WordPerfect document requires that the command be correct for that printer.

A third possibility is to use the PTR utility. The PTR utility lets you change the printer definition files. Tip 314 contains more information about using the PTR program.

Use the PTR Program to Further Customize the Way Your Printer Prints WordPerfect Documents

PTR lets you change many of the settings that determine how WordPerfect works with your printer. However, WordPerfect's printer files are designed to work with the widest variety of printers. Usually, you will want to change them only if you are dissatisfied with how WordPerfect uses your printer. Most of the features with which you used the PTR program in a prior release of WordPerfect are now available through WordPerfect's features.

To use the PTR program, switch to the directory containing your printer files, usually the \WP51 or \WPC60DOS directory depending on the release. To use the **PTR** program in WordPerfect 6, you must order the Utilities disk separately from WordPerfect Corporation. Type **PTR** and press ENTER. Many of the keys you use in WordPerfect perform the same function in the PTR program. From the initial screen, press SHIFT-F10 and type the name of the printer file you want to modify, and press ENTER. This is either the .PRS for a specific printer, the .ALL file for a group of printers, or the WP.DRS file that WordPerfect uses for displaying and printing graphics fonts.

If you select the .ALL file, select which printer in the group you want to modify. In WordPerfect 5.1's PTR program, press ENTER after highlighting your choice and then F7 (Exit) to return to the previous menu. In WordPerfect 6's PTR program, you use the same style of menus you use in the Text mode of WordPerfect. For example, when you select Edit after retrieving a .PRS file, you have a menu like the one shown next. When finished with the PTR program, from the main menu, press F7 to leave the program and respond to the prompts for saving the printer file and for exiting PTR.

```
══════════════════════ Edit Printer ══════════════════════
  1.  Attribute Methods...
  2.  Color...
  3.  Default .PRS Filename...
  4.  Default Sheet Feeder...
  5.  Fonts...
  6.  Graphics...
  7.  Information about Printer...
  8.  Miscellaneous       Numbers...
                          Questions...
  9.  Output Trays...
  P.  Paper Size/Type...
  E.  Printer Commands...
  T.  Printer Type...
  R.  Resources...

                                              OK
```

From this menu you select the printer features you want to work with. Don't be surprised if some menu choices are dimmed to indicate commands you cannot select because they do not apply to your printer. The PTR program lets you access the most complex printer features, many of which require that you be very familiar with the printer commands that operate the printer's features. Tips 317 and 319 provide a few examples of some changes you can make with the PTR program. If you plan extensive changes to a printer file with the PTR program, contact WordPerfect to order technical information for the PTR program. (Contact WordPerfect at (800) 321-4566 or (801) 226-6800.)

Many of the PTR program changes may require that WordPerfect update its WP.DRS file. To do this in WordPerfect 6, select Font Font Setup Update Graphics Fonts. WordPerfect 6 may display a message when you start WordPerfect that lets you update the WP.DRS file then.

If You Can't Find the PTR Program, You May Need to Install It

If you try starting the PTR program and you see the message "Bad command or file name", you may need to install it. The PTR program is not installed as part of the default installation because many people never use the program since the printer files contain all the printer features they will use in WordPerfect. Before installing the PTR program, check your \WP51 or \WPC60DOS directory, depending on the release. If either directory does not have a PTR.EXE file, the PTR program needs to be installed. Once you have installed the PTR program, you can use it as described in Tips 316, 317, and 319.

In WordPerfect 5.1, start the Install program from the main Installation screen by selecting **Custom**. You may need to select Install Files From or Install Files To to change where you are installing from and to. When you select Install Disks, you can select **No** for every prompt until you see the question "Do you want to install the PTR Program?" For this one, select **Yes**. When you return to the Custom Installation screen, select Exit.

In WordPerfect 6, start the Install program from the \WP60 directory and select **Yes** or **No** when asked whether you see colored boxes. Select Install Disk(s) and then respond to the prompts for the location where the files will be installed from, and the location where they will be installed to. Select how files will be overwritten. Put the Utilities disk in the requested drive. Press ENTER and then, when prompted to install more files, select No. Select Exit and Yes to leave the installation program. Besides installing PTR, copying all of these files will also install CURSOR.COM (see Tip 942), FIXBIOS.COM, GKDUEN.EXE (Tip 593), GKRDEN.EXE (Tip 593), GRAB.COM (Tip 670), and the SPELL utility (Tip 545). If you don't have the Utilities disk, contact WordPerfect Corporation.

Print Current Settings with WordPerfect 6's PTR Program Before Changing Them

You will feel more comfortable using the PTR program and be able to make changes more easily if you know the current settings. Examining the current settings will help you find the corresponding features in the PTR program and give you an idea of the type of entry the PTR program expects. In WordPerfect 6, the PTR program will create reports containing the current settings for various parts of the printer and font selections. You can move to different parts of the PTR program and add the settings for each section into a file. You can create individual files or add all the settings to the same file.

When you start the PTR program and have selected the file you wish to work with, every time you see a **Text Out** button or option selecting Text Out it displays a dialog box like this:

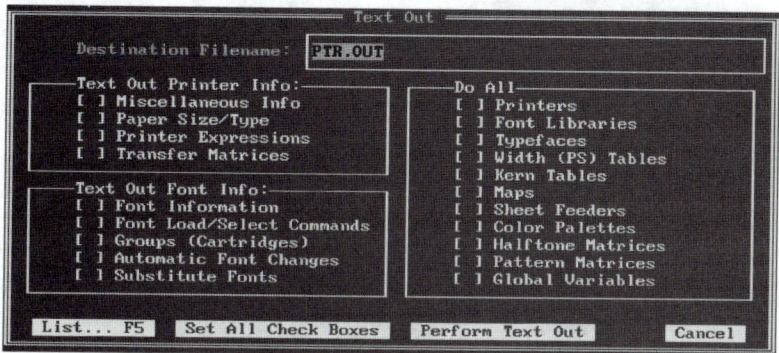

When you provide a filename and select OK, the file selected in the dialog box will contain the current settings. When you select Text Out, the dialog box will contain a filename prompt and an Append check box. If the Append check box is selected, PTR will add the current settings to the end of any existing file with that name. When the Append check box is not selected and a file with that name exists, the current settings PTR is reporting will replace any contents in the file. The file PTR creates is a text file that you can bring into WordPerfect or any other text file editor. As an example, the following shows the section of the PTR report showing the settings for the built-in Univers font for the Hewlett-Packard LaserJet Series III printer:

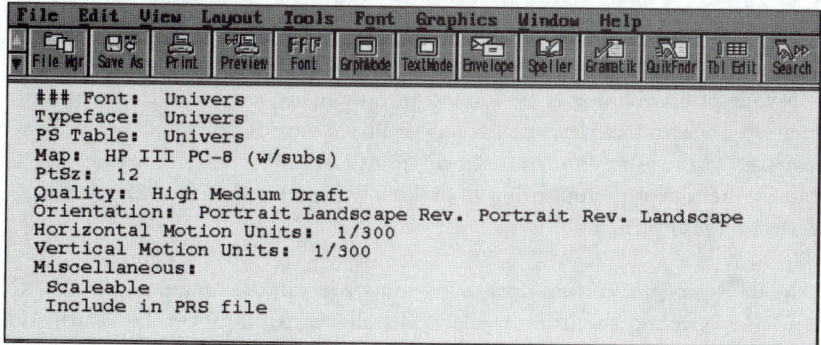

The best way to get the current settings before you change them is to start PTR, go through the different sections of the PTR program you might want to change, and choose the Text Out selection whenever it appears. Then append the current settings to the same file. When you are done generating the file with the current settings, leave the PTR program without saving the file.

Use Go To in WordPerfect 6's PTR Program for Common Printer Changes

Many of the changes you make through the PTR program display when you select **Go To** from the Printers dialog box. When you select **Go To** you will see this dialog box:

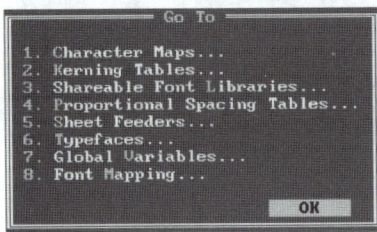

You May Have a Limited Number of Fonts You Can Use on a Page

Depending on your printer, you may be limited in how many fonts you can print on a page. For example, a Hewlett-Packard LaserJet Series II lets you have only 16 fonts on a page. When counting fonts, different sizes of the same font count as different fonts. You will know that you have reached the limit because either the page stops using all of the fonts you have selected or you will see a message from WordPerfect or your printer.

You can use the PTR program to find how many fonts you can use on a page. In WordPerfect 5.1's PTR program, after selecting the printer, select Miscellaneous Numbers. In WordPerfect 6's PTR program, select the printer, select Edit Miscellaneous Numbers. The number after Maximum Number of Fonts/Page is the largest number of fonts you can put on a page. Tips 317 and 319 contain more information about using the PTR program.

Change the Amount of Space Each Character of a Proportional Font Occupies Using the PTR Program

You can change the amount of space characters have. This adjustment is done on a font-by-font basis so if you want the same change to apply to several fonts, you must make the adjustments separately. From the PTR program in WordPerfect 5.1 or 6, you need to retrieve the .PRS file for the printer to change a printer's proportional font or the WP.DRS file to change a graphics font. After this point, the selections depend on which version of the PTR program you are using.

In WordPerfect 5.1's PTR program, select Fonts and the font you want to change. Next, select Size and Spacing Information and Proportional Spacing Table. Select the proportional sizing table you want to use by pressing *. To change the proportional sizing table the font uses, highlight it and press ENTER. The subsequent screen contains a window with each character in the character set, its current width, and any adjustment the character requires.

Usually, you will highlight the character you want to change, press ENTER, type a new width for the character, and press ENTER again. Pressing TAB lets you switch to Units, Point Size, and Kerning Table. Units set the fraction of the inch that the measurements represent, so entering **1200** means each unit of measurement equals 1/1200 of an inch. WordPerfect will convert existing widths to the new measurement system for you. Point Size sets the size for which you are setting the width and adjustment. As you use a larger or smaller font, WordPerfect scales the font widths and adjustments to match the character's size. Kerning Table switches you over to the kerning tables for that font. Tip 187 has more information about kerning.

In WordPerfect 6, after retrieving the .PRS file for the printer to change a printer's proportional font or the WP.DRS file to change a graphics font, select **Go To**. From the Go To menu, select **Proportional Spacing Tables**, highlight the font from the list of proportional fonts, and select **Edit** to display this dialog box:

```
┌──────────────── Proportional Spacing Table ──────────────────┐
│ 1. Character Set [ ASCII                              ↓]      │
│                                                  Width─ Adjust─│
│ * 32      (Space)                                  741      ↑ │
│ * 33   !  (Exclamation Point)                      833        │
│ * 34   "  (Double Quote)                          1157        │
│ * 35   #  (Number/Pound)                          1250        │
│ * 36   $  (Dollars)                               1250        │
│ * 37   %  (Percent)                               2222        │
│ * 38   &  (Ampersand)                             1944        │
│ * 39   '  (Single Quote)                           833        │
│ * 40   (  (Left Parenthesis)                       833        │
│ * 41   )  (Right Parenthesis)                      833      ↓ │
│                                                               │
│ 2. →Edit...          4. Units:         300                    │
│ 3. Search            5. Point Size:    600                    │
│                      6. Kerning Table...CG Times              │
│                                                     ┌────┐    │
│                                                     │ OK │    │
│                                                     └────┘    │
└───────────────────────────────────────────────────────────────┘
```

Character Set selects the character set for which you change the spacing. The middle section has three columns for the character, the width the character occupies, and the adjustment made for the character. Usually, you will highlight the character you want to change, select Edit, type a new width for the character, and select OK. Point Size sets the size you are setting the width and adjustment for. As you use a larger or smaller font, WordPerfect will scale the font widths and adjustments to match the character's size. Search lets you find characters in the list. Kerning Table switches you over to the kerning tables for the font. Tip 187 gives more information about kerning. When finished setting the width or adjustment, select OK.

The measurements you enter for width and adjustment use the number of units set by the printer and the PTR program. Since the units of measurements might be similar to 1/300 of an inch or 1/1200 of an inch, don't be surprised if the increments you are using seem unfamiliar.

Font Attributes Are Set with the WordPerfect Program or the PTR Program

WordPerfect uses Automatic Font Changes, or AFCs, to set how the font changes when you add an attribute such as boldfacing, underlining, or a change in relative size. As Tip 192 mentions, you can change the AFCs for printer and graphics fonts within WordPerfect or the PTR program. First retrieve the .PRS file to change AFCs for printer fonts or WP.DRS to change AFCs for graphics fonts and select the printer or resource file. In WordPerfect 5.1, select Fonts, the font you want to change, Automatic Font Changes, the attribute to change, and the font to use for the AFC. In WordPerfect 6, select Edit from the PTR's Printers dialog box Fonts Edit, highlight the font to change, select Edit Automatic Font Changes, highlight the attribute you want to change, select Edit, highlight the font to use for the AFC, and select Change to Highlighted Font. With WordPerfect 6, whether you change the AFCs through WordPerfect or the PTR program, the results are the same.

Check that the Installed Printers Match the Ones You Plan to Use

For WordPerfect to use your printer's features correctly, it must know the instructions to send to the printer. WordPerfect selects the printer instructions to use when you install and then select a printer.

When you install WordPerfect, add all of the printers you plan to use. As you use WordPerfect, select the correct printer (as described following). Before a printer is available to be selected, it must be installed. Installing a printer copies the .ALL file that contains the printer information from the WordPerfect disk to the disk with your WordPerfect files.

If you want to install a printer that is similar to one already installed, you do not have to leave WordPerfect to do it. The same .ALL files that are installed already for the other printers have the printer information for additional printers. You can install one of these printers from within WordPerfect.

In WordPerfect 5.1, select File Print Select Printer Additional Printers. In WordPerfect 6, select File Print/Fax Select Add Printer. WordPerfect will list the printers that have their printer definitions stored in the same .ALL files as the printers already installed. From the list of printers, highlight the printer you want to add and choose Select. You can then supply a name for the .PRS file this printer will use or accept its default. Press ENTER. WordPerfect will create the .PRS file the printer uses and displays printer information for the printer. When you press F7 you get the screen or dialog box in which you can make any changes to the printer's setup. When you press F7, you will return to the screen or dialog box to select the printer you want to use.

You Can Use Landscape and Portrait Orientation on the Same Page

If you have text that you want to appear sideways on a page that also has text in the regular, portrait orientation, put the text that will appear sideways in a graphics box. When you add the graphics box, select Create Text and type the text to be shown sideways, press ALT-F9, and select Rotate Box Contents.

From the next dialog box, select 0°, 90°, 180°, or 270° rotation. 0° places the text upright and 180° places the text upside down. 90° rotates the text so the top is on the left side and the bottom on the right. 270° rotates the text so the top is on the right side and the bottom is on the left. The following previewed page shows a page that uses rotated text:

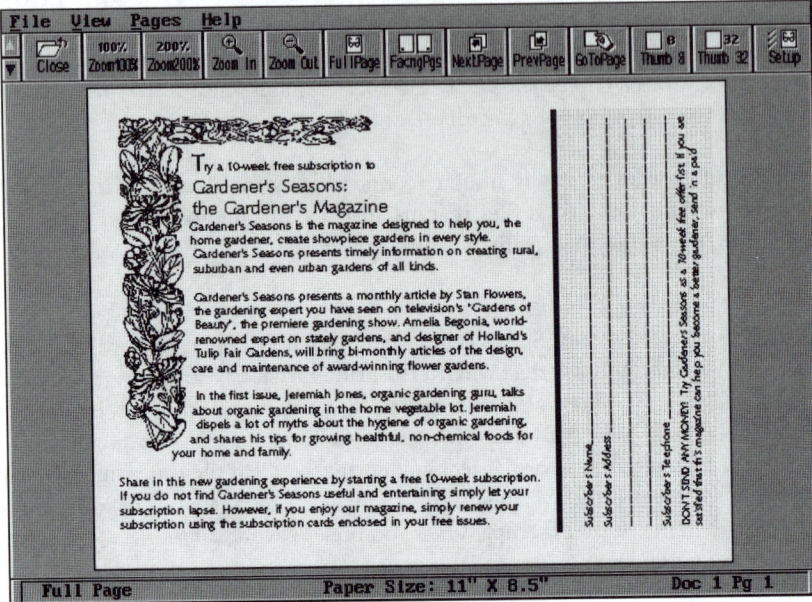

In this illustration, the page size is set to landscape; the text on the right was first placed in a graphics box, and the graphics box was then rotated 90°.

Some printers cannot print both orientations at once. Other printers will require that you use all graphics fonts rather than printer fonts for this to print correctly.

When Printing Double-Sided Pages, Tell WordPerfect 6 How the Page Is Flipped

When printing a document in WordPerfect using a printer that can print on both sides of the page, you need to tell WordPerfect how the page is flipped. The setting you select should match your printer's

capability. To do this in WordPerfect 6, select Layout Page and then Double-sided Printing. If the page will be flipped along the long side of the page, like the pages in a book, select Long Edge. If the pages will be flipped along the short side of the page like pages in a pad of paper, select Short Edge. In WordPerfect 5.1, select Layout Page Paper Size/Type and Double Sided Printing, then select Yes. Depending on where the book is to be bound, select Binding Edge then Left or Top. See Tip 984 for information about adding space along the side of the page where the pages are bound.

CHAPTER 7

Working with Blocks

Use CTRL-HOME CTRL-HOME with the Block Feature to Do Two Things to the Same Text

It is easy to select text and change the text attribute. If you want to add two different attributes to the same text, you normally need to select the text twice. A shortcut to selecting the same text a second time is to press the Block key F12 again and press CTRL-HOME twice.

You can use a macro to handle the task for you. Since you want to be able to execute the macro quickly, you should assign the macro to one of the ALT-key sequences. To assign the macro the key sequence ALT-Q, for example, you would press ALT and Q together in the name box. The macro name would then display as ALTQ. The macro code might look like this:

```
DISPLAY(Off!)
BlockOn(CharMode!)
PosGoPrev
```

You can use the ALTQ.WPM macro on the accompanying disk to perform the task for you.

ALTQ.WPM

Copying to Multiple Locations Requires Different Strategies in WordPerfect 6 and 5.1

WordPerfect 6 allows you to select text once, then copy it to as many locations as you like. Because WordPerfect 6 writes the selected text to a special area in memory, you can continue to access it until you replace it by copying or cutting other text.

In WordPerfect 5.1, once you place copied text in its new location, you can make another copy by moving to a new location, pressing CTRL-F4 (Block), and selecting **Retrieve Block**. Another method

is to delete the text from its original location and immediately put it back with the Undelete feature (F1 or **Edit Undelete**). You can then move to as many additional locations as you want and, by continuing to undelete the text, copy the text to each location. (Although this approach also works in WordPerfect 6 using the ESC key instead of F1, it is not necessary.)

You can actually make additional copies of your last three deletions using the ESC *key strategy.*

Be Careful Not to Press ENTER Before You Have Copied or Moved Text

TIP 326

When you copy or move text with WordPerfect 5.1 or WordPerfect 6's **Edit Copy** and **Paste** or **Edit Cut** and **Paste** commands, the second part of the procedure requires you to position the cursor at the new location where you want the text to appear and press ENTER to insert the text. Therefore, as you move through the document to relocate the text, refrain from pressing ENTER for any reason unrelated to the copy procedure (to insert a blank line, for example) or else the text will appear at the location where you pressed ENTER. If you make a mistake, you will need to select the text, cut it from its current incorrect location, and paste it to the new location.

In WordPerfect 6 you can avoid this potential problem by using the **Edit Cut** and **Edit Copy** commands followed by **Edit Paste**. This way you store the text you want to move or copy; you can add extra blank lines to the document with ENTER and invoke a command to paste the text when you need it. It is worth using this approach if you want to copy or move the text to the end of the document and have not as yet added the blank lines that need to precede it.

Copying Part of a Style to Another Style

TIP 327

WordPerfect provides an option for copying one style to serve as the basis for another style. Sometimes you do not want the entire style, but only a small section of the codes it contains. It is possible to copy

codes from one style to another to get just the codes that you need. The steps are similar whether you use WordPerfect 5.1 or 6:

1. Select **L**ayout **S**tyles.
2. Highlight the desired style.
3. Select **E**dit.
4. Select Style **C**ontents in WordPerfect 6 or **C**odes in WordPerfect 5.1.
5. Move to the location where you want to start including codes.
6. Block the text by using the mouse or the F12 key combination (the same techniques used with text).
7. Select **E**dit Cop**y** and Paste in WordPerfect 6, or **E**dit **C**opy in WordPerfect 5.1.
8. Select OK or press F7 twice.
9 Select **C**reate and type a name for a new style.
10. Select Style **C**ontents or **C**odes.
11. Press ENTER
12. Complete any additional code entries for the style and select OK or press F7 twice.

Deleting and Undeleting Has the Same Effect as Moving

328

Deleting text and using the undelete option to restore it in a new location produces the same effect as moving it. You might prefer the delete/undelete option, since it has fewer keystrokes.

To move text you must block it and choose Edit Cut. Then you must move to the location you want the text to appear and either press ENTER (WordPerfect 5.1) or select Edit Paste (WordPerfect 6). You can also move text by blocking it and using the CTRL-F4 function key shortcut.

To move text with delete and undelete, select the text and press the DEL key. Move to the new location and press the Undelete key (ESC in WordPerfect 6 and F1 in WordPerfect 5.1). Select option 1 to restore the text. You do not need to remember a combination key sequence or which menu you need with this approach.

You Are Limited to Working with One Block at a Time

A *block* in WordPerfect is a continuous group of entries. A block can be defined with F12, ALT-F4, or the mouse. After pressing the Block key, you can highlight as much text as you want. Since it works with on and off toggle settings, pressing the Block key again will turn the Block feature off.

In WordPerfect 5.1 and 6 you can use the Append feature to gather text together in a Clipboard (if you have the Shell program). This is discussed in more detail in the next tip.

Once you turn block mode on you can type a letter, instructing WordPerfect to define the block from the cursor location to the next occurrence of that letter. If, for example, you type m, all the text from the cursor location to the first m is blocked. You can also use symbols. You can, for instance, type ?, . (period), or , (comma), and WordPerfect will define the block from the cursor location to the first occurrence of the symbol.

With the Shell Installed, Gather Blocks of Text by Appending Them to the Clipboard

WordPerfect does not allow you to block text from more than one area of the document at a time. If you want to move six items from page 1 to page 10 in a document, and they are in different locations, you will need to perform six different operations.

If you are running Shell, you can avoid some of this work. To save time, you can append the data to a special storage area in memory called the Clipboard. After all of the entries have been placed in the Clipboard, you can then paste them to page 10. (The Clipboard is created by the Shell program, which is included in WordPerfect 6, and can be purchased from WordPerfect Corporation to work with WordPerfect 5.1.) If you are using WordPerfect 6, you should know that the Shell is automatically installed in the \WPC60DOS directory if you select a standard installation of WordPerfect.

Another option for simplifying the process of moving text is to set a bookmark on page 10, allowing you to copy or move each individual piece of data there quickly. Bookmarks are discussed in Tip 42.

Using Block to Save Part of a File

If you have a section of a document that you would like to store on disk as a separate file, one approach is to copy the file and delete the parts you don't need. A much quicker alternative is to block the text in the current document that you want to put in the file. Next, select File Save in WordPerfect 5.1, or File Save As in WordPerfect 6. Because text is blocked, WordPerfect knows that you only want to save the block and prompts for a name for this file.

Short entries such as a letter closing or salutation are best stored as styles, which are part of your style library. You will learn more about styles in Tips 390 and 404.

Use the Block Feature to Recheck the Spelling in a Newly-Edited Section of Text

WordPerfect provides options to check the spelling of a word, the current page, or the entire document. If you want to spell-check a paragraph or two (in the current document) that you have just edited, none of these options meet your particular need. What you need to do instead is move to the beginning of the text that you want to check, block the section of text using F12 and the arrow keys, and invoke the spell-check feature with Tools Writing Tools Speller in WordPerfect 6 or CTRL-F2 in either WordPerfect 5.1 or 6. Only the blocked section will be spell-checked.

Changing the Appearance of Blocked Text in Text Mode

When you block text, it is normally shown in a reverse video on a monochrome monitor or a different color combination in a color monitor. If you find it difficult to discern which text is normal and which text has been included in the block, you will want to change the way that blocked text is shown.

To make this change, follow these steps in WordPerfect 6:

1. Select **F**ile Se**t**up **D**isplay.
2. Select **T**ext Mode Screen Type/Colors **C**olor Schemes.
3. Highlight a color scheme that you have created and select **E**dit or select **C**reate, type a new color scheme name, and select OK.
4. Select **A**ttributes.
5. Highlight Blocked.
6. Select **C**olor.
7. Move the box to the desired combination, select OK twice, and Close twice.

To change the appearance of blocked text in WordPerfect 5.1:

1. Select **F**ile Se**t**up.
2. Select **D**isplay **C**olors/Fonts/Attributes.
3. Select **S**creen Colors.
4. Move to the line for Blocked in the Foreground column and type a letter that corresponds to the color you want to use.
5. Move to the Background column of the same line and type the letter that corresponds to the background color you want to use.
6. Press F7 twice to return to editing your document.

Text that you blocked will appear in the newly-selected colors.

Blocking a Rectangle of Text Looks Different

TIP 334

Working with a rectangle of text is an excellent way to remove or move part of a tabular column of entries. It is particularly useful when entries in a column contain repeated words or characters that would be better placed in a column heading, since it will allow you to reduce the space allocated to the column of entries. The table that follows has information repeated in entries. The ", 1993" entered with each date, as well as "Part No.", are not needed; each can be removed and incorporated into a column heading. To block a rectangular column follow these steps:

1. Move to the first character to be blocked.
2. Press F12 to begin the block operation.

3. Move down and then to the right to include the last character to be included in the block.

    The shape of the block looks like this right now:

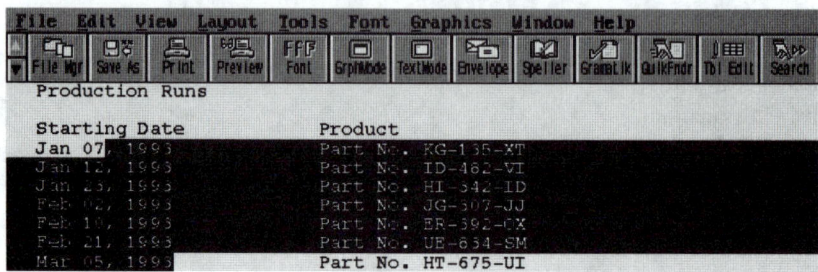

4. Select **E**dit **S**elect (or **S**elect in WordPerfect 5.1) **R**ectangle. The text that you want to work with is now highlighted.
5. Select the proper option to move or delete this text.

If the two sets of text entries discussed are removed (in two separate operations) and replaced with heading entries, the final table looks like this:

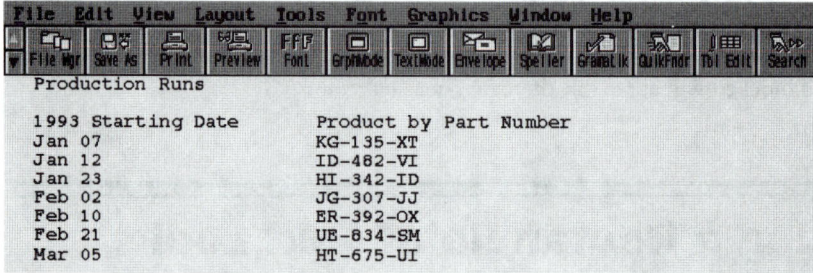

Block Tabular Columns and Move, Delete, or Copy Them

You cannot work with a regular block of text to move, delete, or copy columns of data displayed at tab stops. A regular block will include entire lines of data, rather than the entries in a single column. WordPerfect does, however, provide a way to work with columns of data that affects only the entries

in that column. WordPerfect assumes that each column is separated by one tab stop and when you start and end your blocking within a column, it includes the tab stop that precedes the column when selecting the text. What you need to do after blocking the entries you are interested in is to choose Tabular Column, rather than Block, before selecting Copy, Move, or Delete.

Let's say you want to move the entries in the second column of the following table so that they follow column 3:

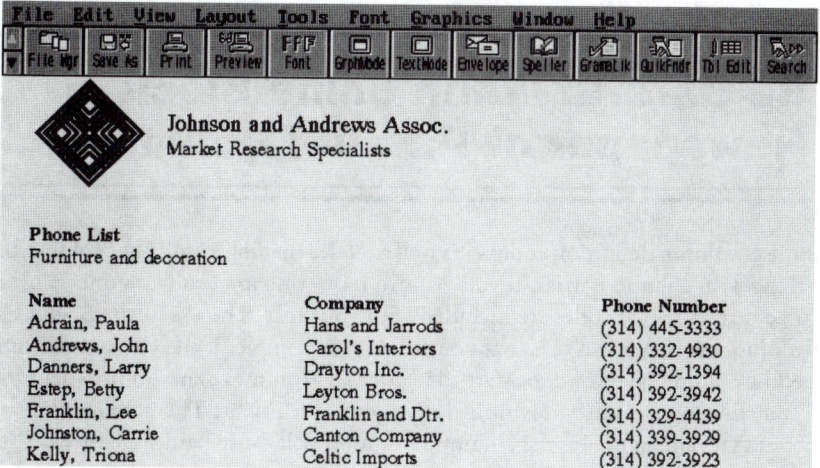

You can follow these steps:

1. Position your cursor anywhere in the first line in column 2.
2. Press F12 and move anywhere on the entry in the last line of column 2.
3. Press CTRL-F4 and choose Tabular **C**olumn.
   The highlighted area now covers just the entries in column 2 and the tab stop that precedes it.
4. Select **M**ove in WordPerfect 5.1 or Cu**t** and Paste in WordPerfect 6.
5. Move the cursor to the end of the entry in what now appears as the first line in column 2.
6. Press ENTER to place the column you removed in this new location.

If you have multiple tab stops between columns, you might find it easier to use the rectangular block feature to define what you need.

Tables offer much more flexibility than tabular columns. See Tips 684, 689, and 705 for ideas about using tables rather than tabular columns.

The graphic used as the logo on this client list is called LOGO_06.WMF and is included on the accompanying disk. The graphics file was rotated and changed to black and white with the Image Editor in WordPerfect.

LOGO_06.WMF

TIP 336 — Be Careful When Using Block in Newspaper or Parallel Columns

WordPerfect uses column definition codes—as well as codes that indicate a hard column break—when you are working with column entries. If you want to move or copy text from one column to another you need to be certain which codes are included with your text. The use of the Reveal Codes display lets you select just the codes and text that you need. For example, if the column definition is in the wrong place, the column layout might start too early. You can move the column definition to a new location to start the column entry down further in your document. The hard column codes used to split the entries that remain before the column definition will cause hard page breaks.

In WordPerfect 5.1 there are codes for column definition, column on, and column off. You will need to select the column on code when you want to change the start location for a table. The column definition code can remain until you redefine what columns will look like, since each new column used in the document does not require another definition code.

The tabular column option discussed in Tip 334 will not work in newspaper or parallel columns.

TIP 337 — Moving Block-Protected Column Text Is More Difficult in WordPerfect 5.1

WordPerfect 6 streamlines the way columns work, with a column definition code affecting the entries that follow until the end of a column section. If you create columns with block-protected text in

WordPerfect 6, the column definition code at the beginning and end of the column section conveys this information to WordPerfect. WordPerfect 5.1 works differently and requires that you become much more involved with codes that are added to your document when you move entries. With 5.1 you will need to reveal codes and be sure to include the [Block Pro:On][Col On] and [Block Pro:Off] and [Col Off] codes that enclose each set of entries.

WordPerfect 6 Provides Some Mouse Shortcuts for Selecting Text

When you click the left mouse button once, WordPerfect 6 moves the cursor to the current location of the mouse pointer. A second click to the same location causes WordPerfect to select the current word. A third click selects the current sentence and a fourth click selects the current paragraph.

WordPerfect continues to cycle through these options if you continue clicking. Thus, the fifth click removes the selection from the current paragraph and places the cursor at the current location. Although you can click in rapid succession creating double- and triple-clicks, a series of single clicks has the same effect.

Use Block to Apply Format Changes to a Section

If you want to apply the same format changes to a section of text, block it first. After blocking, you can request font, margin, and text attribute changes (among others) that affect the entire selection.

WordPerfect 6 makes it easier to apply multiple changes to a section of text. Once a dialog box is opened, you can make as many selections as you need from it and all of the selected text will be affected.

With Block Off, WordPerfect Can Move Sentences and Paragraphs

A quick way to select a sentence, paragraph, or page is to press CTRL-F4 without blocking any text. If you prefer, you can use Edit Select (Select in WordPerfect 5.1) and choose the same options. To move or copy the text, you can select the desired action next.

Use the F12 Shortcut for Blocking When You Have an Enhanced Keyboard

In WordPerfect 5.1 and 6 you can use the ALT-F4 key to block text. If you have an enhanced keyboard, you will have two extra function keys that are not on the standard keyboard (F11 and F12). Use the F12 key to request the Block function, since it is quicker to press than the combined keystroke.

Reveal Codes Before Copying, Moving, or Deleting Text

If you want to be certain that you are working with the desired set of data and codes, the simplest approach is to display the Reveal Codes screen before selecting your text. Once you become proficient with the program, you can always use the special key sequences that move your cursor to the left of the codes on a line or above the codes at the top of the page, but revealing the codes eliminates the need to remember to use the special key sequences.

There Are a Number of Ways to Reclaim the Last Cut You Made

If you cut text from your document with Edit Cut, WordPerfect stores this text in a special location in memory. You can use Edit Paste to add this text back to your document. You can also use CTRL-V

or press SHIFT-F10 to request Retrieve, leave the filename blank, and select OK. The results are the same regardless of the process, it just depends on which approach you prefer.

Copying the Graphics Box Code to Copy the Graphic

If you select a graphics box and activate the Edit menu, the options for copying and moving the current selection are not available: you cannot move or copy graphics images in this way. To copy a graphics image to a second location, display the Reveal Codes screen. Block and copy or move the code to a new location. The graphics image and all of the features defined for the original image will appear in the new location.

If you want graphics images to precede certain sections of text, you might find it simpler to define a style that displays the image. You can define all of the options normally used with graphics images and cause them to display in a specific location. You might use a small image as an icon to mark tips or warnings in a document, like this:

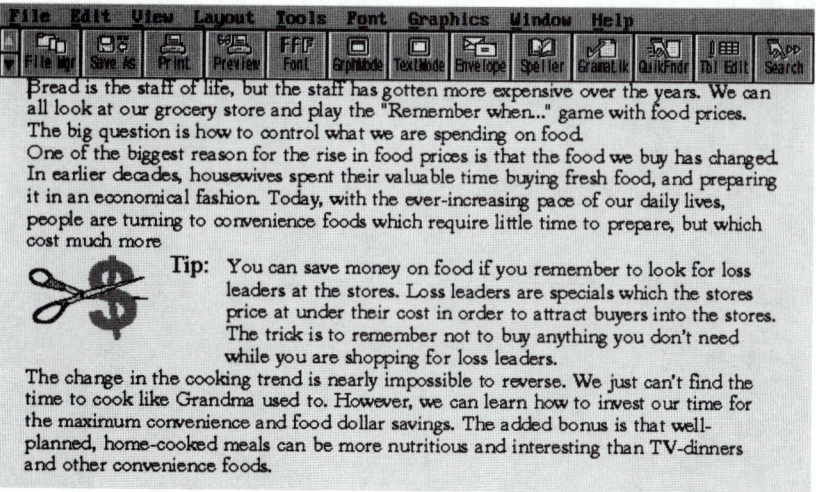

The style TIP is used to define this graphic element and other settings. To save storage space, this graphic is not included in the style definition. You will need to edit the graphics box for the style and replace the current text placeholder with the name of the graphics file containing the symbol.

COST_CUT.WMF
TIP.STY

The COST_CUT.WMF graphic used in this tip is included on the accompanying disk. The style TIP is also found on the disk, without the graphic in the style library, as TIP.STY.

Searching and Sorting

Use Wildcards to Find Similar Words in Your Search Strings

You can use wildcard characters as part of your search strings to help you find words that are similar. Wildcards are characters that take the place of one or many characters in the search string. In WordPerfect 5.1, you can only use a wildcard to take the place of a single character. In WordPerfect 6, there are two wildcards, one that takes the place of a single character and the other that can take the place of any number of characters. You cannot simply type in the wildcard characters; they must be inserted as special codes.

As an example, suppose that you want to find the words "gray" and "grey" in your document. You can use a wildcard to find both of these words with the same search. The search string would be "gr?y", in which ? is the single-character wildcard code.

For WordPerfect 6:

1. Press F2 or select **E**dit Sear**c**h.
2. Enter the string you want to search for.
3. Where you want to use wildcards, select Codes.
4. Highlight the code [?] for a wildcard that takes the place of a single character, or [*] for a wildcard that takes the place of many characters.
5. Press ENTER or choose **S**elect to insert the code.
6. Select S**e**arch to start searching the document for the search string.

With WordPerfect 5.1:

1. Press F2 to start the search.
2. Type the string you want to search for.
3. Press CTRL-V CTRL-X to insert the wildcard code ^X.
4. When you have finished entering the search string, press F2 again.

Press CTRL-HOME Twice to Quickly Return to the Place Where You Started a Search

When you use the Search feature to find text in your document, WordPerfect moves the cursor so that it appears after the last character in the text string that is found. Having found this text, you might want to return quickly to the location where you started the search, either because you searched for the wrong text, or because you wanted to review the text to determine how to change, or continue entering, text at your original location.

To return to the place where the cursor was before you began the Search procedure, press CTRL-HOME CTRL-HOME. For example, you can search for the name "Jon" in your document if you know that you misspelled the word once. You can then edit the name to add an H so that it is now spelled "John". To return the cursor to the place where it was before you searched for the error, press CTRL-HOME CTRL-HOME.

A Search Can Be Extended to Include Headers, Footers, Endnotes, and Graphics Boxes

Normally, when you search for a string in WordPerfect, WordPerfect only checks for that string in the main body of the document. However, the string might be found in a header or a footnote, or in a pull quote in a graphics box. To search these elements, you need to do an *extended search*, which includes the text in headers, footers, footnotes, endnotes, and graphics boxes.

To start an extended search in WordPerfect 6:

1. Select **E**dit Searc**h** or press F2.
2. Select the **E**xtended Search check box.
3. Continue with the search as usual.

To start an extended search in WordPerfect 5.1:

1. Press HOME.
2. Press F2.
3. Continue with the search as usual.

For example, suppose that you want to search for the word "society" in the newsletter shown here. Only an extended search would find the word, which is in the graphics box at the center of the page.

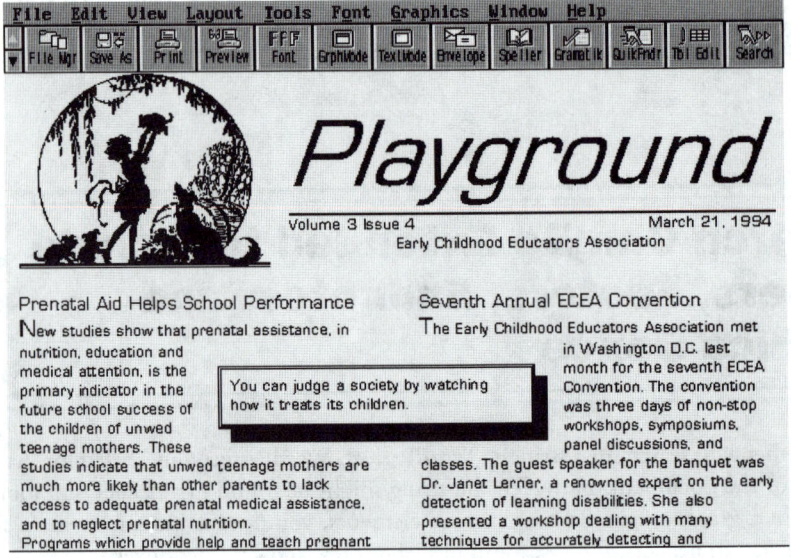

The PUPPIES.PCX graphic that you see in the above document is included on the accompanying disk.

PUPPIES.PCX

Block Text to Limit the Scope of a Search

TIP 348

You will not always want to search the entire document. At times, you will want to search only a section of the text, such as the introduction of a report. In order to limit the search to a specific block of text, simply block that text before starting the search. Only the blocked text will be searched.

Search Backward to Find Text Before the Cursor

TIP 349

You do not need to search from the cursor location to the end of the document. Depending on which version of WordPerfect you are using, there are several ways to search backward, from the cursor's location back toward the beginning of the document. This feature is useful when you have just finished typing a long document and want to find some text without first having to move to the beginning of the document. It is also useful for limiting the search to a specific part of the document.

To start a backward search with WordPerfect 6:

1. Select **E**dit Searc**h** or press F2.
2. Select the **B**ackwards Search check box.
3. Continue with the search as usual.

In WordPerfect 6, you can also start a backward search by pressing SHIFT-F2. This opens the Search dialog box with the Backwards Search check box already selected.

To start a backward search with WordPerfect 5.1:

Press SHIFT-F2 and continue with the search as usual.

Hidden Codes Can Be Located with Search

You might think of using the Search feature only to find text. Sometimes, however, you will want to use the feature to locate hidden codes in your document. For example, you might want to search your report for all second-level headings, which you have formatted with small caps. You can search for the hidden code [Sm Cap On], which will move you directly to each heading so that you can edit it or change its formatting.

When Searching in WordPerfect 5.1, You Must Use Function Keys to Specify Codes

In WordPerfect 5.1, when you want to use the Search feature for locating hidden codes, you must use the function keys to enter the hidden codes. If you are accustomed to using WordPerfect's menu options instead of the function keys, you might want to double-check the function key assigned to a hidden code before searching for it. Otherwise, you might not remember the correct function key when you need to use it.

In WordPerfect 6, You Can Select the Code You Are Searching For

In WordPerfect 6, when you want to search for hidden codes using the Search feature, you must select the hidden code from a dialog box, as shown in the following:

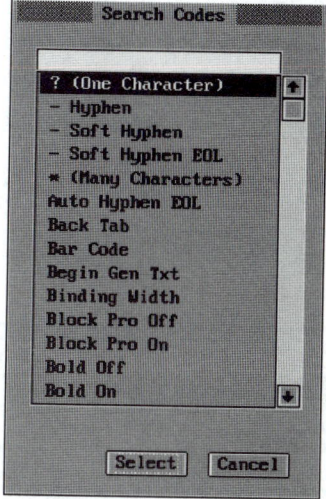

However, the codes appear in this dialog box exactly as they do in the Reveal Codes screen. Since some of the codes are a trifle cryptic, you might want to double-check what your hidden code looks like before you start the Search feature.

You can also select the code by pressing the function key or shortcut key associated with it. For example, you can press CTRL-I to search for the [Italc On] code in your document.

Use the Replace Feature with the Confirm Option to Check for Words the Speller Did Not Catch

As useful as the Speller can be, it will not help you locate words that are spelled correctly but used incorrectly. For example, you might run into problems substituting "their" for "there", or "files" for "fields".

You can use the Replace feature with the Confirm option to find words that you need to replace. For example, you might know that you routinely type "there" when you really mean "their". Use the Replace feature to search for "there" and substitute "their"; activate the Confirm option to ensure that you do not replace "there" when it is used correctly.

The grammar checker Grammatik included with WordPerfect 6 can provide some assistance with problems of usage.

Replace Can Remove Entries as Easily as It Can Change Them

You can use the Replace feature to delete repeated instances of text, just as you can replace text with other text, by replacing the search string with nothing. By default, the Replace With text box contains the code <Nothing>. If you do not replace this code, WordPerfect will remove the text you search for, and simply not replace it with anything.

Alter Hidden Codes with the Replace Feature

You can change hidden codes by using the Replace feature to find them and to replace them with some other code. For example, you can change boldface text in your document to italics by searching for the [Bold On] code and replacing it with the [Italc On] code.

Remember that you have to insert the hidden codes in your search string by selecting Codes and then selecting the hidden codes you want. If you are not sure what a code looks like, you might be at a disadvantage. Remember that you can also press the function key or shortcut key that activates the feature associated with the code.

Perform a Case Sensitive Search to Limit the Number of Items Found

TIP 356

Sometimes, you will want to limit the matches the Search or Replace features find to a specific case. For example, you might want to find "Green," for Mr. Jonathan Green, but not every instance of "green," the color. You can limit the search to find text that matching the exact case of the search string, as well as its characters.

To make the Search or Replace features case sensitive in WordPerfect 6:

1. Select **E**dit Searc**h** or **E**dit Replace, or press F2 or ALT-F2.
2. Select the **C**ase Sensitive check box.
3. Proceed as usual with the Search or Replace procedure.

In WordPerfect 5.1, you cannot make a search case sensitive in the same way. These features are already partially case sensitive. Lowercase characters can match lowercase characters, but capitals only match other capitals. For example the string "wordperfect" will match "wordperfect", "WordPerfect", and "WORDPERFECT", but "WordPerfect" in a search string will only locate "WordPerfect".

Selectively Remove Redline and Strikeout Codes with the Replace Feature

TIP 357

When you use the Compare Documents feature, WordPerfect compares an open document to a document on disk, and marks where the new document is different from the stored document. WordPerfect marks deletions by applying the Strikeout text attribute, and marks additions by applying the Redline text attribute. WordPerfect also offers a feature for removing all redline and strikeout codes from the open document when you have finished comparing the two.

You might not want to remove all instances of strikeout or redlining. One way to quickly remove only specific instances is to search for these codes and replace with nothing those codes that you want to remove, as described in Tip 354.

To selectively replace certain instances of a search string, you can use the Confirm Replacement option.

There Is a Special Way to Search and Replace Codes with Specific Settings in WordPerfect 6

Sometimes it is not enough to simply search for general codes, such as the bottom margin code. You might need to search for a specific code, such as the hidden code that sets the bottom margin to 1.75 inches. WordPerfect 6.0 offers a special feature that lets you find certain codes with specific settings. The number of codes you can search for in this way is limited, but it includes the codes you most likely need to locate.

For example, if you are searching for the code that sets the bottom margin to 1.75, follow these steps:

1. Select **E**dit Search or **E**dit Replace, or press F2 or ALT-F2.
2. With the cursor in the **S**earch For text box, select Specific Codes by clicking on the button or pressing SHIFT-F5.
3. Highlight the general code you want to look for, such as Bot Mar, in the dialog box shown here:

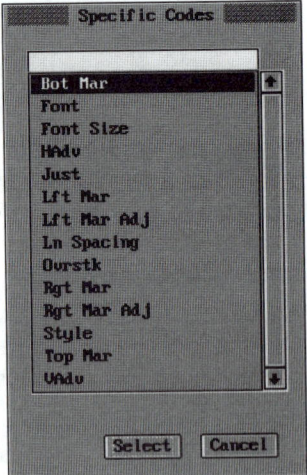

4. Choose Select.
5. When WordPerfect displays the next dialog box, make the selections, or type the entries, for the specific elements of the code you are searching for. For example, type **1.75** if you selected Bot Mar.
6. Continue as usual with the Search or Replace process.

You Can Search for Soft Page Breaks and Soft Returns in WordPerfect 5.1

TIP 359

Most of the codes that you will want to search for are codes that you have entered into your document yourself. You can include these codes in a search string by pressing the function keys that insert the codes in a document. However, searching for a soft return or soft page break code is not quite as simple, because you do not insert these codes into a document; WordPerfect does.

To search for a soft return or soft page break code in WordPerfect 5.1:

1. Press F2.
2. Press CTRL-V CTRL-K to insert a soft return code, or CTRL-V CTRL-M to insert a soft page break code.

In WordPerfect 6, you can select both of these codes from the search dialog box.

Save Typing Time by Using Replace to Make Your Own Glossary Feature

TIP 360

When you are typing a document that frequently uses a certain long word or title, you can use a shortcut. When you type the document, enter some unique abbreviation of the word or title. For example, you might abbreviate "Masterson School of Accounting" as MSA. Before finalizing the document, you can simply use the Replace feature globally to replace all incidences of the abbreviation with the complete word or title.

 *It is important to use an abbreviation that will not be used as part of another word. Otherwise you will need to put spaces on either side of it in WordPerfect 5.1, or use the Whole Word option in WordPerfect 6. (See Tips 366 and 367.)*

WordPerfect comes with the GLOSSARY macro, which you can use to replace abbreviations with words. This feature lets you create glossary definitions in which a specific abbreviation is assigned to its full form. You can then use the GLOSSARY macro to replace the abbreviation. The glossary feature is designed for use with long terms that you commonly abbreviate in your documents. The macro does not perform a global replacement, however; you must move to each instance of the abbreviation you want to replace. Still, this macro can prevent misspelling errors and save some typing time. To use the GLOSSARY macro:

1. Select **T**ools **M**acro **P**lay.
2. Type **glossary** and press ENTER.
3. Select **L**ist All.
4. Select **C**reate. The macro opens a Glossary Definition dialog box.
5. Type the abbreviation in the Abbreviation text box and press TAB.
6. Type the full form of the word in the Expanded Form text box, and press TAB once more.
7. Select OK.

The macro replaces the instance of the abbreviation with the complete expanded form.

 # Pressing ENTER in a Search String Makes WordPerfect 5.1 Look for a Hard Return

In WordPerfect 5.1, you have to be careful about pressing ENTER while specifying your search string. If you press ENTER while specifying the search string, WordPerfect inserts a hard return code into the search string.

Use the Search Feature to Look for Words That You Commonly Misuse

TIP 362

One common typing error is simply typing the wrong word. For example, you might regularly type "files" for "fields". WordPerfect's spelling feature is not going to catch this type of error, because the word is correctly spelled, just incorrectly used. Many such mistakes are made regularly with words that we use often. If you know that you commonly mistype or misuse a word, you can easily check the document and selectively replace this word with the correct word, using the Replace feature.

The Search Feature Is Available in the WordPerfect 5.1 Look Screen

TIP 363

In WordPerfect 5.1, you can look at a document on disk while using the List Files feature to help you decide whether you should open the file. While using the Look screen, you can use the Search feature to help you find certain text in the highlighted document. For example, you can check to see if a name you need to look at is included in a long file; this way, you can determine whether that file is the one that you want to open.

Be Careful with Spaces in a Search String

TIP 364

It is very easy to inadvertently add spaces to a search string. For example, you might type **green**, and then a space. The problem with this is that WordPerfect will then find "green" only if it is followed by a space. Instances where "green" is followed by a comma or a period will be passed over. Make sure that you remove any unnecessary spaces when you create a search string.

Type a Keyboard Character Instead of a Frequently Used Composed Character, and Then Do a Global Replace

You might use various composed characters regularly, such as the pound or yen characters. Creating these composed characters takes many more keystrokes than simply entering a character. One way to speed up the process is to use a keyboard character when you are entering text, and then use a global replace. For example, you might enter the tilde (~) in place of the yen symbol (¥) in your text. Since the tilde can be easily entered from the keyboard, the time it takes you to type your document is greatly reduced.

When you have finished entering text into your document, you can use the global replace feature to replace each tilde with the yen symbol, following these steps.

In WordPerfect 5.1:

1. Press ALT-F2.
2. Type N to avoid confirming each replacement.
3. Press UP ARROW to search backward.
4. Type ~, and press F2.
5. Press ALT and type **157** on the numeric keypad.
6. Press F2.

In WordPerfect 6:

1. Select **E**dit and then select Rep**l**ace, or press ALT-F2.
2. Enter ~ in the **S**earch For text box.
3. In the **R**eplace With text box, enter a yen symbol by pressing ALT and typing **157**.
4. Select the **B**ackwards Search check box.
5. Select R**e**place.

Enter Your Search String Carefully When Doing a Global Replacement

Global replacements occur when you use the Replace feature, without confirmations, to replace every occurrence of the search string with the replacement string. Global replacements can be dangerous; when performing a global replacement, you must be very careful not to accidentally change words, or portions of words, that you do not want to replace. For example, if you were to replace the string "tab" with the string "bill" in a document, you would want to make sure that the document did not include the words "database" ("dabillase"), "tables" ("billles"), or "accountable" ("accounbillle").

When you want to do global replacements, therefore, make sure you include enough characters in the string to adequately identify the text you really want replaced. In this example, you might use the SPACEBAR to enter a space on either side of "tab"; this would prevent WordPerfect from replacing the string "tab" when it is used as part of a word.

In WordPerfect 6, You Can Use Special Features to Limit Global Replacements

Global replacements are dangerous because if you are not careful performing them, you can accidentally change words that you do not want to change. For example, if you were to replace the string "the" with the string "one" in a document, you would want to avoid making the replacements in "theatre" ("oneatre"), "theft" ("oneft"), and "thenceforth" ("onenceforth").

WordPerfect 6 offers you several special features that prevent you from making such mistakes. You can make WordPerfect sensitive to the case of your search string, or tell WordPerfect to recognize the search string only when it comprises a whole word, rather than part of one.

When you make the search case sensitive, WordPerfect will locate only those text strings that match the case, as well as the characters, of the original search string. For example, if the search string is "WordPerfect", WordPerfect will not recognize "wordperfect", "WordPerfect", or "WORDPERFECT" as being the same as the search string.

When you tell WordPerfect to search for whole words only, WordPerfect will locate only those instances in the text where the search string is a whole word, with a space before and after the word or with some surrounding combination of space and punctuation. Using this option is preferable to entering a search string with a space on either side, because with this method WordPerfect recognizes the word even if it is at the end of a sentence, or is followed by a comma or some other punctuation mark.

To specify that WordPerfect be case sensitive or look only for whole words:

1. Select **E**dit, Rep**l**ace or press ALT-F2.
2. Enter the search string in the **S**earch For text box, and press ENTER.
3. Enter the replacement string in the **R**eplace With text box, and again press ENTER.
4. Select the **C**ase Sensitive Search check box.
5. Select the Find **W**hole Words Only check box.
6. Select R**e**place.

If You Normally Use Only One Space After Periods, Remember to Check for Double Spaces

When you first learned to type, it is likely that you learned "French spacing", which means entering two spaces after each sentence. However, now that most people use computers with proportional fonts, one space after the end of each sentence is becoming the standard. You can see here the difference in how documents appear with double or single spaces at the end of each sentence:

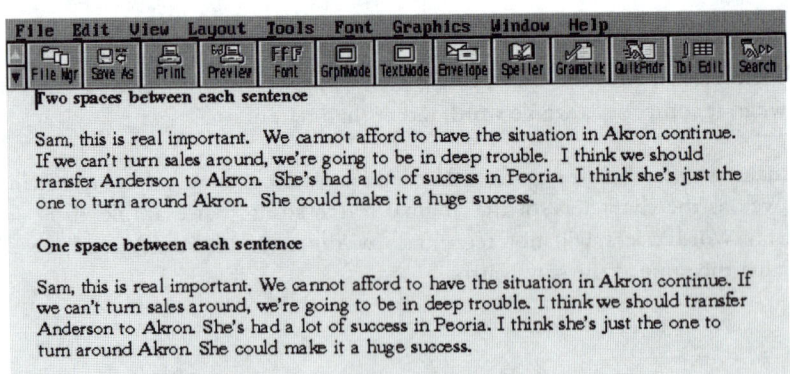

Even if you plan to enter only one space at the end of each sentence, you might fall back on your old training at times and find yourself inadvertently typing two spaces instead of one.

To avoid this, remember to use the Replace feature after typing every document. Specify a search string of two spaces, and a replacement string of one space. If you've accidentally entered three or more spaces, you might have to search the document more than once to remove all the duplicate spaces. However, Replace is still the quickest way to eliminate extra spaces.

Before You Perform a Sort, Make Sure You Know How WordPerfect Will Divide Your Document into Records

TIP 369

If you attempt a sort without being certain how WordPerfect will divide your documents into records, you are likely to find that your file has been missorted. Records are sets of information. For example, a record in a merge file might include the name, address, and telephone number of your client.

WordPerfect 6 has five different kinds of records, depending on how your data is organized. WordPerfect 6 can sort lines, paragraphs, merge data, parallel columns, and tables. WordPerfect 5.1 is limited to sorting lines, paragraphs, and merge records. The way WordPerfect divides data for sorting will differ according to the data's type of organization.

For the purpose of sorting, WordPerfect defines a line as any unit of text that ends with a hard or soft return. If you want to sort text items that wrap over more than one line, sort them as paragraphs. A paragraph is defined as a block of text followed by two or more hard return codes. You will notice that this is a different definition of paragraphs than the one you use when editing or formatting a document. It is important that you recognize the difference; otherwise, you might missort your document.

A merge data record is made up of a number of fields and is followed by an ENDRECORD merge code. WordPerfect defines these records the same way it defines merge records for merging. When you are sorting data arranged in parallel columns, each row of columns is a single record. This is similar to tables. WordPerfect 6 considers each row in a table to be a single record.

Before you attempt to sort a document, be sure that you have it organized so that WordPerfect will define the records correctly. You can specify how your document or block should be sorted by selecting the type of sort from the Record Type pop-up selection box in the Sort dialog box.

When you are ready to sort, follow these steps in WordPerfect 6:

1. Select **T**ools **S**ort.
2. Select OK to accept the default source and destination locations.
3. Select the options you want from the Sort dialog box.
4. Select **P**erform Action.

In WordPerfect 5.1 follow these steps for sorting:

1. Select **T**ools **S**ort.
2. Press ENTER twice to indicate that you want to sort the document currently on the screen and that you want the output displayed on the screen.
3. When the Sort menu appears, select the keys and other options you want to use.
4. Select **P**erform Action.

The Edit Undo feature in WordPerfect 6 can undo a sort if you make a mistake. In WordPerfect 5.1, you should save a copy of the file before sorting so you will have an unsorted version that you can restore if you need to.

Make Sure You Know How WordPerfect Will Divide Your Records Before Proceeding with a Sort

WordPerfect sorts records by keys, which reference smaller parts of each record. You will want each division of a record to be a single unit of information. There are five ways to divide records in WordPerfect 6: fields, lines, words, columns, and cells. WordPerfect 5.1 supports the use of fields, lines, and words. For example, in a file that includes the names, addresses, and telephone numbers of many clients, the name is one unit of information.

Fields are used in two ways. In regular text, such as a series of paragraphs, each line is considered a field. You can divide a single line into more than one field by using tabs and indents to separate the fields. A field in a merge data file is a unit of text followed by the ENDFIELD merge code. Fields are

numbered from first to last, starting at the top or left side of the text. Fields are used for sorting lines, paragraphs, and merge records.

A line is a unit of text followed by a hard return. When you are sorting a paragraph, a soft return marks the end of a line. Be careful when sorting a paragraph by lines; simply changing the font can change where the lines break. Lines are numbered starting from the top. Lines are used for sorting paragraphs, merge records, parallel columns, and tables.

A word is a unit of text separated from other text by spaces, forward slashes, or hard hyphens. Because of this, you can sort records by the month part of a date when the data is formatted as 12/31/99 or 12-31-99. WordPerfect recognizes the 12, the 31, and the 99 as separate words. Words are numbered starting from the left side of the text. Words are used to sort lines, paragraphs, merge records, columns, and tables.

When you are sorting parallel columns, you sort the rows, according to the contents of the columns in each row. Each column is separated by a hard page break. These columns are numbered from left to right. When you are sorting in tables, you sort the rows, according to the contents of the cells in each row. Cells are numbered starting on the left.

Many of these divisions of records can be combined when you are creating a key that specifies what piece of information to sort the record by. All of this can be very confusing to understand, but an example should help.

Suppose you want to sort the merge data file shown here by the city name:

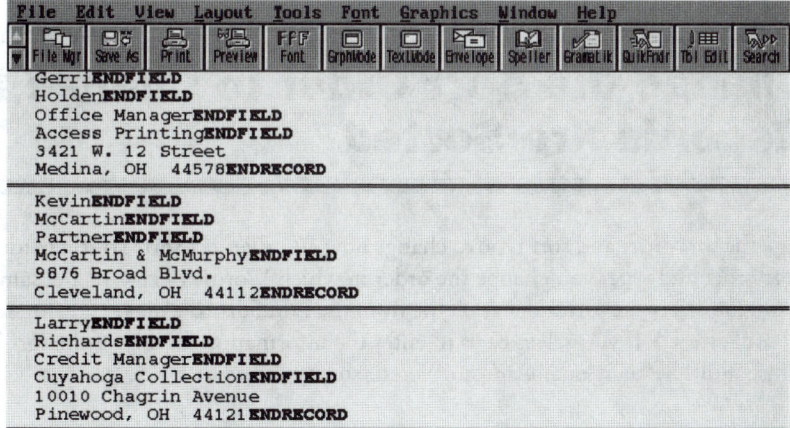

The city name is not a single field, nor is it a line. It is the first word on the second line of the fifth field in each of these merge records. If you want to sort the file on the screen according to this word, follow these steps:

1. Select **T**ools So**r**t.
2. Select OK to accept the defaults for the source and destination of the sort data. (In WordPerfect 5.1, press ENTER twice.)
3. Select Sort **K**eys and **E**dit to create the first sort key. (In WordPerfect 5.1, you can select **K**eys.)
4. Select **F**ield and type **5** to indicate that you want to sort by the fifth field. (In WordPerfect 5.1, type **5** in the Field column.)
5. Select **L**ine and type **2** to indicate that you want to sort by the second line in the fifth field. (In WordPerfect 5.1, type **2** in the Line column.)
6. Select **W**ord and type **1** to indicate that you want to sort by the first word in the second line in the fifth field. (In WordPerfect 5.1, type **1** in the Word column.)
7. Select OK. (Skip this step in WordPerfect 5.1.)
8. Select **P**erform Action.

Sorting might rearrange your format codes. See Tip 376.

Change the Sort Order to Change How Records Are Sorted

371

You can change the sort order and sort type to change how WordPerfect sorts your records. When you change the sort order and type, you change the order in which WordPerfect sorts the same characters or numbers. You can select the sort order and type from the Edit Sort Key dialog box for each different sort key. In WordPerfect 5.1, you select Keys to enter the information for any of the sort keys. In one sort, you can use multiple keys, each using a different sort type or sort order.

WordPerfect has two sort types: numeric and alphanumeric. Select alphanumeric when you are sorting words. This arranges the words in alphabetical order. (Numbers sort oddly when you select alphanu-

meric.) When you sort alphanumerically, WordPerfect sorts all the words starting with A together, then all those starting with B, and so on. Inside each letter set, WordPerfect sorts according to the second letter, then the third, and so on. When you use an alphanumeric search on numbers, numbers are sorted the same way. Therefore 12,500 comes before 174 because 2 comes before 7, even though the first number is much more than the second.

When you use a numeric search, WordPerfect sorts according to the actual value of numbers. Therefore 12,500 comes after 174 because it is a much higher number. All words using alphabetic characters come before all numbers, but in a random order.

In addition to changing how the records are sorted, you reverse the order in which they are sorted. You can choose ascending or descending order. Ascending order sorts letters from A to Z, and numbers from negative to positive. In descending order, WordPerfect sorts from Z to A, and from positive numbers to negative.

You have one further option for changing the order in which your records are sorted. You can choose to put capital letters before their equivalent lowercase letters (or after them, if you are using a descending sort). If you choose to sort capitals and lowercase letters separately, you must do so for all sorting keys. The Sort Uppercase First check box is found in the Sort dialog box, rather than the Edit Sort Key dialog box.

Save Your Document Before Sorting to the Screen

TIP 372

In WordPerfect you can choose the source and destination of the sort process. If you consistently choose destination separate from the source of the data being sorted, you will run no risk of accidentally missorting a file. However, you may find that you want to sort an open document on the screen, or that you want to sort a file on disk.

To prevent the disaster of losing information because its format is ruined by a misdefined sort, be careful never to write over your only clean copy of the information. This means that if your document is on the screen and you want to sort to the screen, save the document first. Then, if the sort goes wrong, you can simply exit without saving, or select Edit Undo (in WordPerfect 6 only), reopen the document, and try the sort again. If you are sorting to a file, make sure that your destination filename is not the same as that of your source file. If you do a lot of sorting, you might even want to set up a filename (such as SORTTEMP) that you will use to sort to. Then you can open this file, double-check that the sort went correctly, and save it either under a new filename or under the old one.

The Sort feature can also be used to select files. You have to be even more careful when you are selecting files because the files that are not selected are simply deleted from your document. Take all precautions to ensure that those records are not permanently lost.

A Global Sort Can Locate Files That Contain a Specific Word

You can use the Sort feature to separate out specific files of interest. One way to do this is to use the global sort key. When you use a global sort to select files, WordPerfect retains those files that contain the text you assign to the global sort key, at any place in the record. Files that do not contain the text you have specified are deleted from your document.

For example, if you have a list of clients, you might want to send a specific flyer only to those clients who live in Akron. To select only the files with the word "Akron" in them and delete the rest, follow these steps:

1. Select **T**ools Sort.
2. Select OK to accept the default source and destination for the sorting or selection process.
3. Choose **S**elect Records.
4. Type **keyg=Akron** .
5. Select **P**erform Action.

Use Selection Keys to Select Specific Records

You can use *selection keys* to select specific records from a file. You can use selection keys as simple as one specifying that a specific merge field is equal to "Akron", or as complicated as one that finds every client in Ohio whose first name is "Adelaide", whose credit limit is over $3000, and who has a current outstanding bill of under $500. You can use these selection keys to separate out merge records or other records when you want to work with only certain records in your file.

Be careful when selecting records, because WordPerfect will delete the records that are not selected. You can use Edit Undo to reverse the process of selection, but you must do so immediately. An even safer idea is to specify a destination file, open that file after sorting, and check to see whether the sort

was acceptable. If you take this precaution before writing over your original file, you will not need to worry about inadvertently losing data.

You create selection keys by combining sort keys and selection operators. You define which text or numbers the key should refer to, just as you normally would for a search, using Edit under Search Keys in the Sort dialog box. However, to specify your selection conditions, choose Select Records and then enter your selection statement, using the appropriate symbols.

Symbol	Meaning
=	Equal to
<>	Not equal to
&	And
:	Or
<	Less than
>	Greater than
<=	Less than or equal to
>=	Greater than or equal to

For example, to find Ohio clients named Adelaide with credit limits over $3000 and credit balances of under $500, enter this code:

```
key1=adelaide & key2=OH & key3>3000 & key 4<=500.
```

Hard Spaces Prevent Records with Differing Numbers of Subdivisions

TIP 375

Suppose your records consist of single lines, each with the client's name, credit limit, and outstanding credit separated by hard hyphens. If you wanted to search the document by the clients' credit limits, you could create a sort key using the second word. However, all client names might not be one word. ABM might be one word, but what about Allen & Associates, or XYZ Company?

You can avoid this difficulty with the careful use of hard spaces. If you include a hard space between words, the two words are joined and treated as one word. If you use a hard space between "ABC" and "Company", for example, then "ABC Company" will be treated as one word. By using hard spaces

carefully, you can be sure that you have the same number of subdivisions in each record, making it easier to select records accurately.

Document Initial Codes Let You Avoid Moving Codes When Sorting

When you sort your document, WordPerfect moves entire records at one time, including the codes to be found in those lines, paragraphs, or other records. For example, if a [Tab Set] code appears in the first record in your document, and if, when you sort that document, that record is now last, then the changed tab settings are now valid only for that last record. They will not affect the other records.

Because of this, you should make a point of storing as much formatting as possible with Document Initial Codes. Because Document Initial Codes sets the default formatting for the entire document, the formatting you specify with this feature will stay the same, no matter how your document is sorted.

To access the Document Initial Codes feature:

1. Select **L**ayout **D**ocument.
2. Select Document Initial **C**odes.
3. Enter any of the codes you want used for the document, just as if you were entering them into the document. You can use the menus or the shortcut keys.
4. Press F7.
5. Select OK.

In WordPerfect 6, You Can Sort Using Foreign Language Conventions

Some foreign languages arrange their alphabets differently, or use characters that we are unfamiliar with. For example, in Spanish, (double) "ll" and (double) "rr" are letters in their own right. Words beginning with "ll" would appear alphabetically after words that begin with "lu", even though in English the opposite is true.

You can instruct WordPerfect to sort using the conventions of a foreign language. To do this, insert a foreign language code in your document before the text that you want to sort. If you want to sort the

entire document, put this foreign language code in the Document Initial Codes. To enter a foreign language code:

1. Select **L**ayout **O**ther.
2. Select **L**anguage.
3. Highlight the language you want to use and select OK.
4. Select OK to return to the document.

You Must Define Sort Keys Before Selecting Records

When you tell WordPerfect how to select records, you do so by defining sort keys. A *sort key* is your specification for the sequence you want. You must define the sort key before telling WordPerfect how to select records. You cannot enter the selection statement and then go back and enter the sort keys.

You Can Sort Blocks of Text Rather Than Entire Files

You can choose to select the document currently on the screen or another document when you first start the Sort feature. Sometimes, however, you will only want to sort a small part of the document. You can do this by blocking the text and selecting the Sort feature. WordPerfect will then sort only the block that you have selected.

Use a Macro for Repeated Sorts

If you perform the same sort repeatedly, consider creating a macro to do the sorting for you. Using a macro enables you to be sure that the sort will be done correctly, because you will have had a chance to test the sort settings and can ensure that the exact same keystrokes are used each time. Using a macro eliminates the errors of forgetfulness or mistyping, and ultimately saves you time.

For example, suppose you can have a to-do list, in which you assign priorities to the tasks that you must complete. Routinely sorting this list by the assigned priorities and due dates will give you a clearer view of what tasks need to be done first. Since the to-do list will have to be periodically updated, creating a macro to sort it will save you time in the long run, because you will not have to re-create the sort commands each time you sort.

Margaret Smith's to-do list is shown here. It contains columns for the tasks, the date each task should be started, the date each one should be completed, and a priority level for each task. You would probably want to sort this kind of list by priority level first, so that high-priority projects would appear first on the list, and then by date, so that the projects with the earliest due dates would appear first within each priority level.

File Edit View Layout Tools Font Graphics Window Help

File Mgr Save As Print Preview Font GrphMode TextMode Envelope Speller Graselik QuickFndr Tbl Edit Search

Alleyn and Laney, LPA
Margaret Smith's
To Do List

Task	Start Date	Due Date	Priority
Finish Carlson brief	2/13/93	3/10/93	1
Letters to Kenners, Lyons and Phipps		3/11/93	3
Respond to discovery on "Smith vs. US Corporation"	2/20/93	3/10/93	1
Prepare for Johnson deposition	3/8/93	3/16/93	2
Contact Sam about settlement on "Kenners vs. Jones"		3/16/93	2
Research eminent domain for Lyons case		4/1/93	3
Respond to discovery on "Layton vs. Truebody"	3/3/93	4/1/93	3
Contact George Fein about settling "Drayton vs. Long"		3/1/93	1
Research tenant law for Ms. Myrtle Langdon	3/3/93	3/15/93	2

You can use the macro SORTLIST to sort this kind of table. SORTLIST sorts the table first according to the contents of the priority column, in ascending order. Then, within each level of priority, SORTLIST sorts the tasks in descending order according to the due dates. This way, the first priority task due yesterday should be the first item on your list, unfortunately. The macro code looks like this:

```
DISPLAY(Off!)
SortType(TableSort!)SortAction(Sort!)
SortKeys(4;1;1;Numeric!;Ascending!;3;1;3;Alphanumeric!;
Descending!;3;1;2;Alphanumeric!;Descending!;3;1;1;
Alphanumeric!;Descending!)
Sort()
```

The macro SORTLIST's first key is a numeric key. Therefore, the two heading rows are not moved in the sorting process. If you change the to-do list's header rows to include numbers in the fourth cell, WordPerfect might sort the header along with the tasks you have to complete. To avoid this, block the tasks before starting the macro. This will limit the macro to sorting the blocked tasks.

The to-do list on the accompanying disk does not look like the one shown here. Margaret Smith has modified her to-do list to include her name and the two graphics boxes, which use the PEN-PUSH.WPG graphics image file that comes with WordPerfect 6. You, too, can personalize your to-do list by adding your name, your company's name, your company's logo, or some other personalizing feature.

The graphics and other personalizing features are not added solely for your amusement. To-do lists often disappear under other papers. Adding graphics, or printing your to-do list on a different-colored paper, will help your list stand out so that you can find and use it more easily. You might want to invest in a ream of brightly colored paper, to be used only for your to-do list, so that you can always be sure of finding the list in the pile of white papers on your desk.

This sample macro form and the template are available on the accompanying disk as SORTLIST.WPM and TODOLIST.TEM.

SORTLIST.WPM
TODOLIST.TEM

Use Sort with Your Merge Files to Order Your Merge Records

TIP
381

Many people store mailing lists in WordPerfect merge data files to create letters and labels for large mailings. This is an efficient use of WordPerfect, but have you considered combining the merge feature with the Sort feature to save money and time as well?

The post office will give you a discount on large mailings when the mail is presorted by ZIP code. In addition, when you presort the mail, it is easier for the postal service to get it to the right post office for delivery, and this means that your mailing might get to your customers a little faster. However, organizing your mailing by ZIP code can be very difficult when done by hand.

If you sort your merge data file before you run the merge, you can presort the mailing. Then, all you have to do after preparing the envelopes or brochures is to bind the mail for each different ZIP code together.

The WordPerfect 6 macro, SORTMAIL, can sort a merge file for you. This macro assumes that the ZIP code is the last word in the second line of the third field of each merge data record. In this setup, you could have the customer's name and company name first, then the street address and city, state, and ZIP code as one field on two lines. Other information you might use would be stored in the subsequent merge fields.

The macro sorts your files by the ZIP code in ascending order. Then, within each ZIP code, your customers will be sorted alphabetically by the customer's company name, which is field 2. The macro looks like this:

```
DISPLAY(Off!)
SortType(MergeSort!)
SortAction(Sort!)
SortKeys(3;2;255;Numeric!;Ascending!;2;1;1;Alphanumeric!;Ascending!)
Sort()
```

SORTMAIL.WPM

This sample macro is available on the accompanying disk as SORTMAIL.WPM.

CHAPTER 9

Styles

WordPerfect's Sample Styles Might Give You Ideas

WordPerfect 6 and 5.1 come with a sample style library that you can use as the basis of ideas for the kinds of styles you can use. This style library is called LIBRARY.STY and is automatically copied to the directory that contains your WP.EXE file. This style library includes both normal styles and outline styles.

Making Instant Changes When You Alter a Style

One of the great advantages of using styles is that you can easily change the entire appearance of a document. You can create instant changes throughout your document, if you have used styles to edit text in the document, simply by editing the codes assigned to the style. For example, you might have used a style to format the subheads in your report. You can quickly change to a completely different format for your subheads by changing the style.

Creating Special Papers with Styles

You might have seen, from various paper supply companies, special printed papers used for memos or other communications that include either graphics or text to signify the importance of the document. You can use WordPerfect's styles to create your own special papers for use in your company. By using styles, you can be sure of keeping the same form for the same type of documents. The following special papers are included on the accompanying disk.

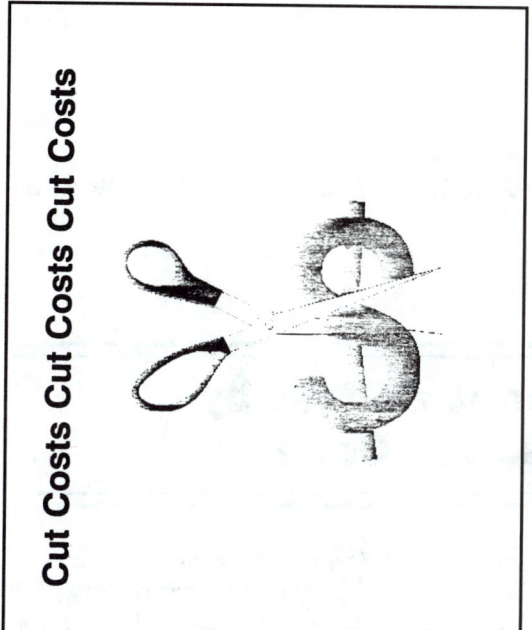

ESPPAPER.STY

The Bulletin, Cost Memo, and FYI styles are in the style library available on the accompanying disk as ESPPAPER.STY.

CUT_COST.WMF
DINGBT36.CGM

The graphics shown above are in the files CUT_COST.WMF and DINGBT36.CGM on the accompanying disk.

T I P 385

Learning More About a Style by Highlighting Its Hidden Code

A quick way to learn about the formats a style sets is to show the Reveal Code screen and then move the cursor on top of the code turning the style on. When you highlight this code, it expands to show the hidden codes for the formatting it applies. If there is a lot of formatting or text in the style, you might not be able to see all of it.

T I P 386

Use a Style Library When You Want to Use a Style in All Documents

If you want a style available for all documents, save it in a *style library*. A style library is a file that contains the setting for files. You can assign style libraries to any document. By saving a style to a style library and assigning that style library to other documents, you make the best possible use of the time and effort you put into creating the style. When you change the style in the style library, you automatically change the formatting for all of the documents that use the style library.

You Can Create Style Libraries for Different Types of Documents

TIP 387

You are not restricted to just one style library. You can create as many style libraries as you think you will need. If you create a variety of documents, you might have a different style library for each type of document you create. This way you keep each type of document consistent in format because you are using the same styles consistently, but without the investment in time of continually creating new styles and double-checking them against old documents for consistency.

You will find style libraries a great boon if you type for several different people. Create a style library for each person, using the settings and formatting each of them prefer. You can quickly create documents without having to remind yourself of the different formatting each person prefers.

You Can Standardize Your Papers with Styles

TIP 388

You might want to standardize the way your papers are written. You can to do this to maintain a unified corporate identity in your printed material or to match an academically required style. One way to do this is to use styles. Use styles for each element of your papers that needs to be formatted.

The accompanying disk includes a sample style library called PAPERS.STY. To use this style library after retrieving it in a document, use Title Page at the beginning of the document. Start the rest of the document with the Document style. Use Topic for main headings and Subtopic for secondary headings. Use Foreign Term style to mark text you want to italicize. Complete the document using Endnote Page for the page where you want the endnotes placed.

PAPER.STY

TIP 389

You Can Insert Styles for Existing Text

You do not have to apply styles to text when you first enter it. You can apply styles to text you have already typed. For example, you might want to use a style library given you by a friend or coworker to format a report after you have created it.

When you insert an open style, simply move the cursor to where you want the open style to take effect, and select it. If you want to format text with a paired style (character or paragraph styles in WordPerfect 6), you need to block the text to be affected first, just as if you were inserting a paired code, such as Bold, to text you had already entered. After blocking the text, select the style just as you would normally, and it will affect all of the selected text.

TIP 390

Styles Can Only Be Altered by Editing

You can remove a style easily by displaying the Reveal Codes screen and deleting the style code. However, you cannot change the settings of the style from the main document. Instead, you need to edit the style. You can edit a style in WordPerfect 6 by selecting Layout Styles, highlighting the style name, and selecting Edit. This opens the Edit Style dialog box, shown here:

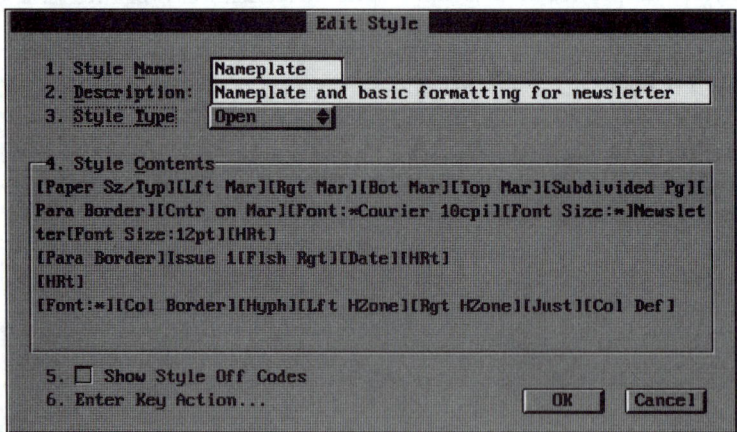

You can edit a style in WordPerfect 5.1 by selecting Layout Styles Edit.

Every Document Can Have Its Own Unique Set of Styles

You can create unique styles for each document you create, if this is the most sensible solution for you. Use unique styles if each document you are creating is very different. For example, if you are creating brochures or newsletters for a number of different companies, use unique styles so that you do not inadvertently format a document for XYZ Company in the formatting you have set up for True Fun Rock Promotions, Inc.

Styles Only Work for Features Used Often

You will not want to create styles that you only need to use once. Doing so would be a waste of time. Styles are a time-saving feature, however, if you are using the same formatting repeatedly in a document, such as for subheads throughout a long report, or if you are going to use them frequently in many documents by saving them to a style library. Remember that styles are meant to be a time-saving feature. Don't use them if they aren't going to save you time.

You Can Use ENTER in Different Ways When You Use Paired Styles

Paired styles are styles that have an on and an off code. In WordPerfect 6, there are two types of paired styles, character and paragraph styles. You can use ENTER in a variety of ways when you are using paired styles. You can have ENTER function normally, in which case it enters a hard return code. You can have ENTER turn the style off. You can have ENTER turn the code off and then turn it back on again. In WordPerfect 6 you can also have ENTER turn a style off and turn on another style.

In WordPerfect 6, you set what ENTER is going to do by selecting Enter Key Action in the Edit Style dialog box. You can use any of the four options if you are creating a character style. However, if you are creating a paragraph style, you cannot set ENTER to simply insert a hard return and leave the style on.

In WordPerfect 5.1, you select Enter in the Edit Style menu to set what action pressing ENTER carries out. In WordPerfect 5.1, you cannot set ENTER to turn one style off and turn a different style on.

The Style Comments Box Marks the Location of Text to Be Used with Styles

When you create a paired paragraph or character style, you only need to insert the codes that will be in effect for this text formatted with the style. WordPerfect will automatically turn off any paired codes when the style is turned off. However, you might want certain other formatting or text to appear for the text after the style is turned off. You can introduce codes to be turned on when the style is turned off.

To do this, you need to insert the codes to be used after the style is turned off, after the document comment box in the Codes or Style Contents screen. In WordPerfect 5.1, this box automatically appears. In WordPerfect 6, you must select the Show Style Off Codes check box before this comment box, shown here, appears:

```
┌──────────────────────── Edit Style ─────────────────────────┐
│                                                              │
│   1. Style Name:     Headline 1                              │
│   2. Description:    First level head lines                  │
│   3. Style Type:     Paragraph ◆                             │
│                                                              │
│  ┌ 4. Style Contents ──────────────────────────────────────┐│
│  │[Para Border][Color][Font:*Courier 10cpi][Font Size:*][Cntr on Mar││
│  │]                                                         ││
│  │  ┌──────────────────────────────────────────────────┐   ││
│  │  │ Codes above take effect when the style is turned on.│  ││
│  │  │ Codes below take effect when the style is turned off.│ ││
│  │  └──────────────────────────────────────────────────┘   ││
│  │[Para Border]                                             ││
│  └──────────────────────────────────────────────────────────┘│
│                                                              │
│   5. ⊠ Show Style Off Codes                                  │
│   6. Enter Key Action...  Off/On           [ OK ] [ Cancel ] │
└──────────────────────────────────────────────────────────────┘
```

Cancel and Delete a Style to Discard It

While you are in the process of creating a style, you might find that you want to cancel the process and discard the file. However, you cannot simply cancel the process. Instead, you must first cancel it and then actually delete the style from the style library by highlighting it and selecting **Delete** from the Style dialog box or menu. Once you have begun creating the file, you cannot simply not create it. You must delete it.

In WordPerfect 5.1, the Style Comment Box Does Not Appear If You Have Set Comments to Be Hidden

In WordPerfect 5.1, a comment appears on the screen when you are entering codes for a style. This comment takes the place of the text that will be formatted by the style. Any codes you enter before it are turned on for the style, and any codes inserted after it are turned on when the style is turned off.

However, if you set WordPerfect to hide all comments, this comment box is hidden as well. Because of this, you will be unable to insert codes to occur after the style is turned off.

Save the Document After Creating the Style In Order to Save the Style

When you create a style, you have to save the document you create it in afterward if you want to use the style in that document again. WordPerfect saves styles you create in a document as part of that document. If you do not save the document again, it is like adding text to your document and not saving it afterward. The text or the style is lost.

Another way to save a style is to save it as part of a style library. Saving it as part of a style library by using the Save command from the Style dialog box or menu has the advantage of letting you use it with any other document you might create.

Use Styles to Make Sure Your Letters Are Formatted Correctly

There are a number of standard formats used for letters and correspondence. Your company has probably chosen one to be the standard format for the entire company. To simplify the process of creating correspondence that matches your company's standard, use styles that conform to these standards.

The accompanying disk includes a sample style library called MODBLOCK.STY. Once you retrieve this style library into a document, you can use the Body Text, Closing, Return Add, and Send Address paragraph styles for the text of the letter, the closing greeting, the return address, and the sending address, respectively.

MODBLOCK.STY

When You Use Paired Codes in a Paired Style, the Ending Code is Inserted Automatically

When you insert a code that is paired in WordPerfect 5.1's paired styles, and WordPerfect 6's character and paragraph styles, you do not need to insert both the on and the off codes. Insert the on codes for the style, and WordPerfect will automatically turn the codes off when the style is turned off.

Creating a Style from Formatting in Your Document in WordPerfect 6

TIP 400

You might already have documents formatted in a way that you want to use repeatedly. In WordPerfect 6 , you can create a style using the formatting you have already applied to the document. To do this, move your cursor to a section of text with the formatting you want to save as a style. Then create the style normally. In the Create Style dialog box, select the **C**reate From Current Paragraph/Character check box. You cannot create an open style from formatting in the document.

Creating Open Styles by Copying Existing Codes from Your Document

TIP 401

You can create a style based on an existing document by copying codes and text from the document and pasting them into the style. You can use this method to create open styles easily. This method is also very effective if the style you are creating uses graphics or text that needs to be formatted. By creating it in the document first, you can see the effect of the formatting changes that are made to ensure that they are what you want. While you enter codes while creating the style, you cannot see the effect of the formatting changes that you make.

You Can Simplify Creating a Newsletter with Styles

TIP 402

When you create a newsletter for your company, church, or group, you want to create a professional and consistent appearance that will make your readers want to read your newsletter. One way to do this is to use consistent formatting, so that the readers know how to recognize the elements of your newsletter that they want to read and see. One way to simplify this process is to use styles for the various newsletter features.

The NEWSLTR.STY style library on the disk includes several styles (one is shown in the following) used in creating a brochure style newsletter. This newsletter style creates a booklet newsletter sideways on 8 1/2 × 11 paper. Remember to use the Print as Booklet option for printing this document to receive the pages in the correct order.

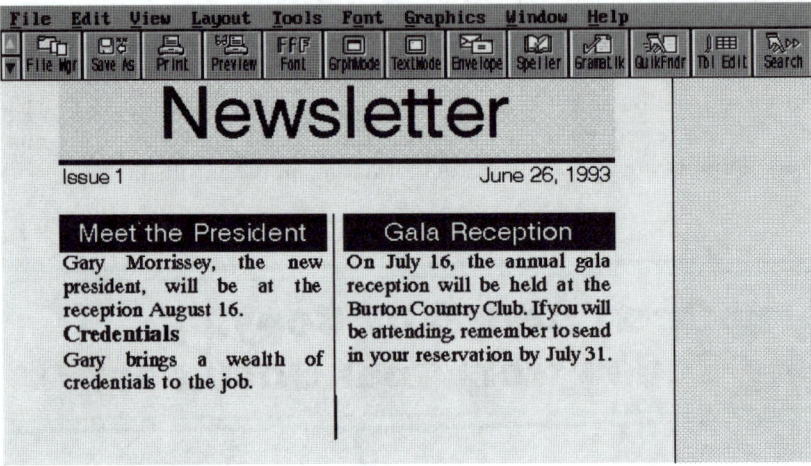

This sample style library is available on the accompanying disk as NEWSLTR.STY. You will want to change Newsletter in the Nameplate style to the name of your newsletter.

NEWSLTR.STY

Creating a Letterhead Style for Yourself

You can use styles to create many types of documents. For example, if you want to use a letterhead for your stationary, but don't want to go to the expense of having one printed up, why not create your own? With WordPerfect's graphics features and styles, you can easily create a letterhead. The accompanying disk contains several letterhead styles, including those shown in the following:

These style libraries are available on the accompanying disk as LTHD1.STY, LTHD2.STY, LTHD3.STY, and LTHD4.STY. The graphics used are on the accompanying disk in the files BORDER24.CGM, BORDER4.CGM, FAIRY.PCX, and WOODCARV.PCX.

TIP 404 — Using a Style to Provide a Letter Opening or Closing

Styles are not limited to providing formatting in your document. You can also include text, graphics boxes, or tables in your styles. You can then use the style consistently to reduce the amount of time you have to spend typing. For example, if you create a lot of correspondence, you might find yourself repeating the same text over and over again, such as the opening address and date of the letter, or a closing paragraph and signature line. You can store the text and formatting for these parts of the letter as open styles and insert the style code into the document, saving you time.

On the disk you will find a style library that includes some opening and closing styles for your letters. Customize these styles to suit your needs and simplify the typing of your letters.

LETTER.STY

This style library is available on the accompanying disk as LETTER.STY. This style library has three styles to use for closings: Closing, Closing 2, and Closing 3. By changing from one of these styles to another, you can alter the appearance and text of the letter's closing.

TIP 405 — Using Styles Instead of Macros to Add Flexibility

The capabilities of styles and macros in WordPerfect overlap to a great degree. Where it is possible, use styles instead of macros, especially for entering text and formatting. Styles provide a much greater

flexibility than macros can. Macros repeat specific keystrokes, but a style can adjust more easily to formatting already in the document, the amount of text you have and other variable conditions.

Using Styles from Three Sources with WordPerfect 6 to Add Variety to Your Documents

T^{IP} **406**

In WordPerfect 6, you can use styles from three locations at one time. You can use the styles saved as part of the document, styles saved in a personal style library, and styles saved in a shared style library. *Personal libraries* are those saved on your computer system or in your own directory on a network, while *shared libraries* are available on a network system. You can use a personal library as a shared library if you want.

The advantage of using multiple sources is the flexibility it allows you. For example, you can use a shared style library that offers standard styles used by your company. Use a personal style library to access those styles that you use frequently in your work, but aren't relevant to the entire company. Then you can also use the styles saved with the document for document specific information or formatting. Having three sources for styles allows you a great deal of flexibility at a minimal time cost.

WordPerfect 6 Uses a Specific Hierarchy When Styles in Style Libraries Have the Same Name

T^{IP} **407**

You may assign style libraries to your document that contain different styles with the same names. For example, a shared style library might have a letterhead style used throughout the company. You could then copy this style, customize it to yourself, and save it with the same name in your personal style library.

Styles that are stored with the document are used first. So if you have styles saved with the style libraries and create a style with the same name in the current document, WordPerfect 6 will use the style as saved in the document. Second in the hierarchy are personal style libraries. If you have the same style name in both personal and shared style libraries, WordPerfect will use the style saved in the personal

style library, rather than the one in the shared style library. Styles saved in the shared style library are used only when there are no styles with the same name in the document or the personal style library.

If you want to prevent some styles from being overridden by styles with the same name in other libraries, use a library specific name, such as P_*name* for styles in the personal library or S_*name* for styles in a shared library.

When You Edit a Library Style It Becomes a Document Style

When you edit a library style, it becomes a style saved with the document. This is to prevent your style library from changing when you have to modify a file to suit a particular document. If you actually want to keep the changes that you make to the style, you will have to save the style to the style library again.

Applying Paragraph Styles Without Blocking Text

When you apply a WordPerfect 6 paragraph style to an existing paragraph, you do not actually have to block any text. Instead, simply place your cursor in the paragraph to be formatted and select the paragraph style. WordPerfect 6 automatically moves the paragraph style code to the beginning of the paragraph, because the Auto Code Placement feature is the default. However, if you want to format more than one paragraph, you must select some text from each of the paragraphs you want to format. Remember that if you want to apply a character style to existing text, you have to block the text first.

In WordPerfect 6, You Can Carry Out Actions with Multiple Styles with the Mark Command

You might want to carry out an action on more than one style at once, such as deleting or copying them. You can do this by marking all of the styles you want to work with and selecting the Mark command. You cannot use this feature to edit or select the styles, but it does let you save, copy, or delete multiple styles at once. To use the Mark command, highlight the style name, and select Mark. Marked styles have an asterisk (*) before them.

Linking Paragraph Styles That Naturally Follow Each Other in WordPerfect 6

WordPerfect 6 offers you the chance to simplify the formatting of your document even further. When creating a paragraph style, you can choose what happens to the style when you press ENTER, as discussed in Tip 393. One option is to have WordPerfect turn off the current style and start a new paragraph style. This is called *linking* the paragraph.

For example, if you were to create a report, you might want to follow paragraphs formatted as headings with paragraphs formatted as text. By changing the definition of the ENTER key, you can make this transition without having to select the style.

Selecting the Style You Last Selected Quickly in WordPerfect 6

You can quickly reselect the last style selected after it is turned off by pressing ALT-F8 twice from the document window. When you do this, WordPerfect 6 opens the Style dialog box and highlights the last selected style. You can immediately select some action, such as Select, to use the style with.

You Can Nest Paragraph and Character Styles

In WordPerfect 6, you can insert some style codes inside other style codes. For example, you can use a character style within a paragraph formatted with a paragraph style. You might use a character style for your company name within a paragraph formatted for newsletter text. You can also nest character styles. You might have a sentence formatted with a character style for emphasis and one word within it formatted for your company name. If some element of the styles is in direct conflict, the setting for the inside style code is used. You cannot nest two paragraph styles because WordPerfect 6 automatically replaces the first paragraph style code with the second one entered even if the Auto Code Placement feature is turned off.

When You Retrieve One File into Another, Styles with the Same Name Are Not Replaced

You can retrieve one document into another using the File Retrieve command. These files might have styles with the same name. When you retrieve one document into another document, the styles in the original document are not replaced. Therefore, the entire open document is formatted with the styles of the first document. If you want to retrieve files from another document or a style library to replace the styles in the currently open document, you need to access the Style feature and use that retrieve command.

You Can Use WordPerfect 5.1 Styles in WordPerfect 6

When you upgrade from WordPerfect 5.1 to WordPerfect 6, you don't have to re-create your styles. WordPerfect 6 will automatically convert your 5.1 styles into 6 styles when you retrieve them into a document. You might need to retrieve a style library into an empty document and save it again, to make sure that you will not have to undergo the conversion process each time you try to access those styles.

You Can Display Styles from Only One Source at a Time in the WordPerfect 6 Style Dialog Box

You must select the source of the styles displayed in the Style List dialog box: the document, a personal library, or a shared library. You can only display the styles in one source at a time in the Style List dialog box, as shown here:

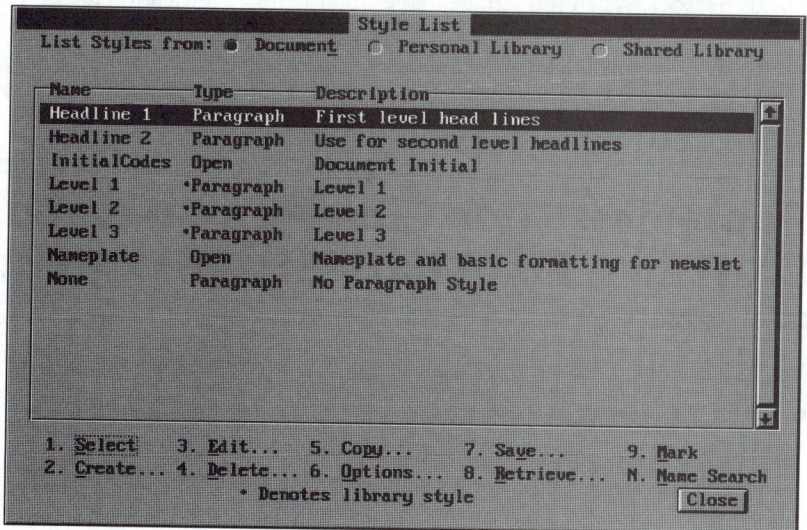

However, you can use the styles from all three sources at once in the document. To simplify the process of formatting your document, try to add all of the styles from one source before displaying the styles of the next source.

In WordPerfect 6, Retrieve Style Libraries Only to Change the Document Styles

Usually you will access the style saved in style libraries by assigning those style libraries to the document. To assign style libraries:

1. Select **L**ayout **S**tyles.
2. Select **O**ptions.
3. Select **L**ibraries Assigned to Document.
4. Type the filename for the personal library and press ENTER.
5. Type the filename for the shared library and press ENTER.
6. Select OK to return to the Style dialog box.

WordPerfect 6 does, however, offer the ability to retrieve the styles into the document, just as you had to do with WordPerfect 5.1. When you retrieve a style library into a WordPerfect document, any styles in the document are replaced by styles with the same name from the style library. This replacement is irrevocable, so the styles originally in the document are destroyed.

Replacing Style Libraries Changes a Draft to a Final Version Quickly

You probably use very different formatting for creating a document as a draft and creating a final version of the document. You can use styles and style libraries to make this change quick and painless.

The trick is to use the same style names in two different style libraries, one for the draft formatting and the second for the final version formatting. When you are ready to go from the draft versions to a final version, you can simply replace the draft style library with the final style library by assigning the final style library to the document in WordPerfect 6, or retrieving the styles into the document with WordPerfect 5.1. The formatting or text actually applied by the styles changes to that of the new library immediately.

For example, the draft version of your paper might be double-spaced to make it easier to write revisions and comments on it. When you print your final draft, you will want to use a new style that single-spaces the document. There would be other changes probably, including how headings are formatted and the header and footer to be used.

Finding One Style in the List Using Name Search

TIP 419

When you create a document or style library that contains many styles, you might not be able to find the one that you are looking for easily because the entire style list is too long to show in the Style List dialog box at once. A shortcut for locating the style that you want to use is to select Name Search and start typing the name of the style. As you type each letter, WordPerfect moves the highlight to the first word that matches what you have typed. When the style you want is highlighted, press ENTER.

Choose Default Style Libraries in WordPerfect 6

TIP 420

If you find that you use one or two style libraries consistently, assign them as the default style libraries. Remember that you can use a second personal style library by assigning it as a shared library.

Select File Setup Location of files Style Files. Then enter the name of the default files in either the Default Personal Library or the Default Shared Library text boxes and select OK.

Create Consistent Formatting with a Shared Style Library

Creating and maintaining a strong corporate identity in all written materials is difficult when everybody is using their own styles. You can create a style library and make it available over your network to ensure that everyone uses the same styles, making your corporate identity in printed materials more consistent.

Shared Style Libraries Without a Network Are Just Like Personal Style Libraries

You can still use the shared style library feature even if you are not on a network system. Without a network, you can attach a second personal style library to your document, using the steps you would use to attach a shared style library. Once you have done so, you can use this second personal library to supply new styles to your document. If this is a style library that you want to share, you can still pass the library file around on disk and let people copy it onto their systems.

View and Edit WordPerfect 6's System Styles to Change Formatting for Features Indirectly

WordPerfect uses certain system styles to format items such as footnote numbers, footnote text, headers, and other types of text. To edit the formatting or contents of these features, you can edit the system style itself. To do this, select Options in the Style List dialog box and select the List System Styles check box. When you return to the Style List dialog box, you will see the following greatly expanded list of styles used for features such as footnote text, tables of contents, and outlining levels.

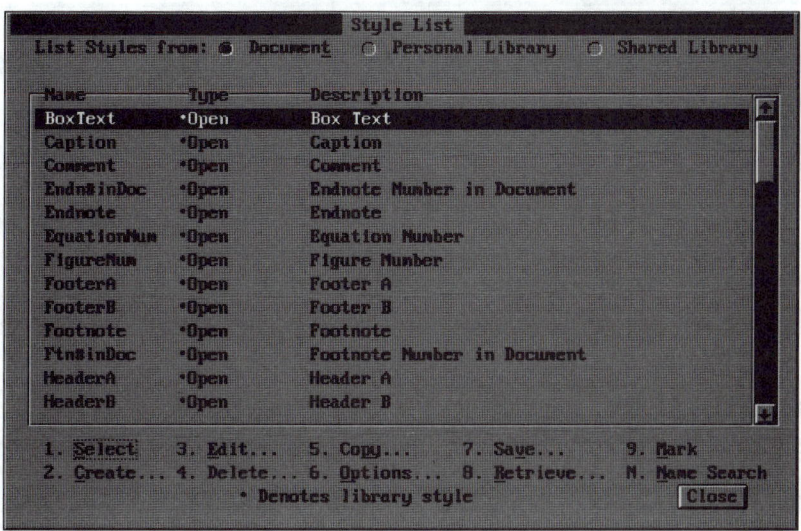

Edit WordPerfect 6's InitialCodes Style to Change the Defaults for the Document

TIP 424

In WordPerfect 6, every document begins with an open style code, inserting the InitialStyles open style. This style sets all of the default settings for your document. When you edit this style, you change the default settings used in your document. The great advantage of editing this style rather than inserting the changes at the beginning of the document is that you eliminate code clutter at the beginning of your document. *Code clutter,* which is created when you insert several different codes to format the document, can make it difficult to avoid putting text or codes in the wrong place. You can edit this style in two ways. One is to edit it like any other style, by selecting Layout Styles, highlighting this style, and selecting Edit. The second is to select Layout Document Document Initial Codes, and edit the settings there.

Use WordPerfect 6's Character Styles When Formatting Specific Text

WordPerfect 6's character styles are designed for formatting short sections of text. For example, you can use a character style for words in a foreign language. You can format foreign words in italics or with another format that distinguishes them from words in your main language. You will not want to use character styles when you are changing the format of an entire paragraph, such as a heading or bulleted list style.

Use WordPerfect 6's Paragraph Styles When Formatting Complete Paragraphs

WordPerfect 6's paragraph styles are designed for formatting paragraphs of text. For example, you can use a paragraph style to create headings or bulleted list items. You cannot use paragraph styles to format short stretches of text. Do not use paragraph styles to format entire documents because paragraph styles insert specific on and off codes.

Use Open Styles When Changing the Formatting of the Entire Document from the Current Point

WordPerfect uses open styles to change the formatting of a document from the point it is inserted to the end. You cannot use an open style for a block of text by blocking the text and inserting this style any more than you can use a paragraph style for a single sentence. For example, if you include a bibliography in your document, you might want to change several page formatting features, such as margins, that will effect the remainder of the document.

Set Default Style Libraries to Save Time

When you set a default library to use with each new document, you speed up formatting new documents by making a specific set of styles immediately available. This keeps you from having to re-create the formatting for each document you create, and lets you take advantage of the time you spent creating the format in the first place. If you set a default shared style library, you take advantage of the time that someone else has spent in creating those styles, reducing the amount of time you have to spend on the documents you need to create.

Be Careful with the Styles Used in Master Documents

You can create *master documents* containing links to subdocuments, as described in Tip 462. Each subdocument can have its own styles saved with the document. If you expand a master document and each of the subdocuments have different styles, all of the styles are read into the expanded document. When there are document styles with the same name in different subdocument files, the style in the subdocument closest to the beginning of the master document is used.

Remember That Auto Code Placement Will Affect Your Style Settings

The Auto Code Placement setting automatically places certain codes in the position they need to be in. Be careful when using styles that you assign codes appropriately to the different style types to ensure that the codes are correctly placed. Character style codes are not moved from the location where they are entered. Paragraph style codes automatically move the top of the paragraph you are in when they are inserted. Open style codes can be inserted at any point. If they include codes that must appear at the top of the page, they will insert a soft page break and start a new page at their location.

Use Styles to Format Long Documents to Ensure Consistency

When you are creating a very long document, such as a long report or brief, or when you have several different people assisting in creating the document, be sure to use styles for all formatting in the document. That way you can ensure consistency, and can easily change the formatting when the creation phase of the project is over. If you do not use styles, you run the risk of someone, possibly you, having to sit down and integrate all the work done at different times or by different people, to ensure that the parts of the document are completely consistent.

Copying a Style to Another Style Source to Make It Available

After creating a style in your document, you might find it useful in other documents. With WordPerfect 6, you can quickly copy this style to a style library, or from a library to your document, without having to reenter the codes. To copy a style, highlight the style and select Copy. Enter the name of the style location, either the library or a document, and select OK. WordPerfect copies the style to the new source.

CHAPTER
10

Date and Time

JAN
1994

In WordPerfect 5.1, the % Symbol in a Date Format Pads Numbers and Abbreviates Days and Months

In WordPerfect 5.1, you create a date format by entering characters that take the place of elements of the date or time. You can abbreviate months and days to three letters, or add zeros in front of numbers less than ten by adding a percent sign (%) before the code for that character. To add a space before numbers less than ten, use a dollar sign ($) instead of a percent sign before the code for the character.

You Can Create Default Date Formats

You may find that you usually use a specific date format that differs from the default that WordPerfect sets, either because you usually write to foreign companies, which may use a different date format as the standard, or because you work for the military, which uses a different date format. You can create a new default date format in both WordPerfect 5.1 and 6.0.

In WordPerfect 6:

1. Select **L**ayout **D**ocument Initial Codes Se**t**up.
2. Select **T**ools **D**ate **F**ormat.
3. Create the date format using the dialog box shown here:

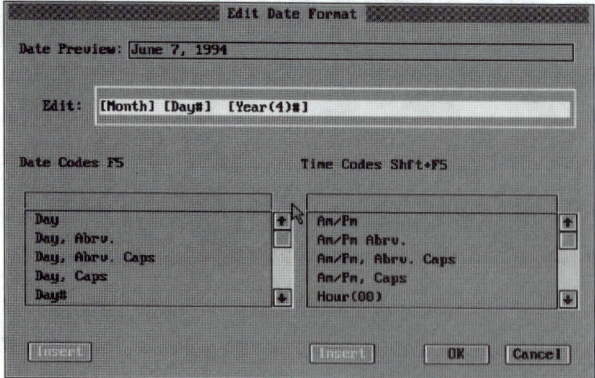

Press F5 to access the codes for elements of the date or SHIFT-F5 to access the codes for elements of the time.

4. Select OK to return to the document.

All new documents will use the newly created format as the default. However, the current document default date setting has not been changed.

In WordPerfect 5.1:

1. Select **F**ile Se**t**up **I**nitial Settings.
2. Select **D**ate Format.
3. Enter the codes to create the date format.
4. Press ENTER three times to return to the document.

Use the Date Feature to Add Both the Date and Time to a Document

You can use the date feature to insert a date, a time, or a date and time combination. You switch to inserting the time or time and date by creating a date format that includes the time, or, in WordPerfect 6, by selecting an option that includes both.

You can select a new date format in WordPerfect 6:

1. Select **T**ools **D**ate **F**ormat, opening the dialog box shown here:

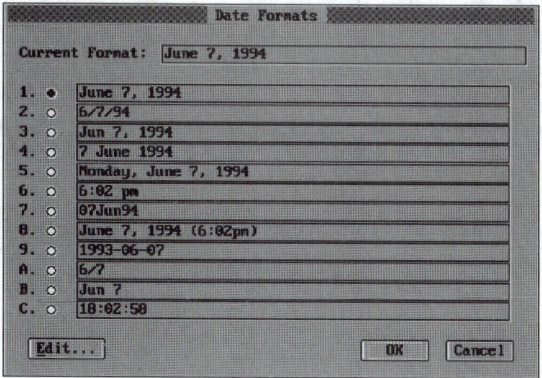

2. Select the radio button for the format you want to use.
3. Select OK.

Have WordPerfect Insert the Current Date and Time to Timestamp Documents

It may be important for readers to know when a document was created. For example, if you have several drafts of a document, you may want to add the current date and time to ensure that the readers or editors know which draft copy they are working from. You could type the current date and time each time you edited and printed the document (if you remembered), but an easier solution is to have WordPerfect substitute the correct date and time each time you open or print the document.

To do this, you insert a date code. WordPerfect will update this code each time you open or print a document. This way, you do not have to do the typing each time, and you can be sure that the date is correct (unless your computer's internal clock has lapsed).

To insert a date or time code in WordPerfect 6:

1. Position your cursor where you want the date code.
2. Select **T**ools **D**ate **C**ode.

WordPerfect inserts the appropriate code, which now shows the current date or time. If you do not want to use the default date format, select Tools Date Format and choose a different format, or create a new one as discussed in Tip 434, and follow the steps just given to insert the code using this format.

To insert a date or time code in WordPerfect 5.1:

1. Position your cursor where you want to insert the date code.
2. Select **T**ools Date **C**ode.

Again, if you do not want to use the default format, you can change it by selecting Tools Date Format.

Use a Date or Time Code in Your Text in Forms

In form or primary documents for use with merges, remember to insert a date code rather than inserting the date text or typing a date. When you merge your data file with this form file, WordPerfect will automatically update the date code for you, which ensures that all of your merge documents will have the correct date. If you do not take this step, you run the risk of forgetting to update the date before printing, which either results in a lot of documents that you have to print again or in you looking very unprofessional when your client receives a letter dated three weeks earlier.

Use Date Codes Rather Than Date Text for Frequently Updated Documents

If you have documents that you have to update frequently, such as sales reports, production results, or cover letters for résumés, insert a date code rather than inserting or typing date text. You will never have to retype the date in that document because WordPerfect will automatically update it for you, ensuring that the date is always correct.

Create a Graphic to Accompany Month Names in Newsletters or Calendars

When you create newsletters, calendars, or other monthly publications, you may want to call attention to the timely nature of the document, and increase its "eye appeal" by adding graphic elements to the month name. Using the month names as graphics adds visual interest to your publication and increases the chances that a customer or client will pick it up and take a look, not only at the graphic, but at the message you are trying to convey. You can see how the following document attracts interest with the use of the month name graphic. You will find this graphic and one for each of the other eleven months, on the accompanying disk.

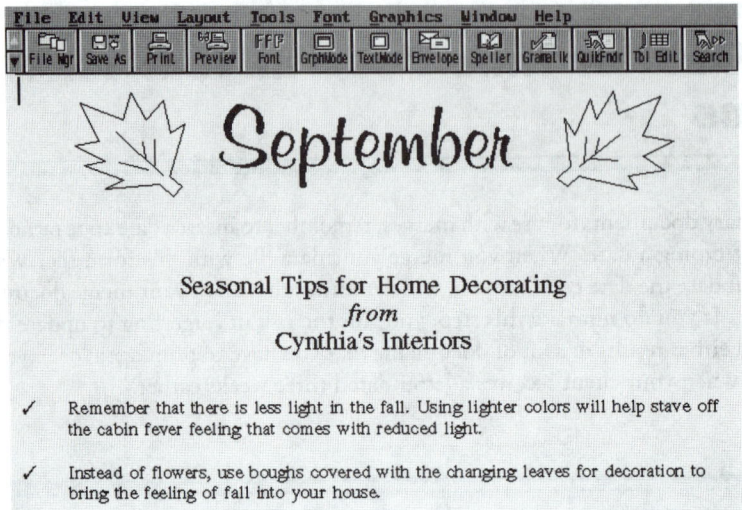

This graphic is available on the accompanying disk as SEPTEMBE.WPG.

SEPTEMBE.WPG

TIP 440
Remember to Change Date Formats When Preparing Military or Foreign Correspondence

If you prepare correspondence or forms for the military, you will want to change the document's default date format. The military uses a different standard date format, which places the day before the month. For example, members of the military use 6 March 1994, while the civilian standard would be March

6, 1994. Also note that the military standard does not use commas. Even for short date formats, day and month are reversed: 31/12/94 is used rather than 12/31/94. The military standard time format uses a 24-hour clock rather than the standard 12-hour clock, which means, for example, that your dinner appointment might be at 18:30 in the military but 6:30 P.M. in the civilian world.

If preparing correspondence with foreign countries, you will find that those countries may also use a different standard date format than the U.S. The standard used depends on the country. Before preparing correspondence to a foreign country, find a handbook about the style of that country to ensure that you are using a format that can be easily understood by a citizen of that country. For example, if you are writing to someone who is accustomed to seeing the day before the month in the short format, and you do not change from the U.S. standard of month before day, you may create a problem. What date does 03/04/94 mean, March 4, 1994 or April 3, 1994?

Spell the Date in Legal or Formal Documents

TIP 441

When entering dates or times in legal or formal documents, completely spell out all numbers—both for the sake of formality and to ensure that the date or time is precisely understood. If you do not spell out the entire date or time, you run the risk of creating confusion, particularly when you are working across cultures.

For example, some countries place the day before the month in dates, whereas in the U.S. the month comes before the day. If you use 5/6/94 in a contract, you may understand this to mean the sixth of May, while the other party may understand it to mean the fifth of June. To avoid the complications and possible lawsuits that can be generated from such a misunderstanding, write out the date as Friday, May sixth, 1994. This extra step can prevent grave misunderstandings.

In documents such as wedding announcements or formal invitations, it is simply customary to spell out dates and times. For example, in the wedding announcement shown in the following, the date and time are completely spelled out:

William Wilson Long

and

Adora Lillian Roth

request the honor of your presence at

their wedding

at

eleven'o'clock in the morning

on

Saturday, the fourteenth of May

in the year of our Lord

one thousand nine hundred and ninety-four

at St. Paul's Episcopal Church

in Lowesville

These graphics are available on the accompanying disk as ROSES.PCX and BRIAR.PCX.

ROSES.PCX
BRIAR.PCX

Use WordPerfect's Default Date Format for Most Business Correspondence

TIP 442

WordPerfect comes with a specific date format set for inserting date codes and date text. This format is the standard style for dates in business correspondence within the U.S. You should be able to insert date codes and text in most contexts without having to change the date format.

Use Parentheses When Referring to a Date of Publication or the Date of an Event

TIP 443

When you use a date in a document as secondary information, describing something such as the date of a publication, the dates should appear within parentheses. For example, in the sentence "The first edition of the *English Dancing Master* (1651) reversed the men's and women's symbols in the explanation," the date 1651 is enclosed in parentheses. You would also use parentheses when referring to upcoming events, as in "The management meeting (June 3) will cover the changes in management style brought on by the merger."

Create Different Date Formats with Macros in WordPerfect 5.1

In WordPerfect 5.1, you have to create a new date format each time you want to change the date format, while in WordPerfect 6 you can select from a few standard formats. If you are creating a document in WordPerfect 5.1 in which you need to switch date formats frequently, you may want to create a macro with which you can change from the default format to another one quickly. For example, the macro shown here will switch from the default date format to a format that shows the current time, and then insert a date code:

```
{Date/Outline}3
{Del to Eol}
%8:%9 {Enter}
2
```

Use the Date You Printed the Letter, Not the Date You Created the Letter

Often, you will create a letter that will not be printed and sent for a day or two to allow time for it to be edited. In this case the creation date and the final date will differ. They may also be different if you have a form letter created for merges that are done after the original letter is created.

You do not want to send a letter dated weeks before it actually was sent. This makes it look as though your office forgot to mail the letter. In addition, in business correspondence, you may find that you have inadvertently caused legal difficulties if your letter appears to have been created long before it was sent.

To avoid these difficulties, use date codes instead of date text in letters that will be used in merges or letters slated for revisions. This way you can be sure that the letter shows the date that it was printed.

Use Hard Spaces in Date Text to Keep the Date from Breaking Incorrectly

TIP 446

When you add date text in the default format of *month, day, year,* you may want to insert a hard space between the month and day. If you do not, WordPerfect may insert a soft return between them to wrap the date. Standard usage requires that the month and day appear together, although the year may be wrapped to a separate line. To insert a hard space, press SHIFT-SPACEBAR.

You cannot add a hard space inside a date inserted as a date code. If you look at the Reveal Codes screen, you will see that there is nowhere to insert the space. However, WordPerfect may still wrap a date inserted incorrectly with a date code. The only way to prevent this is to change text on the line to set where WordPerfect wraps the line, or to press SHIFT-ENTER to enter an end-of-line code before the date.

In Date Text, Use Commas to Offset the Year

TIP 447

When you add a date in the default format, which is *month, day, year,* standard usage requires a comma after the year. Do not include the comma in the date format because you could not insert the date at the end of a sentence or as part of a table or date line that did not require the comma after the year.

Use Month and Day Abbreviations Only When Space Is Tight

TIP 448

As a rule, you should not abbreviate months and days except when space is tight. Therefore, do not use abbreviations when the date appears within the text of a letter or report. Do abbreviate in a table or a form where there is very little space. For example, you can see in the following table that spelling out the days of the week would have created spacing problems, but the abbreviations make the table quite easy to read.

Jones and Jones, LPA

Room Reservation Schedule
for week of 3/19/94

Room	Sun		Mon		Tue		Wed		Thu		Fri		Sat		Authorizing Partner
	a	p	a	p	a	p	a	p	a	p	a	p	a	p	
1st Fl. Conference															
1st Fl. Lounge															
Teleconferencing															
2nd Fl. Conference															
2nd Fl. Lounge															
McHaley Hall															
3rd. Fl. Conference															

LAW2.CGM

This graphic is available on the accompanying disk as LAW2.CGM.

TIP 449
Include Time Zone References to Ensure Accuracy

In today's global economy, many businesspeople must schedule appointments or create itineraries or schedules that cross time zones. For example, if you are in Boston, and create an itinerary that has the traveler arrive at Los Angeles at 10 A.M., does this mean you can make a 9 A.M. appointment, Los Angeles time? To maintain accuracy, make a point of adding the time zone designation to times in your documents.

These are the standard abbreviations for the various time zones:

Time Zone	Abbreviation	Region
Eastern standard time	EST	East Coast: New York City, Tallahassee
Eastern daylight time	EDT	
Central standard time	CST	Midwest: Chicago, Houston
Central daylight time	CDT	
Mountain standard time	MST	Far West: Denver, Phoenix
Mountain daylight time	MDT	
Pacific standard time	PST	West Coast: Seattle, Los Angeles
Pacific daylight time	PDT	

If you are writing to someone within your own time zone, but are writing about events that may occur after daylight savings time takes effect, include the abbreviation *DST* to indicate the time change.

Use the Default Format for the Date Line of Business Letters

TIP 450

Most business letters call for a date line that appears above the text of the letter indicating the date that the letter was sent or created. The standard form used for date lines is the default form used by WordPerfect. Therefore, you can simply insert the date, either as a code or as text, when you want to create the date line.

Remember to Set the Date and Time on Your System Correctly to Ensure That Date Codes Are Displayed Correctly

TIP 451

When WordPerfect inserts date text, or when it updates a date code, it uses the time set by your computer's internal clock to indicate the correct date and time. On older systems, the date and time

have to be set each time you start your computer. Most newer systems include an internal clock that maintains the current date and time for your computer. After being set with a time or date in the factory, it keeps counting the time, just like a clock. Just like a clock, however, you may find it necessary to reset the date occasionally. For example, leap years and changes to daylight savings are not programmed into most internal clocks. When you switch from standard to daylight savings time and back, you will have to change the date and time setting on your computer. You also will need to change the date and time if you change the battery in your computer.

To change the date:

1. At the DOS prompt, type **date**.
2. Type the correct date, in the format shown.
3. Press ENTER.

To change the time:

1. At the DOS prompt, type **time**.
2. Type the correct time, in the format shown.
   You do not need to include hundredths or thousandths of a second.
   (Entering these fractions correctly is nearly impossible.)
3. Press ENTER.

With Times in Tables or Columns, Align the Times on Their Colons

When you have numeric times, such as 8:30 or 4:14, in a table or tabular column, align them on the colon by using a decimal aligned tab and changing the decimal alignment character to a colon. When you add times such as 12 noon or 3 P.M. into a table or column, you want to align them on the space between the number and the letters. You also can do this by using decimal alignment and setting the alignment character to a space.

CHAPTER 11

Working with
Large Documents

Add Footnotes and Endnotes to Indicate Your Source of Information

When a document contains cited material or comments that are not part of the main document, you want to indicate your source. Footnotes and endnotes let you add text indicating where you got your information. Footnotes normally are at the bottom of the page and endnotes are at the end of a document. You can use both in the same document; for example, use footnotes for explanatory notes and endnotes for the sources you cite in the document. All of the options described for footnotes are also available for endnotes.

Use the Correct Format for Referencing Source Materials

When you use footnotes and endnotes for bibliographic entries, follow a consistent format for the type of information you are presenting. While there are many variations of format, you want to present the reference in a format your readers expect, such as that suggested by the Modern Language Association. For example, the following shows the format for a reference to a book and to a magazine.

The graphic shown is on the accompanying disk as SURFER.CGM. It is attached to the page and does not overlap with the text in the endnotes because the Endnote style that controls the appearance of endnotes has the right margin set to 4.25 inches.

SURFER.CGM

You Can Set When WordPerfect Restarts Numbering Footnotes

TIP 455

Footnotes and endnotes can either be numbered from the beginning to the end of a document or they can start with 1 on every page. You can select one of these numbering styles by selecting Layout or pressing CTRL-F7, selecting Footnote or Endnote, and then selecting Options. In WordPerfect 5.1, select Start Footnote Numbers each Page and Yes. In WordPerfect 6, select the Restart Footnote Numbers each Page check box. Then, with both releases, press F7 to return to the document.

The other type of renumbering for footnotes and endnotes is to change the number used by the next footnote or endnote. To set the next number used in WordPerfect 5.1, select Layout or press CTRL-F7, select Footnote or Endnote, and select New Number. Type the number of the next footnote or endnote and press ENTER. To set the next number used in WordPerfect 6, select Layout or press CTRL-F7, select Footnote or Endnote, and select New Number. From the dialog box, you can select New Number and enter the number of the next footnote or endnote. You can also change the numbering style, increase or decrease the footnote or endnote number, or display it in the document. Select OK until you return to the document.

You Can Set How Footnotes and Endnotes Are Separated

TIP 456

WordPerfect has several defaults for how footnotes or endnotes appear in the footnote or endnote section. WordPerfect will add a two-inch line separating the document from its footnotes. The text for each note is single spaced with .167-inch space between notes. Also, when the page has more space than needed for the document text and its footnotes, WordPerfect puts the footnotes right after the end of the text rather than at the bottom of the page. If you want to use different settings, you can change them.

To change these footnote settings, select Layout or press CTRL-F7 and select Footnote Options. Select Line Separating Text and Footnotes in WordPerfect 5.1 or Footnote Separator Line in WordPerfect 6 to change the line from a two-inch line to no line or another type of line. WordPerfect 6 has several options for the type of line, position, length, and spacing of any line you use. You can select Spacing Within Footnotes to change how footnotes are spaced and Spacing Between Footnotes to change how much space separates footnotes and endnotes. Amount of Note to Keep Together sets the vertical space of a footnote that must be treated as a unit. You can also select Footnotes at Bottom of Page (and select Yes in WordPerfect 5.1) to have the footnotes printed at the bottom of the page even when there is space after the document text to put the footnotes higher. When you are finished, press F7 to return to the document.

You Can Set the Style of Footnotes or Endnotes

The footnote or endnote numbers are superscript and indented. You can change the appearance of the footnote or endnote number indicator. The character and codes that you use for the footnote or endnote are at the beginning of the entry for every footnote or endnote added after this point. When you change the footnote or endnote style, you can use function keys and, in WordPerfect 6, menus, to add formatting that the footnotes or endnotes should include.

To customize the footnote/endnote indicator in WordPerfect 5.1:

1. Select **L**ayout or press CTRL-F7 and select **F**ootnote or **E**ndnote.
2. Select **O**ptions Style for Number in **N**ote.
3. Type the entry you want each note to start with and press ENTER.
   The code for footnote and endnote numbers can be added by pressing CTRL-F7, selecting **F**ootnote or **E**ndnote, and selecting Number **C**ode.
4. Press F7 (Exit) to return to the document.

In WordPerfect 6, follow these steps:

1. Select **L**ayout or press CTRL-F7 and select **F**ootnote or **E**ndnote.
2. Select Edit **S**tyle in Note.
3. Type the entry you want each note to start with.
   The code for the footnote and endnote numbers can be added by pressing CTRL-F7, selecting **F**ootnote or **E**ndnote, **N**umber **D**isplay in Document, and then OK.
4. Press F7 until you return to the document.

Let WordPerfect Indicate When Footnotes Will Extend Beyond One Page

WordPerfect will only use about two-fifths of a page for footnotes. When the contents of a footnote are long, it will be split across several pages. To make sure your reader understands that the footnote continues on to the next page, you can have WordPerfect print a "continued" message in the footnote. Select Layout or press CTRL-F7, select Footnote Options, select the Print Continued Message check box, and press F7 to return to the document.

You Can Change the Way Footnotes Are Identified in the Document

The footnote or endnote numbers in a document are superscript but you can change their appearance by changing the style of the note's number in the document. When you edit the note's style in the document, you will see a code for the location where WordPerfect inserts the number of the footnote or endnote.

In WordPerfect 5.1, select Layout or press CTRL-F7, select Footnote or Endnote, select Options Style for Number in Text. Change the entry to what you want to appear for each note. You can add codes with the function key combinations that invoke the feature. You can add the code for the note number by pressing CTRL-F7, selecting Footnote or Endnote, and selecting Number Code. Press ENTER and F7 to return to the document.

In WordPerfect 6, select Layout or press CTRL-F7, select Footnote or Endnote, select Edit Style in Document, and type the entry you want to use for each note. You can use the keys and menus to add the codes for the features you want to add. Footnote and endnote numbers can be added by pressing CTRL-F7, selecting Footnote or Endnote, selecting New Number Display in Document, and then OK. Press F7 until you return to the document to complete the change.

You Can Delete Footnotes by Deleting the Footnote Character in the Document

When you want to remove a footnote or endnote, all you have to do is move to the character in the document marking the footnote or endnote and press DEL. WordPerfect handles removing the text of the footnote and renumbering the remaining footnotes or endnotes in the document.

You Can Create Footnotes Using Different Symbols

Besides using numbers or letters to indicate footnotes and endnotes, you can use symbols. For example, you can have the footnotes use the *, dagger, double dagger, section, and paragraph symbols. To use different symbols instead of numbers, you must follow an extra three steps. Before you add the footnote, you must reset the number to 1, tell WordPerfect you want to use characters to indicate footnotes, and select the character to use.

In WordPerfect 5.1, select Layout or press CTRL-F7, select Footnote or Endnote, select Options Footnote Numbering Method Characters, type the character to use, and press ENTER. Then select Layout or press CTRL-F7, select Footnote or Endnote, and select New Number, type 1, and press ENTER.

In WordPerfect 6, select Layout or press CTRL-F7, select Footnote or Endnote, and select New Number. Select New Number, type 1, and press ENTER. Then select Numbering Method and Characters. Finally, select Character, type the character to use, press ENTER, and select OK. You can also create a macro to perform these three steps for you. The FONTCHAR macro shown here will perform these steps for footnotes in WordPerfect 6.

```
DISPLAY(Off!)
FootnoteNewNumber(1)
GETSTRING(Character;"Press Ctrl-W for a list";"Enter character to
      use as the footnote";2)
FootnoteNumberMethod(Characters!;Character)
FootnoteCreate
```

When you perform this macro, you will be prompted for the character to use as the footnote. When you select the character, the macro adds the footnote using the character and waits for you to enter the text for the footnote.

This sample macro is available on the accompanying disk as FONTCHAR.WPM.

FONTCHAR.WPM

If You Are Working with a Large Document, Consider Making It a Master Document

T I P
462

If you prefer working with smaller documents, consider breaking up your large documents into a master document and its subdocuments. A master document is a document that is a placeholder for where other documents are inserted. For example, you can create one master document for this entire book and have the separate chapters be the master document's subdocuments. When you want to work on a section, you retrieve the document used as a subdocument or edit the document when the master document is expanded. When you want to print the entire master document, you expand the master document, as described in Tip 467.

To add another document as a subdocument of the current document, select Mark in WordPerfect 5.1 or File Master Document in WordPerfect 6. Next, select Subdocument and then enter the filename of the document to use as a subdocument. When you add the subdocument, it looks like the following, in WordPerfect 5.1 and in WordPerfect 6's Text and Graphics display modes:

```
 File  Edit  View  Layout  Tools  Font  Graphics  Window  Help
                        Schedule of Activities

  ┌──────────────────────────────────────────────────────────────┐
  │ Subdoc: EVENTS                                                 │
  └──────────────────────────────────────────────────────────────┘
 |
                                Map
```

You Can Use Many Types of Documents as WordPerfect 6 Subdocuments

WordPerfect 6 lets you use files as subdocuments that are not in a WordPerfect 6 format. For example, you can have Word for Windows documents as subdocuments for a WordPerfect 6 master document. When you expand the master document, you will be prompted to select the format of the file you are using as a subdocument; just as when you open a document that is not in WordPerfect's format. Since WordPerfect has such extensive features for working with subdocuments, the master document must remain a WordPerfect format document. Some of the WordPerfect features, such as indexes, that you might want to use with subdocuments will not work when you keep the subdocuments saved in a format other than WordPerfect.

You Can Make an Entry in the Master Document for a Subdocument That You Have Not Created Yet

When you select a document to use as a subdocument, you can enter the name of a document that does not exist yet or one that exists in a different location. However, when you expand the master document, you will see a message that WordPerfect could not find a subdocument. At that point, you can select New Filename and supply a new filename to use in place of the file WordPerfect does not find. Or you can select Skip, and WordPerfect will skip over expanding the document it cannot find.

WordPerfect Documents Can Be Either Master Documents or Subdocuments

Every WordPerfect document can be a master document or subdocument. The only difference between a master document and a subdocument is that a master document contains codes indicating where another document should be inserted. Other than the codes for the subdocument, the documents are the same.

Subdocuments Can Also Have Subdocuments

Just as a master document can have a subdocument, a subdocument can be a master document to other documents. When you expand the initial master document, both its subdocuments and the subdocuments of its subdocuments are expanded. For example, the document ANNUAL.RPT can have the subdocument SALESRPT. The SALESRPT document can have subdocuments named DIVIS1 and DIVIS2. When you expand ANNUAL.RPT, it includes the contents of the SALESRPT document as well as the DIVIS1 and DIVIS2 documents.

You Must Expand a Master Document Before You See the Subdocuments

When you add a subdocument to a master document, WordPerfect only displays a box indicating the document's position. You will not see the contents of the subdocuments until you expand the master document.

To expand a master document in WordPerfect 5.1, press ALT-F5 (Mark Text) and select Generate Expand Master Document, or select Mark Master Documents Expand. To expand a master document in WordPerfect 6, select File Master Document Expand, select OK, and select Yes as confirmation. From the Expand Master Document dialog box, you can also select Subdocuments and select which documents to expand. Move to the subdocument name and press the SPACEBAR, or click the subdocument name to add or remove the mark next to the filename. The subdocument names with a mark are expanded while the others are not.

You Can Edit Subdocuments by Themselves or as Part of a Master Document

When you want to change a subdocument, you have two choices. You can retrieve the document into a window, edit it, and then save it again after making the changes. You can also edit the subdocument

when it appears in the master document. When you compress the master document, you can save the subdocuments, as described in Tip 474. Changes you make to the subdocument within the master document that you subsequently save, have the same effect as opening the subdocument separately and making the change there. Decide how to edit your subdocuments by the method that is convenient for you, based on whether you want only to modify the subdocument or you want to work with the master document as well as the subdocument.

You Must Select How Subdocuments Are Separated

TIP 469

If you want subdocuments that are part of a master document to start on a new page, add a page break before the code that inserts the subdocument. The master document will use any page breaks in the subdocument, so you can also add page breaks as part of the subdocument that you want the master document to use.

To Eliminate a Subdocument, Delete the Codes from the Compressed Master

TIP 470

When you no longer want a subdocument in a master document, compress the subdocument out of the master document, as described in Tip 474. Next, move to the box that indicates the beginning or end of the subdocument (you do not want to do this from Page Display mode in WordPerfect 6). Delete the box and the code, which represents where WordPerfect inserts the document. The next time you expand the master document, the subdocument for the code you just deleted is not included. Remember to compress the subdocument you want to delete. Otherwise, you will convert the subdocument text into text that is part of the master document, as described in Tip 477.

If you use the File Manager to delete the master document, you are prompted for whether or not you want to delete the subdocuments. Selecting Yes deletes the subdocuments of a master document and selecting No deletes only the master document while leaving the subdocument files intact.

Printing an Expanded Master Document Numbers All Pages, Footnotes, and Endnotes Sequentially

TIP 471

When you expand subdocuments that are part of a master document, WordPerfect handles numbering in the document from beginning to end. Any page numbers, footnote numbers, endnote numbers, graphics boxes, and other WordPerfect substructures are numbered sequentially. This means that you can print a subdocument separately, and everything is numbered starting with 1. However, when you include this subdocument in a master document, the subdocument will start with whatever page it is within the master document.

As an example, suppose you have a two-page master document that includes a two-page subdocument and a three-page subdocument. When you print the subdocuments separately, the first page in each subdocument is numbered page 1. When you expand the master document and print it, the master and subdocuments are numbered sequentially, as shown here:

Document	Page Number When Printed Separately	Page Number When Printed in Master Document
Master: 1st page	1	1
Subdocument 1	1	2
	2	3
Subdocument 2	1	4
	2	5
	3	6
Master: 2nd page	2	7

Footnotes and Pages Can Be Numbered Within Master or Subdocuments

TIP 472

As Tip 471 mentioned, WordPerfect numbers substructures in a master document sequentially, including the substructures in the subdocuments, as if they were part of their own document. You

may want a subdocument within the master document to use its own numbering system. For example, you may want each chapter of a master document to number footnotes or pages separately. Tip 135 describes using multiple page levels in WordPerfect 6, which you may want to use in a master document to create page numbers that include chapter numbers as well. To restart counting structures for each subdocument, you need to add codes with numbering instructions for the particular structure. The easiest place to do this is right before the code that puts the subdocument into the master document. Once you put the codes here, you can copy them and place them before the other subdocument codes in the master document. See Tip 136 for more information about resetting the next page number; Tip 642 for resetting the next graphics box number; and Tip 455 for how to reset footnote numbers.

As an example, suppose you have a two-page master document that includes a two-page subdocument and a three-page subdocument. Before each subdocument code is the [HPg] code for the page break. The master document also has the codes for setting and incrementing chapter page numbers before the code that adds each subdocument. An overview of the structure of the document and the codes it uses looks like this:

> *Master Document*
> Table of Contents
> [code for chapter and page number]
> [HPg - Hard Page Break]
> [Set Chapter Number]
> *Subdocument 1*
> [Increment Chapter Number and Reset Page Number]
> [HPg - Hard Page Break]
> *Subdocument 2*
> [HPg - Hard Page Break]
> Index

You Don't Have to Hide Subdocument Comments

TIP 473

When you print a master document, the comments indicating where subdocuments begin and end do not appear (nor do the subdocuments appear if you have not expanded the master document). Subdocument comments are the same as comments you create in documents, so they are never printed.

You Can Select Which Subdocuments Are Saved when You Compress a Master Document

When you compress a master document so it no longer shows the contents of a subdocument, you can select which of the subdocuments are saved. If you make changes to a subdocument within the master document and do not save the document when you compress the master document, the next time you expand the master document or use the subdocument, the changes you have made will not be included.

In WordPerfect 5.1, after you select **Mark Master Documents Condense** or press ALT-F5 (Mark Text) and select **Condense Master Document**, you can select **Yes** when prompted to save the subdocuments. For each subdocument, you are prompted for replacing the version on the disk with the version of the subdocument in the master document. To save the subdocument changes made in a master document, select **Yes**. To save every subdocument in the master document without further prompts, select **Replace All Remaining**. To skip over saving the one currently displayed, select **No**.

In WordPerfect 6, after you select **File Master Document Condense**, the Condense Master Document dialog box lists all of the subdocuments in the current document. You can select **Subdocuments** and select the subdocuments you want saved. When you select OK, only the subdocuments that have the X are saved.

Expand a Master Document when You Want to Be Sure You Are Using the Latest Version

Before you print a master document, you will want to be sure that it contains the latest version of any subdocuments. When you repeat the expansion process described in Tip 467, WordPerfect will update every subdocument in the master document.

Save the Compressed Master Document to Save Disk Space

When you save a master document, it can be saved either with the subdocuments in the master document or with the subdocument codes only. Saving the master document with the subdocuments compressed, as described in Tip 474, makes the version of the master file smaller. Saving the master document with the subdocuments expanded will of course make the document larger and use more disk space; however, the next time you retrieve the document, the subdocuments are already expanded.

In WordPerfect 5.1, when you save a master document that is expanded, you will see a prompt to compress the documents. Selecting Yes compresses the documents to make the saved version of the master document smaller; selecting No saves the master document with the subdocuments.

In WordPerfect 6, if the master document you are saving has uncompressed subdocuments, you will be prompted to compress the documents. Selecting Yes brings up the Condense Master Document dialog box. When you select OK, WordPerfect will compress the documents to make the saved version of the master document smaller. If you select No from the first prompt, WordPerfect saves the master document with the subdocuments.

Once an expanded master document is saved, you will not see the prompt for compressing the document when you save the document again, until you compress the document.

You Can Convert a Subdocument to Text Within the Original Master Document

You can put a subdocument in the master document as though you were retrieving the subdocument's contents into the master. When the subdocument is expanded into the master document, simply delete the comment indicating the beginning or ending of the subdocument. This deletes the [Subdoc Begin] and [Subdoc End] codes, and the contents between the codes remain and are now part of the text in the master document.

Give All the Documents in a Master Document a Consistent Appearance

TIP 478

You can use styles for all of the documents in a master document to give a consistent appearance to the overall document. Rather than develop the styles in each document separately, develop the styles in one of the documents and then save the styles in a style library. In the other documents that you want to have the same appearance, attach the style library or retrieve it. Attaching and retrieving style libraries are described in Tip 415. All of the documents that use the style library will use the same styles. Also, in WordPerfect 6, changing the style saved in the style library will change how that style appears in every document that uses the style library.

Beware of Conflicting Styles in Subdocuments

TIP 479

A master document acquires all of the styles in the subdocuments expanded into it. The subdocument will pick up all of the styles from the master document if you save the subdocument from the master document. Otherwise, formatting changes done in the master document will have no effect when you open the subdocument separately. If a style is used by more than one subdocument, the master document and all subdocuments saved while using the master document will use the first style with that name expanded into the document.

If two subdocuments use different styles with the same name, both uses of the style will use the style set by the first subdocument opened with that name. Styles in the master document have preference over styles with the same name in the subdocuments.

For example, if you have a document named MASTER with two subdocuments named SUB1 and SUB2, the named styles in the MASTER document include the ones you created in this document along with the ones you created in SUB1 and SUB2. If you save SUB1 or SUB2 from MASTER, the subdocument includes all of the styles in MASTER (and by attribution, the styles in the other subdocuments). If SUB1 or SUB2 have a style named Title1 that is also used by the MASTER document, all text that uses the Title1 style uses the style contents of the Title1 style in the MASTER document even if the text using the Title1 style is in a subdocument. Also, if SUB1 and SUB2 have a style named Important, both subdocuments will use the style contents of the Important style in the SUB1 document.

Document Formatting Changes Both the Master Document and the Subdocuments

When you expand subdocuments into a master document, the document formatting in the master document will affect the subdocument. For example, if a master document is double spaced and you expand a subdocument that does not have its own spacing set, the subdocument will also have double spacing. Formatting changes set by the master document are in effect for the subdocuments. However, this is only until one of the subdocuments has a competing code that changes the formatting for the rest of the document, including other subdocuments. Also, the subdocuments will not adopt the formatting changes until they are expanded into the master document. Formatting changes made with the master document do not affect the subdocument when you open the document separately. Formatting changes you make between the [Subdoc Begin] and [Subdoc End] codes will be included in the subdocument if it is saved from the master document.

As an example, suppose you have a document named MASTER with two subdocuments named SUB1 and SUB2. If MASTER has the font set to Dutch 801 Roman, when you expand the document, the SUB1 and SUB2 documents will also use this font—if they do not have their own font setting. However, suppose SUB1 has the font set to Swiss 721 Roman. From the point of the code for the Swiss 721 Roman font until the end of the document (or another font code), SUB1, SUB2, and MASTER will use the new font. When you open SUB2 separately, it will not use either font (unless you have set the initial font to one of these fonts) because the codes that set the font to Dutch 801 Roman or Swiss 721 Roman are not part of that document.

When you expand a master document, its document initial codes will override conflicting subdocument's initial codes. If you save a subdocument from the master document, the subdocument will include the initial codes of the master document as part of its own initial codes.

Master and Subdocuments Have Separate Passwords

As Tip 847 mentions, you can protect a document with a password. Master and subdocuments have their passwords set separately. When you expand a master document that has password-protected subdocuments, WordPerfect will prompt you for the correct password before expanding a protected document.

Use Generated Entries to Create Indexes, Lists, Cross-References, Tables of Contents, and Tables of Authorities

If you need to create indexes, lists, cross-references, tables of contents, or tables of authorities, you will want to use WordPerfect's generated entries. Generated entries use text from a document the way the text for each tip in this book is used for the table of contents. WordPerfect handles the page references. As text shifts between pages, you can regenerate the text, and page numbers are updated in the entry. For each type of generated entry (index, table of contents, and so on), you have three steps. First, you select the text used to generate entries. Second, you select where you want the generated entries. Third, you generate the entries, as described in Tip 484. The first and second steps can be performed in any order. The types of generated entries you can create and their purposes are

- ❑ *Indexes* to give the page where a term or idea is used.

- ❑ *Lists of items* in a document; for example, lists of all of the graphics or tables in a document with their page numbers.

- ❑ *Cross-references*, which include the page or graphics box number in the text of a document.

- ❑ *Tables of contents* to reference headings used in a document.

- ❑ *Tables of authorities* to list legal citations divided by the source of the citation, such as a type of court or legislative ruling.

If a Document Contains Generated Entries, Regenerate Entries Before Saving Them

Since WordPerfect only updates generated entries when you regenerate the entries in a document, you want to regenerate the entries as described in Tip 484 before you print them. When you print a document containing generated entries, if you have not generated the entries just before printing, WordPerfect will remind you to do so.

Indexes, Lists, Cross-References, Tables of Contents, and Tables of Authorities Do Not Appear Until You Generate Them

As you are setting up indexes, lists, cross-references, tables of contents, and tables of authorities, you will not see these entries. The document will not contain them until you generate the entries. Generating entries generates all of the entries you have defined for a document at the same time; you cannot generate only one type of entry at a time.

To generate indexes, lists, cross-references, tables of contents, and tables of authorities in WordPerfect 5.1, select **Mark** or press ALT-F5 (Mark Text), then select Generate Generate Tables, Indexes, Cross-References, etc., and **Yes**. To generate the entries in WordPerfect 6, select Tools Generate. You will be prompted for whether WordPerfect should save any modified subdocuments. When you select OK or **Yes**, WordPerfect generates the entries for you.

If you have changes you consistently make every time you generate entries (such as deleting some of the index entries), put a reminder of the changes to make in hidden text (see Tip 170) or a document comment (see Tip 71). This will help you remember to make any changes after you regenerate the index.

Generated Entries Can Be Put in Master or Subdocuments

When you are defining the indexes, lists, cross-references, tables of contents, and tables of authorities for a master document and subdocument, you need to decide which document contains the generated entry definition. Where you place the definition decides where the compiled information is placed. Most of the time, the generated entries definition will be placed in the master document in a section outside of the subdocuments. For example, you will usually put a table of contents and index in a master document, since you want it to include the table of contents and index entries for the master document and its subdocuments.

Be Careful Putting Text Around Generated Entries

Put any labels, headings, or graphics for an index, list, cross-reference, table of contents, and table of authorities before the code that defines it. If you put entries between any [Begin Gen Text] and [End Gen Text] codes, these entries are removed the next time you generate entries in the document. Every time you generate entries, WordPerfect deletes everything between the [Begin Gen Text] and [End Gen Text] codes. The entries you want before the generated text should be placed before the [Def Mark] code that marks the placement of the generated entries. The entries you want after the generated text should be placed after the [Def Mark] or the [End Gen Text] code, whichever comes later. As an example, suppose you create the following table of contents:

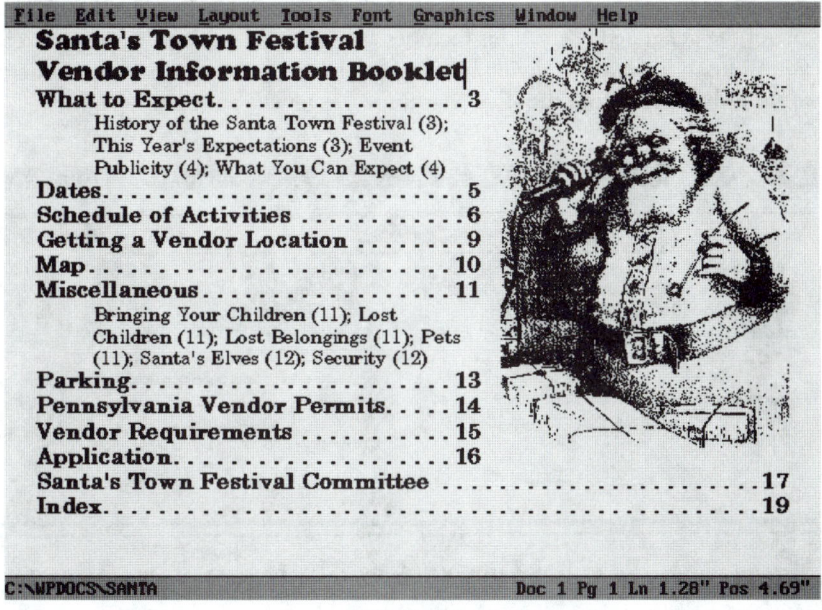

The two lines of heading text and the graphics are added before the [Def Mark] code. If you accidentally put them after the code, when you generate the table of contents, they are placed after the table of contents. Or, if you put them in between the [Begin Gen Text] and [End Gen Text] that WordPerfect uses to mark the boundaries of generated text, the text and graphics will be deleted. Remember, when you generate entries, WordPerfect deletes everything between the [Begin Gen Text] and [End Gen Text] codes.

SANTA.PCX

The graphic shown previously resides on the accompanying disk as SANTA.PCX.

Put Any Formatting You Want to Apply to a Generated Entry Before the Code That Defines the Entry

If you want generated entries (indexes, lists, cross-references, tables of contents, and tables of authorities) to include formatting of their own, place the formatting before the [Def Mark] code that marks the start of the generated entry. This includes tab stops, fonts, page breaks, and columns. For example, if you want an index to be divided into two columns, as shown here, the code that sets the newspaper columns belongs before the [Def Mark] for the generated entry.

| File | Edit | View | Layout | Tools | Font | Graphics | Window | Help |

Index

Activities		
Creating Your Own 6		Parking
Provided by Festival 8		General 13
Admission		Vendor 13
General Public. 4		Pennsylvania
Vendor. 9, 15, 16		Vendor License 14
Advertisements 4		Food Service Requirements. . 14
Application. 15, 16		Pets. 11
Attendance. 4		Planning Committee 17
		Publicity 4

You Do Not Have to Expand a Master Document Before You Generate Entries

When you are generating entries in a master document, you do not have to expand a master document first. When you generate indexes, lists, cross-references, tables of contents, or tables of authorities for a master document, WordPerfect expands the master document behind the scenes. After the entries are generated, the document is again compressed. Since WordPerfect must expand and compress the master

document when you generate entries, generating them will take longer if the document is compressed. In WordPerfect 5.1, you will also see a prompt about updating the subdocument. In WordPerfect 6, this prompt instead appears as the Save Modified Subdocuments check box. You will want to save the modified documents if, during the generation process, WordPerfect changes text in the subdocuments.

Save a Document Before Generating Entries

Before you generate entries in a document, especially the first time, save the document. If you don't like what you get, it is easy enough to close the document and return to the version before you generated the data. The first few times you generate entries, you can easily forget to put text outside of the area where WordPerfect will generate the entries. It is easier to regenerate entries than to handle misplaced codes.

Make Sure to Look Over Entries You Have Just Generated

Most of the biggest mistakes in generated entries can be discovered by scanning the entries as soon as you generate them. Don't be surprised if, after you generate entries the first time, you close the document and return to the prior version. It is very easy to make a mistake in how the generated entries are shown. In an index, for example, you will want to check that you have consistent capitalization and whether you have any entries that should be combined.

Change WordPerfect 6 System Styles to Change Many Features of Generated Entries

Most generated entries in WordPerfect 6 use system styles. For example, in a table of contents the first level headings use the TableofCont1 style. Rather than changing the format of these entries yourself,

change them by changing the system styles. Changing the system styles has another advantage since when you regenerate the entries, the regenerated entries continue using the modified styles; but if you change the generated entries without changing the styles, the entries return to their original appearance. The codes for the different generated entries are Index# for indexes, List for lists, TableofCont# for tables of contents, and TableofAuth for tables of authorities. The # represents the level of the generated entry, so it is replaced by a number. By changing the contents of the system style, you change the appearance of the generated entry. Tip 423 has more information about changing system styles.

Make Sure to Delete All Text and Codes when Removing an Index or Table of Contents

If you want to delete an index or table of contents that you have generated, make sure to remove all of the text from the [Def Mark] code to the [End Gen Text] code. If you do not delete the [Def Mark] code, the next time you generate entries, the generated entries you removed will reappear, although they will be more up to date than the ones you deleted.

You Can Convert Generated Entries so They Will No Longer Be Generated

You can convert generated entries so they will no longer be generated by deleting the [Def Mark] and [Begin Gen Text] codes. This puts a table of contents permanently into a document without further adjustments. After you delete the [Def Mark] and [Begin Gen Text] codes, the generated entries are in the document just as if you entered the data in yourself. However, the entries will continue to use the styles WordPerfect added when WordPerfect generated the entries. If you forget to delete the [Def Mark] code, WordPerfect will regenerate the generated entries. If you forget to delete the [Begin Gen Text], which also removes the [End Gen Text], when you generate entries in the document again, WordPerfect will delete everything between the [Begin Gen Text] and the [End Gen Text] codes.

Generated Entries Can Use Different WordPerfect 6 Page Levels

When a WordPerfect 6 document uses multiple levels of page numbers, as described in Tip 135, you do not have to do anything special to have these page numbers included in your indexes, lists, cross-references, tables of contents, and tables of authorities. WordPerfect automatically uses the page numbers in the same format that they appear in the document. If you want to change the format of the page numbers, you can do it when you define where WordPerfect places the generated entries. Most generated entries have a Page Number Format. Selecting this and then **Different** from Document, lets you enter the format you want the generated entries to use. For example, if you are using chapters in a document and each chapter has its own table of contents, you may want to exclude the chapter numbers.

You Must Redefine Generated Entries to Change the Definition

If you want to change the definition of an index, list, table of contents, or table of authorities, you will have to redefine how WordPerfect generates the entries. You cannot edit the code that defines the generated entries.

Use Text in a Document for Index Entries

Before WordPerfect can generate an index, you must select the text used for index entries. Creating an index entry adds an [Index] code to the document. Concordance files described in Tip 505 provide one method of creating index entries. Another method is to block the text to use, or if it is only one word, move to the word to use as the index entry.

Next, in WordPerfect 5.1, select Mark or press ALT-F5 (Mark Text) and select Index. The selected text appears as the heading entry. You can modify this entry if you want. Press ENTER to complete the heading for the index entry. Next, you can type any subheading entry if you are using more than one level. Press ENTER.

In WordPerfect 6, select Tools Index Mark or press ALT-F5 and select Mark Text Index. The text will appear as the heading in the index. You can replace the entry as well as make an additional entry in the Subheading text box if you want to create a second level index entry. Select OK.

Before you can generate an index for the entries you have added, you must define where the index is to be placed. Tips 499 and 504 have more information about defining an index. Once an index is defined and you have index entries to include, you are ready to generate the index, as described in Tip 484.

As an illustration of how an index is created, when WordPerfect generates an index, it searches the document for codes for index entries. (These codes do not appear in the text, but surround text in a document to indicate text that WordPerfect should include as an index entry.) It also searches for text that matches entries in a concordance file, as described in Tip 505. WordPerfect takes these entries, alphabetizes them, and combines multiple references for the same index entry. A diagram of what WordPerfect is doing looks like this:

Code for
index
entries

Concordance file

Lost Children
Lost Belongings
Security

Santa's Elves

All during the festival, you will see Santa's Elves. They are here to wander around, amuse the children, and keep an eye on the festival. The elves are also present to provide many services (see Lost Children, Lost Belongings, Security). All the elves will be dressed in the same outfits with the bright red and green sacks. Their sacks contain candy, information sheets, and a walkie talkie. If you encounter problems, call them. As they are present for everyone's safety, treat them kindly (a nasty elf is no fun).

Index

Lost Belongings _____
Lost Children _____
Santa's Elves
Security _____
Walkie Talkie

You Do Not Have to Use Text That Appears in the Document for the Index Entry

TIP 497

You can have different text for an entry, such as when you want an index entry to include its abbreviation. For example, you might want to add an index entry for What You See Is What You Get (WYSIWYG) and have it reference text that either has What You See Is What You Get or WYSIWYG. To create these index entries, move to the point in the text where you want the index entry to reference but do not select the text. Instead, select Mark Index in WordPerfect 5.1 or Tools Index Mark in WordPerfect 6, and edit or type the text to make the entry you want in the index.

You Can Add Page References to Existing Entries in WordPerfect 6 Indexes

TIP 498

A quick method of adding another page reference to the same WordPerfect 6 index entry is to select the index entry from a list of those you have already defined. When you use this method to have more than one page reference for the same index entry, you ensure that you do not have discrepancies between similar entries you want treated as the same.

To do this, move to where you want the index entry to reference. Next, select Tools Index Mark or press ALT-F5 and select Mark Text Index. In the dialog box, press F5 or click the List Index Marks button. From the list of existing index entries, highlight the one you want. Select either Select Complete Mark to use both the heading and subheading for the index entry you are creating or Select Heading Only to use the heading for the index entry. Select OK to complete adding the current location as another page reference to the same index entry.

To Define the Index, Tell WordPerfect Where You Want It Placed

Besides telling WordPerfect the entries you want in the index, as described in Tips 496 and 497, you must also tell WordPerfect where you want the compiled index placed. This step defines the index. You can select the options the index uses. After you define the index's location, as described below, you can generate it (as described in Tip 484) using the entries you have created or using the entries automatically generated with a concordance file.

To tell WordPerfect 5.1 where you want the index placed, move to the location where you want the index to begin and select Mark Define Index. Type the name of any concordance file. Press ENTER. From the next screen, select how you want the page numbers indicated. When you select one of these choices, WordPerfect adds the [Def Mark] code that indicates the location of the index.

To tell WordPerfect 6 where you want the index placed, move to the location where you want the index to begin and select Tools Index Define. From the Define Index dialog box, you can select how the page numbers are indicated, the styles to use for the two levels of index entries, whether a series of pages are joined (for example, 1,2,3 or 1-3), whether you use the same page numbering style as the entire document uses, and any concordance file. When you select OK, WordPerfect adds the [Def Mark] code that indicates the location of the index.

Any index heading must be put above the [Mark Def] code. As Tip 487 mentions, you want text to appear above the generated text.

Search For Words Like *Named* and *Called* to Find Text That Should Be in the Index

When you are reviewing a document for entries to index, one quick way to find entries you might want to include is to look for words that draw attention to new terms. This often includes words like *named* and *called,* as in the phrase "a graphical interface called WYSIWYG." You may also want to look for the underline or italics codes that frequently mark new terms. You can find both the words and the codes using the search feature available when you press F2.

Unusual Index Entries Are Caused by the Source of the Index Reference

TIP 501

If you see any unusual characters in your index entry when you generate it, look at the location it references. You will see the same unusual characters in the document where the [Index] code is located. This includes soft returns and page breaks. If you want to remove these characters from the index entry, change the entry's definition (or change the highlighting of the entry) so that instead of including the unwanted characters as part of the blocked index entry, it only references a single point—then you can type the correct index entry.

A frequent cause of problems in an index is varying punctuation or singular versus plural words. WordPerfect will not combine index entries of "deadline" and "deadline." for example. Nor will it join "deadline" and "deadlines" index entries; they will be two separate entries if you mark them both. When you look through the generated index, look for these types of problems. You will want to replace the index entry to be consistent or change the index entry's heading to match.

Case Differences Can Make Index Entries Confusing

TIP 502

Another frequent cause of problems in an index is varying capitalization. WordPerfect picks up the capitalization style of an index entry the first time it appears. When you use a concordance file, the index entry will use the capitalization style of the concordance file. If you want to change the capitalization style of the entries in the generated index, replace the first instance of an index entry with the capitalization that you want.

Include Multiple References to the Same Topic when You Want a Reference to Span Pages

TIP 503

When you want an index entry to span several pages, use the same index entry on all of the pages. WordPerfect joins pages to span a range when you have three or more consecutive page numbers

containing the same index entry. This means that if the same index entry is used on pages 4, 5, and 6, WordPerfect puts it in the index as 4-6.

You can quickly have the same index entry in multiple locations by copying the [Index] code for the entry. Block the entry and copy it to the other locations that you want included in the range.

You Can Create Your Own Index Styles or Use One of the Styles in WordPerfect 6

In WordPerfect 6, you can change the appearance of the generated entries in the index by changing the styles. The entries in the generated index use the Index1 and Index2 styles by default. You can modify these styles or create your own. Select Tools Index Define to define the index; then to set the index entry appearance, select Index Level Styles. For either the Heading or Subheading index level, you can select Edit and Style Contents to change the contents of the style the index entry uses. You can also select Create to create a style used by the index entry and then define the style, as described in Tip 491. You can also select another style by choosing Select and the style to use. When you select Close, the index entries for the index you are defining will use the styles you have chosen.

In WordPerfect 5.1, use ALT-F2 *(Replace) to replace the [->Indent][->Indent<-][<-Mar Rel][<-Mar Rel] codes with the codes you want the index entries to use.*

Use Concordance Files to Pick Up Index Entries Automatically

A concordance file is a file containing lines of text, which speeds up generating index entries by providing selected words or phrases that are automatically included as index entries. When WordPerfect creates an index and finds one of the words or phrases in a concordance file in a document, it picks up that location

as an index entry. WordPerfect picks up index entries that you create and those created from the concordance file. After you generate an index, you will not notice any difference in the document by using a concordance file, because WordPerfect does not mark the document for the index entries generated by a concordance file.

To create a concordance file, enter the index entries on separate lines in a WordPerfect document, as shown here:

```
File  Edit  View  Layout  Tools  Font  Graphics  Window  Help

    Children
    Dates
    Day Passes
    Deadlines
    Displays
    Drop off
    Permits
```

These entries will be separate headings in the index. If you want to create subheadings, you must add codes to the concordance file for the subheading entry by typing the entry, as described in Tip 497. The text in the concordance file must match exactly, except for case. For example, "DATE" in the concordance file will match "date" in a document, but it will not match "DATES". The entries in the index will have the capitalization style of the entries in the concordance file. Use the concordance file entries to give the index entries a consistent capitalization style.

You need to tell WordPerfect that the index will use a concordance file as part of the process of defining the index. In WordPerfect 5.1, when you select Mark Define Index, type the name of the concordance file and press ENTER. In WordPerfect 6, when you select Tools Index Define, select Concordance Filename and enter the name of the concordance file.

Make Index Generation Faster by Sorting Your Concordance File

When you create an index using a concordance file, WordPerfect will create the index faster if the concordance file is in alphabetical order. Sort the entries by selecting Tools Sort and selecting OK twice. This works if you do not have any subheadings in the concordance file.

Define the Table of Contents By Telling WordPerfect Where You Want It Placed

Besides telling WordPerfect the entries for a table of contents, as described in Tips 509 and 510, you must also tell WordPerfect where you want the table of contents by defining it. Defining the table of contents also selects the options it uses. After you define the table of contents, as described below, you can create it by generating the entries in the document as described in Tip 484.

To tell WordPerfect 5.1 where you want the table of contents, move to the location where you want it and select **Mark Define** Table of Contents. Select **Number** of Levels, type the number of levels you want, and press ENTER. Select **Display** Last Level in Wrapped Format and **Yes** if you want the headings for the last level wrapped into one paragraph. Select **Page** Numbering to change the style of each level used to one of those presented. When you press F7 (Exit) to return to the document, WordPerfect adds the [Def Mark] code, which indicates the location of the index.

To tell WordPerfect 6 where you want the table of contents, move to the location where you want it and select **Tools** Table of Contents **Define**. From the Define Table of Contents dialog box, you can select how many levels the table of contents shows, the styles to use for each level of entries, where page numbers appear, and whether you use the same page numbering style as the entire document uses. When you select OK, WordPerfect adds the [Def Mark] code, which indicates the location of the table of contents.

The following is an example of a WordPerfect 6 table of contents showing two levels, with the second level wrapped. The text looks different from the default because the TableofCont1 and TableofCont2 styles are edited. The two lines of heading text and the graphics box at the top are entered before the [Def Mark] code.

Create Styles That Create Table of Contents Entries for You

A shortcut for creating entries for tables of contents is to create a style that adds the codes for the entry. Every time you use the style on text, the text will appear as a table of contents entry when you generate a table of contents.

To create a style that generates entries for a table of contents in WordPerfect 5.1:

1. Select **L**ayout **S**tyles or press ALT-F8 (Style) and select **C**reate.
2. Select **N**ame, type the name of the style, and press ENTER.
3. Select **C**odes.
4. Press ALT-F4 (Block) and press DOWN ARROW.
5. Press ALT-F5 (Mark Text) and select To**C**.
6. Type the level number for the table of contents and select OK.
7. Add any other formatting you want the style entry to use.
8. Press F7 (Exit) until you return to the document.

To create a style that generates entries for a table of contents in WordPerfect 6:

1. Select **L**ayout **S**tyles **C**reate.
2. Type the name of the style and select OK.
3. Select Show Style **O**ff Codes and Style **C**ontents.
4. Press ALT-F4 and press DOWN ARROW.
5. Select **L**ayout Ta**b**le of Contents **M**ark.
6. Type the level number for the table of contents and select OK.
7. Add any other formatting you want the style entry to use.
8. Press F7 until you return to the document.

WordPerfect does not care if some table of contents entries are from styles and others are added directly. The table of contents will include all table of contents entries for each level regardless of whether you use styles or not.

Use Predefined Styles in WordPerfect 6 to Create a Table of Contents

WordPerfect 6 has some styles that already have codes to include their contents in a table of contents. You can use these styles to quickly create a table of contents. To do this, change a document's outline style to Headings by selecting Tools Outline Outline Style and the Headings outline style. Then use the Heading 1, Heading 2, and Heading 3 styles for the headings in your document. You do not have to mark text for the table of contents because these styles already include the codes for the different heading levels you can use in a table of contents. You can customize these styles so your headings have the appearance you want. Using styles for the headings and table of contents entries also ensures a consistent appearance between a master document and its subdocuments. When you generate the table of contents, as described in Tip 484, WordPerfect will pick up the headings using the Headings outline style as the appropriate level of table of contents entries.

Select All the Text for Table of Contents when You Are Adding Entries Yourself

Before you use the Tools Table of Contents Mark command or press ALT-F5 and select Table of Contents, you must select the text for the table of contents entry. Unlike index entries, WordPerfect will not pick up text based on the current position within the document. You cannot even select Tools Table of Contents Mark unless you have a block selected. The only exception is when you include it as part of a style, as described in Tip 508. When you apply the style to a paragraph, WordPerfect picks up the paragraph as the entry for the table of contents.

The Table of Contents Can Use Your Styles or Those in WordPerfect 6

In WordPerfect 6, you can change the appearance of the generated table of contents by changing the styles. You can either change the styles the table of contents entries use or you can change the format of the styles. By default, the table of contents entries use the TableofCont1 through TableofCont4

styles for the different levels. To modify the TableofCont# styles, see Tip 423 about changing the system styles. You can change the TableofCont# system styles to change the appearance of the tables you have already created.

The other option is to change the style that the different levels of the table of contents use. To set the styles for the different levels, when you select **Tools Table of Contents Define** to define the table of contents, select Table of Contents Styles. To change the style of a level in the table of contents, highlight it and select one of the choices on the right. Select **Edit** and Style **Contents** to change the contents of the style just as if you were changing the style definition from the Style List dialog box. You can also select **Create** to create a style and then define the style as you would any other WordPerfect style you create. You can also select another style by choosing **Select** and the style to use. When you select Close, the different levels of the table of contents will use the styles you have chosen.

In WordPerfect 5.1, use ALT-F2 *(Replace) to replace the [->Indent<-][<-Mar Rel] codes with the codes you want the entries to use.*

You Must Select Each Piece of Text You Want in a List

TIP 512

Unless you are creating a list of graphics boxes, as described in Tip 514, you must select the text to put in the list. Block the text to be the entry in the list. In WordPerfect 5.1, select Mark List or press ALT-F5 (Mark Text) and select List. In WordPerfect 6, select **Tools List Mark** or press ALT-F5 and select List. Next, you must enter the list you want the entries included in and press ENTER. In WordPerfect 6, a quick method of doing this is to press F5 and select the list to use. In WordPerfect 5.1, you can have as many as ten lists, labeled 1 through 10. The last five automatically pick up captions from figures, tables, text, user-defined boxes, and equation boxes, as described in Tip 514. In WordPerfect 6, you can have more lists and use both text and numbers for the names you assign to each one.

Set a List's Appearance when You Define It

TIP 513

Before you define a list, you must move to where you want the list placed. When you define it, you also set how the list appears.

In WordPerfect 5.1, select Mark Define List. Next, type the number of the list that you want displayed and press ENTER. Then select the format for the page numbers in the list. When you select a page numbering option, WordPerfect adds the [Def Mark] code for where the list will be generated.

In WordPerfect 6, select Tools List Define to define the list. You can highlight the list to use and choose Select. If you do not see the list you want to use, select Create to create one. When you create one, you can enter the name of the list after Name. You can also select the page number appearance and how page numbers are formatted to use a different format than the document. You can set the formatting for each entry in the list by selecting Style. From the List Style dialog box, you can choose Select to select another style for generated entries or Create to create one that you can subsequently select. When you select Close, the entries in the list you are defining will use the style you have chosen.

Use Lists to List the Captions of Graphics Boxes

TIP 514

WordPerfect can automatically include the captions for figure, table box, text box, user box, and equation box graphics box styles in a list. When you create a list to automatically include the captions, you do not have to mark the text to appear in the list, as described in Tip 512. The captions in the list have the same formatting as the captions in the graphics boxes.

In WordPerfect 5.1, select Mark Define List or press ALT-F5 (Mark Text) and select Define and Define List. Type **6** for figure boxes, 7 for table boxes, **8** for text boxes, **9** for user boxes, and **10** for equation boxes. Press ENTER. Select the style of page numbers for the list.

In WordPerfect 6, select Tools List Define Create. Type the name of the list and then select Include Graphics. WordPerfect lists the counters used for graphics box styles. Select one, and the graphics boxes that use that graphics box counter are included in the list. You can make additional changes to the list, such as the page numbering style and style of the entry in the list, to add formatting on top of formatting used in the caption. When you are finished, select OK to create the style, then choose Select to add the definition for this list to the document.

Summarize Blocks of Text by Putting Them into Graphics Boxes

TIP 515

When a document contains tables or other blocks of text that you want to summarize by listing the table or block's title, put the text in a text box or other graphics box style with the

title as the caption of the graphics box. Then define a list that will automatically pick up the titles in the captions.

You Can Share Lists and Tables of Authorities Between Documents

TIP 516

If you want to use lists or tables of authorities that you have defined in one document in another document, you do not have to define them again. In the document that you want to use the lists or tables of authorities created in another document, select Tools, Lists or Table of Authorities, and Define. From the Define List or Define Table of Authorities dialog box, select Retrieve, enter the document containing the list or table of authorities you want to use, and press ENTER. Under Definition is a list of the lists or tables of authorities defined in the other document. You can select the ones to add to the current document by marking them with a *. When you select OK and then Yes, WordPerfect adds the selected definitions of lists and tables of authorities to the current document. Once the definitions are retrieved, they are available in the Define List or Define Table of Authorities dialog box to select to add to the document. When you select them from the Define List or Define Table of Authorities dialog box, WordPerfect adds the [Mark Def] code that marks where the list or table of authorities is placed when you generate entries in the document.

Use a Table of Authorities to List Citations

TIP 517

A table of authorities provides a listing of citations, statutes, and regulations used as part of a legal document. Each citation, statute, and regulation is grouped by its source, such as the type of court. When you use a table of authorities, the citations, statutes, and regulations are listed in full once and then as an abbreviated form in other locations. Like other generated entries, you must mark the entries that you want to reference, as described below; then define the table of authorities, as described in Tip 520; and then generate the table of authorities by generating entries in the document, as described in Tip 484.

In WordPerfect 5.1, block the text containing the full form of a citation, statute, or regulation. Select Mark Table of Authorities Mark Full or press ALT-F5 (Mark Text) and select ToA. Type the number

for the section it belongs to and press ENTER. Edit the text as you want it to appear in the generated table of authorities and press F7 (Exit). Next, edit the entry for the short form and press ENTER. Now you have the long form and the short form of the citation, statute, or regulation defined. To mark other instances of the case, move to the cases where the short form appears and select **Mark Table of Authorities Mark Short** or press ALT-F5 (Mark Text) and select ToA Short Form.

In WordPerfect 6, block the text containing the full form of a citation, statute, or regulation. Select **Tools Table of Authorities Mark Full** or press ALT-F5 and select Table of Authorities. From the ToA Full Form dialog box, select Section Name and type the section you want the full citation listed under. Select Short Form and edit the entry for the short form and press ENTER. Select Edit Full Form, edit the text as you want it to appear in the generated table of authorities and press F7. Now you have the long form and the short form of the citation, statute, or regulation defined. To mark other instances, move to the locations where the short form appears and select **Tools Table of Authorities Mark Short** or press ALT-F5 and select **Mark Text ToA Short Form** and then OK.

When Creating a Table of Authorities, Decide Which Sections to Have and Print a Listing

Since using a table of authorities requires that each entry is included in the correct section, you will want a list of the sections you will use. That way, you know which section to select when marking references. This is especially true for WordPerfect 5.1, which uses the numbers 1 through 16 to identify the different lists. WordPerfect 6 lets you use more descriptive names than the numbers 1 through 16, so it is not as important. A sample listing might look like this:

```
 File  Edit  View  Layout  Tools  Font  Graphics  Window  Help

   Supreme    Supreme Court
   Appeals    Federal Court of Appeals
   Ohio       Ohio Supreme Court
   IRR        Internal Revenue Rulings
   Code 86    Tax Code of 1986 |
```

The list does not have to match the order they will appear in a document.

Search for Court Names to Find Entries for Tables of Authorities

519

To help find entries for a table of authorities, search for words that appear as part of the citation. For example, looking for "Appeals" or "Supreme Court" will help you quickly find the cases you want to include. Searching for "vs." or "versus" is another way to quickly find court cases. You can find the words using the search feature available when you press F2. Remember to search the document substructures. In WordPerfect 5.1, this means pressing HOME before you press F2. In WordPerfect 6, select the Extended Search check box.

Define the Sections of the Table of Authorities in the Order You Want Them to Appear

520

In a table of authority, each section is defined separately. Regardless of the order that you create sections, it is the order of the definition codes in the document that determines the order of the sections of the table of authorities in the document.

To define any section in WordPerfect 5.1, select **Mark D**efine **T**able of **A**uthorities. Type the number of the section and press ENTER. Then change any part of the definition you want. These changes include using dot leaders between the text and the page number, including underlining from the long form of the citation in the section, and adding an empty line between entries in the section.

To define any section in WordPerfect 6, select **T**ools **T**able of **A**uthorities **D**efine. You can highlight the section to use and choose **S**elect. If you do not see a section for the one you want to use, select **C**reate to create one. When you create one, you can enter the name of the section of the table of authorities after **N**ame. You can also change any part of the section's definition. These changes include using dot leaders between the text and the page number, including underlining from the long form of the citation in the section, adding an empty line between entries in the section, and the style of the entries. When you select **S**tyle, you can edit the style that the table of authorities entries use or select a different one.

Use Cross-References to Keep Page References Up to Date

You can use cross-references when you reference another page and you want the page to be adjusted as the text is edited. To create cross-references for this purpose, follow either set of steps. When you create a cross-reference, you are creating two halves. The place containing the reference to the other location is called a *reference*. The other location is called the *target*. WordPerfect uses a name for the target. This target name will not appear in the document and is solely used to help you and WordPerfect keep track of the references in a document.

To create a cross-reference in WordPerfect 5.1:

1. Move to where you want to put the page reference.
2. Select **M**ark Cross-**R**eference **B**oth, or press ALT-F5 (Mark Text) and select Cross-**R**ef Mark **B**oth Reference and Target.
3. Select **P**age Number to include the page number.
4. Type a name for the reference and press ENTER.
5. Move to the location that you want to reference and press ENTER.

To create a cross-reference in WordPerfect 6:

1. Move to where you want to put the page reference.
2. Select **T**ools Cross-Re**f**erence **B**oth or press ALT-F5 and select **M**ark Text **B**oth Reference & Target.
3. Select Tie **R**eference To and **P**age to include the page number.
4. Select **T**arget Name and type a name for the reference.
5. Select OK.
6. Move to the location that you want to reference and press ENTER.

After performing either set of steps, WordPerfect adds the codes for the cross-reference and adds the contents of the cross-reference. The examples tell you to select the page number in step 3, although you can select a different type of reference by selecting one of the other choices listed.

WordPerfect does not constantly update cross-references. Before you print a document containing cross-references, you will want to regenerate the cross-references as well as other generated entries, as described in Tip 484.

Search for Codes to Find Cross-References

TIP 522

Generated cross-references appear in the document as text just like the text you have entered, but when you look at the document's codes you will see a code in place of the text that appears in the document. When you are searching a document for the text created by a cross-reference, do not search for the text generated by the cross-reference; search for the code instead. The codes WordPerfect uses for cross-references include

[Ref Box]	Reference to a WordPerfect 6 graphics box
[Ref Chap]	Reference to a WordPerfect 6 chapter number
[Ref Count]	Reference to a WordPerfect 6 counter
[Ref Endnote]	Reference to a WordPerfect 6 endnote
[Ref Footnote]	Reference to a WordPerfect 6 footnote
[Ref Para]	Reference to a WordPerfect 6 paragraph number
[Ref Pg]	Reference to a WordPerfect 6 page number
[Ref Sec Pg]	Reference to a WordPerfect 6 secondary page number
[Ref Vol]	Reference to a WordPerfect 6 volume
[Ref]	Reference in WordPerfect 5.1
[Target]	Target

Type Text to Appear Next to the Cross-Reference

TIP 523

Cross-references can supply page numbers and graphics box caption names, but if you want more text than that, you have to enter it. This includes adding text such as "page" or "(See ...)". The only exception is text that appears as part of the item you are referencing, as described in Tip 524.

Some Cross-References Include Additional Text

References to some targets will include the text that is part of the item you are referencing. For example, if you are referencing a page number, the reference will include any text that is part of the page number format (Tip 133 describes how to set this). Graphics boxes include the text that is part of their captions' style. That is why references to figure boxes will include "Figure" in front of the figure number.

A Cross-Reference to the Same Location Can Be Used More Than Once

If you want to reference the same location more than once, you can do so by having multiple references to the same target. Each time you want to reference a defined target, add the reference as described here.

In WordPerfect 5.1, move to where you want to put the reference. Select **Mark Cross-Reference Reference** or press ALT-F5 (Mark Text) and select **Cross-Ref Mark Reference**. Select the type of reference to add. Type a name of the target and press ENTER.

In WordPerfect 6, move to where you want to put the reference. Select **Tools Cross-Reference Reference** or press ALT-F5 and select **Mark Text Cross-Reference**. Select the type of reference to add. Select **Target Name** and type a name for the reference, or press F5 and select one of the targets defined in the document. Select OK.

You Can Have More Than One Target for a Reference

You can use the same target name for more than one target location. When you use the target name as the source for a reference, WordPerfect includes each location of the target name separated by a comma. For example, if you have assigned the target name "Reports" to text that appears on pages 5,

7, and 10, when a cross-reference has Reports as the target name to reference, the document will contain 5, 7, 10. As this example shows, the different locations in a target are separated by a comma.

The Type of Cross-Reference Is Set by the Reference, Not the Target

TIP 527

WordPerfect has different types of cross-references depending on the type of information you want from the target. In WordPerfect 5.1, the reference can be to the page number, paragraph or outline number, footnote number, endnote number, or graphics box style number of the target. In WordPerfect 6, the reference can be to the page number, secondary page number, chapter number, volume number, paragraph or outline number, footnote number, endnote number, graphics box style number, or counter number of the target. Of course, some of the types are illogical for some target locations, such as referencing the figure number of a target that is not a figure. Other targets can be used for more than one type of reference. For example, you can have a target and use different types of references, as shown here:

```
 File  Edit  View  Layout  Tools  Font  Graphics  Window  Help
```
Dealing With Lawyers
```
As the graph in Figure 3 on
page 4 of Chapter 2 indicates,
the number of lawyers is
increasing. You will be
dealing with lawyers at some
point.
```

In the sample document, the chapter number, page number, and graphics box number are all created with cross-references. The cross-references use the same target, which happens to be a graphics box on page 4 of Chapter 2. The three cross-references are created in the same way, with the only difference being what the reference is tied to.

The graphic shown above resides on the accompanying disk as CLICHE02.CGM.

CLICHE02.CGM

Unmarked Targets Will Be Noted After You Generate Cross-References

When you generate cross-references, you will want to check them over (see Tip 522 about using codes to find cross-references). If you have references to a target that WordPerfect cannot find, these cross-references will appear as a question mark. Usually the cause is a misspelled target name, you forgot to define the target, or you deleted the target. Changing the reference or selecting the cross-reference target and regenerating the cross-references will handle this problem.

Use Document Summaries to Provide Quick Information About Files

Document summaries provide summary information about a document. When you list files or use File Manager to look at a document that has a document summary, WordPerfect shows the document summary. This is like "Cliffs Notes" for the contents of a document.

To create a document summary in WordPerfect 5.1, select File Summary or press SHIFT-F8 (Format) and select Document Summary. WordPerfect displays a list of fields. For any field you want to change, select the field, type the new entry, and press ENTER.

To create a document summary in WordPerfect 6, select File Summary or press SHIFT-F8 and select Document Summary. WordPerfect displays a list of fields. You can use TAB or the mouse to move between fields to make entries in them. When you are finished, click OK or press F7 and select OK.

Use Document Summaries with File Lists to Select the Correct File

With documents that have defined document summaries, when you look at the document using the files list or File Manager, WordPerfect shows you the document summary, as shown in the following:

```
File:  C:\WPDOCS\SANTA                          WP 6.0        Revised:  06-18-93 12:41p
Name:  Vendor Information Booklet for Santa Booklet           Created:  06-18-93 12:37p

Author:                      Jude Hardy                                              ↑
Typist:                      Nell Dickens
Subject:                     Vendor Booklet
Account:
Keywords:                    Vendor Booklet
Abstract:                    This document is the booklet that is mailed to all vend
```

At this point, you can select **Look at text** to switch to seeing the document text.

Let WordPerfect Supply Some of the Document Summary Entries

Rather than entering the value of every field in a document summary, WordPerfect can supply some of the entries. Some of the entries are automatically supplied, such as the revision and creation dates. When you press SHIFT-F10 or select the Extract button in WordPerfect 6, and then select Yes, WordPerfect picks up the Typist, Author, Subject, and Abstract fields. WordPerfect picks up the typist and author from the last entries made in these fields. The subject comes from text in the document that follows a specific phrase, RE: by default. The abstract comes from the beginning of the document.

You cannot change the revision date. WordPerfect sets the revision time and date to the time and date when you save the document.

You Can Print and Save Document Summaries

WordPerfect lets you easily print and save document summaries.

You can print the document summary for the current document by displaying it and then pressing SHIFT-F7 or clicking the Print button in WordPerfect 6. In WordPerfect 5.1, you can print the

document summary of a document on disk by looking at the file in the files list and selecting Print Summ. WordPerfect 6 will also let you print the document summary in other ways. When you select Multiple Pages or Document on Disk from the Print/Fax dialog box, or highlight the file in the File Manager and select Print, you will see the Print Multiple Pages dialog box. Selecting the Document Summary check box prints the document summary before printing the current document.

You can put the contents of a document summary into a WordPerfect document. First display the document summary either in the current document or by looking at the file in the files list or File Manager. Next, press F10, select Save to File, or click the Save button in WordPerfect 6. You will need to select Yes in WordPerfect 6 to confirm. Type the filename and press ENTER. If you open the document, you will see the document summary fields and the entries for each of the fields.

Delete the Document Summaries You No Longer Want to See
TIP 533

If you have a document summary you want to get rid of, you can delete it. To delete a document summary, display it. Then in WordPerfect 5.1, press DEL and in WordPerfect 6, press F9 or select the Delete button. You will need to select Yes to confirm that you want to remove the document summary. After selecting Yes, the document summary is removed and you return to the document. After you delete the document summary, when you look at the document in the files list or File Manager, you will see the document rather than an empty document summary.

You Can Tell WordPerfect to Prompt You for a Document Summary Every Time You Save a File
TIP 534

When you are using document summaries, you will want to have WordPerfect prompt you for the information for the document summary when you save the file.

To have WordPerfect 5.1 prompt for a document summary when you save a file, select File Setup or press SHIFT-F1. Select Environment Document Management/Summary Create Summary on Save/Exit Yes.

To have WordPerfect 6 prompt for a document summary when you save a file, display the current document's document summary and press SHIFT-F1. Select the Create Summary on Exit/Save check box and OK.

You Can Set the Descriptive and Subject Fields' Default Values

TIP 535

You can select the information WordPerfect enters for the Descriptive Type or Document Type field and the text WordPerfect looks for when you extract data for the Subject field. The default entry for the Descriptive Type or Document Type field is entered for all new document summaries. The subject search text is the text that WordPerfect should search for when you extract entries, as described in Tip 531. The text that comes after this entry is the text WordPerfect enters into the Subject field.

To set the default values for the Document Type and Subject field in WordPerfect 5.1, select File Setup or press SHIFT-F1 and then select **E**nvironment **D**ocument Management/Summary. Select Default Document **T**ype, type the text for the document type, and press ENTER. You can also select Subject Search Text, type the text that WordPerfect should search for, and press ENTER.

To set the default values for these fields in WordPerfect 6, display the current document's document summary and press SHIFT-F1 or select the Setup button. Type the text for the descriptive type after **D**efault Descriptive Type. Type the text that WordPerfect should search for after Subject Search Text. Select OK to return to the document summary.

Set the Fields Used in WordPerfect 6 Document Summaries

TIP 536

WordPerfect 6 has more fields available for document summaries than appear in the Document Summary dialog box. Instead of listing every one available, you can select which fields one document or all documents use in their document summaries. The fields you use in the document summaries are set by pressing F4 or clicking the Select Fields button in the Document Summary dialog box. In the Select Summary Fields dialog box, WordPerfect lists the fields currently shown in the left box and the list of all the fields available in the right box. You can add and remove fields from the first list by highlighting field names and selecting the buttons in the middle of the dialog box. If you want the fields you have selected to be used for all document summaries you subsequently create, press F10 or select the Use as Default button.

CHAPTER 12

Grammar and Spelling

Focus on Conveying Your Message, Then Improve the Document with WordPerfect's Writing Tools

Many people complain that it takes them a long time to create written documents. The best strategy you can use to become a prolific writer is to divide the process into two distinct steps: write your message, then improve the way it's worded. If you let yourself struggle for the perfect words, you will lose six others in the process. Write your message as quickly as possible, then use the writing tools WordPerfect provides to polish the document. With WordPerfect you can use the copy and move feature to reorganize your first draft. Next, you can use writing tools like the Speller and Thesaurus with either WordPerfect 5.1 or 6. With WordPerfect 6, you also have a grammar checker, called *Grammatik*, that can locate partial sentences, passive voice, and other grammar and style problems. Grammatik can also analyze the level of your writing to ensure that it is targeted to the audience you are trying to reach.

Use Multiple Dictionaries to Make Your Job Easier

WordPerfect 5.1 and WordPerfect 6 both allow for the use of more than one dictionary, although there are a few differences between the releases. In addition to being able to use several WordPerfect dictionaries, you can even acquire specialized dictionaries from third-party vendors. Before looking at a few options available from third parties, a brief overview of what comes with WordPerfect will help you understand all the options you already have.

With WordPerfect 6 you can have as many as six main dictionaries, six supplemental dictionaries, and a document-specific dictionary. If you want to use more than one main or supplemental dictionary at the same time, you must link or *chain* them together. When you chain multiple dictionaries, WordPerfect 6 can search each dictionary when it performs a spell check. WordPerfect 6 also supports the use of foreign language dictionaries for sections of a document that you indicate are written in a foreign language. Foreign language dictionaries are not chained to the main language dictionaries.

Third-party dictionaries compatible with WordPerfect 6's main dictionary can be chained together. WordPerfect will then check each dictionary in the chain. Use the Setup option in the Speller dialog

box to access options for chaining main or supplemental dictionaries. Once chained, the dictionaries function as one.

In WordPerfect 6, the main dictionary can be a word list or a set of algorithms that are processed for each word. The type of dictionary used depends on the language. The United States English dictionary is a word list that has both a common and a main word list. The common word list, which contains frequently-used words, is checked first for a more efficient spelling check. Main dictionaries are .LEX files. The main file has a name such as WPUS.LEX, where "US" indicates the United States English version. Other two-character codes in front of the filename extension indicate a different language. Supplemental dictionaries in WordPerfect 6 have names such as WP{WP}US.SUP. You can add others with names that have a .SUP filename extension. In WordPerfect 6, words skipped within a document—that is, recognized as valid for that document—are added to a document-specific dictionary, which is saved as part of the document file.

In WordPerfect 5.1, you can use a main and a supplemental dictionary. There is no document-specific dictionary and no ability to chain multiple dictionaries together. Third-party dictionaries are used as supplemental dictionaries and can be merged with your own dictionary. When you merge these dictionaries, they become one file and cannot be separated later.

Although WordPerfect has more features than most users ever access, there are some third-party dictionaries that supplement WordPerfect's features and that you might be interested in. Most of these products are designed to meet the needs of a specific group of users and are therefore not provided with WordPerfect. If you can benefit from any of these third-party dictionaries, you will normally find them to be a cost-effective answer to your needs. A few of these products are

- ❏ Reference Software Black's Legal Dictionary
- ❏ Spellex Development Spellex Modules (available for various industries and applications)
- ❏ Williams & Wilkins Stedman 25 (medical)
- ❏ Geo Comp Tech Words

To explore other products that might be helpful to you, check the advertisements in *WordPerfect Magazine*. This magazine is available at many libraries or by a subscription. For information, write to *WordPerfect Magazine*, 270 West Center Street, Orem, Utah, 84057 or call *WordPerfect Magazine* at (801) 228-9626.

You can use the Speller utility, available through WordPerfect, to convert WordPerfect 5.1 .LEX dictionary files to WordPerfect 6 dictionary files.

WordPerfect Will Count the Number of Words in a Document

Whether you are entering a contest or responding to your boss's request for a 500-word summary, WordPerfect can tell you how many words there are in the current document. When you select **Tools Writing Tools Document Information**, WordPerfect 6 returns various statistics about your document, including the word count. To count the words in a WordPerfect 5.1 document, you can choose **Tools Spell Count**. In WordPerfect 5.1, spell-checking the entire document also provides a word count. If you block a portion of text and use the same steps, WordPerfect will tell you how many words are in the block.

WordPerfect 5.1 and WordPerfect 6 do not provide the same word count for some documents because WordPerfect 6 uses Grammatik's counting method. For example, Grammatik counts an entry of 1213 as a word, but WordPerfect 5.1 does not because the text consists entirely of numbers.

WordPerfect Corrects the Spelling of a Word in All Subsequent Occurrences

If you select a corrected spelling for a word flagged as potentially misspelled, WordPerfect remembers your correction and applies it to all future occurrences of the misspelling. For example, if you misspell the word "scuff" as "suff" and select "scuff" from the list of options when WordPerfect offers choices, WordPerfect will replace all occurrences of "suff" with "scuff".

In WordPerfect 6, you can change the automatic replacement for subsequent occurrences. If you are concerned that you might not always want automatic replacement, you can set WordPerfect to prompt you before it makes automatic replacements. After requesting the Speller feature, you can press SHIFT-F1 with WordPerfect 6 and select the **Prompt on Auto-Replace** check box.

You Can Use the Speller While Entering a Header or Footer

TIP 541

As you are typing text in a header or footer, you can check its spelling. If only the current word is in question, you can select the Word option from the Speller menu to make this check.

To check all the text in the header or footer in WordPerfect 6:

1. Move to the top of the header or footer text and choose **T**ools Writing Tools **S**peller.
2. Choose the option for **H**eader or **F**ooter, which is presented in the Speller menu.

To check all the text in the header or footer in WordPerfect 5.1:

1. Select **T**ools Sp**e**ll or press CTRL-F2 (Spell).
2. Choose **P**age or **D**ocument to check the spelling of the header or footer.

The Speller Checks More Than Document Text

TIP 542

You do not have to worry about separately checking the spelling of nondocument entries such as captions for graphics boxes, headers, footers, watermarks (in WordPerfect 6), and footnotes. WordPerfect automatically checks the spelling of these entries, as well as the document itself, when you choose the Document option from the Speller menu. WordPerfect does not check style text entries or equations in equation boxes.

Password-Protect Your Supplemental Dictionaries

TIP 543

If you do not want either to add or change the entries in your supplemental dictionaries, you can password-protect them. To add a password in WordPerfect 6, select File Save **A**s and choose Password.

In WordPerfect 5.1 you need to use CTRL-F5 (Text In/Text Out) and select **P**assword. Remember that you need to remember this password or risk being unable to edit these dictionaries yourself. Try thinking of a password that's obvious to you but would be unfamiliar to most of the others who might use your system.

Passwords can be up to 24 characters and are not case sensitive.

You Can Select Specific Sections of Text to Be Spell-Checked

WordPerfect provides options for checking the spelling of a word, a page, or an entire document. In WordPerfect 6, you can also spell-check forward from the cursor location.

If you add a new paragraph or page of text, you can block the text and check just that text. If you have a section of text that you do not want to check, WordPerfect 6 will let you block it and choose **T**ools **W**riting Tools and select the Disable Speller/Grammatik check box. To enable the spell check again for the same text you need to choose **T**ools **W**riting Tools and clear the Disable Speller/Grammatik check box.

Perform Maintenance on the Dictionary Itself with the Speller Utility

WordPerfect provides a utility program, SPELL.EXE, to perform maintenance on your dictionaries. WordPerfect 5.1 is shipped with the Speller utility. In WordPerfect 6, you must request the Spell and Hyphen Utility from WordPerfect separately.

To use the Speller utility in WordPerfect 5.1:

1. In the WP51 directory, type **spell** to start the Speller utility. The utility automatically locates your main dictionary (WP{WP}US.LEX) in order to edit it.

2. Select **2** - Add Words to Dictionary when you want to add new words to the dictionary. You can add words to the common word area or the main word area. You can either type in the words from the keyboard, or you can specify a file you previously created that contains the words you want to add.

3. Select **3** - Delete Words from Dictionary to specify the words you want to remove. Again, you can remove words from the common word area or the main word area. You can also enter the words to delete at the keyboard or from a file.

4. Select **4** - Optimize Dictionary to optimize the dictionary. When the dictionary is optimized, WordPerfect can find words in the dictionary more quickly.

5. When you are finished with the Speller utility, select **0** - Exit from the main menu.

To use the Speller utility in WordPerfect 6:

1. Type **spell** at the DOS prompt from the \WPC60DOS directory to start the Speller utility.
    The utility automatically locates your main dictionary (WPUS.LEX) in order to edit it if it is in the directory. If it is not, the utility prompts you if you want to create it. If you select No, the utility then prompts you for the location of the dictionary. and you can enter the correct pathname.

2. Select **A**dd Word(s) to Dictionary when you want to add new words to the dictionary. You can add words to the common word area or the main word area. You can either type in the words from the keyboard, or you can specify a file you previously created that contains the words you want to add.

3. Select **D**elete Word(s) from Dictionary to specify the words you want to remove. Again, you can remove words from the common word area or the main word area. You can also enter the words to delete at the keyboard or from a file.

4. Select **O**ptimize Dictionary to optimize the dictionary. When the dictionary is optimized, WordPerfect can find words in the dictionary more quickly.

5. When you are finished with the Speller utility, select Exit from the main menu.

The dictionary has two main areas for storing words, the common word area and the main word area. WordPerfect checks the common word area first because these are words that it finds frequently. If you find that you do not use a word from the common word area frequently, delete it from the common word area and add it to the main word area.

When you add or delete a large number of words from the dictionary, optimize the dictionary so the words can be put back in the most efficient order.

Utilize the Supplemental Dictionary Effectively

Both WordPerfect and the Speller utility offer maintenance features for the supplemental dictionary. Not only can you add many words at once, but you can also delete words added by accident. With WordPerfect 6, new options allow you to specify words or phrases to skip, word or phrase replacements, and alternative spelling options for words or phrases.

Before looking at the steps needed to perform these maintenance tasks, some applications for the new WordPerfect 6 features should be discussed. When you chose to edit the supplemental dictionary in WordPerfect, you can insert specific replacement words and phrases. These words and phrases will be automatically substituted for other words or phrases in your document, providing another glossary-like feature. You might, for example, use the initials **CWRU** in your document and specify that it be replaced with **Case Western Reserve University** during the spell check. When you spell-check the document, all occurrences of "CWRU" will be changed to "Case Western Reserve University."

Alternative words and phrases provide a list of suggested replacements that the Speller uses when it encounters a word or phrase that you have added replacements for. You might use these features to provide replacement words for gender-specific words. For example, instead of using the word "mailman," you might prefer "postal worker," "letter carrier," or "mailperson." You can add these replacements words for "mailman" and enter a comment to indicate why you are asking the user to pick a replacement word.

Each entry that you make to the WordPerfect 6 supplemental dictionary is coded to tell what type of entry it is. You can see an example of each of the three types of changes in the following:

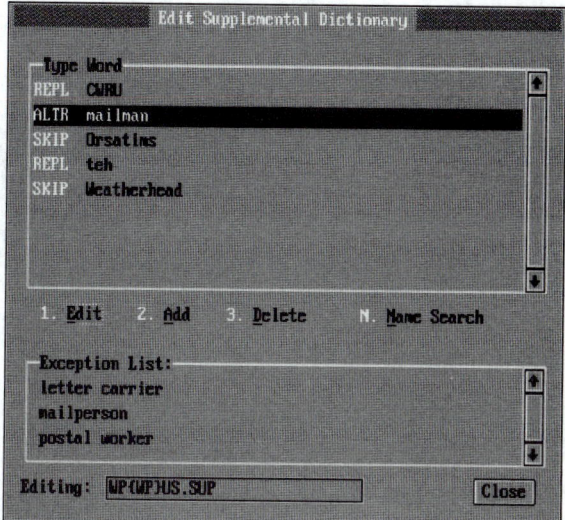

You can use the replacement word option to correct for your own repeated typographical errors. For example, I frequently type "the" as "teh". I have entered "teh" with a replacement of "the" so that WordPerfect will fix these occurrences for me.

To change to supplemental dictionary in WordPerfect 6:

1. Select **T**ools **W**riting Tools **S**peller.
2. Select **E**dit Supplemental Dictionary.
3. Highlight the filename of the supplemental dictionary and select Edit.
4. Modify the dictionary by adding, editing, changing or deleting words.
   The special options for entering replacement or alternative words
   and phrases are available when you choose to edit the supplemental
   dictionary.
5. Select Close to return to the Speller menu.

In WordPerfect 5.1 you can use the Speller utility to maintain your supplemental dictionary.

1. Type **spell** at the DOS prompt in the \WP51 directory.
2. Select **1** - Change/Create Dictionary.
3. Select **2** - Change/Create Supplemental Dictionary.
4. Enter the filename of the supplemental dictionary you want to work with.

5. Select **2** - Add Words to Dictionary when you want to add new words to the dictionary.

    You can add words to the common word area or the main word area. You can either type in the words from the keyboard, or you can specify a file you previously created that contains the words you want to add.

6. Select **3** - Delete Words from Dictionary to specify the words you want to remove.

    Again, you can remove words from the common word area or the main word area. You can also enter the words to delete at the keyboard or from a file.

7. Select **B**-Compress/Expand Supplemental Dictionary to compress the supplemental dictionary.

    When a dictionary is compressed, less disk space is required to store it, and words from it can appear as replacement words.

8. Select **4** - Optimize Dictionary to optimize a compressed supplemental dictionary.

9. When you have finished with the Speller utility, select **0**-Exit from the main menu.

You can use the Speller utility SPELL.EXE, which you can obtain from WordPerfect, to add a list of words to a supplemental dictionary quickly. Check the spelling of these words first. Any words not flagged as not found can be removed from the supplemental dictionary, as they are already in the main dictionary.

TIP 547
You Can Edit a WordPerfect 6 Document-Specific Dictionary

In WordPerfect 6, when you choose to skip a potential misspelling, WordPerfect ignores this word throughout the document. It stores this word in a document-specific dictionary so that whenever you spell-check the document, WordPerfect 6 will ignore this word. Although this is a great time saver, if you inadvertently ignore a misspelled word, WordPerfect will always ignore it in this document. To remove the misspelled word from the document-specific dictionary:

1. Select **T**ools **W**riting Tools **S**peller.
2. Select **E**dit Supplemental Dictionary.
3. Highlight Document Specific and select **E**dit.

4. Modify the dictionary by adding, changing, or deleting words.
5. Select Close to return to the Speller menu.

You Can Use the Speller Utility to Transfer Words from Your Supplemental Dictionary to WordPerfect's Dictionary

If you regularly use a number of words that have been included in your supplemental dictionary, you might find that the Speller is checking your document more slowly. This slowness is due to the fact that the Speller has to look through two different dictionaries. To increase the speed, you can add the contents of your supplemental dictionary to your main dictionary.

To add words from your supplemental dictionary to your main dictionary in WordPerfect 6:

1. At the DOS prompt, type **spell** from the \WPC60DOS directory to start the utility.
2. Select Convert **S**upplemental Dictionary.
3. Type the name of the supplemental dictionary and press TAB.
4. Type the name of the file you want to use, such as **JUNK.LEX,** press TAB, and select OK.
5. Select **A**dd Word(s) to Dictionary **M**ain Word Area or **C**ommon Word Area to determine where in the document to add the words.
6. Select Add Word(s) from a **F**ile.
7. Type the name of the converted file you created and in step 4 select OK.

To add words from your supplemental dictionary to your main dictionary in WordPerfect 5.1:

1. At the DOS prompt, type **spell** to start the utility.
2. Select **2**-Add Words to Dictionary.
3. Select Add to common word list (from a file) or Add to main word list (from a file).
4. Type the name of the supplemental dictionary you want to add and press ENTER.
5. Select Exit.

When you exit, the Speller utility updates the dictionary you are adding words to. This process takes the same amount of time—up to 20 minutes, depending on the speed of your system—whether you are adding 2 words or 200 words.

After adding a whole file's worth of new words to your main dictionary, optimize it with the 4-Optimize Dictionary command.

WordPerfect's Speller Lookup Feature Does a Phonetic Lookup for a Word

You can use the Lookup feature in the WordPerfect 5.1 or WordPerfect 6 Speller to perform either a phonetic lookup or a pattern match lookup. If you type an entry after selecting the lookup option, WordPerfect checks for other words that sound the same. If you look up "rest", WordPerfect 6 finds 29 different word options, including a close match like "wrest," as well as others, such as "raced," "reset," "razed," "reseat," and "wrist."

If you include the wildcard characters * and ? in your entry, WordPerfect will perform a pattern match. The ? is used to represent any one character. For example, if you look up "?ay", WordPerfect would find "pay," "lay," "may," "say," and so on. The * represents any number of characters (including no characters). For example "day*" would provide "day," "daylight," and "daytime" among its word options.

If You Plan to Use Words in Multiple WordPerfect 6 Dictionaries, Chain, or Link, the Dictionaries

You can link together up to six main or supplemental dictionaries, as long as they are all for the same language. To chain dictionaries follow these steps:

1. Select **T**ools **W**riting Tools and select **S**peller.
2. Select Setup.
3. Select Chain **S**upplemental Dictionaries or Chain **M**ain Dictionaries.

4. Highlight the dictionary in the chain you want to add to.
5. Choose **A**dd Chain, **D**elete Chain, or **E**dit.
6. Select Close until you return to your document.

The Main Dictionary Is Organized into a Main Word List and a Common Word List

TIP 551

There are two different sections in WordPerfect's main dictionary: a common word list and a main word list. The common word list includes the most frequently used words found in a typical document. By checking the common word list before the main word list, WordPerfect performs a more efficient search.

You can increase your spell-checking efficiency by removing words you don't use often from the common word area and adding them to the main word area instead, or by adding words you do use frequently into the common word area.

If you delete a word from the common word list, it is deleted from the dictionary completely. Therefore, when you delete a word from the common word list, you should add it to the main word area. Just because you don't use the word frequently doesn't mean you will not be using it at all; it is safer to have the word available somewhere in your dictionary.

When you add words to WordPerfect's dictionaries, add hyphens to mark the location of syllables. WordPerfect uses these hyphens to split words between lines when you turn on hyphenation as described in Tip 826.

Use the Same Supplemental Dictionary for a Related Group of Documents

TIP 552

If you are preparing a lengthy report for a client or working on another specialized task, you might want to set up a special supplemental dictionary that will contain the special terms that are used by a project. When the project is completed, simply remove the supplemental dictionary.

To create and use a new supplemental dictionary in WordPerfect 6, follow these steps:

1. Select **T**ools **W**riting Tools **S**peller.
2. Select **E**dit Supplemental Dictionary.
3. Select **C**reate New Sup.
4. Type the filename for the new supplemental dictionary and select OK.
5. You can add words to the dictionary immediately. If you don't want to, select Close.
6. Select an option for checking your document, **W**ord, **P**age, or **D**ocument.
7. Select Select Dictionar**y**.
8. Highlight the dictionary you want to use and select OK.

In WordPerfect 5.1 select a new supplemental dictionary with these steps:

1. Select **T**ools Sp**e**ll.
2. Select **N**ew Supplementary Dictionary.
3. Type the filename of the dictionary you want to use and press ENTER.

To Spell-Check a Document That Uses Multiple Languages, Indicate Where the Language Changes

553

If you have a document that uses a word or phrase from a different language, you can block the foreign words, indicate the foreign language used, and WordPerfect will automatically check the spelling using the appropriate foreign language dictionary. After blocking the phrase, select Layout Other Language and select the desired language from the list. After selecting OK and Close, appropriate codes are added to your document. If you were to select "Croatian," which has a code of HR, the foreign word in your text would be enclosed by these codes [+Lang:HR] and [–Lang:US] (when the codes are highlighted in the Reveal Codes screen).

In WordPerfect 5.1, enter a language code by selecting Format Other Language. Type the two-letter code for the language you want to use and press F7 twice.

If you spell-check the document, WordPerfect looks for the appropriate dictionary and displays a message if it cannot find it. For the Croatian language, the dictionary file that it tries to find is WPCC60HR.DTL. You can choose to skip checking the spelling for this language when the dictionary file is not available.

If Your Document Has Many Numbers, Turn Off the Check for Numbers in Words Option

WordPerfect recognizes some of the common numeric representations, such as "1st," but it will flag entries such as "25th" as potentially misspelled. If you do not want numeric abbreviations like these included in the spell check, disable the Check for Numbers in Words option. In WordPerfect 6, after invoking the Speller, you can select Setup and clear the check box for Check for Numbers in Words by selecting the option. You can then proceed with your spell check; words containing numbers will be ignored. In WordPerfect 5.1, you cannot disable the check before you start a spell check. You must wait until WordPerfect finds the first occurrence of a number. You can then select Ignore Numbers to have WordPerfect skip them in the rest of the document.

If Unusual Capitalization Is the Norm, Disable the Irregular Capitalization Check in WordPerfect 6

If you regularly use unusual capitalization (such as in the word "WordPerfect,") you might prefer not to have WordPerfect check for improper capitalization. To prevent WordPerfect 6 from searching for improper capitalization:

1. Select **T**ools **W**riting Tools **S**peller.
2. Select Setup.
3. Clear the Check for **I**rregular Capitalization check box and select OK.
4. Continue the spell check of the document.

In WordPerfect 5.1, you can tell WordPerfect to stop checking for irregular capitalization only after the first occurrence of irregular capitalization is found.

When Spell-Checking an Outline, Don't Check for Repeated Words

It is not uncommon for words to repeat within an outline. Although the Speller's ability to flag repeated words in a document can be a big help, it can be an annoyance when checking outline entries like this:

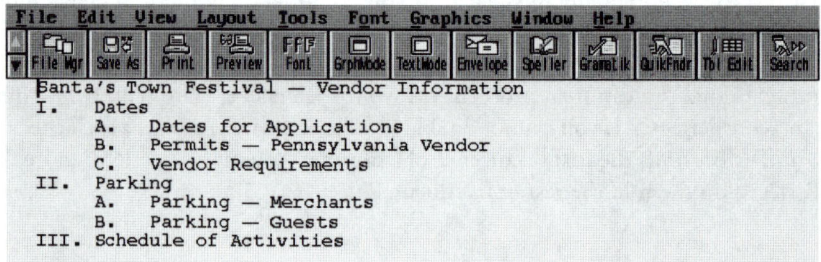

To stop checking for repeated words in WordPerfect 6, you have two choices: you can choose Disable Duplicate Word Checking after the first repeated word is found, or you can select Setup from the main Speller menu and clear the Check for Double Words check box. In WordPerfect 5.1, you can disable the repeated word check (by selecting Disable Double Word Checking) only after WordPerfect finds the first occurrence of a repeated word.

There is another difference between the two versions of WordPerfect. WordPerfect 6 notes repeated words even when they are flagged as potential misspellings that you choose to ignore. WordPerfect 5.1 does not flag these entries as repeated words.

You Can Have Multiple Supplemental Dictionaries If You Do Different Types of Writing

If you do several different types of writing, you might need several different dictionaries. If you find yourself doing both medical and legal typing, you might want to use two supplemental dictionaries

and change them when the circumstances arise. You might also want to use different supplemental dictionaries if you type for more than one person or if more than one person uses your computer. That way, the supplemental dictionaries are specifically tailored to the individual person's needs.

Make Your Writing More Interesting by Using the Thesaurus to Find Synonyms

Using the same word repeatedly in a document is boring and soon loses the interest of the reader. If you notice that a word has been repeated many times (see Tip 588), see if there are synonyms in WordPerfect's Thesaurus that you can use to add variety to your writing. Often the synonyms have subtle nuances that add color and interest to your writing. Consider the difference between these two paragraphs using WordPerfect's Thesaurus replacements for the word "sound".

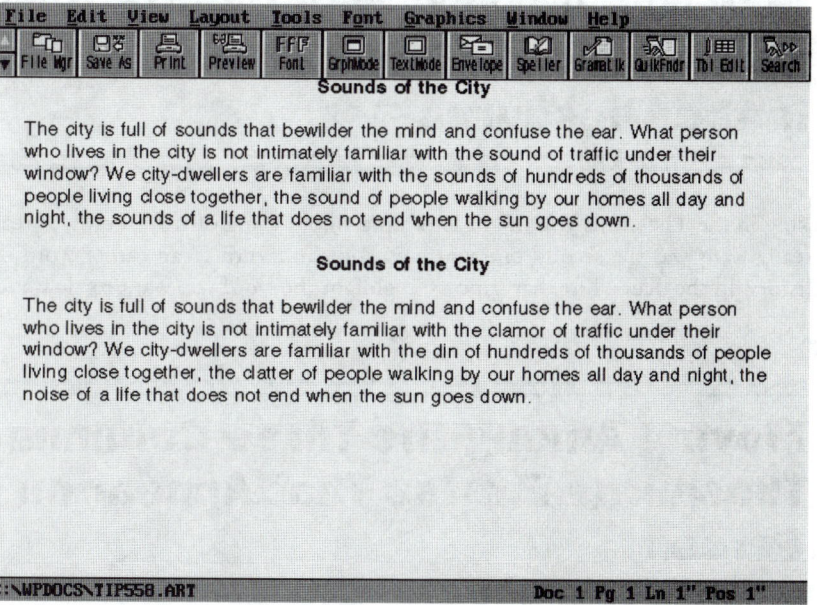

While Using the Thesaurus, View More of Your Document to See the Words in Context

It can be difficult to choose the best synonym without considering the sentence or paragraph that the word is in. After activating the Thesaurus, choose View (View Document in WordPerfect 5.1). In WordPerfect 6, WordPerfect expands the display of the document by lopping off the top half of the Thesaurus dialog box. In WordPerfect 5.1, the display of the Thesaurus is not affected. In both releases you can move around in the document using the usual cursor movement keys, exploring the text around the word in question. When you are finished looking at the text, press F7 to use the dialog box again.

In WordPerfect 6, You Can Go Back to Look at a Word You Looked Up Before in the Thesaurus

While working in the Thesaurus you might look up a whole string of words, only to realize that the word you really want was the second one you saw. You can return to an earlier word in the list by selecting History. In the dialog box that appears, highlight the word you want to view and select OK.

Moving Among the Three Columns of Thesaurus Entries That Appear on the Screen

Each time you look up a new word in the Thesaurus, the word is added at the top of a new column, to the right of the previous columns, with its synonyms and antonyms displayed in that column. Only three of these columns can be displayed on the screen at one time. You can move from column to

column by pressing the RIGHT ARROW and LEFT ARROW keys. If you move right or left to a column that is not currently displayed, WordPerfect scrolls the display to show the column you want.

Headwords Are Marked with a Dot and Provide Additional Synonyms

Any of the Thesaurus entries can be used as replacement words for the word that you are looking up. Some suggested replacements can provide another set of potential replacement words. These words are called *headwords* and have their own set of entries in the Thesaurus. If you highlight one of these words and press ENTER, a list of words will display in the next column, as described in Tip 561.

You Can Purchase Foreign Language Dictionaries and Thesauri from WordPerfect

WordPerfect Corporation creates Speller and Thesaurus dictionaries for many different languages. If you want a Speller dictionary or Thesaurus for another language, you need to contact WordPerfect (as described in your documentation) about ordering them.

Clear the Current Thesaurus Entries To Eliminate Old Options

You might want to clear the current column of Thesaurus entries to eliminate options that are no longer of interest. To do this, select Clear Column to eliminate the current column. Any columns to the right of the current one slide over to fill the empty space.

TIP 565

You Can Purchase Grammatik Separately if You Have WordPerfect 5.1 and Are Not Ready to Upgrade

Grammatik is a grammar-checking program that can be purchased separately from WordPerfect. The upgrade pricing for WordPerfect 6 is attractive, making it the best way for most users to obtain Grammatik, although you can buy it separately if you do not want to buy the upgrade yet.

TIP 566

WordPerfect 6 Provides a Quick Overview of Your Document's Readability

In addition to checking for grammar errors, WordPerfect 6 can provide an overview of document readability with Grammatik. When you choose Tools Writing Tools Grammatik and request a statistics check by typing T, you will see an overview of your document's readability, as well as paragraph, sentence, and word statistics. The Readability section has several indices that measure readability. These indicate popular measure such as the Gunning's Fog Index, Flesch Reading Ease, and Flesch-Kincaid Grade Level. An explanation of the document's ratings is provided on the second page of statistics that displays when you press ENTER. The other statistics sections provide average sentence, paragraph, and word length.

TIP 567

To Change the Readability Statistics of a Document, Look at the Paragraph, Sentence, and Word Statistics

If you want to make your document easier to read, check whether your paragraphs, sentences, or words are too long. You can edit your document, make the necessary changes, and run the statistics check again.

You Can Print the Errors Grammatik Finds

TIP 568

You can print a copy of the errors Grammatik encounters as it reviews your documents. You can review this list and Grammatik's advice later or keep it as a target for future documents. All you need to do is select Preferences Options and choose the Print errors on printer check box.

Paragraph Length Statistics Are Skewed If You Have Tables in the Document

TIP 569

If you check the statistics on paragraph length in a document, then add several tables and run the check again, you will find a considerable difference. Because tables have hard returns at the end of each line, WordPerfect counts each line of a table as a paragraph when it computes paragraph statistics, giving a skewed picture of paragraph lengths in the document.

Match One of Grammatik's Writing Styles with the Style of Your Document

TIP 570

Grammatik provides specific style checks for a number of predefined writing styles. When you select one of these style checks, you are actually selecting a set of rules that will be applied to your document as it is checked for potential problems.

There are four different categories of rules for each style: Grammar Rules, Mechanical Rules, Style Rules, and Writing Thresholds. Each category provides a set of standards that are applied to your document. As an example, one threshold rule governs the number of words necessary before a sentence is considered too long. Your choice of a style automatically decides which rules are applied.

The predefined writing styles available are Business Letter, Memo, Report, Technical Document, Proposal, Journalism, Advertising, and Fiction. An example of the differences between style selections is the number of words allowed before a sentence is considered too long. In the Technical style, 40 words is the maximum, but in the Memo style 25 is the maximum, and in the General style 30 is the limit.

Remember That Grammatik's Suggestions Are Only Suggestions

Sometimes you will see suggestions that are inappropriate for your document. You need to review each suggestion and determine if you want to make the change or leave the text alone. You might, for instance, want to keep a slang or colloquial expression that Grammatik suggests you change.

You Can Turn Off Grammatik's Spell Check

Grammatik's spell check does not utilize the document supplemental dictionary created when you spell-check with WordPerfect's Speller—unless you use the utility program mentioned in Tip 593. Every word that you ignored with WordPerfect's Speller will be flagged again as a potential misspelling. You can either create your own writing style that has Speller disabled, press F6 the first time Grammatik flags a misspelling, or use the utility to include WordPerfect's supplemental dictionary entries in the spell check.

Use Grammatik Interactively to Correct Problems Immediately

Correct problems as they are detected when you use Grammatik interactively. Function keys make quick work of the changes. The following keys can be used when a problem is presented:

Key	Action
F1	Displays help information
F2	Replaces the highlighted error with a suggested correction
F3	Performs the same action as F2 and moves to the next problem
F4	Shows the parts-of-speech analysis
F5	Ignores a potential spelling error
F6	Ignores the rule class permanently or in the current session
F7	Adds a word to Grammatik's dictionary
F8	Marks the problem for later review
F9	Lets you edit the problem
F10	Moves to the next problem

Use WordPerfect to Apply Grammatik's Suggestions

574

If you want to use WordPerfect to apply Grammatik's suggestions, have Grammatik mark the document for grammatical errors. In Grammatik, select Checking Mark. After the document is marked, select Quit Grammatik. While back in WordPerfect, you can review the document and make the changes you want. Do not remove the Grammatik comments. When you have finished working with the Grammatik comments in a document, start Grammatik and select Checking Unmark. Grammatik removes its comments, but does not remove the editing you have done to the document. When Grammatik finishes unmarking the document, press ESC and select Quit Grammatik.

Print the Grammatical Errors or Save Them in a File

575

You have other options if you do not want to make the grammatical changes interactively. You can choose Preferences Options and mark the check box for either Print errors on printer or Write errors to .ERR file.

Postpone Handling Grammatical Problems by Marking Them for Later Review

You can either mark all grammatical problems at once or you can mark selected ones as you review the document. To mark the current problem for later review, press F8 when the problem is noted. To mark the entire document and look at it in WordPerfect, select Checking Mark.

You Can Stop Grammatik's Interactive Check and Begin Again Where You Left Off

If you decide that you cannot finish working on a document interactively, you can choose **Quit Quit Place Bookmark**. Once a bookmark is added you will be able to resume interactive checking from the Checking menu, where you select Resume Interactive. Grammatik automatically handles moving to the bookmark it has added.

Grammatik Will Display Definitions of Grammatical Terms You Do Not Understand

Grammatik may sometimes note a problem or display advice about the parts of speech that you don't understand. When this happens, you can find general grammatical information and definitions of grammatical terms at the Help menu. You can also press F4 to get more information on parts of speech.

Use Grammatik's Advice on Writing Styles to Help You When a Document Does Not Have the Style You Want

TIP 579

If Grammatik is finding many errors, you might find it best to let it mark all the errors; you can then study them in more detail. After you have checked a few of these documents you will notice that, as you write a new document, you are finding errors and applying Grammatik's advice yourself rather than having to wait for Grammatik to do it.

You Can Save Different Preference Files

TIP 580

Once you customize your preference settings, you can choose File Save Preferences File. When you want to use the file again choose File Get Preferences File.

You Can Leave Grammatik Without Saving Any Changes You Have Made

TIP 581

If you want to discard the editing changes made while using Grammatik, you can choose Quit Cancel Ignore work so far. This is a good solution if you want to study the overall suggested changes before making permanent changes to your document.

You Can Instruct Grammatik to Temporarily Ignore a Specific Rule

TIP 582

When Grammatik flags an error, you can stop the display of future suggestions for that rule class. Use F6 to begin ignoring the rule class. To start using it again select Edit Restore Rule Classes.

You Can Run Grammatik Separately from WordPerfect

You can use Grammatik separately from WordPerfect by typing **GMK** at the DOS prompt—if the software is installed and your path statement has the directory where the Grammatik programs are stored.

If You Are Left-Handed You Can Switch the Mouse Buttons for Grammatik

The left/right mouse button settings in Grammatik are set separately from those in WordPerfect, so if you have changed the settings in WordPerfect, you'll have to change them in Grammatik as well. To change the mouse buttons to a left-handed setting, select Preferences Options and make sure there is an X in the check box for Swap left/right mouse buttons. Select this option if the X is missing to add it.

You Can Set Grammatik's Screen Colors

Grammatik does not use WordPerfect's screen color settings. To customize Grammatik's screen colors, select Preferences Screen Attributes. Six different color options are available.

Use a Predefined Writing Style or Create One Yourself

The default style preference in Grammatik is General. This style provides a set of rules that can be applied to multipurpose documents. In addition to General, there are other predefined writing styles, as discussed in Tip 570, as well as styles you can create yourself.

You can also change the level of formality while defining a writing style by pressing F3.

You will probably want to try several of the styles to see which best meet your needs. You can choose among the writing styles as follows:

1. Select **P**references **W**riting Style.
2. Highlight the desired style and press ENTER.

You can also create your own style, using one of the predefined styles as your starting point. Follow these steps to create your own writing style:

1. Choose **P**references **W**riting Style after starting Grammatik.
2. Highlight one of the predefined styles and choose F2: Create Custom Style.
3. Highlight a custom style placeholder and select OK.
4. Type a new style name and select OK.
5. Modify the specific rule classes on each of the next four screens.
6. Choose OK twice.

When You Want to Check the Grammar of a Specific Section of a Document, Block the Section First

By blocking a section of text before you run a grammar check, you can limit the scope of the grammar check to that section of text. Press F12, block the text you want to check, and request the grammar check. This allows you to check new paragraphs or other additions without having to check the entire document again.

Use Grammatik to Find Out Which Words You Frequently Repeat

You can use Grammatik to list how frequently you use words in a document. Select Statistics Historical profile. (You can also select Statistics Single-document profile.) Scan this list for words that appear frequently (look for large numbers next to the words), ignoring words like "the" and "an". Then use the Thesaurus to find alternatives to the words that are used too often in your text.

You Can Compare the Statistics of One Document to the Statistics of Another Document

Grammatik initially provides comparison statistics from three different documents: the Gettysburg Address, a Hemingway short story, and a life insurance policy. The statistics presented are the Flesch-Kincaid Grade Level, the Flesch Reading Ease, the average words per sentence, the average words per paragraph, and the average letters per word.

If, however, you have another document you would like to base your comparisons on, simply make that document active and choose Statistics Comparison Charts, type + to customize the charts, and type a description of your file. You can substitute the values from your file for the Gettysburg Address, the Hemingway story, and the insurance document. If you decide you would like to go back to the original comparisons, choose Statistics Restore default comparisons and the original values will be in place next time you use Grammatik.

Many Grammatik Menu Options Can Be Activated with Shortcut Keys

TIP 590

A few of the Grammatik options—and the letters that activate them—appear at the bottom of the initial screen, but many other menu options can be invoked by typing a single letter. The complete list of letters that activate features is shown in the following:

Letter	Action
O	File Open
Q	File Quit
I	Checking Interactive
R	Checking Resume Interactive
G	Checking Grammar and Mechanics
E	Checking Spelling only
D	Checking Read only
M	Checking Mark
U	Checking Unmark
W	Preferences Writing style
H	Statistics Historical profile
N	Statistics Comparison charts
T	Statistics Show Statistics

In WordPerfect 6 You Can Check the Grammar of a Document That Is Not Open

TIP 591

After starting Grammatik, simply select File Open and select the desired file from the subsequent list. Grammatik will then check the document.

Readability Is the Key to Delivering Your Message—Let Grammatik Help

The three readability scores that Grammatik provides can help you present information that is understandable to your audience. The three scores are Flesch-Kincaid Grade Level, Flesch Reading Ease, and Gunning's Fog Index. All three scores indicate a grade level or convert to one. They all look at the number of words per sentence and the number of syllables, though each uses a slightly different formula.

The Flesch-Kincaid Grade Level provides an approximate grade level with this formula:

$$(.39)\times(\text{average words per sentence})+11.8\times(\text{average syllables per word})$$

This total is subtracted from 15.59 to give a grade level.

The Flesch Reading Ease score is measured on a scale of 1 to 100 and calculated with this formula:

$$1.015\times(\text{average sentence length})+.846\times(\text{number of syllables in 100 words})$$

Subtract the total above from 206.835 to calculate the score.

Grammatik provides these approximate conversions to grade level for the following Flesch Reading Ease scores:

Score	Grade
90-100	4
80-90	5
70-80	6
60-70	7 & 8
50-60	Some high school
30-50	High school to college
0-30	College and above

The Gunning Fog Index provides a grade level with this formula:

$$(\text{average words per sentence})+(\text{number of words with three or more syllables})$$

Multiply this total by .4 to arrive at Gunning's Fog Index.

There Are Two Additional Grammatik Utilities

TIP 593

Two additional Grammatik utilities are the Rule Designer, which lets you create your own rules for document checking, and the Dictionary Utility, which lets you add WordPerfect supplemental dictionaries to Grammatik's spelling check. You can get these and other WordPerfect utilities by contacting WordPerfect Corporation.

CHAPTER 13

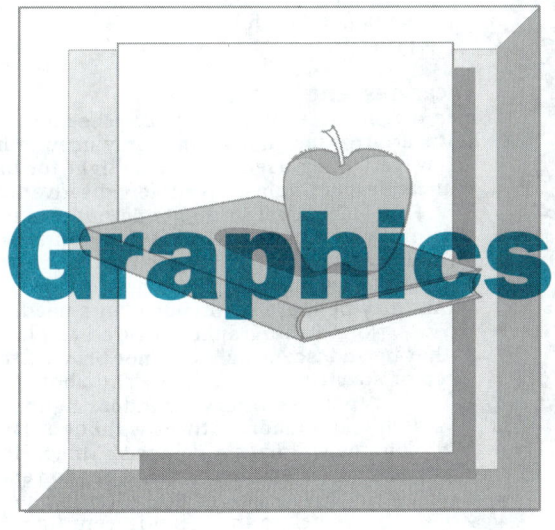

Graphics

TIP 594

Liven Up Your Documents with Clip Art

Your documents will look more interesting and keep the reader's attention if they are enhanced with pictures or other graphical elements. WordPerfect has many pieces of clip art that you can include in your documents. The following document contains text that has been livened up with clip art.

Lighting Your Plants

When you have indoor plants, you will want to consider the type of lighting these plants receive. The right light will encourage your plants' growth, and without the correct type of light, some plants will not grow.

The two types of indoor lighting are incandescent and fluorescent lights. These two types of light have different effects on plants. Most of the cause of the difference between the types of lighting is the color spectrum of light each type of light provides. Light is made up of many different colors that combine to give the white color associated with light. For example, when you direct sunlight through a prism, you will see many colors ranging from red on one end to blue on the other. Neither incandescent nor fluorescent lights provides the full spectrum. Plants need both red and blue light to prosper.

Incandescent Lights

Since incandescent light bulbs are cheaper, these bulbs are the ones most commonly used in homes. However, when used to provide light for plants, incandescent lights have a few disadvantages. First, incandescent lights do not provide the full color spectrum. They frequently lack the blue end of the color spectrum. They are also less energy efficient. They generate a lot of heat that may be more than your plants need.

Note: Photographers as well as plants know that incandescent lights do not provide the full color spectrum. If you know any photographers, ask if they use filters for indoor lighting. When you take indoor pictures without a flash, the photos will have a yellowish tinge. However, you can use an 80A or 80B filter to remove this yellow tinge. The 80A or 80B filter is blue to add the blue back to the incandescent light's color

You can add a graphics box in WordPerfect 5.1 by following these steps:

1. Press ALT-F9 or activate the **G**raphics menu.
2. Select **F**igure, **T**able Box, Text **B**ox, **U**ser Box, or **E**quation.
3. Select **C**reate.
4. Select the contents of the graphics box.
   - If the graphics box will contain an image or text that is copied from a file on disk into the document, select **F**ilename, type the name of the file, and press ENTER.
   - If the graphics box will contain an image that you keep on disk, select **F**ilename, type the name of the file, and press ENTER. Next, select Co**n**tents, and then select Graphic on **D**isk.
   - If the graphics box will contain text, select Co**n**tents, and then select **T**ext. Select **E**dit, type the text, and press F7 (Exit).
   - If the graphics box will contain an equation, select Co**n**tents and **E**quation. Select **E**dit, enter the equation, and press F7 (Exit).
5. Select additional graphics box options as described next.
6. Return to the document by pressing F7.

You can add a graphics box in WordPerfect 6 by following these steps:

1. Press ALT-F9 or activate the **G**raphics menu.
2. Select Graphics **B**oxes **C**reate.
3. Select the contents of the graphics box.
   - If the graphics box will contain an image or text that is copied from a file on disk, select **F**ilename, type the name of the file, and select OK.
   - If the graphics box will contain an image that you keep on disk, select **F**ilename, type the name of the file, and press ENTER. Next, select Co**n**tents Image on **D**isk.
   - If the graphics box will contain text, select Co**n**tents **T**ext Cr**e**ate Text, type the text, and press F7.
   - If the graphics box will contain an equation, select Co**n**tents, **E**quation Cr**e**ate Equation, enter the equation, and press F7.
4. Select additional graphics box options as described next.
5. Return to the document by pressing F7.

Some of the options you can select for graphics boxes include

- ❏ Adding a caption, whose placement and appearance can be customized as described in Tip 643.

- ❏ Setting the image or text placement relative to the graphics box size.

- ❏ Setting the height and width of the graphics box, as well as keeping or ignoring the original height-to-width ratio.

❏ Adding shading to the graphics box at the percentage you desire, as described in Tip 647.

❏ Changing the appearance of the border around the graphics box.

❏ Adjusting how the graphic is placed on the page relative to the text. Tip 644 describes how you can select Anchor Type to change the graphics box position relative to the surrounding text.

❏ Setting how the graphics box fits relative to the page.

❏ Setting how text flows around or through the graphics box. Tip 634 has more information on how you can use this feature.

❏ Setting the graphics box style for WordPerfect 6 graphics boxes. Tip 633 has more information about changing the style of graphics boxes.

FLOWERS.PCX
BORDFLOW.PCX

The graphics shown above are in the files FLOWERS.PCX and BORDFLOW.PCX on the accompanying disk.

The graphics images you see in this book come from one of two sources. They are either the images that WordPerfect 5.1 or 6 provides, or they are included on the disk that accompanies this book. Appendix D includes a complete listing of the images available on the accompanying disk.

If You Have Extra Room on a Page, Consider Jazzing It Up with Graphics or Text

Large areas of empty space at the beginning or end of a report can be improved by adding a graphic to the extra white area. Since you can use many different types of graphics files in your WordPerfect documents, you can choose from almost any clip art you have available. See Tip 664 for a list of the many graphics file formats that can be used with WordPerfect.

WordPerfect Lets You Add as Many Graphics Boxes as You Want

You can add multiple graphics boxes to a WordPerfect document. The constraint is memory. You can continue to add graphics boxes of any sort as long as WordPerfect has enough memory. If your system runs out of memory, try replacing graphics boxes containing images with images on disk.

Choose the Graphics Box Style Based on the Box's Default Settings

Each type of graphics box has a different set of default settings. The default settings specify the graphics box's caption, numbering style, border, size, and alignment. By choosing the type of graphics box that best matches the caption, numbering style, border, size, and alignment you want, you save yourself from having to change the options of your graphics box. The different graphics box types and some of their default settings are as follows:

❑ *Figure boxes* are used for displaying clip-art images and other graphics. Figure boxes use the caption "Figure", followed by the figure number. These boxes have a thin border on all sides, with a width of 3 1/2 inches and automatic height. Each figure box is attached to a paragraph, and appears at the right of the paragraph.

❑ *Table boxes* are used for displaying tables, spreadsheets, and other statistical data. They use the caption "Table", followed by the table number. Table boxes have a thick border on the top and bottom; they have a width of 3 1/2 inches and automatic height. Each table box is attached to a paragraph, and appears at the right of the paragraph.

❑ *Text boxes* are used for displaying text that you want set off from the main document. They use a caption consisting of the text box number. Text boxes, by default, contain text and are shaded. They have a thick border on the top and bottom, a width of 3 1/2 inches, and automatic height. Each text box is attached to a paragraph, and appears at the right of the paragraph.

❑ *User boxes* are used for displaying clip-art images and text when no border is desired. They use a caption consisting of the user box number. User boxes have no border; they have a width of 3 1/2 inches and automatic height. Each user box is attached to a paragraph, and appears at the right of the paragraph.

❑ *Equation boxes* are used for displaying mathematical or scientific equations. The default caption consists of the number of the equation box, surrounded by parentheses and placed on the right side of the box. Equation boxes, by default, contain an equation; they have no border. Each equation box is attached to a paragraph but is fully justified.

❑ *Button boxes* are used to display buttons for the user to press or click. Hypertext uses button boxes to allow the user to move to the text. Button boxes do not have a default caption. Button boxes have shading and borders that make them look like buttons in the Button Bar; they have a width of 1 inch, with automatic height. Each button box is attached to a character, and appears at the right of the character.

❑ *Watermark image boxes* are used for displaying images behind areas of text in a document. By default, these boxes contain images but do not have captions or borders; they have a brightness of .75. Each watermark image box is attached to a page, and is sized and positioned to fill the page; the text of the document prints right over the box and its contents.

❑ *Inline equation boxes* are used for inserting equations within the document's text, rather than set apart from the other text. By default, these boxes contain equations, and have no captions or borders. Each inline equation box is attached to a character; both the width and the height of the box are set automatically.

If you want to change the settings for a graphics box, you can change the graphics box style options, as described in Tip 633. In WordPerfect 6, you can also change the style of a graphics box, as described in Tip 600.

The initial selection of a graphics box style is more important in WordPerfect 5.1 than in WordPerfect 6. As Tip 600 mentions, WordPerfect 6 can reassign the graphics box style of any graphics box. WordPerfect 5.1 does not have this feature.

TIP 598
Create Your Own WordPerfect 6 Graphics Box Styles

In addition to the eight graphics box styles available in WordPerfect 6, you can create your own styles. Select **Graphics Graphics Boxes Styles**, or select Based on Box Styles from the Edit/Create Graphics

Box dialog box, and the Graphics Box Styles dialog box will appear. From this box, you can select Create, and the Create Graphics Box Style dialog box will appear. Initially, the style you create will adopt the settings of the currently highlighted graphics box style. However, after you type a name for the style you wish to create, you can use the Create Graphics Box Style dialog box to edit many of the settings for your custom style. You can select Contents to select the default contents of the graphics box. Tips 643, 647, 644, 651, 654, and 634 have more information about the changes you can make to the caption options, the border and fill styles, the attachment options, the size and position of graphics boxes, and the placement of text around them.

WordPerfect 5.1 and WordPerfect 6 Number Graphics Boxes Differently

TIP 599

WordPerfect 5.1 and 6 keep track of graphics boxes in different ways. WordPerfect 5.1 keeps separate lists of each graphics box style. WordPerfect 6 has a master list of every graphics box in a document; it uses this list to determine how many of each graphics box style are used in the document.

For example, if you have a document that has four graphics boxes, two using the figure graphics box style and two using the table graphics box style, WordPerfect 5.1 will use one counter for figure graphics boxes and another counter for table graphics boxes, as shown here:

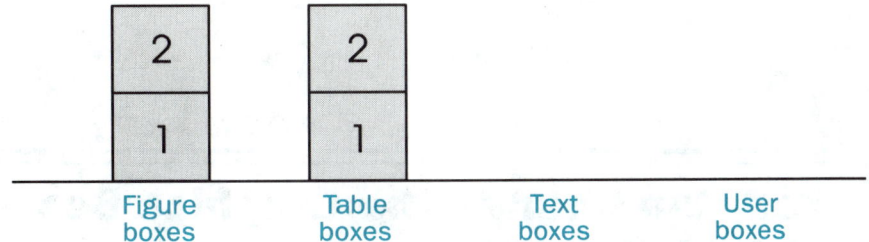

The same document in WordPerfect 6, on the other hand, has one counter that keeps track of all the graphics boxes in a document. Each of the graphics boxes is also included on a separate list that includes all the graphics boxes of a particular style, as shown in the following:

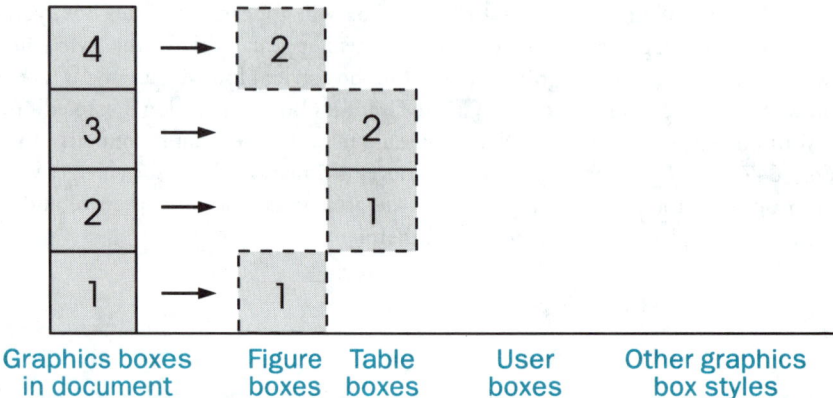

Graphics boxes   Figure   Table   User   Other graphics
in document   boxes   boxes   boxes   box styles

This difference in methods of numbering graphics boxes in a document is why, when you edit a graphics box in WordPerfect 5.1, you must select the appropriate graphics box number for the graphics box style. To edit a graphics box in WordPerfect 5.1, select Graphics or press ALT-F9 (Graphics), select the type of graphics box, select Edit, type the number of the graphics box you want to work with, and press ENTER. In WordPerfect 6, when you select Graphics Graphics Boxes Edit, you have two ways of selecting the graphics box to edit. You can select Document Box Number and enter the number of the graphics box within a document. You can also select Counter Number, the graphics box style, and the number of the graphics box within the subset of graphics boxes using that style.

WordPerfect 6 has two shortcuts for working with graphics boxes: You can change which graphics box you are editing by pressing HOME PGUP *or* HOME PGDN *to edit the previous or following graphics box. Also, if you are using a mouse you can edit a graphics box by double-clicking it when you are in Page or Graphics display mode.*

You Can Change the Graphics Box Style in WordPerfect 6

Since it uses a single list for all of the graphics boxes in a document, WordPerfect 6 will let you change the style of a graphics box. Select Graphics Graphics Boxes Edit, select the graphics box to edit, and select Edit Box. From the Edit Graphics Box dialog box, you can select Based on Box Style. Then,

from the Graphics Box Styles dialog box, you can select one of the graphics box styles. You can also edit the settings of the graphics box style (see Tip 633), create new styles (see Tip 598), save them to a file, retrieve a file of graphics box styles, and establish libraries. Selecting the graphics box style and then clicking the Close button returns you to the Edit Graphics Box. When you leave the Edit Graphics Box, the currently selected graphics box is assigned the style you have selected.

Changing the graphics box style changes the counter in which the graphics box is included. For example, changing a graphics box style from a table box to a figure box only reassigns the graphics box from the list of text boxes to the list of figure boxes.

WordPerfect 5.1 does not let you change a graphics box type. If you want a graphics box to use the same settings as another graphics box style, you will need to change its options, as described in Tip 633.

You Can Add Graphics Box Numbers to Your Text in WordPerfect 6

TIP 601

If you are creating graphics boxes that are referenced in their adjoining text, you can use WordPerfect to insert the graphics box numbers. If you rearrange the graphics boxes in a document, both the graphics box numbers in the captions and those in the text will be updated. To insert the graphics box number, select **Graphics Graphics Boxes Numbering**. From the Counters dialog box, you can see the system counters that WordPerfect has set up. WordPerfect has separate counters for each of the graphics box styles that uses a caption and that includes the number of the graphics box. Next, highlight the counter for the graphics box style you want to add to the document. Select **Display in Document** and OK. The number WordPerfect adds to your document is the number of the last graphics box of that style.

Use Another File as the Contents of a Graphics Box

TIP 602

You can fit one document into another by inserting the file into a graphics box. When you create the graphics box and select Filename, you can type the name of the file you want to use. Most of the time

when you add graphics to a document, you copy the graphics image from the disk to your document. However, you are not limited to graphics images. You can also insert another document's text into a graphics box by supplying the document's filename.

Add Graphics to WordPerfect 6 by Retrieving Graphics Files

You can quickly create a graphics box by retrieving a graphics file. Select **G**raphics, or press ALT-F9 and then select **R**etrieve Image, and a prompt for a filename will appear. Enter a filename, being sure to include its extension. WordPerfect 6 will attempt to bring the image into the document, using a figure box graphics style and the default settings.

You Can Retrieve Graphics Files the Same Way You Retrieve WordPerfect 6 Documents

When you select File Retrieve or press SHIFT-F10 twice in WordPerfect 6, you can enter the name of a graphics image you want to use. You will see the prompt for the type of image contained in the file. After you select the file's format, WordPerfect 6 brings the image into the document using a figure box graphics style and all of the default settings.

When you retrieve a graphics image file the same way you would retrieve a document, make sure to include the extension and path. WordPerfect 6 assumes that the file has only the extension you provide. WordPerfect 6 also assumes that the file is in the same directory as your other WordPerfect documents, unless you specify a different location.

Make Your Documents Smaller by Using Images on Disk

If disk space is at a premium, you can make the documents that use graphics images smaller by not saving the graphics images as parts of the documents. When you retrieve a graphics file into a document,

WordPerfect copies the graphics image into the document. The document file will then be larger by the size of the image file. You can choose to keep the image in its own file, separate from the document. When you edit a graphics box, select Contents and Graphic on Disk in WordPerfect 5.1. In WordPerfect 6, select Contents, and then select Image on Disk. Now, although the image is used in the document, it will not be copied into the document. Remember, however, that if you move the document to another computer, you will also need to move or copy the image files used by the document.

Update Graphics Images If They Have Changed

If one of the images used in a graphics box has changed, you need to tell WordPerfect to update the version of the graphics file included in the document. When you edit the graphics box, select Filename and press ENTER. When WordPerfect asks if you want to replace the current contents of the graphics box, select Yes. However, if the contents of the box is an image on disk, and has not been saved into the document file, WordPerfect will automatically update the graphics image when you retrieve the document that uses it.

You Can Place One Graphics Box on Top of Another for a Different Look

You can create new graphics by combining others. For example, in the following you can see a graphics box created with two copies of BORDER4.WPG and one copy of TIGERHD.WPG. These files are included with WordPerfect 6.

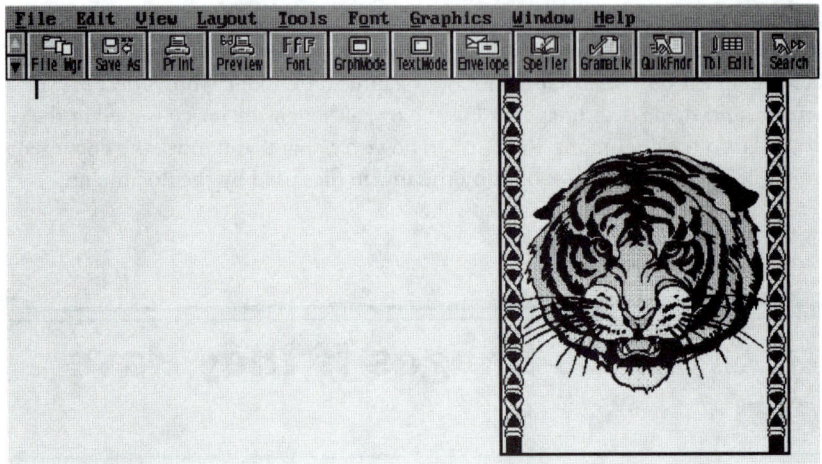

When you combine multiple graphics into one, each part is a separate graphics box. Set all of the graphics boxes except the last to let text flow through the box as described in Tip 634. Also, you will either want to use user graphics box styles or set all of the graphics boxes you use for one image to the same size so you do not have different boundaries. If a graphic is not the appropriate size, you can increase or decrease its size within the graphics box as described in Tip 651. You can also change the graphics position within the graphics box, as described in Tip 654.

The graphics shown above are in the files BORDER4.WPG and TIGERHD.WPG that are included with WordPerfect 6.

BORDER4.WPG
TIGERHD.WPG

Use an Empty Graphics Box to Keep Text from Wrapping in a Given Area

If you need to keep text out of an area on a page, do so by adding a user graphics box. For example, when you are creating a document that will have a seal imprinted on it, add a user graphics box where you expect the seal to be placed. Make the user box the size of the area you want text to skip over. You will

also want to use position options for specifying the location of the user box on the page. Use the user box graphics box style so you do not have a border around the empty area filled by the graphics box.

When You Integrate Text and Graphics into a Single Document, Add the Text and Then the Graphics

You will find that the final result looks better when you create the text for a document and then add the graphics. Adding the graphics afterward lets you focus on the document's appearance without having to look at the text. Also, if you add the graphics and then make major adjustments to the text, you will find yourself having to rearrange the placement of the graphics box. You might want to add the graphics boxes as you go along but hold off making placement and sizing adjustments until you have finished working with the text. Tip 629 offers suggestions for arranging graphics boxes to improve a document's appearance.

Use List Files or the File Manager to Select the Intended Graphics File

When you are adding a filename to a document in a graphics box, you can press F5 to use the WordPerfect 5.1 List Files feature or the WordPerfect 6 File Manager. Selecting a filename from a list of files is easier than remembering the correct name to type. After you press F5, you might need to select the directory where your graphics files are stored. For example, in WordPerfect 6, you can type **\WP60\GRAPHICS** to have the File Manager list the graphics files in this directory. From the list of files, you can highlight the file containing the graphic to use and select Retrieve. The highlighted file is added as the filename for the contents of the graphics box.

WordPerfect 6 has two shortcuts. First, from the File Manager, you can highlight a file and select Look. WordPerfect displays the image in the file. This feature works with the graphics files WordPerfect can directly accept. Second, when prompted for the directory of files to look at, you can press F6 for QuickList and select Graphics Files Personal. WordPerfect has this QuickList set up for the location where the .WPG files included with WordPerfect 6 are stored.

In WordPerfect 6, Display Mode Selects Whether You See the Contents of Graphics Boxes

When the graphics appear in your WordPerfect 6 document in Graphics or Page display mode, moving around in the document is slower because WordPerfect must use more of your computer's resources for displaying the graphics. You can speed things up by using Text mode rather than Graphics mode for displaying your document. In Text mode, you will see the box where the graphics will ultimately appear, but the box will be empty. You can return to the Graphics or Page display mode when you want to see the contents of the graphics boxes. To switch between the display modes, select **P**age Mode, **G**raphics Mode, or **T**ext Mode from the View menu.

The Contents of WordPerfect 5.1 Graphics Boxes Don't Display Until You View or Print Your Document

WordPerfect 5.1 does not have the graphics display modes available in WordPerfect 6. When you add a graphics box to a WordPerfect 5.1 document or a WordPerfect 6 document using the Text display mode, WordPerfect will draw a symbol for the graphics box. When a graphics box is attached to a character, the graphics box appears as a rectangle character. When a graphics box is attached to a page or paragraph, WordPerfect will draw a box indicating the boundary of the graphics box. The exception is when a WordPerfect 5.1 graphics box uses full justification. Fully justified graphics boxes use a diagram that spans the page but does not indicate how far down a page the graphics box extends. The following illustration shows some different ways that graphics boxes can appear on a Text mode screen:

```
Hours █
9 a.m. - 8 p.m. Monday through Saturday
9 a.m. - 5 p.m. Sunday

How to Order                     ┌USR 2─────────────────────────┐
By Mail - Complete and mail      │                              │
the attached order form. If      │                              │
there is insufficient time to    │                              │
mail your tickets, they will     │                              │
be held for you at the Box       │                              │
Office. If you do not receive    │                              │
your tickets, please call the    │                              │
Box Office to confirm your       │                              │
order.                           └──────────────────────────────┘

By Telephone - Complete the following form:
┌TXT 1─────────────────────────────────────────────────────────┐
Once the form is completed, you can call one of the Box Office
phone numbers shown below to place your order.

Rush Tickets

C:\WPDOCS\TIP612                          Doc 1 Pg 1 Ln 5.55" Pos 5.6"
```

In the above document, the square after "Hours" is a user graphics box attached to a character. The box with "USR 2" at the top is another user graphics box attached to a character. The box with "TXT 1" at the top is fully justified horizontally.

You Can Move Graphics Boxes to Specific Positions

When you want a graphics image to start at a specific location, you need to determine two measurements. First, measure the distance from the top of the page to the point where you want the top of the graphics box to appear. Second, measure the distance from the left side of the page to the point where you want the left side of the graphics box to appear. Once you have these measurements, you can set the graphics box position by following the appropriate set of directions below.

To move a graphics box in WordPerfect 5.1, follow these next steps:

1. Select Anchor **T**ype **P**age.
2. Select Vertical **P**osition **S**et Position.
3. Type the distance from the top of the page to the top of the graphics box and press ENTER.
4. Select **H**orizontal Position **S**et Position.
5. Type the distance from the left side of the page to the left side of the graphics box and press ENTER.

To move a graphics box in WordPerfect 6, follow these steps from the Edit Graphics Box dialog box (see Tip 599 if you need help getting to the Edit Graphics Box dialog box):

1. Select **A**ttach To **F**ixed Page Position.
2. Select Edit **P**osition.
3. Select Distance from **L**eft of Page and type the distance from the left side of the page to the left side of the graphics box.
4. Select Distance from **T**op of Page and type the distance from the top of the page to the top of the graphics box.
5. Select OK.

Pages That Print Incompletely When You Are Printing Graphics Indicate Insufficient Printer Memory

TIP 614

If you see the message "Not enough memory to print graphics", or if a printed page has incomplete graphics, your printer might not have enough memory. As described in Tip 308, page printers require enough memory to store all of a page. When your printer does not have enough memory, you will not be able to fill all of a page with graphics. If you run into this problem, try the following solutions:

❏ Reduce the size of the graphics images. For example, if a graphic occupies the whole page, resize it so it only uses half of the page.

❏ Change the fonts the document uses to printer fonts.

❏ Remove any watermarks.

❏ Try printing graphics and text separately, as described in Tip 272.

❏ Reduce the resolution of the graphics, as described in Tip 272.

You Can Set Graphics Printing Settings

TIP 615

Your printer has several options for printing colors and shades in graphics boxes. The three methods you can select from include halftoning, error diffusion, and ordered dither. To select the one used to print the contents of the graphics box, edit the graphics box (see Tip 599) and then select Image Editor. From the Image Editor window, select Edit Print Parameters, or select Edit All Print Parameters. You can select how the colors or shades are created by selecting one of the dithering methods. To see how the different dithering methods will print on your printer, create a document containing a graphic and try printing the document after changing the current dithering method to another one of the available choices.

Create Borders by Using Multiple Graphics Boxes

TIP 616

You can create your own borders by repeating graphics images in multiple locations, rotating the images as necessary. An example of such a border is shown here:

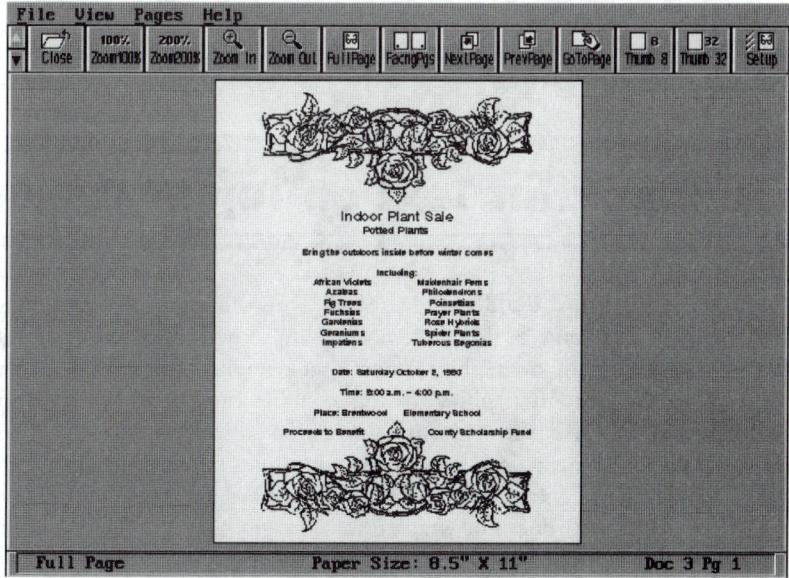

You can create this same border by using the graphics in ROSES.PCX and following these steps:

1. Add the graphics to a user-defined box. A user-defined box is used because by default, this style does not draw a line around the image it contains. The image is in the file ROSES.PCX. Make sure that the graphics box is attached to the page, rather than to the paragraph, and that the horizontal position is set to Full.

2. Make copies of the graphics box for each side of the page where you want your border to appear. You can block the code for the first box, press CTRL-INS to copy it, and press ENTER to make the second copy. If you want four copies, for example when you are putting a graphics box in each corner of the page, you can press CTRL-F4 and select **R**etrieve and then **B**lock in WordPerfect 5.1, or **P**aste Block in WordPerfect 6.

3. Edit each graphics box so that it appears where you want. For this example, you need to edit the second box to have a bottom vertical position.

4. Rotate or flip the images by editing the graphics box as described in Tips 655 and 656. For this example, in WordPerfect 5.1, select **E**dit, and then **R**otate, type **180**, press ENTER, and select **N**o to choose not to mirror the image. In WordPerfect 6, select **E**dit and use the Flip **V**ert check box to adjust the image. Pressing F7 twice returns you to the document.

5. Type the text that will appear on the page.

ROSES.PCX

The clip art used in this example can be found on the accompanying disk in the file ROSES.PCX.

You Can Print Text on Top of Graphics

TIP 617

Most of the time when you add graphics to a file, you will want the document's text to flow around the text. However, there may be times when you want to overlay text and graphics. You have two options for printing text on top of graphics. You can set a graphics box so that text does not wrap around it, or you can create a second graphics box that contains the text you want to appear on top of the graphics image, and then place the box containing the text directly on top of the box containing the graphic. Tip 607 has more information about putting multiple graphics boxes in the same location. The beginning of the document pictured in the following shows an example of text and graphics combined. In this document, text does not wrap around the graphics box. To achieve this effect in WordPerfect 5.1, when you edit or create the graphics box, set the Wrap Text Around Box option to

No. In WordPerfect 6, select Text Flows Around Box Text Flows Through Box. The image is from the file SHIPPING.PCX.

In this document, the horizontal position of the graphics box is set to Full. Once you add a graphic to your document, you can use features such as line spacing, line height, and advance to move the text to the place where you want it to appear on top of the graphic. This text can be part of the main document, or if the document includes other text that you do not want to place on top of the graphic, you can create a separate text box to contain the text to be overlaid. With this method, any changes made to the line spacing or line height of the overlaid text will not interfere with the remaining text in the document.

If you use WordPerfect 5.1, or the Text display mode in WordPerfect 6, you will need to check the document frequently with Print Preview to see how well the text overlaps the graphics. When you use Graphics mode in WordPerfect 6, the text is printed first, and then the graphics are drawn. Often the graphics cover the text. If you want to see both, use the Page display mode.

The clip art used in this example is on the accompanying disk in the file SHIPPING.PCX.

SHIPPING.PCX

You Can Create Watermarks in WordPerfect 5.1 Using Graphics Boxes

WordPerfect 5.1 does not have the watermark features available in WordPerfect 6; however, you can create your own watermarks. To do so, add a user-defined graphics box or a figure graphics box, depending on whether you want a border. For this graphics box, set the Wrap Text Around Box option to No. Change the size so the vertical and horizontal positions are full. A point to remember is that the image should be rather faint. For example, if you want to use the SHIPPING.PCX image shown in Tip 619 for a WordPerfect 5.1 watermark, edit it with a program such as DrawPerfect or Windows Paintbrush, changing the black in the image to gray so that you can still see the text above it. Then use the modified image for your watermark. You will also need to copy the code for the graphics box to use as a watermark on each page.

Use the Button Box Graphics Box Style for Documentation in WordPerfect 6

If you are using WordPerfect 6 to create instructions for a computer application, and you want to tell the reader to press a button, you can make the button stand out by putting it in one of WordPerfect's button box graphics boxes. A sample of a document using the button box graphics box style looks like this:

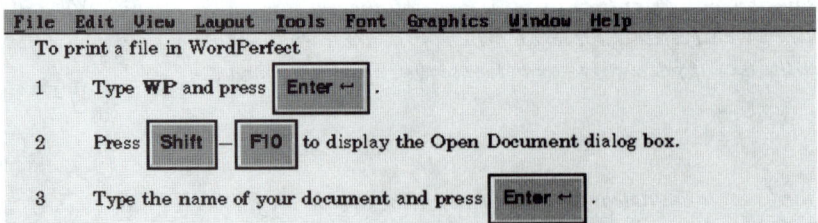

For each of these buttons, the width and height are set automatically. The BoxText system style has been changed, as described in Tip 423, so that the font is now set to Swiss 721 Bold (Speedo). To make entering the document quicker, once one button is created for a specific key, it is copied to every location where that key is used.

When you use the button box graphics style, add a space between the graphics box and any adjacent punctuation so that periods and commas do not look like they are part of the graphics box. Also, when you are joining keys (as in SHIFT-F10 in step 2), you will want to use an em dash created with CTRL-W (or Font WP) Characters. The em dash is character 4,34. CTRL-W has also been used here to create character 5,20, the arrow symbol which appears on the ENTER key.

Start Newsletters with Graphics

TIP 620

You can make your newsletters look more inviting by adding graphics images at the beginning. Using the same graphics on each version of the newsletter helps your readers quickly recognize your newsletter. It also makes the newsletter more pleasing to read. An example of such a newsletter is shown here:

You can also try combining the newsletter title with the graphics by having the text of the title overlay the graphics. Tip 617 has more information about combining text and graphics.

The graphic used in the newsletter is in the file HORNS.PCX, included on the accompanying disk.

HORNS.PCX

Create Calendars Using Tables and Clip Art

TIP 621

The following shows a calendar for December 1995 created with WordPerfect:

| File | Edit | View | Layout | Tools | Font | Graphics | Window | Help |

December

Sunday	Monday	Tuesday	Wednesday	Thursday	Friday	Saturday
				1	2	3
4	5	6	7	8	9	10
11	12	13	14	15	16	17
18	19	20	21	22	23	24
25	26	27	28	29	30	31

The art at the top is stored in the file DECEMBER.WPG on the accompanying disk. The calendar is created by adding a table with seven columns and seven rows. The days of the week are entered in the second row and the dates are entered in the bottom rows. Once you have this calendar, you can add information about events occurring on various dates. The table's height will expand to hold each new entry that you make. You might also want to switch to a smaller font, smaller margins, or landscape orientation to provide more space for the calendar.

The accompanying disk has clip art for each of the twelve months; you can incorporate this art into your own calendars. Each of these images uses the month's name, or at least the first eight characters, and a .WPG file extension.

DECEMBER.WPG

Create Greeting Cards by Using a Graphic on the Front

TIP 622

You can use WordPerfect to create greeting cards. A sample graphic that you can print and fold in half to create a card is shown here. The lines that you see should not be printed; they are shown only to indicate where you should fold the paper to create the card. The text that appears upside down has been put into graphics boxes to make it easier to rotate and place in the document.

The clip art used in this example is on the accompanying disk in the file PICNIC.PCX.

PICNIC.PCX

Graphics Boxes Can Be Used in Headers, Footers, and Footnotes

In addition to including graphics in the text of your documents, you can also place them in the document's headers, footers, endnotes, comments, and footnotes. As you create these elements, you can add graphics to them by pressing ALT-F9 or selecting the Graphics menu, and then continuing to make selections just as if you were adding graphics to the main part of your document.

Sidebars and Pull Quotes Add Visual Interest to Documents

You can highlight a point mentioned in your document by putting that text into a sidebar or pull quote. The text to appear in the sidebar or pull quote should be put into a text box, as shown here. The text box here has been attached to the page so it appears between the two columns of body text.

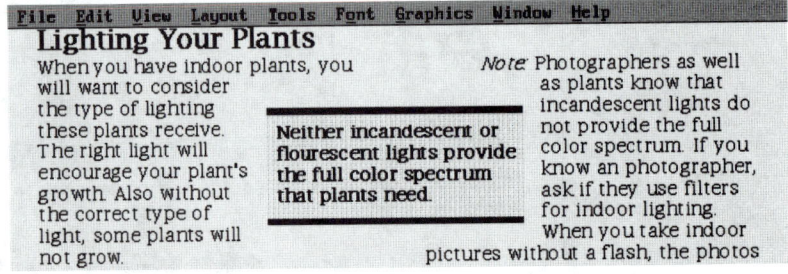

Large Initial Capitals Add Visual Interest

You have probably seen magazine articles that use large letters to begin sections of text. You can add the same feature to your documents, as shown in the following, by placing the initial character in a graphics box that is attached to a character position:

```
File  View  Pages  Help
One of the most important reference books available will soon
be celebrating its Fifteenth Edition. As a performer, you will
understand and appreciate the importance of a publication such as
the Internation
```

Use Clip Art from Third Party Sources to Have More Graphics for Your Documents

TIP 626

You can order clip art for your documents from many vendors. Many clip-art companies create specialized clip art, such as medical symbols or pictures of well-known individuals. Purchasing clip art from outside sources can save you time and money. With the more elaborate drawings, the cost of the clip art is usually less than the value of the time you would use to draw it yourself. You can locate sources of clip art by reviewing advertisements in computer periodicals. If you have a scanner, you can scan images into a computer files and use those images as clip art.

WordPerfect Comes with Several Pieces of Clip Art That You Can Use in Your Documents

TIP 627

Both WordPerfect 5.1 and WordPerfect 6 provide sample graphics that you can incorporate into your documents, just like any other graphics. The following illustration shows WordPerfect's DRAGON.WPG incorporated into a document:

Clip Art from WordPerfect 5.1 Can Be Used in WordPerfect 6

The same .WPG files used by WordPerfect 5.1 will work with WordPerfect 6. If you are upgrading to WordPerfect 6 from an earlier version, keep the old .WPG files so that you can use them in your WordPerfect 6 documents. After installing WordPerfect 6, enter **COPY \WP51*.WPG \WP60\GRAPHICS** at the DOS prompt (assuming that your WordPerfect 5.1 files are in the \WP51 directory).

After Adding Graphics, You Can Adjust the Page Breaks in a Document to Improve its Appearance

After you add all of the text and graphics you want to include in your document, you will be spending time flipping though the pages to ensure that you are happy with the layout. If you are not satisfied with the placement of the graphics relative to the page breaks, you have several options:

- ❑ Work from the beginning to the end of the document as you adjust its appearance. Changes you make in the beginning might shift the contents later in the document. You do not want to spend lots of time making the end of the document look fantastic, only to undermine your efforts later by making substantial changes at the beginning of the document.

- ❑ Change the anchor of the graphics box. You might want to keep a graphics box anchored to a particular paragraph or character while you are working on the text, and then change its anchor point to the page. When you change the anchor to the page, you can easily move the graphics box to the top or bottom of the page.

- ❑ Move the graphics box to another paragraph, or place it next to another character, to change its location on the page.

- ❑ Change the vertical and horizontal placement relative to the point where the graphic is anchored. For example, if you have a graphic anchored to a paragraph, you might want to change its vertical placement to the bottom of the page.

- ❑ Consider resizing a graphic if it is too large or small for your needs.

❑ Move large graphics images to the top or bottom of a page when they would otherwise break up the flow of the document.

❑ If the document has facing pages, remember that it is better to have a reference to a graphic on an even page, with the graphic on the following odd page, than to have the reference on an odd page with the graphic on the following even page. When the reference is on an odd page and the graphic is on the next page, the reader has to turn the page to see the image being referred to. When the reference is on an even page, however, and the graphic is on the following odd page, the reader need only glance to the right to see the image in question.

❑ Finally, if you still end up with large blocks of empty space on a page, consider using more clip art.

Graphics boxes only appear on one page. You cannot put part of a graphics box on one page and part on another. If a graphics box will not entirely fit on the page where it is inserted, the box will be bumped to the next page. (You cannot make a graphics box larger than a single page.)

When You Want Text to Be Treated as a Unit, Put the Text in a Box

TIP 630

With text that should be kept together as a unit, you have a couple of choices. You can use Block Protect, described in Tip 140, or Conditional End of Page, described in Tip 141. A third option is to put the text in a graphics box; the text will then be separated from the rest of the document. This method works well if you are making lots of formatting changes to the text that you do not want applied to the rest of the document. When you create a graphics box for storing the text, select Edit in WordPerfect 5.1 or Create Text in WordPerfect 6. Then type the text you want in the graphics box.

You Can Rotate Text in WordPerfect

TIP 631

You can add rotated text to a document by adding a graphics box. When you create the graphics box, select Edit, and then type the text that should be placed at an angle. Rotate the text by pressing ALT-F9, selecting the angle at which the text should appear, and pressing ENTER. An example is shown in the following:

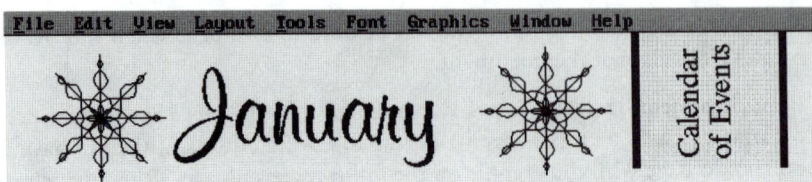

 *Some printers cannot print in two directions at once. Other printers will require that you use all graphics fonts, rather than printer fonts, in order for your angled text to print correctly. You will have to test this feature on your printer to see if you can use it.*

 *The accompanying disk has clip art for each of the twelve months, including the January graphic shown here, that you can incorporate into your own calendars.*

JANUARY.WPG

TIP 632 — Use 100 Percent Shading and White Text to Create a Reverse Box

You can use graphics boxes to create a black box with white text, like the one shown here:

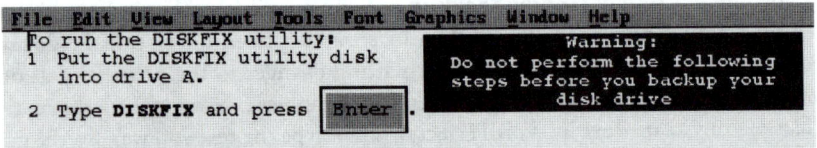

To create a black background box with white text in WordPerfect 5.1, follow these steps:

1. Press ALT-F9, or select **G**raphics.
2. Select the type of graphics box.
3. Select **O**ptions **G**rey Shading
4. Type **100** and press ENTER.
5. Press F7 (Exit) to return to the document.
6. Press ALT-F9, or select **G**raphics.
7. Select the type of graphics box.

8. Select **C**reate **E**dit.
9. Press CTRL-F8 (Font), select Print **C**olor **W**hite, and press F7 (Exit).
10. Type the text for the graphics box.
11. Press F7 (Exit) twice to complete the graphics box.

To create a black background box with white text in WordPerfect 6, follow these steps:

1. Press ALT-F9 or select **G**raphics, and then select Graphics **B**oxes **C**reate.
2. Select Edit **B**order/Fill **F**ill Fill St**y**le.
3. Select 100% Shaded and choose **S**elect, OK, and Close.
4. Select Cr**e**ate Text F**o**nt **P**rint Color, highlight White, and choose **S**elect.
5. Type the text for the graphics box.
6. Press F7 and select OK to complete the graphics box.

By changing the style of the graphics box as described in Tip 633, you can make all of the graphics boxes of a selected style reversed. The following BLACKBOX macro will cause the user graphics box style to have white text, and will then add a user graphics box with a black background.

```
DISPLAY(Off!)
BoxCreate(UserBox!)
BoxFillStyle(Fill100!)
BoxContentType(Text!)
BoxContentEdit
TextColor("White";255;255;255)
SubstructureExit
BoxEnd(Save!)
StyleEditBegin(BoxTextStyle!)
StyleCodes()
TextColor("White";255;255;255)
AttributeAppearanceOn(Bold!)
SubstructureExit
StyleEditEnd(Save!)
```

The accompanying disk has the BLACKBOX.WPM macro shown here.

BLACKBOX.WPM

If You Don't Like the Default Settings of a Graphics Box Type, Change Them

The default settings for a graphics box type sets the border, the space between the border and the box's contents, the space between the border and the surrounding document contents, the numbering of graphics boxes, the default figure caption, the caption position, and the shading level of graphics boxes.

To change a graphics box setting in WordPerfect 5.1:

1. Press ALT-F9, or select **G**raphics.
2. Select the type of graphics box.
3. Make changes to the graphics box settings.
4. Press F7 (Exit) to return to the document.

The new graphics box settings affect all of that type of graphics box, from the point in the document where the new code is entered until the end of the document.

To change a graphics box setting in WordPerfect 6:

1. Press ALT-F9 or select **G**raphics, and then select Graphics **B**oxes Styles.
2. Highlight the type of graphics box you want to use, and select **E**dit.
3. Make changes to the graphics box settings.
4. Select OK and Close to complete the graphics box settings.

WordPerfect 6 is more flexible about changing the settings of graphics boxes of any style. The graphics box style sets the defaults for how the box looks, but you can make changes to individual graphics boxes. In WordPerfect 5.1, you would have to change the settings for the graphics box style, add the graphics box, and return the graphics box style to the original settings.

Text Can Flow Around WordPerfect 6 Graphics

Instead of wrapping the text around the graphics box area, the default in WordPerfect 6 is to adjust the text so that it flows around the graphic inside a graphics box. However, if you select the Contour

Text Flow check box below the Text Flows Around box, WordPerfect 6 will wrap the text around the graphics box area, just as WordPerfect 5.1 does. An example is shown here:

The clip art used in this example is on the accompanying disk in the file TOON28.CGM.

TOON28.CGM

Use Graphics to Emphasize Your Point

You can highlight any point in your text by including graphics that illustrate the point in question. For example, you can purchase clip art to illustrate many clichés. The following document shows a graphic used to emphasize the topic of cutting travel costs.

The clip art used in this example is on the accompanying disk in the file CUT_COST.WMF.

CUT_COST.WMF

You Can Set the Amount of Space Between a Graphics Box and Surrounding Contents

Graphics boxes usually have space between the contents of the graphics box and any border, and also between the borders of the box and the text of the document. You can use more space to keep graphics box contents further away from the document's text, or less space to bring the text closer to the graphics box.

To change the amount of space in the border in WordPerfect 5.1, edit the graphics box settings for the graphics box style as described in Tip 633. From the Options menu, select **Outside Border Space** or **Inside Border Space**, depending on where you want to change the space. Type the measurements for the sides of the graphics box, pressing ENTER after each one.

To change the amount of space in the border in WordPerfect 6, select Edit Border/Fill Spacing from the Edit Graphics Box dialog box. You can clear the **Automatic Spacing** check box and select whether you want to change either the inside or outside spacing. When you select OK and Close, the graphics box will use the new spacing.

You Can Change the Style of the Graphics Box Number in a Figure Caption

When you add a caption to a graphics box, WordPerfect uses the default caption. You can change the appearance of the default caption. Changing the default caption actually changes the meaning of the code that WordPerfect adds to the caption.

In WordPerfect 5.1, press ALT-F9 or select **Graphics**, then select a type of graphics box, and select **Options Caption Number Style**. Edit the caption, using the function keys to add formatting. Add the text that you want to appear in the caption, and place a 1, A, or I, depending on the numbering style, at the location where you want the graphics box number to appear.

In WordPerfect 6, press ALT-F9 or select **Graphics**, then select **Graphics Boxes Create**, and Create or Edit **Caption Number**. From the screen for entering the caption, press ALT-F9, and select **Caption**

Number Style and Edit. In the Caption Number Style dialog box, you can type the text around the [Box Num Disp] code exactly as you want to appear around the graphics box number. You can use the menu or function keys to add formatting.

You Can Alter the Numbering Style for a Graphics Box Style

TIP 638

Each graphics box style has a numbering style as one of its characteristics. You can change the numbering style between using numbers, using letters, and using roman numerals.

In WordPerfect 5.1, press ALT-F9 or select Graphics, then select a type of graphics box, and finally select Options First Level Numbering Method. You can select from numbers, letters, or Roman numerals, or you can turn the numbers off. If you need a second level of numbers for identifying graphics boxes, you can select Second Level Numbering Method, and then specify how you want the second-level item labels to appear.

In WordPerfect 6, press ALT-F9 or select Graphics, and select Graphics Boxes Numbering. From the dialog box, highlight the counter for the graphics box caption number you want to change, and select Edit. Select Numbering Method and one of the available choices. You can select OK twice to return to the document. If you will need more than one level of numbers, you will set the numbering style for each level separately.

You Can Change the Caption for a Single Graphics Box Without Changing All of Them

TIP 639

When you edit the caption of a graphics box, you will see the default caption for that style of graphics box. You can delete the default caption and replace it with another caption by typing new text. When you press F7, that graphics box will use the new caption. However, all other graphic boxes of that style will continue to use the default caption.

You Can Change a Caption Back to the Default Caption

You can add the code for the default caption to any location while you are editing a caption. Use this feature if you change the default caption and want to change it back again. In WordPerfect 5.1, press ALT-F9. In WordPerfect 6, press ALT-F9, and then select **Caption Number Style** and **Insert**.

You Can Have Several Numbers in a Caption

A caption such as "Figure 1A" has two levels. You can use multiple levels in WordPerfect. When you use multiple levels, each graphics box increments the lower level each time you add a graphics box of that style. However, if you increment the number of the upper level, WordPerfect automatically restarts the lower level numbers.

In WordPerfect 5.1:

1. Press ALT-F9, or select **G**raphics.
2. Select a type of graphics box.
3. Select **O**ptions **S**econd Level Numbering Method, and select an option for identifying the second level.
4. Select **C**aption Number Style, and type **2** where you want the second-level caption identifier placed.

Press ENTER, and then press F7 (Exit) to return to the document. When subsequent graphics boxes of the style you have modified appear, you will notice that they have two identifiers. When you want to change the first-level caption number, use the command for setting a new number, as described in Tip 642. When you reassign the first-level number, the second-level numbering automatically starts over.

In WordPerfect 6, you make the change by modifying the caption style for the graphics box style. The different graphics box styles that use captions have different system styles. You can modify the system style so that it uses more than one numbering level. To make such a change, follow these steps:

1. Select **L**ayout **S**tyles, or press ALT-F8.
2. Select **O**ptions List S**y**stem Styles, and then select OK.
3. Highlight the style for the caption, and select **E**dit.
4. Select Style **C**ontents **G**raphics Graphics **B**oxes **N**umbering.
5. Move to the location at which you want to add the additional counter to the caption.
6. Highlight the counter for the graphics box style, and select **E**dit.
7. Select **L**evels, type the number of levels, and select OK.
8. Select Dis**p**lay in Document, and select OK.
9. Press F7 until you return to the document.

After you complete these steps, any caption you add (for a graphics box of the style you have modified) will use the multiple levels you have specified. To increment a level, and restart counting of the lower levels, move to the location in the document where you want the incrementing to take place. Select Graphics Graphics **B**oxes Numbering Increment, and click OK.

You Can Renumber Graphics Boxes

TIP 642

There may be occasions when you need to restart the numbering of figures at some point within a long document. When you need to change the next number used for identifying a graphics box in a document, move to the point where you want the change to take place. (This should be before the next graphics box to use the new number.)

Next, in WordPerfect 5.1, select **G**raphics or press ALT-F9, and select the graphics box style and New Number. Type the number that you want the next graphics box to use, and press ENTER.

In WordPerfect 6, select **G**raphics or press ALT-F9, and select Graphics **B**oxes and Numbering. Highlight the counter for the graphics box style you want to change, and select Set Value. Type the number you want the next graphics box to use, and press ENTER.

In WordPerfect 6, You Have Several Options for Caption Locations

TIP 643

In WordPerfect 5.1, captions are placed automatically (if you choose to use them). In WordPerfect 6, you can choose a caption placement to achieve the look that you want. You can place captions on any

side of a graphics box by choosing Options Caption Options, and then choosing Side of Box from the Captions Options dialog box. You can choose Top, Bottom, Right, or Left. Once a side is selected, you can choose the desired position on the side. Select Position, and then if you have selected the top or bottom side, you will have choices of Center, Left, or Right. If you have selected the left or right side, you can position the caption vertically at the top, middle, or bottom of the box.

You can refine the Position placement even further by selecting Offset from Position, and then choosing either Set (for a specific position) or Percent (for a shift based on a percentage of the height or width). You can also choose Offset Direction, and then select from Top or Bottom and Left or Right, depending which side of the box the caption is on.

You can also position the caption in relation to the border around the graphics box. After selecting Relation to Border you can choose On, Outside, or Inside.

There Are Different Ways of Anchoring Graphics Boxes

A *graphics box anchor* controls how a graphics box moves and where it is positioned as you edit your document. You can set the type of anchor by selecting Anchor Type in WordPerfect 5.1 or Anchor To in WordPerfect 6, and then selecting one of the available options. The anchor type sets the position options available for a graphics box. When you select Vertical Position or Horizontal Position in WordPerfect 5.1, or select Edit Position in WordPerfect 6, the available options for placing the graphics box are listed.

You can have a graphics box anchored to a character, and as that graphics box's character position moves, so will the graphics image. A character-anchored graphics box has position options that move it relative to the character position of the graphics box. A graphics box anchored to a paragraph moves with the top of the paragraph. A graphics box anchored to a page moves according to the placement of the code for the graphics box. This anchor type has options for placement that control where the box appears on the page. WordPerfect 6 has a fixed-page-position attachment option that lets you position a graphics box solely by its distance from the upper-left corner of the page. The following illustration shows some of the position options for the different attachment types:

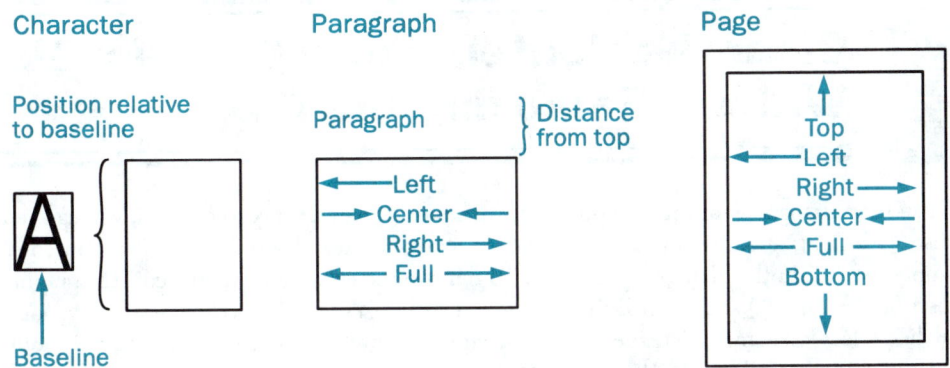

You Can Make a Graphic Smaller or Larger by Changing the Size of Its Box

The size of a graphics image is set according to the size of the graphics box and the size setting for the graphics image relative to the graphics box. (Scaling a graphics image according to the size of its box is described in Tip 651.) To quickly change the size of a graphics image, you can change the size of its graphics box.

To change the size of a graphics box in WordPerfect 5.1, edit the graphics box as described in Tip 599 and select Size. You can choose to set the width and let WordPerfect set the height, to set the height and let WordPerfect set the width, to set both, or to let WordPerfect set both. If you select one of the first three options, you will need to supply the measurement for the height and/or width.

To change the size of a graphics box in WordPerfect 6, edit the graphics box as described in Tip 599 and select Edit Size. You can select Set Height or Set Width, and enter the height or width that the graphics box should use. You can also select Automatic Height or Automatic Width to let WordPerfect set the height or width, based on the other dimension that you set and on the size of the image. Select OK to save the new size settings and return to the Edit Graphics Box dialog box.

Clear the Contents of a Graphics Box Without Removing the Box

If you have changed your mind about what you want a graphics box to contain, you can remove the existing contents and leave the box empty. Later, when you decide on the box's new contents, you can simply insert it in the blank graphics box. To remove the existing contents, edit the graphics box as described in Tip 599 and select Edit or Edit Text. If the graphics box contains an image or an image on disk, select Filename, delete the current filename, and press ENTER. When prompted about deleting the box's contents, select Yes. If the graphics box contains text, edit the text, select all of it, and delete it. If the graphics box contains an equation, select Contents Text and select Yes to respond to WordPerfect's prompt about deleting the contents of the box. In WordPerfect 6, you have the additional option, regardless of the box's contents, to select Contents None and select Yes to respond to WordPerfect's prompt about deleting the box's contents.

Use Gray Shading for Images and Text to Produce a Different Look

Graphics boxes can include shading on top of the text or graphics in a graphics box. By default, text graphics box styles use light shading.

To add shading to one of the graphics box styles in WordPerfect 5.1, follow these steps:

1. Press ALT-F9, or select **G**raphics.
2. Select the type of graphics box you want to use.
3. Select **O**ptions **G**rey Shading.
4. Type the percentage of shading you want and press ENTER.
5. Press F7 (Exit) to return to the document.

The next graphics box of the style you selected in step 2 will have the shading you added in step 4. If you want to remove the shading, repeat the steps, this time entering **0** in step 4.

In WordPerfect 6, you can perform the following steps for adding shading as you create or edit a graphics box:

1. Select Edit **B**order/Fill **F**ill Fill Style.
2. Highlight one of the shading options and choose **S**elect, OK, and Close.

The appearance of each different shading level will depend on your printer. Try a sample document using the different shading levels to see how they affect your document's appearance.

Use the Status Box in WordPerfect 6 to Simplify Editing of Graphics Images

WordPerfect 6 has a status box for the Image Editor that appears when the Status Box option in the View menu is active. (When this option is active, a check mark appears next to it on the menu.) The status box is located at the bottom of the Image Editor; it looks like this:

In this status box, you can see many of the editing changes that are discussed in other tips. When the status box appears, you can select any option in it either by typing the underlined letter or by clicking it.

Use Keystroke Shortcuts While Editing a Graphics Image

WordPerfect has several key combinations that you can press while editing an image. These keys are listed here, along with a brief description of each one's function:

Key	Function
PGUP	Increases scaling, as described in Tip 651
PGDN	Decreases scaling, as described in Tip 651
F10	Saves image to a .WPG file
CTRL-HOME	Resets the image's settings to the default
+	Rotates 36 degrees clockwise, as described in Tip 656
–	Rotates 36 degrees counterclockwise, as described in Tip 656
./,	Increases or decreases brightness, as described in Tip 658
>/<	Increases or decreases contrast, as described in Tip 657
INS	Changes increment percentage

Graphics Can Be Stretched or Squeezed Vertically or Horizontally

If you want to stretch a graphics image by its height or width, you can do so by telling WordPerfect to ignore the height-to-width ratio. WordPerfect normally maintains the height-to-width ratio of a graphic so that the image does not appear distorted. When you intentionally want to stretch or squeeze an image, you can do it by adjusting the ratio. Initially both the horizontal (X axis) and the vertical (Y axis) directions are set to 100 percent. When you select Edit or Image Editor, you can change the scaling. In WordPerfect 5.1, you can select Scale and type the new percentages for the X and Y axis. In WordPerfect 6, you can select Scale Height or Scale Width and type a new percentage to change the scaling in the direction you have chosen. For example, if you set the height scaling to 50 percent and leave the width scaling to 100 percent, the image will appear flattened.

WordPerfect 6 has a shortcut. You can select **O**ptions **C**ontent Options and clear the **P**reserve Image Width/Height Ratio check box. The image will stretch to fit the size of the graphics box.

You Can Adjust the Size of a Graphics Image to Better Fit its Graphics Box

Changing the size of a graphic does not automatically change the proportion of the graphics box. However, you can enlarge or reduce a graphics image until it fits in the box the way you want it to.

Use this feature when the graphic is too small or too large. Select Image Editor from the Edit Graphics Box dialog box. Next, select Scale Height or Scale Width, and type the percentage of the graphics image's original size that you want to use, with 1.0 equaling 100 percent.

An alternate method changes the graphics image's size gradually, according to a percentage you specify. When you use this method, you increase or decrease the size of the image within the graphics box by the increment amount. To increment or decrement the size of the image, press PGUP or PGDN, select Enlarge % or Reduce % after selecting Edit Position, or click one of these two buttons:

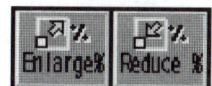

Color Images Can Be Converted to Black-and-White

TIP 652

If you do not want a document to use colors, you can have WordPerfect convert the colors to black-and-white. Light colors convert to white, and dark colors convert to black. You can convert the image to black-and-white when you want to create silhouettes.

To convert an image to black-and-white in WordPerfect 5.1, edit the graphics box as described in Tip 599 and select Edit. From the Graphics Editor, you can select Black & White, and then Yes. If you want to return to color, repeat the steps, selecting No instead of Yes, select Black & White, and then select No.

To convert an image to black-and-white in WordPerfect 6, edit the graphics box as described in Tip 599 and select Image Editor. From the Image Editor, you can select the B/W check box, or select Edit Attributes Black and White. Clearing the check box or repeating the command returns the image to color. You can also select Edit Attributes B/W Threshold, enter a number between 1 and 255 for the cutoff point, and select OK. Colors with a luminosity lower than the threshold convert to black, and colors with a luminosity above the threshold convert to white.

Graphics Images Can Be Inverted

TIP 653

Images in graphics boxes can be inverted. Inverting an image that has only black lines on a white background will change it so that it has only white lines on a black background. With colors, the result appears similar to photographic negatives.

To invert the colors in WordPerfect 5.1, edit the graphics box as described in Tip 599 and select Edit. From the Graphics Editor, select Invert On. To return to color, edit the image, and select Invert Off.

To invert the colors in WordPerfect 6, edit the graphics box as described in Tip 599 and select Image Editor. From the Image Editor, you can select the Invert check box or select Edit Attributes Invert Color. Clearing the check box or repeating the command returns to normal colors.

A Graphics Image in a Graphics Box Can Be Repositioned

TIP 654

The default for most graphics boxes is to center the graphics image in the graphics box. You have one option in WordPerfect 5.1, and two options in WordPerfect 6, for repositioning an image in its box.

In either version, when you select Edit or Image Editor, you can press the arrow keys to shift the image within the graphics box. The arrow keys move the image within the graphics box area, so pressing the UP ARROW moves the graphics image higher in the graphics box. In WordPerfect, pressing the arrow keys has the same results as entering values after X and Y in the Status Box. You can also position the graphics image in WordPerfect by dragging the boxes on the scroll bars.

The additional option available in WordPerfect 6 is to use Content Options to shift the image. To do so, select Options Content Options from the Edit Graphics box. You can have the graphics box contents placed in the graphics box shifted to the top or bottom and to the left or right by selecting different radio buttons. If you want this change to apply to all graphics boxes of a graphics box style, select Options Contents Options when you edit a graphics box style.

Flip an Image When You Want It Reversed

TIP 655

You can take an image in a graphics box and reverse it so that what is on the top flips to the bottom, or what is on the left side flips to the right. To reverse an image this way, edit the graphics box.

In WordPerfect 5.1, select Edit and Rotate. When prompted for the angle, you can type the angle at which you want to rotate the image, and press ENTER. Next, select Yes for Mirror Image, and WordPerfect will redraw the image.

In WordPerfect 6, select Image Editor. Then select the Flip Horz check box to reverse the image from left to right, or select the Flip Vert check box to reverse the image from top to bottom.

Graphics Images in a Graphics Box Can Be Rotated

You can rotate an image in a graphics box. In WordPerfect 5.1, select Edit and Rotate. When prompted for the angle, type the angle that you want to rotate the image and press ENTER. Next, select Yes or No to the Mirror Image prompt. The Mirror Image prompt is asking if you want the image flipped at the same time you rotate it.

In WordPerfect 6, select Image Editor and Rotation. Type the angle to rotate the image and press ENTER. Another option is to select the Rotate button in the button bar or select Edit Position Rotate. This displays a small diagram, as shown here:

You can drag either opposite end of the diagram to the angle at which you want the image to turn.

For either release of WordPerfect, you can also rotate the image by pressing + or − to rotate the image in 36-degree increments.

STOP.PCX

The image used here is on the accompanying disk in the file STOP.PCX.

Make Graphics Images Sharper by Changing the Contrast

You can often make WordPerfect 6 images stand out more by changing their contrast. To do this, edit the graphics box as described in Tip 599 and select Image Editor and Contrast in the Status Box, or select Edit Color Adjust Contrast. Next, type a number between 1 and −1, and press ENTER. 1 is for the highest contrast and −1 is no contrast, with 0 as the default. You can also adjust the contrast by the percentage shown after Increment by typing a period or comma.

Darken or Lighten WordPerfect 6 Images by Changing the Brightness

You can make images in WordPerfect 6 darker or lighter by changing the brightness setting. To do this, edit the graphics box as described in Tip 599 and select Image Editor, then **Brightness** in the Status Box, or select Edit Color Adjust Brightness. Next, enter a number between 1 and −1, and press ENTER. 1 is all white, −1 is all black, and 0 is the default. You can also adjust the brightness by the percentage shown after Increment by typing < or >.

A watermark automatically uses a brightness of .75. This faint level of brightness allows you to see the text printed on top of the watermark.

In WordPerfect 6, You Can Change the Fill Style for Some Graphics images

TIP 659

A quick way to convert an image with shading into a line drawing is to let WordPerfect 6 handle it. This feature only works with vector images, such as those with the .WPG or .CGM format. When you select Image Editor from the Edit Graphics box, you can select Fill from the Status Box, or Edit Fill. Next, select one of the fill options. Normal uses the normal colors in the image. Transparent outlines the image without filling in the shades, so that anything behind the image can show through. White outlines the image in black, filling in the shape with white so the document area behind it is covered by the white fill and the black lines. The different fill selections, and their effects on a graphics box at a fill of 10 percent, are shown here:

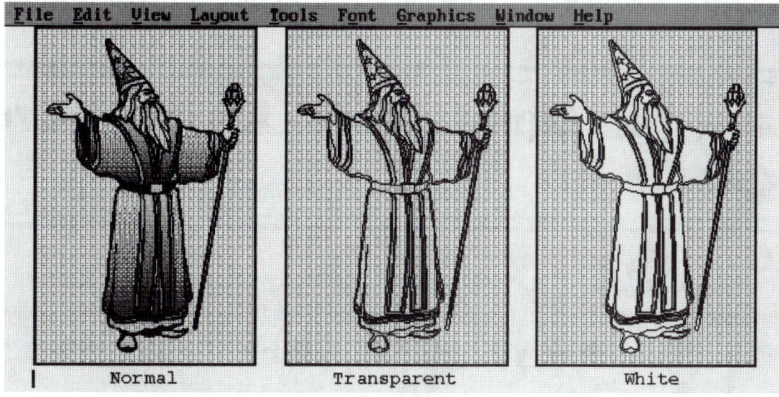

The images shown are in the file WIZARD.WPG which is included with WordPerfect 6.

WIZARD.WPG

Create Equations in Graphics Boxes Rather Than Using Compose

TIP 660

While composing characters lets you add many characters to an equation, you are better off using the Equation Editor, available when you set the contents of a graphics box to an equation. The Equation

Editor is more flexible than Compose because it has more placement options that match standard equation formats. If you do not use the Equation Editor, getting a formula to look correct requires a lot of work with line spacing and advance.

Equations Are Not Updated Until You Press CTRL-F3

661

After you set a graphics box to contain an equation and you select Edit or Create Equation, you can type the equation that you want to appear in the graphics box. When you are creating or editing an equation, your latest work will not appear in the box until you press CTRL-F3. At this point, WordPerfect draws at the top the equation you have entered at the bottom of the Equation Editor. If you have typed something WordPerfect cannot understand, you will see a message about it.

Use { } in Equations to Indicate Group Boundaries

662

When an equation has several parts that you want treated as a single item, those parts must be enclosed in braces ({ }). Several entries in the Equation Editor will affect only the next entry or an entry enclosed in braces. An example using braces is $4a$ times $\{2b\}$ over $\{1+3c\}$, which could be used to create the following equation:

$$4\,a \times \frac{2\,b}{1+3\,c}$$

Transfer Equations to the Equation Editor Using the File Retrieve or Restore Command

663

When you have an equation in another area, you can transfer it into the Equation Editor. To do so, put the equation in a file. Then, from the Equation Editor, select File Retrieve, and enter the name

of the file containing the equation. Another option is to delete the equation where it appears in a document in WordPerfect, and switch to the Equation Editor. Press F1 (Cancel) in WordPerfect 5.1 or ESC in WordPerfect 6 to display the deleted equation, and then select Restore.

WordPerfect Supports a Wide Variety of Graphics File Formats

TIP 664

In addition to the default WPG format, WordPerfect handles many graphics formats, including the following:

BMP	Bitmapped Graphics (WordPerfect 6 only)
CGM	Computer Graphics Metafile
DHP	Dr. Halo PIC format (WordPerfect 5.1 only)
DXF	AutoCAD format (WordPerfect 5.1 only)
EPS	Encapsulated PostScript
GEM	GEM Draw Format (WordPerfect 5.1 only)
GIF	CompuServe Graphics (WordPerfect 6 only)
HPGL	Hewlett-Packard Graphics Language Plotter File
IMG	GEM Paint Format (WordPerfect 5.1 only)
MNTG	Macintosh Paint Format (WordPerfect 5.1 only)
MSP	Microsoft Windows Paint Format (WordPerfect 5.1 only)
PCX	PC Paintbrush Format
PIC	Lotus 1-2-3 PIC Format
PICT	Microsoft PICT (WordPerfect 6 only)
PPIC	PC Paint Plus Format (WordPerfect 5.1 only)
TIFF	Tagged Image File Format
WMF	Windows Metafile (WordPerfect 6 only)

To use one of the formats WordPerfect supports, supply the filename, including the extension after you select Filename. WordPerfect 5.1 converts the image's format to its own, based on the file's extension. WordPerfect 6 prompts for the correct format to use for the conversion.

If You Have Graphics That Are Not in a Format WordPerfect Understands, Don't Despair

If you want to use a file in a format not supported by WordPerfect, you might be able to convert it. Tip 664 includes a list of supported formats. Check the documentation of the program that created the image to see if it can convert the image into one of those shown in Tip 664. Harvard Graphics for Windows, for example, can save charts in the .CGM, .PCX, and .TIF formats.

Another option is to purchase a utility that converts graphics files from one format to another. For example, Hijaak takes graphics from other applications and converts them to one of many formats, including the .WPG format preferred by WordPerfect.

Convert Images to the .WPG Format in WordPerfect 5.1

The .WPG format is WordPerfect's preferred format for graphics files. When you import a graphic into WordPerfect, the document stores the image using its .WPG format. You can use the graphic conversion program provided by WordPerfect 5.1 to convert graphics yourself, rather than having WordPerfect do it for you. You can control how the conversion is made, as described in Tip 667; you can also convert some file types with the conversion program that you cannot convert within WordPerfect, as well as converting groups of files at once. To use the graphics conversion program, follow these steps:

1. Type **GRAPHCNV** at the DOS prompt and press ENTER.
2. Type the name of the file to be converted, and press ENTER.
3. Type a name for the new file to be created, or keep the default name, and press ENTER.

In step 2, you might need to supply the pathname if the file is in a different directory. You will also need to include the extension. You can convert multiple files by including the wildcard symbols * and ? in the filenames in steps 2 and 3.

You Can Cutomize the Conversion of Graphics Files in WordPerfect 5.1

TIP 667

The graphics conversion program in WordPerfect 5.1 lets you customize the appearance of a graphics file as you convert it to a WPG file. To use the graphics conversion program for customizing the conversion process, type **GRAPHCNV**, the name of the file to convert, the resulting file you will create, and the options to be used during the conversion process. An example is typing **GRAPHCNV SCREEN01.TIF SCREEN01 /L**. The graphics conversion program has the following options:

Option	Function
/l	Prints the conversion status of each file, or if you follow /l with =*filename*, puts the conversion status of each file in the named file.
/o	Overwrites any existing files without prompting for whether you want to overwrite them.
/W	Sets the widths of lines in HPGL files to the minimum rather than the plotter's pen thickness.
/b=#	Sets the background color of the graphic for a .WPG file. Replace # with one of the following numbers: 1 for black, 2 for blue, 3 for green, 4 for cyan, 5 for red, 6 for magenta, 7 for brown, or 8 for white. The default background color is intense white.
/c=w	Converts all colors in input file to white.
/c=b	Converts all colors in input file to black.
/c=2	Converts all colors in input file to black-and-white.
/c=16	Converts colors in input file to WordPerfect's 16-color palette.
/c=256	Converts colors in input file to WordPerfect's 256-color palette.
/g=16	Converts colors in input file to WordPerfect's 16 shades of gray palette.
/g=256	Converts colors in input file to WordPerfect's 256 shades of gray palette.
/f=#	Converts colors of filled objects to the color set by #. # ranges from 1 to 16 or 1 to 256, depending on whether you are converting the graphic to WordPerfect's 16- or 256-color or grayscale palette.
/n=#	Converts colors of lines to the color set by #. # ranges from 1 to 16 or 1 to 256 depending on whether you are converting the graphic to WordPerfect's 16 or 256 color or grayscale palette.

Use the Graphics Conversion Program in WordPerfect 6

The WordPerfect 6 conversion program, CV, handles the conversion for word processing and graphics file formats. Usually, this program works in the background when you select a format other than a WordPerfect 6 document or a .WPG graphics file. You can run this program from the DOS prompt if you want to change how the conversion is made. To run the program, type **CV** at the DOS prompt and press ENTER. Then, in the ConvertPerfect dialog box, select **I**nsert Job. Type the name of the file to be converted, and press ENTER; then type the name of the file to contain the converted image, and press ENTER once more. Select **S**ource File Format, and then select **G**raphics to ensure that the selections are graphics images, and not word processing documents. Select OK and Convert to perform the conversion. Finally, select Exit to return to the DOS prompt.

What To Do if the Graphic in Your Graphics Program Does Not Look the Same Way in WordPerfect

When you import a graphic into WordPerfect and you do not like the way it looks, here are a couple of ideas you can use to get the results you want:

❑ Try a different format. For example, the .CGM format picks up the fonts of the program you are using the graphic in, replacing the fonts of the program that created it. If you want to keep the original fonts, try switching to a .PCX format.

❑ Use GRAPHCNV or CV to convert the graphics file into a .WPG graphics file, using the customizing options to adjust the conversion process, as explained in Tip 667.

Transform the Contents of Your Computer Screen into a WordPerfect Graphic

WordPerfect's GRAB utility will capture the screen's contents and put the contents in a .WPG file. You can use GRAB to capture screens in WordPerfect, or in any other application. Use GRAB to

capture screens created by any software that does not support one of WordPerfect's acceptable graphic formats. GRAB is not included as part of WordPerfect. Contact WordPerfect Corporation for information about obtaining GRAB and several other utilities.

Once you have saved the screen contents in a .WPG file, you can add the file to a document. This utility would be useful, for example, if you were preparing documentation for your coworkers explaining how the computer system works. GRAB captures screen images when the screen is in a graphics mode, such as when you are previewing a document to be printed, or using WordPerfect's Graphics or Page display mode. GRAB does not work in text mode; it will not work, for example, with the document editing screens or menus in WordPerfect 5.1, or with the Text display mode in WordPerfect 6.

To load GRAB, first remove any programs you are running from memory. Type **GRAB** at the DOS command prompt, along with any options, and press ENTER. (The options you can use are made available when you use the /H switch, as described in Tip 671.) Next, go to the program and screen from which you want to capture the image. Now you are ready to capture a screen, following these steps:

1. Press ALT-SHIFT-F9; you should hear two tones. (If you hear a buzz, GRAB is telling you that it cannot capture the image.) GRAB displays a box on your screen, indicating the size and position of the image it will capture.
2. Press the arrow keys so the box covers the area to be captured. You can also press SHIFT and the arrow keys to change the size of the box. Change the size of the box when you want to include only a portion of the screen in the file. You can also change the increment by which the arrow keys move by pressing INS.
3. Press ENTER to capture the screen. You should hear the same two-toned pitch indicating that GRAB has stored the image in a .WPG file.

The file that stores the image will normally be called GRAB.WPG in the current directory. After using GRAB.WPG, GRAB uses GRAB1.WPG, increasing the number after "GRAB" for every subsequent screen capture. You can change the default location and name of the files using GRAB's startup options. If you press ESC before you press ENTER a second time, you will cancel the screen capture.

The GRAB utility will remain in your system's memory until you turn your computer off, or until you type **GRAB /R** and press ENTER at the DOS prompt.

You Can Get Help with the Screen Capture Utility

TIP
671

If you type GRAB /H at the DOS prompt and press ENTER from the directory containing GRAB, you will see a screen of help information on GRAB's other / options. You can load GRAB with any of these options to change the images you capture with GRAB.

You Can Create Your Own Clip Art Using Graphics Programs

WordPerfect documents can include clip art that you create, as well as clip art supplied with WordPerfect or acquired from third-party sources. If you have DrawPerfect, use it to create .WPG files to add to your WordPerfect documents. If you have Windows, use the Windows Paintbrush accessory and save your files in a .PCX format or, for WordPerfect 6, a .BMP format.

Since WordPerfect will accept a variety of formats that popular programs use and create, your choice of programs for creating artwork is based on the programs that are available to you and, more importantly, the ones you are most comfortable using.

When Given a Choice, Save Graphics in a Vector Format

Most graphics files save their images using either the raster or the vector format. *Raster images* are ones created with Paintbrush programs, where you apply colors to any area of the drawing surface. Raster images remember an image by the dots of each color that make up the image. When you draw a line, the program remembers the line by the series of dots that looks like a line. *Vector graphics*, on the other hand, record the lines and endpoints of shapes used in an image. Instead of remembering every point on a line, a vector format remembers the end points of the line and the line's features, such as colors and styles. Vector graphics make certain types of editing easier, such as changing the line style, changing its size, or moving just the line without moving anything below it. Vector graphics look smoother than raster graphics, especially when enlarged. Vector graphics files usually also have the advantage of being smaller than raster files.

A third way graphics images are stored is using a metafile format, such as .WMF or .CGM files. Metafiles store both vector and raster data used to create an image.

Sketch a Drawing on Paper Before Drawing It in a Graphics Program

A brief sketch on paper will help you draw an object in a graphics program. The sketch will help you break up an object into the lines and shapes you will draw in the graphics program (see Tip 675). It

will also provide a guideline to the relative size and placement of objects in the drawing. The sketch is only a simple guide, so don't spend a lot of time drawing it. The following sketch and final drawing show how one leads to the other.

When You Create Graphics, Break Them Up into Lines and Shapes

TIP 675

Many drawing programs let you draw lines, circles, rectangles, and polygons. To make drawing pictures easier, convert the mental image or the rough sketch of what you want to draw into the lines and shapes that create it. Break the overall object into the lines and shapes that make it up. The following indicates how a picture of a coffee mug could be represented by lines, arcs, and shapes.

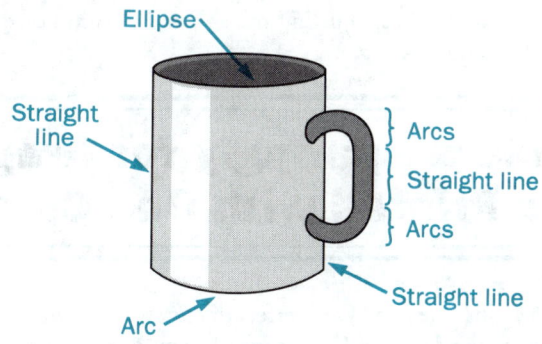

It usually helps to imagine what the object would look like on the screen. Then you can follow the lines you have imagined on the screen as you actually draw lines and shapes.

Use Light Colors Rather Than Dark Colors

The visual difference between shades of gray are more noticeable with lighter shades. The higher the percentage of black used in shading, the less difference you will see between percentages. For example, the difference between 10 percent and 20 percent black is much more noticeable than between 70 percent and 80 percent. When you are selecting gray scales, use the lighter shades. To give you a better idea of how the differences in shading appear, the following shows various shading percentages:

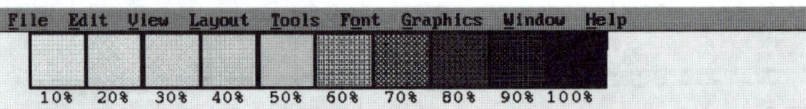

Make the Graphics Image Fill the Work Area in the Graphics Program

When you finish creating your drawing, resize it to fill the entire work area. Enlarging the drawing to fill the work area means that there will be less empty space in the graphic when you bring it into a WordPerfect document. If the image has a lot of empty space when you bring it into WordPerfect, you may have to spend several minutes adjusting the size and position of the image in the graphics box, as described in Tips 651 and 654.

Use Colors Sparingly for Graphics That Will Be Printed with One Color

When you create graphics to include in a WordPerfect document, you will be tempted to use colors to differentiate different parts of the drawing. Unfortunately, when you convert the document into black

and white, all of your colors might convert to the same shade of grey. You could end up with a gray blob, rather than the object you have drawn. When you create designs that will eventually be used in a monochrome format, such as a printer, you might want to stick to black, white, and varying shades of gray.

You Can Draw Simple Line Drawings in WordPerfect

TIP 679

WordPerfect lets you create quick line drawings with its line feature. To use this feature, press CTRL-F3 and select Line Draw. In WordPerfect 5.1, you can also select Tools Line Draw. In WordPerfect 6, you can also select Graphics Line Draw. Now as you press the arrow keys, you are drawing lines where the cursor moves. You can set the character used to draw the line by typing **1**, **2**, or **3**. The third character option is set by selecting Change and choosing one of the characters shown or selecting Other and typing the character to be used. If you need to skip over an area, select Move so that, as you press arrow keys, you will not draw lines. The final option, Erase, causes lines to be removed wherever the cursor moves. When you have finished drawing lines, press F7 to return to your document.

You can use line drawings to create a diagram like the one shown here:

File	Edit	View	Layout	Tools	Font	Graphics	Window	Help

Combine Line Drawings with Text

TIP 680

The lines you draw in a document can have text added around the lines. Switch to Typeover mode so the characters you type do not shift the drawn lines. Ideally, you want to put the text in the document and then add the lines. By combining lines and text, you can create a document that looks like the following:

Organization Chart

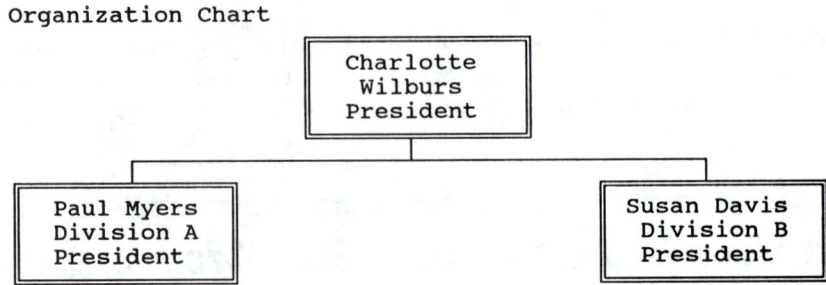

Use Only Monospace Fonts with Line Draw

TIP 681

In a monospace font, every character uses exactly the same amount of space. Line draw works by using characters that are part of the available character set to create lines. If WordPerfect used a font that was not a monospace font, the lines would never match, because each character would use different spacing. WordPerfect will not let you draw lines unless the current font is a monospaced font, such as Courier. However, if you should switch the font to a non-monospaced font in a document containing line drawings, don't be surprised if your document looks something like this:

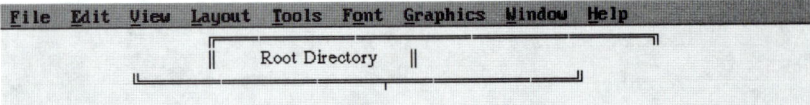

Use the Graphics Feature to Add Lines and Bars to Your Documents

TIP 682

You can use WordPerfect's graphics feature, instead of Line Draw, to add lines to your document. Graphics lines have several advantages over lines created with Line Draw. Graphics lines are easier to add to a document, and you can set them to adjust automatically to fit the page. Keep in mind, however,

that graphics lines do not appear in the editing screen in WordPerfect 5.1, or in Text mode display in WordPerfect 6.

To add graphics lines to a WordPerfect 5.1 document, follow these steps:

1. Press ALT-F9 or activate the **G**raphics menu, and select **L**ine.
2. Select **H**orizontal or **V**ertical to select the direction of the line.
3. Change any options for the line you want to add.
4. Press F7 (Exit) to complete the line.

To add graphics lines in a WordPerfect 6 document, follow these steps:

1. Press ALT-F9, or activate the **G**raphics menu.
2. Select Graphics **L**ines **C**reate.
3. Select Line **O**rientation, and then select **H**orizontal or **V**ertical.
4. Change any options for the line you want to add.
5. Select OK to complete the line and return to the document.

Some of the options for creating lines include the following:

❑ *Horizontal Position* For horizontal lines, you can set whether a line goes from one margin to the other, or is left aligned, right aligned, centered, or set to a specific position. For vertical lines, you can set whether a line appears on the left side or the right side, is centered, or is positioned between columns.

❑ *Vertical Position* For horizontal lines, you can set whether the line appears on the baseline of the current line (where the bottoms of the characters are), or appears at a set position from the top of the page. For vertical lines, you can set whether the line appears at the top or the bottom of the page, is centered, stretches from the top to the bottom, or is a set distance from the top of the page.

❑ *Line Length* When the horizontal or vertical position is not full, you can set the length of the line.

❑ *Line Width* You can set the width of the line by entering a new measurement.

❑ *Line Style* WordPerfect 6 has several line styles that you can use to alter the appearance of a graphics line.

❑ *Color or Shading* You can change the color of the line, or control how dark the line appears, by setting the shading percentage.

❑ *Spacing* WordPerfect 6 lets you adjust the space on either side of the line.

Once you add the line, you can modify it by editing the line. In WordPerfect 5.1, perform the steps just shown, but select Edit Horizontal or Edit Vertical in step 2. In WordPerfect 6, perform the same steps, but select Edit instead of Create in step 2, and then select the line to edit. A document that uses graphics lines might look like this:

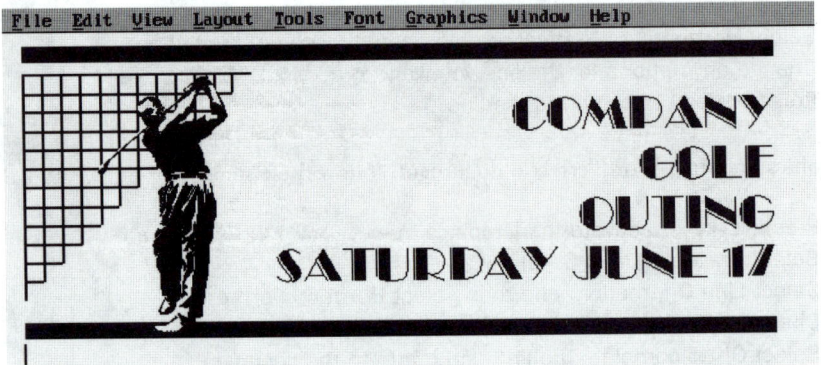

These graphics are in the file SPORT38.CGM on the accompanying disk.

SPORT38.CGM

TIP 683
Don't Use Line Draw or Graphic Lines for Paragraph Borders

If you want to create a border around a paragraph, use the paragraph borders feature, described in Tip 110. If you use Line Draw or graphics lines, then change the paragraph, the lines will not adjust to the paragraph's new size. While WordPerfect 5.1 does not have paragraph borders, you can create a similar effect by putting the text in a text box.

CHAPTER 14

Tables

WordPerfect 6 Tables Give You All the Power of a Spreadsheet

WordPerfect tables have always supported computations, but the new features in WordPerfect 6 give you all the power of a spreadsheet. New *floating cells,* which can be anywhere in a WordPerfect document, can be used to reference data in table cells, rows, or columns. WordPerfect 6 also provides almost 100 different predefined formulas called *functions.* These new functions extend the power of WordPerfect well beyond the totaling functions that were introduced in WordPerfect 5.1. See Tip 687 for more on floating cells.

WordPerfect 5.1 and WordPerfect 6 Support Different Operators and Precedence

WordPerfect 5.1 supports four operators: +, −, *, and / representing addition, subtraction, multiplication, and division. When a formula contains more than one operator the operators are computed from left to right unless you use parentheses. Anything in parentheses has a higher priority and is computed first.

WordPerfect 6 supports many new operators, and the operators have a defined priority sequence much as they do in spreadsheet programs. WordPerfect scans formulas many times, performing operations for those operators with high priority before those with a lower priority. Parentheses override the sequence, with operations inside parentheses receiving the highest priority. A complete list of WordPerfect operators and what they do, from highest to lowest priority, is shown in the following table:

! %	Factorial, percent
! −	Not, negative
^	Exponentiation
* / %	Multiply, divide, mod
+ −	Add, subtract
< <= > >=	Less than, less than or equal to, greater than, greater than or equal to

= <>	Equal, not equal
&	Logical AND
^ ^	Logical OR
|	OR

Use Functions to Create Date and Time Entries in WordPerfect 6 Tables

TIP 686

WordPerfect 6 has a number of functions that support the use of date and time entries. You can use these functions to record dates and times that can be used in calculations. The date and time functions and what they do are shown here:

DATE()	Returns the current date
DATETEXT(date value)	Returns the date as a text entry with a format matching the current date format
DATEVALUE(text)	Returns a date number for text that has a date format
DAY([date value])	Returns a day of the month for the current day or a specified date
HMS([hour], [minute], [second])	Returns a specified or current time of day
HOUR([time value])	Returns the current hour or the hour from a specified time
MDY(month, day, year)	Returns the date value of the specified date
MONTH([date value])	Returns the number of the month for the current month or the date specified
SECOND([time value])	Returns the second of the current second or a specified time
TIME()	Returns the current time as text
TIMETEXT(time value)	Returns the specified time as text
TIMEVALUE(text)	Returns the decimal value of the time specified
YEAR([date value])	Returns the current or specified year

You might use these functions in a document like the one shown in the following:

Weekly Time Sheet for Carol Jones					
	Morning In	Lunch Out	Lunch In	Evening Out	Hours Worked
Monday	8:00 am	12:00 pm	1:30 pm	5:15 pm	7.75
Tuesday	8:15 am	11:30 am	12:15 pm	6:30 pm	9.50
Wednesday	9:30 am	2:00 pm	2:30 pm	7:30 pm	9.50
Thursday	8:30 am	1:00 pm	1:30 pm	7:00 pm	10.00
Friday	9:15 am	2:15 pm	2:45 pm	8:00 pm	10.25
Total					47.00

Your pay for the week at your current hourly rate of $6.00 per hour is $282.00.

Floating cells

These functions are essential when you want to perform calculations with dates and times. The table in the document shown allows the user to enter start and end times for morning and afternoon work hours and computes the total hours worked each day. The formula for Monday's hours is

$$((TIMEVALUE(C3)-TIMEVALUE(B3))+TIMEVALUE(E3)-TIMEVALUE(D3))*24$$

The clock picture is one of the graphics images that accompanies WordPerfect 5.1. As Tip 628 mentions, WordPerfect 6 can use the clip art used in WordPerfect 5.1.

TIP 687

You Can Put Formulas in Your Document That Reference Data Stored in a WordPerfect 6 Table

Floating cells, a new feature in WordPerfect 6, allow you to put formulas in your document that reference data stored in tables. Floating cells are not surrounded by table lines and they appear within your document text. Upon closer examination on the Reveal Codes screen you will see that they are surrounded by [Flt Cell Begin] and [Flt Cell End]. Floating cells can reference data in other floating cells or tables. In the illustration shown with the previous tip, floating cells were used to record the hourly pay rate and calculate the total pay.

Follow these steps to create a floating cell in WordPerfect 6:

1. Place the cursor at the desired location for the cell.
   If you want to edit rather than create, the cursor should follow the [Flt Cell Begin] code.
2. Select **L**ayout **T**ables Create **F**loating Cell.
3. Select **N**ame and type a name.
4. Select Number **T**ype and select the appearance you want.
5. Select **F**ormula and enter your formula.
   To tell WordPerfect the table and cell you want to use, type the name of the table, a period, and the name of the cell. The name of the cell is the column letter and row number, or it is a name you have given to the cell using **N**ames in the table editing window.
6. Select OK twice.

Use TAB *and* SHIFT-TAB *to move off of a floating cell to the next position to the right or left.*

If you want to enter formulas in floating cells from your document window, Formula Recognition at Document Level must be on.

Some Entries Are Not Recognized as Formulas Unless Placed in the WordPerfect 6 Formula Box

Although you can turn Formula Recognition at Document Level on to enter formulas in the document editing window, there are a few types of entries that will not be accepted as formulas. You will have difficulty entering formulas that look like phone numbers, a ten-digit ZIP code, social security numbers, or dates. You can enter these in the formula box to overcome the problem or place the formula in parentheses if you want to enter it directly in your document.

Tables Without Lines Have the Same Effect as Tabbed Entries but Offer Advantages

If you want to create a few simple entries like this, you might think of using tabs rather than a table:

Sales of Widgets by State

State	Widget Sales
Maryland	950
Nevada	560
Ohio	430
Wisconsin	865

You can create the same type of entries in your document with a table where the lines do not show. One advantage of a table is that it is easy to add another column if you want to retain additional information, such as the manager of the sales territory. It is also easy to format entries in tables to add currency indicators, commas, or special text attributes. Computations such as totals can also be added easily. You may have seen tables with lines separating the entries and avoided them because that was not the look you wanted. You can use tables and delete the lines around the outside as well as the inside. After creating a table, you might want to enter your data with the lines still visible and then remove them. To do this, follow these steps in WordPerfect 6 from the table editing window:

1. Select **L**ines/Fill **D**efault Line.
2. Select **L**ine Style.
3. Highlight None, choose **S**elect, and select Close.
4. Select Bord**e**r/Fill **B**order Style.
5. Highlight None and choose **S**elect, then select OK and select Close.

In WordPerfect 5.1, follow these steps:

1. Block the entire table from the table editing window (ALT-F7 **T**able **E**dit).
2. Select **L**ine **A**ll **N**one.

The task seems much shorter in WordPerfect 5.1 because there are fewer options affecting the lines used in tables.

You Can Use Financial Functions in WordPerfect 6 Tables

TIP 690

WordPerfect 6 supports the use of financial functions. You can use the Table Functions dialog box to add the functions to any cell where you want to perform these computations. Since arguments are used to define the data used in the computations, you will need to fill in the specific arguments after the function is added to the cell. The financial functions supported are given in the following table.

DDB(cost, salvage, life, period)	Returns a double-declining balance method depreciation
FV(rate%, payment, periods, [,type])	Returns the future value of a loan or investment
IRR(cashflow list, rate%)	Internal rate of return
NPV(list, rate%)	Calculates present value of a list
PMT(rate%, PV, periods, FV [,type])	Payment for a loan or an investment
PV(rate%, periods, FV [,type])	Present value of a loan or investment
RATE(PV, payment, periods, FV [,type])	Periodic interest rate for a loan
SLN(cost, salvage, life)	Straight-line depreciation
SYD(cost, salvage, life, period)	Sum-of-years-digits depreciation
TERM(rate%, PV, payment, FV [,type])	Term for a loan or investment

The document shown in the following illustration is on the accompanying disk and contains the PAYMT function needed to compute the payment for a home loan. You can plug in new numbers after retrieving the file, then recalculate the formulas with Layout Tables Calculate All.

Monthly Payment Estimator

Cost of Home	$150,000
Down Payment	$50,000
Loan Amount	$100,000
Interest	7.50%
Term	30
Monthly Payments	**$699.21**

—— Formula B1 – B2

—— Function PMT (B4/12, B3, B5*12, 0)

Type a new entry for Cost of Home, Down Payment, Interest, and Term, then select Layout Tables Calculate All. Amounts are typed without dollar signs and a percentage of 8.25% is typed as 8.25 with Typeover mode on. Without Typeover mode, you will need to delete the old entry and respond Yes, that you want to replace the formula, in order to have your entry formatted. There are formulas stored for the Loan Amount and the Monthly Payments.

You can point to WordPerfect 6 cells rather than type their names. Just press F4 when using the formula box for entries and highlight the cell you want to use.

This sample template is available on the accompanying disk as LOANPAY.TEM.

LOANPAY.TEM

T^{IP} 691

WordPerfect's 5.1 Functions Are Still Supported in WordPerfect 6

WordPerfect 5.1 supports only three functions. They do not have names like the more sophisticated functions that are part of WordPerfect 6. The WordPerfect 5.1 functions are represented by the symbols +, =, and *. The + represents the subtotal function, which adds the numbers in the column directly

above it. The = represents the total function, which adds the subtotals used above the function. The * represents the grand total function, which adds all of the totals above the grand total. The table below shows a table using the + and = operators to place totals and subtotals. The placement of the + and = operators is indicated. You can see from the table how Quattro Pro totals the values in the table:

MIDWEST REGION CADILLAC SALES DURING 1993		
OHIO		
	Cleveland	$23,456,321.00
	Columbus	$34,521,356.00
OHIO TOTAL		$57,977,677.00
MICHIGAN		
	Detroit	$45,675,438.00
	Lansing	$13,454,329.00
MICHIGAN TOTAL		$59,129,767.00
MIDWEST TOTAL		$117,107,444.00

OHIO TOTAL ——— +

MICHIGAN TOTAL ——— +

MIDWEST TOTAL ——— =

To enter one of these functions in WordPerfect 6 you do not use the Table Functions dialog box as you do with other functions. To enter one of these functions in a cell:

From the table editing window, type the special symbol in the cell.
These functions are not available in the Table Functions dialog box. You can type these symbols in a cell when you are on the regular editing screen if the Formula Recognition at Document Level option is checked.

To enter one of these functions in WordPerfect 5.1, follow these steps:

1. Select **M**ath from the Table Edit menu.
2. Select the function.
   Typing *, =, or + will not work; you must add them with these steps.

Use Block Protect to Ensure That a Table Stays Together on a Page After Editing

TIP 692

If you have a table that you do not want split between two pages, you can use the Block Protect feature to ensure that if any of the table needs to be moved to the next page, the whole table will be moved.

To keep a table together in WordPerfect 6:

1. Block the table.
2. Press SHIFT-F8
3. Select **O**ther.
4. Select **B**lock Protect.

To ensure that a table is not split between pages in WordPerfect 5.1:

1. Block the table.
2. Press SHIFT-F8
3. Press Y for Yes.

TIP 693

Crossfoot Entries Easily with a Table and Sum

As you prepare reports for budgets, sales projections, and financial forecasts, numbers are likely to change from your first draft to the final document. In the past this often meant that you needed to recompute totals both down and across to crossfoot the numbers on the report. (*Crossfooting* is adding the numbers across the bottom of a table and down the last column to make sure they agree. For example, if you have a table containing your budget for each of the next six months, the total for all of the items should equal the total for each month.) With tables, the recalculation on a table like the one here can be quick:

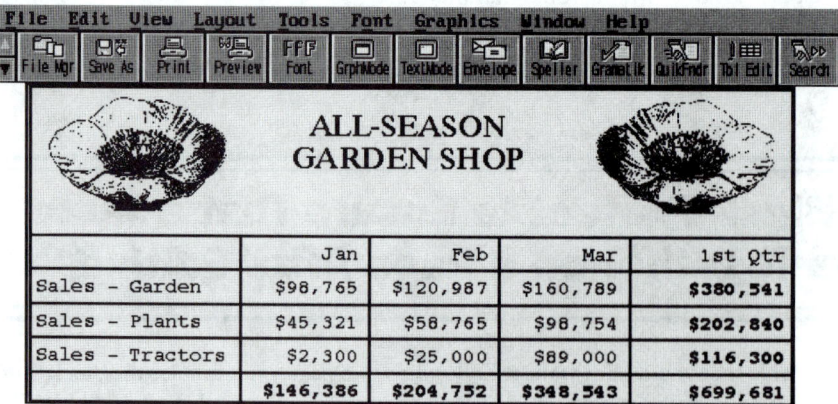

	Jan	Feb	Mar	1st Qtr
Sales – Garden	$98,765	$120,987	$160,789	**$380,541**
Sales – Plants	$45,321	$58,765	$98,754	**$202,840**
Sales – Tractors	$2,300	$25,000	$89,000	**$116,300**
	$146,386	**$204,752**	**$348,543**	**$699,681**

To enter a sum to compute a total, follow these steps:

1. In the table editing window, move to the cell to contain the sum.
2. Select **F**ormula, type **SUM(**, and type a block range, a name assigned to the block, or a list of individual cells.
3. Type **)** and press ENTER, then select OK.

The document shown had names assigned to B3:D3, B4:D4, B5:D5, B3:B5, C3:C5, and D3:D5. In Tip 718, you will learn how to create a list of your table names. In addition, the block B2:E5 was selected before selecting Cell Justification Center, Number Type Currency, and Options Digits after decimal 0. Cells containing the formulas are locked from the table editing window with **Cell Lock**.

This sample document (without the flowers) is available on the accompanying disk as SUM. The flower graphic is available on the accompanying disk as BLOSSOM.PCX and can be added to SUM to create the sample document shown.

SUM
BLOSSOM.PCX

You Can Control How Much of a Table Is Deleted

TIP
694

You can delete a row or column from the table structure or you can delete the text it contains. You can also delete an entire table with all the data or delete only the table structure, placing the entries in tabular columns. Save yourself the frustration of potential mistakes by saving your table before starting on the deletions. You can always retrieve the saved copy if something goes wrong. In WordPerfect 6, you have another lifesaver in Edit Undo, which can eliminate the effect of your last action.

To delete a row or column:

1. Move to the first row or column.
2. Select **D**el from the WordPerfect 6 table editing window, or press DEL from the same window in WordPerfect 5.1 or 6.
3. Specify whether you want to delete rows or columns.
4. Indicate how many rows or columns you want to delete.
    In WordPerfect 6, if you block the rows or columns to be deleted first, you will not be asked to specify how many you want to delete.

To delete data from a row or column:

1. Block the data to be deleted from the document editing window.
2. Press CTRL-F4.
3. Select **B**lock **D**elete.

To delete the table structure:

1. Press ALT-F3 to display Reveal Codes.
2. Highlight the code, [Tbl Def], that precedes your table entries.
3. Press DEL. The table structure disappears but the table entries remain.

To delete the entire table:

1. Press ALT-F3 to display Reveal Codes.
2. Block the entire table, including the codes.
3. Press DEL.

CTRL-Z *or* ESC *will undo a change from the table editing window.*

Deleting a row or column may affect your formulas, but most adjustments can be handled by WordPerfect.

Set Up Frequently Used Tables as Forms

If you have tables that you need to complete once a week or once a month, you will save time if you store the empty table as a form. You can write-protect the document that contains it, then save it under a new name after completion, or copy the table to another document. The invoice shown in the following is a good example of a table that should be write-protected to prevent overwriting the master copy:

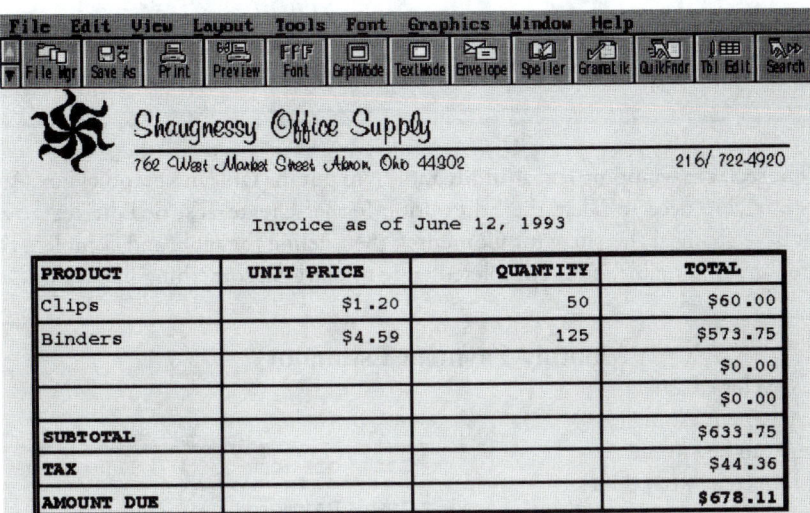

To write-protect a document, it cannot be open. You must enter the ATTRIB command at the DOS prompt (DOS is the operating system that is active in your computer when you are running WordPerfect) to write-protect a file. Follow these steps in WordPerfect 5.1 or 6:

1. Press CTRL-F1.
2. Select **G**o to DOS.
3. Type **ATTRIB +R** *filename*, where filename is the actual name and path of the file that you want to protect.
4. Type **exit** and press ENTER.

To remove protection from a file, repeat the steps, typing a +R in step 3 instead of a –R.

The symbol shown in the document is available on the accompanying disk as DINGBT36.CGM.

DINGBT36.CGM

TIP 696

You Can Wrap Text Around a Table

The secret to wrapping text around a table is to put the table in a graphics box. After defining the graphics box, you need to select the Edit option (either Create Text or Edit Text, depending on whether you have changed the entry for Contents), then define the table and complete the entries as you would for any other table. Your completed table might look something like this:

Monthly Payment Estimator

We have developed a new monthly payment estimator. Customers can key in their information to see what their monthly payments will be under different scenarios. No other real estate forms in the Cleveland area are offering a service like this. Other estimators that are now in the development stage include a closing cost estimator, a commission estimate, and an advertising cost breakout by news publication. Sales agents with ideas for new products that would give us a competitive edge should contact Sally Smithson at 543-9999. Sally will work with you to develop products to increase your business.

Cost of Home	$150,000
Down Payment	$50,000
Loan Amount	$100,000
Interest	7.50%
Term	30
Monthly Payments	**$699.21**

Sample Loan Estimator

To create a graphics box and add the table in WordPerfect 6:

1. Select **G**raphics Graphics **B**oxes **C**reate.
2. Select **C**reate Co**n**tents **T**ext.
3. Select **E**dit Text. (Note, the first time you will need to select Cr**e**ate Text.)
4. Select **L**ayout **T**ables **C**reate and specify the size.
5. Use the table editing window to make changes to the table structure and format.
6. Select Close and complete your table entries.
7. Press F7 to complete the editing of the graphics box.

The steps required to create a graphics box in WordPerfect 5.1 are similar:

1. Select **G**raphics or press ALT-F9 (Graphics) and select **T**able Box **C**reate **E**dit.
2. Select **L**ayout **T**ables **C**reate and specify the size.
3. Use the table editing window to make changes to the table structure and format.
4. Press F7 (Exit) and complete your table entries.
5. Press F7 (Exit) until you return to the document.

You Can Move or Copy Information in a Table

TIP 697

Once you enter table information, you can use it to make copies of the data, or you can move it to a new location to correct mistakes or rearrange the way it is represented. The same WordPerfect 6 procedure works for copying and moving cells, rows, columns, or blocks. Follow these WordPerfect 6 steps from the table editing window:

1. Block the data to be moved or copied.
2. Select **M**ove/Copy, then choose **M**ove or Co**p**y.
3. Move the cursor to the new location.
4. Press ENTER.
5. Select Close to return to your document.

If you want to copy or move data between tables, temporarily move the tables to an adjacent location with no intervening text or codes between the [Tbl Off] code for the first table and the [Tbl Def] code for the second table.

Block the Columns and Rows You Want to Work With

TIP 698

When you are selecting table columns and rows from the table editing window, you can block the columns and rows and the How Many option in the dialog box will be dimmed. However, if you haven't defined the block as you want it, you will need to leave the command and change the size of the block or eliminate the blocking before selecting the command again.

Tables for Drawing Boxes

TIP 699

Line draw and the repeat feature provide a good way to draw boxes. You can also create a table when you need many adjacent boxes that are all the same size. If you want to create an office layout or a tic-tac-toe game for your children, a table may offer the quickest approach. You create the table shown in the following illustration in WordPerfect 6 as a simple three-column and three-row table, then return to the document editing window. Next, increase the number of lines in each box by moving to the first box in each row and pressing ENTER a sufficient number of times to create the desired look. Now select Layout Tables Edit to display the table editing window. Borders are removed from the table by selecting Lines/Fill and then Border/Fill. The next selection needed is **Border Style**. Highlight None, choose Select, then select OK and Close. The top row is blocked and the lines at the top are changed to none. The first column is blocked and lines are removed from the left. The remaining two sides are handled in a similar fashion. The table with text at the top is shown here:

TIC-TAC-TOE

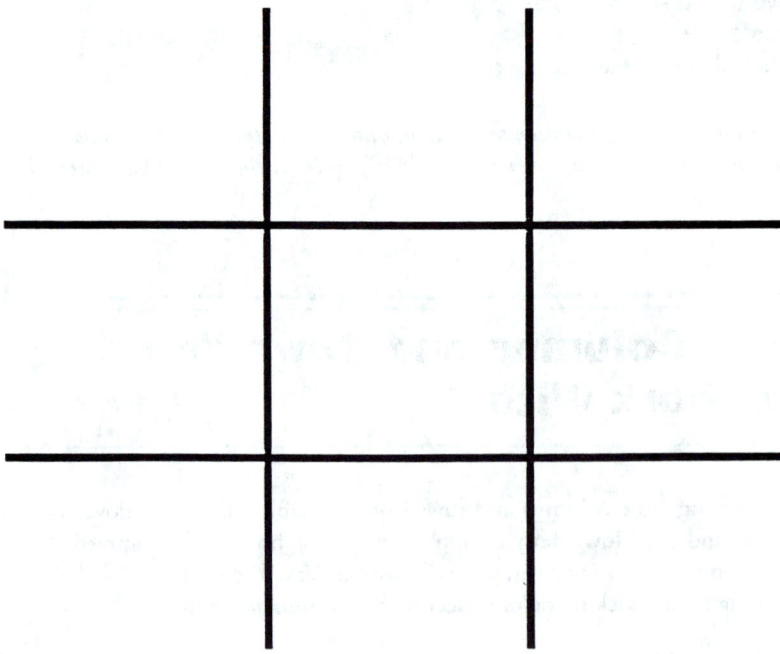

WordPerfect Can Create a Link to a Spreadsheet File to Obtain Table Data

You can use the Spreadsheet Create Link option to obtain data from a spreadsheet for a WordPerfect table. The Spreadsheet command is located on the Tools menu in WordPerfect 6 and can be found by pressing CTRL-F5 (Text In/Out) in WordPerfect 5.1. An added advantage is that WordPerfect can update the data in the table either upon retrieval or request.

To create a link to a spreadsheet in WordPerfect 6:

1. Select **T**ools **S**preadsheet **C**reate Link.
2. In the **F**ilename text box, enter the name of the file you want to link to.
3. Type the range to show in the document in the **R**ange box or leave the default of <Spreadsheet>.
4. Select **L**ink.

Performing these same steps—but selecting Import instead of Create Link in step 1—places a copy of the spreadsheet in the document *without* creating a link that you can subsequently update. You can set WordPerfect to update the spreadsheet values in the document by selecting Tools Spreadsheet Link Options Update on Retrieve and OK. To have WordPerfect update the spreadsheet data that appears in the document immediately, select Tools Spreadsheet Link Options Update All Links.

To create a link to a spreadsheet in WordPerfect 5.1:

1. Press CTRL-F5 (Text In/Out) and select **S**preadsheet **C**reate Link.
2. Select **F**ilename, enter the filename you want to link to, and press ENTER.
3. Leave **R**ange empty to use all of the spreadsheet, or select **R**ange, type the range to use, and press ENTER.
4. Select **P**erform Link.

Performing the same steps—but selecting Import instead of Create Link in step 1—places a copy of the spreadsheet in the document *without* creating a link that you can subsequently update. You can set WordPerfect to update the spreadsheet values in the document by pressing CTRL-F5 (Text In/Out) and selecting Spreadsheet Link Options Update on Retrieve Yes. To have WordPerfect update the spreadsheet data that appears in the document immediately, press CTRL-F5 (Text In/Out) and select Spreadsheet Link Options Update All Links.

Spell-Check Tables Before Locking the Cells

You can lock cells in a table to prevent changes to the cells. This is a good safeguard for cells that contain formulas. If you spell-check a table, WordPerfect cannot correct mistakes that it finds in locked cells. The best approach is to spell-check the table before locking the cells. This way you are certain that the entries are finalized, and you can take advantage of the features offered by the Speller to make corrections quickly.

To lock cells in WordPerfect 6:

1. Block the cells you want to lock in the table editing window.
2. Select **C**ell **L**ock.

To lock cells in WordPerfect 5.1:

1. Block the cells you want to lock from the table editing window.
2. Select **F**ormat **C**ell **L**ock.

You Can Make Headings for WordPerfect 6 Tables Stand Out by Reversing the Text

When you want a table's headings to stand out, you can reverse the colors so the heading has white letters on a black background. The following table shows the results of this:

Weekly Sales Totals						
Product	Monday	Tuesday	Wednesday	Thursday	Friday	Total
BY-7865	88	54	32	78	67	319
CL-7621	56	121	68	42	88	375
DG-4504	43	32	23	54	45	197
KH-9987	67	45	89	28	93	322
	254	252	212	202	293	1213

To change the top row of a table to inverse colors, follow these steps:

1. Block the top row from the table editing window.
2. Select **L**ines/Fill, then select **F**ill and Fill St**y**le.
3. Highlight 100% Shaded Fill and choose **S**elect.
4. Choose Foreground **C**olor and choose Black.
5. Choose Background Color and choose White.
6. Return to your document by selecting OK, then Close twice.
7. Block the top row of the table, then select F**o**nt **P**rint Color.
8. Highlight White and choose **S**elect.

Print the Heading for Multipage Tables on Each Page

TIP 703

In WordPerfect 5.1, you can specify the number of rows that will print at the top of each page with the following selections from the table editing window.

To set rows as header rows that will appear on multiple pages in WordPerfect 5.1:

1. Select **L**ayout **T**ables **E**dit.
2. Block the rows you want to use with F12.
3. Select **R**ow **H**eader Row.

To set rows as header rows that will appear on multiple pages in WordPerfect 6:

1. Select Header.
2. Type the number of rows at the top of the table that will repeat on each page.

If You Want to Insert a Hard Tab in a Cell, Remember to Press HOME and Then Press TAB

Since pressing TAB causes the cursor to move to the next cell, you need a special way to insert a hard tab code into a cell entry. Just press HOME and then press TAB. WordPerfect 6 also supports the following hard tab entries in addition to the left tab:

Right tab	HOME ALT-F6
Decimal tab	HOME CTRL-F6
Center tab	HOME SHIFT-F6

Any of the WordPerfect 6 hard tabs can be made into a dot leader tab by pressing HOME *twice instead of once before entering the other key sequence.*

WordPerfect Can Convert Parallel Columns or Tabular Text to a Table

If you decide that entries in parallel columns would look better in a table, or if you would like to take advantage of some of the table formatting options, you can make the conversion without retyping any text. All you need to do to convert the data is follow these steps:

1. Block the parallel columns.
2. Select **L**ayout **T**ables **C**reate.
3. Select **T**abular Text or **P**arallel Columns.

If your tables contain cells with extra lines, use the Join option in the table editing window to remove them.

If you try to convert tabular text with different numbers of tabs between columns into a table, you will not get the results you expect—the data will not line up in columns. To prevent this problem, establish tab stops for each column.

It is not possible to include a table in a parallel column unless you first place the table in a graphics box.

You Can Rearrange the Entries in a WordPerfect Table by Sorting

TIP
706

You can sort the rows of a table using Tools Sort to rearrange the table's contents. The only glitch is that WordPerfect 5.1 reorganizes the table lines along with the data. If you sort a WordPerfect 5.1 table, be prepared to spend time redefining the lines around cells when you are finished sorting.

You Can Change Which Column in a Table Is Used for Sorting

TIP
707

You can define which cell of a row you want to use to control the sort. The default setting is to use the first column of the table.

Remember Not to Sort Top Rows That Have Identifying Data Unless They Are Header Rows

WordPerfect will automatically skip header rows when you sort a table, even if you accidentally include them in the block of rows you want sorted. If your table is smaller than a page, it is possible that you have not designated header rows to appear at the top of each page in the table. One or more of your rows may still contain identifying information even if you have not labeled them as header rows. If you include such header rows in the block to be sorted, they will be sequenced with the data rows, depending on the entry in the column that controls the sort.

Create a WordPerfect 6 Bookmark That Contains the Entire Table

When you want to select the entire table, you can display the Bookmark dialog box, select the bookmark for the table, and select Find and **B**lock. If you have never created a bookmark, it is easy. Follow these steps:

1. Block the table.
2. Select **E**dit Boo**k**mark.
3. Select **C**reate, type a name, and select OK.

You Can Set a WordPerfect 6 Table Cell to Use the Column Defaults for Formats

When you select an attribute, number type, or justification option for a cell, the cell no longer uses the column option for that setting. You can remove the specific cell setting from the table

editing window by selecting Cell and then selecting Use Column, followed by Attributes, Justification, or Number Type.

You Can Change the Lines That Appear in the Table

You can change any of the lines that make up the table grid. You might, as an example, want to add emphasis to the rows containing header information or highlight rows at the bottom of the table containing totals.

To change the lines in WordPerfect 6 from the table editing window:

1. Select **L**ines/Fill from the table editing window.
2. Select **D**efault Lines or the specific line.
3. Select **Li**ne Style and make the appropriate selections.

You can also change the lines in WordPerfect 5.1, but there are not as many variations as in WordPerfect 6.

You Can Add Shading to the Cells in a Table

In WordPerfect 5.1, you can add gray shading to cells in a table after blocking the cells. In WordPerfect 6, the options are even more sophisticated. In WordPerfect 6, you can not only choose shading but you can choose to use a color, pattern, or gradient to vary the amount of shading within the selected area where it is applied. Gradient options include a choice of a linear, radial, or rectangular gradient, a rotation angle, an offset from center for a radial or rectangular gradient, and the smoothness of the color blend for background and foreground colors. The last option, to set the number of shades, is only available when Calculate Number of Shades is not selected. To change from a pattern fill to a gradient fill in WordPerfect 6, follow these steps:

1. Block the cell to be affected from the table editing window.
2. Select **L**ines/Fill **F**ill Fill St**y**le.

3.   Highlight a style and then choose **E**dit.
4.   Select Fill **T**ype **G**radient.
5.   Select OK, choose **S**elect and OK, and then select Close.

You Can Count Table Entries with a WordPerfect 6 Function

You may want to know how many cells in a row or column of your table contain entries. If you have a table that contains monthly sales totals, you can quickly check the count to see if each salesperson has completed his or her table entries rather than checking the form line by line.

COUNT(list) is the function that you select from the function list. After copying the function, the table cell will contain COUNT(). Between the parentheses you can place entries that refer to the cells you want to include. The list can include values, cell addresses, name references, and ranges. A simple range reference might look like this: COUNT(A2:A25).

Mark Rows as Header Rows to Appear at the Top of Every Page

You will not see a header row repeat on every page except when you print or preview the document. You can choose more than one row for a header row if you want. If the row you select is not at the top, it is only repeated on pages after the page where it originally appears.

Use a Shortcut to Edit a Table in WordPerfect 6

In WordPerfect 6, use the Tbl Edit button in the Button Bar, or press ALT-F11, to make changes to the table. It is a shortcut for the Layout Tables Edit command. The Tbl Edit button looks like the following:

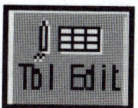

You Can Change the Name of the Table from the Default Name WordPerfect Provides

WordPerfect gives the name Table_A to the first table you create, with subsequent tables named with the next consecutive letter, as in Table_B, Table_C, and so on. You can rename the table by selecting Names Table in the table editing window, typing a new name, and pressing ENTER.

You Can Assign Names to Cells, Columns, and Rows in WordPerfect 6

Once you have named cells, columns, and rows, you can use the names to quickly move to that part of the table after pressing CTRL-HOME. These names are different from the bookmark names you see when you press CTRL-B or select Edit Bookmark. You can also use these names in formulas.

To name a cell or block:

1. Highlight the cell, or block a group of cells, from the table editing window.
2. Select **N**ames.
   If you select a block in step 1, your choices are **B**lock, **C**olumns, **R**ows, Cells **D**own, or Cells **R**ight. If no block was selected in step 1, your choices are **C**ell, Co**l**umn, **R**ow, or **T**able.
3. Select the option indicating what you want to assign the name to.
4. Enter a name and select OK.

You can reference intersection rows and columns that both have names with a combined entry. Type the column name followed immediately by a period, then type the row name. For example, if the column is called "Ohio" and the row is called "Sales," the intersection can be specified as Ohio.Sales.

You Can See a List of All the Names You Have Assigned to Table Elements

You can select F5 from the Names dialog box for a list of all the names assigned to the current table, or all the names assigned in the current document if you select List all Names in Document.

You Can Tell WordPerfect 6 to Ignore Cells in a Column When Performing Calculations

If you use a column for a formula that WordPerfect calculates, you may need to tell WordPerfect which cells in the column are to be ignored. You need to do this when cells contain numbers that you do not want WordPerfect to use in calculations. From the table editing window, select the cell you want to exclude. Choose Cell Ignore When Calculating to make this change.

You Can Control the Appearance of Numbers in a Table

WordPerfect 6 provides many options for controlling the appearance of numbers in a table. This is one of the advantages of using table entries over tabular columns. You can choose from a variety of Number Type options after selecting Cell to control the way numbers look. Options are similar to the ones that you find in popular spreadsheet programs and include General, Integer, Fixed, Percent,

Currency, Accounting, Commas, Scientific, Date, and Text. You can access these number type changes at the Cell, Column, or Table level in the table editing window.

Both WordPerfect 5.1 and WordPerfect 6 allow you to change the size and appearance of entries as well.

There Is a Precedence to the Formats Set for a Table

721

You can set formats for cells and columns in WordPerfect 5.1 and 6. In WordPerfect 6, you can also change the format of tables. The cell formats have the highest precedence. Next, changes made to column formats will take effect. In WordPerfect 6, cells and columns are not affected by settings changed with table format options.

Cells in a Table Can Have Both Horizontal and Vertical Alignment

722

In WordPerfect 6, you can determine whether entries in a cell are right-aligned, centered, or left-aligned with the Justification option available in the Cell Format dialog box. You can also control the vertical alignment in WordPerfect 6 with options for top, bottom, and center under Vertical Alignment in the Cell Format dialog box. In WordPerfect 5.1, you would choose Cell Format, then select either Justify or Vertical Alignment.

Formulas Are Copied Differently in WordPerfect 5.1

723

To copy a cell containing a formula in WordPerfect 5.1, you must use the Math Copy Formula command. In WordPerfect 6, you can use the Move/Copy option in the table editing window for any type of entry, including formulas.

In WordPerfect 6, cell addresses placed in brackets, such as [A1], are not updated when they are copied. These are referred to as absolute cell addresses.

You Can Set the Distance Between the Entries and the Top and Bottom of a Row

To change the top and bottom cell margins in WordPerfect 6, you can select Row Top or Bottom from the table editing window. The default settings are .083 for the top and .4 for the bottom. In WordPerfect 5.1, the default settings are .1 for the top and 0 for the bottom. To make a change in WordPerfect 5.1, select Options Spacing Between Text and Lines.

You Can Truncate the Text That Appears in a Table so That Each Row Only Uses One Line

You can accept either single or multiple line entries. If you accept multiple line entries, WordPerfect automatically word-wraps the text you enter. If you accept only a single line, the text is truncated at the end of the display. This text is not lost and will appear if you change the setting to multiple line. To make the change in WordPerfect 6, select Row, and then select Single or Multiple. In WordPerfect 5.1, select Format Row Height and Fixed under the Single option.

A Table's Position on the Page Is Set as a Property of the Table

When you create a table, it is positioned at the left margin. The table is then formatted to fill all of the available space extending to the right margin. Changing the table alignment at this point will not

have any effect, since it occupies the entire width of the line. If you narrow the width of any of the table columns, changing the position of the table will allow you to provide a different look for the table. Centering, for example, provides a more balanced look, with extra space on both sides of the page. You can use CTRL-LEFT ARROW to shrink the width of any column.

To change the position of a table in Word Perfect 6:

1. Select **T**able from the table editing window.
2. Select **P**osition and then select **L**eft, **R**ight, **C**enter, **F**ull, or **S**et.
   If you choose **S**et, you must also enter the fixed offset from the left side of the page.

To change the position of a table in WordPerfect 5.1:

1. Select **O**ptions from the table editing window.
2. Select **P**osition of Table.
3. Select **R**ight or **C**enter if you have made the original table smaller and want to align it at the right or center. A selection of **F**ull allows the table to use the space between margins, even if it is related to a place in the document where the margins are different. **L**eft is the initial setting.

Enter Table Formulas in WordPerfect 6 from the Document Editing Window

TIP 727

You can use the formula box to enter formulas, or you can enter them directly in the WordPerfect 6 document editing window. To enter formulas while typing the rest of your document, you need to set Formula Recognition at Document Level on. To make this change, select Formula from the table editing window, then select Formula Recognition at Document Level to switch its setting. Next, choose OK and Close.

Placing quotes around a formula prevents its calculation even if WordPerfect is set to recognize formulas entered in the document.

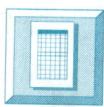

WordPerfect 6 Supports the Use of Functions for Many Mathematical Operations

You can make many of your formulas more concise with the use of mathematical functions in WordPerfect 6. In WordPerfect 5.1, computation that required basic computations such as rounding or the use of an integer portion of an entry were complicated since you had to record the formula. The mathematical functions in WordPerfect 6 and the results they provide are given in the following table.

ABS(number)	Returns the absolute value of the number
EXP(number)	Calculates the base of the natural log e
FACT(number)	Returns the factorial of the number
INT(number)	Returns the whole number portion of a number
PI()	Returns 3.1415926535897932
POWER(number1, number2)	Calculates number1 raised to the number2 power
PRODUCT(list)	Returns the product of all the numbers provided
QUOTIENT(list)	Divides the first number by the second, then continues to divide the result by each subsequent number
ROUND(number, precision)	Returns the number rounded to a specified decimal place
SIGN(number)	Returns a –1 if the number is negative, a 1 if the number is positive, and a 0 if the number is 0
SQRT(number)	Returns the square root of the number
SUBTRACT(list)	Subtracts the second number from the first, then subtracts subsequent numbers from the result

Width Changes Made with CTRL and the Arrow Keys Depend on the Font Used

You can use CTRL-LEFT ARROW and CTRL-RIGHT ARROW from the table editing window to decrease or increase the width of the current column. Each time you press the key sequence, the column can

contain one less or one more character in the font currently used. You can use the Column or Table Width option available from the table editing window to specify a precise measurement.

You Can Join Cells Both Horizontally and Vertically

For appearance you might want to make multiple adjacent cells into one large table cell. This is particularly useful when you want to put a heading at the top of a table. The procedure to use is as follows:

1. Activate the table editing window. Press ALT-F7, then select **T**able Edit if you are not there.
2. Block the cells to be joined (F12).
3. Select **J**oin, then press Y to confirm.

In WordPerfect 6, you can join two tables as long as they have the same number of columns. You need to move the tables so they are adjacent to each other. Delete any hard returns separating the tables, then select Layout Tables Join.

You Can Split a Cell into Multiple Cells Either Horizontally or Vertically

You can split a cell, making either another row or column entry from the cell. If you block cells in either a row or a column before choosing Split, all the cells in the block will be split. The split that you create can cause a section of the table to have a column that another section does not. This is quite unlike a spreadsheet but may give the effect you want. In the following table, several cells were split into two columns to allow for the entry of both a total and an average:

Weekly Sales Average/Totals						
Product	Mon.	Tues.	Wed.	Thurs.	Fri.	Avg/Total
BY-7865	88	54	32	78	67	63.8
						319
CL-7621	56	121	68	42	88	75
						245
DG-4504	43	32	23	54	45	39.4
						197
KH-9987	67	45	89	28	93	64.4
						322
	254	252	212	202	293	1213

The extra cells are only available in the last column.

To split a cell from the table editing window of WordPerfect 5.1 or 6:

1. Move to the cell to be split or block the group of cells to be split.
2. Select **S**plit.
3. Select **R**ows or **C**olumns.
4. Specify the number of rows or columns for the split.
5. Choose OK.

You Can Prevent WordPerfect 6 from Adjusting Column Widths

Changes in the width of adjacent columns or changes in margin settings affect the width of the current column. From the table editing window you can choose Column Fixed Width to prevent this from happening in the future.

You Can Use a Shortcut for Inserting Rows

Although there is a menu command, Layout Tables Insert Row, to insert rows, other approaches are shorter. From your document screen you can press CTRL-INS or TAB at the end of the table. Pressing INS in the table editing window is another quick approach.

You Can Use a Shortcut for Deleting Rows

In addition to using the command Layout Tables Delete Row or Del in the table editing window, you can press CTRL-DEL to delete a row.

Settings for a Cell in WordPerfect 6 Are Revealed in the Address in the Status Line

When you lock a cell, ignore a cell, or specify it as a header cell or a filled cell, an indicator appears for the cell address in the status line. The address of a header cell is followed by an asterisk (*), as in C1*. An ignored cell is preceded by quotation marks ("), as in "C1, indicating that it is not used in computations. Square brackets surround a locked cell that cannot be changed, as in [B2]. The address for a filled cell is shown in reverse video. If C1 is both locked and ignored, its cell address will look like this:

"[C1]

Remember to Update Any Calculations You Have in Your Table Before You Save or Print

Table calculations are not automatically reevaluated as you replace entries in cells. Once a formula is entered and calculated, it will not be recalculated until you select a command to make WordPerfect recalculate it. In WordPerfect 6, you need to select Layout Tables Calculate All. In WordPerfect 5.1, select Math from the Table Edit menu, then select Calculate.

Since you may want to recalculate frequently as you look at what-if options, a macro is the most efficient solution. This macro is entered and stored as ALTC to place the recalculate feature a keystroke away:

```
DISPLAY(Off!)
TableCalculateAll
```

ALTC.WPM

This sample macro is available on the accompanying disk as ALTC.WPM.

CHAPTER 15

Columns and Math

In WordPerfect 5.1, Turn Off Automatic Reformatting for Columns While Editing

You can save time and computer memory when working with columns in WordPerfect 5.1 if you turn off the feature that displays columns side-by-side. While columns are displayed side-by-side, Word-Perfect is spending more than the usual amount of memory on maintaining the display accurately. Instead, you can turn off this feature so that the columns are displayed one after the other, vertically, with the line indicating a page break between each column. They occupy the correct location on the page, but they are not all on the same page. To change the display:

1. Select **F**ile Se**t**up **D**isplay.
2. Select **E**dit-Screen Options.
3. Select **S**ide by Side Display and press N.
4. Press F7 to return to the document.

In WordPerfect 6, You Can Add Borders and Shading Around Columns

In WordPerfect 6, you can add borders and fill patterns to columns, just as you can add them to paragraphs and pages. When you add column borders, they affect all of the text formatted as columns in that area. Therefore, if your entire document is formatted as columns, the entire document uses the column formatting that you set. However, if you switch in and out of column format within your document, using columns, then none, then a different number of columns, only the columns affected by the current column setting will be affected by the column border. The column border setting turns off when the columns turn off.

The following illustration shows how column borders are used to set off the information about a new investment manager.

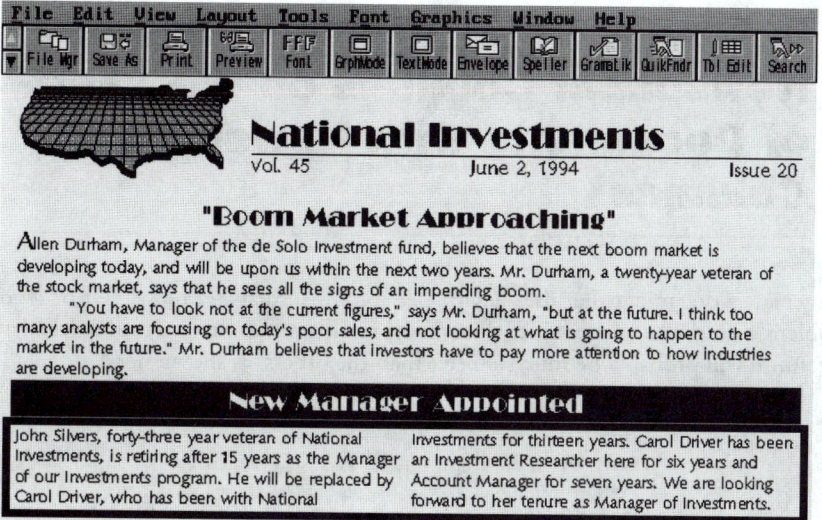

The National Investments logo is stored on the resource disk as USA4.CGM.

USA4.CGM

To add column borders or fill:

1. Select **L**ayout **C**olumns.
2. Select Column **B**orders.
3. Choose the option you want to use for column borders.
4. Select OK to return to the document.

If you simply select OK, instead of choosing a specific option, WordPerfect uses the default column border setting, which is to have a single line serve as the separator line between columns. Closing the Column Border dialog box turns the columns on, unless you select Off in step 3.

In WordPerfect 6, Use Balanced Newspaper Columns on the Last Page of Documents with Newspaper Columns

When you create a document that uses newspaper columns, such as a newsletter or report, you may find a problem with the last page. Since documents rarely end up precisely filling the last page, your very last column will probably be much shorter than the others, as shown here:

This last dangling column leaves the document looking unprofessional and slightly unfinished. WordPerfect 6 provides an easy solution, called balanced newspaper columns. When you choose Balanced Newspaper Columns, WordPerfect adjusts columns so that each column ends at the same distance down the page. Using this feature prevents those end-of-document dangles.

If you are concerned about space, you may not want to use balanced newspaper columns. Since the primary purpose is to balance the column lengths, WordPerfect will move one line onto the next page, even if there was room for it on the original page, if doing so will better balance the columns. Because WordPerfect is concerned with position on page rather than number of lines, a column with a heading in a large font will have fewer lines of text than a column with no heading—but the columns will be the same length.

In WordPerfect 5.1, Change the Bottom Margin to Balance the Columns

TIP 740

WordPerfect 5.1 supports newspaper columns, but not balanced newspaper columns, which ensure that the columns on a page are of equal length. To create balanced columns on the last page of a report or other document using columns in WordPerfect 5.1, you would change the bottom margin setting.

Changing the bottom margin setting is better than inserting a hard page break to shift the remaining text to the next page because you can easily see when formatting makes the columns uneven. Extra text goes directly to the next page. If you insert a hard page break, and then edit or add text before it, you may make the columns uneven again without realizing it.

Use Lines Between Columns If You Are Forced to Reduce the Space Between Columns

TIP 741

If you must reduce the distance between columns to a small amount to save space, consider adding a single line between the columns to make it easier for your readers to know where each column begins and ends. Without the line to distinguish columns, readers tend to skip across, from line one of column one to line one of column two, instead of down, as they should.

You can see in the following illustration how, without the rule between columns, the article might be difficult to read. You will find this especially true when you use full alignment, as is used here.

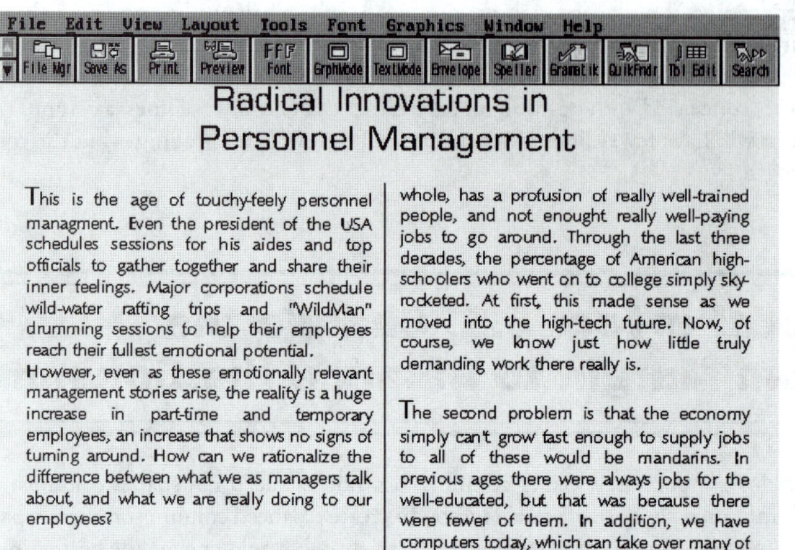

Tip 738 explains how to use the column borders feature in WordPerfect 6 to create a line between columns. To create a line between columns in WordPerfect 5.1, you have to use the graphics features, as described in these steps:

1. Select **G**raphics **L**ines.
2. Select Create **V**ertical.
3. Select **B**etween Columns.
4. Type in the appropriate column number at the WordPerfect 5.1 prompt, "Place line to right of column: ".
5. Press F7.

You Can Change the Space Between Rows in Parallel Columns Using WordPerfect 6

WordPerfect adds a blank line between each row of entries in parallel columns. This extra line helps you differentiate where rows begin and end. In WordPerfect 6 you can remove or increase this space between rows by changing the Line Spacing Between Rows setting. To do this, follow these steps:

1. Position your cursor in the parallel columns you want to edit.
2. Select **L**ayout **C**olumns.
3. Select Line **S**pacing Between Rows.
4. Enter the number of lines of space you want between rows. Enter 0 if you want no space between rows. Enter a number greater than 1 if you want more space between rows. You can also enter fractions.
5. Select OK until you return to the document.

You Can Set the Widths of Each Column and Space Between Columns

T^{IP}
743

In both WordPerfect 5.1 and 6, you can easily set the width of each column and the space between columns. This offers you unparalleled flexibility in choosing how to set up your document. You are not restricted to having columns of equal width, or even to having equally wide spaces between your columns.

To set column width and space between columns in WordPerfect 6:

1. Select **L**ayout **C**olumns.
2. Select Custom **W**idths.
3. Select **E**dit.
4. Enter the width for the first column in the **W**idth text box.
5. Select **N**ext to move to the space after the column.
6. Repeat steps 4 and 5 until you have set the widths of all the columns and all the spaces between columns that you want to adjust.
7. Select OK twice to return to the document with the new column definition in effect.

To set column width and space between columns in WordPerfect 5.1:

1. Select **L**ayout **C**olumns **D**efine.
2. Select **M**argins.
3. Enter the margins for each column, pressing ENTER after each measurement. The margins are the margins for each column, as measured from the left edge of the page. Each column will have two margins, the left and the right. You do not specifically set the distance between the columns when you use this method, but the distance will be what is

left between the right margin of one column and the left margin of the next.

4. Press F7 until you return to the document.

It is advisable that the right column's right margin be the same as the right margin for the page, and the left column's left margin the same as the left column for the page.

You Can Set Whether WordPerfect 6 Adjusts Columns When the Page Size or Margins Change

When you change page size or margins, WordPerfect tries to keep columns the same size in relationship to each other. In WordPerfect 5.1, you cannot change this feature; therefore, you cannot keep any one column at one precise width. However, WordPerfect 6 offers a feature that sets the width of columns so they cannot change.

When you open the Column # dialog box, which lets you specify the width of the column, as described in Tip 743, you can select the Fixed check box. If this check box is selected, the width of that column or space between columns will not change.

CTRL-ENTER Has New Uses in Newspaper and Parallel Columns

You are probably used to pressing CTRL-ENTER to insert a hard page return into your document. When you work with columns, you will find that CTRL-ENTER works somewhat differently.

In newspaper columns, pressing CTRL-ENTER inserts a [HCol] (WordPerfect 6) or [HPg] (WordPerfect 5.1). These codes are hard column break codes that end the current column and move the cursor directly to the top of the next column. This column may be on the same page as the column you pressed CTRL-ENTER in, or it may be on the next page.

In parallel columns, pressing CTRL-ENTER also inserts a [HCol] code (WordPerfect 6) or a [Col Off][HRt][Col On] code (WordPerfect 5.1). This moves you to the next column in the row, or the

first column in the next row, depending on where you are. Because of this, you will find yourself using the CTRL-ENTER code quite frequently in parallel columns, because it is the easiest way to create the next column you want to enter text into.

You Can Use CTRL-HOME as a Shortcut to Switch Between Columns on a Page

WordPerfect's CTRL-HOME key combination is a shortcut for switching between columns. Simply press CTRL-HOME, then the arrow key for the direction you want to move. WordPerfect moves the cursor to the next column in that direction.

Use the Ribbon in WordPerfect 6 to Set Up Newspaper Columns Quickly

WordPerfect 6 offers a convenience for mouse users called the Ribbon. The Ribbon is displayed between the pull-down menus and above the Button Bar (assuming you have these enabled). You can only access the Ribbon with the mouse. The third element on the Ribbon is used to quickly create standard newspaper-style columns. To use the Ribbon to create columns:

1. Point the mouse at the third element in the Ribbon and click once. The drop-down selection box is displayed, showing the selections you can make.
2. Point your mouse to the selection you want to make and double-click the mouse.
     WordPerfect inserts the code to turn the columns on using the settings you have chosen. The columns will spread from the left to the right margin with approximately .5 inches between each column.

The Reveal Codes Screen Will Only Show One Column at a Time

In both WordPerfect 6 and 5.1, you can display your columns side by side on the screen, just as they will appear when they are printed out. However, this is not how the codes will appear in the Reveal Codes screen. Instead, the columns appear sequentially, separated by the code symbolizing the end of the column.

You Can Insert a Page Break at a Specific Point in Columns

If you want a page break at a specific point in a document with columns, you can insert a hard page break code, [HPg]. You do not press CTRL-ENTER to insert this code, since this key combination has a different purpose in columns, as explained in Tip 745. Instead, you press CTRL-A then CTRL-ENTER.

Create a Document More Easily by Entering the Text and Then Formatting for Columns

The easiest way to create a document that you want to format with columns is not to set up the column format first. It is usually easier to enter and edit the actual text without multiple columns. WordPerfect does not have to allocate the memory necessary to maintain the display of the columns, and you can see more sequential text at one time.

After entering and editing the text, including such steps as checking spelling or applying character styles or formats to individual words, move to the top of the text to format in columns. Then make final changes such as adding graphics boxes and positioning text on the page.

In WordPerfect 6, Use the Layout Columns Custom Widths Command to Get Information About Column Definitions

Because the hidden code for columns in WordPerfect 6 does not display much information about the settings, you need to find the information about column margins and other settings in some other way. You can do this by selecting Layout Columns Custom Widths. The right half of the Text Columns dialog box shows the defined columns and the spaces between each one, as you can see here:

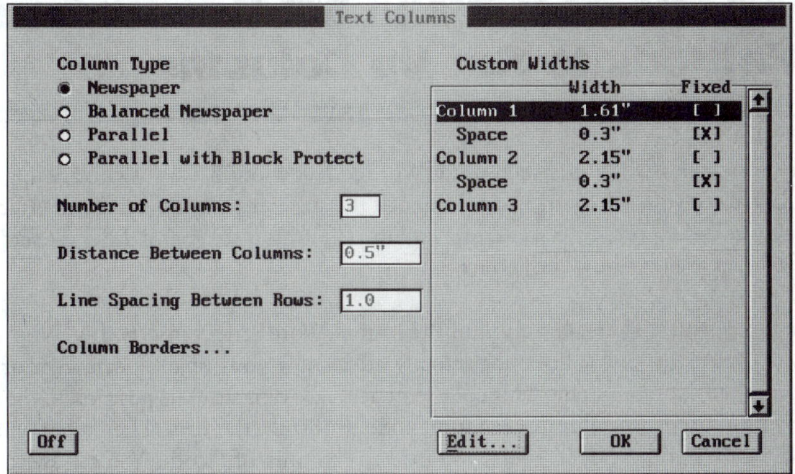

In WordPerfect 5.1, this is not as much of an issue because the hidden column definition code shows the margins for each of the columns.

Use Graphics to Add Interest to Columns

You can use graphics boxes within columns to add interest to the column format. For

example, you can use a *pull quote*—a snippet of text from the article or document—in a text box. When you use graphics boxes with columns, you can have one graphics box overlap two columns so that the text in the columns has to wrap around it. Using a graphics box to break up the gray lines of text in columns brings liveliness to your document.

You can also use column borders in WordPerfect 6 to add interest to your document. With column borders, you can add lines around the columns, a line between them, or a fill as a background for the text in the columns. You can use the graphics lines feature in WordPerfect 5.1 to add lines between columns.

By adding lines, background fill, or a few graphics, either created by yourself or using clip art from a graphics package, you can increase the level of attention your reader is going to bring to your document.

WordPerfect 6 and 5.1 Use Different Methods to Set Up Columns

If you find it necessary to switch between using WordPerfect 6 and 5.1, or if you are upgrading from WordPerfect 5.1 to 6, you will want to know about the different ways that WordPerfect 6 and 5.1 work with column codes. You cannot use one column definition for many different sets of columns in WordPerfect 6, as you can in WordPerfect 5.1.

In WordPerfect 5.1, you first create a column definition. WordPerfect inserts this column definition code into your document, but it does not actually affect how your text appears in your document. Then you insert a "column on" code. This code searches backward from its position to the last column definition code and uses that column definition code to format the text. Then when you no longer want that column definition code in effect, you insert a "column off" code. You can switch in and out of columns throughout your document, using the same column definition code to define how the columns appear.

WordPerfect 6 works somewhat differently. In WordPerfect 6, you define and turn on the column at the same time. When you are finished with the column formatting, you insert a code to turn it off. When you next want to use columns, you need to either copy the beginning column code, or create a whole new definition for the next set of columns. Instead of searching backward for the last column definition code, WordPerfect 6 requires that you re-create that column definition code.

As you can see, WordPerfect 6 is going to be easier to work with if your document uses many different column settings. You do not have to be careful about keeping the location of the column definition codes in relationship to the "column on" codes straight. However, if you are switching between one

column definition and regular text in a document, WordPerfect 5.1 would be easier to use because you wouldn't need to redefine the column definition or find and copy the beginning column code.

WordPerfect Offers Many Special Key Combinations for Moving in Columns

Columns are a little more difficult to get around in than normal text. In normal text, to get to the right margin, you simply press the keys that will take you to the right margin. In columns, you first have to move to the rightmost column, then move to the right margin. This may not be intuitively obvious.

The following table shows a set of shortcut keystrokes that you can use to move around in text formatted for columns.

Keystrokes	Moves the Cursor
CTRL-HOME RIGHT ARROW	To the next column on the right
ALT-RIGHT ARROW	To the next column on the right
CTRL-HOME LEFT ARROW	To the next column on the left
ALT-LEFT ARROW	To the next column on the left
CTRL-HOME END	To the last column
CTRL-HOME HOME RIGHT ARROW	To the last column
CTRL-HOME HOME LEFT ARROW	To the first column
CTRL-HOME UP ARROW	In parallel columns, to the top line in the current column in the current row
CTRL-HOME DOWN ARROW	In parallel columns, to the last line in the column in the current row

Sometimes You Will Want to Use Tabular Columns Instead of WordPerfect Columns

WordPerfect columns are used for arranging information in a specific way on the page. On some occasions, however, it may be much easier to use tabular columns than the column feature. Tabular columns are columns of data arranged using tab stops or indents.

For example, if you want to include three lines with names, job titles, and phone numbers in the middle of a memo, there is no reason to create and format parallel columns. It will be much quicker to simply press TAB before each type of information to arrange it in columns by the tab location.

In WordPerfect 6, You Can Add Tables to Your Column Formatted Text

In WordPerfect 5.1, if you want to add a table to a column formatted document such as a newsletter, you have to create the table in a graphics box and place the graphics box in the columns. With WordPerfect 6, this extra step is no longer necessary because you can create a table within the columns, as you can see here:

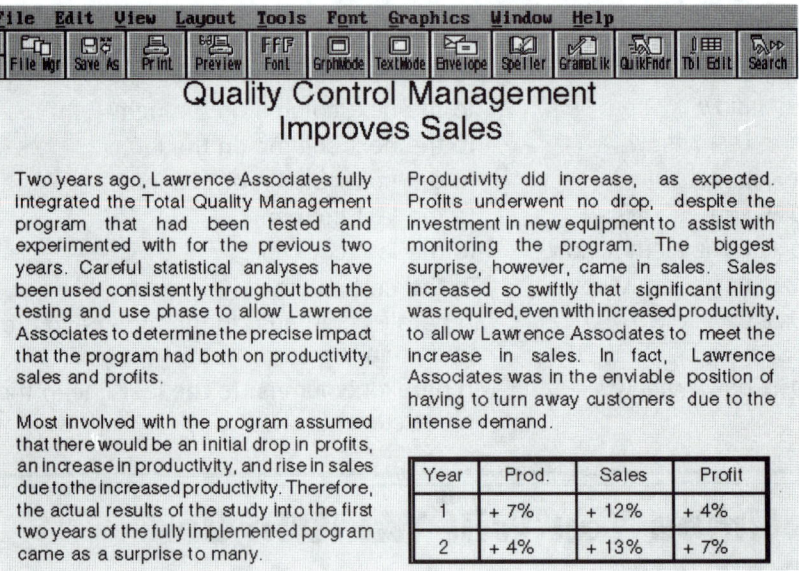

When you add a table to a column, the table uses the column margins to define its own limits. Therefore the table will not print across column margins, as a graphics box can be placed across column margins. If you want to include a table in your document that crosses column margins, you will have to place it in a graphics box first.

Use tables in columns to provide visual relief. Remember that long stretches of gray text with no relieving graphics or other visual elements can make retaining a reader's interest difficult. Tables not only present information concisely and clearly, they provide a graphic element that helps prevent boredom.

Limit the Number of Columns You Put on the Page

757

WordPerfect allows you to put up to 24 columns, either newspaper or parallel, on a page of any size. However, you will probably never want or need to put so many columns across a single page. If you have too many columns across the page, the text becomes difficult to read.

If you want to arrange short bits of information such as times or numbers in many columns and rows, consider using tables instead of parallel columns. Tables can support more columns across the page. The lines that you can use to outline tables make it easier to locate and read information than in parallel columns.

Use a Macro to Create WordPerfect 6 Columns

758

With WordPerfect 6, each time you want to turn columns on, you have to redefine them. If you regularly use the same column definition, you may find this inconvenient. You can simply copy the "column on" code, but this involves having to display the hidden code, find the code, and copy it. An easier solution is to create a macro that defines and turns on the column feature. Then you simply run the macro each time you want to turn columns on. The macro THREECOL.WPM on the disk defines and turns on three newspaper-style columns.

```
DISPLAY(Off!)
ColumnsDefinition(Newspaper!;1.0;{1.5";NotFixed!;0.25";Fixed!;
2.25";NotFixed!;0.25";Fixed!;2.25";NotFixed!})
```

THREECOL.WPM

This sample macro is available on the accompanying disk as THREECOL.WPM.

You Can Use WordPerfect's Math Feature to Include Calculations in Your Document

WordPerfect offers two ways to do math in your WordPerfect document, Tables and Math. Math works with data entered into columns created using tabs. You can easily do subtotals, totals, and grand totals using the math feature. You can also create more complicated formulas that calculate across tables.

To use the math feature, you first need to determine what you want to do with math. If you simply want to do totals down columns, you create the columns, insert the codes to do the calculations, and have WordPerfect calculate. If you want to use formulas that can calculate across or down columns, you need to use an extra step.

When you are doing complex math calculations, you need to create a column definition that tells WordPerfect what each column contains—numbers, calculations, text, or totals. Then you can create your formulas and insert them in the proper locations. Only after you have created and defined the columns do you tell WordPerfect to calculate the formulas contained in these columns.

You Can Continue a Math Column Beyond the Page Break Without Affecting Calculations

The math feature will work even if the columns of numbers are broken across two or more pages. However, if the column is short, you may want to use the block protect feature to keep the column on one page, making it easier for your readers to read and understand the entire list of numbers.

Math Columns Are Tabular Columns Rather Than WordPerfect Columns

TIP 761

You cannot arrange values using WordPerfect's column feature and then use those columns as math columns. The columns that you create for use with the math feature must be created using tabs rather than other features. If you want to use a parallel column format for your data and still do math with it, you will want to use a table, which incorporates mathematical features and allows you to arrange your data in columns.

Create Headings for Math Columns After Setting Up the Columns

TIP 762

It is a good idea to add headings to your math columns after you create the columns and enter the information rather than before. You will want to create the column headings using different tab settings than the math columns, because the math columns will probably all align on the decimal point. Headings usually align differently; for example, centered over the columns to make them more readable. Furthermore, you may need to move the math columns around to make them appear their best. Rather than changing two tab settings each time you adjust a column, wait until the math columns are set and then add the heading.

Pay Attention to Calculation Order in Math Formulas

TIP 763

WordPerfect 6 and 5.1 calculate formulas using different calculation orders. It is important that you know in which order WordPerfect is going to calculate your formula so you write the formula correctly.

WordPerfect 6 calculates formulas by calculating operations in parentheses, then multiplication and division, then addition and subtraction. For example, in the formula $3+(2*4)*3$, WordPerfect 6 first calculates $2*4$, which is 8; then $8*3$, which is 24; then it adds 3, making the solution 27.

WordPerfect 5.1 calculates operations within parentheses first, then performs operations from left to right. For example, in the formula 3+(2*4)*3, WordPerfect 5.1 first calculates 2*4, which is 8; then 3+8, which is 11; then 11*3, making the solution 33.

You can see that you would not want to use the same formulas in WordPerfect 6 and 5.1, because you get different results due to the different order of calculation. However, you do not need to rewrite the formulas in your WordPerfect 5.1 documents when you upgrade to WordPerfect 6. When you convert your 5.1 documents to 6, WordPerfect automatically edits the formulas, using parentheses to ensure that the results of the calculation will be the same. You can also add parentheses to your formulas to ensure you get the correct order of calculations.

Change the Decimal/Align Character and the Thousands Separator to Change the Display of Math Results

By default, WordPerfect assumes that a comma separates the thousands in a number, while the decimal point is a period. WordPerfect also uses the characters this way when displaying the results of math calculations.

You may want to use different characters for these symbols. Your company may use different standards, or you may be creating a foreign language document and want to use the math standards of that country. For example, in much of Europe, the thousands separator is a period and the decimal point is a comma, the exact reverse of the U.S. standard. To avoid confusion you should stick with the standard format of the person or people who will be reading the document, just as the European standards are used here:

File Edit View Layout Tools Font Graphics Window Help
File Mgr Save As Print Preview Font GrphMode TextMode Envelope Speller GramLik QuikFndr Tbl Edit Search

Budget Variances in US Dollars (12/31/93)

European Division

	Percentage	Total
Spain	2,45%	12.320,34
Portugal	(3,45%)	(10.394,39)
France	3,70%	23.392,49
Germany	1,01%	2.390,20
Italy	2,22%	39.209,69
Britain	3,21%	14.392,03

To change the decimal/align character or thousands separator in WordPerfect 6:

1. Select **L**ayout Cha**r**acter.
2. Select **D**ecimal/Align Character or **T**housands Separator.
3. Type the character to use.
4. Select OK to return to the document.

To change the decimal/align character or thousands separator in WordPerfect 5.1:

1. Select **L**ayout **O**ther.
2. Select **D**ecimal/Align Character.
3. Type the character to use as the decimal/align character.
4. Type the character to use as the thousands separator.
5. Press F7 to return to the document.

Enter Fractions as Decimals or Within Parentheses

TIP 765

WordPerfect uses the / character in math formulas to indicate division. You use the same character when creating fractions. Depending on your formula, this may be a problem because of how WordPerfect calculates formulas.

In WordPerfect 6, multiplication and division calculations are performed first, starting from the left. If you wanted to divide 6 by 3/2, and entered **6/3/2**, WordPerfect 6 would first calculate 6/3, which is 2; then 2/2, which is 1. If you entered **6/(3/2)**, WordPerfect would first divide 3/2, which is 1.5; then divide 6 by 1.5, which is 4. As you can see, not using the parentheses here creates a large error. The other solution would be to enter the fraction as a decimal fraction (1.5), which would eliminate the confusion.

In WordPerfect 5.1, all calculations are performed starting on the left and going across. Therefore, if you wanted to add 2 and 1/2, and entered the formula **2+1/2**, WordPerfect 5.1 would first add 1 and 2, which is 3; then divide this by 2, giving you a result of 1.5. If you used the parentheses, as in **2+(1/2)**, WordPerfect 5.1's answer would be 2.5, which it should be. The other solution to this is to use decimal fractions, entering **2+.5**, which eliminates the confusion.

Add Text to Math Columns for Readability

When creating math columns remember that not only do you need to be able to calculate the numbers, you need to be able to read them easily. To increase readability, one easy formatting change you can make is to add text. You can enter characters such as % and $ to make the meaning of your columns clearer.

Change the Display of Negative Numbers and Decimals

When you define math columns, you can change how math results are displayed. You can choose how negative numbers will be indicated and the number of digits that will appear after the decimal point.

You can select to use either parentheses or a negative sign to indicate when numbers are negative. While the negative sign is most common in scientific or technical papers, the parentheses are commonly used to indicate negative numbers in financial documents.

You can also select how many digits may appear after the decimal point. If you are displaying currency, you will want to display only two digits after the decimal point, even if calculations yield a result that goes to four digits. Alternatively, you may want to display no digits when performing other types of calculations.

WordPerfect Has Six Functions You Can Use in Math Columns

You can use six functions in numeric, total, or calculation columns to calculate down math columns. When you insert these functions a special character appears. When you print the document after calculating, however, only the results appear, not the function characters.

Symbol	Function	Purpose
+	Subtotal	Adds the numbers above it
=	Total	Adds the subtotals above it
*	Grand Total	Adds the totals above it
t	Extra Subtotal	Adds the number following itself to the next total
T	Extra Total	Adds the number following itself to the next grand total
N	Math Negative (WP 6 only)	Tells other functions to treat the number following it as a negative

When the + (Subtotal) function appears in a total column, it is used to calculate the total of the numbers above itself, and one column to the left. Total columns are used because in many financial documents, the total of a column of numbers should appear to the right of the column.

WordPerfect Has Special Functions That Can Be Used in Math Formulas

TIP 769

WordPerfect offers four special functions that you can use as formulas when defining a calculation column. These functions cannot be combined with anything else in the formula, such as other functions, operators, or numbers. They must appear alone, as the entire calculation.

Symbol	Purpose
+	Adds the numbers in numeric columns to the left
+/	Averages the numbers in numeric columns to the left
=	Adds the numbers in total columns to the left
+/	Averages numbers in total columns to the left

If you want to create elaborate formulas, you may prefer to use the table feature for math. When you use the table feature, WordPerfect offers you many advanced functions for calculating, including financial functions, as explained in Tip 690.

Be Careful About Using Negative Numbers for Subtraction

You will want to be careful when you use negative numbers in math calculations and then create formulas to work with those negative numbers. For example, suppose that the first column is sales, entered as a positive number, and the second column is expenses, entered as a negative number. If you create a third calculation and calculate sales minus expenses, your result will be much higher than it should be because subtracting a negative number is the same as adding a positive one. Make sure that you use an addition sign when you want to subtract a number you have already entered as negative.

Include Row Titles in Text Columns or Before the First Column

When you create math columns, you may find that you want to insert titles or headings for different rows within the columns. You can do this in two ways. You can define a column as a text column. The contents of text columns are not used in calculations or functions. Instead these columns allow you to add labels to your data without upsetting your calculations.

If you want to add titles to the beginning of rows, you can also enter the text at the left margin, before the first tab stop. Since WordPerfect's math feature does not use the space between the margin and the first tab stop for storing data, you will not confuse your calculations by including text in this location.

Remember not to accidentally include a column of data you want to access in calculations at the left margin. If you do, it will be ignored by the math feature. Because of this, your row titles can include numbers such as times and dates as well as strictly text, as you can see in the following:

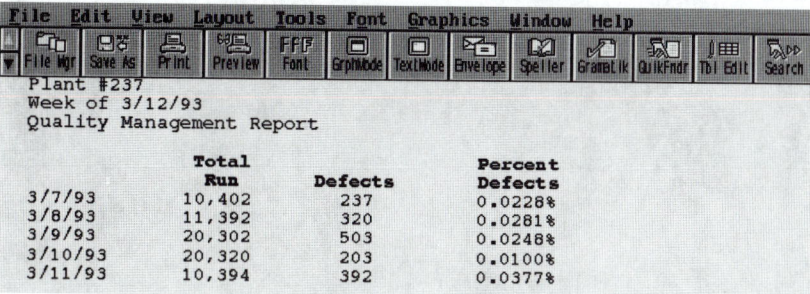

You Can Stop WordPerfect from Calculating a Formula in One Row of a Calculation Column

TIP 772

When you press TAB to create a column already defined as a calculation column, a ! character appears in that column. Like the function characters, which you enter in numeric or total columns, this character indicates that a result can be calculated for that column. This character will not print, but does appear on the screen.

If you do not want to calculate the formula for that row, delete this character. For example, you may have used a blank line to separate two sets of data. To avoid having WordPerfect calculate a null result for that blank row, simply delete the ! character.

CHAPTER 16

Outlines

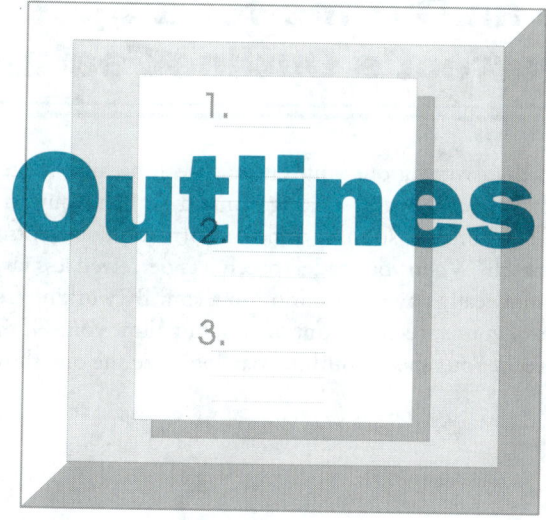

Add Body Text to WordPerfect 6 Outlines

Unlike WordPerfect 5.1 outlines, the outline feature in WordPerfect 6 allows you to add paragraphs of body text to your outlines. Properly speaking, body text is not part of the outline. Instead, it is text that fully explains the actual outline entries. One way to think of this is to think of a paper you have to write. You first create an outline to specify what topics you are going to cover, and in what order. These outline entries are like the headings you might use in the paper. Then, after the appropriate outline entries, you add body text, which actually explains the topics and presents your information. When you are done, you have a paper with headings and text under the headings. The headings, however, are the entries in your original outline.

The quickest way to set a paragraph as body text, after turning the outline feature on, is simply to move the cursor into that paragraph and press CTRL-T. CTRL-T switches the paragraph between being an outline entry and being body text.

Create an Outline for a Speech Using WordPerfect's Outline Features

Using an outline is better than writing out your entire speech because it prevents you from simply reading your speech directly. Since you are working from an outline, you can more easily respond to your audience's reactions, new time constraints, or new information or events that may have occurred since you first wrote the speech. When you read a speech it is perceived less favorably by the audience, because they feel you are not really paying attention to them. By working from an outline, you can still have the major points of your speech in front of you, but allow yourself the looseness and vitality of an extemporaneous speech. Your speech outline may look like the one shown in the following:

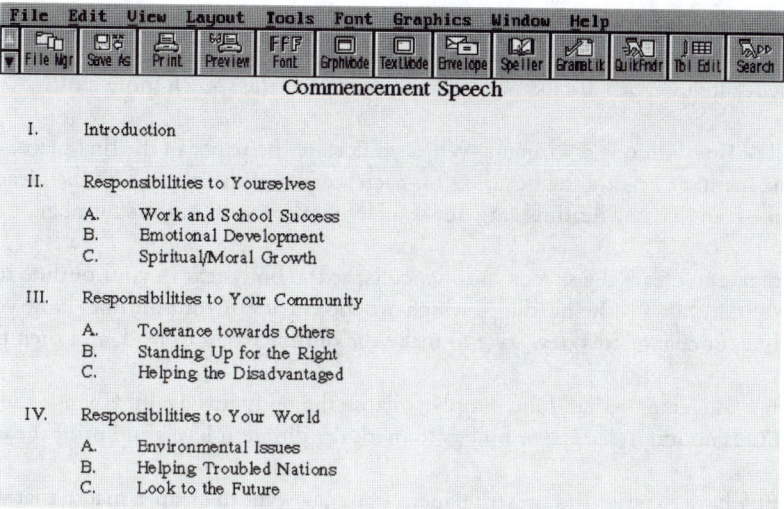

Do not make your outline all capitals if you are using it to present a speech. Text that is all capital letters is harder to read than text that mixes capital and lowercase letters, because we use the height of the letters as part of recognizing words. If you are having trouble reading your outline, you will fall right back into the problem of having to pay more attention to the paper on the podium than to the audience. Try using a large font size so that you can read the outline easily at arm's length.

Create a Speech Outline, Paper, and Handout with One Document in WordPerfect 6

TIP 775

WordPerfect 6 includes some outlining features not available in WordPerfect 5.1 that can be used to take one document and create three separate printouts from it. Some of these features are to include body text in your outline and to expand or collapse the levels shown in your outline's display. Other features, used in WordPerfect 6 and 5.1, include outline styles, which you can use to quickly change how the outline and outline numbers appear. You can use all of these features to create a speech outline, paper, and handout from one document.

For example, you may be publishing a professional paper, and have been invited to present it at a conference. You won't want to just read the paper at the conference, since the attendees can presumably

just read it when it is published. Instead, you will want to give a speech that covers the same general issues, but in a more timely fashion. You will also want to present a handout at the presentation to help the audience follow your discussion and later remember the speech more clearly.

You can do all of this with one document. When you create the paper in the first place, remember to use the outline feature to create the headings for each section of the paper. Use the Headings outline style or one like it so that the headings are not actually marked with outline numbers.

When you prepare to create the speech outline, collapse the body text in your outline so that it does not appear. All that shows is the headings, which are the entries in your outline. Now you can either print the outline, or change to a new style to make the outline easier to read, and then print it.

When you want to create the handout, simply collapse the body text again. Change the outline style to a style that uses numbers, letters, or bullets to mark the different levels and print the outline again.

If you frequently have to write and present papers, you may want to create a macro that will make this part of the preparation a little easier. For example, the following macro, which is saved as HAND-OUT.WPM on the accompanying disk, does three things: It collapses a document so that only the first and second level headings are displayed; it switches to the Outline outline style and prints the resulting documents; then it expands the document to show all body text and outline entries again.

```
DISPLAY(Off!)
OutlineShow(2;ShowBodyText!)
OutlineStyleSelect(OutlineStyle!)
PrintFullDoc
OutlineShow(8;ShowBodyText!)
```

HANDOUT.WPM

The sample macro is available on the accompanying disk as HANDOUT.WPM.

Do Not Worry About Renumbering Outlines

One of the great advantages of using WordPerfect's outline feature instead of typing an outline yourself is that WordPerfect will maintain and update the correct numbers for each paragraph in the outline for you. When you insert a new outline paragraph, WordPerfect renumbers the paragraphs for you.

Add Paragraph Numbers to a Document Using the Outline Feature in WordPerfect 6

In WordPerfect 5.1, you added paragraph numbers to a document using the Tools Paragraph Number command. In WordPerfect 6, you add paragraph numbers using the outline feature.

To add paragraph numbers using WordPerfect 6:

1. Move to the beginning of the first paragraph you want numbered.
2. Select **T**ools **O**utline **B**egin New Outline.
3. Highlight the Numbers outline style and choose **S**elect.
4. At the beginning of each paragraph you want numbered, press CTRL-T.

Pressing CTRL-T makes that paragraph an outline entry. Only paragraphs that are outline entries are counted; other paragraphs are simply skipped in the numbering process. If you change to a different outline style, the format of your numbered paragraphs may change.

Change How Paragraph and Outline Numbers Appear by Changing the Outline's Style

In both WordPerfect 6 and 5.1, you can change the appearance of an outline by changing its style. You can also create your own outline style instead of using one that comes with WordPerfect.

To change an outline style in WordPerfect 6:

1. Move your cursor within the text in the outline.
2. Select **T**ools **O**utline Style.
3. Highlight a style name.
4. Choose **S**elect.

To change an outline style in WordPerfect 5.1:

1. Press ALT-F3 to display the hidden codes.
2. Find the [Para Num Def] code closest to the beginning of the outline or paragraph numbering and delete it.
3. Select **T**ools **D**efine.
4. Select one of the formats given for the outline or page numbers, or select Outline Style **N**ame, highlight the style you want to use, and choose Se**l**ect.
5. Press ENTER twice to return to the document.

Change the Bullet Characters for an Outline Style in WordPerfect 6

In WordPerfect 6, you can quickly create an outline style that uses bullets, and then change the default bullets that WordPerfect uses to any character in the WordPerfect character set. Use fanciful bullets to add personality to your document by following these steps:

1. Select **T**ools **O**utline **O**utline Style.
2. Select **C**reate. If you are editing a style, select **E**dit with the style highlighted, and skip to step 4.
3. Type a name for the style and select OK.
4. Select Number **F**ormat **B**ullets.
5. Select N**u**mbers and highlight the text box for the outline level whose assigned bullet you want to change.
6. Press F5 to display a list of standard bullets, then highlight a bullet and choose **S**elect.
    Alternatively, you can use a compose sequence or press CTRL-W to select any character in the WordPerfect character sets to use as a bullet.
7. When you are finished changing the bullets, select OK.
8. Choose **S**elect to select this bulleted style and return to your document.

Add Paragraph Numbers in WordPerfect 5.1

TIP 780

When you want to number your paragraphs, as in a legal document or for a paper, rather than entering the numbers yourself, let WordPerfect enter them for you. The greatest advantage to having Word-Perfect enter them is that you do not have to worry about misnumbering, or about editing a document and having to reenter the paragraph numbers. WordPerfect will automatically number the paragraphs correctly.

To enter paragraph numbers in WordPerfect 5.1:

1. Move to the beginning of the first paragraph you want to number.
2. Select **T**ools **P**aragraph Number.
3. Either type the number to insert and press ENTER, or press ENTER to have WordPerfect calculate the correct paragraph number for you.

When you insert a paragraph number, WordPerfect uses the style or format of numbering specified by the last [Par Num Def] code. If you want to use a different style of numbering, you will have to enter a new [Par Num Def] code by selecting Tools Define and selecting a new format or style.

Create Numbered and Bulleted Lists Using the Outline Feature

The outline and paragraph numbering features are easy ways to create numbered or bulleted lists in WordPerfect. You simply select the appropriate style or format for the paragraph numbers, then include the paragraph number or outline codes before each paragraph that is an item in the list. WordPerfect will keep the list formatted correctly and maintain the numbering on numbered lists. This is decidedly less cumbersome than adding the bullet character for each item or renumbering the items on the list when you add a new one. For example, the bulleted list shown in the following illustration was created with the outline feature using bullets from the WordPerfect Iconic character set.

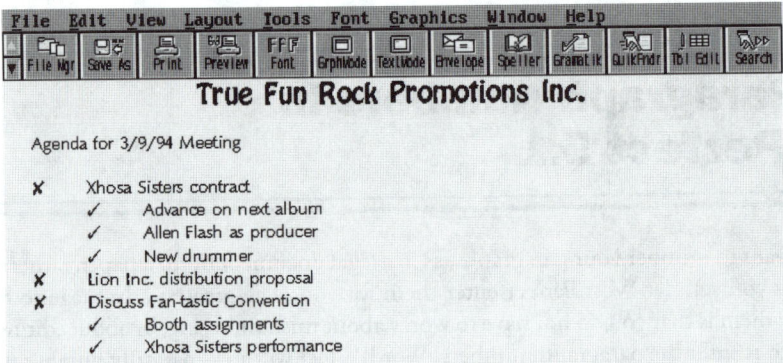

WordPerfect Has Several Options That You Can Use for Numbering Paragraphs

In WordPerfect 6 and 5.1, there are several options for adding numbers to all paragraphs. You can choose the paragraph numbering option that is simplest for you to use and provides the features you want.

In WordPerfect 6, you can add paragraph numbers using the outline feature or by creating a counter. Using the outline feature of WordPerfect 6 to number paragraphs is discussed in Tip 777. Counters allow you to keep track of any type of item in your document; they can have up to eight levels. To create a counter:

1. Select **L**ayout Cha**r**acter **C**ounter.
2. Select **C**reate.
3. Type the name of the counter, such as **Paragraph** .
4. Select **L**evels and type the number of levels you want to use.
5. Select Numbering **M**ethod and choose the numbering method you want to use.
6. Select OK.
7. Select OK to return to the document.

You can now increment the counter each time you enter a new paragraph to count. WordPerfect displays the counter's paragraph numbers only when you choose to display them in the document. If you choose to have more than one level in the counter, you will have to go back, select the levels, and edit them to choose a different numbering method for each.

In WordPerfect 5.1, you can add paragraph numbers using the outline feature or the paragraph numbering feature. Using the paragraph numbering feature is discussed in Tip 780. To create a WordPerfect 5.1 outline:

1. Select **T**ools **O**utline.
2. Select **O**n.
3. Enter the text of the outline, using TAB and SHIFT-TAB to change outline levels.
4. Select **T**ools **O**utline Off.

Use WordPerfect's Outline Feature to Number Paragraphs in Contracts and Agreements

TIP 783

When you are creating a contract, agreement, or other legal document, you may need to number the paragraphs so that the lawyers can specify which part or article in the document they are referring to. When you include these paragraph numbers in a legal document, you do not simply number the paragraphs from one to as many paragraphs as you have. Instead, the paragraphs are arranged into sections. You can see how this is done using the outline feature in the document shown in the following:

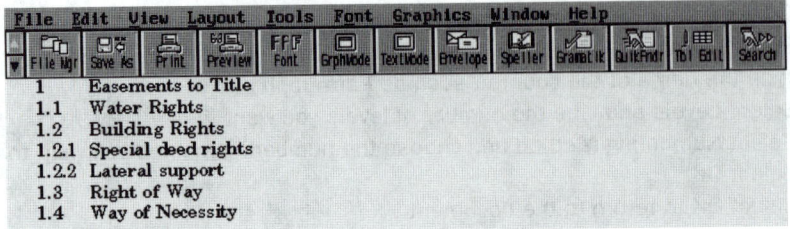

To number these paragraphs in WordPerfect 6:

1. Select **T**ools **O**utline **B**egin New Outline.
2. Highlight the legal style.
3. Choose **S**elect.
4. Create your agreement or contract.

Each time you press ENTER a new paragraph number will appear. To make the paragraph number one level lower, press TAB; to make it one level higher, press SHIFT-TAB.

To number these paragraphs in WordPerfect 5.1:

1. Create any introductory text you do not want to number.
2. Select **T**ools **D**efine.
3. Select **L**egal.
4. Press ENTER twice.
5. Select **T**ools **O**utline **O**n.
6. Create your agreement or contract.

You Can Change the Paragraph Levels After You Have Typed a Document

The levels of the paragraphs entered when you are creating an outline are not set forever after you finish typing them. You can always change the level of the paragraph in the outline, even if the document was created and saved some time ago. Simply move the cursor to directly after the paragraph number or style code that inserts the paragraph or outline number, then press TAB or SHIFT-TAB to change the level of the paragraph.

You do not need to move to the beginning of the outline when you want to change the style of an outline. Instead, just move your cursor to some position within the outline. You can even position your cursor in a paragraph of body text within the outline. The trick is to make sure that the cursor is between the codes that turn the outline feature on and off when you change the style.

Use the Outline Bar When Editing Outlines in WordPerfect 6

WordPerfect 6 has a bar much like the Ribbon especially designed for working with outlines. After displaying it, you can use the mouse to select many options and commands that relate to outlines. To display the bar:

1. Select **V**iew Scree**n** Setup.
2. Select **S**creen Options and the **O**utline Bar check box.
3. Select OK to return to the document and display the following bar:

The Outline Bar, shown here, contains several options for use with the WordPerfect 6 outline feature. The bar's elements and their purposes are given in the following table.

Element	Purpose
#	Changes body text into an outline entry
T	Changes an outline entry into body text
←■	Moves each entry in the current family up one level
■→	Moves each entry in the current family down one level
−	Hides the current family below the level the cursor is on
+	Displays the hidden family beneath the entry the cursor is on
Show	Lets you select the lowest outline level to show
Hide/Show Body	Hides or displays the body text
Style	Lets you select the outline style to use such as "Paragraph" in the bar shown above
Options	Opens the Outline Options dialog box

You Can Collapse or Expand the Outline in WordPerfect 6

786

A new feature with WordPerfect 6 is the way that you can collapse or expand outlines. When you collapse an outline, you do not display all of the text in the outline. When you expand it, you show more of the text in the outline. For example, this document has a fully expanded outline with all of its entries displayed:

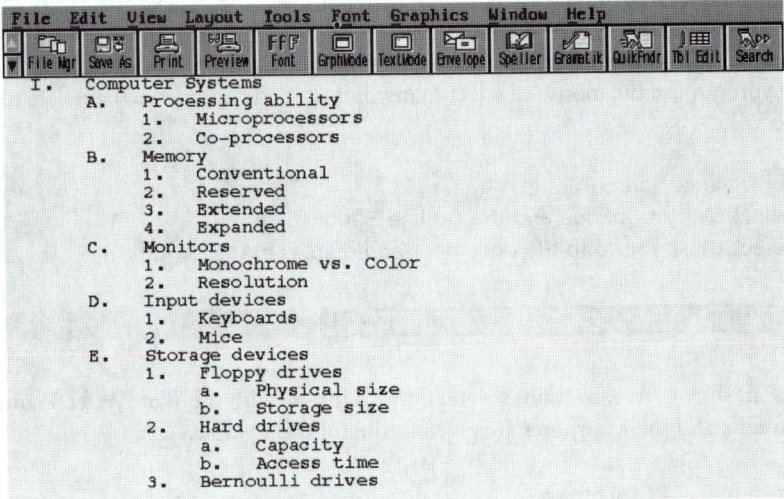

After changing the settings so that only the first two levels of the outline are displayed, the same document looks like this:

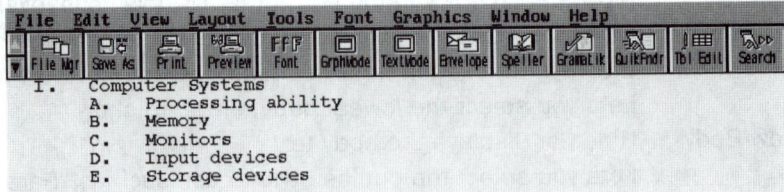

To hide all body text:

1. Select **T**ools **O**utline.
2. Select Hide Body **T**ext.

To show a specific number of levels:

1. Select **T**ools **O**utline Outline Options.
2. Select **H**ide/Show.
3. Select **S**how Levels.
4. Select the lowest level that you want to display.

To hide all outline entries, but show body text:

1. Select **T**ools **O**utline Outline Options.
2. Select **H**ide/Show.
3. Select Hide **O**utline.

In outlines, you have families, which are an outline entry and all of the outline entries that appear under it in the hierarchy of levels. You can hide or show a specific family of an outline.

To hide an outline family:

1. Place your cursor in the lowest outline entry you want to display.
2. Select **T**ools **O**utline **H**ide Family.

To display an outline family:

1. Place your cursor in the lowest outline entry in that family that is displayed.
2. Select **T**ools **O**utline **S**how Family.

You can also use the Outline Bar to change the display of the outline, as explained in Tip 785.

You Can Share Your Own Custom Outline Style Definitions Between Documents

In WordPerfect 6 and 5.1, you can create outline styles that determine how outlines appear and then save them to a style library. You can use that style library in any document so that the outline style becomes a resource for all files that you create.

To create a style library in WordPerfect 6:

1. Select **T**ools **O**utline **O**utline Style.
2. Create the outline style you want to save.
3. Select Sa**v**e.
4. Type the filename for the style library file.
5. If you want to save the files you have created in the style library, make sure the Save **U**ser-Created Styles check box is selected.
6. If you want to save WordPerfect's standard outline styles, make sure the Save WP **S**ystem Styles check box is selected, or clear it if you don't want to.
7. Select OK.

You can access these styles in two ways, either by assigning the style library as a personal or shared library, or by retrieving the styles from the style library directly into the document as document styles.

To retrieve the styles into the document:

1. Select **T**ools **O**utline **O**utline Style.
2. Select **R**etrieve.
3. Type the filename of the style library you want to retrieve the styles from.
4. Select the Retrieve **U**ser-Created Styles check box to retrieve the styles you created.
5. Select the Retrieve WP **S**ystem Styles check box to retrieve the styles that come with WordPerfect.
6. Select OK.

If you already have styles by that name in your document, WordPerfect prompts you with the message "Style(s) already exist. Replace?". You can replace the styles in the document with those you are retrieving or you can keep the existing document styles.

To assign a style library as a personal or shared library:

1. Select **T**ools **O**utline **O**utline Styles.
2. Select **O**ptions.
3. Select **L**ibraries Assigned to Document.
4. Enter the name of the style library in the Personal or Shared text box.
   Personal style libraries are those stored on your computer system, while shared ones are those available to all users of a network. If you are not part of a network, or just don't want to use a style library from the network, you can enter a library stored on your system in the Shared text box, allowing you to assign two personal style libraries to the same document.
5. Select the List **U**ser Created Styles check box to have WordPerfect display the styles in the library that were created by you or another WordPerfect user.
6. Select the List **S**ystem Styles check box to have WordPerfect display the styles in the library that were created by WordPerfect.
7. Select OK to return to the Outline Styles dialog box.

To create a style library in WordPerfect 5.1:

1. Select **T**ools **D**efine Outline Style **N**ame.
2. Create the styles you want to save, if necessary.
3. Select **S**ave.
4. Type the filename for the style library and press ENTER

To retrieve a style library in WordPerfect 5.1:

1. Select **T**ools **D**efine Outline Style **N**ame.
2. Select **R**etrieve.
3. Type the filename of the style library and press ENTER

You Can Set the Default WordPerfect Outline Style

TIP
788

You can determine which of the WordPerfect outline styles is the default. The default when you receive WordPerfect is Paragraph. To set the default outline style:

1. Select **L**ayout **D**ocument.
2. Select Initial Codes Se**t**up.
3. Select **T**ools **O**utline **O**utline Style.
4. Highlight the outline style you want as the default and choose **S**elect.
5. Press F7.
6. Select OK.

Move or Copy Outline Families with a Special Command

TIP 789

An outline consists of families or branches. Each family is an outline entry and all the outline entries and body text that appear under it, before the next outline entry of the same level. When you move or copy entries in an outline, you often want to move or copy an entire family rather than just the text of a single outline entry. You cannot do this easily with the standard move and copy commands, so WordPerfect offers you some special commands for moving or copying outline families. When you use these commands, you can be sure of moving all the text in the family at once, and of preserving the outline codes correctly.

To move or copy outline families in WordPerfect 6:

1. Position your cursor in the highest level of the family that you want to move or copy.
2. Select **T**ools **O**utline.
3. Select Cop**y** Family to copy it or Cut **F**amily to move it.
4. Position the cursor where you want the family to appear.
5. Select **T**ools **O**utline **P**aste.

To move or copy outline families in WordPerfect 5.1:

1. Position your cursor in the highest level of the family that you want to move or copy.
2. Select **T**ools **O**utline.
3. Select **M**ove Family to move it or **C**opy Family to copy it.
4. Use the arrow keys to move the cursor to where you want the family inserted and press ENTER

CHAPTER 17

Merges, Form Letters, and Templates

Use WordPerfect to Create Forms Instead of Paying a Print Shop to Create Them for You

You use many forms in the business world, including invoices, fax sheets, press releases, proposals, and mailing labels. You might have these forms created by a printer so they include your logo and graphics elements such as lines, boxes, and reverse coloring. You can use WordPerfect to create these forms instead, reducing the cost to you. With WordPerfect's graphics features you can add the lines, boxes, and other graphics elements. You can then either print the forms and photocopy them, or give the camera-ready form to the printer to print for you, at a reduced cost.

Use Different Colors or Reverses in a Form to Make Sections Identifiable

Using different background or text colors in particular parts of a form will help make the different parts more immediately visible. For example, on an employment application, there may be areas you want set aside for the interviewer to record comments. To avoid having the applicant write in that section, add a screen. A screen is a block of background color, which you can add by changing the fill for the paragraph border.

When you create a form with several lines of information, such as an invoice form, use a screen to help the user of the form clearly see how the left and right sides of the form are related. If you simply use lines, it is easy for the eye to slip down or up a line while moving from the left to the right side of the line. When you use screens on alternating lines, skipping lines is more difficult.

The following invoice is an example of how you can use screens to make a form more readable:

Davidson Illumination Company

32473 Magnolia Lane ⚬ Akron, OH 44302
216/762-1212
216/762-1231 (fax)

Invoice Date: June 22, 1993
Invoice No.: 342494
Purchase Order: AP-X392

Shipping Date: 6/28/93
Via: UPS Ground

Bill To: James Bros. Manufacturing
231 South Exchange St.
Akron, OH 44302

Ship To: James Bros. Manufacturing
342 Devonshire Road
Cleveland, OH 44114

Qty	Item #	Description	Price	Cost

Please call if there are any questions about your order

1-800-342-9304

Subtot.	
Tax	
Total	
Balance	

This sample template is available on the accompanying disk as INVOICE.TEM. The invoice uses the lightbulb graphic as a logo, which is not included in the template, but is available as BULB.PCX on the disk.

INVOICE.TEM
BULB.PCX

Use Different Colors in an Onscreen Form

When you create a form to be filled out onscreen, remember to use the color abilities of your monitor. You can use bright colors on your screen to alert the user of the form to information that needs to be filled in. For example, on an information form for new employees, there may be some fields that must be filled in, such as name, social security number, and exemptions on the W2 form and other fields that are optional, such as race, marriage status, or home phone number.

To make it easier for the person filling in the form to be sure they have not accidentally missed some of the required fields, it helps to show these fields in red or some other bright color that contrasts with the rest of the form. There are two ways to do this. One is to change the color assigned to the text in that location. The other is to create a border for the paragraph or table cell, and assign a fill of red.

Create Distinctive Fax Forms to Help Recognition

With so many documents being faxed now, it is easy for any one fax to get lost or mixed in the pages of another fax. To prevent this, you can create a striking and distinctive fax cover sheet. If the cover sheet catches the eye of the recipients, they are less likely to mix it in with other faxes. You can use one of the sample fax form templates included on the accompanying disk (and shown following), or use them as a source for other ideas.

FAXFORM1.TEM
FAXFORM2.TEM
FAXFORM3.TEM
DOG.PCX
MOON.PCX

These sample templates are available on the accompanying disk as FAXFORM1.TEM, FAX-FORM2.TEM, and FAXFORM3.TEM. FAXFORM1.TEM uses the MOON.PCX graphics image, while FAXFORM2.TEM uses the DOG.PCX graphics image.

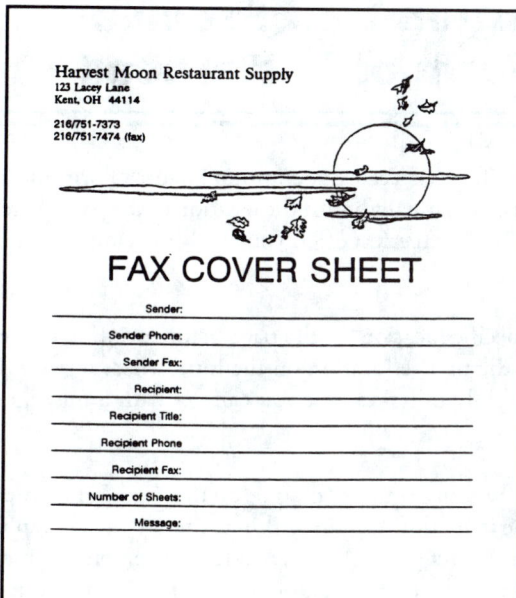

Cover Sheet

Sender:	Jane Stewart
Sender Phone:	216/739-9340
Sender Fax:	215/739-9341
Recipient:	Carol Jamison
Recipient Title:	Partner
Recipient Phone:	216/934-2945
Recipient Fax:	216/934-2966
Number of Sheets:	30
Message:	Hi Carol, this is the big one. Hope we can get complete approval of the bid, but call me if you have any questions or problems with it. Say hello to Jerry for me.

Advance Can Position Text Precisely on a Preprinted Form or Letterhead

Filling out preprinted forms with the computer is difficult, because you cannot be sure of printing the text in the correct location. With a typewriter, you can manually adjust the location of the paper before typing on a form, but you can't do that with a printer. WordPerfect offers you nearly the same flexibility, however, with its Advance feature.

The Advance feature moves the printhead to a specific location on the page before printing the text that follows it. You can use Advance to move to the precise location on the form where text should appear, and then enter it. This prevents the unsightly mistakes that you can get with a misaligned typewriter or printer.

Another use for the Advance feature is to align text within a frame or graphic on the page. For example, in the page of postcards shown here, the text of the invitation appears within the scroll on the graphic. To make sure that the text appears in precisely the correct place, Advance codes were entered to move the cursor to the location, rather than trying to approximate the position using hard returns and tabs.

This graphic is available on the accompanying disk as SHIPPING.PCX.

SHIPPING.PCX

To use the Advance feature with WordPerfect 6:

1. Select **L**ayout **O**ther.
2. Select **A**dvance.
3. Select one of the option buttons under Horizontal Position:
    Left from Cursor, **R**ight from Cursor, or **F**rom Left Edge of Page;
    then enter the measurement.
4. Select one of the option buttons under Vertical Position:
    Up from Cursor, **D**own from Cursor, or From **T**op of Page; then
    enter the measurement.
5. Select OK.

To use the Advance feature with WordPerfect 5.1:

1. Select **L**ayout **O**ther or SHIFT-F8 (Format).
2. Select **A**dvance.
3. Select **U**p, **D**own, **L**eft, or **R**ight to move to a position relative to the
    cursor's current location, type a measurement, and press ENTER.
4. Select Li**n**e or **P**osition to move to a position measured from the edge
    of the paper, type the measurement, and press ENTER.
    When you select Li**n**e, enter the measurement from the top of the page,
    setting the vertical position. When you select **P**osition, enter the
    measurement from the left side of the page, setting the horizontal position.
5. Press F7 to return to the document.

WordPerfect inserts a code wherever your cursor is. This code tells WordPerfect to move the cursor, or the printhead when you are printing, to that precise location. Any text that you insert after this appears in the new location.

Use a Similar Design on Envelopes to Match Letterhead

You probably spent some time in designing your letterhead. Since you use your letterhead for most of your communications with clients and other business associates, the image or message that it conveys is very important. To help this image, use a design on your envelopes that matches your letterhead. This ties your envelopes and letterhead together, conveying a professional image of consistency and attention to detail. Your messages will stand out from the normal run of communications, and will bring instant recognition from people used to seeing your letterhead already.

You can tie your envelopes and letterhead together by re-creating a logo on your envelopes or by using the same paper or style of printing. If your letterhead uses graphics elements that are not your logo, repeating one part of this design on the envelope is effective. If your letterhead is preprinted for you, then have your envelopes preprinted for you. If your letterhead is created in WordPerfect, you can use WordPerfect for creating the design on your envelopes as well.

Spell-Check Form and Data Files Separately

Be sure to spell-check both your form and data files before doing a merge. Wait till after you have done the merge, and the spell-checking process will take much longer, because the resulting merge document is much larger than either file alone.

Spell-check your data files, even if they consist primarily of names and addresses. WordPerfect will find some misspelled city and state names. This provides another defense against incorrect spelling and mistakes, even though it is a tedious process, because WordPerfect will stop at every word or name that is not in its dictionary.

Match Your Form to the Order in Which Entries Are Received

When you design a form to be filled out either by hand or on the screen, consider how the person is going to get the information to fill it out. You can increase speed and accuracy by creating a form that follows the progression of the information as it is presented.

For example, when people are filling out onscreen forms for phoned-in complaints, create a form that requests information in a reasonable order. Most companies require that their phone operators request a phone number first so that if they are disconnected, the operator can call right back and continue taking the message. If the phone number is halfway down the form, the operator is going to have to move to it, fill it out, and then move back to the top of the form to complete other information. If operators are in a hurry, they might enter information in the wrong area. By matching your form layout to the way information is requested, you can assure that the process of filling out the form is easier and faster.

Use Standard Forms to Present a Professional Image

Part of creating a professional image is attention to details. When different people in your organization send out the same form, but with different formats, you present an image that suggests that you do not pay attention to the details of your work. To present a more professional image, make sure you use standard forms throughout your company.

You can ensure that forms are standardized in several ways. You can use templates to create standardization. *Templates* are files that contain all the correct formatting and dummy text that can be replaced with correct text. You can also create keyboard merge files to ensure that everyone puts the same information in the same locations. You can use styles to ensure consistent formatting.

Quickly Create Business Cards Using a Template

You can create business cards quickly and consistently by using a business card template and business card paper. You can create a template that formats the page into business card-sized logical pages and includes the elements that need to occur on the business card in the correct locations. Then print this onto a page of business cards. Many paper supply houses carry sheets of heavy paper that is perforated or marked for dividing into business cards.

You can use the template BUSICARD.TEM on the accompanying disk to create business cards. The first card of the template looks like this:

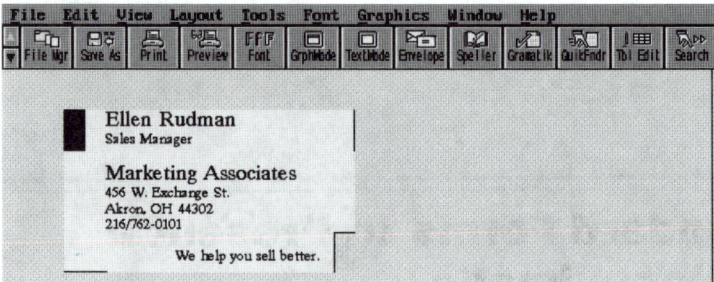

BUSICARD.TEM

This sample template is available on the accompanying disk as BUSICARD.TEM.

This template assumes that you are going to print the cards on paper that is designed to be divided into ten standard 2-by-3-1/2-inch business cards, and that this paper has no designs already printed on it. You can purchase paper that is preperforated to be divided into business cards, or you can print, using this template, onto heavy paper or card stock and cut it into parts yourself. The thin lines on the left and bottom of the first card are there to show you where to cut. Only the first card shows, but all you need to do is copy its contents to the other nine cards printed on the page.

Merge Terminology Can Be Confusing at First

T^{IP} 800

There is a lot of terminology, or jargon, associated with doing merges. Once you are familiar with how merges work, the meaning of these terms will appear obvious, and be of great use to you. At first, however, the terms can be very confusing, and may make doing merges seem tremendously technical. In addition, some terms have changed between WordPerfect 5.1 and WordPerfect 6, so even if you are familiar with the terms used with 5.1, you will have to adjust to a few new ones.

In a basic merge, you have WordPerfect take information from one file and put it into another file, in specific locations. The file that the information is put into is called the *form file* (WordPerfect 6) or the *primary file* (WordPerfect 5.1). The file that stores the information is called the *data file* (WordPerfect 6) or the *secondary file* (WordPerfect 5.1). This is illustrated here:

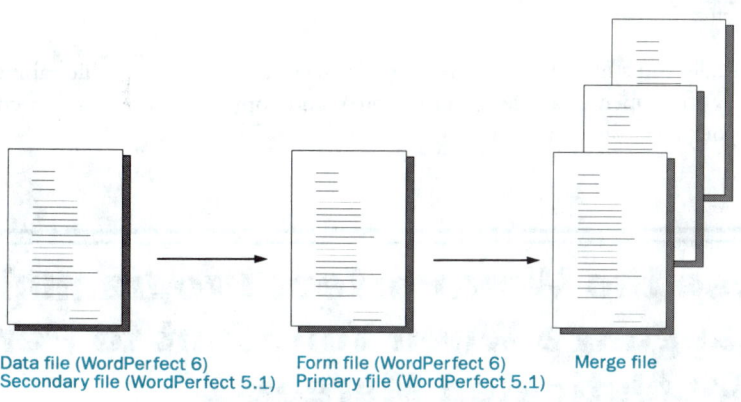

Data file (WordPerfect 6)   Form file (WordPerfect 6)   Merge file
Secondary file (WordPerfect 5.1)   Primary file (WordPerfect 5.1)

When you think about these files, think of a form letter. The form (primary) file is the text of the letter itself. The data (secondary) file is the file of names the letter will be addressed to.

The data in the data (secondary) file is arranged into records and fields. Records are made up of several fields. Each field is the smallest part of information in the data file. For example, in a data file that lists your clients, the client's first name is a single field. A record consists of all the fields referring to a specific unit. In that client list, all of the fields that refer to the client "Beatrice Smith", such as name, address, or phone number, make up one record.

When you think of fields and records, try visualizing a file folder. Each of the papers in the file folder contains one piece of information. These papers are fields. The file folder, which contains all of the information about one person, place, or thing, is the record. Your data (secondary) file is like a file cabinet drawer, because it contains many different records or file folders, as you can see here:

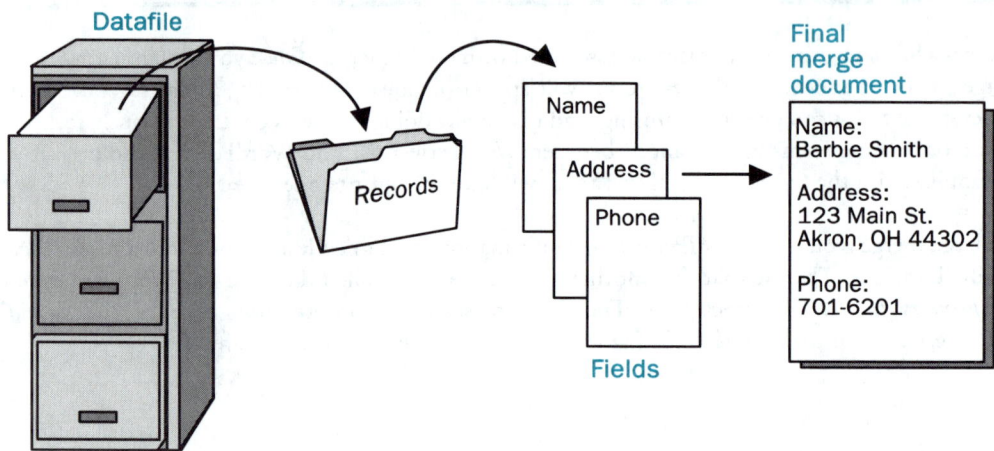

When you actually run a merge, you are telling WordPerfect to go into the file cabinet, which is your data (secondary) file, open each file folder (record), and copy the contents of specific pages (fields) onto a form (your form file).

Use the WordPerfect Programming Language When You Want to Perform Sophisticated Merges

WordPerfect is capable of much more sophisticated merges than described in Tip 800. When you use the WordPerfect Merge Programming language, you can create complex merges that take into account blank lines, different coding categories, and other contents of either file to let you create even more personalized documents.

For example, suppose you are sending out a sales letter to your clients and potential clients. You may want to send a letter with different text to clients who have never placed an order, clients who only placed small orders, and clients who placed very large orders. WordPerfect's Merge Programming

language would enable you to create three varied sections of text, then have WordPerfect choose the text and add it to a base letter, depending on a code in the records of the secondary file.

In the following illustration, you can see the base form letter and the merge codes that enable you to change the text of the letter depending on the type of client.

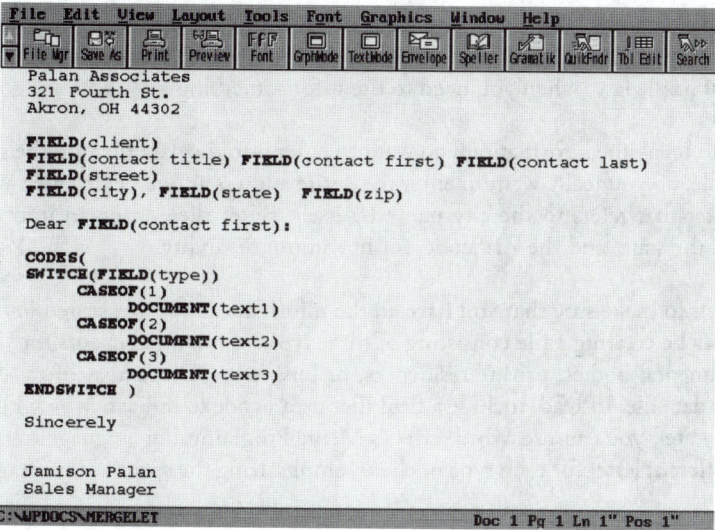

The CODES command contains the commands used to select the text. The CODES command lets you enter your merge codes, and organize them using hard returns and tabs without affecting the format of your document. If you enter the merge codes, using hard returns and tabs to organize them logically, those hard returns and tabs will appear in your document, even though the merge commands will not.

The SWITCH command examines the contents of the Type field. The CASEOF commands specify what is to happen when the Type field is equal to specific options. The DOCUMENT commands tell WordPerfect to retrieve the contents of those files into this document in this location to fill out the letters.

Plan Your Data File Before Entering Its Contents

Before you create a data file, take some time to sit down and plan what you want to be able to use it for. A few minutes spent carefully planning how the file will be used before you actually create it will save you hours of hassle later when you need to use it for something new.

The first step is to break the information you want to enter into the data file into the smallest possible parts. For example, do you really want to enter the entire address as one field? Later, you may want to write a form letter that refers to the city name by itself. Enter the address in four parts, the street address, the city, the state, and the ZIP code, for maximum flexibility.

The second step is to make sure that you have all the information possible stored in the data file. For example, you may be creating a file consisting of three types of potential clients for your landscaping business: governmental bodies, private residences, or businesses. Don't just throw all three types of clients into your data file. Instead, include a field that uses a code to indicate which kind of client that record refers to. Later, you can use WordPerfect's Merge Programming language to run a merge that uses a slightly different letter for each type of client, emphasizing the specific advantages you can offer to each one.

When you first create a data file, don't worry about entering more information than you are planning to use in the near future. Taking the extra time to enter the data now will save you time later on when you want to use that information to create better documents.

Name the Fields in Your Data File to Make Creating Form Documents Easier

WordPerfect has a merge command that lets you assign names to fields in your data (secondary) file. This command does not actually change any features of the data file, it simply lets you refer to the same fields by name. When you have names assigned to these fields, you will find it easier to create form (primary) documents that use the information stored in this secondary file. Names simplify the process of creating a form document because you don't need to continually double check which field contains which bit of information. Instead, you can be sure of getting the correct field in the correct location because the name assigned to that field has some meaning to it.

To assign names to the fields of a data (text) file in WordPerfect 6, start at the beginning of the data file. Select **T**ools **M**erge **D**efine. If you have not yet started adding data to the file, you will have to select the Data (Text) option button. Select Field Names. Enter the name for the first field and press ENTER. Continue until all fields are named, and select OK. You will see a merge code like this in your document, if you are displaying full merge codes:

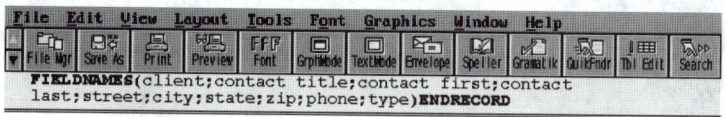

To assign names to the fields of a data (table) file in WordPerfect 6, start at the beginning of the data file. Select **T**ools **M**erge **D**efine Data (Table). Choose **C**reate a Table with Field Names. Type the name for the first field, press ENTER; repeat until you have named all of the fields, then select OK. WordPerfect creates a table with the field names you have specified in the top row of each column.

To assign names to the fields of a secondary file in WordPerfect 5.1, start at the top of the secondary file. Select **T**ools **M**erge **C**odes **M**ore. Highlight the code {Field Names} using the arrow keys or by typing the code, then press ENTER. Type the name of the first field and press ENTER. Repeat until all fields are named, then press F7.

You Can Use Merge to Create Mailing Labels in WordPerfect

TIP 804

You can set up a merge that uses your data file of addresses to create mailing labels for each address. To do this, create a form file that sets up mailing labels. Instead of entering an actual address, enter the appropriate merge codes to merge in the information for the addresses.

WordPerfect 6 offers a new Merge Programming code that you can use to include a POSTNET bar code on your mailing labels. The POSTNET bar code can reduce your costs for bulk mailings, and may increase the speed and accuracy with which the U.S. Postal Service processes your mail. To include POSTNET bar codes on your merge mailing labels, move to the line where you want the bar code to appear on the label. Then follow these steps:

1. Select **T**ools **M**erge **D**efine.
2. Select **M**erge Codes.
3. Highlight the POSTNET merge command and press ENTER.
4. Select OK in the Parameter Entry dialog box without making an entry.

5. In the document, move the cursor between the two parentheses after the word *POSTNET* in the code.

    If you are not displaying full merge codes, you should display them. You will always want to display the full merge code when adding or editing merge codes in your document.

6. Select **T**ools **M**erge **D**efine and **M**erge Codes again.

7. Highlight the FIELD command this time, and press ENTER.

8. Type the name or number of the field containing the ZIP code and select OK.

The label with the merge codes now looks something like this:

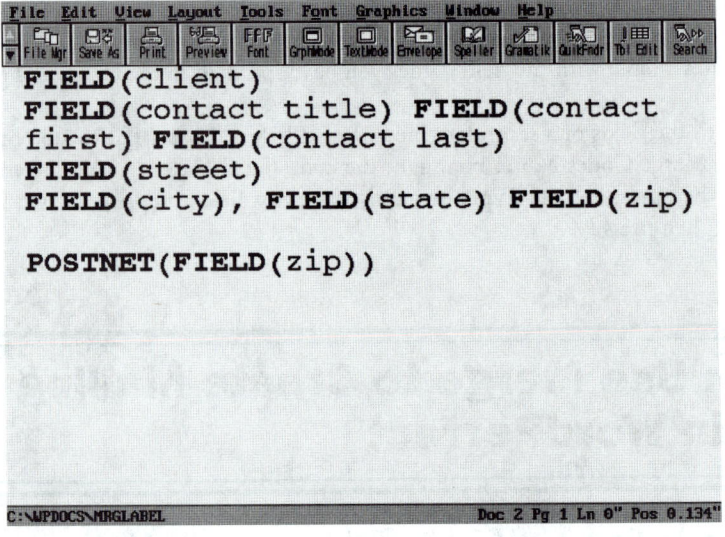

The POSTNET merge code will take the contents of the ZIP code field and create and insert the POSTNET code that matches that ZIP code on your mailing labels. When you run your merge, the first few labels will look like the following:

Hide or Show the Merge Codes in Your Document

TIP 805

You can set WordPerfect to hide or to show the codes that mark the end of fields, end of records, and field placement in data and form files. In WordPerfect 6, you can also display these codes as icons. While creating the form letter to use the merge codes, you will want to show the merge codes to make sure you know they are located correctly. However, when formatting the document, you may prefer to hide them, since the codes do not actually affect the formatting of the document. It will be easier to see how the document is formatted without them.

To change the display of merge codes in WordPerfect 6:

1. Select **T**ools **M**erge **D**efine.
2. Select **D**isplay of Merge Codes.
3. Select the **S**how Full Codes, Show Codes as **I**cons, or **H**ide Codes option button.
4. Select OK to return to the document.

When you select the new Show Codes as Icons option, your merge codes appear as diamond-shaped characters in the document. This eliminates the extreme clutter of a number of merge codes in your document, but doesn't let you forget where your merge codes are placed.

To change the display of merge codes in WordPerfect 5.1:

1. Select **F**ile Se**t**up **D**isplay.
2. Select **E**dit-Screen Options.
3. Select **M**erge Codes Display.
4. Press **Y** to show merge codes or **No** to hide them.
5. Press F7 to return to the document.

You Can Sort Out Merge Records with Blank Fields

You may have a data (secondary) file in which some records do not contain entries in all fields. For example, you may have a client list that contains company names and contact person names. If a company is new, or if you have no specific contact person there, you may not have an entry in the field for the contact person's name.

You may create a form (primary) file, which is a letter with the salutation line that reads "Dear" followed by the contact person's name. Your letter will look unprofessional and somewhat silly if you use this letter with the merge records that don't have a contact person's name, because they would be addressed to "Dear :". To prevent this, you can use the Sort command to select all those files that have entries in the fields for the contact people's names. Run the merge with only these records. Sort the original file again to select those files with no entries in these fields, and run the merge with a different form letter.

When you select specific records from a client list like this, you can either save the selected records to a new filename, or simply show them on the screen, and then not save the secondary file when you are done. Don't save the new file over the old file, or you will lose the records that were not selected.

Use Merge Programming Commands to Work with Blank Fields

Sometimes, you may have blank fields in your document because the information that should go in the field is unavailable or not applicable for that record. For example, as explained in Tip 806, you may have a client list that includes the name of your usual contact person with that client. If the client is new, or you don't have a usual contact person, you may not have an entry in that field.

This creates a problem when printing documents. For example, you would look foolish if you sent a letter to "Dear *blank*.", just because that one field of your data file was empty. You can use WordPerfect's advanced merge commands to correct this problem easily. You can tell WordPerfect to create a different salutation letter for records with blank or nonblank contact person fields. The beginning of the letter using these advanced merge commands, including the commands used to create the salutation line, is shown here:

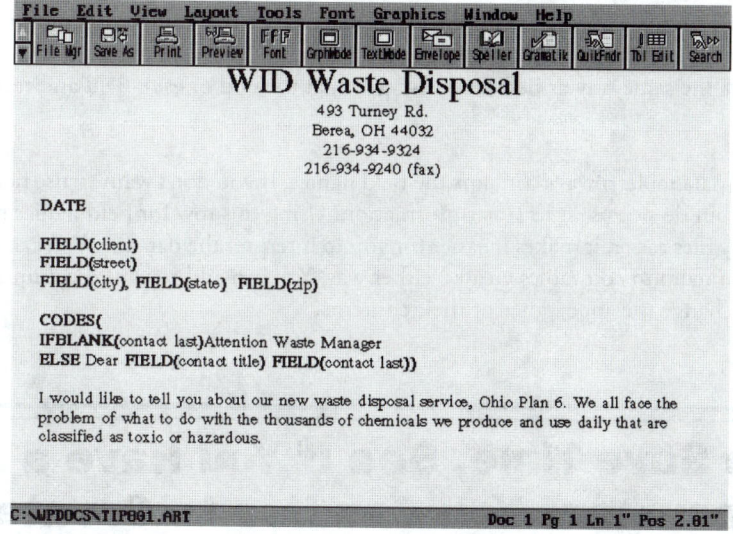

Use Tables to Arrange Data with the Merge Feature in WordPerfect 6

A new aspect of the merge feature in WordPerfect 6 is the ability to store data for use with the primary file within a table, rather than using the end of field and end of record merge codes that you use in a normal data file. The advantage of locating information in a table is twofold. The table makes information you enter easier to see and proof for missing or incorrectly entered fields because of how the information is visually arranged. Second, you can bring a spreadsheet file into a WordPerfect table, letting you use the information you have already stored in a spreadsheet instead of retyping it.

You can create a table to use with the merge feature in two ways, using the merge feature itself, or by creating a table normally. When you use the merge feature to create a table for merge data, you start by selecting Tools Merge Define. Then select Data [Table] and Create a Table with Field Names. Type the field names, pressing ENTER after each, select OK, and start entering data. When you reach the end of each row, or record, press TAB to create a new row to enter the next record's information. When you create a table normally, select Layout Tables Create, enter the number of columns or fields, and select OK. Press F7 to leave the Table Edit screen, then enter the field names in the first row of the table. Enter data the same way as before, pressing TAB at the end of each field and record to proceed to the next.

The first row of data tables always contains the field names. If you don't want to use field names, leave this row blank, but do not use it to store information. Using this row for field names not only makes creating primary files easier, it makes it easier for you to interpret the data file. You can use the Layout Tables Edit command to edit tables created either way. You can add rows and columns, change their appearance, or change the appearance of their contents.

To Save Time, See If You Have a Document You Can Use to Create a Form Letter

When you create a form letter or other document for use as the form or primary file of a WordPerfect merge, you don't have to start from scratch. You have probably already sent out letters much like the one you want to use as a form letter for the merge. If you do have a letter you can use, simply copy

this letter and add the requisite merge codes to do the merge correctly, using the same text and formatting as before. You may need to do some editing of the text to make it applicable to the many people you will now be using it for; but using a previously created letter will still save time.

Make Sure Your Data File Is Consistent

TIP 810

Inconsistencies in your data (secondary) file can wreak havoc with your merge documents. This is because of the way that WordPerfect finds the information to merge into the form (primary) file. Whether your fields are named or numbered, WordPerfect works the same way.

To understand the damage this can do, imagine that your data file is set up like this:

Field	Contents
Field 1	Mr/Ms
Field 2	First Name
Field 3	Last Name
Field 4	Address
Field 5	City
Field 6	State
Field 7	ZIP
Field 8	Classification

In your third record, you didn't know what title the person preferred, so you simply left that field out. WordPerfect, of course, doesn't know this. When you run a merge, the letter created for the third record is going to be very confused.

For example, the address will read:

Lee Godwin 123 Elm Street
Cleveland
OH 44302

The salutation of your letter may read:

Dear Lee 123 Elm Street:

You will have the same problem if you simply reverse fields. For example, you may accidentally enter a last name in field 2, and a first name in field 3, if you receive a form with the name in that order. Then your address might read:

Carruthers Carol
543 Forsythia Blvd.
Akron, OH 44115

Your salutation would read:

Dear Ms. Carol:

To avoid this type of problem, remember to proofread your entries in the data file after you make them. If your data file is short enough, you may want to proof the entire file occasionally. If it is larger, try spot-checking it occasionally, or running dummy merges with a blank form file containing only one or two fields, and then just looking over the fields. You should quickly find mistakes like these if you create a form document consisting only of field 7 (ZIP codes), and you find a telephone number in the merge document.

Use {STEP ON} to Find Bugs in Your Merge Codes

811

Sometimes when you run a sophisticated merge that uses Merge Programming codes, you may find that your end product is not what you expected. At some point in your merge program, you have a *bug*, or a flaw in the programming logic, which is telling your computer to do something you didn't really want it to do. To find and correct this error, use the {STEP ON} Merge Programming code.

All commands after the {STEP ON} code execute one at a time. After each step is executed, WordPerfect displays a message explaining what the next step will be. The user must press a key for the next step to execute. When you run the merge, you watch to make sure that the merge program is executing correctly. At the point when it stops executing correctly, you will find the error. Usually, the error is as simple as a missing tilde in WordPerfect 5.1, which makes the command function improperly, or a command that has been left out.

To use the {STEP ON} command, enter it as you do other merge commands in the primary file. If you have no idea where the mistake is occurring, enter the command at the beginning of the file. If you suspect what section of the primary file contains the commands that are producing the error, insert the command just above these other commands. If you only want to check a section of your merge program in the middle of a document, you can also enter a {STEP OFF} command after the section you believe has the bug. This allows WordPerfect to execute the rest of the program quickly, so that you only spend time examining the part of the program that is fallacious.

Keyboard Merges Make Sense for
Small Batches of Merge Documents

All data that merges into a form (primary) file in a WordPerfect merge does not have to come from a data (secondary) file. You can also do keyboard merges, in which WordPerfect stops and prompts you to make the entries at the merge fields. Keyboard merges enable you to create standardized documents without first creating a data file.

For example, your manufacturing company may send out three or four letters a week to local residents who want to know what your plant does, what kind of pollutants are or can be emitted, and other safety factors about your facility. There is no real reason to keep these names and addresses on file, so you don't want to create a data file of them. You do want to use a standard letter containing all of the necessary information so that you don't have to rewrite the letter three or four times a week.

For this, you can use a keyboard merge. At all the locations where you would usually insert a FIELD code to tell WordPerfect to go to the data file and retrieve the required information, you set up a prompt that tells WordPerfect to pause the merge while you insert the necessary information.

By using a keyboard merge, you keep the main advantage of a merge: the ability to create customized copies of a single document. But you do not have to bother setting up a data file when you create only a few such documents and do not want to save the information.

Use Data Files When You Have Multiple Uses for the Data

Keyboard merges can save you time when creating a small number of documents. However, no matter how small the number of documents you are planning to create, never use a keyboard merge if the data is such that you want to use it again later.

You probably already understand that merges are time-saving because you do not need to re-create a single document for hundreds of people. You can save hours, if not days, with a good form (primary) document. Another great time-saving feature, one that is often forgotten, is the data (secondary) file. Once you save data in a data file, it is always available. This means you can use the same data file over and over and over, increasing its efficiency and the worth of the time you invested in it.

If you ever think that you will need certain data again, be sure to enter it into a data file before doing the merge. Don't go with a keyboard merge, even if it is just a single document you are currently creating. The savings in time will come when you are creating a second, third, fourth (and so on) document, and do not need to enter that information yet again.

Use Comments to Show Further Merge Instructions

When you create a merge that uses keyboard input, you will want to prompt the user for the correct information to key in. Most user input commands can display a message, or you can use the PROMPT command to display a one- or two-line message about what the user is supposed to key in.

Sometimes, you will want to present more information to the user than can be shown using the keyboard merge command messages or the PROMPT command. To do this, insert a comment just above where the keyboard entry will be made. When you do the merge, be sure that WordPerfect is set to display comments. When you reach the point in the merge where text is to be input, the comment will be displayed on the screen. You can include instructions, such as what the choices mean, to make possible selections clearer to the user.

Don't confuse the Merge Programming command COMMENT with the document comments you can include to add instructions. Document comments, which are entered with Layout Comment

Create in WordPerfect 6 or Edit Comment Create in WordPerfect 5.1, appear within a box in the text of the document while merging, but do not print or otherwise affect your merge. The merge command COMMENT is used to insert text that does not appear during a merge, and does not affect the merge process. You can use the COMMENT command in documents with complicated merges to provide documentation or an explanation as to how the merge functions. This information would be of use if someone tried to modify or correct your merge program, but not to the person who uses your merge to create merge documents.

Use Keyboard Merges to Fill Out Onscreen Forms

TIP 815

You can set up a keyboard merge file for creating several documents consecutively from the keyboard. For example, you can create a keyboard merge where the form file is an onscreen form that must be filled out. By sending the merge process back to the top of the form, you can have WordPerfect display the next form as soon as the first one is finished. This allows the user to enter the contents of several forms one after the other.

You may use a merge document like this for taking complaints or requests for service over the phone. The advantage of creating a repeated keyboard merge is that users don't have to close a file and reopen a new file for each phone call. Instead, they can just quickly progress to the next call without a pause.

To create a keyboard merge form of this type, first create and format the form. Then enter the KEYBOARD merge command, requesting input from the keyboard at each location an entry is needed in the form. At the very beginning of the form, enter a LABEL command, labeling that position with a name. At the end of the file, include a GO command, which moves the execution of the command back up to the top of the form. Set up this way, every time the user reaches the end of the form, the merge restarts at the top of a fresh copy of the form. Remember to include a hard page return at the end of the form before the GO command, or all the forms will blend together.

When you create a looping onscreen form like this, the merge feature itself will never stop. There is never a command that tells it to stop. Instead, users will have to stop the command when they leave for lunch, have to do something else, or leave for the day. To stop it, finish filling out the form, press SHIFT-F9, and select OK. WordPerfect finishes writing the remainder of that form to the merge document and stops the merge process. The merge document will then need to be saved or printed.

Style Codes Affect File Size Differently in WordPerfect 5.1 and 6

When you save formatting as styles in either WordPerfect 6 or 5.1, the document you save the styles with becomes larger because more space is required to save the codes as styles than to simply include them in the document. However, after you run a merge, repeating those codes many times, WordPerfect 6 and 5.1 split ways. In a WordPerfect 6 document, using styles saves file space, whereas in WordPerfect 5.1, using styles will cost you file space when you merge.

In WordPerfect 6, for example, a merge document (the document after the merge is completed) that is 38,691 bytes when you use manual coding for the formatting, is only 24,543 bytes if you use styles instead. In this case, both the form and data files are fairly small and use limited formatting. If you run a merge with a large data file and a long or heavily formatted primary file, your savings could amount to a great deal. Keeping files smaller helps you print them faster and frees up space on your hard disk or other storage medium.

In WordPerfect 5.1, the reverse is true. A small merge document that is 4271 bytes with manual coding expands to 6153 bytes with styles. In a WordPerfect 5.1 document, then, you may prefer to go with manual formatting so that your file does not become so large.

Use a Macro to Print Your Data File Without Hard Page Breaks

Don't create your data files and then forget about them. Your data files require ongoing maintenance to be reliable and useful. Remember to print them out occasionally to review their contents. This will make it easier for you to find duplicate entries, old entries with incorrect names, dates, amounts, or addresses, and other entries that you do not want to keep.

Use the macro HARDDATA.WPM on the accompanying disk to help you print your data files. WordPerfect automatically inserts a hard page break after each end of record merge code. This code means that simply printing your data file will take much more paper than necessary. The HARD-DATA.WPM macro removes the hard page breaks and replaces them with a blank line between each record. It adds a header that indicates the path and filename of the data file so that you do not mix up

the printouts of multiple files, prints the document using your defaults and then restores the hard page breaks to your file.

```
DISPLAY(Off!)
PosDocVeryTop
SearchString("[ENDRECORD][HPg]")
ReplaceString("[ENDRECORD][HRt]")
ReplaceForward()
PosDocVeryTop
HeaderA(Create!)
Type("This is the merge data file ")
InsertFilenameWithPath
SubstructureExit
PrintFullDoc
HeaderA(Edit!)
BlockOn(CharMode!)
PosDocBottom
DeleteCharNext
SubstructureExit
SearchString("[ENDRECORD][HRt]")
ReplaceString("[ENDRECORD][HPg]")
ReplaceForward()
```

This sample macro is available on the accompanying disk as HARDDATA.WPM.

HARDDATA.WPM

Use Spreadsheet Data as a Data File for a Merge

Many companies maintain a database with a spreadsheet package to store information about clients' orders and sales, or production numbers. Much of the information in that spreadsheet file may be information you want to use in your WordPerfect data or secondary files for a merge. It would be a true nuisance to have to type the information again. WordPerfect has a way for you to use the data stored by this other program as your data file.

In WordPerfect 6, you can simply open the spreadsheet file with WordPerfect. As long as WordPerfect can recognize the format, WordPerfect 6 will read the file into a table in a WordPerfect document. You can then use that table as the data file for running WordPerfect merges.

In WordPerfect 5.1, using spreadsheet data as a data file for a merge is somewhat more difficult. If the file is in a .DIF format, which is a common format for exchanging information between spreadsheet programs, you can use the Convert program in WordPerfect 5.1 to convert the .DIF file into a WordPerfect secondary merge file automatically. If you have the program saved in the spreadsheet's normal format, you can try retrieving it directly into WordPerfect, if it is a format that WordPerfect recognizes. When you retrieve a spreadsheet program into WordPerfect, it appears in a table. You will then need to edit the file to make it a secondary merge file, including the end of field and end of record codes.

If your spreadsheet can save text as an ASCII delimited file, as most can, you can use this ASCII delimited file as a data file without any conversion or setup at all, as described in Tip 819.

Use ASCII Delimited Files for Data Files

ASCII delimited files contain only text and characters that mark the end of fields and records. ASCII delimited files can be created by most spreadsheets and database programs. You will need to check the documentation of your program to see how to create an ASCII delimited file.

Using an ASCII delimited text file as a data or secondary file for a WordPerfect merge is quite easy. First, you start to run the merge as usual. When WordPerfect prompts for a data file, enter the name of the ASCII delimited file. When WordPerfect attempts to open this file, it will recognize the file's format. Then WordPerfect will prompt you to verify the delimiters being used to mark the divisions between fields and records. By default, WordPerfect believes that commas will appear between fields, and a carriage return or line feed character between records. You can change these settings if you need to. After this, WordPerfect runs the merge as usual.

If you frequently access a spreadsheet saved in ASCII delimited text format as a secondary merge file, and that program uses some other delimiters when it saves as ASCII delimited text, then you may want to change the default delimiters to match the ones this program uses. You can change the delimiters using the File Setup Environment menu or dialog box.

Merge Fields Can Contain Multiple Lines

TIP 820

When you enter the contents of a merge field in a merge data or secondary file, you are not restricted to entering one line. A careful use of lines can prevent your having to find other ways to remove blank lines in your final merge document.

For example, some businesses have mailing addresses that use three lines instead of two. The following are examples of both:

127 Southern Way   Chapel Hill Mall
Akron, OH 44302   127 Southern Way
                         Akron, OH 44302

When you enter the text for the field containing the street address for a three-line address, you really need to use two lines, not one. With WordPerfect, instead of defining two fields and then having to find a way not to display a blank line for addresses that only need one line for their street address, you can enter the two lines, including the hard return, within the text of the field.

When WordPerfect runs the merge, it will simply enter the two lines and the hard return between them in this location. This may throw your merge off if you are printing to mailing labels and don't have room for the extra line, but otherwise this solution makes it easier for you to create consistent merge documents even when your data cannot be completely consistent.

Use Merge Codes in Headers, Footers, and Other Secondary Text Locations

TIP 821

You are not confined to using merge codes within the main body of your form document. Instead, add merge codes to the headers, footers, footnotes, and other secondary merge locations if you feel it is appropriate. For example, you may have a two-page legal document as a form document. You may want to include the name and court number of the case on the second page as part of the header, using merge codes, to help make sure that the pages of the document do not become separated or lost.

Double-Check Your Tildes in WordPerfect 5.1 Merges

WordPerfect 5.1 uses tildes (~) as punctuation in advanced merge commands. If your merge is not functioning correctly, your first step should be to check that all of the necessary tildes are present and in the correct location. As a rule, you need a tilde between each expression within the command and after the command as a whole. Some commands will have two tildes at the end, one as punctuation for the expression and the second as punctuation for the command.

You Can See the Field Names in a Data File While Creating a Form File

WordPerfect 6 offers a new feature that will help you create your form files for merges. When you are entering FIELD commands in your form file to reference text in a data file, you may not be able to remember precisely what the name of the field you are looking for is. If you need to double-check, WordPerfect 6 offers an option.

Select Tools Merge Define. Select Form if this is the first time you have selected this in the current document. Then select Field. If you want to see a list of the field names used in your data file, select List Field Names by pressing F5. Then type the name of the data file you are using and select OK. Highlight the name of the field you want to use in the dialog box, like the one shown in the following, and choose Select to enter a FIELD command into your document using that field name.

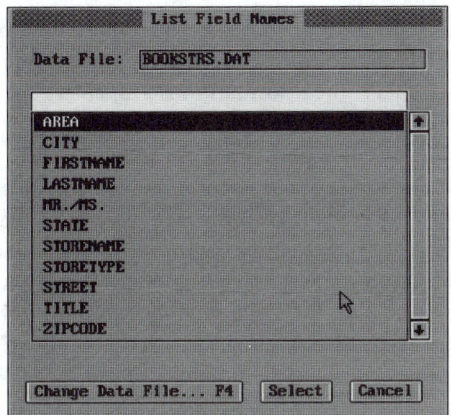

Understanding Variables and Expressions Is Essential to Programming Sophisticated Merges

When you create complicated macros that use the WordPerfect programming language, you are quite literally programming in a very sophisticated way. If you are familiar with programming concepts and terminology, then learning to use the WordPerfect programming language to create merges shouldn't be very difficult. If you are unfamiliar with programming, don't worry. Learning to use these merge features is going to be harder than learning other WordPerfect features, but there is nothing inherently impossible about it, and the payoffs will be tremendous.

Two features that you have not had to deal with elsewhere are variables and expressions. *Expressions* are terms used as part of merge commands that evaluate something. For example, you can use an IF command in merges. The IF command tells WordPerfect to evaluate an expression and then choose one of two actions based on the results of that evaluation. For example, if a field contains the number

1, the letter should begin "Dear Sir or Madam"; but if it contains anything else, the letter should begin "To Whom It May Concern". Expressions can be math formulas, comparative operations like the last one, or they can simply check that some information is available.

Variables are different. Variables are like the boxes your mail goes in at the front desk of a hotel. Each bin has a name. You can put any kind of information in a variable, just as the desk clerk can put any type of mail in your bin. WordPerfect will keep the information in that bin, so that you can use it at any time in the merge. For example, at the very beginning of the iteration of the merge, the variable may contain a piece of information that tells you if the person receiving the letter is male or female. This variable may be used in expressions of IF commands throughout the letter, to change how certain things are phrased in the letter. Each time WordPerfect needs to know if the recipient is male or female, it checks this mail bin to find out.

Variables are important in merges because they let you introduce more variety by customizing your document in several places based on a single piece of information. Expressions are important to understand because they are used as part of a variety of advanced commands to let those commands choose a reaction based on a calculation or a comparison.

You Can Have WordPerfect Sort the Records for a Data File

TIP 825

There are many reasons for sorting the records in your data file. One reason might be to order documents for mailing by ZIP code, to make it easier to create a bulk mailing. Another reason would be to simplify using only certain records. A third reason could be to double-check for duplicate entries in a specific field. The Sort command can sort your records just as it can sort lines. See Chapter 8 for a variety of tips to help you sort your data file.

CHAPTER 18

Hyphenation script

Using Hyphenation Improves the Look of the Finished Page

The use of hyphenation can improve the appearance of your finished document. Technical or scientific writing that contains many long words will often show the most dramatic improvements. Without hyphenation, any word that spans the hyphenation zone and does not fit within the right margin is moved to the next line. This can leave lines that are very short.

The use of columns can heighten the need for hyphenation since the number of short lines will increase in these narrow columns. The following passage was entered without turning hyphenation on:

Short lines without hyphenation

```
 File   Edit   View   Layout   Tools   Font   Graphics   Window   Help

 File Mgr  Save As  Print  Preview  Font  GrphMode  TextMode  Envelope  Speller  Gramatik  QuikFndr  Tbl Edit  Search

Bacteriology is        animals. They are      often the
the study of           studied and grown      development of
single-celled          within                 vaccines. Vaccines
organisms. These       laboratories.          may be made from
organisms are          These bacteria         killed or live
called bacteria        cultures may be        bacteria.
and can be helpful     injected into          Some bacteria
or cause serious       healthy animals        produce serious
diseases.              experimentally.        diseases by the
Bacteriologists        The bacteria are       toxins produced as
study harmful          isolated from the      they grow.
varieties to           experimental
develop vaccines       animals and
for them.              compared against
Pathogenic             the original
bacteria are           strains.
frequently             These result of
obtained from dead     these studies is
```

You can turn on hyphenation by selecting **Layout Line Hyphenation**. After doing so and responding to the prompts, the passage now looks like this:

Manu-script

File	Edit	View	Layout	Tools	Font	Graphics	Window	Help

File Mgr	Save As	Print	Preview	Font	GrphMode	TextMode	Envelope	Speller	Gramatik	QuikFndr	Tbl Edit	Search

Bacteriology is the study of single-celled organisms. These organisms are called bacteria and can be helpful or cause serious diseases. Bacteriologists study harmful varieties to develop vaccines for them. Pathogenic bacteria are frequently obtained from dead animals. They are studied and grown within laboratories. These bacteria cultures may be injected into healthy animals experimentally. The bacteria are isolated from the experimental animals and compared against the original strains. These result of these studies is often the development of vaccines. Vaccines may be made from killed or live bacteria. Some bacteria produce serious diseases by the toxins produced as they grow.

WordPerfect Uses a Multistep Process When Deciding Whether or Not to Hyphenate

WordPerfect has to make several assessments before hyphenating a word or prompting for your help with hyphenation. The first check is whether hyphenation is on or off. If hyphenation is off, no further checks are performed and the word is wrapped to the next line. If hyphenation is on, WordPerfect next checks to see if the word spans the hyphenation zone. (Refer to Tip 829 for more information on the hyphenation zone.) If the word does not span the zone, no further checks are made. If it spans the zone, WordPerfect determines where to put the hyphen and uses the hyphenation prompt settings to help determine the action it takes. You will see more on the hyphenation prompt settings in Tip 828.

Manu-
script

WordPerfect Does Not Force You to Hyphenate a Word with Hyphenation On

Even when you turn hyphenation on and WordPerfect finds a word that is a candidate for hyphenation, the end result is not always a hyphenated word. The hyphenation prompt settings determine what happens.

You can choose Never, Always, or When Required for the prompt setting. When you select **Never**, you are telling WordPerfect to handle hyphenation without your help whenever hyphenation is on. If found in the WordPerfect dictionary, the word will be hyphenated depending upon other hyphenation criteria.

Choosing **Always** tells WordPerfect that you want to be involved in every hyphenation decision and are not willing to delegate this to WordPerfect. You will be prompted to position the hyphen, or to confirm its current location by pressing ESC.

Choosing **When Required** lets WordPerfect handle hyphenation when the word that meets hyphenation criteria is in its dictionary. If it cannot find the word, it prompts you to take an action. In WordPerfect 5.1, the prompt reads, "Position Hyphen, Press Esc." In addition to positioning the hyphen you can also press F1 to cancel hyphenation for the word. In WordPerfect 6, you are presented with a dialog box that offers options for inserting hyphens and/or spaces, suspending hyphenation, ignoring the word and wrapping it to the next line, and adding a hyphenation soft return.

Words That Do Not Span the Hyphenation Zone Are Not Candidates for Hyphenation

The *hyphenation zone* defines which words are candidates for hyphenation when hyphenation is on. The zone is a percent of the line length and has a left and a right edge. The default settings for the left edge of the zone are established at a point that is 10 percent of the line length from the right margin.

The right zone has a default location 4 percent of the line length from the right margin. With a line length of 6.5 inches, the left edge of the zone is .65 inches from the right margin, and the right edge is .26 inches from the right margin. You can change the hyphenation zone by selecting Layout Line Hyphenation Zone.

A word that starts before the left edge of the zone and ends within the zone remains on the current line. A word that starts before the left edge of the zone and extends beyond the right edge of the zone is hyphenated as long as hyphenation is on. (If hyphenation is off, WordPerfect's word-wrap feature moves the word to the next line.) A word that starts inside the zone and extends beyond it is word-wrapped to the next line. These three examples are illustrated here:

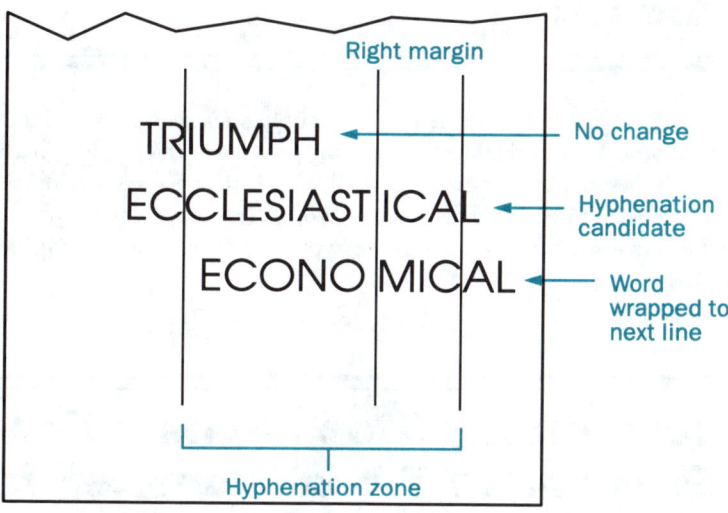

A Hyphenation Soft Return Is an Option When You Want Words Split Without a Hyphen

Both WordPerfect 5.1 and WordPerfect 6 support the separation of words without a hyphen. This is useful for entries separated by a slash such as "On/Off," "True/False," and "and/or." In WordPerfect

5.1, this is referred to as an *invisible soft return* and in WordPerfect 6, it is called a *hyphenation soft return*. In both releases, Hyphenation will separate the word at the marked location without adding a hyphen if the word spans the hyphenation zone. To add a hyphenation soft return at any location, press HOME-ENTER.

Hyphenation Methods Depend on Which WordPerfect Release You Are Using

In WordPerfect 5.1, you can select whether you want hyphenation to be an internal or external event. Internal hyphenation in WordPerfect 5.1 bases the position of the hyphen on a set internal algorithm that calculates the best hyphen location. External WordPerfect 5.1 hyphenation uses the syllable-based hyphenation of words stored in a dictionary. In WordPerfect 6, you no longer have to choose between internal and external hyphenation; words are hyphenated based on the syllables stored in the .LEX dictionary files.

Temporarily Stop Hyphenation By Pressing F7 When Prompted for a Hyphen Location

Since hyphenation can interrupt tasks such as spell checking, you might want to turn it off at least temporarily. In WordPerfect 6, you can select Suspend Hyphenation when prompted about hyphenating a word. In WordPerfect 5.1, you can press F7 (Exit).

Manu-script

Use CTRL- - to Add a Soft Hyphen When You Want to Hyphenate a Document Yourself

WordPerfect automatically inserts a soft hyphen when it hyphenates a word. A *soft hyphen* is used when needed but can disappear if the document is edited and the word no longer spans the hyphenation zone. You can add your own soft hyphens to words as you type from the keyboard to mark the location where you want the word hyphenated, if hyphenation is required. To add a soft hyphen all you need to do is press CTRL- -.

In WordPerfect 6, Mark Syllables in Chained Dictionaries

Dictionaries from other sources that are merged with or chained to WordPerfect's dictionary might not have syllables marked for the placement of hyphens. You can edit these files using the Speller-Hyphen Utility.

You Can Turn On Hyphenation Right Before Printing

If you do not want to be interrupted with hyphenation prompts while you are typing, leave hyphenation off. Then, right before printing, turn hyphenation on and use the DOWN ARROW to move through your document. Your document will then be hyphenated.

You Can Add a Hard Space Instead of a Hyphen

WordPerfect 6 provides an option for adding a hard space. (A *hard space* looks like a regular space; the hard space, however, keeps the words on either side together so they aren't broken over two lines.) The dialog box for this option displays when WordPerfect 6 requests your assistance with hyphenation. In WordPerfect 5.1, you will need to press HOME-SPACEBAR to insert the hard space. You can press HOME-SPACEBAR when you are editing a document to add a hard space. In WordPerfect 6, you can also add a hard space by selecting Layout Special Codes Hard Space and then choosing OK.

You Can Relocate Hyphens After WordPerfect Inserts Them

In both WordPerfect 5.1 and WordPerfect 6 you can relocate hyphens when WordPerfect prompts for how you want a word hyphenated. From the dialog box or prompt at the bottom of the screen, all you need to do is use the arrow keys to reposition the hyphen. When you press ENTER or select Insert Hyphen, WordPerfect adds the hyphen at the location you have moved it to using the arrow keys.

There Are Restrictions on Hyphen Placement

Although you can move the location of the hyphen with the LEFT ARROW and RIGHT ARROW when in the Hyphen dialog box, there are some limitations. You can move the hyphen anywhere between the first letter of the word and the right edge of the hyphenation zone. It will not move any further to the right or left.

Manu-script

WordPerfect 5.1 Will Give Better Hyphenation Results If You Use the External Dictionary

WordPerfect 6 always uses external dictionary hyphenation, but WordPerfect 5.1 lets you decide. In WordPerfect 5.1, you can choose to use an internal algorithm or an external dictionary. The results are generally better using the external dictionary unless you have added thousands of specialized terms, such as medical terms that do not show hyphenation. In this case, the algorithm-based methods work the best. The change is made with File Setup Environment Hyphenation. You can then choose between External Dictionary/Rules or Internal Rules.

The Prompt Settings for Hyphenation Affect How Hyphenation Works

Both WordPerfect 5.1 and WordPerfect 6 allow you to decide how involved you want to be in the hyphenation decisions. You can choose one of the following options after selecting File Setup Environment Prompt for Hyphenation:

❏ *Never* Only uses the dictionary; if not in the dictionary, word wraps

❏ *When required* Uses dictionary if available; otherwise prompts

❏ *Always* Prompts for placement

Change the Hyphenation Zone to Control the Amount of Hyphenation

If you make the hyphenation zone smaller, more words will span the zone and become candidates for hyphenation. If you make it larger, fewer words will span the zone and will result in fewer hyphenated words.

Changing the Hyphenation Zone Settings After Hyphenation Is On Can Cause Problems

If you change the hyphenation zone and then make some editing changes, you might get hyphenation prompts as you move through the document. The rules that control hyphenation have changed, and different words may now be candidates for hyphenation.

Manu-script

CHAPTER
19

Change WordPerfect's Default Delimiters to Match Those Used by Your Delimited Text Files

Delimited text files have a defined format with elements separated by special characters called *delimiters*. The program that writes the data to the file determines which characters are used as delimiters. The default settings in WordPerfect are to use a comma (,) as a delimiter between fields, quotation marks to encapsulate a field consisting of characters, and a carriage return or line feed at the end of a record. A record that fits this description might look like this:

> "Smith","Jane",13,45321,"Accounting"

It is possible for programs to use other delimiters, and WordPerfect allows you to specify what these characters are with the File Setup Environment Delimited Text Options selections. Codes for line feed, tab, and other special options can be added by pressing F5 and entering them in the proper format.

You Can Link One Section of Text to Another with WordPerfect 6 Hypertext

Hypertext is highlighted text in a document that provides a link to other text or a macro. When other text is used, it can be text in the current document or another document. Bookmarks are used to mark the locations to which hypertext is linked. The text itself can be used as an object that you can click to invoke the link, or a button can be generated. The following screen shows five hypertext buttons, as well as the text "financial condition," which are connected to text in other locations.

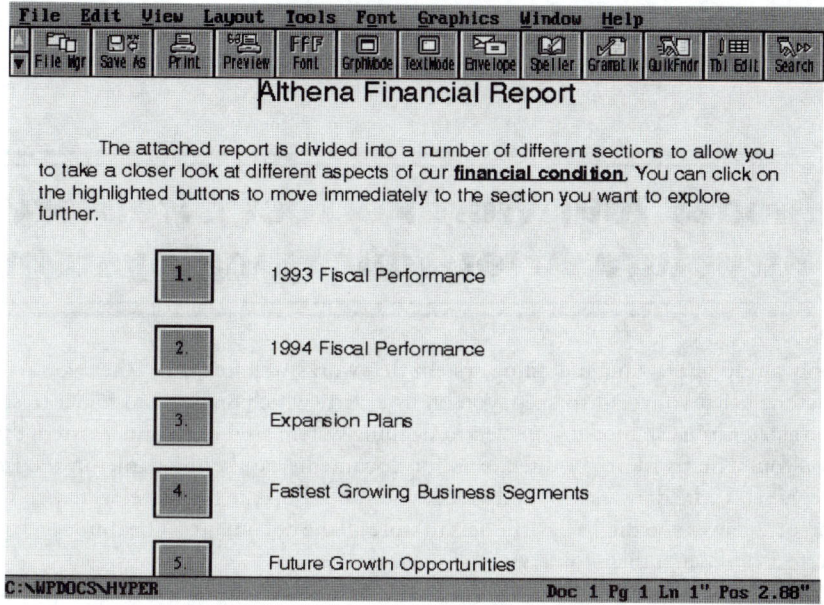

The procedure for creating hypertext is simple. All you need to do is block the text and select **Tools Hypertext**. You can choose whether you want to link to the current document's bookmark, another document's bookmark, or run a macro. You can also choose either to have the text marked as hypertext or to have a button box placed to the left of the text.

There is an option in the Hypertext dialog box to activate all the hypertext in a document. After the text is active you can highlight a button or text and press ENTER to move to the link. TAB moves to the next link and SHIFT-TAB moves to the previous link. When hypertext is off, these keys perform their normal functions.

You can also work with one link at a time by highlighting it and selecting Tools Hypertext Jump/Run rather than activating all hypertext.

The default style of hypertext is bold with underlining, although you can use any style you like with Tools Hypertext Edit Hypertext Style.

Model Your WordPerfect Directory Structure After Your Filing System

You probably already have a manual filing system that works well for you. When you receive a letter or other materials that you want to keep, you know exactly which drawer and folder to store it in for quick retrieval later. You can model your electronic filing system after the manual system that is already working for you. The first level of directories for documents can be the name on the front of each drawer or cabinet. If the drawers are subdivided, you can set up the next level to match that. Within each section of a drawer you might have folders to store all the documents. The third level of directories in WordPerfect can match these folders.

You Can Add Directory Descriptions in WordPerfect 6

WordPerfect 6 supports the use of descriptive names for your directories. If you want to use these descriptive names you will have to create a special file in the root directory of drive C that contains the path information and its descriptive replacement. The name you must use for this file is WP{WPC}.DLN.

This file is created in a new WordPerfect 6 document file with the full path descriptions on the left. These path entries are separated from the description text to the right by a single tab entry. Your file entries might look something like this:

C:\WP60\CLMEMO   Client letters and memos
C:\WP60\BRPTS   Budget and financial reports

Once you make your entries in the blank document file to correspond to your needs, save the file as C:\WP{WPC}.DLN. When you reboot WordPerfect, you will see the more descriptive names in the File Manager window.

Store Confidential Documents on a Floppy Disk

If you want to restrict access to confidential information you can password-protect the file, but unauthorized users may be lucky and guess your password or overwrite your file. The best protection against unauthorized use of a file is to store the file on a removable disk. You can then lock this disk in a safe place and be certain that no one can access it. It is still a good idea to password-protect the file, in case you inadvertently leave it in the disk drive.

Use Timed Backups to Save Work After System Failures

You can minimize the amount of work that you lose when your system crashes suddenly, by allowing WordPerfect to help you recover some of what was entered since the last time you saved. This will only work if you are using WordPerfect's automatic timed backup feature. Also, the amount of what you can recover depends on the timing of the backup. By default, WordPerfect 6 is set to back up your work every ten minutes. Leaving this setting in place ensures that you can never lose more than ten minutes of entries.

When WordPerfect is restarted, you will be prompted about renaming, deleting, or opening the backup file if you were using the timed backup feature when your system crashed. You should choose Rename or Open. You can look at the file and decide whether to replace your last version of the document with it.

If your system is not set to do automatic backups, you can select File Setup Environment Backup Options to make a change. See Tip 867 for complete steps for setting timed backups.

Keep WordPerfect Documents in a Separate Directory

WordPerfect documents should never be placed in the directory with WordPerfect programs. It is too easy to delete a program file by mistake, and it makes the list of filenames you have to look at much

longer than necessary when you use List Files or File Manager. WordPerfect 6 makes it easy for you to store files in a location other than the program directory by setting up this extra directory, called WPDOCS, for you. WordPerfect 5.1 does not provide a default location for document files. Whatever directory is active when you start the system is the directory used as the default. This means if you start WordPerfect 5.1 from the WP51 directory, it assumes that you want to use that location when saving and retrieving files unless you indicate otherwise. You can set up a new directory for WordPerfect 5.1 and use File Setup Location of Files to define this location to WordPerfect. You can also create a batch file that starts WordPerfect from a specific directory that contains only data files.

Use a Batch File to Start WordPerfect and Set a Default Data Directory

If you want to use a different directory for documents in most WordPerfect sessions, the best approach is to leave the file location for document files blank after selecting File Setup Location of Files. You can then create a batch file that will start WordPerfect from different directories. Whatever directory it is started from will be the default directory used. You will need to modify your AUTOEXEC.BAT file to include a path statement that has the location of the WordPerfect program files as part of it. For WordPerfect 5.1 your path statement might look like this:

PATH C:\DOS;C:\WP51

The batch file that you use to start WordPerfect from C:\REPORTS would look like this:

```
CD\REPORTS
WP
```

You can also put the path statement at the beginning of this batch file to ensure that WordPerfect's directory is in the current path. If you name this batch file REPORTS.BAT, you can type **REPORTS** at the DOS prompt no matter which directory on drive C is active (assuming the current PATH command includes the directory REPORT.BAT is in) and still start WordPerfect with REPORTS as the active directory.

You Can Change the Format That WordPerfect 6 Uses When Saving Documents

If you are providing WordPerfect 6 documents to someone who has not as yet upgraded to the package, you may prefer to save your documents in the format they need. You can choose a format compatible with one of the popular word processing packages or choose one of the text formats that most programs will read. To make the change follow these steps:

1. Select **F**ile **S**ave.
2. Type the name for the file in the **F**ilename text box. Remember to use the default extension for the format you want to save the file in.
3. Select Fo**r**mat.
4. Highlight the format you want to use and press ENTER.
5. Select OK to save the file.

You Can Create a New Directory from Within WordPerfect

To create a new directory in WordPerfect 6 follow these steps:

1. Select **F**ile **F**ile Manager.
2. Select OK to accept the default directory for display.
3. Select C**h**ange Default Directory.
4. Type the full pathname of the directory you want to create and select OK.
5. When WordPerfect asks if you want to create the directory, select **Y**es.

A shortcut method is to press F5, type =, type a new directory name, and press ENTER.

To create a new WordPerfect 5.1 directory:

1. Select **F**ile List **F**iles.
2. Press ENTER to accept the default directory for display.
3. Select **O**ther Directory.
4. Type the complete pathname of the new directory and press ENTER.
5. When WordPerfect asks if you want to create the new directory, select **Yes**.

After creating a new directory this way, WordPerfect displays the contents of the empty directory.

Keep an Archive Copy of Important Documents

You should regularly back up the data on your hard disk to protect yourself from hardware failures. Important documents that are finished but must be retained can be stored as an archive or long-term record. Archival copies can be made using the File Manager (WordPerfect 6), or the List Files feature (WordPerfect 5.1), or from DOS using the COPY or BACKUP commands. Since disks can become defective after long storage periods, you will want to make copies of your archived files on a regular basis. Keep a copy of the archived material off-site to provide you with a backup if your house or office is burned, flooded, or otherwise damaged or destroyed.

WordPerfect 6 Automatically Converts Most WordPerfect 5.1 Files

Macros, styles, and documents created in WordPerfect 5.1 are automatically available for use in WordPerfect 6. Only complex macros and WordPerfect 5.1 keyboard files that define new assignments for keyboard keys are not usable in WordPerfect 6.

Some DOS Commands Are Useful Supplements to WordPerfect Features

TIP 855

Both WordPerfect and DOS are programs. DOS is an operating system program that controls your computers resources and must be loaded in memory before you can run WordPerfect. While you are running WordPerfect you may want to use a DOS command for a feature that WordPerfect does not provide, such as formatting a disk. You can temporarily exit from WordPerfect and execute DOS commands if you choose File Go to Shell, Go to DOS (WordPerfect 6) or **File Go to DOS Go to DOS** (WordPerfect 5.1). You might use a command such as FORMAT to prepare a disk for data storage. You should avoid commands such as CHKDSK or starting memory resident programs that will affect what is in memory, or files that WordPerfect is using. When you are ready to use WordPerfect it is important to remember that it is still in memory. If you were to type **WP**, another copy of WordPerfect would be started in memory. To use the copy that is already in memory all you need to do is type **EXIT** and press ENTER.

If you started WordPerfect from the DOS Shell, you may be surprised that, when you go to DOS from WordPerfect, you are not in the DOS Shell, but at the command prompt. It is not recommended that you start the DOS Shell again.

To Prevent Editing Changes, Use a Password or Make the File Read-Only

TIP 856

There are two different ways to deny users access to updating one of your documents. One method requires you to add a password to the document. Only users who can supply the password can access the file. The other method requires you to work from DOS to make the file *read-only*. Any user can retrieve the file, but with a read-only setting they cannot save any changes over the file. To add a password to a file, follow these steps:

1. Select **F**ile Save **A**s.
2. Select **P**assword.
3. Type the password twice, pressing ENTER after typing it each time.
4. Select OK.
5. If the file has been saved before, select Yes.

Adding a password to a file in WordPerfect 5.1 is a separate procedure from saving it, and can be done before saving it. Of course, adding a password is useless if you do not also save the file. To add the password:

1. Press CTRL-F5.
2. Select **P**assword.
3. Select **A**dd/Change.
4. Type a password of up to 24 characters and press ENTER; re-enter the password when prompted.

Remember you must be able to supply the password yourself when you attempt to use the file. You will not even be able to look at the document with the List Files or the File Manager unless you can supply the password.

You can enter the DOS command ATTRIB (available in DOS versions 3 and above) to prevent other users from saving to a file that you want to use as a template. They can access the file but will need to save to a file with another name. To make a file read-only, make this entry at the DOS prompt:

```
ATTRIB FILENAME +r
```

To remove the read-only status, type

```
ATTRIB FILENAME -r
```

TIP 857 Optimize Your Hard Disk Occasionally

As your hard disk gets fuller, it may no longer be possible to store a file in one contiguous location on the disk. The file is then broken into fragments and stored in different locations. These fragments are put back together when you need to work with a file. Although you can use the file as before, splitting the file into pieces when saving it and putting it back together again takes time, degrading your system's performance. You can use a utility program like Speed Disk, that is part of Norton Utilities, to perform hard disk optimization for you.

When you optimize—or *defragment*—your hard disk, your files are rearranged on your hard disk so that each file occupies one continous stretch of space on the disk. When a hard disk is optimized, the hard disk reading head does not have to move around as much in order to access files. Accessing files on your hard disk thus becomes a much faster, more efficient process. Many programs for optimizing your hard disk are available, usually as part of a set of disk utility programs.

Compress Large Files to Save Space

TIP 858

When you compress a beach ball, you squeeze all the air out of it and flatten it so that it uses less space. Compressing a file is similar. The spaces and repeated occurrences of characters are squeezed from the file. You cannot use files in their compressed format with most programs, but they do require much less disk space. Unlike the beach ball, it is easy to inflate the file again to use it with your programs.

There are a number of popular programs on the market that can compress files, including PKZIP and MGZIP. Both create compressed files, referred to as *zipped* files, with .ZIP filename extensions.

If you have a copy of a 100-page report on your system, you may find it more convenient to zip the file. You can always unzip it again when you want to work with it. Zipping and unzipping files is a good way to conserve space when you have files that are used infrequently; it is not a good idea for files used every day.

Extra fonts and graphics used infrequently are good candidates for compression. You will get a greater compression percentage than for most text documents.

Another space-saving option is to copy all .BK! files to a disk, then delete them from the hard drive to free space. These files are created when you elect to have WordPerfect save the original copy of a file you have edited. WordPerfect saves it with the .BK! extension, and you save the edited version under the original filename.

Use Document Compare to See the Differences Between Two Versions of a Document

You can see the differences between a current document and a document on your disk by having WordPerfect compare them. In the comparison process, WordPerfect will mark text that does not appear in the document on disk with the redline attribute. Text from the document on disk that was not in the document onscreen is added with the strikeout attribute. The first step of comparing two documents is displaying one of them as the current document. The other document is on disk. Even if the other document is open in another document window, WordPerfect will compare the current document with the version of the document on disk.

In WordPerfect 5.1, select **Mark Document Compare Add Markings**, or press ALT-F5 and select **Generate Compare Screen and Disk Documents and Add Redline and Strikeout**. Then type the name of the other document and press ENTER.

In WordPerfect 6, select **File Compare Documents** or press ALT-F5 and select Add Markings. Then select **Document on Disk**, type the name of the other document, and select OK.

One of the most common uses for document compare is to find the latest version of documents when your computer is not set to the correct date and time. Keep the date and time set correctly in your system to minimize the use of this feature.

Use WordPerfect to Remove the Strikeout and Redline Markings Added by Document Compare

Rather than removing the strikeout and redline markings yourself, you can tell WordPerfect to do it for you.

In WordPerfect 5.1, select **Mark Document Compare Remove Markings**, or press ALT-F5 and select **Generate** and **Remove Redline Markings and Strikeout Text From Document**. Then select **Yes** to confirm that you want the redline and strikeout text and codes removed.

In WordPerfect 6, select **File Compare Documents** or press ALT-F5 and select **Remove Markings**. Then select either to remove only the strikeout text or the strikeout text and the codes for redline before you select OK.

Change Compare in WordPerfect 6 by Setting How Much of a Difference Between Documents WordPerfect Marks

TIP 861

WordPerfect 6 allows you to set the way different documents should be compared. "Phrase" is the default, but you can work with smaller or larger groups of text by selecting a different radio button under Compare By in the Compare Documents dialog box that you use to enter the filename of the document you are comparing to the current one.

Document comparisons ignore formatting differences; they focus solely on the text in the document.

Document Comparisons Also Compare Substructures

TIP 862

WordPerfect does not limit itself to comparing document text for two documents. All substructures such as headers and footers are included in the compare operation.

If Disk Space Is Scarce, Place Backup Files on a Diskette

If you are having WordPerfect create regular backup files, you can also specify a location for the backup. If you are concerned about running short on disk space you may want to use a high-density removable disk to store these files. You can set the location for backup files by selecting File Setup Location of Files. Select **Backup Files** and specify the desired location.

Use the QuickList Feature in WordPerfect 6 to Save Time

WordPerfect 6 offers the new QuickList feature to help speed up all sorts of file maintenance tasks. QuickList is a list of items—directories or files—that you can select from. WordPerfect 6 automatically includes the default file locations established in File Setup Location of Files, but it allows you to add other directories and individual files to the list of entries that you want to be able to access quickly. To add entries to QuickList, select File File Manager, then choose QuickList and Create, and complete the entries for the files and directories you want in your list in the Create QuickList Entry dialog box shown here:

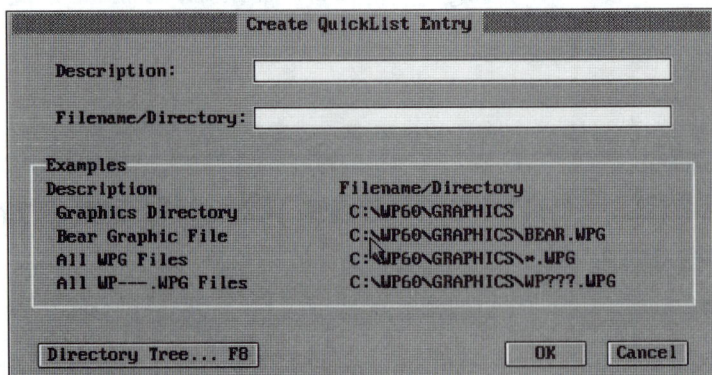

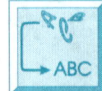

In QuickList, the item's name can be longer than a filename, so it can be used to explain exactly what the directory or file is. For example, if you frequently work with a directory that contains the letters created for the accounting department of your company, you may have a QuickList item that reads "Accounting Letters." The directory that this item references could be the C:\WPDOCS\ACCNTING\LETTERS\ directory.

You can access the QuickList feature from a number of locations by selecting it in dialog boxes. The QuickList button appears in all dialog boxes where you may have to enter a filename or directory, such as the Save or Retrieve dialog boxes. To use the QuickList to open a file from the C:\WPDOCS\ACCNTING\LETTERS\ directory, for example, select File Open. Then select the Quick-List button in the Retrieve dialog box. Highlight the Accounting Letters item and select Use as Pattern. WordPerfect returns to the Retrieve dialog box, but the name of the directory now appears in the Filename text box. Simply add the name of the file to the end of the directory name and select OK to retrieve the file.

Using QuickList this way saves the time used in typing this pathname, and prevents you from making mistakes in the pathname. Another reason to use QuickList is when you have a system that may be used by different people at times, such as when you share one computer system, or someone is using your system while you are gone. Having an up-to-date QuickList that includes the directories and files that you use most often will make it easier for those other people to access the correct items. This way, they will not need to know the actual directories involved, just the item names in the QuickList dialog box that will get them there.

Check the Contents of Your CONFIG.SYS and .BAT Files from WordPerfect

TIP 865

CONFIG.SYS and files with a .BAT extension are files used by the DOS operating system to configure your system and provide operating instructions for DOS. While working in WordPerfect, you may have reason to look at the contents of these files and determine which exact settings you are using. In WordPerfect 6, simply select File File Manager, enter the directory containing the files you want to look at and select OK. Highlight the file you want to see, and select Look. In WordPerfect 5.1, select File List Files, type the correct pathname, press ENTER, highlight the filename, and select Look.

You Can Create Batch Files as Long as You Save Them as ASCII Text Files

Batch files contain a series of DOS commands that you can execute at any time just by loading the batch file into memory. You can use batch files to carry out all sorts of tasks. For example, a very sophisticated batch file will assign commands to some of your function keys while you are at the DOS prompt, letting you start a program you use frequently by pressing that function key. A batch file to do this is saved as F.BAT on the accompanying disk, but you will have to edit the batch file, perhaps in WordPerfect, to make its settings match the directory structure of your disk.

You can create and save a batch file in WordPerfect by saving the file in ASCII text format. Working in WordPerfect will let you create long and complicated batch files easily. To save a file in ASCII text format in WordPerfect 6, select File Save, type the filename, select Format, highlight ASCII text (Standard), press ENTER, and select OK. To save a document as a batch file in WordPerfect 5.1, select File Text Out, then DOS Text. Type the filename and press ENTER. Remember when creating a batch file to give the file a .BAT extension.

F.BAT

This sample batch file is available on the accompanying disk as F.BAT.

Create Automatic Timed Backups to Prevent Data Loss

If something should happen to your system, such as a power surge or drop, or someone tripping across your power cord, making it lose power for a moment, you will lose whatever is currently in memory. Losing the programs is usually not too serious, because of course you have those programs saved on disk. However, if you have not recently saved, you will also lose the document you are creating, and any changes made to that document since you last saved it.

While virtually everyone will tell you to remember to back up your document about every 10 or 15 minutes, very few of us remember this while we are working. Therefore, WordPerfect offers an automatic backup option. You can tell WordPerfect to save your document every so many minutes.

Then, as you are working, every so many minutes, WordPerfect will stop what you are doing for the time it takes to back up your open files. This usually takes only a few seconds. If you do lose your power, or otherwise have to restart WordPerfect without exiting correctly or having a chance to save your file, you will have that backup.

When you do restart WordPerfect, WordPerfect tells you that it has a backup copy, and asks if you want to delete it, rename it, or, in WordPerfect 6, open it. Don't select **D**elete, because if you do, then the data is lost forever (unless you immediately recover it with the Undelete command). You can select **R**ename and WordPerfect will save the backup file under a new name, letting you use it again. In WordPerfect 6, select **O**pen to open the file, check which file it is, and then save or delete as necessary.

To set the period of timed backups:

1. Select **F**ile Se**t**up.
2. Select **E**nvironment.
3. Select **B**ackup Options.
4. Select the **T**imed Backup Options radio button to have WordPerfect create timed backups. (Make sure you don't clear this button.)
5. Select **M**inutes Between Backups and type how often you want to back up.
6. Select OK or press ENTER, then press F7 to return to the document.

There Are Some Special Considerations when Installing WordPerfect 6 on a Network

TIP 868

One of your decisions when installing WordPerfect on a network is whether to keep all files in one directory or multiple directories. In most cases, multiple directories are best because they provide better file organization, flexible access, flexible security level assignments, and the ability to customize settings.

The Installation procedure for networks is similar to the Install procedure used for a single copy of WordPerfect. After you complete it, you will need to make some decisions about rights and privileges.

Each network program will have its own unique set of commands for granting rights and privileges. In general, you will want to select the commands for your network that provide the following rights:

File	Privileges
WordPerfect program	Read and execute
Writing tools, macros, Button Bars, backups	Read, execute, write, and delete
Printer files	Read and execute
Temporary and setup files	Read, write, create, delete, and execute

You will need to set up printer files first.

After setting directory rights, secure all WordPerfect files with these extensions: .COM, .DRS, .EXE, .FIL, .HLP, .IRS, .LEX, .LRS, .MRS, .ORS, .SPW, .SRS, .TRS, .VRS, and .WPF. The .PRS files should not be secured until you have edited them. Use the DOS ATTRIB command to set printer files as read-only. See Tip 856.

WordPerfect 6 Network Users Can Have Master and Personal Setup Files

WordPerfect allows for the creation of a company-wide setup file. This master setup file is called W{WP__}.SET. It is created by starting WordPerfect with the network administrator's initials. It is also possible to use the program NWSETUP to select any user's setup file to use as the master.

Personal setup files initially get their settings from the master file. As individual users change settings, the settings are saved to a file that includes their initials, such as WMVC__}.SET. It is important for users to use the same initials each time or they could have several setup files. One way to take care of this is to use a SET command in their AUTOEXEC.BAT file that specifies their initials. It might look something like this:

    SET WP=/U-MVC

SHARE Affects the Use of Multiple Copies of the Same File

SHARE is a DOS command that provides support for file sharing. It can be loaded at system startup when it is part of your CONFIG.SYS file. Your system will react differently to opening a second copy of a file depending on whether or not SHARE is loaded. Without SHARE, you can open as many copies of a file as you want. With SHARE loaded, the second and subsequent copies can only be opened as read-only.

Insert a Filename with WordPerfect 6

You can insert the name of the current file within your document text, header, or footer without typing it. To add the filename, position the cursor on the desired location, then select Layout Other Insert Filename, then select either Insert Filename or Insert Path and Filename. Select OK and Close.

View Document Summaries of Multiple Files

In both WordPerfect 5.1 and 6, you can view the document summaries of files using the File Manager or List Files feature. You can use this to quickly find files when you are not sure of the filename. To use this feature, select File, then File Manager (WordPerfect 6) or List Files (WordPerfect 5.1), and press ENTER to select the default directory for display. Highlight the file whose document summary you want to look at. Select Look. If the document has a document summary, WordPerfect will immediately display the document summary. To look at the text, select Look at Text. If the document does not have a document summary, you will see the text instead. If after looking at the text, you want to see the document summary again, you can select Look at Summary to switch back to that display.

If you need to search through many files for a particular document summary, consider using a QuickFinder index to index these document summaries beforehand. Then the process of searching for specific text in the document summaries can go much faster. See Tip 893 for more information about how to create and use a QuickFinder index.

Narrow Your Search for Documents Using WordPerfect's Find Feature

WordPerfect will help you find your files by searching through a series of files for text. You can set conditions to help find the precise file that you want.

To set conditions, start by opening the File Manager dialog box (WordPerfect 6) or the List Files window (WordPerfect 5.1). Select **Find**, then **Conditions**. Select where you want to search for text. You can choose to search in fields of the document summary, in the entire document, or on the first page. Then enter the text you want to search for.

You can enter operators with the text you want to search for to control how WordPerfect searches. If you simply enter a word by itself, WordPerfect will search for any files that contain the word, even if it is part of another word. If you enclose the word or phrase in quotes, WordPerfect will only find files that have exactly that word or phrase, as you typed it.

You can also use wildcards with the text that you enter to create a word pattern. Wildcard characters take the place of one or more characters in the text. If you enter **?** as part of the text, as in **s?n**, WordPerfect will find files containing *sun, son,* or *sin,* since the ? wildcard character takes the place of a single character. If you enter **s*n**, WordPerfect will find words such as *satisfaction, slain,* and *strewn,* since the * wildcard takes the place of any number of characters.

If you put a semicolon or a space between words, WordPerfect will look for any document that contains all of these words. If you put a comma between words, WordPerfect will find files that contain any of them. If you add a hyphen before a word, WordPerfect will find documents that do not contain that word. To include a hyphen, enclose it in quotation marks. You can combine all of these operators into a single condition if you need to.

Timed Backups Are Not a Substitute for Saving

Don't think that because you have set timed backups you don't need to worry about saving regularly. The timed backup feature in both WordPerfect 5.1 and 6 only saves the contents of the file the cursor is currently in. If you are working in two document windows in WordPerfect 5.1, or have multiple documents open in WordPerfect 6, the timed backup feature will not save the contents of those other windows. It only saves the contents of the document the cursor is in when it backs up. This could be unfortunate if the document you have put all your work into was the one you happened not to be in when the timed backup was done, and then your system died.

Consider Using the Document Initial Codes Screen to Format Subdocuments

You will want to use the Document Initial Codes option to format subdocuments if you do not want these codes to override master document settings. If you place the codes directly within the document, these codes will take effect once the subdocument text is expanded in the master document.

The Look Screen Scrolls Through a File Quickly if You Press S

While you are looking at a document using the Look command from the File Manager dialog box or the List Files window, you can cause the file to automatically scroll to the end for you, by pressing S.

You Can Mark Files to Define a Group to Work With

When you are in the File Manager dialog box or the List Files window, you can mark the files displayed. When you next select an action to perform using a file, all of the marked files are included in this command. Marked files are indicated with an asterisk before the filename in the list.

You can mark files in WordPerfect 6 by highlighting the file and selecting (Un)mark. If the file is already marked, then selecting this merely removes the mark. If you want to mark or unmark all of the displayed files, select (Un)mark All. If the file that is currently highlighted is marked, this unmarks all the files, but if it is unmarked, all files are then marked.

In WordPerfect 5.1, you can mark files by highlighting them and typing *, even though no command is shown for this purpose. You can press HOME-* to mark or unmark all the files in the directory, in the same way that selecting (Un)mark or (Un)mark All in WordPerfect 6 does.

Override the Fast Save Option

By default, WordPerfect saves files using the Fast Save option. The Fast Save option means that WordPerfect only saves the changes you have made to the file. Since WordPerfect calculates the changes to formatting as you see them on the screen, when you use the Fast Save option, only that part of the document you have looked at is formatted. When you use Fast Save, therefore, printing will take a little longer than normal because WordPerfect must format the entire document before printing. The advantage, of course, is that saving documents is much faster because formatting does not need to be done each time you save, and you save more often than you print.

To override this, without turning the Fast Save feature off, simply move to the end of the document before saving. In the process of moving the cursor to the end of the document, WordPerfect must calculate the effect of all the formatting changes you have made. When you save the document, even though you are using the Fast Save option, all of the formatting changes are saved as calculated.

Use the Directory Tree in WordPerfect 6 to Find Other Directories Easily

879

WordPerfect 6 includes a new feature, the directory tree, that you can access from several different dialog boxes, including the File Manager. The directory tree shows you a graphic diagram of the directory structure of your hard disk. You can move through this directory structure using your arrow keys.

You can highlight a directory in the directory tree and choose Select Directory. This adds the directory to the current text box in the dialog box you were in, and lets you continue working. Use the directory tree when you aren't sure of where a particular subdirectory is located, or cannot remember the correct name of the directory.

WordPerfect 6 Bookmarks Can Move the Cursor to a New Location Quickly

880

You can establish bookmarks with WordPerfect 6 that assign a name to a location or block of text. Bookmarks work just like bookmarks you might put in a book you are reading—they give you a way to return to a particular location quickly. To set a bookmark:

1. Move your cursor where you want the bookmark, or block the text you want to mark this way.
2. Select **E**dit Boo**k**mark.
3. Select **C**reate.
4. Type a name for the bookmark in the Bookmark **N**ame text box.
5. Select OK.
6. Select Close to return to the document.

Originally, this text box contains a bit of the text immediately after the cursor, or text at the beginning of the blocked text. To return to the position of a bookmark, press F5 or select Edit **G**o to, then type

the bookmark name. If the bookmark was placed on a block of text, then when you go to the bookmark, the entire block of text is blocked again so that you can do something with it.

You Can Quickly Locate Where You Were When You Saved a WordPerfect 6 Document

You can move quickly to your location in a WordPerfect 6 document when you saved it. WordPerfect 6 places a bookmark at the current cursor location each time a file is saved. You can press CTRL-F to move immediately to this location in the file as soon as you retrieve it. This allows you to pick up exactly where you left off.

The Smart Prompting Installation Option in WordPerfect 6 Affects How Files Are Replaced

When you use WordPerfect's Install program to install or update WordPerfect or install new printer files or utilities, at some point the Install program will ask you how you want to be prompted about replacing files. You have three choices: One is to always be prompted before replacing a file; another is to never be prompted. The third and usually the best choice is Smart Prompting.

When you select the Smart Prompting option, the WordPerfect Install program considers the date of the two files and the type of file, before replacing a file. If the dates and times of the two files are the same, you will not be prompted. If the file is likely to contain data, then you will be prompted.

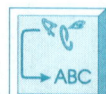

Backup Your Original Copies of AUTOEXEC.BAT and CONFIG.SYS Before Editing Them

Since these files are essential to starting your system properly, it is a good idea to rename the existing files AUTOEXEC.OLD and CONFIG.OLD before beginning your modifications.

If you are willing to invest a few extra minutes of time you can prepare a disk that allows you to boot your system from drive A in case anything goes wrong with your modifications. You will use the DOS FORMAT command, which you must enter from the DOS prompt. See Tip 855 about exiting to DOS temporarily. Place a new disk in drive A and enter the following at the DOS prompt:

```
FORMAT A: /S
```

The /S option copies essential system files to the disk. You can then copy AUTOEXEC.BAT and CONFIG.SYS to this disk, along with any files that these look for, such as device drivers or memory managers. If you mess up the edits of the files and cannot reboot your system with the new versions, you can place the disk you prepared in drive A, reboot your system, and reedit these files to make corrections.

ConvertPerfect Allows You to Convert More Than One File at a Time

In WordPerfect 6, it is easy to work with files in different formats. When you attempt to open these files, WordPerfect prompts you for the format in which they are saved. When you select a format, or confirm WordPerfect's selection, WordPerfect begins to convert the file so that it can be opened. If

WordPerfect cannot convert the program with the built-in conversion feature, it will open Convert-Perfect, let this more powerful conversion program convert the file, then return you to WordPerfect.

At times you may want to use ConvertPerfect directly, especially when you have several files to convert at once. You may want to convert files saved with the word processing program you used to use, or given to you by someone else but created with another word processor. It will be easier to convert the files as a group, rather than to open and save each of them individually. In addition, it will be easier to change the extension of the files consistently to a new extension indicating WordPerfect 6 format files.

To use ConvertPerfect to convert many files:

1. Move to the directory the ConvertPerfect program is in, which should be C:\WP60.
2. Type **CV** and press ENTER.
3. Select **I**nsert Job.
4. Type the path and filename of the file you want to convert and press ENTER. You can use the wildcard characters to select more than one file in the same directory. The files must be named similarly, so that the wildcard characters can be used to create a pattern for all of them, and they must be in the same format.
5. Type the path and filename to use for the converted files and press ENTER. You can use the wildcard characters here, too.
6. Highlight the format the files to convert are saved in and choose **S**elect.
    Depending on the type of file to convert, you may want to choose **W**ord Processing, **G**raphics, or **Sp**readsheets to display the possible formats for each type of document. You can also choose Auto-Detection, the default format selection, to let WordPerfect determine what format the files are in.
7. Highlight the format you want to convert the files to and choose **S**elect.
8. Choose OK.
9. Repeat steps 4 to 7 until you have inserted all the files you want to convert.
10. Select **C**onvert.

In WordPerfect 5.1, the Convert Program Lets You Access Data Saved in a Different Format

In WordPerfect 5.1, you cannot just retrieve a file with a different format into a WordPerfect document. If you want to use a file saved with 1-2-3, Microsoft Word, or WordStar, for example, you need to

convert the file into the WordPerfect 5.1 format using the Convert program, which is a utility program that comes with WordPerfect.

To use the Convert program:

1. Move to the directory that contains the Convert program. This should be the C:\WP51 directory, or, if you are using floppy disks, the Utilities disk. If you did not install the Convert program when you installed WordPerfect, you will have to do this first.
2. Type **CONVERT** and press ENTER.
3. Type the path and filename of the file to convert and press ENTER.
4. Type the path and filename for the converted file and press ENTER.
5. When the Convert program displays a menu of conversion choices, type the number that corresponds to how you want the file converted.

The Convert Program Is Not a Menu Option in WordPerfect 5.1

886

WordPerfect 5.1 allows you to access files created with a different format by providing the Convert program (see Tip 885). However, you cannot do such conversions from within WordPerfect. The Convert program must be run from outside WordPerfect.

Do not run the Convert program after going to the DOS prompt using the File Go to DOS command. The Convert program uses a great deal of memory in the conversion process, which may disturb the memory used by WordPerfect. Instead, exit WordPerfect and use the Convert program, then return to WordPerfect.

You Can Work with Multiple Files Using the Convert Program in WordPerfect 5.1

887

You are not restricted to converting one file at a time to the WordPerfect 5.1 format when using the Convert program. Instead, you can convert several files at once. This might be useful if you are

switching from another program to WordPerfect and want to convert the document files you used before, or if you need to send several files to someone who uses another program.

To convert several files at once, simply enter a filename pattern, using the wildcard characters, when entering the file to be converted and the name of the converted file. The wildcard characters are ?, which takes the place of a single character and *, which takes the place of multiple characters. For example, if you use the extension .TXT for all of your word processing files, and you now want to convert them to WordPerfect 5.1 format, enter *.**TXT** to have the Convert program convert all files with the .TXT extension in the given directory. If you enter *.**WPD** as the name of the converted files, all of your new WordPerfect 5.1 format documents will use that extension.

View Files by Long or Descriptive Names

You can assign a Descriptive Filename (WordPerfect 6) or Long Document Name (WordPerfect 5.1) to a file by making an entry in that field of the document summary. You can then view these filenames in the File Manager or List Files window, to help you locate the files you want to work with. The advantage of using these names is that you can add more text than the eight-character limit for DOS filenames, making your names more precisely descriptive of their contents.

To display descriptive names in the File Manager in WordPerfect 6:

1. In the File Manager dialog box, select Setup.
2. Select Display List **M**ode.
3. Select the **D**escriptive Names and Types radio button.
4. Select OK.

The File Manager dialog box now changes so that it can easily display the longer descriptive filenames.

To display long document names in the List Files window in WordPerfect 5.1:

1. Select **S**hort/Long Display from the List Files window.
2. Select **L**ong Display.
3. Press ENTER to display the same directory as before.

The display is now changed to show the long document names.

You Can Print a List of the Contents of the Displayed Directory

TIP 889

When you use the File Manager in WordPerfect 6 or List Files in WordPerfect 5.1, you are viewing the contents of a directory. You may wish to have a printout of the files in the directory to use as documentation or for use in setting up a new system. You can use special commands to print a list of the directory contents.

To print the directory contents in WordPerfect 6:

1. Display the contents of the directory you want to print in the File Manager dialog box.
2. Select Print List.

To print the directory contents in WordPerfect 5.1:

1. Display the contents of the directory you want to print in the List Files window.
2. Press SHIFT-F7 (Print).

What exactly is printed depends on what you have displayed. If you are displaying descriptive or long document names, then those are what will be printed. If you are displaying the shorter DOS filenames, then those will be printed.

Use Name Search to Move to a File Beginning with the Letters You Type

TIP 890

In the File Manager dialog box (WordPerfect 6) or List Files window (WordPerfect 5.1), you see a long display of filenames. To move quickly to one of those names, or to one in the same directory that you cannot see, select Name Search, then begin typing the name of the file. WordPerfect moves to the first file that begins with the characters that you type.

TIP 891

Select Different Files for Display

You can change which files are listed in the File Manager or List Files window by using wildcard characters to create a filename pattern. Then only the files that match this pattern will be displayed.

To display certain files in WordPerfect 6:

1. In the File Manager dialog box, select Current Directory.
2. Type the pathname and the pattern for the filename.
3. Select OK.

To display certain files in WordPerfect 5.1:

1. In the List Files window, press F5.
2. Type the pathname and pattern for the filenames.
3. Press ENTER.

For example, type C:\WPDOCS*.TEM to find all the files in the WPDOCS directory that have a .TEM extension.

TIP 892

You Can Set a New Default Directory for the Rest of Your Session

WordPerfect has a default directory which it automatically displays when you open the File Manager dialog box or List Files window. You can easily change the default directory so that the new directory will be used automatically until you exit and restart WordPerfect.

To change the default directory in WordPerfect 6:

1. Select File File Manager and select OK.
2. Select Change Default Dir.
3. Type the pathname of the directory to use as the default.
4. Select OK.

A shortcut to changing the default directory in WordPerfect 6 is to press F5, type =, type the name of the directory to use as the default, and select OK.

To change the default directory in WordPerfect 5.1:

1. Select **F**ile List **F**iles and press ENTER.
2. Select **O**ther Directory.
3. Type the pathname of the directory to use as the default.
4. Press ENTER.

A shortcut in WordPerfect 5.1 is to press F5, type =, type the pathname of the directory to use as the default, and press ENTER.

Use QuickFinder's Indexes in WordPerfect 6 to Help You Find Files Quickly

TIP 893

QuickFinder is a new WordPerfect 6 feature designed to help you find files on the basis of the contents or document summaries. You can assign files to a QuickFinder index, then have the files indexed, which means that WordPerfect has indexed all of the text in the file or its document summary. When you search a QuickFinder index, WordPerfect quickly locates which files were associated with the words and displays those files.

To create a QuickFinder index:

1. Select **F**ile File Manager.
2. Select Use QuickFinder. The QuickFinder File Indexer dialog box is displayed:

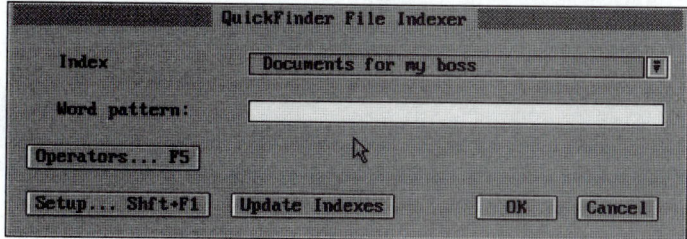

3. Select Setup.
4. Select Location of **F**iles.
5. Select **P**ersonal or **S**hared Path.
6. Type the path where you want your index files stored and press ENTER.
7. Select OK.
8. Select **C**reate Index Definition.
9. Type a description of the contents of the index in the Index **D**escription text box and press ENTER.
10. Type a filename and press ENTER.
11. Select **A**dd.
12. Type the pathname for the files to index. Include a filename pattern using wildcards if you wish. Select **I**nclude Subdirectories to have WordPerfect index the contents of this directory's subdirectories as well.
13. Select OK twice.
14. Select steps 11 and 12 until all the files you want in the index are selected.
15. Highlight the description and select **G**enerate.
16. Select Close, then OK, to return to the document.

To search an index:

1. Select **F**ile **F**ile Manager.
2. Select Use QuickFinder.
3. Choose **I**ndex.
4. Highlight the index you want to search.
5. Select **W**ord Pattern.
6. Type the word you want to search for.
7. Select OK.

At this point, the File Manager window displays the files that contain the text you are searching for.

This is just the beginning of what QuickFinder can do for you. Make sure to fully explore this feature to find out how to harness its power for your needs.

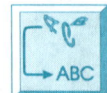

Fast Save Lets You Save Quickly but Printing Takes Longer

TIP 894

WordPerfect uses the Fast Save option by default, which makes saving files faster because WordPerfect only saves the changes you have made to the file, and does not calculate the effect of formatting changes before saving. This saves time, especially if you create long or heavily formatted files, which take longer to save because there is so much more data in them.

The problem with the Fast Save option comes when you try to print. When you print, WordPerfect has to finish the formatting that it did not do when the file was saved. This means that your printing is going to take longer, particularly if your document is long, has a lot of formatting, or contains graphics.

You should be saving more often than you are printing, because you want to be saving frequently to make sure that you do not lose data. This is why the Fast Save option is the default, to make it easier for you to save. You will have to consider how you use WordPerfect, and the kind of time pressures you tend to be under, before choosing to use the Fast Save option or not.

Check Which Directory Is Being Used When WordPerfect Cannot Find the File You Want

TIP 895

At some time, you will probably attempt to open a file and receive a message telling you that WordPerfect cannot find the file. Don't panic. The first step is to check which directory is the current default by pressing F5. If you accidentally changed the default drive, you will want to change it back, and then try reopening your file.

Search for Some Unique Text when You Forget the Filename

You can ask WordPerfect to scan all the files on the current directory for identifying text. For example, if you wrote a letter to Forsythia Plumbing Supply but do not remember the name that you used to save the letter, search for the name of the company. To search for a specific occurrence of text from the File Manager dialog box in WordPerfect 6:

1. Select **F**ind.
2. Select First **P**age or another option for where the text should be found.
3. Type **Forsythia Plumbing Supply** or other text you want to find.
4. Select OK.

WordPerfect will display the files containing this text.

To locate text in a file in the List Files window in WordPerfect 5.1:

1. Select **F**ind.
2. Select **T**ext
3. Type the text to find.
4. Press ENTER.

In WordPerfect 5.1, Use Text In/Out for Text Files

In WordPerfect 5.1, you will want to reserve File Save and File Retrieve for WordPerfect documents. ASCII text files should be read and written using File Text In and File Text Out. You can also use CTRL-F5 to invoke these features. If you use the same commands that are used with WordPerfect documents, they will have initial codes and other formatting that will interfere with their use as DOS files or with other programs expecting nothing more than text entries.

Use the Save Feature Frequently While You Are Working to Minimize Risk

Even though you have WordPerfect making backups for you every ten minutes you might want to save the file on your own more frequently. If you are about to make a major change to the document, such as major restructuring or other alterations, saving it first means that you can always return to the pre-save condition.

Use File Save As Immediately After Retrieving a File You Plan to Save Under a New Name

Sometimes, you will use one document as a template for another document. For example, you may retrieve a letter you used last week for acknowledging a sales order, and plan to make a few changes, then send it to another client. To prevent yourself from saving the new version over the old version, remember to save the document under its new name, using the File Save As option, immediately after opening the template document. Otherwise, you may lose your original copy of the document by accidentally saving your edited copy to the same filename.

Don't Forget to Update Your WordPerfect 6 QuickFinder Indexes

When you create a QuickFinder index in WordPerfect 6, you index the contents of the files you selected at that time. However, as you create new files in those directories, or edit and change the files that are indexed, your index will become out of date. You need to update or regenerate your QuickFinder index so that it is useful again.

 *Updating indexes is usually faster, but the indexes are larger than if you regenerate them. You may want to update your indexes regularly, and regenerate them only occasionally. For example, if you are busy, you can update your indexes every Friday, and regenerate them the last Friday of every month.*

To update all QuickFinder indexes:

1. Select **F**ile **F**ile Manager.
2. Select Use QuickFinder.
3. Select **U**pdate Indexes.
4. Select OK to return to your document when the updating is finished.

To regenerate a specific index:

1. Select **F**ile **F**ile Manager.
2. Select Use QuickFinder.
3. Select Setup.
4. Highlight an index in the **I**ndex Description list box.
5. Select (Un)mark to Regenerate.
6. Repeat steps 4 and 5 to mark all indexes to regenerate.
7. Choose **G**enerate Marked Indexes.

You Can Make Your Directory Change Temporary, for the Current Session, or Permanent

When you make a temporary change in the current directory, the change is in effect only while the directory listing is displayed on the screen.

To change the current directory in WordPerfect 6:

1. From the File Manager dialog box, select C**u**rrent Directory.
2. Type the new directory.
3. Select OK.

To change the current directory in WordPerfect 5.1:

1. Select **F**ile List **F**iles.
2. Type the pathname for the new directory.
3. Press ENTER.

You can also change the default directory for the remainder of the current WordPerfect session. The steps needed to do so in WordPerfect 6 and 5.1 are given in Tip 892.

A permanent change to the directory means that the new directory will be the current directory in subsequent WordPerfect sessions. To make the change permanent follow these steps:

1. Select **F**ile Se**t**up **L**ocation of Files.
2. Select **D**ocuments.
3. Specify a new location for document files.
4. Select OK or press F7 until you return to your document with the new directory active.

Remember to Delete Excess Files Regularly

As you work with WordPerfect, you will be creating many files. You already know to back up the files to protect against damage to your data disks. You may not know to delete the files from your default directory when they are no longer in use. The advantage is twofold. First, it makes it easier to find the files that you do want to use, since there are not myriad other files in the way. Second, your system will run faster, because you will not have as much fragmentation of files, as described in Tip 857.

Develop a Set of Rules for Naming Your Files

A consistent approach to creating filenames helps you locate needed data. Create a set of rules for yourself and post it near your computer to make assigning new filenames easier. For example, if you need to create reports on budget data for each month in 1993, you might want the first four digits of

the filename to contain the characters BUDG; the next two, the month number; and the last two, the year. This would give you filenames like BUDG0193, BUDG0293, and BUDG1293. This is much better than BUDGET01, BUDGT932, and B199312, where none of the names follow a pattern. If you use consistent filenames, you can use wildcards, as in BUDG??93.*, to find them.

It Is More Efficient to Edit Several Small Files Than One Large File

A very large document can slow your system down. You might want to split a large file into parts. You can use the master/subdocument options discussed in Tips 453 through 536, or you can save the file in separate parts until it is near completion.

Change the Order in Which Files Are Sorted in the File Manager

When you are in the File Manager in WordPerfect 6, you can change the order used to sort the files that are displayed. By default, files are sorted alphabetically by name. You may want to look at the last two files you created yesterday, however. To find them, select Sort by Sort List By, then the Date/Time radio button, and select OK to return to the File Manager.

Don't Go to DOS to Execute One DOS Command

As explained in Tip 855, you can go to DOS from WordPerfect, execute a series of DOS commands, and then return to WordPerfect. However, when you only need to execute one command in DOS, there is an even easier way to do this. Select File, then **Go to Shell** (WordPerfect 6) or **Go to DOS** (WordPerfect 5). Then select **D**OS Command, type in the command, and press ENTER. Only this one DOS command is executed. After it is executed, the first key you touch returns you to WordPerfect.

Delete Unneeded Files when You Run Out of Space

TIP 907

If you ever attempt to save a file and receive the message that there is insufficient space on your disk, you will need to delete some of the documents on the disk in order to save the file. To do this quickly, use the File Manager (WordPerfect 6) or the List Files window (WordPerfect 5.1) to quickly locate and delete unneeded or extra files. A good place to start is to see if you have original backup files or other early copies of files that you have current copies of.

WordPerfect Does Not Eliminate Current Screen Data Before Retrieving

TIP 908

When you choose the File Retrieve command in WordPerfect while in a document, the retrieved file is added to the current document at the cursor location. The formatting of your retrieved document may be lost if the formatting of the current document overrides it. For example, if your current document has margins of 2 inches set as initial codes, but your retrieved file has margins of .5 inch on the sides and 1 inch at top and bottom set as initial codes, after retrieval the entire document will have margins of 2 inches.

To retrieve a document without bringing it into a current document in WordPerfect 6:

1.   Select **File O**pen.
2.   Type the filename.
3.   Select OK.

To retrieve a document without bringing it into a current document in WordPerfect 5.1:

1.   Press SHIFT-F3 to switch to the second document.
2.   Select **File R**etrieve.
3.   Type the filename.
4.   Select OK.

There Is an Easy Way to Convert a WordPerfect 6 Document to the Format for Another Word Processor

WordPerfect 6 supports the direct creation of text files as well as files in a format suitable for immediate use with another word processor. This is especially useful when you are working in a mixed computing environment and want to share files with other users. All you need to do is use the File Save As command and change the format using the pull-down list box.

To Convert to WordPerfect 6, Select WordPerfect 5

Most other applications will not have WordPerfect 6 as a choice for exporting their documents, since it is so new. You can export their documents to WordPerfect 6 anyway, by selecting WordPerfect 5 or 5.1 as the format in which to save the file. Then bring the WordPerfect 5 or 5.1 document into WordPerfect 6. WordPerfect 6 automatically detects that the file is saved in a format for an older version of WordPerfect, and converts it as it opens it.

When You Change a Document to Another Format, You May Lose Features

You may lose formatting not supported by both programs when you convert a file from one program to another. Conversion programs take the smaller of the two feature sets and use that set to decide which features will transfer. This means that if you use some custom WordPerfect 6 features and convert the document into a WordPerfect 5.1 document, you may lose the WordPerfect 6 features that are not part of the WordPerfect 5.1 feature set. If you know your files are going to be converted to another format, try to minimize the use of features in your document.

You Can Add Data to the End of a Document on Disk

TIP 912

You can use WordPerfect's append feature to add text from the current document to the end of a file on disk. This is useful if you want to open a new file each day and record your daily transactions in the new file. At the end of the day you can append these transactions to the end of the transaction history file on disk.

To append to the end of a disk file, follow these steps in both WordPerfect 6 and 5.1:

1. Block the text in the current document that you want to append.
2. Select **E**dit **A**ppend.
3. Select To **F**ile.
4. Type the name of the file you want to add the text to.
5. Select OK or press ENTER.

With the Correct Hardware You Can Record and Play Sound Clips with WordPerfect 6

TIP 913

If your computer has a sound board and a set of compatible sound files, you will be able to include sound clips in your documents to create a multimedia presentation with WordPerfect 6. WordPerfect will support both MIDI (Musical Instrument Digital Interface) and digital audio sound files. You can also create your own sound files.

The accompanying disk offers a sampling of four exciting sound files from Voyetra Technologies. This company has been selected by WordPerfect to provide audio enhancements to WordPerfect 6 and has an array of sound-related products. You can add the sound clips on the accompanying disk to any document when you want to enhance presentations, meetings, or training sessions with music. Voyetra offers a variety of other sound files to enhance your documents and can be contacted at the following address: Voyetra Technologies, 333 Fifth Avenue, Pelham, NY 10803, or you can phone (800) 233-9377.

To play the sound clips, you must first setup your sound hardware. To do this, choose **Tools Sound Clip Hardware Setup**. You will need to select both OK and Close after making selections for your system. Your next step is to add a sound clip to your document by choosing **Tools Sound Clip Add**. You can specify the name of the sound clip and a location before selecting OK. To play the sound, choose **Tools Sound Clip Play**. You can choose a sound clip from the list and select Play.

The accompanying disk contains four sound files that you can use if your computer is equipped with a sound board compatible with WordPerfect 6.

WASHPOST.MID
ACTION3.MID
50SROCK1.MID
TURKISH.MID

TIP 914

Setting Changes Alter Both the Quality and File Size for WordPerfect 6 Sound Clip Files

You can alter the Recording Quality options after selecting Tools Sound Clip Sound Setup to affect both sound quality and the size of the files that are recorded. Each setting that you select to improve the quality of the sound recorded has a negative effect on the size of the file. You can select either Good or Better for quality sufficient for voice recording, but Better is needed for recording music. You can also choose a sample rate from 5.5 KHz to 44.1 KHz, depending on your sound board, with a higher setting improving the sound quality. You can also choose an 8-bit a 16-bit sample size. You can choose either Stereo or Mono for mode. Stereo automatically doubles the size of the sound file.

CHAPTER 20

Initial Settings

Switch the Mouse Buttons If You Are Left-Handed

If you are left-handed, the normal assignment of buttons on the mouse may be uncomfortable if you attempt to use the mouse with your left hand. The standard setting for the mouse was defined for right-handed people. You can easily switch the mouse buttons, however, to make the mouse easier to use with the left hand.

To switch the mouse buttons in WordPerfect, select File Setup Mouse, then Left-handed Mouse. In WordPerfect 6, selecting this check box makes the mouse left-handed by switching the functions of the left and right mouse buttons. In WordPerfect 5.1, press Y for Yes to do the same.

Change the Time WordPerfect Will Allow Between Two Clicks and Still Recognize a Double-Click

You have to make the two clicks of a double-click within a certain time for WordPerfect to recognize a double-click. If your clicks are farther apart in time, WordPerfect recognizes your two clicks as just that, two separate clicks. If you have difficulty making the two clicks in the standard amount of time, you will want to adjust WordPerfect's settings to allow more time between the two clicks of the double-click.

To change the double-click speed, select File Setup Mouse and Double-click Interval. Then enter the maximum time that can elapse between the two clicks that are part of a double-click. You specify this time in 1/100ths of a second. The default is 50. You may have to experiment with this setting a little to find the interval that is appropriate for you. If you set it too short, you will not be able to double-click with the mouse, but if you set it too long, your double-click may not be distinguishable from two separate clicks.

You Can Set How Quickly the Mouse Pointer Changes Position

When you move the mouse on your desk, the mouse pointer moves across the screen. However, the mouse pointer usually does not move one inch for every inch you move the mouse on your table. You can set how quickly the mouse pointer will respond to your movement of the mouse.

If you make the setting faster, you will get much better responsiveness, and will not need to move the mouse as much. However, every little jiggle of the mouse will move your mouse pointer significantly. If you make the setting too slow or insensitive, you will have very good control over the mouse pointer, but you will need more space in which to move the mouse itself.

To change the speed of the mouse pointer's response to the mouse, select File Setup Mouse Acceleration Factor. Enter a measurement between 0 and 100. The lowest setting means that the mouse pointer will not move at all, while 100 means that it will move very quickly. The default setting is 24.

Change What Conditions Cause WordPerfect to Beep

At different points, WordPerfect beeps to alert you to a situation on the screen. You can change what conditions cause WordPerfect to beep. To change these settings, select File Setup Environment Beep Options. You are presented with three choices of when WordPerfect will beep: Beep on Error, Beep on Hyphenation, and Beep on Search Failure. By default, WordPerfect is set to beep on hyphenation but not on error or search failure. You can set these options to on or off.

Not All Setup Options Are in the Same Location in WordPerfect 6

In WordPerfect 5.1, all setup options are available by selecting File Setup or pressing SHIFT-F1. However, in WordPerfect 6, many of the setup options are found elsewhere. For example, the options

for setting up the screen are now accessed by selecting View Screen Setup, while initial settings are entered by selecting Layout Document Initial Code Settings. If you can't find the setup option you want by selecting File Setup, check your documentation or online help for where that option can be found.

Have Documents Automatically Reformatted for the Default Printer If You Print Most Documents Retrieved

If a document was created with one printer, say a dot matrix printer, selected, and then given to you on disk, you would need to reformat it for your laser printer. If you frequently print documents that are not originally formatted for your default printer, you will want to set WordPerfect so that it automatically reformats documents for your printer as you retrieve them. To do this in WordPerfect 6, select File Setup Environment and set Format Document for Default Printer on Open. This is the default for WordPerfect 6. For WordPerfect 5.1, select File Setup Initial Settings, and Format Retrieved Documents for Default Printer. When you make these selections, WordPerfect will display a message when you retrieve or open a document, that it is formatting it for the default printer. Depending on the document size and your system, you may not even see this message as it flits by.

Change How Distances Are Measured by WordPerfect

You may find that you want or need to change the default measuring system used by WordPerfect. You can change the unit of measurement used in the status line display, or you can change the unit of measurement used in displaying and entering numbers for things like margins, tabs, and Advance. To change the settings, select File Setup Environment Units of Measure. Then in WordPerfect 6, select Display/Entry of Numbers or Status Line Display. In WordPerfect 5.1, select Display and Entry of Numbers for Margins, Tabs, etc. or Status Line Display. Enter the character that indicates the unit of measurement you want to use in those circumstances.

WordPerfect offers you six possible units of measurements. You can use inches, where inches are marked with inch marks ("). You can use inches, where inches are marked with an i. You can use centimeters

(c), points (p), 1200ths of an inch (w), or the units used by WordPerfect 4.2, which were lines and columns (u).

Many magazines, newspapers, and publishers may request items such as advertisements by their size in picas. WordPerfect does not have a unit of measurement for picas. However, a pica, used in this way, is equal to 12 points. You can select points to create your advertisement, and simply remember this conversion.

You Can Make WordPerfect 6 Use the Key Assignments of WordPerfect 5.1

If you are accustomed to the keyboard in WordPerfect 5.1, you may not want to change your habits just because WordPerfect 6 uses some different key assignments for features. You can set the assignments of the function keys in WordPerfect 6 to match those in WordPerfect 5.1. To change to the WordPerfect 5.1 key assignments in WordPerfect 6, select File Setup Environment. Then select the WordPerfect 5.1 **Keyboard** (F1=Cancel) check box.

If you use the WordPerfect 5.1 key assignments with WordPerfect 6, you will not be able to access new features that have new key assignments. You will have to use the menu commands instead of the function keys to access those options.

You Can Make WordPerfect 6 Move Through Text and Hidden Codes Like WordPerfect 5.1

WordPerfect 5.1 always moves through both text and hidden codes even when the Reveal Codes screen is hidden. This occasionally means that the cursor appears not to move as you press an arrow key, because it is moving between the hidden codes in that place. WordPerfect 6 only moves through the hidden codes when the Reveal Codes window is displayed. In WordPerfect 6, the cursor simply skips over the codes and moves between the displayed characters only. Because of this, you cannot delete a hidden code using DEL or BACKSPACE without displaying the Reveal Codes screen. To set WordPerfect

to move through both text and hidden codes at all times, select File Setup Environment. Then select the WordPerfect 5.1 Cursor Movement check box.

You Can Change How WordPerfect 6 Places the Codes That You Insert

WordPerfect 6 uses auto code placement, which is a new feature. Auto code placement means that WordPerfect does not place codes wherever your cursor is when you insert them. Instead, WordPerfect inserts codes where they are appropriate. Therefore, most codes that format an entire page, such as margin codes, are automatically inserted at the top of the current page when you insert them. Codes that format paragraphs, such as margin adjustments, are inserted at the beginning of the paragraph. The problem with the old way of placing codes is that some codes, if inserted in the middle of a unit such as page, do not take effect until the next page. With auto code placement, formatting is more accurate.

However, there may be times when you want a code inserted at a particular location instead of being moved by WordPerfect to its "correct" location. To prevent this, turn the auto code placement feature off by selecting File Setup Environment and clearing the Auto Code Placement check box.

Customize Your Keyboard by Assigning Different Characters or Functions to Keys

You can change what happens when you press certain keys on your keyboard by creating a new keyboard definition. The keyboard definition tells WordPerfect what is supposed to happen when keys are pressed either alone or in combination. You can assign certain keys or key combinations to start macros, enter text, or activate certain features. You can use this to make WordPerfect match another word processor you are familiar with, to match keyboards for another language or setup, or to make the features and macros that you use frequently more accessible.

WordPerfect is shipped with a few different keyboard definition files. For example, the MAC-ROS.WPK keyboard file has several macros assigned to different keys. The EQUATION.WPK file assigns to keys the characters used in constructing scientific or mathematical equations, such as the Greek letters epsilon and sigma. You can select any one of these files to use the keyboard in a special way. To select a new keyboard definition file:

1. Select **F**ile Se**t**up.
2. Select **K**eyboard Layout.
3. Highlight the keyboard definition file you want to use.
4. Choose **S**elect.

You can also create your own keyboard definition file. There are two ways to do this; they have exactly the same effect, but are just two methods to the same end. You can either *edit* or *map* the keyboard layout. If you edit the layout, you see a different display than if you map the layout. The map display shows you the keys and the types of things—commands, macros, or text—that are assigned to them, as you can see here:

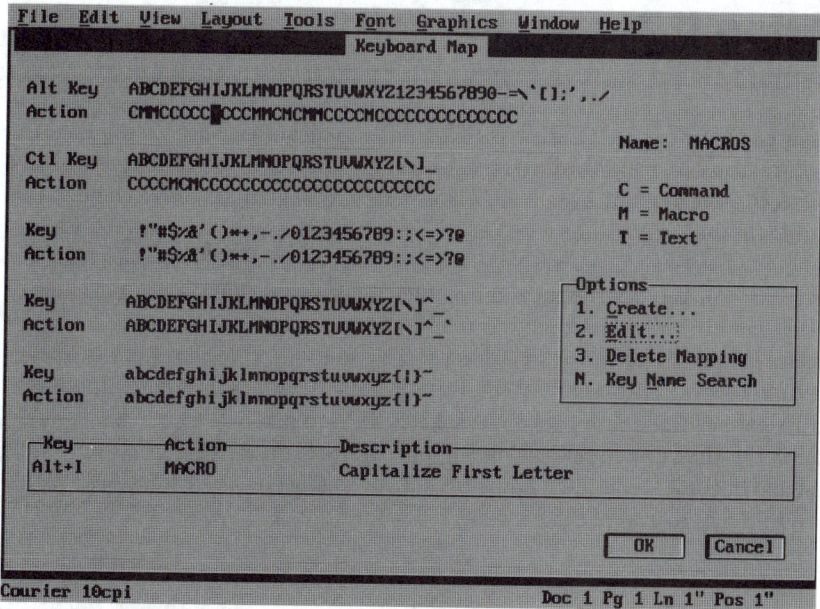

When you edit the keyboard definition, you see a screen and can add new definitions to the keys, but you don't see a listing of the current key assignments.

To create a keyboard definition:

1. Select **F**ile Se**t**up.
2. Select **K**eyboard Layout.
3. Select **C**reate.
4. Enter the name for the file and press ENTER.
   In WordPerfect 6, you now see the Edit Keyboard dialog box. In WordPerfect 5.1, you need to select either **E**dit or **M**ap to move to a menu to start creating the keyboard definition.
5. Create key assignments as explained in the documentation.
6. When finished assigning keys, press F7 to return to the Keyboard Layout menu or dialog box.

Tell WordPerfect Where to Find the Files It Uses

TIP 926

WordPerfect uses a number of different files for different features, such as the dictionary files for checking spelling. You can help WordPerfect function more efficiently by telling it where to find these files. WordPerfect 6 creates and installs files in several different directories, while WordPerfect 5.1 installs most files in the \WP51 directory.

For either release, you can set the location of files by selecting File Setup Location of Files. For WordPerfect 6, you can then assign the location for backup files; macro, keyboard, and Button Bar files; writing tool files; printer files; style library files; graphics files; documents; spreadsheet files; QuickFinder indexes; WP.DRS and *.WFW files; and the Graphics font data files. For WordPerfect 5.1, you can assign the location for backup files; keyboard and macro files; the main and supplemental dictionaries for the thesaurus, spelling, and hyphenation features; printer files; style library files; graphics files; and document files. Remember that if you change these file locations, WordPerfect may not be able to find files that were correctly located before.

When you define the default location of style files, in either release, you can define the name of the default style libraries as well.

Set Where WordPerfect Saves and Searches for Documents by Default

When you set the location of document files, as described in Tip 926, you set the default location where WordPerfect saves and searches for document files. The directory you specify is where WordPerfect saves your document files when you save them without specifying a pathname. When you attempt to retrieve a file, WordPerfect will look for it in this path first if you do not enter a pathname. If you have one document directory that you use more than others, specify this directory in the location of files. If time is an important factor, save all documents that are currently being edited or in use in this directory, even though you may normally store files in separate directories based on who they were created for, or what their purpose was.

You Can Create a Custom Printing Palette

A printing palette creates the colors that WordPerfect uses when you select colors for your text or fills. How closely your colors match what you define depends on the capabilities of your printer. WordPerfect comes with two color palettes. You can also create custom color palettes and custom colors. You may want to do this to access new colors with your printer, or to match more closely the colors your printer is capable of creating.

When you create colors, you have a choice of three systems for defining colors, called units. The default is RGB (Red, Green, Blue), which combines these three colors to create other colors. HLS (Hue, Luminosity, Saturation) creates colors by defining their hue, adjusting their luminosity (amount of white), and their saturation (the intensity of the color). The third system, CMYK (Cyan, Magenta, Yellow, Black), creates colors by combining these colors. HLS parallels the method of creating colors on the monitor. CMYK is the system used in most print shops, because these are the four standard colors used to create color art, such as your Sunday comics.

To select a new color palette:

1. Select **F**ile Se**t**up.
2. Select **C**olor Palette.
3. Highlight the name of a color palette.
4. Choose **S**elect.

To create a new color palette:

1. Select **F**ile Se**t**up.
2. Select **C**olor Palette.
3. Select **C**reate.
4. Type a name for the palette and select OK.
5. Highlight the new color palette name and select **E**dit.
    Each new color palette starts with the basic colors Black, Red, Green, Blue, Cyan, Magenta, Yellow, and White.
6. To create a new color, highlight the closest color and select **C**reate.
7. Enter the values for each color or setting in the appropriate text box, depending on the color units you are using, or use the mouse to select a position on the color wheel and luminosity bar.
8. Enter a name for the color in the Color **N**ame text box.
9. Select OK.
10. Repeat steps 6 through 9 until you have added all the colors you want to use.
11. Select Close twice to return to the document.

You Can Run WordPerfect Within Windows

WordPerfect is a DOS-based program, but you can run it within the Windows environment. Windows is a graphics-oriented interface, which provides a different way of communicating and working with your computer. In Windows you can start a program by selecting a graphical icon. To install WordPerfect as an icon in Windows:

1. Start Windows by typing **WIN** at the DOS prompt.
2. Move to the program group window you want to add the icon to, probably Applications, by selecting **W**indows and the number of the program group.
3. Select **F**ile **N**ew.
4. Select the Program **I**tem option button, then choose OK.

5. Type **WORDPERFECT 6** or **WORDPERFECT 5.1** in the **D**escription text box and press TAB.

6. Type the path and filename of the .PIF file included with your copy of WordPerfect. .PIF files contain settings that let WordPerfect run more efficiently under Windows. If you have WordPerfect 6, your .PIF file is in the same directory as your WordPerfect files and is called WP60.PIF. If you are using WordPerfect 5.1, you have two possible .PIF files, depending on whether you are using a 286, or 386 or higher, computer. These files are in the same directory as the WordPerfect program files, and are called WP51-286.PIF and WP51-386.PIF.

7. Select Change **I**con. WordPerfect 6 comes with a library of icons to use for WordPerfect and its utility programs. Type **C:\WP60\WPICONS.DLL** and press TAB, then select OK. WordPerfect 5.1 does not come with any icons. You can use the default DOS program icon by skipping this entire step; or, if you are using Windows 3.1, enter **C:\WINDOWS\MORICONS.DLL** and press TAB, use the RIGHT ARROW key to move to a WP icon included in this dictionary of icons, and select OK.

8. Select OK to return to the program group window.

Retrieve a File as You Start WordPerfect

You can open or retrieve a file with the same command you use to open WordPerfect. If you know which file you want to work with, this saves the extra keystrokes of choosing to open the file and entering the name. To retrieve a file as you start WordPerfect, type **WP** and the filename, then press ENTER. When WordPerfect is loaded, the file is also opened, if it already exists, before you do anything else in WordPerfect.

Load WordPerfect and Start a Macro with One Command

WordPerfect has a startup option that lets you specify a macro that begins running as soon as WordPerfect is loaded into memory. For example, you may have an onscreen form using a keyboard merge that you fill in as you answer the phones. If the first thing you do each morning is start this merge

file, you can create a macro that sets up the merge for you. Then when you start WordPerfect each morning with the macro, it will read the macro and execute those steps faster than you could set up the merge.

To load WordPerfect and start a macro, type **WP /M=** followed by the name of the macro file. For example, if the macro that starts the merge is called MRGSTART.WPM, you would type **WP /M=MRGSTART.WPM** and press ENTER.

WordPerfect May Require Changes in Your CONFIG.SYS file

932

Your CONFIG.SYS file, which should be in the root directory of your hard disk or startup disk, contains commands that establish settings for your computer. One of these settings is set with the FILES command, which specifies how many files may be open on your system at any one time. WordPerfect 6 requires that FILES be set to 30, while WordPerfect 5.1 requires that it be set to 20. If this setting is below these minimum levels, or if you are running other programs with open files and then start WordPerfect, you may receive a message telling you that there are too few "file handles" to run WordPerfect. WordPerfect's Install program will change the FILES command if you tell it to modify your CONFIG.SYS file while installing WordPerfect. However, this setting may be changed again when you create a new CONFIG.SYS or install another program that alters the FILES command.

If your FILES command is set to a lower number, you need to change the FILES command back to the higher number for WordPerfect to run properly. You can use the DOS Editor, or even WordPerfect, to make the change, remembering that the CONFIG.SYS file must be in the root directory of the hard or startup disk and that it must be saved in a standard ASCII format. The FILES command should appear on a single line and read FILES=n, where n is the number of files you want to allow to be open at one time. After changing this setting and saving the file, you must reboot your system by pressing ALT-CTRL-DEL or turning it off and back on.

Save Original Documents When You Save the Edited Version

933

You can set WordPerfect to create an original backup. When you have this setting, and save an edited file, WordPerfect first changes the name of the original file, giving it a .BK! extension with the same

filename. Then it saves the edited version of the file to the original filename. Original backups can help you if you use one document as a template for another, then accidentally save the document back to the template's filename. To set WordPerfect to save original backups, select File Setup Environment Backup Options. In WordPerfect 6, select the Back Up Original Document (.BK!) on Save or Exit check box. In WordPerfect 5.1, select Original Document Backup and press Y for Yes. Then press F7 until you return to the document.

Hide the Filename in the Status Line to Promote Security

You may not want people walking by your system to see what file you are working with. For example, if you are working with confidential material, it would be a good idea to keep the actual filename hidden, so that even if people can see some part of the information in the file while passing by, they cannot see the filename, which might allow them to later locate and retrieve the file.

To hide the filename in WordPerfect 6, select View Screen Setup Window Options Status Line. Then choose Filename, Font, or Nothing as an option for what to display on the left end of the status line. In WordPerfect 5.1, select File Setup Display Edit-Screen Options and Filename on Status Line. You can then press Y for Yes or N for No.

Use the Left and Right Mouse Buttons to Perform Different Tasks

Most mice have at least two buttons. The tasks that you perform with the left and the right mouse buttons are somewhat different. If you have an older mouse with just one button, that button will function like the left mouse button. If you have a mouse with three buttons, the center button is ignored by WordPerfect and performs no functions. Remember that you can switch the mouse buttons, so that the left performs as the right and vice versa. If you reversed your mouse buttons, then reverse the assignments explained here:

Mouse Button	Functions
Left	Click
	Double-click
	Drag
Right	Activate or cancel menu bar
	Scroll through text
	Select OK in dialog boxes

Change the Screen Settings When You Cannot Tell Formatted Text from Normal Text Onscreen

In WordPerfect 6 in Text mode and WordPerfect 5.1 at all times, formatting that is applied to text is signified on the screen by a change in the color of the text or of the background of the text. If these text attribute settings have been changed, then you will need to change them again to see where you have formatted your document.

To change the text attribute settings in WordPerfect 6, start in Text mode. Select File Setup Display, then select Text Mode Screen Type/Colors. You can highlight another choice in the Color Schemes list box and choose Select to use a different set of colors. Alternatively, you can select Create, type a name, and select OK, or highlight a color scheme and select Edit. Then you can select Text Attributes, highlight a selection in the Attributes list box, select Color, move the cursor to a combination of text and background colors that you like, and press ENTER. After changing all the colors, select OK, highlight the color scheme, choose Select, and press F7 to return to the document.

To change the text attribute settings in WordPerfect 5.1, select File Setup Display Colors/Fonts/Attributes. Select Screen Colors. Use the arrow keys to move the foreground or background column for each text attribute whose assigned color you want to change. Type the letter corresponding to the color you want to use. These colors and corresponding numbers are displayed near the top of the screen. When you are done, press F7 until you return to the document.

Set WordPerfect to Activate the Pull-Down Menus When You Press ALT

Many programs with pull-down menus use the ALT key to activate the pull-down menus. In WordPerfect ALT-= always activates the menu when accessible, but you may prefer to switch WordPerfect to activate the menus as soon as you press ALT, to match your other programs.

To change this setting in WordPerfect 6, select View Screen Setup, then Screen Options. Select the Alt key activates menus check box, then select OK. In WordPerfect 5.1, select File Setup Display Menu Options Alt Key Selects Pull-Down Menu, and then press Y for Yes.

When these settings are on, pressing the ALT key on either side of the keyboard activates the menu. You can then simply press the mnemonic letter in the title of the menu you want to open it, and then the mnemonic letters of the commands to select them.

You Can Start WordPerfect with Many Different Settings

WordPerfect provides special startup options that can be used when you start it from DOS, in addition to those mentioned in Tips 933 and 934. These options allow you to make better use of your hardware or WordPerfect's software features. They are also useful when you want to emulate an environment, such as monochrome, that your users may be working with. Each option you want to use is entered immediately after **WP** at the DOS prompt. For example, you might type **WP /M=MYMAC** to run the macro MYMAC.WPM at startup. You can also combine these options. The following startup options are available for WordPerfect 6:

Startup Option	Effect
/?	Displays the startup options
/bp=*printing output buffer*	Memory allocated to the printing output buffer (0-63K)
/cp=*code page number*	Specifies code page to determine keyboard layout and ASCII character set
/d-*path*	Specifies a location for temporary and overflow files
/du	Prevents use of high memory to reduce TSR conflicts
/f2	Allows your monitor to use its extended text mode for more than 25 lines
/h	Displays startup options
/l=*language code*	Specifies the text resource file to use (.TRS)
/ld-*path*	Specifies a local directory for the .TRS and WP.FIL files
/ln	Allows you to change the WordPerfect license number
/m=*macroname*	Specifies the macro to run at startup
/mono	Simulates a monochrome monitor
/nb	Prevents the use of backup when a file is saved
/nd	Disables the fix for a SHIFT key on enhanced keyboard that sticks
/ne	Does not allow the use of expanded memory
/nx	Does not allow the use of extended memory
/nf	Stops the screen from flashing with some software
/nh	Disables the startup call to BIOS that enables you to be able to print to a hardware port
/nk	Disables enhanced keyboard calls
/no	Disables CTRL-6, which returns a keyboard to its normal mapping
/np	Disables the power down feature on a laptop
/nt=*network #*	Specifies your network software
/pf=*path*	Path for temporary print queue files
/ps=*path*	Tells WordPerfect the path for the SET file you want to use
/r	Places 1.7Mb of WordPerfect information into extended memory
/re	Loads 1.7Mb of WordPerfect information into expanded memory
/rx	Loads 1.7Mb of data into WordPerfect's extended memory
/sa	Tells WordPerfect to use stand-alone mode
/sd=*path*	Directs temporary stand-alone print files to specified path
/sp=*number*	Specifies time for processing the print job

Startup Option	Effect
/ss=*rows,columns*	Sets the screen size
/tx	Sets the display to Text mode for all WordPerfect sessions
/u=*user initials*	Supplies user initials for a network
/@u=*userid*	Overrides network returned user name if /u is not entered and no USERID.FIL file is present
/w=*workspace*	Lets you specify size of the workspace in K for conventional, expanded, and extended memory. An entry of **WP /W=300,1000, 1500** indicates 300K of conventional, 1000K of expanded, and 1500K of extended memory. If you use an asterisk, WordPerfect will use all the available memory
/wo=*kk*	Size of the workspace overlay in K
/ws	Shows the amount of conventional and expanded memory at startup
/x	Restores setup defaults
/32	Use LIM 3.2 calls only for expanded memory drivers that are not LIM 4 compatible

WordPerfect 5.1 also provides startup options, although they are more limited than those in WordPerfect 6. The following are available in WordPerfect 5.1: /cp, /d, /f2, /m-*macroname*, /mono, /nb, /ne, /nf, /nk, /no, /ps=*path*, /r, /ss=*rows,columns*, /w=*workspace*, and /x. All of these options are supported in WordPerfect 6. In addition, WordPerfect 5.1 provides the /nc option to disable the cursor speed feature.

You can use the DOS SET command to include startup options every time you use WordPerfect. For example, SET WP=/M=MYMAC would run MYMAC.WPM every time you started WordPerfect, unless you overrode the SET options with other entries.

Use Text Mode Display in WordPerfect 6 When Text Is Small or Very Ornate

You may have difficulty reading the text in the Graphics or Page mode screen, because the text is shown as it actually appears. If the font that you are using uses light lines or is very ornate, it may be fairly difficult to read on the screen for long periods of time. Also, if you have changed the zoom percentage to something large, the text size may be reduced to make it difficult to read the text.

When you have difficulty reading the text in the WordPerfect 6 Graphics or Page mode, consider switching to Text mode. While the display may not be as attractive, Text mode is easier to decipher because all of the characters appear in the same size of the same clearly readable font. Your formatting will appear as changes in the text or background color rather than making the text difficult to read.

Use Text Mode Display in WordPerfect 6 to Ease Eyestrain

The Graphics mode display used in WordPerfect 6 is very useful and attractive. It lets you see your document as it will print. You can clearly see all of the formatting on your page. However, the Graphics mode display can be tiring to your eyes. This is because the background is always a bright white color, which promotes good contrast, but also can help cause glare. Also, since text displays as it will print, small text actually appears small, making it difficult to read at times. If you are using decorative fonts, these may also make the screen easy to read. The Text mode display is easier to read because you can change the background color to something more soothing to your eyes, and because the text is of an even size in an easily readable font.

WordPerfect 6 and 5.1 Use Different Default Justifications

A small but possibly annoying surprise, if you are upgrading from WordPerfect 5.1 to 6, is that the default justification has changed. In WordPerfect 5.1, the default justification was full. However, in WordPerfect 6, the default justification is left. If you prefer full justification, and use it more often, you can change the default by selecting Layout Document Initial Codes Setup Layout Justification Full, and pressing F7 twice.

Use CURSOR.COM to Change the Size of the Cursor

You can change the appearance of the cursor used in Text mode in WordPerfect 6 or WordPerfect 5.1 using the CURSOR.COM utility program. This program lets you select a new cursor for use with WordPerfect, DOS, and other DOS-based programs that do not create their own cursor definition.

CURSOR.COM comes with WordPerfect 5.1, but must be requested, along with other utility programs, from WordPerfect Corporation if you have purchased WordPerfect 6.

To use CURSOR.COM, move to the directory that contains the program (\WP51 or \WP60), type **CURSOR**, and press ENTER. Use the arrow keys to move around the displayed grid, shown here:

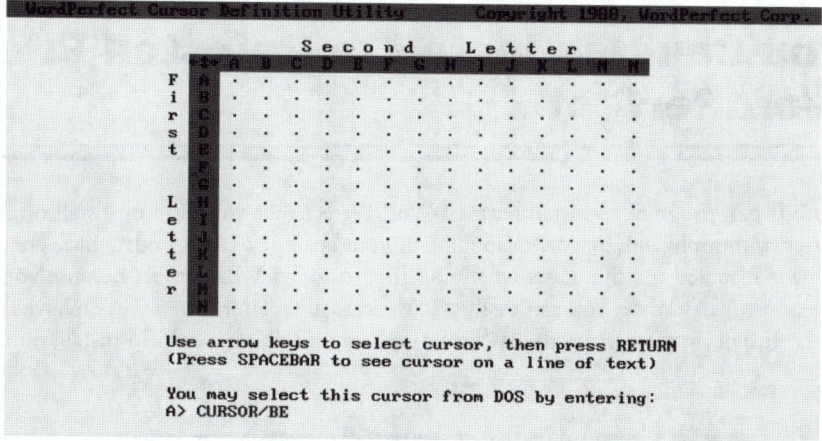

Each position you move to will display a different cursor. Some positions on the grid will make the cursor invisible. Other parts of the grid, depending on your graphics card, may not be available. To see the currently highlighted cursor in a row of text, press SPACEBAR. When you have highlighted the cursor you want to use, note the command at the bottom of the screen, which tells you how you could enter the change in cursor from the DOS prompt at some later time.

Your computer system will go back to the default cursor when you reboot the system. If you want to use the same cursor in every DOS session, enter the command **CURSOR /** followed by the two grid letters in your AUTOEXEC.BAT file, and DOS will automatically run CURSOR.COM to load the new cursor style each time you reboot your system.

Undo and Undelete Are Not the Same

WordPerfect 5.1 provides the F1 (Undelete) feature, which lets you restore up to three deletions. Undo, which is a new feature offered by WordPerfect 6, is not the same as Undelete. In fact, WordPerfect 6 offers both Undelete and Undo. Undo is used to reverse the last action you took with WordPerfect. For example, if you just copied a family within an outline to a new location, then realized you copied the wrong family, you could just select Edit Undo.

You Can Use Install to Reinstall Bits of WordPerfect

You can use the Install program to install parts of WordPerfect that you did not install originally, or to install updates, without having to worry about losing your current settings or data files. For example, you may not have installed the thesaurus when you first installed WordPerfect because you did not have the space on your hard disk. You can easily add the thesaurus later, when you do have the room, by restarting the Install program from the \WP60 directory and doing a custom installation.

Don't Give Up on TSRs When You Run into Problems

TSRs are programs that work in the background on your computer. TSR stands for Terminate and Stay Resident. This means that when you exit those programs, they stay in memory. TSRs do many

different things. Some common TSRs are programs that provide a calculator, a calendar, grammar-checking, spell-checking, or connecting with a modem and sending files.

You may run into problems with TSRs because WordPerfect is designed to be the only program running in memory at a given time. Therefore, depending on the TSR, you may find that the two programs in memory are fighting for the same spaces in memory.

One way around this is to load one program into high memory, and the other into conventional memory. You can load WordPerfect into a specific memory, high or conventional, by using startup switches, as explained in Tip 938.

Depending on the TSR, it may let you define where it is to load, or you may have to check the documentation for where it is set to load, and then make sure WordPerfect loads elsewhere.

You Can Get New Printer Files, Fonts, or Utilities from WordPerfect Corporation

WordPerfect Corporation not only provides WordPerfect itself, it also provides other files that help make WordPerfect even better, such as new printer files, fonts, or utility files. For example, with WordPerfect 6, you can request a Spell utility, which lets you update and modify your Speller dictionary files, and an Additional Fonts disk, which provides an array of new soft fonts to use with WordPerfect.

WordPerfect Corporation provides a program for certifying WordPerfect instructors and training materials for instructors to use in teaching other people how to use WordPerfect's features. To find out about resources available through WordPerfect, call one of the numbers labeled as Information Services in your copy of the WordPerfect *Reference*.

Don't Install All of WordPerfect 6 When You Are Short on Space

You may realize that you are short of space when attempting to install WordPerfect. WordPerfect 6, for example, needs 16Mb to install completely. One solution is to use the Minimal Installation option,

which installs those files necessary to running WordPerfect itself, but nothing else. Another way is to use the Custom Installation option, and choose which files to install.

You should not install any of the files that you won't have a use for. For example, do not install the Fax files if you do not have a fax. If you have an EGA or VGA monitor, you will not need to install any other graphics drivers. Don't install the Sound Drivers or Sound Clips files unless you have a sound card and have a use for sound when working with WordPerfect.

The Shell 4.0 files are only useful if you plan to use WordPerfect's shell for starting WordPerfect and other programs, and will free up about .5Mb of space. You can free another half megabyte by not installing the Graphic Images files. If you don't install the Grammatik and Thesaurus files, you can save a little over 1Mb. You can save another half megabyte by not installing the Learning files. If you don't install the Keyboard files, which include the keyboard, macro, and Button Bar files, you can save almost 2Mb, but you will be unable to change the keyboard layout, will not have macros available, and cannot create new Button Bars.

Use WPINFO.EXE to Get Useful Information About Your Computer

The WPINFO program examines your computer and provides you with information about how it is set up. You can use this program when you are encountering difficulty with WordPerfect to make sure you know what your system consists of. When you run this program, which is found in the same directory as the WordPerfect program files, it tells you what type of machine you have, what type of BIOS you are using, what memory you have available, the keyboard supported, the disk drives available, and other information. Press any key and WPINFO shows you the contents of your AUTOEXEC.BAT file and then your CONFIG.SYS file.

Use Help WP Info in WordPerfect 6 Before Calling the Software Support Line

WordPerfect 6 offers an option that you should be aware of before you try diagnosing any problems with WordPerfect, or before calling a WordPerfect support line. Select Help WP Info, and WordPerfect

displays a dialog box that displays many bits of information about WordPerfect and your system. Chief among these is the registration number. You will need your registration number before calling a WordPerfect support line, and this is an easy way to find it. Depending on the problem you are having with WordPerfect, the person on the support line may need some of the other information in this dialog box as well, to help them figure out how to help you.

When Short of Memory, Try to Free Some Up with These Hints

TIP 950

If you frequently receive a message in WordPerfect saying that there is insufficient memory on your system, you will want to reduce any other calls on your computer's memory so that there is enough for WordPerfect. Remember, WordPerfect 6 requires a minimum of 480K of conventional memory, while WordPerfect 5.1 requires 384K. However, the more memory you have available, the faster WordPerfect will run, the larger and more complicated documents you can create, and the more other programs, such as Shell or Spell Checker, you can run.

Some steps to follow when you receive insufficient memory messages:

❏ Remove other programs from memory, including any Terminate and Stay Resident programs. For example, close Shell, Windows, or DOS Shell. You may need to close WordPerfect, then close these programs and restart WordPerfect. Unload any MOUSE.COM files.

❏ Turn off WordPerfect features that use a lot of memory. For example, switch to Text mode, turn off the Ribbon, Button Bar, Outline Bar, or scroll bars. Turn off Hyphenation. Remove some graphics boxes.

❏ Use default settings instead of custom settings, which use more memory. Use default display drivers. Select a printer that has few fonts.

❏ You may receive insufficient memory messages when you have plenty of memory available for most functions. You may be working with very large files, or those containing a lot of graphics, which use a great deal of memory. You may be carrying out an operation that WordPerfect uses conventional memory for, with a large file. You can free up some conventional memory by changing where TSRs load, or by starting WordPerfect 6 with the /du option, which disables the 6K of conventional memory it usually reserves for memory tables and buffers.

WordPerfect May Not Use All of Your Extended or Expanded Memory

WordPerfect has limits on the amount of extended and expanded memory it can use under certain situations. You may want to be aware of this, so that you can either change the setup options or your system to match what WordPerfect requires. WordPerfect can use 87.5 percent of your expanded memory capacity. It can use 100 percent if you use the /w startup option. WordPerfect can only use 50 percent of expanded memory if you started it using Shell.

Expanded memory is usually administered by a memory manager, which handles integrating this memory with DOS and your conventional memory. A standard set of specifications used by memory managers is LIM. WordPerfect is limited in the amount of expanded memory it can use by different versions of LIM. For example, if you use LIM 4, WordPerfect can use up to 32Mb of expanded memory. If you use LIM 3.2, however, WordPerfect can only use up to 16Mb.

WordPerfect can use up to 256Mb of extended memory when you use a memory drive that meets XMS standards. The file HIMEM.SYS, which comes with DOS, meets these standards.

Various startup options affect what part of memory WordPerfect loads into, or is forbidden, as described in Tip 938. If you are running into memory conflicts, consider using one of these startup options.

WordPerfect 6 Comes with Shell 4.0

One of the programs that comes with WordPerfect 6 is WordPerfect Shell, previously available only as a separate program. The Shell is a utility used for creating menus, from which you can start programs. Shell also enables you to have multiple programs open at once, and to switch between these programs without having to exit any of them. Shell also provides a Clipboard, which lets you transfer information between the different programs that it opens.

For details about setting up and using the Shell, see the WordPerfect Shell User's Guide included in your WordPerfect documentation. If you are using WordPerfect 5.1, you can also purchase the Shell from WordPerfect Corporation as a separate program.

CHAPTER 21

Macros
→ PLAY

Look at WordPerfect's Keyboard Definition for Macro Shortcuts

WordPerfect allows you to customize your keyboard, as discussed in Tip 64. WordPerfect also provides several alternative keyboard definitions for you to use. You can look at the keyboards defined on your system by selecting File Setup Keyboard Layout. You can move to the desired keyboard and choose Select or Edit. Select chooses the one you have highlighted and closes the dialog box. Edit displays the settings of the highlighted choice so you can modify it. If you select a new keyboard, certain keys will be redefined. If you are modifying a keyboard layout, you can redefine the use of the function-key combinations, the character keys, and the ALT, SHIFT, and CTRL combinations. As an example, the following definitions are part of the MACROS keyboard for WordPerfect 6:

Key Combination	Effect When the MACROS Keyboard Is Selected
ALT-R	Add or replace attributes
ALT-I	Use initial caps
ALT-P	Legal pleading
ALT-S	Change spaces to tabs
ALT-X	Return to main edit screen
ALT-C	Pop-up calculator
ALT-B	Insert bullet
ALT-N	Convert to notes
ALT-M	Memo, letter, or fax cover
CTRL-E	Edits a code
CTRL-G	Glossary

The WordPerfect 5.1 keyboard options are a little different for MACROS. You can take a look at any of them onscreen before deciding which one you want to use by selecting Edit after displaying the keyboard layout options.

WordPerfect 5.1 and WordPerfect 6 Macros Look Very Different

TIP 954

WordPerfect 5.1 and WordPerfect 6 macros look very different. The WordPerfect 5.1 macros are recorded as the actual keystrokes that you type. WordPerfect 6 macros are recorded as the result of your entries rather than the keystrokes themselves, meaning that several keystrokes may be represented by a single command. Programming commands to add logic and other more rigorous tests are part of both the WordPerfect 5.1 and WordPerfect 6 macro entries.

WordPerfect 5.1 Macros Are Compatible with WordPerfect 6

TIP 955

WordPerfect provides a conversion program that allows you to use your WordPerfect 5.1 macros with WordPerfect 6. The conversion program is executed from the DOS prompt, and is located in the WP60 directory. It can be executed by typing **MCV** when the WP60 directory is active. To convert WordPerfect 5.1 macros and store the resulting macros on drive B, enter the following:

    MCV C:\OLDMAC*.WPM B:

You can use the following switches with MCV:

- ❏ /b   Indicates macro is designed to run only when a block is on
- ❏ /h   Displays help
- ❏ /l-logfile   Provides a filename for logging conversion messages
- ❏ /o   Replaces the destination file if it exists without prompting
- ❏ /q   Removes quotes from strings
- ❏ /s   Uses short names

When you use a switch, make sure it precedes the source designation. The command MCV /L-MAC_LOG \WP51*.WPM \WP60\MACROS, for example, converts the macros in the \WP51 directory and puts the resulting macros in \WP60\MACROS. After the conversion is finished, the file MAC_LOG will list the warnings and errors encountered during the conversion process.

You Can Use Different Types of Macro Names

There are three different options for naming macros. If you want to be able to execute macros from the keyboard, you can use the ALT key in combination with a letter key. You can then press ALT with the letter to invoke the macro. If you use the letter *A* (for a key combination of ALT-A), the macro name will be ALTA.WPM.

The second option for naming a macro is to assign it a filename of from one to eight characters. WordPerfect will add the macro extension (.WPM) automatically. You will need to type the name or select it from a file list when it is time to execute the macro.

The last option for naming a macro actually involves no name at all: you simply create the macro and press ENTER. This unnamed macro is temporary and is discussed in Tip 972.

Use the Repeat Key to Run a Macro More Than Once

A macro that is assigned to a key combination can be executed multiple times if you press the Repeat key first. For example, in WordPerfect 6 you would first press CTRL-R, then press the ALT-*letter* combination that invokes the macro. You follow the same procedure in WordPerfect 5.1, except that ESC is the Repeat key.

You can change the repeat setting before you run a macro repeatedly to control how often the macro is performed. Type the number of times you want to repeat the macro before you press the key combination that runs the macro.

Use Mnemonics Rather Than Numbers When Recording WordPerfect 5.1 Macros

TIP 958

WordPerfect 5.1's macro recorder records the keystrokes that you type, rather than the commands invoked by those keystrokes. Although you can make your selections with numbers or the mnemonic letters on all menus except the first pull-down menus, you should choose the letters when recording a macro. When you look back at a macro later you will find that it is easier to decipher when you see the mnemonic letters.

There Are Three Different Parts to WordPerfect Macro Commands

TIP 959

The WordPerfect 6 macro language has a syntax similar to a programming language. There are three different parts to the command entries, as shown in the following command:

DLGCONTROL(CtrlOption!;;"Small ~Circle";;;;;1)

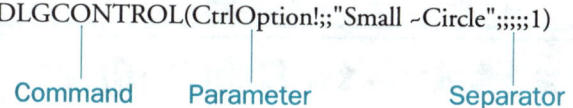

Command   Parameter   Separator

The *command name* indicates the action you want taken. *Parameters* qualify the action you want to take. A parameter can specify a dialog box component, a specific font, or anything else that defines the way the command is to be used. Some commands do not require parameters. Parameters that can accept only a specific set of options use *enumerated types*. All of these entries end with an exclamation point, as in Display(Off!). *Separators* indicate where one parameter stops and another begins. They can also be used to mark the place of missing parameters. With only one parameter, as in Type-over(On!), no separator is needed.

WordPerfect Lets You Edit the Macros You Create

In WordPerfect 5.1, you cannot edit macros in the document editing screen—it is necessary to press HOME CTRL-F10 (Macro Define), enter the macro name, press ENTER, and press ENTER again for the description to reach the macro editing screen. You must remain in the macro editing screen until you are finished editing, then perform the steps again to return to the macro.

In WordPerfect 6, you can select Tools Macro Record, indicate the name of the macro, then select Edit Macro and OK. Once you select OK, you see the same document screen you see for other documents and you can switch between other documents and the macro. Retrieving the file containing the macro is an alternative for editing the document containing the macro. Either way, when you save the macro, WordPerfect checks that the macro commands have the correct syntax. Although the process seems a bit longer, it offers you the advantage of being able to switch back and forth between editing and recording by simply pressing SHIFT-F3, which lets you record part of a macro, look at what you have recorded, and record some more. It is a good idea to add a macro command for a menu command by having WordPerfect record your selections, rather than remembering yourself the macro command you want. In WordPerfect 6 you can also retrieve the macro file and edit it as you would any other file. You must conform to the syntax rules for macro entries, regardless of which WordPerfect 6 method you choose.

You Can Set a Macro to Run Using Typeover Mode or Insert Mode

When a macro adds or replaces text, it is important that you know whether you are in Insert mode or Typeover mode. If you are in Typeover mode, for example, and run a macro that should add text to your document, the macro will actually replace—type over—existing text. If you are in Insert mode, and run a macro that should replace text, the macro will actually add—insert—text and not replace existing text. To have a macro switch to Typeover mode regardless of whether WordPerfect was in Insert or Typeover mode to begin with, press HOME-INS.

Create a Variety of Macros for Simple Menu Tasks

TIP 962

To create a variety of macros for simple menu tasks, all you need to do is turn on the macro recorder, supply a name, and begin selecting menu options. Start the macro recorder in WordPerfect 6 by selecting **Tools Macro Record**. In WordPerfect 5.1, select **Tools Macro Define** or press CTRL-F10 (Macro Define). The recorder will remember all of your selections. You can stop the recorder by selecting **Tools Macro Stop** in WordPerfect 6, or pressing CTRL-F10 (Macro Define) in WordPerfect 5.1. When you want to use the macro again you can play it from the macros menu. You can edit the macro to make corrections or to add logic and other checks that cannot be added while recording. The macro that follows blocks the current paragraph, selects it, and invokes the Speller:

```
DISPLAY(Off!)
BlockOn(ParagraphMode!)
SpellerDoc
```

This sample macro is available on the accompanying disk as SPELPARA.WPM.

SPELPARA.WPM

You Can Add a Dialog Box to Macros

TIP 963

Macros can create dialog boxes that you will see and complete when you run the macro. WordPerfect 6 uses dialog boxes because they make it easy to define numerous options without many levels of menus. When you create macros you can create dialog boxes to make it easier for the users of your macros to define exactly how they want to use a macro that will handle several different tasks.

Three commands are necessary to add a dialog box to a macro. The first command is DLGCREATE. This command allows you to specify the title for the dialog box, its position, and its style. The next command is DLGCONTROL. You will use one DLGCONTROL command for each object in the dialog box. (A list box or radio button, for example, each count as one object.) A DLGEND command lets WordPerfect know it is at the end of the dialog box definition.

The macro that follows is designed to move quickly to one of three locations in your document. A dialog box is constructed to allow you to choose between moving to the first page, last page, or a specific page.

```
Page=0
DLGCREATE(Chosen;"Quick Go To";16;;;;)
DLGCONTROL(1;;"~First Page")
DLGCONTROL(1;;"~Last Page")
DLGCONTROL(5;Page;"Specific ~Page")
DLGEND
IF(Chosen=-1)
     QUIT
ENDIF
IF(Chosen=1)
     PosDocTop
ENDIF
IF(Chosen=2)
     PosDocBottom
     PosPageTop
ENDIF
IF(Page>0)
     DISPLAY(Off!)
     PosPage(NoneSpecified!;NoneSpecified!;Page)
ENDIF
```

ALTG.WPM

This sample macro is available on the accompanying disk as ALTG.WPM.

Mnemonics for dialog box objects are established by preceding the mnemonic letters with a tilde (~).

Try out and look at the contents of some of the sample macros that contain code for dialog boxes. You'll see how these macros work and see the effects of the commands. You can also use the sample macros as templates when creating your own macros.

Create a Library of Common Routines for Use in Many Macros

TIP 964

If you become proficient with macro building, you might want to create a library of macro *procedures* and *functions*. Both procedures and functions are groups of macro commands. Rather than included in the macro, these macro commands are grouped into a procedure or function because they are the same commands performed by several macros. Grouping the macro commands together into a procedure or function lets you share the same macro commands across multiple macros. Procedures and functions differ from macros in that they are designed to be called *from* a macro, rather than run by themselves. The difference between procedures and functions is that when a function is done, it returns information. Procedures are more often used for macro commands that perform a task but do not need to return information to the macro that ran the procedure.

Putting procedures and functions into a file that all macros can access saves time because whenever you want the macro to perform commands that you have grouped in a procedure, you simply have the macro run the procedure, rather than enter the macro commands yourself into the macro. The sample WordPerfect macros in \WP60\MACROS share the procedures and functions stored in LIBRARY.WPM. The macros know to look for procedures and functions in LIBRARY.WPM because the macros have a USE statement. A macro that uses the Message procedure stored in LIBRARY.WPM looks like this:

```
USE("LIBRARY.WPM")
IF(?BlockActive)
     DISPLAY(Off!)
     CutAndPaste
     SwitchDoc(2)
     MoveModeEnd
     SwitchDoc(1)
ELSE
     Message("You must select a block first")
ENDIF
```

In this macro, Message is a procedure in LIBRARY.WPM. The Message procedure displays a dialog box onscreen with the message you provide as this macro command's parameter.

MOVETEXT.WPM

This sample macro is available on the accompanying disk as MOVETEXT.WPM.

Sophisticated Macros Often Contain Extra Commands

When you use the Macro Recorder, you are recording commands that provide the same functions as menu selections. You may want to add a bit more sophistication and check for various conditions, such as whether or not you are in the document edit window. Sophisticated macros will make decisions about what to do next. For example, you may have a simple macro, like the one shown here, that centers the current page horizontally:

```
DISPLAY(Off!)
BlockOn(PageMode!)
Justification(Center!)
CenterCurrentPage(On!)
BlockOff
```

You can enhance this macro in many other ways. For example, you can have a dialog box that prompts for common entries that you want to include on a title page after picking up the current entries on the page. The macro can also set the font size for the title page based on the font used by the rest of the document. When you add these enhancements, you will need extra commands. These will include commands that get text from the document and ones that decide on the formatting to add to the page.

CENTERPG.WPM

This sample macro is available on the accompanying disk as CENTERPG.WPM.

You Can Assign Macros to the WordPerfect 6 Button Bar

TIP 966

You can assign either menu options or prerecorded macros to the Button Bar. To make the assignment, select View Button Bar Setup Select Create Add Macro, highlight the name, and select OK.

It is a good idea to give short, meaningful names to macros that you assign to the Button Bar. The key combination names are not necessary since you will be executing the macros from the Button Bar. The name you choose will be placed on the button for your selection.

The WordPerfect 6 Compiler Can Provide Assistance in Debugging Macros

TIP 967

Removing the errors in macros is a procedure known as *debugging*. Finding your mistakes can be difficult because the compiler only tells you that an error exists—it does not mark the error for you (although it may provide some general information about your problem). When you save a macro, WordPerfect 6 will compile the macro to test that it does not contain syntax errors. If WordPerfect 6 finds a syntax error, you have the choice of editing the macro or saving it with the error, although it is not compiled. (WordPerfect normally compiles a macro so it can run faster.) You can save the uncompiled version of the macro and work with it later or edit it. If you edit the macro, the cursor will be placed after the error. If you are still stumped about the location of the problem, you can ask a friend to take a look or try copying sections of the macro to a new macro and testing each piece separately to try and locate it.

When you write a long macro, it can be difficult to locate and correct even a few bugs. Therefore, testing a macro section-by-section as you write it is a good strategy for creating an error-free macro.

Look at the Macros That Come with WordPerfect 6 for Ideas

There are 13 macros that are part of your WordPerfect 6 package. For the most part, these are sophisticated macros that build dialog boxes and provide rigorous error-catching code. If you want to progress from building simple macros to the more complicated variety, you can learn a number of useful techniques by studying the macro code in these WordPerfect 6 macros. The macros and the tasks they accomplish are listed here:

- ❑ **ALLFONTS.WPM** Creates a list and sample of every font you can use with WordPerfect.

- ❑ **BULLET.WPM** Adds the bullet character of your choice to the current paragraph or, if several paragraphs are selected, each selected paragraph.

- ❑ **CALC.WPM** Displays a calculator to make quick calculations.

- ❑ **EDITCODE.WPM** Lets you edit the setting for the code at the cursor's location. The macro determines what the code is and how to edit it.

- ❑ **EXITALL.WPM** Returns to the document from any dialog box or substructure.

- ❑ **GLOSSARY.WPM** Creates and expands glossary entries so you can enter an abbreviation and have WordPerfect substitute the unabbreviated version.

- ❑ **INITCAPS.WPM** Converts first letter of current word to uppercase, the rest of the word to lowercase.

- ❑ **LIBRARY.WPM** Contains many functions and procedures used by other WordPerfect macros that you can include in your own macros.

- ❑ **MEMO.WPM** Creates a fax, letter, or memo using your responses to the dialog boxes displayed by this macro.

- ❑ **MOD_ATRB.WPM** Finds paired font attributes or replaces one paired font attribute with another.

- ❑ **NOTECVT.WPM** Converts footnotes to endnotes (and vice-versa) for all footnotes/endnotes forward from the point in the document where the macro was begun, or those footnotes/endnotes within a selected block.

- ❑ **PLEADING.WPM** Creates a Pleading style based on your responses to a dialog box and sets up a Pleading in the current document.

- ❑ **SPACETAB.WPM** Converts spaces to tabs based on the selections you make in a dialog box.

You Can Use Logical Tests in Your Macros

T I P 969

Logic is an important element in macros since you will need to test to see if certain conditions are true or false and alter the macro results depending on what you find out. The macros that follow both test to see if there is an active block and perform a series of steps if a block is active. The first macro, COPYTEXT.WPM, copies blocked text from document 1 to document 2. The second macro, SORT.WPM, sorts lines in the currently selected block.

```
USE("LIBRARY.WPM")
IF(?BlockActive)
     DISPLAY(Off!)
     CopyAndPaste
     SwitchDoc(2)
     MoveModeEnd
     SwitchDoc(1)
ELSE
     Message("You must select a block first")
ENDIF
```

The Else condition is only executed when a block is not selected.

The following macro is similar to the first macro but executes a completely different set of steps when a block is selected. This macro will sort the lines in the selected block.

```
USE("LIBRARY.WPM")
IF(?BlockActive)
     DISPLAY(Off!)
     SortType(LineSort!)
     SortAction(Sort!)
     Sort()
ELSE
     Message("Select the block to sort first")
ENDIF
```

These sample macros are available on the accompanying disk as COPYTEXT.WPM and SORT.WPM.

COPYTEXT.WPM
SORT.WPM

TIP 970

You Can Execute One Macro from Within Another Macro

In Tip 632 you saw a macro that created a black box with white text. You can execute this macro from within another macro. The macro that follows places a black box with a pull quote inside into your document. Rather than rewrite the code, you can use the existing macro BLACKBOX.WPM. Notice that all you need to do is place the macro name in the macro you are running—assuming that the macro name is in the current directory (in this case, assuming that BLACKBOX.WPM is in the same directory as PULLQUOT.WPM).

```
USE("LIBRARY.WPM")
IF(?BlockActive)
     DISPLAY(Off!)
     CutAndPaste
     BLACKBOX
     GraphToEdit=?BoxNumber
     BoxEdit(GraphToEdit)
     BoxContentEdit
     MoveModeEnd
     SubstructureExit
     BoxEnd(Save!)
ELSE
     Message("Select the block to put in a box first")
ENDIF
```

PULLQUOT.WPM

This sample macro is available on the accompanying disk as PULLQUOT.WPM.

You Can Use the Mouse to Make Menu Selections, but Not to Select Blocks, in a WordPerfect 6 Macro Recording

When the macro recorder is running, you can make menu selections with the mouse and have WordPerfect 6 record them for you. You cannot, however, select a block with your mouse and have that selection recorded. To make a block selection that WordPerfect 6 will record, you must use the keyboard.

You Can Create Temporary Macros with WordPerfect

You can create a temporary macro that corrects a specific problem in your current document—performs a text replacement or changes the formatting in different areas of the document, for example. You create a temporary macro by first recording the macro, then pressing ENTER when you are prompted for the macro name. If you create another temporary macro, the previous one is destroyed.

You Can Reuse Macro Names If You Use a Different Directory

You cannot use the same name for more than one macro if the macros are stored in the same directory. You can, however, use the same name for more than one macro if you store each of the macros in different directories.

WordPerfect 6 Provides Additional Macro Information in the Online Help Manual

The WordPerfect 6 manual provides limited information on the new programming language that you use for macros. You can select Help Macros to use online help and get additional information.

You Can Type Any WordPerfect 6 Macro Commands Yourself

You do not need to use the Macro Recorder when you need a new macro. Although the recorder is a great feature when you are first starting out (because it remembers the correct syntax for you), once you know the commands for the task you want to accomplish, you might find it easier to type them yourself. It is easier to add the logic commands and other extra commands that cannot be added with the recorder. While you are typing the macro commands, you can use tabs, spaces, and special formatting without affecting the operation of the macro. If you look at any of the WordPerfect sample macros you will see that they use indentation to show the structure of the macro. They also use bold for parameters, variable values, and some names of dialog box controls. You will also see two slashes (\\) and text after macro commands for comments describing the tasks the macro commands perform. These extras should be used consistently and make the macros you write easier to understand.

Adding comments is just as important as recording the macro instructions. Without comments, you will not remember the function of each macro line in a month or two. Macro comments can be added to each line of a macro in only a few extra seconds. Just add a few spaces, two slashes (//), and type your comment after the macro command.

WordPerfect Has Special Support Numbers for Macros

WordPerfect has a macro support number specifically designed to provide help to all licensed users of WordPerfect 6 who have macro questions. The toll free number is (800) 228-9013. At present these support lines are available Monday through Friday from 7:00 A.M. to 6:00 P.M Mountain Standard Time.

If you need to contact WordPerfect outside the normal support hours, you can call (801) 222-9010; this is *not* a toll free number. No support is available on Sundays, Saturdays after 4 P.M., and Fridays after 10 P.M.

Chapter 22

Desktop Publishing

Use WordPerfect to Create Newsletters and Other Professional Publications

WordPerfect contains many desktop publishing features that you can use to create publications. Printed material that you would not have dreamed of tackling without the services of a professional printer can be handled in your office. Advertisements, flyers, or newsletters can now be done in-house.

Don't think that you can immediately create these publications simply because you know the rudiments of WordPerfect. Desktop publishing requires not only entering the text or graphics, but creating a professional layout and printing the document, or having the document printed. You need to practice laying out documents, and you need to learn how to arrange for the printing services you need. There are many new details to consider, which you do not need to consider when simply creating correspondence. But your investment of time can eventually result in a sense of satisfaction and significant cost savings.

A good first step for learning more about effective desktop publishing is to find a book that deals with all aspects of the subject: the system, the software, and design and printing issues. With some experience, you can create attractive publications like this:

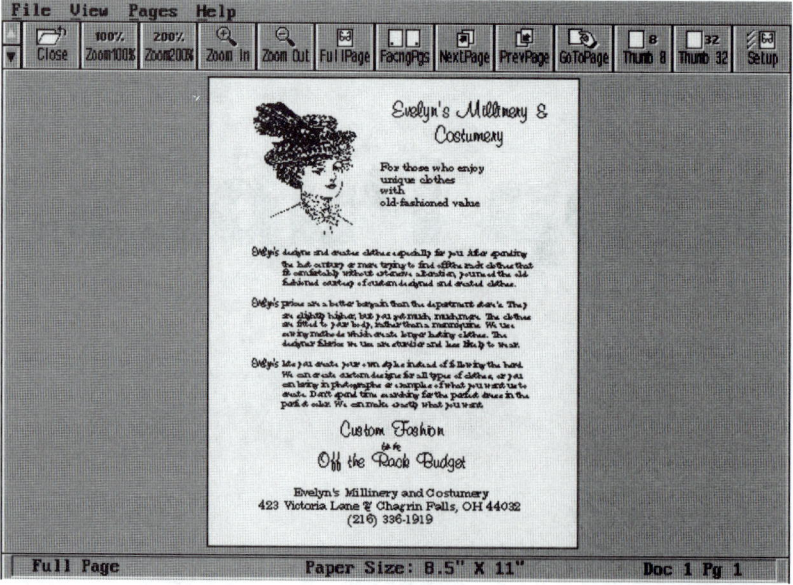

This graphic is available on the accompanying disk as HAT.PCX.

HAT.PCX

You Can Set Line Spacing in Fractions of a Line

TIP 978

Most line spacing you think of is either single or double spacing. However, WordPerfect lets you increment line spacing by fractions of a line. For example, you can have 1.5 spacing. When you select Layout or press SHIFT-F8 and select Line Line Spacing, you can enter the line spacing to use. WordPerfect accepts most fractions. For example, you can try a document with 1.25, 1.5, or 1.75 spacing to see how small changes in the line spacing affect the document's appearance.

When Printing Double-Sided Pages, Preview the Document as Facing Pages

TIP 979

When a document has two facing pages, like this book, you want to look at both pages when creating their appearance. If you are creating a document that will be printed on double-sided paper, you will want to preview the document with facing pages. Readers see the facing pages as a unit rather than as two separate pages, so you will want to look at the pages in the same way. Facing Pages always puts the odd page on the right and the even page on the left. Display facing pages by selecting 4 Facing Pages in WordPerfect 5.1 or View Facing Pages in WordPerfect 6. Or select the following button in the Print Preview window's Button Bar:

For example, you may have facing pages that look like the following:

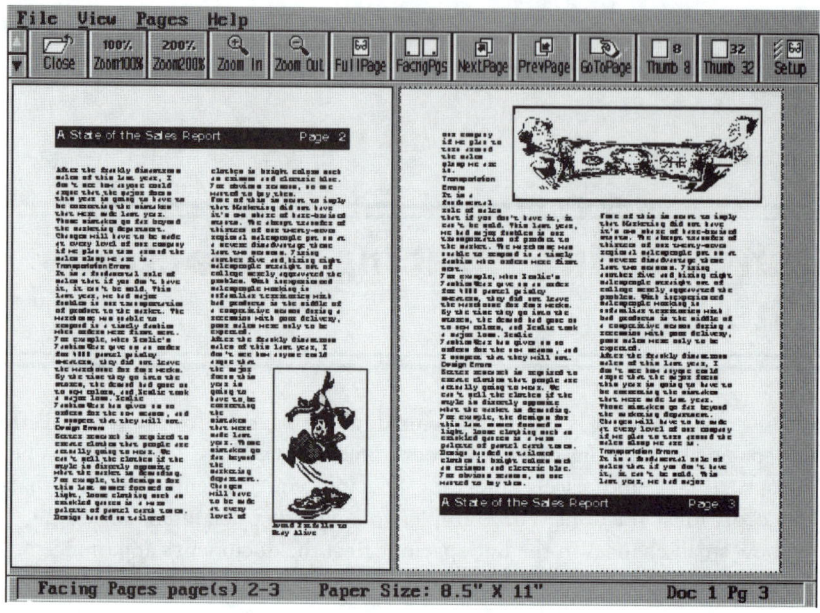

These graphics are available on the accompanying disk as JUNGLE10.CGM and STRETCH.PCX.

JUNGLE10.CGM
STRETCH.PCX.

In this example, you can see how the pages seem to have different margins because of where text and graphics are placed. You can adjust the text and graphics placement to give a more balanced appearance to both pages. If you did not look at facing pages, you might not notice this.

 **Clip Art Provides Inexpensive Graphics Images**

980

Nothing makes a document look better than the well-conceived use of good graphics images. WordPerfect comes with some graphics images, but you will probably find that these are not enough,

or that they are not exactly what you need. You can purchase inexpensive collections of clip art software that will suit your needs.

Clip art is just art, stored in a file, that you can pull into any document. Packages of clip art are fairly inexpensive. For example, you should be able to find about 50 images for approximately $20. You can choose sets of clip art with images useful to you. The greatest advantage of computer clip art is that you can change it as needed, employing WordPerfect's Image Editor to change its size, rotation position, or other features.

The examples in this book use clip art from WordPerfect and from three clip art companies. In the back of this book, you can find advertisements from the companies who supplied the clip art. These would be a good place to start expanding your supply of graphics images.

Sketch Your Document Format First

981

The advantage of working with the computer is that you can try many different types of formatting without very much work involved. However, when you need to get a document done quickly, this versatility will only distract. To get a document done quickly and easily, start without the computer. Sketch out the basic format you want to use for the document. Use squiggly lines to indicate text and boxes to indicate graphics. What you are trying to create is not the exact finished document, but a guide for how you want things arranged so that you know where to start. This is another way to get a good feel for the overall impact of the page.

You Can Use WordPerfect 6 to Produce a Booklet

982

If you want to produce a booklet with WordPerfect, the program will handle many of the steps in creating the finished product. To create a booklet, follow these steps:

- ❑ Set the page size. For example, if you are using standard 8-1/2-by-11-inch paper sideways, you would change the page size to Letter (Landscape).

- ❑ You need to subdivide the page. To do this, select Layout Page Subdivide Page. Enter two columns and one row to specify how you want the page divided.

❑ If you want a page in the booklet to be on the right side of the physical page, remember to select Layout Page Force Page **Odd**.

❑ Preview the document to make sure that margins and page breaks are what you want. Often what looks good on a full page looks wrong when you put it on only half of a page.

❑ Print the document as a booklet. From the Print/Fax dialog box, select **Multiple Pages Print as Booklet**. When you select OK and then **Print**, WordPerfect prints the outside page of the booklet and works inward; it then works its way out again. During the printing process, you may be prompted to reinsert previous pages.

As an example, suppose you have a booklet that, when finished, will have the following pages:

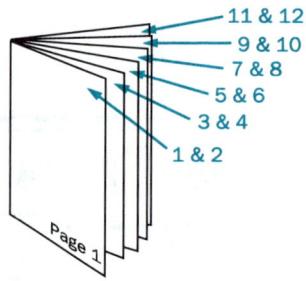

When you print this booklet, WordPerfect will print the pages in the following order:

Page 1 on the right and page 12 on the left

Page 3 on the right and page 10 on the left

Page 5 on the right and page 8 on the left

Page 6 on the left and page 7 on the right, after prompting you to reinsert the third piece of paper

Page 4 on the left and page 9 on the right, after prompting you to reinsert the second piece of paper

Page 2 on the left and page 11 on the right, after prompting you to reinsert the first piece of paper

Notice how WordPerfect figures out what combination of document pages are printed on each piece of paper. Also, WordPerfect prompts for the correct page when it is time to print on the back of the page.

 *If you are creating a master document to use to print copies, you may want to print the two sides of pages on different pieces of paper. Some of the print from the other side may show through during copying.*

You can use the two macros BOOKLET1.WPM and BOOKLET.WPM, on the accompanying disk, to automatically set up and print your document as a booklet. BOOKLET1.WPM selects Letter paper with landscape orientation, subdivides the page, changes the margins to .25, and adds a header that prints a single line and two footers that print a single line, with the page number on the outside edge.

The BOOKLET1.WPM macro is as follows:

```
DISPLAY(Off!)
PaperSizeSelect("Letter (Landscape)")
SubdividePage(2;1)
MarginLeft(0.25")
MarginRight(0.25")
MarginBottom(0.25")
MarginTop(0.29")
HeaderA(Create!)
TextBorderCreate(SingleBorder!;NoFill!;ParagraphBorder!)
BorderLeftLine(NoLine!)
BorderRightLine(NoLine!)
BorderTopLine(NoLine!)
BorderBottomLine(NoLine!)
BorderSeparatorLine(NoLine!)
BorderBottomLine(SingleLine!)
TextBorderEnd(Save!)
SubstructureExit
FooterA(Create!;OddPages!)
TextBorderCreate(SingleBorder!;NoFill!;ParagraphBorder!)
BorderLeftLine(NoLine!)
BorderRightLine(NoLine!)
BorderTopLine(NoLine!)
BorderBottomLine(NoLine!)
BorderSeparatorLine(NoLine!)
BorderTopLine(SingleLine!)
TextBorderEnd(Save!)
FlushRight
Type("Page - ")
PageNumberDisplayFormat
SubstructureExit
FooterB(Create!;EvenPages!)
TextBorderCreate(SingleBorder!;NoFill!;ParagraphBorder!)
BorderSeparatorLine(NoLine!)
BorderTopLine(SingleLine!)
BorderLeftLine(NoLine!)
```

```
BorderRightLine(NoLine!)
BorderTopLine(NoLine!)
BorderBottomLine(NoLine!)
BorderSeparatorLine(NoLine!)
BorderTopLine(SingleLine!)
TextBorderEnd(Save!)
Type("Page - ")
PageNumberDisplayFormat
SubstructureExit
```

The BOOKLET.WPM macro, which automatically prints all the pages of the document in booklet format, is as follows:

```
DISPLAY(Off!)
Type(" ")
PrintMultiplePages("(all)";;;;PrintAll!;NoDocSummary!;Booklet!;Forward!)
```

These sample macros are available on the accompanying disk as BOOKLET1.WPM and BOOKLET.WPM.

BOOKLET1.WPM
BOOKLET.WPM

TIP 983

Make Your Sales Document a Keeper

So much paper flows through peoples' mail that they are accustomed to throwing out advertisements if they do not have a prior interest in them. All the effort and time that went into creating that document disappears when it is filed immediately in the trash can. To prevent this, create a document worth keeping.

For example, create a calendar filled with special events, and mentions of your product or service. Include a list of important events occurring in the next few months in your community. Include a schedule of the local sports team. You can also create an advertisement that includes a set of money-saving tips, recipes, or other items that people will want to keep. The longer they hold on to your document, the more chances there are that they will pay attention to the sales message and purchase your product or service.

Add Extra Space on the Side Where You Are Binding Papers

T^{IP} **984**

If you are printing a document that will be bound, you will want to let WordPerfect know so you can add extra space to the binding side of the document. For example, in this book, the page on the left has a larger right margin than left, and the page on the right has a larger left margin than right. The larger margins provide the extra space needed to bind the book. If the extra margin on the inside of the book were missing, the text closest to the binding would be harder to read. When you create a publication that will be bound, all you need to do is tell WordPerfect the additional margin to put on the side with the binding. In WordPerfect 6, you can set the side of the page where the binding is on the left side, like this book, or on the top side like a notepad.

In WordPerfect 5.1, select **F**ile **P**rint **B**inding Offset. In WordPerfect 6, select **L**ayout **O**ther Printer Functions **B**inding Offset Binding Offset. Type the additional amount of margin you want on the side where the binding is. For example, if you want a margin of .5 inch on the side away from the binding and 1 inch on the side with the binding, set the margin to .5" and the binding to .5". In WordPerfect 6, you can select From Edge and select the side of the page where the binding is located on the first page. If you are printing pages on both sides of the paper, selecting one side automatically adds the binding to the opposite side on the next page. If you are not printing on both sides of the paper, include the additional binding offset in the other side's margin. For example, if you want a margin of .5 inch on the side away from the binding and 1 inch on the side with the binding—with the binding on the left side—set the left margin to 1" and the right margin to .5".

Use Leading to Stretch or Squeeze Text on a Page

T^{IP} **985**

Changing the leading adds just a little bit of vertical space or removes just a little bit of vertical space between every line. This adds or removes space between lines in addition to the line spacing. Leading in WordPerfect starts at the location where you add the code and continues until you change it with another code. An example of using leading is to make articles in magazines always end at the bottom of a column. Tips 739 and 740 describe some typesetting features you can use to get columns to end evenly; changing the leading is one of these methods. Leading is normally changed by small amounts such as .05 inch. Unlike line spacing, it is measured by actual distance rather than lines of text.

To change the leading in WordPerfect 5.1, select Format Other Printer Functions Leading Adjustment. After Primary Leading, type the vertical space to add between lines that end with a [SRt] code. After Secondary Leading, type the vertical space to add between lines that end with a [HRt] code.

To change the leading in WordPerfect 6, select Format Other Printer Functions Leading Adjustment and type the vertical space to add between all lines. If you want to add extra space after [HRt] codes, use Layout Margins Paragraph Spacing.

TIP 986

Consider the Style of Art You Are Using

A document that uses different styles of art will appear confusing to the reader, even at first glance. When you create a document that contains graphics, first decide on the type of graphics you are going to use. For example, in the following document, both a modern gray-scale graphic and an old-fashioned line art graphic are used. While each graphic is attractive on its own, the combination is not pleasing.

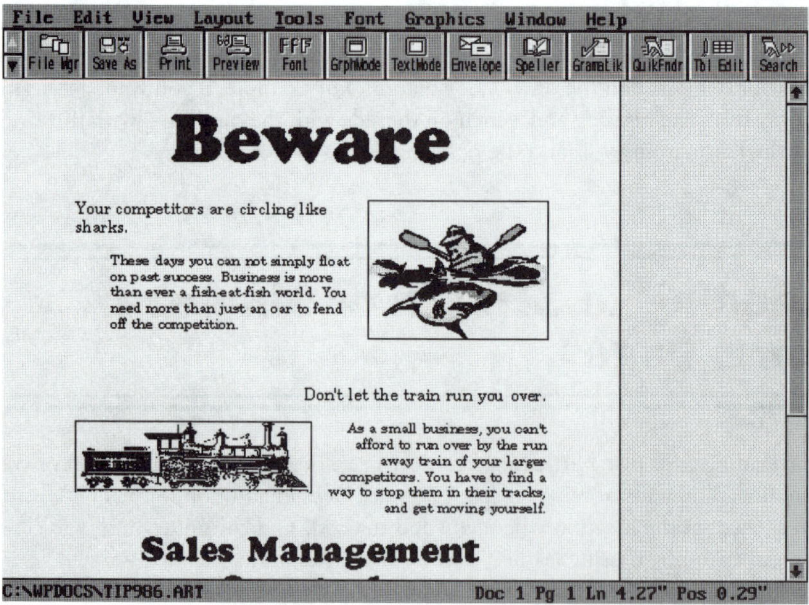

These graphics are available on the accompanying disk as TRAIN.PCX and CLICHE02.WMF.

Consider Using Nonstandard Paper

Besides using standard white paper for your printer, consider other paper options. Some of these options include

- ❑ Paper that includes your company's letterhead.

- ❑ Brochures that you can run through the printer and then fold. Brochures can add color and pizazz that your printer may not be able to supply.

- ❑ Preprinted paper that includes color graphics at little cost. You can find sets of letterhead, envelopes, presentation papers, notebooks, brochures, business cards, and postcards with related graphic elements. Use these complete sets to inexpensively create a vibrant and professional corporate image.

- ❑ Transparencies. You can create documents containing the information you want on transparencies, then print the transparencies. You can use all of WordPerfect's printing features for creating transparencies that look like they took you hours instead of minutes to prepare.

Local office supply stores and print shops may have other types of materials that you can print on. You may be able to reduce outside printing requirements by adapting and using some of these materials for your in-house printer.

Make Sure You Know Who You Are Writing For

You create a document, of any kind, because you have a message to give. Your message can be to buy your brand of toothpaste, or it can be that your company has a new health plan. Your role as the creator

of the document is to make sure that the person who reads your document clearly understands your message. To do this well, you need to know who you are writing for.

Before creating a document, take the time to figure out who you are writing to. If the document is meant for advertising, you may already have done some market research to find out the age, sex, or income of your readers. If you are creating a newsletter for your company, you should already have a good idea who you are writing for.

You may want to actually write a description of an average member of your audience to use as a guide throughout the process of creating the document. When you run into a question of how something in the document should be handled—phrasing, art choices, or even design—refer to this profile. Consider how that person might like it.

Some things to consider in creating this profile are the age, sex, and income of your audience. Do they have anything in common, such as membership in your group or living in the same city? Do they already know who you are, or are you introducing your group, company, or product? Are they favorable to you, or do you need to overcome a negative feeling? What effect do you want to have on them; for example, do you want them to buy your product, join your group, or vote for your proposal?

TIP 989

Using Color for Your Printing

While black ink is something of a standard for documents, you are not confined to using only black ink. With a little ingenuity, you can bring a lot of visual interest to your documents with just a bit of color.

Most computer printers cannot print in color. If your printer can, then you already know how to get color for your document. If you do not have a color printer, you have two solutions. One is to have your black-and-white original photocopied using a color copier or a standard copier using colored toner. You may need to call a few photocopying stores to find those that do color copying. Alternatively, you can take your documents to a printer. Using a nonstandard ink color in place of black won't make your work too much more expensive, and it will add a great deal to the effectiveness of your document if presented correctly.

Another alternative, (available through some paper supply companies), are color foils, which are foils you attach to a page that is already printed, then run through the laser printer once. The metallic color on the foil is attached to the toner on the page. Peel the foil off, and the printing that was black is now a metallic color.

Creating Brochures

You can use WordPerfect and a laser printer to create professional-looking brochures. Paper supply stores carry paper that is specifically designed for printing brochures.

The advantages of using paper designed for brochures include

- ❏ The paper is already marked for where you will fold it or is prefolded.
- ❏ The paper can include graphics, such as those using colors, that you might not otherwise be able to add to your printouts.

To create the brochure in WordPerfect, you first need to know how you want it folded. A tri-fold brochure, using an 8-1/2-by-11-inch sheet folded twice is fairly standard. You can easily create brochures by subdividing the page with the Layout Page Subdivide Page command. WordPerfect will treat each of the three parts as an individual page.

You Can Fold Your Own Paper with a Straight Edge, or Have It Done Professionally

When you create documents that are to be folded, such as brochures or some newsletter formats, you want that fold to be a straight line in the correct location. If your document looks as if it were folded by a group of elementary school children because you were trying to get a mailing out quickly, part of your message will be lost. The first impression your readers will have is of unprofessionalism.

You can have the paper folded professionally, usually by the company that handled the printing. This can be done quickly, since it is done by machine, and fairly accurately. If you only have a few documents to fold, you can do it yourself using a straight edge. To make sure that you are folding in the correct location, measure the distances to the folds on a document that is folded correctly. Then copy these marks onto a straight edge. You don't want to mark the pages themselves because it will disturb your layout. Use the straight edge to measure where you want to make your folds.

Limit the Use of Reverses and Blocks on Your Page

When you create a document such as a newsletter or brochure, you may be tempted to use all of the graphics features you can to make the document look professional and interesting. Remember, however, that the purpose is to get people to read your document, not to admire your technical skill at putting it together.

The overuse of graphics, graphics boxes as blocks, graphics lines, and other visual elements makes it difficult to read your document, and detracts from its appearance. Remember to keep your layout simple. Unless there is a good reason to add a graphic element, don't. For example, in the following document, the overuse of reverse text, graphics lines, and graphics makes the newsletter look cluttered and poorly thought out.

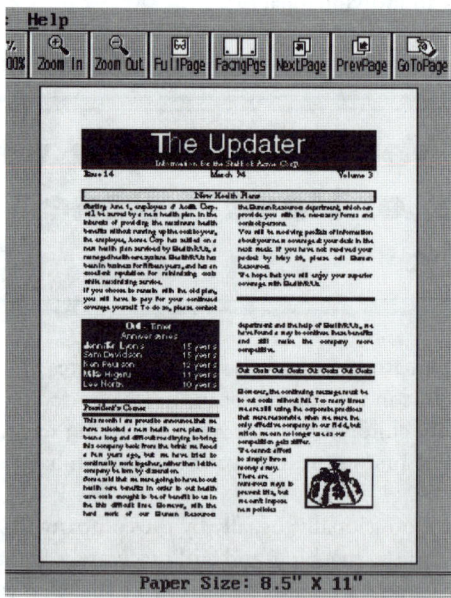

MONBAGS1.CGM

This graphic is available on the accompanying disk as MONBAGS1.CGM.

Make Sure Your Documents Are Consistent

Whether you are creating brochures for your company or a newsletter for your church group, you want to turn out the most professional and useful document you can. One important point, which can get lost in the fun of playing with the format, is to maintain a consistency in your documents. If you are creating a variety of documents for your company, make sure you use the same base font and the exact same logo consistently. If you are creating a newsletter, use the same format for all headings at the same level, mark articles that jump to another page the same way each time, and try to keep regularly appearing articles in the same location in each issue.

The advantage of consistency is that it makes it easier for your readers to identify what they need to know. If you are continually using different logos or formats in similar documents, your clients or readers will never develop a strong image for your company. They may feel that you are disorganized. If your newsletter uses inconsistent headline format, or if the features move around each month, it will take longer for them to find each item, and they will lose interest in hunting for what they want.

Remember that styles can help a great deal in establishing consistency in document formatting.

Use a Service Bureau and Printer for Large or Important Documents

You can create excellent documents using WordPerfect. However, the weak link in getting the message to your readers or clients is your printer. Printers come in varying *resolutions,* or the number of dots per inch you can print on the page. The lower the resolution, the more jagged the text and graphics print. The higher the resolution, the better your final document will look. While you may create a beautiful document in WordPerfect, if your printer cannot match it, your document can never have a fully professional appearance.

To resolve this, you can use a service bureau. Service bureaus can take your WordPerfect document and print it using printers capable of vastly greater resolution than your office printer. For example, a

standard office laser printer can print at about 300 dpi (dots per inch). A service bureau's printer can print at 12,500 dpi or higher.

Service bureaus can also take your color graphics and separate them into plates. Your professional printer uses these plates to accurately print color graphics. Plates are like negatives of your color graphics, telling the printer where to use each of the four standard ink colors to re-create the graphics accurately.

For large runs of documents or for very important documents, use a professional printer rather than your office printer. A professional printer can create more documents in less time than it will take you when you are creating hundreds or thousands of flyers. When you are creating important documents such as annual reports, you will want your document to look as good as possible, and using the higher resolution and improved printing techniques available by using a service bureau and a good printer, you can make these documents look better than ever.

One way to find a good service bureau is to ask your professional printer first. This way the printer can recommend someone he or she has already used and worked well with, and you can minimize any potential problems.

TIP 995

Your Lead-in Paragraph Can Span Columns

When you create a newsletter or other documents, you may want your first paragraph to span the columns. You can use this either as emphasis in a paper or to highlight important information in a newsletter. This is also an effective layout for a flyer or brochure.

You can create an initial column-spanning paragraph by making sure that this paragraph is entered before you define columns, in WordPerfect 6, or before you insert the "column on" code in WordPerfect 5.1. When creating a newsletter, for example, your first paragraph (or more) may be the nameplate containing the name of the newsletter, the issue and date, and other publishing information. You will want to make sure that this is created before the columns for the newsletter are defined.

Use Thumbnails to Get a Quick Idea of How Your Document Looks

Thumbnails are small sketches of your page. They are too small to let you read text or see graphics clearly, but they give you a feel for the overall appearance of the document. When viewing your document as a thumbnail sketch, you may discover that you have several different types of page formats and that they do not flow well together, or that the general appearance of the page is confusing. You might not notice this while working with the document because you are too close to it, but the general appearance of the document is going to be the first thing to strike your reader.

In WordPerfect 6, you can see thumbnails while using the Print Preview screen, as shown here. You can select the number of pages you want to appear on the screen at one time by selecting View **Thumbnails** and selecting an option.

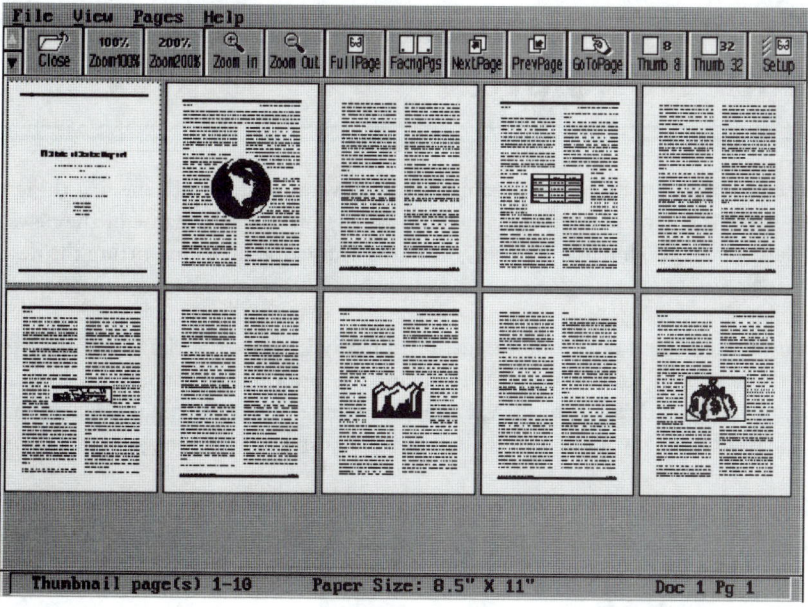

Use an Empty Graphics Box for Graphics You Paste into Your Document

When you create a newsletter or flyer that you want a graphic to appear in, and you are either going to paste it into your original before photocopying it, or you are taking it to a printer to be added to your document, use an empty graphics box in the location of the photo. The graphics box reserves that space on the page so that you do not accidentally let text appear in that location, or overlap another graphic. If you also use a light fill or graphics box borders, this technique will help you paste the photo or other graphic accurately into the document, since it will be easier to see exactly where it belongs.

Create a Distinctive Nameplate for Your Newsletter

When you create a newsletter for your organization, you want to start with the first thing readers will see with each issue, the nameplate. The nameplate usually includes the name of the newsletter and a publication date. It can also include a motto, the name of the organization putting the newsletter out, or a graphic element.

The nameplate should stand out from the text. Ordinarily it appears at the top of the first page, but you can vary its position if you feel that it will enhance the appearance of your newsletter. Remember that readers will use the nameplate to identify your newsletter, though, so put it where they can see it and immediately know what your newsletter is. Confusion can lead to having your newsletter promptly thrown out.

Study Other Printed Materials for Ideas on Effective Layout

TIP 999

The easiest way to learn about good page layout is no further away than the nearest magazine rack. Professionals spend thousands of dollars creating the layout for these magazines and the ads that appear in them. When you read a magazine or receive a flyer or other ad from a company, examine it. Ignore its message and try looking at it simply as an example of layout. If it is one that you like, save it for reference when you are creating similar documents. This way, you can take advantage of the effort and money that the company spent to create that document.

Change Leading and Type Size to Make Columns More Readable

TIP 1000

When you create columns, you will want to check both the size of the font you are using and the leading between lines to ensure readability and attractiveness of the page. Some rules for this are obvious. You do not want to use a very large font in a very narrow column because it will be hard to read. As a rule, the bigger the column, the larger the font you can and should use. If you want to cram a lot of text in a very small font onto a page, use multiple columns.

Remember that people read groups of words rather than single words. If there are many groups of words on a line, your readers must move their eyes in several jerks across the page, and then from the end of the line to the beginning of the next. Each time the eyes have to move to a new word cluster, and especially when they have to move to the beginning of the next line, there is the risk of missing, and skipping, a few lines. This sounds innocuous, but it works subliminally to make your document less easy to read.

You want to adjust the leading, or space between lines, to help ensure that the document is clearly readable. If the lines are too close together, it becomes even easier to skip lines because the reader's eye is registering a large gray blur. You want the leading to be distinctive enough to clearly differentiate the lines. On the other hand, if the lines are too far apart, readers are getting a visual cue that the lines of text do not relate to one another, and they will read in a jerky fashion.

Usually, you will not have to adjust leading. WordPerfect automatically selects a leading that is quite readable. However, this setting is not always perfect, and you should adjust it when you see the need.

Font Size Adjustments May Not Allow Adequate Space on Documents Requiring Manual Completion

When you create documents, such as order forms, that include areas that must be filled in by hand, make sure that there is plenty of space to do so. For example, if you use a 12-point font to label where you need information added, you will have to adjust the line spacing to make sure that there is enough room for someone to write in the information legibly. You can do this in three ways: by actually changing the height of the line, as part of line formatting; by changing the line spacing, which changes the amount of space WordPerfect puts between lines, and which is also a line format; or by changing to a larger font.

APPENDIX A

WordPerfect 6 Codes

This appendix contains a list of the hidden codes used in WordPerfect 6 and their meanings. This list includes many new codes for features not available in WordPerfect 5.1, and new versions of old codes. If you are using WordPerfect 5.1, consult Appendix C in your documentation for a list of the WordPerfect 5.1 codes.

Code	Description
-	Indicates a hard hyphen
[- Hyphen]	Indicates a hyphen character
[- Soft Hyphen]	Indicates a soft or optional hyphen
[- Soft Hyphen EOL]	Indicates a soft or optional hyphen at the end of a line
[Auto Hyphen EOL]	Indicates an automatic hyphen at the end of a line
[Back Tab]	Indicates a back tab (called *margin release* in 5.1)
[Bar Code]	Indicates a PostNet bar code
[Begin Gen Txt]	Marks the beginning of generated text, such as endnotes
[Binding Width]	Indicates a binding width measurement
[Block]	Marks where the Block feature is turned on
[Block Pro Off]	Marks where the Block Protect feature is turned off
[Block Pro On]	Marks where the Block Protect feature is turned on
[Bold Off]	Marks where boldfacing is turned off
[Bold On]	Marks where boldfacing is turned on
[Bookmark]	Indicates the location of a bookmark
[Bot Mar]	Indicates a new bottom margin measurement
[Box (Char)]	Indicates a graphics box attached to a character
[Box (Page)]	Indicates a graphics box attached to a page
[Box (Para)]	Indicates a graphics box attached to a paragraph
[Box Num Dec]	Marks where the graphics box counter has been decremented
[Box Num Disp]	Marks where a box number is displayed
[Box Num Inc]	Marks where the graphics box counter has been incremented
[Box Num Meth]	Indicates that a new method of numbering a graphics box list has been selected
[Box Num Set]	Marks where a list of graphics boxes is set to a specific number
[Calc Col]	Marks a WordPerfect Math calculation column

Code	Description
[Cancel Hyph]	Indicates the word is to be ignored by the hyphenation feature
[Cell]	Marks the cell of a table
[Change BOL Char]	Indicates a new beginning of line character
[Change EOL Char]	Indicates a new end of line character
[Chap Num Dec]	Marks where the chapter counter has been decremented
[Chap Num Disp]	Marks where a chapter number is displayed
[Chap Num Inc]	Marks where the chapter counter has been incremented
[Chap Num Meth]	Indicates that a new method of numbering is used for a list of chapter numbers
[Chap Num Set]	Marks where a list of chapters is set to specific number
[Char Shade Change]	Marks where a new shade of the chosen character color was selected
[Char Style Off]	Marks where a character style is turned off
[Char Style On]	Marks where a character style is turned on
[Cntr Cur Pg]	Indicates the current page is centered between its top and bottom margins
[Cntr on Cur Pos]	Indicates that text that follows is centered on the cursor's current position
[Cntr on Mar]	Indicates that text that follows is centered between the margins
[Cntr on Mar (Dot)]	Indicates that text that follows is centered between margins and has a dot leader to the preceding text
[Cntr Pgs]	Indicates that all further pages are centered between top and bottom margins
[CNTR TAB]	Indicates that text that follows will be centered on the next tab stop, regardless of its setting
[Cntr Tab]	Indicates that the text that follows is centered on the tab stop
[CNTR TAB (DOT)]	Indicates that text that follows will be centered on the next tab stop and preceded by a dot leader, regardless of the tab stop's setting
[Cntr Tab (Dot)]	Indicates that the text that follows is centered on the tab stop and has a dot leader to the preceding text

Code	Description
[Col Border]	Marks where a new column border definition takes effect
[Col Def]	Marks where a new column definition takes effect
[Color]	Marks a change in the color of the text
[Comment]	Marks the location of a document comment
[Condl EOP]	Marks where a page should end, if a soft return is located within the number of lines specified
[Count Dec]	Marks where a counter has been decremented
[Count Disp]	Marks where the current value of a counter is displayed
[Count Inc]	Marks where a counter has been incremented
[Count Meth]	Indicates that a new method of numbering is being used for a counter
[Count Set]	Marks where a counter is set to a particular number
[Date]	Marks where WordPerfect will insert the current date and time
[Date Fmt]	Indicates that a new date or time format is selected
[Dbl Und Off]	Marks where double underlining is turned off
[Dbl Und On]	Marks where double underlining is turned on
[Dbl Sided Print]	Indicates that page setup is changed to make room for double-sided printing
[DEC TAB]	Indicates that the following text will be decimally aligned at the next tab stop, regardless of the tab stop's settings
[Dec Tab]	Indicates that the following text will be aligned by the decimal character at the top stop
[DEC TAB (DOT)]	Indicates that the text that follows will be decimally aligned at the next tab stop and preceded by a dot leader, regardless of the tab stop's settings
[Dec Tab (Dot)]	Indicates the following text is aligned by the decimal character at the top stop, and is preceded by a dot leader
[Dec/Align Char]	Indicates that a new decimal alignment character has been selected
[Def Mark]	Marks where an index, a table of authorities, list or table of contents will be generated
[Delay]	Indicates that there are codes that will not be turned on for some pages

Code	Description
[Delay On]	Marks that delayed codes are now turned on
[Do Grand Tot]	Marks where WordPerfect's Math will calculate a grand total
[Do Subtot]	Marks where WordPerfect's Math will calculate a subtotal
[Do Total]	Marks where WordPerfect's Math will calculate a total
[Dorm HRt]	Marks a dormant hard return
[Dot Lead Char]	Indicates the selection of a character to use in dot leaders
[End Cntr/Align]	Marks the end of a centering or alignment option
[End Gen Txt]	Marks the end of text that is generated
[Endnote]	Marks the location of an endnote reference
[Endnote Min]	Indicates the minimum amount of an endnote that must appear on a page
[Endnote Num Dec]	Marks where the endnote counter has been decremented
[Endnote Num Disp]	Marks where an endnote number is displayed
[Endnote Num Inc]	Marks where the endnote counter has been incremented
[Endnote Num Meth]	Indicates that a new method of numbering endnotes has been selected
[Endnote Num Set]	Marks where a list of endnotes is set to a specific number
[Endnote Placement]	Marks where endnotes should be generated
[Endnote Space]	Indicates the space to appear between endnotes
[Ext Large Off]	Marks where the extra large font size is turned off
[Ext Large On]	Marks where the extra large font size is turned on
[Filename]	Marks where WordPerfect will insert the name of the file
[Fine Off]	Marks where the fine font size is turned off
[Fine On]	Marks where the fine font size is turned on
[First Ln Ind]	Marks a change in the setting for the indentation of the first line
[Flsh Rgt]	Indicates that the following text on the line will be aligned with the right margin
[Flsh Rgt (Dot)]	Indicates that the following text is flush with the right margin and preceded by a dot leader
[Flt Cell Begin]	Marks the beginning of a floating cell
[Flt Cell End]	Marks the end of a floating cell

Code	Description
[Font]	Indicates that the font has changed
[Font Size]	Indicates that the font size has changed
[Footer A]	Indicates that a new footer A has been entered
[Footer B]	Indicates that a new footer B has been entered
[Footer Sep]	Marks how much space should appear between text and footnotes
[Footnote]	Marks the location of a footnote reference
[Footnote Cont Msg]	Indicates a new footnote continuation message has been set
[Footnote Min]	Indicates the minimum amount of footnote text to keep on one page
[Footnote Num Dec]	Marks where the footnote counter has been decremented
[Footnote Num Disp]	Marks where a footnote number is displayed
[Footnote Num Each Pg]	Indicates that further footnotes will restart numbering at the top of each page
[Footnote Num Inc]	Marks where the footnote counter has been incremented
[Footnote Num Meth]	Indicates that a new method of numbering footnotes has been selected
[Footnote Num Set]	Marks where a footnote list is set to a specific number
[Footnote Sep Ln]	Indicates that a new style for the line separating footnotes and text has been selected
[Footnote Space]	Indicates the amount of space to appear between footnotes
[Footnote Txt Pos]	Indicates where footnote text is to appear
[Force]	Indicates that the page has been forced to be odd or even
[Formatted Pg Num]	Marks where page number is displayed
[Graph Line]	Indicates that a graphic line has been added to the document
[HAdv]	Marks where the cursor is moved to a specific location
[HCol]	Marks where you inserted a column break
[HCol SPg]	Marks where you inserted a column break in the last column of the page
[Header A]	Indicates that a new header A has been entered
[Header B]	Indicates that a new header B has been entered
[Header Sep]	Indicates the amount of space between the header and text
[Hidden Off]	Marks where the hidden text character format is turned off

Code	Description
[Hidden On]	Marks where the hidden text character format is turned on
[Hidden Txt]	Marks the location of hidden body text in an outline
[HPg]	Marks where you inserted a page break
[HRow HCol]	Marks where a hard column break is inserted in a table in columns
[HRow HCol SPg]	Marks where a hard column break, inserted in a table, also ends the page
[HRt]	Indicates where you pressed ENTER
[HRt SCol]	Marks where a hard return also ends a column
[HRt SPg]	Marks where a hard return also ends a page
[HSpace]	Marks the location of a hard space
[Hypertext Begin]	Marks where Hypertext feature begins
[Hypertext End]	Marks where Hypertext feature ends
[Hyph]	Marks where hyphenation is turned on or off
[Hyph SRt]	Marks where you inserted a special code telling WordPerfect where to hyphenate a word when necessary
[Index]	Marks text to be included in a generated index
[Italc Off]	Marks where the italics character format is turned off
[Italc On]	Marks where the italics character format is turned on
[Just]	Indicates a change in justification
[Just Lim]	Indicates a new setting for the space that can be added between words to justify a line
[Kern]	Marks where kerning is turned on or off
[Labels Form]	Indicates that a form for labels has been selected
[Lang]	Indicates that text that follows uses a different dictionary
[Large Off]	Marks where the large font size is turned off
[Large On]	Marks where the large font size is turned on
[Leading Adj]	Indicates that space has been added or removed from lines
[Lft HZone]	Indicates a new setting for the left hyphenation zone
[Lft Indent]	Marks a left indent
[Lft Mar]	Indicates a change in the left margin setting

Code	Description
[Lft Mar Adj]	Indicates an adjustment to the left margin for the following paragraphs
[LFT TAB]	Indicates that the following text is left aligned at the tab stop, regardless of the tab stop's settings
[Lft Tab]	Indicates that the text that follows is aligned with the tab stop
[LFT TAB (DOT)]	Indicates that the following text is left aligned at the tab stop and preceded by a dot leader, regardless of the tab stop's settings
[Lft Tab (Dot)]	Indicates that the text that follows is aligned with the tab stop and preceded by a dot leader
[Lft/Rgt Indent]	Indicates that the following paragraph is indented from the left and right margins
[Link]	Marks the beginning of a link to a spreadsheet
[Link End]	Marks the end of a link to a spreadsheet
[Ln Height]	Indicates a change in the line height setting
[Ln Num]	Indicates that line numbering has been turned on or off
[Ln Num Meth]	Indicates that a new line numbering method has been set
[Ln Num Set]	Indicates that the line number has been set to a specific line
[Ln Spacing]	Indicates a change in the line spacing setting
[Macro Func]	Indicates a function that you created
[Math]	Indicates that the Math feature has been turned on or off
[Math Def]	Indicates that settings for Math columns have been made
[Math Neg]	Indicates that the number following is treated as negative when referenced by a function
[MRG:*command*]	Indicates that a merge programming command has been entered
[Mrk Txt List Begin]	Marks beginning of text to include in a generated list
[Mrk Txt List End]	Marks end of text to include in a generated list
[Mrk Txt ToC Begin]	Marks beginning of text to include in Table of Contents
[Mrk Txt ToC End]	Marks end of text to include in Table of Contents
[Open Style]	Indicates that an Open style has been turned on
[Outline]	Indicates that a new outline style has been selected

Code	Description
[Outln Off]	Marks where the outline character format is turned off
[Outln On]	Marks where the outline character format is turned on
[Ovrstk]	Marks where two or more characters are to be printed on top of each other
[Paper Sz/Typ]	Indicates that a new paper definition has been chosen
[Para Border]	Indicates that the following paragraph has a border defined
[Para Num]	Marks where WordPerfect inserts the number of a paragraph
[Para Num Set]	Indicates that paragraph numbering has been set to a specific number
[Para Spacing]	Indicates a change in the spacing between paragraphs
[Para Style]	Indicates that a paragraph style has been turned on
[Para Style End]	Indicates that a paragraph style has been turned off
[Pg Border]	Indicates that the following page has a border defined
[Pg Num Dec]	Marks where the page number counter has been decremented
[Pg Num Disp]	Marks where WordPerfect will display the page number
[Pg Num Fmt]	Marks a change in the format of the page number
[Pg Num Inc]	Marks where the page number counter has been incremented
[Pg Num Meth]	Indicates that a new method of numbering pages has been selected
[Pg Num Pos]	Indicates that a new location for the page number has been selected
[Pg Num Set]	Marks where the page number is set to a specific number
[Ptr Cmnd]	Marks text to be sent to the printer as a printer command instead of part of the document
[Redln Off]	Marks where the redline character format is turned off
[Redln On]	Marks where the redline character format is turned on
[Ref Box]	Marks where WordPerfect will insert the graphics box number of the specified target
[Ref Chap]	Marks where WordPerfect will insert the chapter number of the specified target
[Ref Count]	Marks where WordPerfect will insert the counter number of the specified target

Code	Description
[Ref Endnote]	Marks where WordPerfect will insert the endnote number of the specified target
[Ref Footnote]	Marks where WordPerfect will insert the footnote number of the specified target
[Ref Para]	Marks where WordPerfect will insert the paragraph number of the specified target
[Ref Pg]	Marks where WordPerfect will insert the page number of the specified target
[Ref Sec Pg]	Marks where WordPerfect will insert the secondary page number of the specified target
[Ref Vol]	Marks where WordPerfect will insert the volume number for the specified target
[Rgt HZone]	Indicates a new setting for the right hyphenation zone
[Rgt Mar]	Marks a change in the right margin setting
[Rgt Mar Adj]	Marks an adjustment in the right margin for the following paragraphs
[RGT TAB]	Indicates that the following text is right aligned at the tab stop, regardless of the tab stop's settings
[Rgt Tab]	Indicates that the following text is right aligned with the tab stop
[RGT TAB (DOT)]	Indicates that the following text is right aligned at the tab stop, and preceded by a dot leader, regardless of the tab stop's settings
[Rgt Tab (Dot)]	Indicates that the following text is right aligned with the tab stop and preceded by a dot leader
[Row]	Marks a row in a table
[Row SCol]	Marks where the end of a table row is the end of a column
[Row SPg]	Marks where the end of a table row is the end of a page
[Sec Pg Num Dec]	Marks where the secondary page number counter has been decremented
[Sec Pg Num Disp]	Marks where WordPerfect inserts the current secondary page number
[Sec Pg Num Inc]	Marks where the secondary page number counter has been incremented

Code	Description
[Sec Pg Num Meth]	Indicates that a new format is selected for secondary page numbers
[Sec Pg Num Set]	Marks where the secondary page number is set to a specific number
[Shadw Off]	Marks where the shadow character format is turned off
[Shadw On]	Marks where the shadow character format is turned on
[Sm Cap Off]	Marks where the small caps character format is turned off
[Sm Cap On]	Marks where the small caps character format is turned on
[Small Off]	Marks where the small font size is turned off
[Small On]	Marks where the small font size is turned on
[Sound]	Marks where a sound clip is added to your WordPerfect document
[Speller/Grammatik]	Indicates where the Speller and Grammatik are disabled or enabled
[SRt]	Marks where WordPerfect has ended a line
[SRt SCol]	Marks where a soft return ends a column
[SRt SPg]	Marks where a soft return ends a page
[StkOut Off]	Marks where the strikeout character format is turned off
[StkOut On]	Marks where the strikeout character format is turned on
[Subdivided Pg]	Indicates that a new setting is chosen for subdividing a page
[Subdoc]	Marks, in a condensed master document, where a subdocument will be added
[Subdoc Begin]	Marks the beginning of a subdocument in an expanded master document
[Subdoc End]	Marks the end of a subdocument in an expanded master document
[Subscpt Off]	Marks where the subscript character format is turned off
[Subscpt On]	Marks where the subscript character format is turned on
[Subtot Entry]	Marks where you have manually added a subtotal value
[Suppress]	Marks where a secondary text feature such as headers or page numbers is suppressed
[Suprscpt Off]	Marks where the superscript character format is turned off
[Suprscpt On]	Marks where the superscript character format is turned on

Code	Description
[Tab Set]	Indicates that new tab stops have been defined
[Target]	Indicates a target to be referred to in a cross-reference
[Tbl Def]	Indicates that a table has been defined and turned on
[Tbl Off]	Indicates the end of a table
[Tbl Off SCol]	Marks where the end of a table is also the end of a column
[Tbl Off SPg]	Marks where the end of a table is also the end of a page
[THCol]	Indicates a temporary column break
[THCol SPg]	Indicates where a temporary column break ends the page
[Third Party]	Marks where a code from another program has been entered into the document
[Thousands Char]	Indicates that a new thousands character has been chosen
[THPg]	Indicates a temporary page break
[THRt]	Indicates a temporary hard return
[THRt SCol]	Indicates where a temporary hard return also ends a column
[THRt SPg]	Indicates where a temporary hard return also ends a page
[ToA]	Marks text to appear as part of a table of authorities
[Top Mar]	Indicates a new top margin setting is made
[Total Entry]	Indicates where a total has been manually added to a math column
[TSRt]	Indicates a temporary soft return
[TSRt SCol]	Indicates where a temporary soft return also ends a column
[TSRt SPg]	Indicates where a temporary soft return also ends a page
[Und Off]	Marks where the underline character format is turned off
[Und On]	Marks where the underline character format is turned on
[Undrln Space]	Indicates that spaces between underline codes will now be underlined
[Undrln Tab]	Indicates that tabs between underline codes will now be underlined
[Unknown]	Indicates a code that WordPerfect does not recognize
[VAdv]	Marks where the cursor will advance up or down a specific distance
[Very Large Off]	Marks where the very large font size is turned off

Code	Description
[Very Large On]	Marks where the very large font size is turned on
[Vol Num Dec]	Marks where the volume number counter has been decremented
[Vol Num Disp]	Marks where WordPerfect inserts the current volume number
[Vol Num Inc]	Marks where the volume number counter has been incremented
[Vol Num Meth]	Indicates that a new method of numbering volumes is selected
[Vol Num Set]	Marks where the volume number is set to a specific value
[Watermark A]	Indicates that a new watermark A has been entered
[Watermark B]	Indicates that a new watermark B has been entered
[Wid/Orph]	Indicates that the widow and orphan protection feature is turned on or off
[Wrd/Ltr Spacing]	Indicates a change in the setting that defines the spacing between words and letters

APPENDIX

B

Macros on Disk

The macros described in this appendix are included on the accompanying disk and are referenced throughout this book. The following table lists the macro name, the tip in which the macro is used, and a brief description of the macro's function. To uncompress the file containing these macros, type **A:TIPSMACS** at the DOS prompt in the \WP60\MACROS directory and press ENTER. These macros do not work in WordPerfect 5.1. The TIPSMACS.EXE file also includes a sample Button Bar file as described in Tip 1.

Macro Name	Tip Number	Description
ADD_PAGE.WPM	138	Adds the page number to the current document
ALTB.WPM	202	Returns to the default color scheme
ALTC.WPM	736	Recalculates table computations
ALTD.WPM	115	Switches to double line spacing
ALTG.WPM	963	Presents a menu that lets you move to the beginning, end, or specific page of a document
ALTN.WPM	202	Switches to the "newcolor" color scheme
ALTQ.WPM	324	Re-selects the last selected block
ALTS.WPM	115	Switches to single line spacing
ALTW.WPM	59	Transposes the current and following characters
BLACKBOX.WPM	632	Creates a box with a black background and white text
BOOKLET.WPM	982	Prints the current document as a booklet
BOOKLET1.WPM	982	Makes different formatting changes to use a document as a booklet
CENTERPG.WPM	965	Centers the current page horizontally and vertically
COMMENT.WPM	77	Creates a comment out of the selected block of text
COPYTEXT.WPM	969	Copies selected text from document 1 to document 2
DATETIME.WPM	243	Creates a footer with the date, time, and page number
FIXIT.WPM	11	Changes abbreviated words/phrases to their non-abbreviated forms
FOOTCHAR.WPM	461	Creates a footnote using a character you select instead of a superscript character
HANDOUT.WPM	775	Prints an outline of a document, then returns to a display of the full document
HARDDATA.WPM	817	Prints a merge file without the page breaks
KOALA_HD.WPM	238	Creates a header combining text and graphics
MOVETEXT.WPM	964	Moves selected text from document 1 to document 2

Macro Name	Tip Number	Description
PULLQUOT.WPM	970	Puts the selected block of text in a graphics box using reversed colors
SORT.WPM	969	Sorts lines in blocked text alphabetically
SORTLIST.WPM	380	Sorts a to-do list by priority number and date
SORTMAIL.WPM	381	Sorts a merge file by ZIP code when the ZIP code is at the end of the second line in the third field
SPELPARA.WPM	962	Checks the spelling of the current paragraph
THREECOL.WPM	758	Defines three columns and turns columns on
UNCOMMNT.WPM	77	Converts the current comment to regular text
WORD.WPM	58	Transposes the current and following words

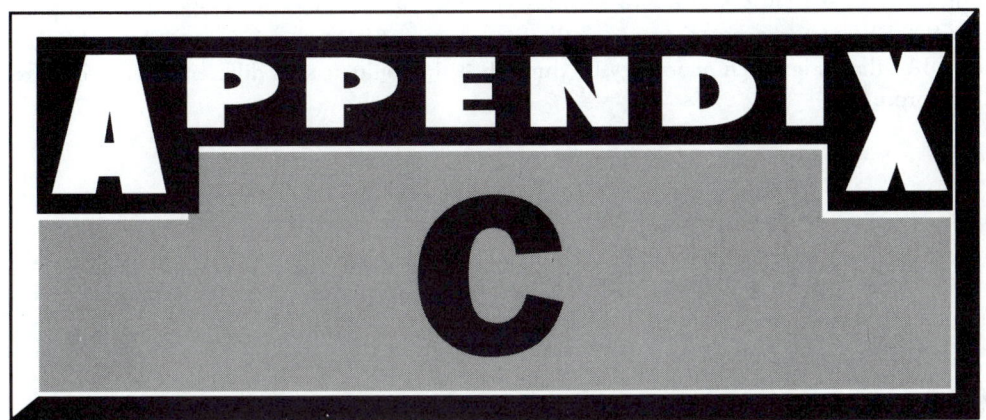

APPENDIX

C

Styles and
Templates on Disk

The following styles and templates are included on the accompanying disk and are referenced throughout this book. To uncompress the file containing these files, type **A:TIPSDOCS** at the DOS prompt in the \WPDOCS directory and press ENTER. Besides the styles and templates, TIPSDOCS.EXE also contains four sound files that have a .MID extension, as well as a batch file named F.BAT that assigns to function keys F5 through F8 the ability to start different applications from the DOS prompt.

Styles

Below is a list of the style libraries on the accompanying disk. Following the style library name is the tip number where that style library is used. Also included are the styles in the style libraries and a brief description of their effects.

BORDERS.STY - Tip 113

Style Name	Effect
Outline	Border style with a single-line box and upper-right shadow
Oval	Border style with a single-line box and rounded corners
Points	Border style with a single-line box, rounded corners, and lower-right shadow

ESPPAPER.STY - Tip 384

Style Name	Effect
Bulletin	Adds a headline of "Bulletin" in large letters, with several graphic symbols
Cost Memo	Adds a side bar containing the words "Cut Costs" and a watermark with CUT_COST.WMF
FYI	Adds a headline of "FYI" and several graphic lines

LETTER.STY - Tip 404

Style Name	Effect
Closing	Adds text for the closing of a letter
Closing 2	Adds text for the closing of a letter

Style Name	Effect
Closing 3	Adds text for the closing of a letter
Opening	Adds text for the opening of a letter

LTHD1.STY - Tip 403

Style Name	Effect
Letterhead	Creates a letterhead for "NightLight Inc.", with a city skyline. User can replace company name
Second Page	Creates a page border for subsequent pages

LTHD2.STY - Tip 403

Style Name	Effect
Letterhead	Creates a letterhead for "Samuel Bros.", with a side border of boxes. User can replace company name
Second Page	Creates a page border for subsequent pages

LTHD3.STY - Tip 403

Style Name	Effect
Letterhead	Creates a letterhead for "Chelsea Fashions", with graphics from FAIRY.PCX on either side. User can replace company name

LTHD4.STY - Tip 403

Style Name	Effect
Letterhead	Creates a letterhead for "Campbell & Associates", with a border and the graphics in WOODCARV.PCX. User can replace company name
Second Page	Creates a page border for subsequent pages

MODBLOCK.STY - Tip 398

Style Name	Effect
Body text	Sets the line spacing to 2 and indents the current paragraph
Closing	Moves the cursor to the appropriate tab stop for the letter closing
Return Add.	Style for the return address
Send Address	Moves the cursor to the appropriate location for the sending address

NEWSLTR.STY - Tip 402

Style Name	Effect
Headline 1	Sets the paragraph as a top level headline
Headline 2	Sets the paragraph as a second level headline
Nameplate	Creates banner across top of newspaper and sets up two columns for articles

PAPERS.STY - Tip 388

Style Name	Effect
Document	Creates a header and footer, sets line spacing and left justification
Endnote Page	Sets up a page for endnotes
Foreign Term	Italicizes foreign terms
Sub Topic	Adds formatting to a subtopic heading
Title Page	Sets justification, line spacing, and the border for a title page
Topic	Adds formatting to a heading

TIP.STY - Tip 344

Style Name	Effect
Tip	Adds a graphic box to the beginning of a paragraph

Templates

The following table lists the template files, the tip in which each template is used, and a brief description of the document each template creates.

Template	Tip Number	Document Created
BUSICARD.TEM	799	Sample business card
FAXFORM1.TEM	793	Sample fax cover sheet using graphics from MOON.PCX
FAXFORM2.TEM	793	Sample fax cover sheet with graphics image of two dogs
FAXFORM3.TEM	793	Sample fax cover sheet with borders and graphic lines
INVOICE.TEM	791	Sample invoice
LOANPAY.TEM	690	Table for calculating house payments
MEMOFORM	9	Sample memorandum slip
PH_NOTE	169	Sample phone message form
SILLY.TEM	233	Sample advertisement
SUM	693	Sample document using cross-footing
TODOLIST.TEM	680	Sample to-do list

Sound Files

The following table lists the sound files located in TIPSDOCS.EXE.

Sound File	Music
50SROCK1.MID	Generic '50s rock tune
ACTION3.MID	Generic action music
TURKISH.MID	*Turkish Rondo* by Mozart
WASHPOST.MID	*Washington Post* by John Philip Sousa

Function Key Batch File

The following table lists the function key assignments (F5 through F8) made possible by the batch file named F.BAT, located in TIPSDOCS.EXE. By using this batch file, you can start different applications from the DOS prompt simply by pressing specific function keys. You need the statement DEVICE=C:\DOS\ANSI.SYS for this batch file to work.

Function Key	Application
F5	dBASE
F6	WordPerfect
F7	Lotus 1-2-3
F8	Windows

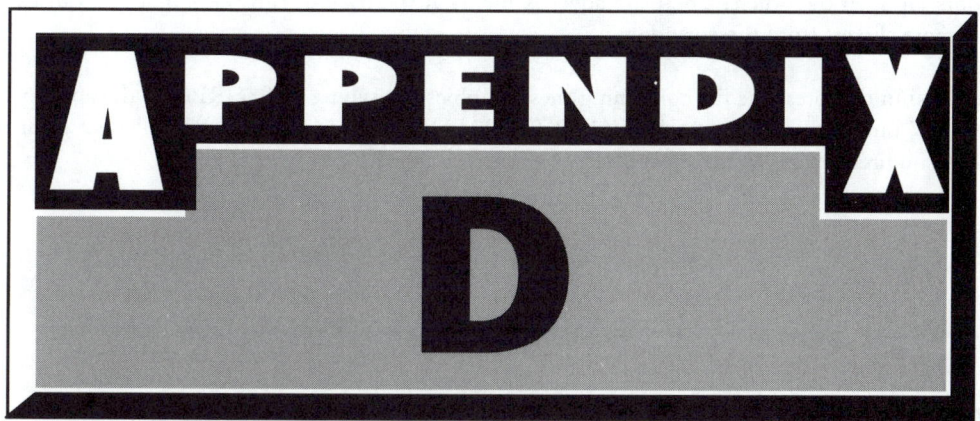

Graphics on Disk

The following graphics are used throughout this book and are included on the accompanying disk. The clip art for each month and the BACK.WPG files were developed by me. Professional clip art vendors supplied the others. There are advertisements at the back of this book that you can use to order more clip art from these vendors.

When you uncompress the file containing these graphics (by typing **TIPSGRPH** in the appropriate directory), uncompress them to the C:\WP60\GRAPHICS subdirectory in WordPerfect 6, or the \WP51 subdirectory in WordPerfect 5.1.

Presentation Task Force by New Vision Technologies

BCKGRD48.CGM

CLICHE02.CGM

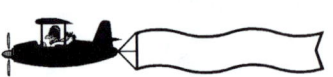

FILLIN12.CGM

JUNGLE10.CGM

MONBAGS1.CGM

PANDA.CGM

SIDNEY.CGM

SPORT38.CGM

TOON28.CGM

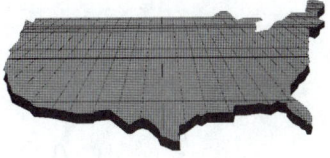

USA4.CGM

Months

JANUARY.WPG

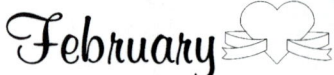

FEBRUARY.WPG

MARCH.WPG

APRIL.WPG

MAY.WPG

JUNE.WPG

JULY.WPG

AUGUST.WPG

SEPTEMBE.WPG

OCTOBER.WPG

NOVEMBER.WPG

December

DECEMBER.WPG

BACK.WPG

ClickArt by T/Maker

BORDER4.CGM

BORDER24.CGM

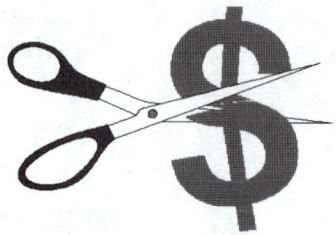

CUT_COST.WMF

DINGBT36.CGM

LAW2.CGM

LOGO_06.WMF

STOP.PCX

STRETCH.PCX

SURFER.CGM

Yesterday's Art by AJ Graphics/PJ Clip/SRL Designs

ACORN.PCX

BLOSSOM.PCX

BORDFLOW.PCX

BRIAR.PCX

BULB.PCX

CAT.PCX

DAISY.PCX

DOG.PCX

FAIRY.PCX

FLOWERS.PCX

HAT.PCX

HORNS.PCX

MOON.PCX

PICNIC.PCX

PUPPIES.PCX

ROSES.PCX

SANTA.PCX

SHIPPING.PCX

TRAIN.PCX

TREES.PCX

WOODCARV .PCX

Index

For more information on the Presentation Taskforce samples included on the disk, contact:

Presentation Taskforce
New Vision Technologies
38 Auriga Drive, #13
Nepean, Ontario, Canada K2E 885
(613) 727-8184

Show Off Your Stuff
Send Us Your Best WordPerfect Tip

If you have a WordPerfect tip that you would like to share with other WordPerfect users, we'd be interested in seeing it. We plan to include the best 25 submissions in the next edition of this book. If we publish your tip in our next edition, we'll send you a free copy of the revised book and give you credit for your submission.

Send your tip to:

> Osborne McGraw-Hill
> WordPerfect Tips
> 2600 Tenth Street
> Berkeley, CA 94710

Please enclose a self-addressed, stamped envelope if you would like your materials returned.

Osborne McGraw-Hill is not responsible for loss of materials. Osborne McGraw-Hill reserves the right to use all submissions for publication and to make copy revisions to your submission. In the event of duplicate submissions, the first submission received will be used.